U.S.
by the Numbers

Also by Raymond J. Keating and Thomas N. Edmonds

D.C. by the Numbers: A State of Failure (1995)

Also by Raymond J. Keating

New York by the Numbers: State and City in Perpetual Crisis (1997)

U.S.
by the Numbers

FIGURING WHAT'S **LEFT**, **RIGHT**, AND **WRONG** WITH AMERICA STATE BY STATE

Raymond J. Keating and **Thomas N. Edmonds**

*FOREWORD BY **JACK KEMP***

CAPITAL
BOOKS, INC.
Sterling, Virginia

As always,
for Beth and David
—R.J.K.

To my wife, Schuyler
daughter, Cathy
and son, Charlie
—T.N.E.

Capital Books, Inc.
P.O. Box 605
Herndon, Virginia 20172-0605

ISBN 1-892123-14-2 (alk.paper)

Printed in the United States of America on acid-free paper that meets the American National Standards Institute Z39-48 Standard.

First Edition

10 9 8 7 6 5 4 3 2 1

TABLE OF CONTENTS

FOREWORD BY JACK KEMP

Ray Keating and Tom Edmonds made a tremendous contribution to the debate over the future of our nation's capital city, the District of Columbia, with their first book, *D.C. by the Numbers: A State of Failure*. Through the use of charts, tables, and numbers, they documented the city's long decline. The book served as a much-needed wake-up call that could not be ignored. I found it invaluable in my own efforts to try to bring about change in the District.

With *U.S. by the Numbers: Figuring What's Left, Right and Wrong with America State by State*, Keating and Edmonds are taking on the entire nation—state by state. Complacent politicians willing to perpetuate the old tax-and-spend model of governing better watch out.

In this one book, the authors provide a comprehensive snapshot of where the nation stands in terms of government spending, taxes and debt; education; the economy and business; health care; the environment; and society in general. Their numbers tell the story for the nation as a whole, as well as for each of the 50 states and Washington, D.C. The rankings and historical trends provide concerned citizens, policy makers, and elected officials with some much-needed perspective. The charts, graphs, and tables assembled by Keating and Edmonds answer questions about how the states have developed in key areas in recent decades, and how each measures up to the others.

Fortunately, the authors provide well-grounded analysis to go along with their numbers. Keating and Edmonds evaluate the nation and the states according to a strong set of principles. Their views on politics and the state of society reveal a solid commitment to the conservative ideas that built this nation. Their take on the economy is unabashedly supply-side, offering a clear understanding that risk taking and entrepreneurship are the engines of economic growth. Indeed, the authors' declaration that we are in the midst of an exciting "Entrepreneurial Revolution" is right on target.

Indeed, it is worth noting U.S. leadership in entrepreneurship. A recent study, the "Global Entrepreneurship Monitor," from researchers at Babson College and the London Business School, measured entrepreneurship among key nations as the percentage of adults that have started a business. The researchers found significant disparities among countries. The United States had the highest rate of entrepreneurship.

Nation	Rate of Entrepreneurship
United States	8.4%
Canada	6.8%
Israel	5.4%
Italy	3.4%
United Kingdom	3.3%
Germany	2.2%
Denmark	2.0%

Nation	Rate of Entrepreneurship (*cont.*)
France	1.8%
Japan	1.6%
Finland	1.4%

The researchers compared levels of entrepreneurship to economic growth rates, and concluded that entrepreneurship accounts for about one-third of the variation in economic growth rates among nations.

Entrepreneurship, of course, is a high-risk endeavor. Keating and Edmonds understand that high taxes, over-regulation, unsound money, and big government raise the costs of entrepreneurship, and pose some of the greatest threats to the continued prosperity and global leadership of the United States.

Therefore, the proentrepreneur policy agenda the authors lay out for the nation and the states is just as valuable as the many numbers and rankings they present. For example, their arguments for eliminating capital-gains and death taxes; rolling back the Clinton and Bush tax increases; cutting the size of government; relinking the dollar to gold; market-based health care reforms like medical savings accounts; school choice; and free trade need to be heeded and implemented as we move into a new century.

U.S. by the Numbers is a significant achievement. This book should sit on the desks of concerned citizens, policy makers, and elected officials at all levels of government, serving as a valuable guide for information, ideas, and policies.

INTRODUCTION

Raymond J. Keating

After coauthoring *D.C. by the Numbers* (1995) and writing *New York by the Numbers* (1997), I periodically have been asked: When are you going to look at my state?

It seems that everybody has a case to make that their state stands out in some way or another. More often than not, they have a particular complaint they want to register.

Well, *U.S. by the Numbers* is an attempt to look at all 50 states, the District of Columbia, and the United States as a whole in terms of politics, taxes and spending, education, the economy and business, crime, health care, the environment, society and demographics, and lifestyle trends.

Obviously, when looking at all of these indicators, some states fare far better than others. And as you will see in the following pages, when looking at the nation as a whole—historical trends, where the United States stands now, and how it compares in some instances to other nations—the United States is in far better shape in most ways than other countries are.

Nonetheless, there is a lot to complain about, and Americans have every right to do so. Indeed, particularly when it comes to government actions affecting the economy, education, crime, business, and our pocketbooks, it is our duty to grouse, complain, and generally make a big stink. Oh sure, it makes perfect sense to pat politicians on the back when they actually do something right, and my coauthor and I do that when appropriate in the following pages. However, when they go astray, we need to come down on them hard.

Why? Well, unlike the private sector, where business performance is assessed on a daily basis by demanding consumers, government faces no such exacting requirements. Every year or two, politicians face the voters; but given the increasing size and complexity of government, only the smallest sliver of voters has any idea what the government is actually doing, and an even smaller number possesses the slightest notion as to whether things are being done well or not.

Factor in that politicians and government bureaucrats are spending other people's money (that is, taxpayers' money), and one thing people can be sure of is that the incentives for waste in government are overwhelming.

However, the situation grows more dire when special interests, with their hands open demanding ever more government largess, are considered. While the average taxpayer does not have the time, resources, or incentives to fight every bit of waste in government, an endless line of special interests exists. These interests know few bounds and include subsidized businesses, public sector unions, private charities taking government money, welfare bureaucracies, the public education establishment, professional sports teams who play in taxpayer-funded stadiums, artists on the government dole, and so on. Since these groups live off the government, they possess every incentive to lobby hard and arm twist for their particular pieces of pork. They are well organized, well financed, and have a specific objective in mind.

In the end, average taxpayers face enormous obstacles in trying to figure out what their government is doing, how much of their hard-earned money is being used, and how well their funds are being spent. It is my hope that this book will help in answering at least some aspects of these questions. Indeed, I would argue that given how skewed our current system is in favor of big, special-interest-driven government, no matter how well your state and our nation might be positioned, there is still plenty of waste to root out.

Look at the numbers, read our analyses, and make life difficult for elected officials.

Thomas N. Edmonds

In the 1950s and early 1960s my father was an Underwood typewriter agent in the historic district of Old Town Alexandria, Virginia, just a few miles south of our nation's capital. The large townhouse where his twenty-some employees worked was in the same block as Gadsby's Tavern and just a few feet away from the site where George Washington reviewed his troops for the final time.

I have many vivid memories of Alexandria Memeo Company: the shiny new electric typewriters in the small display windows and the rows of tall metal repair benches on the second floor that seemed strangely out of place against a backdrop of walls still bearing charcoal drawings made by Hessian troops during the Revolutionary War. But perhaps my most profound memory is the little motto displayed on my father's desk in his cubbyhole office on the first floor: Judge me by What I do, not by what I say.

Even as a young teenager, I could see the irony and significance of that little wooden paperweight. My father was a dark, severe man who seldom smiled. He reminded me of Lyndon Johnson. But he was also an easy touch if you could stomach the inevitable lecture. His employees would routinely ask for advances on their paychecks. My uncles and other family members frequently solicited "loans." Though my dad kept meticulous journals and insisted that each and every dollar would be recovered, it was obvious that these loans were seldom repaid, with the beneficiaries being somehow protected by the little motto on the paperweight.

Ironically, years later, my professional life hinges to no small degree on the converse of that motto. As a political consultant, I depend on surveys and public opinion polls to determine the campaign strategies and advertising content I recommend to my firm's clients. And then, after judging people by what they say, I wait helplessly on election night to see how they'll do. Sometimes what they do and say are one and the same, but often they are not.

Opinion surveys and political polls are the late 20th-century apple pie. A steady stream of sensational results routinely become feature news stories for both print and broadcast journalists. What Americans profess in these numerous polls is the accepted benchmark by which we package, rank, and understand the important issues that punctuate our nation's life. But though modern polling techniques have improved reliability of surveys, they are still only a measure of intent or opinion, not actions. How often have we, as voters, been told by our elected officials, both Republicans and Democrats, that "the era of big government is over," that Pentagon waste will be reduced, or that poverty in the Appalachians will be eradicated? In our private lives, we resolve to lose weight and pay off our credit cards, only to do just the opposite.

U.S. by the Numbers is, in effect, a "survey" of our country by what it does. My coauthor and I have accumulated statistics on the 50 states, our nation as a whole, and other countries around the world in order to better understand who we are, based on what we do. You may disagree with some of our analyses. In fact, I would be surprised if you did not. But without question, you will be empowered by the statistics presented here, for they are the reality, not merely the projections of our society . . . they are the *U.S. by the Numbers*.

ACKNOWLEDGMENTS

A book like this is an enormous undertaking, and is not accomplished without professional and personal assistance as well as some costs. We would like to thank the following people for their understanding and their aid: Beth and David Keating; Sky, Cathy, and Charlie Edmonds; Karen Kerrigan at the Small Business Survival Committee; Matthew Carolan, who coauthors "Carolan and Keating" at *Newsday*; James Slagter, with Capital Hill Research; Mike Smith, Cristie Gates, and Karen Barberie of Edmonds Associates for their countless hours of research, creative input, editing, and proofreading; and all those who gave us interviews, whether directly quoted or not.

UNITED STATES

We currently live in the most exciting economic times man has ever known. Today's "Entrepreneurial Revolution" is overwhelming the "Industrial Revolution" of the late 18th and 19th centuries in terms of tapping into and unleashing man's inherent ability to create, innovate, and prosper.

Fortunately, entrepreneurship always has served as the foundation of the U.S. economy. America's entrepreneurial proclivity—the willingness to take risks and invest in new ideas—has allowed the United States to innovate and adapt like few other nations ever have. Indeed, during its more than 220-year history, the United States developed into and remains a global leader in agriculture and manufacturing. At the dawn of the 21st century, Americans also are leaders in productivity and the unchallenged, dominant force in established and emerging information-based, high-technology industries.

Of course, it was not so long ago that many "experts" were warning the United States to tame its entrepreneurial spirit and to take note of the economic systems of other nations. It was fashionable, for example, in the 1970s and 1980s to urge the United States to mimic Japan's economy with its emphasis on big, cartel-like companies and their close relationships with banks and the government. The proof, these experts said, could be found on America's highways. Japanese cars were small, stylish and superior to Detroit's large, trouble-prone dinosaurs that were manufactured for a captive market. Since the trough of the 1970s, though, American automobiles have closed the gap and now rank among the world's best. The myth of Japanese superiority has evaporated. The Japanese economic model has not held up well, and Japan itself has struggled in recent years to become more entrepreneurial.

Even the Soviet Union's command-and-control economy was seen as a model of efficiency by some, with one leading economist of the latter half of the 20th century, Paul Samuelson, noting in the 1967 edition of his classic textbook *Economics: An Introductory Analysis,* that "all seem to agree that [the Soviet Union's] post-World War II growth rates have been considerably greater than ours as a percentage per year, even though they have not surpassed the performance of such mixed economies as West Germany, Japan, Italy, and France in the last decade." In reality, the Soviet economy was a mess throughout its seven-plus-decade existence, and, of course, no longer exists today.

Peering ahead into the 21st century, it is clear that dramatic advancements in telecommunications, computer, fiber optic, satellite, Internet, and other existing and emerging technologies will more fully empower the individual than ever before. While costs are collapsing, quality and services are expanding. The pace of competition will continue to quicken and grow on a global level. Indeed, U.S. businesses of all sizes will not only have the opportunity to create and fulfill consumer demands around the world, but they also will face more competitors, both domestic and foreign. In terms of communicating, transmitting information, and moving capital, time and distance will have little meaning. Location will be of far less importance.

During the 20th century, Americans tended to migrate from farms and towns to cities and out to the suburbs. In coming years individuals and businesses, mainly as a result of new technologies, services,

1

and products provided by entrepreneurs, will be increasingly free to reside wherever they wish, whether it be country, suburb, town, or city.

The biggest obstacle to economic opportunity will be, as always, government. While costly and misguided government has long taken its toll on the economy, its impact promises to be magnified greatly as both capital and labor become far more mobile in the 21st century. Therefore, the fallout from bad public policy decisions promises to be far swifter and more severe in the future, as individuals, families, and businesses are increasingly able to avoid the costs of big government.

Elected officials and government bureaucrats also will face the great temptation to become more entrepreneurial themselves. We have already seen such attempts in so-called "reinventing government" efforts, stepped up government planning, and taxpayer "investments" in both old and new businesses through subsidies and targeted tax breaks. Unfortunately, the "Entrepreneurial Revolution" will not change the basic incentive structure of government. That is, politicians and government bureaucrats will still lack the proper knowledge, experience, and ownership incentives to become truly entrepreneurial. Indeed, many government entities feel threatened by the rapid changes taking place in our economy. At the federal, state, and local levels, elected officials appear panicked to control information technology, openly expressing their concerns over "lost revenues" rather than acknowledging the inevitable benefit that a vibrant economy means to the very people they are supposed to serve. In the end, politics will still revolve around power, patronage, and pork. And when spending other people's money—that is, taxpayers' money—waste will always rule the day.

What the "Entrepreneurial Revolution" will do for government is provide greater opportunities for privatization of various assets and services, and competitive contracting of other duties whereby private firms compete to provide services currently supplied by the government. Whether or not elected officials take advantage of such opportunities is, to say the least, an open question.

On one level, the "Entrepreneurial Revolution" means that politics and government will face ever diminishing importance, as a dynamic private sector provides greater opportunities, leaves government behind, and more clearly exposes public-sector inefficiencies. On another level, though, getting the policy mix right at the international, national, state, and local levels will never be more important, as policy mistakes promise to be more harshly punished.

POLITICS

Presidential Elections

In the 13 post–World War II presidential elections, Republicans have won seven times, with Democrats taking the other six. Interestingly, while Republican victors grabbed more than 50% of the vote six out of seven times, Democrat winners failed to reach the 50% mark in four out of their six triumphs.

In fact, other than Lyndon B. Johnson's 61.1% in 1964 after the death of John F. Kennedy, the best any Democrat garnered was Jimmy Carter's 50.1% in 1976. From 1980 to 1996, the best percentage garnered by any Democratic presidential candidate was Clinton's 49.2% in 1996, followed by Michael Dukakis's losing 45.6% in 1988.

Meanwhile, other than Nixon's 43.4% in 1968 and Reagan's 50.7% in 1980, the very least that Republican winners gained in their other five wins was 53.4% by Bush in 1988. However, in 1992 and 1996, Republican candidates Bush and Dole gained only 37.4% and 40.7%, respectively, in their losing campaigns.

Year (Since 1900)	Main Candidates	Party	Percentage of Popular Vote	Electoral College Votes	Failed to Complete Term: Successor
1900	William McKinley	Republican	51.7	292	Theodore Roosevelt
	William J. Bryan	Democratic	45.5	155	
1904	Theodore Roosevelt	Republican	56.4	336	
	Alton B. Parker	Democratic	37.6	140	
1908	William H. Taft	Republican	51.6	321	
	William J. Bryan	Democratic	43.1	162	
1912	Woodrow Wilson	Democratic	41.9	435	
	Theodore Roosevelt	Progressive	27.4	88	
	William H. Taft	Republican	23.2	8	
1916	Woodrow Wilson	Democratic	49.4	277	
	Charles E. Hughes	Republican	46.2	254	
1920	Warren G. Harding	Republican	60.4	404	Calvin Coolidge
	James M. Cox	Democratic	34.2	127	
1924	Calvin Coolidge	Republican	54.0	382	
	John W. Davis	Democratic	28.8	136	
	Robert M. LaFollette	Progressive	16.6	13	
1928	Herbert Hoover	Republican	58.2	444	
	Alfred E. Smith	Democratic	40.9	87	
1932	Franklin D. Roosevelt	Democratic	57.4	472	
	Herbert Hoover	Republican	39.7	59	
1936	Franklin D. Roosevelt	Democratic	60.8	523	
	Alfred Landon	Republican	36.5	8	
1940	Franklin D. Roosevelt	Democratic	54.7	449	
	Wendell Wilkie	Republican	44.8	82	
1944	Franklin D. Roosevelt	Democratic	53.4	432	Harry Truman
	Thomas Dewey	Republican	45.9	99	
1948	Harry Truman	Democratic	49.6	303	
	Thomas Dewey	Republican	45.1	189	
1952	Dwight Eisenhower	Republican	55.1	442	
	Adlai Stevenson	Democratic	44.4	89	
1956	Dwight Eisenhower	Republican	57.4	457	
	Adlai Stevenson	Democratic	42.0	73	
1960	John F. Kennedy	Democratic	49.7	303	Lyndon B. Johnson
	Richard Nixon	Republican	49.5	219	
1964	Lyndon B. Johnson	Democratic	61.1	486	
	Barry Goldwater	Republican	38.5	52	

Year (Since 1900)	Main Candidates	Party	Percentage of Popular Vote	Electoral College Votes	Failed to Complete Term: Successor
1968	Richard Nixon	Republican	43.4	301	
	Hubert Humphrey	Democratic	42.7	191	
	George Wallace	American Ind.	13.5	46	
1972	Richard Nixon	Republican	60.7	520	Gerald Ford
	George McGovern	Democratic	37.5	17	
1976	Jimmy Carter	Democratic	50.1	297	
	Gerald Ford	Republican	48.0	240	
1980	Ronald Reagan	Republican	50.7	489	
	Jimmy Carter	Democratic	41.0	49	
	John Anderson	Independent	6.6		
1984	Ronald Reagan	Republican	58.8	525	
	Walter Mondale	Democratic	40.6	13	
1988	George Bush	Republican	53.4	426	
	Michael Dukakis	Democratic	45.6	111	
1992	Bill Clinton	Democratic	43.0	370	
	George Bush	Republican	37.4	168	
	Ross Perot	Reform	18.9		
1996	Bill Clinton	Democratic	49.2	379	
	Bob Dole	Republican	40.7	159	
	Ross Perot	Reform	8.4		

Congress—Political Party Majorities and Minorities

Since the onset of the Great Depression, Congress has been the majority domain of Democrats. In the 35 Congresses from 1931 to 1999, Republicans claimed majorities only five times. Since achieving a majority in the 104th Congress, the GOP's margin slipped in the 105th and the 106th.

Year (Since 1900)	Congress	U.S. House of Representatives Majority	U.S. House of Representatives Main Minority	U.S. Senate Majority	U.S. Senate Major Minority
1899–1901	56	R-185	D-163	R-53	D-26
1901–03	57	R-197	D-151	R-55	D-31
1903–05	58	R-208	D-178	R-57	D-33
1905–07	59	R-250	D-136	R-57	D-33
1907–09	60	R-222	D-164	R-61	D-31
1909–11	61	R-219	D-172	R-61	D-32
1911–13	62	D-228	R-161	R-51	D-41
1913–15	63	D-291	R-127	D-51	R-44
1915–17	64	D-230	R-196	D-56	R-40
1917–19	65	D-216	R-210	D-53	R-42
1919–21	66	R-240	D-190	R-49	D-47
1921–23	67	R-301	D-131	R-59	D-37
1923–25	68	R-225	D-205	R-51	D-43
1925–27	69	R-247	D-183	R-56	D-39

Year (Since 1900)	Congress	U.S. House of Representatives		U.S. Senate	
		Majority	Main Minority	Majority	Major Minority
1927–29	70	R-237	D-195	R-49	D-46
1929–31	71	R-267	D-167	R-56	D-39
1931–33	72	D-220	R-214	R-48	D-47
1933–34	73	D-310	R-117	D-60	R-35
1935–36	74	D-319	R-103	D-69	R-25
1937–38	75	D-331	R-89	D-76	R-16
1939–40	76	D-261	R-164	D-69	R-23
1941–42	77	D-268	R-162	D-66	R-28
1943–44	78	D-218	R-208	D-58	R-37
1945–46	79	D-242	R-190	D-56	R-38
1947–48	80	R-245	D-188	R-51	D-45
1949–50	81	D-263	R-171	D-54	R-42
1951–52	82	D-234	R-199	D-49	R-47
1953–54	83	R-221	D-211	R-48	D-47
1955–56	84	D-232	R-203	D-48	R-47
1957–58	85	D-233	R-200	D-49	R-47
1959–60	86	D-283	R-153	D-64	R-34
1961–62	87	D-263	R-174	D-65	R-35
1963–64	88	D-258	R-177	D-67	R-33
1965–66	89	D-295	R-140	D-68	R-32
1967–68	90	D-246	R-187	D-64	R-36
1969–70	91	D-245	R-189	D-57	R-43
1971–72	92	D-254	R-180	D-54	R-44
1973–74	93	D-239	R-192	D-56	R-42
1975–76	94	D-291	R-144	D-60	R-37
1977–78	95	D-292	R-143	D-61	R-38
1979–80	96	D-276	R-157	D-58	R-41
1981–82	97	D-243	R-192	R-53	D-46
1983–84	98	D-269	R-165	R-54	D-46
1985–86	99	D-252	R-182	R-53	D-47
1987–88	100	D-258	R-177	D-55	R-45
1989–90	101	D-259	R-174	D-55	R-45
1991–92	102	D-267	R-167	D-56	R-44
1993–94	103	D-258	R-176	D-57	R-43
1995–96	104	R-230	D-204	R-52	D-48
		R-236	D-197	R-54	D-46
1997–98	105	R-227	D-207	R-55	D-45
1998–99	106	R-222	D-212	R-55	D-45

Parties: D: Democrat; R: Republican; I: Independent

For the first time in the post-World War II era, the number of public bills actually enacted dipped below the 400 mark in the 104th Congress (1995–96) and stayed below 400 in the 105th Congress (1997–98).

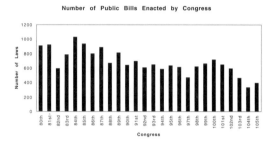

TAXES AND SPENDING

It seems hard to believe today—as at every turn, whether earning a living or buying the smallest item for our families, government is there to take its share—but early last century government once claimed less than 10% of the economy. Today, government grabs more than 30% of the U.S. economy.

Federal government spending as a share of the economy began its long, dramatic ascent (absent World War I) in the 1930s and continued its climb into the 1990s. Interestingly, federal revenues as a share of the economy likewise rose dramatically from the 1930s into the 1950s, but amazingly stayed within the range of 17% to 19.7% from 1960 to 1997. In 1998 and 1999, federal revenues broke the 20% share of gross domestic product (GDP) for the first time since World War II. Before the vast expansion of the federal government that occurred in the 1930s, federal revenues stood at just 3.7% of the economy in 1929.

In terms of the federal government's major revenue raising weapons, payroll taxes have been steadily rising as a share of the economy since their inception in 1934. Individual income taxes spiked dramatically during the 1940s and subsequently fluctuated between a low of 5.7% and a high of 9.4% from 1944 to 1997. In 1998 and 1999, individual income tax revenues as a share of the economy reached record levels of 9.9%. Meanwhile, corporate income taxes as a share of the economy have

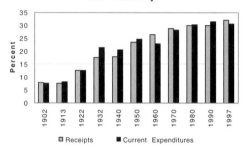

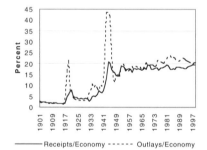

been generally declining since World War II, though rising some in the 1990s.

Compared with other key developed nations and the world in general in 1997, only Japan had a central government that claimed a smaller percentage of the economy.

Finally, U.S. federal debt as a share of the economy was on a long decline after World War II, until it began to climb once more in the 1980s. In recent years, federal debt has again begun to fall as a share of GDP. It is worth noting that the "Federal Revenues and Spending as a Share of the Economy, 1901–99" chart above reveals quite clearly that the source of climbing federal debt during the 1980s was a higher level of federal spending, not a dramatic decline in the level of federal government revenues. That is, the budget deficits and debt of the 1980s resulted from the inability of both Congress and the Reagan White House to restrain spending, not from the Reagan tax cuts.

Showing government revenues, spending, and debt relative to the economy certainly provides some valuable information on the relative burden of government. However, it can also be somewhat deceiving. After all, we do not price any other products or services as a share of the economy. You do not go to the store to see the price of a loaf of bread, for example, quoted as a percentage of your family income. The price is stated in dollars.

When it comes to government, one could be fooled into believing that federal taxes have not increased over the past four decades, for example, because federal revenues have stayed in a fairly tight range as a share of the economy. The charts "Federal Government Receipts, 1901–99" and "Federal Government Outlays, 1901–99" show that the growth in the federal government has been dramatic and consistent since the 1930s.

Federal Individual Income, Corporate Income, and Payroll Taxes as a Share of the Economy, 1934-1999

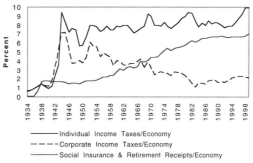

—— Individual Income Taxes/Economy
– – – Corporate Income Taxes/Economy
—— Social Insurance & Retirement Receipts/Economy

Central Government Revenues as a Share of the Economy 1997

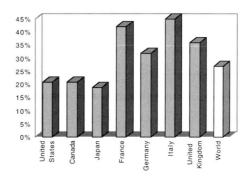

Federal Debt as a Share of the Economy, 1940-1999

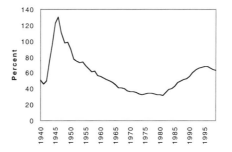

Federal Government Receipts, 1901-1999

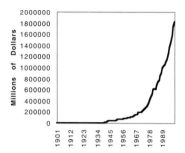

Federal Government Outlays, 1901-1999

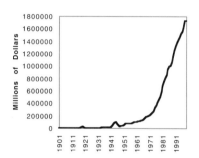

However, an even more accurate picture of the size and growth of government is provided, obviously, when the dollar numbers are adjusted for inflation.

The accompanying charts show the draconian rise in total (federal, state, and local) government spending and revenues, federal spending and revenues, and individual income and payroll taxes in recent decades in real (inflation-adjusted) terms. Only real corporate income tax revenues were relatively steady over this period, though they too have been on a clear rise since the early 1980s.

Note the inflation-adjusted increases in government revenues from 1960 to the late 1990s:

- From 1960 to 1997, real total government revenues increased by 289%.
- From 1960 to 1999, real federal revenues increased by an estimated 236%.
- From 1960 to 1999, real federal individual income tax revenues jumped by an estimated 268%.
- From 1960 to 1999, real federal corporate income tax revenues increased by an estimated 46%.
- From 1960 to 1999, real federal payroll tax revenues increased by an estimated 614%.

Today, 92% of total federal revenues are collected through income taxes—that is, the personal income, corporate income, and payroll taxes. This compares with 89% in 1975, 55% in 1950, 48% in 1925, and 16% in 1916.

Real Federal, State and Local Government Spending and Revenues

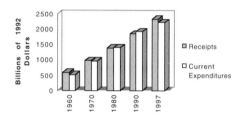

Real Federal Government Receipts, 1940-1999

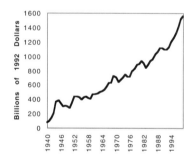

Real Federal Government Outlays, 1940-1999

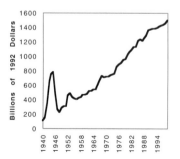

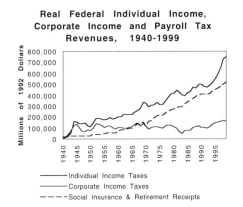

Real Federal Individual Income, Corporate Income and Payroll Tax Revenues, 1940-1999

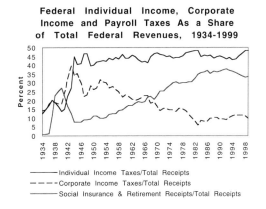

Federal Individual Income, Corporate Income and Payroll Taxes As a Share of Total Federal Revenues, 1934-1999

Below are federal personal income tax rates and the income levels at which they applied in 1998.

Individual Income Tax 1998

Tax Rate (percent)	Single Filer	Married, Filing Jointly
15	up to $25,350	up to $42,350
28	$25,350–$61,400	$42,350–$102,300
31	$61,400–$128,100	$102,300–$155,900
36	$128,100–$278,450	$155,900–$278,450
39.6	over $278,450	over $278,450

The U.S. federal government imposed a personal income tax in 1913, with a top rate of 7%. The top rate quickly reached 77% during World War I, dropped to 24% during the 1920s, climbed steadily to 81.1% during the Great Depression, reached 94% during World War II, and remained at about 91% until the 1960s, when it ranged between 70% and 77%. The top rate stayed at 70% throughout much of the 1970s. In effect, the U.S. maintained wartime tax rate levels from the close of World War II until the 1980s, when the top rate eventually declined to 28%. Subsequent increases pushed the top personal income tax rate back up to 39.6% in the 1990s.

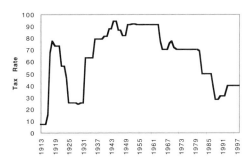

Top Federal Personal Income Tax Rate

Who Pays the Personal Income Tax? (Estimated for Calendar Year 1999)

Income Level	Share of Income	Share of Income Taxes
Above $50,000	29%	90%
Below $20,000	34%	0%

The Tax Code

	Number of Words
Internal Revenue Code:	Over 2.8 million words
War and Peace:	660,000 words
The Bible:	774,746 words

Corporate Income Tax, 1998

Income Range	Marginal Corporate Income Tax Rate
$0–$50,000	15%
$50,000–$75,000	25%
$75,000–$100,000	34%
$100,000–$335,000	39%
$335,000–$10,000,000	34%
$10,000,000–$15,000,000	35%
$15,000,000–$18,333,333	38%
Over $18,333,333	35%

After being imposed in 1909, the federal corporate income tax was on a general climb from World War I into the 1950s. A significant reduction did not occur until the 1980s, with the top corporate rate dropping from 46% to 34%. In 1993, the rate was increased to 35%.

Capital gains taxes are imposed on the profits from the sale of assets, such as the sale of a business, real estate, or shares of company stock. The top tax rate paid by individuals quickly jumped from 7% when first imposed in 1913 to a peak of 77% during World War I. In 1922, however, the top rate plummeted from 73% to 12.5%, where it remained until increased to 25% during the Great Depression. In 1938 the rate was cut back to 15%, but then increased to 25% at the onset of World War II. It remained at 25% (but for a blip up to 26% in two years) until the late 1960s, when the top capital gains tax rate began to climb until it

Top Federal Corporate Income Tax Rate

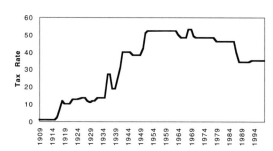

Top Federal Capital Gains Tax Rate For Individuals

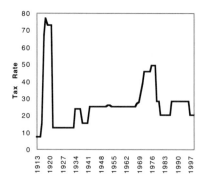

topped 49% in 1976. The rate fell to 28% in 1979, and then dropped to 20% in 1981. In 1987, though, the rate was pushed back up to 28%, where it stayed until returning to the 20% level in 1997.

In the meantime, the top corporate capital gains tax rate has been increasing ever so slowly over the past three decades. In 1987 the rate jumped from 28% to 34% and then rose in 1993 to 35%.

However, when one factors inflation into the equation, the real capital gains tax rate actually climbs much higher than the stated rates. Depending on the rate of inflation, the real capital gains tax rate can climb substantially higher.

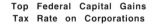

Top Federal Capital Gains Tax Rate on Corporations

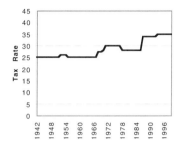

Real Individual Capital Gains Tax Rate, 1982-1998
(Based on Two-Year Investment With a 20% Return)

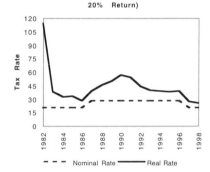

- - - Nominal Rate ——— Real Rate

Payroll taxes collected for Social Security and Medicare have been rising relentlessly over the years, in terms of both the applicable wage bases and rates. Starting in 1993, there was no wage base limit for the Medicare income tax.

Social Security & Medicare—Payroll Taxes Paid by Both Employers and Employees, 1937–99

Year	Wage Base ($)	Tax Rates Paid By Both Employers and Employees	
		Social Security	Medicare
1937–49	3,000	1.000	
1950	3,000	1.500	
1951–53	3,600	1.500	
1954	3,600	2.000	
1955–56	4,200	2.000	
1957–58	4,200	2.250	

Year	Wage Base ($)	Tax Rates Paid By Both Employers and Employees Social Security	Medicare
1959	4,800	2.500	
1960–61	4,800	3.000	
1962	4,800	3.125	
1963–65	4,800	3.625	
1966	6,600	3.850	0.350
1967	6,600	3.900	0.500
1968	7,800	3.800	0.600
1969	7,800	4.200	0.600
1970	7,800	4.200	0.600
1971	7,800	4.600	0.600
1972	9,000	4.600	0.600
1973	10,800	4.850	1.000
1974	13,200	4.950	0.900
1975	14,100	4.950	0.900
1976	15,300	4.950	0.900
1977	16,500	4.950	0.900
1978	17,700	5.050	1.000
1979	22,900	5.080	1.050
1980	25,900	5.080	1.050
1981	29,700	5.350	1.300
1982	32,400	5.400	1.300
1983	35,700	5.400	1.300
1984	37,800	5.700	1.300
1985	39,600	5.700	1.350
1986	42,000	5.700	1.450
1987	43,800	5.700	1.450
1988	45,000	6.060	1.450
1989	48,000	6.060	1.450
1990	51,300	6.200	1.450
1991	53,400	6.200	1.450
1992	55,500	6.200	1.450
1993	57,600	6.200	1.450
1994	60,600	6.200	1.450
1995	61,200	6.200	1.450
1996	62,700	6.200	1.450
1997	65,400	6.200	1.450
1998	68,400	6.200	1.450
1999	72,600	6.200	1.450

The following tables offer a look at how the United States compares to other nations in terms of various key tax rates:

International Tax Rates: Top Personal Income Tax Rate

Nation	Tax Rate (percent)
Germany	53.0
France	52.0
Canada	51.64
Japan	50.0
Italy	46.0
United Kingdom	40.0
United States	**39.6**
Argentina	30.0
Australia	47.0
Belgium	55.0
Brazil	25.0
Chile	45.0
China	45.0
Denmark	60.0
Hong Kong	15.0
India	30.0
Indonesia	30.0
South Korea	40.0
Mexico	35.0
Netherlands	60.0
Poland	45.0
Singapore	28.0
Sweden	56.0
Taiwan	40.0

International Tax Rates: Top Individual Tax Rate on Capital Gains

Nation	Tax Rate (percent)
United Kingdom	40.0 (shares valued at less than $11,225 exempt)
France	26.0 (annual exclusion of $8,315)
Canada	23.5
Japan	20.0 (or 1.25% of sale price)
United States	**20.0**
Italy	12.5
Germany	Exempt
Argentina	Exempt

Nation	Tax Rate (percent)
Australia	48.5 (asset costs indexed for inflation)
Belgium	Exempt
Brazil	15.0
Chile	45.0 (annual exclusion of $6,600)
China	20.0 (shares traded on major exchange exempt)
Denmark	40.0 (shares valued at less than $16,000 exempt if held 3+ years)
Hong Kong	Exempt
India	20.0
Indonesia	0.1
South Korea	20.0 (shares traded on major exchange exempt)
Mexico	Exempt
Netherlands	Exempt
Poland	Exempt
Singapore	Exempt
Sweden	30.0
Taiwan	Exempt (local company shares)

International Tax Rates: Top Individual Tax Rate on Interest Income

Nation	Tax Rate (percent)
France	58.1
Germany	55.9
United Kingdom	40.0
United States	**39.6**
Canada	31.3
Italy	27.0
Japan	15.0
Argentina	33.0
Australia	48.5
Belgium	15.0
Brazil	27.5
Chile	45.0
China	20.0
Denmark	58.0
Hong Kong	Exempt
India	30.0
Indonesia	15.0
South Korea	40.0
Mexico	1.7
Netherlands	60.0
Poland	20.0
Singapore	28.0
Sweden	30.0
Taiwan	40.0

International Tax Rates: Top Corporate Income Tax Rate

Nation	Tax Rate (percent)
Germany	52.5
Canada	46.12
Japan	37.5
Italy	37.0
United States	**35.0**
France	33.33
United Kingdom	31.0
Argentina	33.0
Australia	36.0
Belgium	40.0
Brazil	15.0
Chile	15.0
China	30.0
Denmark	34.0
Hong Kong	16.5
India	35.0
Indonesia	30.0
South Korea	38.0
Mexico	34.0
Netherlands	35.0
Poland	36.0
Singapore	26.0
Sweden	28.0
Taiwan	25.0

International Tax Rates: Top Tax Rate on Dividend Income—Combined Corporate and Individual Rate

Nation	Tax Rate (percent)
France	66.8
Japan	64.0
United States	**60.4**
Germany	55.9
United Kingdom	48.3
Italy	46.0

Nation	Tax Rate (percent)
Canada	45.0
Argentina	33.0
Australia	48.5
Belgium	74.1
Brazil	33.0
Chile	45.0
China	63.1
Denmark	74.7
Hong Kong	16.0
India	54.5
Indonesia	51.0
South Korea	40.0
Mexico	34.0
Netherlands	74.0
Poland	61.6
Singapore	28.0
Sweden	69.0
Taiwan	40.0

International Tax Rates: Top Death Tax Rates

Nation	Tax Rate (percent)
Japan	70.0
United States	**55.0 (60.0 in some cases)**
United Kingdom	40.0
France	40.0
Germany	30.0
Italy	25.0
Canada	0.0
Argentina	0.0
Australia	0.0
Belgium	28.5
Brazil	6.0
Chile	25.0
China	0.0
Denmark	15.0
Hong Kong	15.0
India	0.0
Indonesia	0.0
Mexico	0.0
Netherlands	27.0
Poland	7.0
Singapore	10.0
South Korea	45.0
Sweden	30.0
Taiwan	50.0

Meanwhile, adjusted for inflation, U.S. federal debt was on a very gradual decline from World War II until the early 1970s. From 1974 to 1999, real federal debt increased by an estimated 255%.

The accompanying chart plots real defense spending versus real nondefense spending. Since 1952, nondefense expenditures have been on an inexorable ride ever higher. Meanwhile, since 1968, defense spending has been on a general decline.

- From 1952 to 1999, real federal nondefense spending increased by an estimated 932%, while defense spending actually declined by 26%.
- From 1980 to 1999, real federal nondefense spending increased by 59%, while defense spending rose by 5%.
- More recently, from 1989 to 1999, nondefense spending rose by 32%, while defense spending declined by 29%.

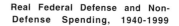

Real Federal Debt

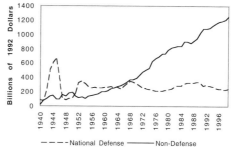

Real Federal Defense and Non-Defense Spending, 1940-1999

- - - - National Defense ——— Non-Defense

Federal Spending by Key Departments or Programs (outlays in millions of 1998 dollars)

Department/Program	1962	1972	1982	1992	1998
Legislative Branch	938	1,680	2,194	3,018	2,600
Executive Office of President	57	128	152	210	237
Judiciary	273	582	1,140	2,602	3,467
Agriculture	30,800	37,215	73,355	63,627	53,947
Commerce	1,029	2,862	3,297	2,894	4,046
Education	3,904	18,643	23,607	29,123	31,463
Energy	13,182	7,741	18,711	17,501	14,483
Health and Human Services	16,885	85,215	141,907	261,060	350,568
Medicare		28,364	75,261	134,135	192,433
Medicaid		15,492	27,915	76,468	101,234
Housing & Urban Dev.	3,952	12,121	24,449	27,587	30,277
Interior	2,900	5,418	6,331	7,372	7,218

Department/Program	1962	1972	1982	1992	1998
Justice	1,431	3,980	4,201	11,051	16,168
Labor	18,727	33,697	48,775	53,076	30,007
State	2,187	2,515	4,308	6,700	5,382
Transportation	19,799	26,707	32,114	36,629	39,463
Treasury	40,957	73,606	177,159	330,312	390,140
Veterans Affairs	26,833	36,071	38,429	38,215	41,773
EPA	335	2,569	8,156	6,708	6,284
FEMA	641	569	634	1,585	2,096
International Assistance	15,172	10,034	12,716	12,523	8,974
NASA	6,014	11,525	9,880	15,740	14,206
Social Security	68,732	136,616	264,417	346,325	408,203
Defense	244,339	274,906	314,143	351,047	287,338

Department/Program	Real Percentage Increase (−Decrease) 1962–98
Legislative Branch	177
Executive Office of President	316
Judiciary	1,170
Agriculture	75
Commerce	293
Education	706
Energy	10
Health and Human Services	1,976
Medicare	578 from 1972 to 1998
Medicaid	553 from 1972 to 1998
Housing & Urban Dev.	665
Interior	149
Justice	1,030
Labor	60
State	146
Transportation	99
Treasury	853
Veterans Affairs	57
EPA	1,776
FEMA	227
International Assistance	−41
NASA	136
Social Security	494
Defense	18

Over the period of 1962 to 1998, federal government employment actually declined by 21%. However, uniformed military personnel declined by 49%, while the number of other federal employees actually increased by 11%.

From 1992 to 1998, incidentally, uniformed military personnel declined by 22%, while the number of other government employees fell by 10%.

Of course, taxes and spending are not the only costs imposed by Congress and the White House. There also are regulations. According to economist Thomas Hopkins of the Rochester Institute of Technology (in a study entitled "Regulatory Costs in Profile," Center for the Study of American Business, August 1996), the real federal regulatory burden was on a steady decline from the late 1970s through 1988. This positive, downward trend, however, was reversed in 1989, and regulatory costs have continued to rise ever since. In 1997 federal regulations were estimated to cost about $7,200 per household.

A study by Dr. Richard Vedder ("Federal Regulation's Impact on the Productivity Slowdown: A Trillion-Dollar Drag," Center for the Study of American Business, July 1996) estimated that rising regulations between 1963 and 1993 explained almost half of the nation's slowdown in long-term productivity. That is, annual productivity growth would be 1 percentage point higher today—2.1 percent versus 1.1 percent—if regulations had remained at 1963 levels. By 1993, GDP would have been $1.27 trillion higher.

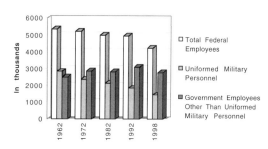

Federal Government Employees

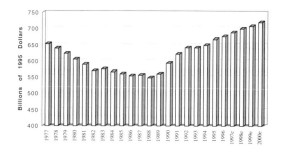

Annual Real Costs of Federal Regulations

EDUCATION

In the United States, per pupil public school total spending, adjusted for inflation, has been on a steady increase throughout most of the 20th century.

Compared with other leading developed countries in 1995, U.S. per pupil spending registered highest.

Per pupil Spending on Public and Private Institutions, 1995

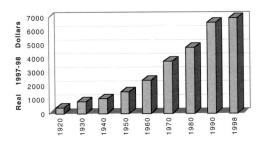

Real Per Pupil Public School Total Expenditures (based on enrollment numbers)

	Primary	Secondary
France	3,379	6,182
Germany	3,361	6,254
Italy	4,673	5,348
Japan	4,065	4,465
United Kingdom	3,328	4,246
United States	5,371	6,812

The U.S. average public school teacher salary increased by 43% from 1960 to 1998. Compared with other leading developed nations, the average elementary school salary in the United States ranked highest, and second highest in terms of high school salaries.

Average Public School Teacher Salaries (in 1997–98 dollars)

	1960	1970	1980	1990	1998
United States	27,496	36,934	33,272	39,956	39,385

Average Public Primary (Elementary) School Teacher Salaries, 1996

	Salary ($)
France	36,409
Germany	38,703
Italy	25,941
United Kingdom	29,948
United States	40,398

Note: Canada not available. United Kingdom data for "public and government-dependent institutions." Germany and Italy only for public institutions.

Average Public High School Teacher Salaries, 1996

	Salary ($)
France	39,218
Germany	47,503
Italy	30,186
United Kingdom	29,948
United States	**41,615**

Pupils Per Teacher in Public and Private Schools, 1995

	Elementary	Junior High	High School
Canada	16.7	19.7	19.2
France	19.5	NA	NA
Germany	20.7	15.8	13.0
Italy	11.0	9.9	9.3
Japan	19.5	16.6	16.4
United Kingdom	21.0	16.0	15.9
United States	**17.1**	**17.6**	**14.7**

8th Grade Students—Hours Each Day Spent on Leisure Activities, 1994–95

	Watching TV/Videos	Playing/ Talking with Friends	Jobs at Home	Playing Sports	Reading for Enjoyment	Playing Computer Games
Canada	2.3	2.2	1.0	1.9	0.8	0.5
England	2.7	2.5	0.8	1.5	0.7	0.9
France	1.5	1.5	0.9	1.7	0.8	0.5
Germany	1.9	3.5	0.9	1.7	0.7	0.8
Japan	2.6	1.9	0.6	1.3	0.9	0.6
United States	**2.6**	**2.5**	**1.2**	**2.2**	**0.7**	**0.7**

While real per pupil public school spending has been on the rise in recent decades, SAT performance has been less than exemplary.

In addition, even as the United States has generally ranked higher than other nations in terms of education spending categories, international performance measures show the United States hovering around the averages or coming in below average.

However, over a lifetime, the United States claims the largest portion of college degree individuals relative to population.

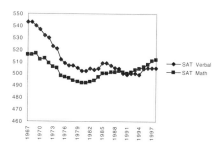

Average Verbal and Math SAT Scores

Average 8th-Grade Math Scores, 1994–95

	Average Percent Correct
Canada	59
England	53
France	61
Germany	54
Japan	73
United States	**53**
International Average	55

Average 8th-Grade Science Scores, 1994–95

	Average Percent Correct
Canada	59
England	61
France	54
Germany	58
Japan	65
United States	**58**
International Average	56

Average 4th-Grade Math Scores, 1994–95

	Average Percent Correct
Canada	60
England	57
Japan	74
United States	**63**

Average 12th-Grade Math Scores, 1994–95

	Average Score
Canada	519
France	523
Germany	495
Italy	476
United States	**461**

Educational Attainment—Between Ages of 25 and 64, 1996

	Percentage with University-Level Education (College Degree)
Canada	17
France	10
Germany	13
Italy	8
United Kingdom	13
United States	**26**

ECONOMY AND BUSINESS

The United States undeniably has been the economic juggernaut of the 20th century. It ranks as the largest economy in the world, and among Organization for Economic Cooperation and Development (OECD) nations, the United States ranks only behind Luxembourg in terms of per capita GDP.

From 1890 through 1998, real annual U.S. economic growth averaged 3.7%. In the post-World War II era from 1948 to 1998, real growth averaged 3.4%, and from 1990 to 1998, real U.S. growth averaged 2.5%. In 1997 and 1998, annual U.S. real growth registered 3.9% in each year—outpacing the postwar average.

Also in the postwar period, U.S. real annual growth averaged 4.1% during recovery years. The economic recovery during the 1990s actually does not compare very well to postwar recoveries, with real growth averaging 3.1% a year from 1992 through 1998.

Meanwhile, among top developed countries, the United States came in only behind Japan from 1980 through 1998 in terms of average annual real economic growth rates. During the 1990s (from 1990 to 1998), the United States ranked very best, leaving Canada, the United Kingdom, Italy, France, Germany, and Japan well behind.

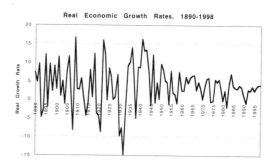

Real Economic Growth Rates, 1890-1998

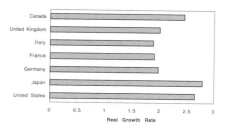

Average Annual Real Economic Growth Rate 1980-1998

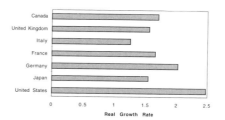

Average Annual Real Economic Growth Rate 1990-1998

The distance between the U.S. economy and the economies of other top developed nations generally reaches massive proportions when it comes to job creation. Only Canada had comparable percentage gains in employment in recent years. Canada's job growth actually outpaced that of the United States in percentage terms from 1960 to 1998 and from 1970 to 1998, but has trailed that of the United States in recent years.

From 1980 through 1998, U.S. employment increased by 32.2 million, while employment for Canada, Japan, France, Germany, Italy, and the United Kingdom increased by just 16.8 million *combined*.

Employment (in thousands)

	1960	1970	1980	1990	1998
United States	65,778	78,678	99,303	118,793	131,463
Canada	6,042	7,919	11,082	13,165	14,326
Japan	43,370	50,140	54,600	61,710	64,400
France	18,250	20,270	21,440	22,100	22,290
Germany	25,710	26,100	26,490	27,950	27,150
Italy	20,060	19,080	20,200	21,080	20,170
United Kingdom	23,600	24,330	24,670	26,740	26,930

	Percentage Changes in Employment			
	1960–98	1970–98	1980–98	1990–98
United States	100	67	32	11
Canada	137	81	29	9
Japan	48	28	18	4
France	22	10	4	1
Germany	6	4	2	−3
Italy	1	4	−0.1	−4
United Kingdom	14	11	9	1

The United States also claims a higher percentage of labor force participation than other leading economies do. This is the working age population employed or seeking employment as a share of the total working age population. Meanwhile, a September 1999 report from the International Labor Organization found that among the 14 developed nations analyzed, U.S. workers put in the longest time on the job each year and also provide the most value added per person employed.

Labor Force Participation Rate

	1997
United States	**67.1**
Canada	64.8
Japan	63.2
France	55.2
Germany	52.2
Italy	47.7
United Kingdom	62.8

The United States also claims a relatively low level of labor union membership as a share of total employment.

Year		Percent
1990	Italy	38.8
1994	United Kingdom	37.7
1994	Germany	30.0
1998	**United States**	**13.7**
1990	France	9.8

Over the period from 1983 to 1998, U.S. total labor union membership as a percentage of total employment steadily declined from 20.1% to 13.7%. Private-sector union membership also fell steadily from 16.5% to 9.4%. Meanwhile, union members as a share of government employment fluctuated narrowly between 35.7% and 38.7%.

Meanwhile, the accompanying charts show fairly solid U.S. employment growth throughout the 20th century, except for a clear slowdown during the Great Depression of the 1930s.

Farming employment has been in freefall since 1910, as a result of dramatic improvements in farm productivity. For example, from 1948 to 1996, farm output per unit of farm labor increased by 715%.

Over the past two decades, we've seen the beginnings of a similar trend in goods producing and manufacturing employment. Manufacturing employment has been on the

Labor Union Membership

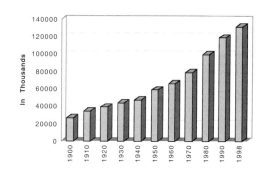

Total Civilian Employment

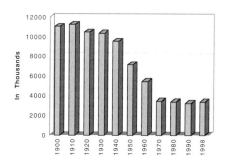

Farming Employment

decline since at least 1980. However, at the same time, manufacturing production has continued on a steady ascent. Obviously, increased productivity, boosts in technology, and efficiency gains have been at work. Much as was the case in agriculture, manufacturing promises to grow less and less labor intensive in coming decades.

The big gains in employment have come in private-sector service industries since 1960, and, especially between 1960 and 1980, in government.

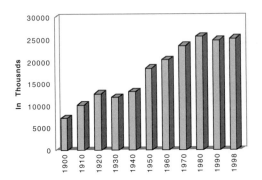

Goods Producing Employment

Manufacturing Production Index vs. Maunfacturing Employment

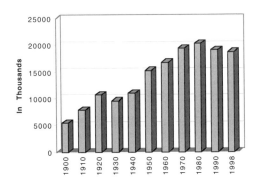

Manufacturing Employment

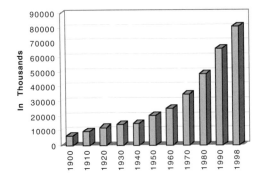

Private-Sector Services Employment

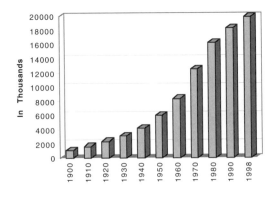

Government Employment

In terms of industrial production, the United States again has well outpaced the world's other leading developed nations over the past two decades. In particular, U.S. industrial production performance has been particularly strong during the 1990s when compared with that of Canada, Japan, France, Germany, Italy, and the United Kingdom.

Another key measure of U.S. economic well-being is the increase in worker productivity. The accompanying chart traces productivity growth (output per hour per person) over the past four decades. From 1959 to 1998, annual productivity grew by 2.03% on average. From 1990 to 1998, average annual productivity growth registered 1.36%. However, productivity growth averaged 2.2% annually from 1996 to 1998.

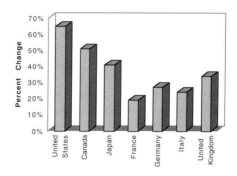

Industrial Production Index: Percent Change 1980-1998

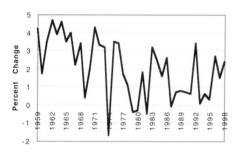

Productivity: Change in Output Per Hour of All Persons

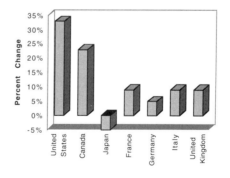

Industrial Production Index: Percent Change 1990-1998

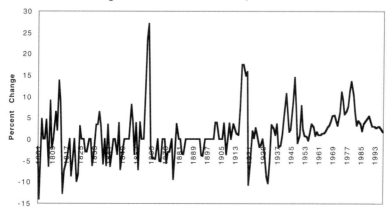

Changes in Consumer Prices, 1801-1998

As for inflation, U.S. history shows that inflation flares up during wartime or when the dollar has been de-linked from gold. When the dollar was linked to gold, U.S. inflation performance was nothing less than stellar.

Interestingly, U.S. inflation performance has registered in the middle of the pack on average—as measured, for example, by changes in the consumer price index (CPI)—when compared with other leading economies over the periods of 1980 to 1998 and 1990 to 1998.

However, in 1997 and 1998, U.S. consumer prices rose by less than 2% annually—the best performance in the post-gold era from the late 1960s to present day.

Increased inflation risks since the United States removed the dollar from its gold anchor in the late 1960s and early 1970s are reflected in higher interest rates, as noted in the chart showing yields on Moody's Corporate Aaa bonds. The relatively tame U.S. inflation environment since the early 1990s translated into a decline in long-term interest rates.

Adjusting for inflation, U.S. per capita disposable income (personal income less the government's take) has continued to increase over the past four decades. However, the rate of increase has been slowing in each subsequent decade. From 1960 to 1970, real per capita disposable income increased by 39%, from 1970 to 1980 by 23%, from 1980 to 1990 by 21%, and from 1990 to 1998 by 6%.

Not only have stock prices risen quite dramatically over the past two decades (see the S&P Composite Index chart), but so has the level of stock ownership in the United States. William H. Peterson, an adjunct scholar with the Heritage Foundation and the Distinguished Lundy Professor Emeritus of Business Philosophy at Campbell University, noted in the June 21, 1999, *Investor's Business Daily* that "a recent Peter Hart survey suggests that the number of U.S. stock-owning adults doubled between 1965 and 1990 and redoubled between

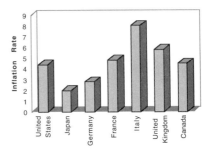

Average Annual CPI Inflation 1980-1998

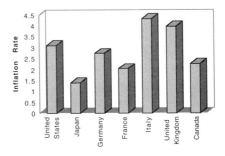

Average Annual CPI Inflation 1990-1998

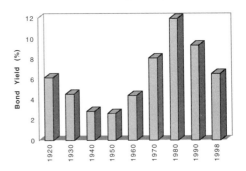

Bond Yield on Moody's Corporate Aaa

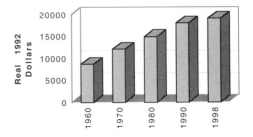

Real Per Capita Disposable Income (1992 Dollars)

1990 and 1997, a 32-year climb from 10.4% to 43%." On the same day, *Investor's Business Daily* reported on Federal Reserve System numbers, showing that equity shares accounted for the largest percentage of household assets at 28%, edging out real estate at 27%.

In the increasingly global economy, of course, U.S. exports and imports have been rising robustly for years. For example, while real U.S. GDP grew by 64% from 1980 through 1998, real U.S. exports rose by 197% and real imports increased by 281%.

A similar disparity existed during the period of 1990 to 1998, with real GDP up 23% versus a 75% increase in exports and a 95% rise in imports.

This trend obviously means that more and more of the U.S. economy is linked to international trade. Indeed, U.S. exports plus imports reached almost 25% of our nation's economy in 1998, rising from below 10% in 1959, for example.

The following tables spell out which nations are the top destinations of U.S. exports and which are the leading sources of U.S. imports.

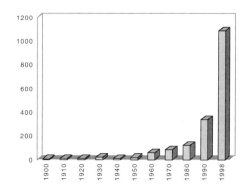

S&P Composite Index

Real U.S. Exports

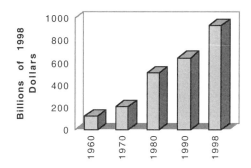

Real U.S. Imports

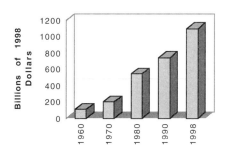

Trade as a Share of the U.S. Economy
(Exports + Imports/Economy)

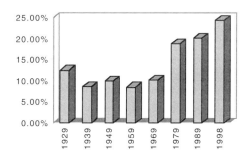

Top Purchasers of U.S. Exports, 1998

Country	Millions of Dollars
Canada	156,603
Mexico	78,773
Japan	57,831
United Kingdom	39,058
Germany	26,657
Netherlands	18,978
Taiwan	18,165
France	17,729
South Korea	16,486
Singapore	15,694

Top Suppliers of U.S. Imports, 1998

Country	Millions of Dollars
Canada	173,526
Japan	121,845
Mexico	94,629
China	71,169
Germany	49,842
United Kingdom	34,838
Taiwan	33,125
France	24,016
South Korea	23,942
Italy	20,959

Interestingly, however, trade as a share of the U.S. economy still comes in at a lower level than in most other leading developed nations, but for Japan.

Finally, when dealing with trade, the subject of the U.S. trade deficit inevitably comes to the fore. The media regularly reports an expansion in the U.S. trade deficit as a negative, and it is viewed similarly by most experts on Wall Street and many economists. Those advocating increased trade protectionism even managed to somehow translate trade deficits and rising imports into lost jobs. Of course, that is not the case. Many "experts" in the 1980s claimed that the U.S. trade deficit was a direct result of U.S. federal budget deficits—ignoring a wealth of contrary historical evidence and further disproved today, as the U.S. trade deficit has risen recently even as the federal government accumulates budget surpluses.

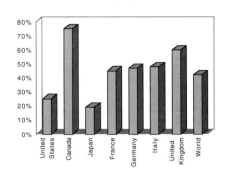

Trade as a Share of the Economy 1997
(Exports + Imports/Economy)

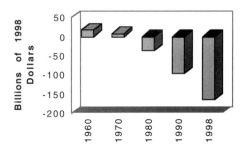

Real U.S. Trade Surplus/Deficit

In reality, throughout U.S. history, shrinking trade surpluses or mounting trade deficits usually have coincided with robust periods of economic growth. This should not be surprising. An increasing current account trade deficit means there must be an offsetting capital account trade surplus. Basically, that means that foreigners view the United States as a hospitable investment environment. In fact, contrary to the prevailing wisdom, the capital account often drives the trade issue—meaning that foreign investment is attracted to the United States, which in turn spurs growth, and of course, an expanding economy means rising consumption and more imports.

Now, we come back to the issue of entrepreneurship in the U.S. economy. Business incorporations offer one measure of entrepreneurship, and the trends reveal solid growth since at least the mid-1950s, with a particularly big jump from the mid-1970s into the mid-1980s and a recent recovery after declines from the late 1980s into the early 1990s.

More comprehensive numbers from the IRS, including corporations, partnerships, and sole proprietorships, reveal a massive surge in entrepreneurship from 1980 into the late 1990s. The total number of businesses filing tax returns increased by 68% from 1980 to 1996, with the number of corporations up by 71%, partnerships by 20%, and sole proprietorships by 74%. Meanwhile, over the same period, the population of the United States increased by just 16%. The rising tide of entrepreneurship is obvious.

Are Rising Imports Bad for Growth? Real U.S. Imports vs. Real GDP Growth

New Business Incorporations

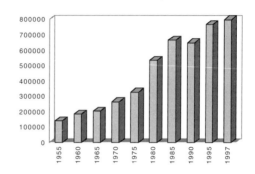

Number of Businesses Based on Those Filing Income Tax Returns (in thousands)

	1980	1990	1996
Corporations	2,710.5	3,716.7	4,631.4
Partnerships	1,379.7	1,553.5	1,654.3
Nonfarm Sole Proprietorships	9,730.0	14,782.7	16,955.0
Total	13,820.2	20,052.9	23,240.7

Again, increased levels of entrepreneurship serve as both a source of U.S. high-tech leadership and a by-product of such technological leaps.

Of course, today's large businesses are doing their share to keep the U.S. economy on top globally as well. For example, a May 1999 report ("Prospects for Success in the Global Marketplace") by economist Murray Weidenbaum for the Center for the Study of American Business, pointed out that U.S. firms in the following industries rank best in the world in terms of sales:

Aerospace	Office Equipment
Airlines	Paper Products
Beverages	Petroleum
Chemicals	Pharmaceuticals
Computer Services	Photographic and Scientific Equipment
Electrical Products	Semiconductors
Entertainment	Soap and Cosmetics
General Merchandise	Tobacco
Motor Vehicles	

Weidenbaum concluded:

> Technology is the bright hope for American competitiveness in the 21st century. Efficiency, quality control, and cost are important factors. Nevertheless, it is the unique ability of American firms to innovate on the basis of technological progress that gives our companies a special edge. Here, the prospects for the United States are buoyed by a silent, strategic crossover that occurred in the early 1980s. For the first time since World War II, company-sponsored research and development began to exceed government-financed R&D. Since then, the gap in favor of the private sector accounted for 70 percent of national financing of R&D and the public sector only 30 percent. The results are positive in many ways, such as the rapid rise of Silicon Valley and other civilian-oriented R&D firms. . . . Although we cannot pinpoint the precise future results of the massive private investment in new technology, it is most likely that an unparalleled array of new products and improved production processes will be brought to market by American firms in the opening decades of the 21st century.

Indeed, a June 1999 report from the U.S. Commerce Department—"The Emerging Digital Economy II"—quantified the increasing importance of information technologies (that is, producers of computer and communications hardware, software, and services) in the U.S. economy. Commerce estimated the following:

- Information technologies as a share of the economy will have risen from 6% in 1993 to 8% in 1999.
- Prices in information technologies have declined on annual basis in recent years:

	Percentage Change in Prices				
	1993	1994	1995	1996	1997
Information Technology Producing Industries	−2.4	−2.6	−4.9	−7.0	−7.5
Rest of the Economy	3.0	2.7	2.8	2.6	2.6
GDP	2.6	2.4	2.3	1.9	1.9

- The contribution of information technology-producing industries to U.S. real economic growth has been impressive:

	Share of Real Economic Growth (Percent)					
	1993	1994	1995	1996	1997(est)	1998(est)
Information Technology-Producing Industries	26	15	41	42	28	29

- Information technology-producing and -using industries accounted for 36% of U.S. employment in 1989 and 41% in 1996, and are estimated to rise to 51% by 2006.
- In 1997, average per-worker earnings in all industries stood at $29,787, compared with $33,532 in information technology-using industries and $52,920 in information technology-producing industries.

Lastly, it is worth noting where the United States is ranked in terms of its international competitiveness. According to "The 1999 Global Competitiveness Report" from the World Economic Forum (as reported in the *Wall Street Journal* on July 14, 1999), which measures include long-term growth, rates of saving and investment, trade openness, low marginal tax rates, and quality education, the top competitive nations ranked as follows:

1.   Singapore
2.   **United States**
3.   Hong Kong
4.   Taiwan
5.   Canada
6.   Switzerland
7.   Luxembourg
8.   United Kingdom
9.   Netherlands
10.   Ireland
11.   Finland
12.   Australia
13.   New Zealand
14.   Japan
15.   Norway

Meanwhile, the "1999 Index of Economic Freedom," written by Byran Johnson, Kim Holmes, and Melanie Kirkpatrick for the Heritage Foundation and the *Wall Street Journal*, gauges nations according to trade policy, taxation, government intervention in the economy, monetary policy, capital flows and foreign investment, banking, wage and price controls, property rights, regulation, and black markets. The top nations ranked as follows:

1.   Hong Kong
2.   Singapore
3.   Bahrain

4.   New Zealand
5.   Switzerland
6.   United States
7.   Ireland
7.   Luxembourg
7.   Taiwan
7.   United Kingdom
11.   Bahamas
12.   Czech Republic
12.   Japan
14.   Australia
14.   Belgium
14.   Canada
14.   United Arab Emirates

The bottom line: The United States ranks among the very best in the world when it comes to competitiveness and economic freedom. However, as we shall see, such rankings are no reason for complacency during the present "Entrepreneurial Revolution," but merely provide a solid foundation on which ongoing improvements can be made.

CRIME

Crime Rates Per 100 Residents

Total Crime	1960	1970	1980	1990	1998
United States	1.04	2.74	5.90	5.82	4.62

From 1960 to 1998, the U.S. total crime rate increased by 344%. From 1990 to 1998, the U.S. crime rate declined by 21%.

Violent Crime	1960	1970	1980	1990	1998
United States	0.14	0.36	0.58	0.73	0.57

From 1960 to 1998, the U.S. violent crime rate increased by 307%. From 1990 to 1998, the U.S. violent crime rate decreased by 22%.

Property Crime	1960	1970	1980	1990	1998
United States	0.90	2.38	5.32	5.09	4.05

From 1960 to 1998, the U.S. property crime rate increased by 350%. From 1990 to 1998, the U.S. property crime rate decreased by 20%.

Compared with various leading nations, as noted in the following table (United Nations data as reported by Don B. Kates in the October 1997 issue of the *American Guardian*), the United States carries a heavy murder rate and a low suicide rate (per 100,000 population).

Nation	Year	Suicides	Murders
Denmark	1991	22.0	5.0
Austria	1991	22.3	1.5
Switzerland	1994–95	20.8	1.1
France	1990	20.2	1.1
Belgium	1987	19.3	1.4
United States	**1995–96**	**11.5**	**7.3**
Sweden	1990	17.2	1.3
Germany	1995	15.8	1.8
Luxembourg	1991	15.1	2.1
New Zealand	1989	13.9	1.9
Canada	1995	12.9	2.0
Israel	1989	7.3	1.2

HEALTH CARE

During the 1990s, much was made of health-care costs in the United States. As noted in the accompanying chart, per capita health-care spending in 1995 far outdistanced levels in other leading developed nations.

However, there are two parts to the U.S. health-care spending story. On the positive side of the ledger, obviously new and improved treatments have resulted in increased health spending.

On the negative side, government has been picking up more and more of the nation's health-care bills, as noted in the accompanying charts and tables. Since at least 1929, private health spending has been declining as a percentage of total health expenditures, while government participation has been steadily rising. From 1960 to 1996, for example, real per capita health expenditures increased by 465%, with real per capita federal health spending up by 1,665%, and state and local up by 431%. Meanwhile, over the same period, real per capita private health expenditures increased by 231%.

Per Capita Health Care Spending, 1995

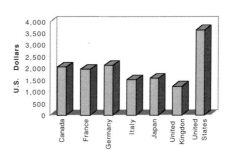

Real Per Capita U.S. Health Expenditures

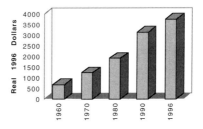

Real Per Capita Federal Health Expenditures

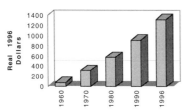

Real Per Capita State and Local Health Expenditures

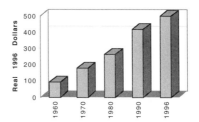

Overall, out-of-pocket payments for health care have been on a long decline. When a third party picks up the tab—whether it be the government or employer-provided health plans—the buyer and seller have few incentives to be concerned about costs.

U.S. National Health Care Expenditures: Private Sector vs. Public Sector

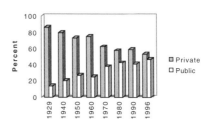

U.S. Personal Health-Care Expenditures (Percentages)

	Private			Public	
	Out-of-Pocket	Health Insurance	Other	Federal	State & Local
1950	65.5%	9.1%	2.9%	10.4%	12.0%
1960	55.3	21.2	1.8	9.0	12.6
1970	39.0	23.2	2.6	23.0	12.2
1980	27.8	28.6	3.6	29.2	10.9
1990	23.5	33.6	3.5	28.9	10.5
1996	18.9	32.2	3.5	35.6	9.9

ENVIRONMENT

Two major environmental issues of late have been government-protected land and the theory of global warming.

Among the top developed countries, the United States ranks third among seven in terms of "nationally protected areas," and comes in far ahead of the world average.

Nationally Protected Areas, 1996

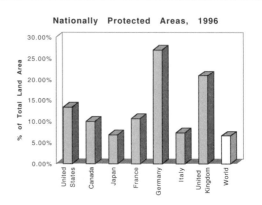

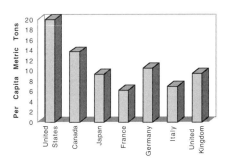

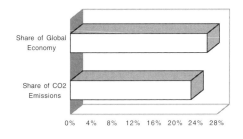

Of course, economic development allows nations to be able to afford to undertake such environmental endeavors as protecting land.

Meanwhile, the global warmers get all hot and bothered over U.S. energy consumption and its level of carbon-dioxide (CO_2) emissions. Global warming theorists assert that a buildup of CO_2 in the atmosphere, as a result of mankind's activities, causes global warming.

However, what the global warming crowd fails to mention is that the United States's share of CO_2 emissions actually comes in below its share of the global economy.

SOCIETY AND DEMOGRAPHICS

A nation's economy is related to its population level. More people, obviously, mean more producers and more consumers. And, of course, people tend to vote with their feet through immigration.

As noted in the accompanying chart, the United States managed to show a steady increase in population throughout the 20th century.

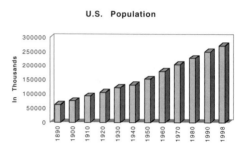

U.S. Population

The table below shows recent immigration trends for key leading nations. The United States regularly lands among the top in terms of percentage population growth, including ranking second only to Canada and outpacing China from 1990 to 1998.

Population (in thousands)

	1950	1960	1970	1980	1990	1998
United States	152,271	180,671	203,302	226,546	248,765	270,299
Canada	14,011	18,267	21,750	24,593	27,791	30,675
Japan	83,805	94,092	104,345	116,807	123,537	125,932
France	41,829	45,670	50,787	53,870	56,735	58,805
Germany	68,375	72,481	77,784	78,298	79,357	82,079
Italy	47,105	50,198	53,661	56,451	56,761	56,783
United Kingdom	50,127	52,372	55,632	56,314	57,507	58,970
China	562,580	650,661	820,403	984,736	1,138,895	1,236,915
World			3,721,311	4,453,832	5,278,640	5,926,467

Change in Population

	Percentage Change 1970–98	Percentage Change 1990–98
United States	33.0	8.66
Canada	41.0	10.38
Japan	20.7	1.94
France	15.8	3.65
Germany	5.5	3.43
Italy	5.8	0.04
United Kingdom	6.0	2.54
China	50.8	8.61
World	59.3	12.30

For those concerned about "overpopulation," the population per square mile data below points to the United States having plenty of room for more people. U.S. immigration levels (as a share of total population) have recovered some over the past two decades after a long decline, particularly from 1930 to 1970.

Population Per Square Mile, 1998

	Population Per Square Mile
United States	76
Canada	9
Japan	826
France	279
Germany	607
Italy	500
United Kingdom	632
China	343
World	117

U.S. Foreign-Born Population (in thousands)

Year	Total Population	Foreign-Born Population	Percent
1890	63,056	9,250	14.7
1900	76,094	10,341	13.6
1910	92,407	13,516	14.6
1920	106,461	13,921	13.1
1930	123,188	14,204	11.5
1940	132,122	11,657	8.8
1950	152,271	10,347	6.8
1960	180,671	9,661	5.3
1970	203,302	9,740	4.8
1980	226,546	14,080	6.2
1990	248,765	19,767	7.9
1997	267,774	25,779	9.6

As for age, the U.S. population generally seems to rate a bit younger than other developed nations, but older than the world as a whole.

Age Distribution, 1998

Nation	Percentage of Population	
	Under 15	65 years and older
Canada	19.8	12.5
France	18.9	15.8
Germany	15.6	15.9
Italy	14.4	17.6
Japan	15.2	16.0
United Kingdom	19.3	15.7
United States	21.6	12.7
World	30.7	6.8

In terms of life expectancy, the United States comes in just below other key developed nations, but far ahead of low- and middle-income nations in general. Indeed, one of the keys to a long life is to live in a high-income nation. Wealth creation does wonders toward making people healthier and allowing them to live longer. Infant mortality rates show the same trend.

Life Expectancy

	1980	1998
United States	73.7	76.1
Canada	75.0	79.2
Japan	76.0	80.0
France	74.0	78.5
Germany	73.0	77.0
Italy	74.0	78.4
United Kingdom	74.0	77.2
China	67.0	69.6
	1980	1997
World	63.0	67.0
Low-Income Nations		59.0
Middle-Income Nations		69.0
High-Income Nations		77.0

U.S. Infant Mortality Rate (Per 1,000 Live Births)

Year	Rate
1950	29.2
1960	26.0
1970	20.0
1980	12.6
1990	9.2
1998	6.4

Infant Mortality Rates (Per 1,000 Live Births)

	1970	1998
United States	20.0	6.4
Canada	19.0	5.6
Japan	13.0	4.1
France	18.0	5.7
Germany	23.0	5.2
Italy	30.0	6.4
United Kingdom	19.0	5.9
China	69.0	45.5

(continued)	1970	1997
World	98.0	56.0
Low-Income Nations		82.0
Middle-Income Nations		34.0
High-Income Nations		6.0

Births to unmarried mothers in the United States have dramatically climbed in recent decades and rank among the worst for key developed nations. In 1997, just about one-third of the babies in the United States were born to unmarried mothers. Interestingly, even as the illegitimacy rate has climbed, births to teenage mothers in the United States (as a percentage of total births) declined from 1970 to 1985 and remained fairly steady thereafter. However, there was a rather strong uptick in births to women younger than 18 years of age between 1990 and 1996.

Percentage of Live Births to Unmarried Mothers in the United States

Year	Percent
1940	3.5
1950	3.9
1960	5.3
1970	10.7
1980	18.4
1990	28.0
1997	32.4

Percentage of Live Births to Unmarried Mothers, 1995

	Percent
United States	32
Canada	26
Japan	1
France	37
Germany	16
Italy	8
United Kingdom	34

U.S. Births to Teenage Mothers (Percentage of All Live Births)

	Percent
1970	17.6
1975	18.9
1980	15.6
1985	12.7
1990	12.8
1996	12.9

U.S. Births to Mothers Under 18 Years of Age (Percentage of All Live Births)

Year	Percent
1970	6.3
1975	7.6
1980	5.8
1985	4.7
1990	4.7
1996	5.1

Meanwhile, low-birthweight births declined rather steadily from 1970 to 1985 but were on the increase over subsequent years. No doubt, though, some of this increase has been a result of improved medical technology, allowing for the survival of younger, smaller babies.

U.S. Low-Birthweight Live Births (Percentage of All Live Births)

Year	Percent
1970	7.93
1975	7.38
1980	6.84
1985	6.75
1990	6.97
1997	7.50

Finally, there is the issue of babies who never get a chance at life. Even though decreasing recently, the number of abortions in the United States is simply staggering, whether measured in the aggregate or as a percentage of live births. In 1995, 31 babies were aborted for every 100 live births in the United States.

Abortions in the United States

Year	Abortion Rate (per 100 live births)	Total Abortions
1973	19.6	616,000
1975	27.2	855,000
1980	35.9	1,298,000
1985	35.4	1,329,000
1990	34.5	1,430,000
1996	31.1	1,211,000

LIFESTYLE

In terms of various lifestyle measures, according to the most recent comparative data, the United States ranks tops among key developed nations when it comes to motor vehicles, radios, televisions, and personal computers per 1,000 people, and it comes in second in terms of cable TV subscribers, mobile phones, and fax machines per 1,000 population. The United States ranks very low among key developed nations when it comes to paved roads and the number of daily newspapers per 1,000 population.

The United States is in the middle of the pack regarding growth in inbound and outbound tourism between 1980 and 1997, and it comes in sixth out of seven in terms of outbound tourists as a share of population.

Motor Vehicles Per 1,000 People, 1997

	1997
United States	773
Canada	563
Japan	547
France	530
Germany	529
Italy	581
United Kingdom	415
China	8
World	121

Paved Roads, 1997

	Percent
United States	60.5
Canada	35.3
Japan	74.3
France	100.0
Germany	99.1
Italy	100.0
United Kingdom	100.0
World	44.4

Daily Newspapers Per 1,000 People, 1996

	1996
United States	215
Canada	157
Japan	578
France	218
Germany	311
Italy	104
United Kingdom	332

Radios Per 1,000 People, 1996

	1996
United States	2115
Canada	1078
Japan	957
France	943
Germany	946
Italy	874
United Kingdom	1445

Televisions Per 1,000 People, 1997

	1997
United States	847
Canada	708
Japan	708
France	606
Germany	570
Italy	483
United Kingdom	641

Cable TV Subscribers Per 1,000 People, 1997

	1997
United States	245.9
Canada	261.4
Japan	114.8
France	27.7
Germany	210.5
Italy	73.0
United Kingdom	40.2

Mobile Phones Per 1,000 People, 1997

	1997
United States	206
Canada	139
Japan	304
France	99
Germany	99
Italy	204
United Kingdom	151

Fax Machines Per 1,000 People, 1996

	1996
United States	78.4
Canada	33.0
Japan	126.8
France	47.8
Germany	68.1
Italy	31.3
United Kingdom	33.8

Personal Computers Per 1,000 People, 1997

	1997
United States	406.7
Canada	270.6
Japan	202.4
France	174.4
Germany	255.5
Italy	113.0
United Kingdom	242.4

Tourism

	Growth in Inbound Tourists, 1980–97
United States	115%
Canada	37%
Japan	400%
France	122%
Germany	42%
Italy	54%
United Kingdom	109%

Growth in Outbound Tourists, 1980–97	
United States	132%
Canada	49%
Japan	222%
France	116%
Germany	245%
Italy	−25%
United Kingdom	194%

Outbond Tourists as a Share of Population, 1997	
United States	20%
Canada	66%
Japan	13%
France	29%
Germany	92%
Italy	31%
United Kingdom	78%

THE POLICY AGENDA FOR THE 21ST CENTURY

Looking at these national trends and the state and local numbers in the following chapters, the United States clearly possesses many positives upon which it can build in the 21st century. Numerous challenges present themselves as well.

"The Entrepreneurial Revolution" that we advocate will demand broad changes in public policy-making, including issues like taxes, government spending, regulations, health care, crime, education, trade and monetary policy.

Taxation

Under the leadership of President Ronald Reagan in the 1980s, the United States finally began seriously paring back an income tax system that had been burdening the economy to varying degrees since the Great Depression. Other than some relief provided by the Kennedy tax cuts (advocated by President Kennedy and implemented after his death in 1964 and 1965), and a capital gains tax cut thrust upon an unwilling President Jimmy Carter by Congress in 1978, little was accomplished in the post-World War II era in terms of dismantling an ugly tax system erected during the confusion of economic depression and world war.

Indeed, war and depression do not foster an environment very conducive to clear economic thinking. The Great Depression itself was ignited and deepened in large part due to bad tax and tariff policies. For example, forward looking markets reacted badly to the Smoot-Hawley Tariff Act that was creeping its way through Congress in 1929. Unfortunately, politicians failed to get the message in October 1929, and Smoot-Hawley was signed into law by Republican President Herbert Hoover in 1930. Predictably, this dramatic increase in tariffs was met with retaliation by other nations, and world trade collapsed. Hoover later worsened matters with a dramatic hike in income taxes. His successor—Franklin Roosevelt—followed a similar course of draconian tax increases.

Meanwhile, the states compounded the misery. From 1929 to 1938, 19 states imposed personal income taxes where they previously had not existed, and 18 states instituted new corporate income taxes. For good measure, 24 states imposed sales taxes.

About a half-century later in the 1980s, however, Reagan signaled that change was finally possible. The top personal income tax rate, for example, declined from 70% to 28%, and the top corporate rate fell from 46% to 34% during Reagan's two terms.

Income tax reduction under Reagan was important for several reasons. Income levies had become the overwhelming source of revenues for government, so serious tax reduction meant that income taxes would have to be cut. Most importantly, income taxes have the clearest impact on the economy. Income taxes directly affect critical economic decisions. Under a high tax rate regime, incentives for working, saving, investing and risk taking—the engines of economic growth—are diminished. Cutting income tax rates means boosting pro-growth incentives. Indeed, each period of substantial income tax relief in the United States during the 20th century—the 1920s, the early-to-mid 1960s, and the 1980s—were also periods of robust economic growth.

Unfortunately, in the immediate years after Reagan left office, some of his progress was rolled back by Presidents George Bush (R) and Bill Clinton (D). The top personal income tax rate was increased to 39.6%, and the Medicare income tax of 2.9% was expanded to all income levels, so that the effective top income tax rate reached as high as 42.5% for many, in particular the self-employed. The corporate income tax rate was bumped up a percentage point as well, to 35%. No doubt, these tax increases in the early 1990s played a part in the below-average rate of economic growth experienced in the first half of the decade.

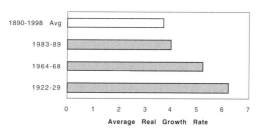

Average Annual Real Rates of Economic Growth During Key Periods of Income Tax Relief

It was not until 1997 that another pro-growth step was taken on the tax front at the federal level. The capital gains tax was reduced from 28% to 20% in 1981; but as part of the price to pay for lower personal income and corporate income tax rates under the 1986 Tax Reform Act, the top individual capital gains tax rate was pushed back up to 28%. In 1997, Congress finally got around to cutting the capital gains rate back to 20%. Economic growth pushed ahead of the post-war average in 1997, 1998, and 1999.

The "Entrepreneurial Revolution" of the next century mandates that the United States, and obviously other nations, establish the most pro-growth tax system possible. Taxes will always have a distorting effect on economic decisions and on the private marketplace in general. The key is to minimize the ill side effects of taxation as best one can.

Given the backlash from the Clinton White House and Democrats in Congress to the very minor Republican tax cut that emerged from Congress in 1999, it is clear that much work needs to be done. Indeed, the GOP tax package that President Clinton vetoed in September 1999 because it was deemed too "massive" and "risky" was, in reality, quite paltry. Its guess-timated 10-year size was $792 billion.

Given that the federal government would probably suck more than $25.5 trillion out of the private sector over that same period, the GOP tax plan was at most a 3% cut in a revenue base that would likely be rising by between 6% and 7% annually.

U.S. policy-makers need to put aside the assumption that the government has a right to ever increasing amounts of people's earnings and profits; leave behind class warfare arguments against tax relief; and focus on making the United States as hospitable as possible for working and investing.

A good first step would be the repeal of the Bush and Clinton tax increases, dropping the top personal income tax rate back to 28% and the corporate rate to 34%. Other immediate measures should be focused on making the United States a haven for growth-generating, job-creating, labor-empowering capital.

For example, the capital gains tax stands out as one of the most antientrepreneur, antijobs, antigrowth taxes ever imposed by man. Understanding that investment, entrepreneurship, innovation, invention, and creativity are the wellsprings of economic growth and job creation, then it becomes quite clear that taxing the returns on such high-risk endeavors—i.e., taxing capital gains—makes absolutely no economic sense.

In addition, capital gains taxes are simply another layer of government taxation. For example, after your salary is taxed, if you then decide to invest part of your take-home pay in a business venture, you face additional taxes at the business level, on any dividends you might earn, and then a capital gains tax when you decide to sell your share. This isn't merely double taxation, it can be triple or quadruple taxation. In contrast, if you decide instead to use all your take-home pay for consumption purposes, the federal government imposes no added taxes. This system is grossly skewed against saving and investment and in favor of consumption. From an economic growth standpoint, this makes no sense whatsoever.

Nonetheless, capital gains have been taxed for decades in the United States—at the federal, state, and even local levels.

In 1999, federal capital gains tax rates stood at 20% for individuals and 35% for corporations. Again, as noted earlier, real capital gains tax rates—i.e., factoring inflation into the equation—reach much higher. Since capital gains are not indexed for inflation, monetary policy plays a direct role in setting real capital gains tax rates at both the federal and state levels. Especially during years of lofty inflation—such as during World Wars I and II, and the 1970s into the early 1980s—real capital gains tax rates could easily top 100%, or individuals could even wind up paying taxes on real capital *losses*. Even during periods of fairly low inflation, the real capital gains tax rate can still climb by a considerable amount.

With capital becoming ever more mobile in our increasingly high-tech, information-based economy, the treatment of capital gains becomes ever more important on the international stage. In an August 1998 policy paper, the American Council for Capital Formation (ACCF) examined capital gains tax rates in 24 nations. The average top rate on individuals registered 15.9%, with nine countries exempting capital gains from taxation. The average corporate rate was 19.6%, with seven nations not taxing corporate capital gains. Also, Australia and the United Kingdom indexed asset costs for inflation for both individuals and corporations, and Chile indexed for corporations. U.S. federal rates come in higher than these 24-nation averages, and gains are not indexed for inflation.

Capital gain tax reductions in 1922, 1978, 1981, and 1997 helped to spur economic growth and job creation, not to mention the stock market. Indeed, these cuts helped set the stage for some of the most robust economic times during the 20th century.

A dynamic analysis of the potential economic impact of various proposals to reduce the federal capital gains tax paid by individuals was performed by Gary and Aldona Robbins for the Institute for Policy Innovation in 1994. (At the time, the top individual capital gains rate was 28%.) The Robbins found:

- Cutting the rate to 15% would add 0.21 percentage points to the long-term annual U.S. growth rate.
- Indexing capital gains retrospectively would add 0.31 percentage points to the long-term annual growth rate.
- Eliminating the capital gains tax would add 0.43 percentage points to the long-term annual growth rate.

In fact, the best capital gains tax policy is not to tax capital gains at all—at the federal, state, or local levels. A torrent of investment and entrepreneurship would be unleashed, pushing the United States ahead in terms of innovation, economic growth, and job creation.

Next in line are death taxes—i.e., estate, gift, and generation-skipping levies. After paying taxes over a lifetime of working, perhaps building a business, the government moves in at death to tax total assets. Indeed, death taxes amount to nothing more than a government hostile takeover of one's business and assets at death—and we mean hostile.

Federal estate tax rates range effectively from 37% up to 55% (plus an additional 5% on certain larger estates). Again, this is not 55% of income, but 55% of *all assets* in an estate.

Death taxes were once primarily a revenue source for state governments. From the late 18th century into the early 20th century, the federal government only imposed death taxes occasionally. However, some kind of federal death tax has been with us since 1916.

In 1998, estate and gift taxes accounted for a mere 1.4% of total federal government receipts. Death tax revenues have stayed within the range of 0.8% and 1.4% of total federal revenues for decades.

Still, for a tax that accounts for such a small share of federal revenues, it causes quite a bit of economic harm. Only in Washington, D.C., for example, could $24.1 billion collected in federal death taxes in 1998 be considered an insignificant number. Between 1988 and 1998, federal death tax revenues grew by 217%, compared with an 88% increase in total federal revenues during the same period. A good portion of death-tax revenues, though, are wasted by the federal government's death tax compliance efforts. Estimates range between 65% and 100% of federal estate and gift tax collections being offset by the costs of collection for the IRS and the Treasury Department, as well as litigation costs.

No sound economic reason exists to impose death taxes; they are purely the creation of government envy. When first imposed in 1916, the federal estate tax was targeted at the very rich, with rates ranging from 1% to 10%. Today, the estate tax takes hold at a very low threshold of total assets, and inflicts far more severe tax rates.

Death taxes stand as obstacles to investment and entrepreneurship. With 55% of a venture essentially slated for a government takeover, few incentives exist to further invest in or expand a family business after the owner reaches a certain age. Instead, every reason exists to sell the business before death to spare heirs the costs and burdens of wrestling with a hostile government takeover. Gordon Gekko has nothing on the tax man.

Still, large amounts of resources are wasted in efforts to avoid the death tax grim reaper. Accountants and lawyers are hired to explore ways to shield assets, and some individuals even purchase life insurance for the sole purpose of paying estate taxes. You know taxes are out of control when people are buying insurance to help deal with them. However, insurance is not cheap, and many can't afford it. As for those who can, insurance payments amount to money wasted that could otherwise be reinvested.

In addition, the U.S. imposes one of the heaviest death tax burdens in the world. Another recent study from the American Council for Capital Formation (ACCF) revealed that among the 24 nations reviewed, the average top death tax rate was 21.6%, compared with the top U.S. rate of 55%.

A host of economic studies have documented the real costs of death taxes to the economy in the United States. A 1993 study by the Center for the Study of Taxation, for example, estimated that under a no-estate-tax scenario, by the year 2000 gross domestic product (GDP) would have been $79.2 billion higher; 228,000 more jobs would have been created; and $630 billion more in savings and capital would have accumulated. A December 1998 study from the Joint Economic Committee, U.S. Congress, concluded: "The existence of the estate tax this century has reduced the stock of capital in the economy by approximately $497 billion, or 3.2 percent."

Obviously, U.S. competitiveness and growth would get a big boost if policy-makers killed death taxes.

Eliminating capital gains and death taxes, and rolling back the Bush and Clinton tax increases of the early 1990s would lay the groundwork for the United States to completely overhaul its tax system. Tax reform should focus on moving away from taxing production, and instead focus on imposing taxes at the final stage of the economic process—consumption. Taxes should be simple, clear, fair, and low.

Back in 1776, the father of modern economics, Adam Smith, spelled out the basics of a sound tax system in his landmark work, *An Inquiry into the Nature and Causes of the Wealth of Nations*. Smith wrote:

> I. The subjects of every state ought to contribute towards the support of the government, as nearly as possible, in proportion to their respective abilities; that is, in proportion to the revenue which they respectively enjoy under the protection of the state. . . .

> II. The tax which each individual is bound to pay ought to be certain, and not arbitrary. The time of payment, the manner of payment, the quantity to be paid, ought all to be clear and plain to the contributor, and to every other person.

> III. Every tax ought to be levied at the time, or in the manner, in which it is most likely to be convenient for the contributor to pay it.

> IV. Every tax ought to be so contrived as both to take out and to keep out of the pockets of the people as little as possible, over and above what it brings into the public treasury of the state. A tax may either take out or keep out the pockets of the people a great deal more than it brings into the public treasury, in the four following ways. First, the levying of it may require a great number of officers, whose salaries may eat up the greater part of the produce of the tax, and whose perquisites may impose another additional tax on the people. Secondly, it may obstruct the industry of the people, and discourage them from applying to certain branches of business which might give maintenance and employment

to great multitudes. While it obliges the people to pay, it may thus diminish, or perhaps destroy, some of the funds which might enable them more easily to do so. Thirdly, by the forfeitures and other penalties which those unfortunate individuals incur who attempt unsuccessfully to evade the tax, it may frequently ruin them, and thereby put an end to the benefit which the community might have received from the employment of their capitals. An injudicious tax offers a great temptation to smuggling. . . . Fourthly, by subjecting the people to the frequent visits and the odious examination of the taxgatherers, it may expose them to much unnecessary trouble, vexation, and oppression; and thought vexation is not, strictly speaking, expence, it is certainly equivalent to the expence at which every man would be willing to redeem himself from it." (Adam Smith; *An Inquiry into the Nature and Causes of the Wealth of Nations*, Volume I, The University of Chicago Press, 1976, page 351–352.)

A flat tax or a retail sales tax certainly would fit the bill. From the perspective of sound economics, unencumbered by politics, a flat tax of 10% sounds about right. After all, if the Lord doesn't ask for more than 10%, then why should government? Such a flat tax would work best if double taxation were eliminated by excluding dividends and capital gains from taxation.

Even better, the U.S. should cease taxing income altogether, and shift to a low retail sales tax. However, in order for such a levy not to become merely an add-on, in addition to income taxes, the 16th Amendment to the U.S. Constitution granting Congress the power to tax personal income would have to be repealed—no easy feat.

The effort though would be worth it! For example, during the post–Civil War period of 1871 to 1912, the United States imposed no personal income tax (a brief one appeared in the mid-1890s, but was quickly struck down as unconstitutional). During that time, the U.S. economy expanded by more than 460% in real terms, while consumer prices actually declined by almost 20%.

If the "Entrepreneurial Revolution" of the 21st century were allowed to break free from the income tax—which acts as high-octane fuel for government's expansion, while causing entrepreneurship and investment to sputter and stall—the economic benefits would be staggering.

Government Spending

Of course, efforts to eliminate various anti-entrepreneur taxes run into a brick wall when one looks at the spending side of the government equation. No matter *how* federal, state, and local governments drain between $2.6 trillion and $3 trillion from the private sector annually, it is not going to be pretty.

The spending numbers laid out above, as well as spelled out in the state chapters that follow, are not encouraging. Government was on a relentless rise throughout the 20th century. The economic pressures to downsize government in coming years, however, promise to intensify greatly.

Economist Richard Rahn has performed some of the most interesting and in-depth analyses of the size of government and its effect on economic growth. In 1986, while chief economist at the U.S. Chamber of Commerce, Rahn looked at the relationship between the total size of government and economic growth in 22 nations. It turns out that government maximized economic growth when it claimed between 15% and 25% of GDP. Today, government in the United States gobbles up more than 31% of GDP.

A more recent study by Rahn and Harrison W. Fox, Jr. ("What is the Optimum Size of Government?" a study sponsored by the Business Leadership Council and the Vernon K. Krieble Foundation) examined the relationship between economic growth and the size of central governments for 57 nations over the period of 1951 to 1993. Growth was maximized when the central government's share of GDP registered between 10% and 15%. The U.S. federal government alone captures about 20% of GDP.

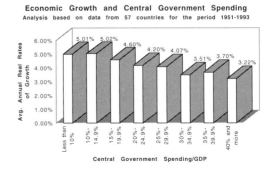

Economic Growth and Central Government Spending

Analysis based on data from 57 countries for the period 1951-1993

Rahn's numbers also reveal that the U.S. economy is grossly under-performing at its current level of central government spending. From 1990 to 1998, U.S. real annual economic growth averaged 2.5%, while Rahn's analysis shows annual average growth rates of 4.2% for nations with similar central government expenditure levels.

This raises additional questions about the size of state and local government in the United States, the overall tax structure, the regulatory environment, as well as the costs of an increasingly litigious society, including lawyers, the proliferation of frivolous lawsuits, less investment, and innovation by business due to the fear of lawsuits. Lavish awards represent a significant deadweight loss to the economy.

Rahn's analysis clearly supports the case for far smaller government than currently exists in the United States. For those with the political will to do so, the options for downsizing government are plentiful. Opportunities for privatization, competitive contracting, department and program eliminations abound at the federal, state, and local levels.

For example, the federal government could eliminate the Department of Education, and leave education issues where they are best handled—at the state and local levels. The federal government should also get out of the businesses of farming, subsidizing large and small businesses, guiding the energy market, subsidizing housing and failed government urban projects, dictating environmental polices better left to state and local governments or individuals, and providing handouts to other nations. These steps would mean that the Agriculture Department, the Commerce Department (leaving the Census Bureau to perform the Census each decade and act as the federal government's statistical service), the Small Business Administration, the Energy Department (moving nuclear programs under the Defense Department), the Department of Housing and Urban Development, the Environmental Protection Agency, and International Assistance programs could all be eliminated.

The Department of Labor could be cut drastically by leaving some labor issues—like training and employment services, welfare-to-work programs, community service employment for older Americans, and the Occupational Safety and Health Administration—to the states and the private sector. The Transportation Department also could be slashed by leaving road and highway spending to states and localities.

The Department of Health and Human Services also is ripe for savings. The federal government, for example, should truly change welfare as we know it by getting out of the welfare business altogether and leaving it either to the states or preferably to private charities. The out-of-control Medicare and

Medicaid programs should not be expanded, but instead phased out and replaced with health-care vouchers for the very poor and needy.

One of the federal government's most glitzy, high profile programs also is ready to fall during the "Entrepreneurial Revolution"—a venture that most assume must be run by the government, but as we look into the future will be better served by private-sector entrepreneurs. That venture is the National Aeronautics and Space Administration (NASA).

Tragically, NASA has become a big government bureaucracy—a huge jobs program for engineers and scientists—operating in a high-risk industry crying out for private-sector entrepreneurs and investors. Beating the Soviets to the moon in 1969 was, in effect, a military feat—a project of the Cold War. Apollo was a political project under which NASA shined. Today, space is about economics.

The record of NASA's failures is a substantial one, for example, most recently, the failed projects to Mars and the Hubble Telescope's faulty mirror, which was not discovered until placed in orbit. Failure permeates most of NASA.

The space shuttle—NASA's jewel—was originally billed as a workhorse shuttling man into orbit some 60 times a year. Instead, the shuttle turned out more like a fine antique, to be handled with great care and only used on occasion (about seven shuttle launches a year). NASA claimed the cost of each shuttle mission would drop to about $15 million with reusable spacecrafts and boosters. NASA now says each mission costs more than $400 million, with outside experts saying the total costs are far closer to $1 billion per mission.

NASA's other big project is the International Space Station. Originally, the space station was called "Freedom" by President Reagan and was to be built by the United States. The Clinton Administration changed its name to "Alpha," and invited the international space community in on the project. Instead of having one government bureaucracy trying to build a space station, the White House thought it best to get several government bureaucracies from around the globe—mainly Russians but 13 total participating nations—in on the project. What a surprise that cost overruns and delays have become the rule.

The space station project began in 1984, and it is now targeted to be completed in about 2002 or later. According to NASA chief Daniel Goldin testifying before Congress in early March 1997, $10 billion was spent on the space station between 1984 and 1993; an added $17.4 billion will be spent between 1994 and 2002; and international partners are kicking in another $10 billion. Then, a decade of operations will cost an estimated $13 billion, with international partners supposedly footing some of the bill. By the way, the original 1984 cost estimate for a space station was $8 billion to be completed by 1994.

A June 1997 Government Accounting Office report identified $291 million in added cost overruns on the space station, and estimated that it would cost $129 million to get production back on schedule, twice the original projection. Russia faces monumental troubles in each of the areas it is committed to for the space station.

NASA's other big project is the next generation of spacecrafts. As it did with the space shuttle, NASA is placing all of its eggs in one basket. And as it has long been prone to do, among the three major competitors seeking to work for NASA on a single-stage-to-orbit (SSTO) space vehicle (i.e., the spacecraft takes off and lands all in one piece, no throw-away booster rockets for example), NASA chose the grandest, most complex, least economical, and least tested of the lot, electing to skip on more proven technologies.

In *Halfway to Anywhere: Achieving America's Destiny in Space* (M. Evans and Company, Inc., New York, 1996), space and rocket expert and veteran G. Harry Stine debunks the myth that NASA and the major aerospace firms perpetuated, and which Congress and the White House accepted, i.e., that "space travel is so difficult, dangerous, and expensive that only the government can afford it." Stine counters: "Actually, space access was difficult, dangerous, and expensive because it was a government monopoly."

Stine has been preaching for some two decades that space entrepreneurs need to understand and speak the language of finance, not necessarily technology, in order to get investors on board. This radical thinking seems to be slowly spreading among those not shackled to NASA in the space community. Indeed, many entrepreneurs are looking to capitalize in space using private investor dollars rather than taxpayer dollars. The private sector is either leading or emerging in areas like satellites, reusable space vehicles, and launch facilities. Space promises additional opportunities for entrepreneurs, including manufacturing (crystals, drugs, and so forth), more satellite applications, as well as energy markets and even tourism (don't laugh—adventure, exploration, hotels, etc.). Private launch pads are being developed in California and other states. Speculation even seems to be growing that the international space station—if it ever gets built—should then be privatized. On September 22, 1999, the Associated Press's Michael White reported that Hilton Hotels Inc. "is looking into the feasibility of a space hotel."

It seems quite likely that NASA eventually will be left behind on the launch pad—probably within the decade relegated to what it does best, i.e., political stunts like sending John Glenn back into orbit—while entrepreneurs continue to launch and expand market-based ventures in space. Though the very existence of NASA and the potential that it could undercut private companies, not through efficiencies but with taxpayer subsidies, restrains the market some. NASA's continuing incompetence, cost overruns, and tight budgets will further whittle away confidence, and combine to restrain the space agency. Eventually, the only serious efforts by the U.S. government in space will be defense-related.

Many government-related questions, though, remain regarding boosting entrepreneurship and investment in space-based ventures, including these on regulations and property rights in space.

One positive step was taken with the passage of the Commercial Space Act in 1998. The key aspect of the Commercial Space Act allows the FAA to license reusable launch vehicles (RLVs). Previously, private industry could only launch vehicles into space, but then not fly them home. This change will help spur much-needed private-sector competition to NASA's government "eggs in one basket" mentality. In addition, the act instructed NASA to make preparations for the possible privatization of the space shuttle fleet. Other aspects include requiring NASA to report on the development of space commerce aboard the International Space Station, encouraging the government to purchase space data from private sources, and requiring the government to purchase space transportation services from the private sector under certain circumstances.

Four mindsets seem to dominate the space industry today: 1) the so-dangerous-only-the-government-can-do-it theory, 2) government should hire the private sector to do more, 3) space should be largely a private-sector venture with government providing basic research and testing of vehicles, etc., and 4) leave it all to the private sector. Right now, we are in between #1 and #3, and we may reach #4 in a decade or so.

Whether on earth or in the heavens, economics does not change. Government is generally wasteful; and provided with the right incentives, entrepreneurs will expand markets and services. Space will not be excluded from the 21st century "Entrepreneurial Revolution."

Social Security

Back on Earth, liberals, Democrats, Republicans, conservatives and even some libertarians are all agreed on one issue—to "save Social Security." While political unity reigns and Social Security remains incredibly popular politically, a closer look supports the assertion that the system actually has been a general failure.

For example, Social Security has been plagued by incessant tax increases. In 1937, the Social Security payroll tax registered 1% paid by employees and 1% paid by employers—for a total tax of 2%—and applied to the first $3,000 in earnings (that was equal to about $33,333 in 1997 dollars, for example). In 1999, the Social Security portion of the payroll tax registered 6.2% applied to both the employee and employer—for a total tax of 12.4%—applied to the first $72,600 in wages and salary. So, since its inception, the Social Security tax rate has risen by 520%, and the earnings threshold has more than doubled in real terms.

If the system proceeds unchanged, more tax hikes will be on the way. As Carrie Lips at the Cato Institute noted in a September 1998 report, "In order to make Social Security solvent in 2032, today's 12.4 percent payroll tax would have to be increased by nearly 50 percent, forcing tomorrow's workers to give up nearly one-fifth of their income just to pay for Social Security."

The number of workers per Social Security recipient tells part of the story. In 1950, there were 16 workers per recipient, with that ratio dropping to 5-to-1 in 1960, 3.3-to-1 in 1996, and is projected at 2-to-1 in 2030.

Meanwhile, after paying big dollars into the system, Social Security offers an abysmal rate of return for most workers. Economist Peter Ferrara of Americans for Tax Reform has estimated that younger workers see an annual real rate of return ranging between −0.45% and 2.13%. In a June 1998 report for the Center for the Study of American Business, economist David Henderson pegged the annual real rate of return on Social Security for an individual born in 1945 at 1.67%, for those born in 1960 at 1.39%, those in 1975 also at 1.39%, and for those born in 1990 at 1.43%. In a November 1996 report, Tax Foundation analyst Arthur Hall concluded that dual-income couples in their 30s and 40s today face annual real rates of return between −1.0% to −1.5%; those in their 20s drop below −1.5%; teenagers below −2.0%; and those born today between −2.5% and −3.0%.

Let's remember, Social Security is not a retirement or pension system, it is a government-imposed, Ponzi-like, inter-generational transfer system. Even the best measure for reforming Social Security will still amount to some form of government-forced savings—meaning that the system translates into a loss of freedom and a continuation of the Nanny State. Social Security clearly acts as a counter to individual responsibility and initiative, with incentives diminished for working, investing, and saving due to the system's high tax rates today and the promise of government support tomorrow.

For good measure, as economist Walter Williams noted in his syndicated column of November 11, 1998, Social Security has worked to break up the institution of the family. Williams observed: "Social Security and Medicare make it convenient for children to forget about their parents' physical and emotional needs." Father Robert Sirico of the Acton Institute for the Study of Religion and Liberty, also noted in the May 20, 1996 issue of *Forbes:* "Thanks to programs like Social Security, children and the extended family have lost much of their economic value. Once there was an implied contract between generations. Parents would take care of helpless children, who, in turn, would take care of the parents when the parents could no longer earn a living . . . Today many parents are horrified at the idea of relying on their children, and the children, even in times of dire need, often resent having to help parents."

Let the government do it." Sirico concluded: "Without Social Security, the young would again be reminded of their obligation to repay the debt they owe to their parents. We would plan for our futures rather than rely on coerced obligation and government programs."

None of these system failures are the reason for an enhanced willingness on the part of politicians to tinker with Social Security. So-called "bankruptcy" of the system looms in the not-too-distant future (as if a government program could actually ever go "bankrupt"). The Social Security Administration projects that the system will begin running annual deficits in 2013, with insolvency occurring in about 2032. After 2032, payroll taxes would cover about 75% of benefits to be paid out.

It is critical that Social Security reforms redress the system's numerous failures. Obviously, lifting the earnings cap and/or increasing payroll tax rates would only make matters worse. Other proposals to have the government invest funds in the private marketplace in order to increase rates of return—whether for the system as it currently exists or for some form of individual accounts—is downright scary. The potential for political mischief in terms of how companies would be run, and where they could invest and do business is painfully apparent. The federal government, in effect, would become the nation's largest shareholder. If reform allows the federal government to become as shareholder, then reform should be rejected out of hand.

If Social Security must continue to exist, then it must be transformed into an individually-controlled savings/investment system of personal retirement accounts. Rates of return would get a big boost, as would individuals' retirement nest eggs. The economy also would likely experience a positive impact, as added capital in the private sector would boost entrepreneurship, economic growth, and job creation.

Transition costs remain a major question when it comes to shifting from the current system to individual retirement accounts. A combination of asset sales, spending reductions, and bonds would probably work best, and faster economic growth also would ease transition costs.

Health Care

In a recent online column written by one of us for the Small Business Survival Committee's website (www.sbsc.org), the "Hundred Years War" that periodically raged between France and England from 1337 to 1453 was compared to today's battle over health care in Washington, D.C. Like that war, one has to wonder if the health-care issue will ever be resolved.

Though there had been several skirmishes since the 1930s, the official start of Washington's health-care war was in the mid-1960s, with the passage of Medicare and Medicaid. Both programs have since become enormously expensive resulting in higher taxes, greater reliance on government, and ever increasing health-care costs.

Periodic battles ensued, until a massive offensive in favor of socialized medicine was undertaken by President Clinton and the First Lady in 1993 and 1994, which was amazingly fought back and at least temporarily defeated.

However, while that battle was won, the war plodded on. Those defending against the expansion of government in health care are still slowly but consistently losing ground. Even though opposition to socialized medicine played a major role in the GOP gaining a majority in the House of Representatives in the November 1994 elections, Republicans are on the defensive when it comes to health care, and have been retreating bit by bit in the fight against expanded health-care programs and more mandates and regulations.

Of course, real market-based reforms present appealing and economically sound alternatives to big government health care. Key measures include the expansion of tax-free medical savings accounts (MSAs), and 100% tax deductibility for health-care expenditures by the self-employed and individuals, placing such spending on par with employer-provided health plans.

Tax-free MSAs were established as a pilot program in 1996. Unfortunately, all sorts of restrictions were placed on them. As we went to press, the number of MSA policies were capped at 750,000 and the pilot program was due to expire on December 31, 2000. They were only available to the self-employed or to businesses with 50 or fewer employees. Deductibles could not be lower than $1,500 for individuals and $3,000 for families, and tax-free deposits into MSAs were limited to 65% of the deductible for individuals and 75% for families. In addition, either the employee or the employer could contribute to an MSA, but not both.

Lifting restrictions on MSAs would create a powerful choice for consumers in the marketplace. And that is the key to improving our health-care system and controlling costs, i.e., more competition and choice.

MSAs, tied to catastrophic insurance plans, allow individuals to make their own health-care decisions with their doctors. Unlike today's predominant third-party payer system (i.e., when government or an employer-provided health plan pays the bills), with MSAs both the patient and the doctor possess incentives to be concerned about costs, since individuals can build up savings. Also, with accompanying catastrophic insurance, individuals and families would be covered when catastrophe and big medical bills hit.

MSA expansion, 100% tax deductibility, and deregulation are the obvious counter-measures to the advancement of big government health care. More government involvement and mandates will only increase costs, boost the number of uninsured, and ration care.

Regulations

The costs of government regulation are more often than not hidden from the view of consumers and voters. Unless you are running your own business, and have to deal with government regulators and the accompanying fines and paperwork, regulations often seem remote. Indeed, to many people, more regulation can sound downright appealing. However, the costs of government regulations and mandates in terms of lost resources, lost jobs, and lost economic growth are quite real. The minimum wage and proposed regulations to battle so-called global warming serve as two prominent examples.

Increasing the minimum wage often holds considerable political appeal, with politicians able to posture themselves as caring and compassionate by expanding government's reach into the workplace without, for example, overtly hiking taxes. Meanwhile, many workers see a minimum wage increase as getting something for nothing.

But make no mistake, like other regulations, the minimum wage has much the same impact as a tax. Some businesses can avoid paying this tax by not hiring young, inexperienced employees. Sometimes automation, outsourcing, or hiring more experienced and productive workers are viable options. Of course, with each choice comes increased costs, as government forces businesses to do something they otherwise wouldn't.

Many labor-intensive businesses, though, simply cannot avoid the direct costs of a minimum wage hike. A minimum wage increase can mean staff cutbacks, fewer work hours, reduced pay or benefits for other employees, canceling expansion plans, or even closing up shop.

Minimum wage supporters, however, have argued that the minimum wage was increased from $4.25 to $4.75 in October 1996 and then to $5.15 in September 1997, and the unemployment rate fell from 5.6% in 1995 to 4.5% in 1998. Therefore, the minimum wage does not hurt employment. The minimum wage, however, impacts a small group of individuals—such as teenagers, welfare recipients, and inner city residents—so the effect is not always evident in economy-wide measures of unemployment. Instead, the impact is seen among select groups.

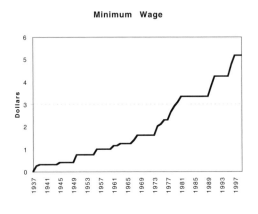

The Reagan years of 1982 through 1989 represent the longest period without an increase in the minimum wage since its inception in 1938. Those eight years saw impressive gains made in terms of the unemployment rates—for teenagers dropping from 23.2% to 15%, for blacks from 18.9% to 11.4%; and for single mothers from 11.7% to 8.1%. In contrast, minimum wage increases in 1990, 1991, 1996, and 1997 put the brakes on such improvements, with the unemployment rates averaging 17.6% for teenagers, 11.7% for blacks, and 8.8% for single mothers over this period.

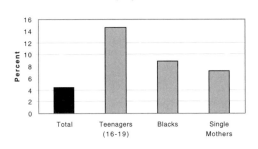

Practically all evaluations of the minimum wage show that it adversely affects employment. For example, a 1995 study for the Employment Policies Institute Foundation, Michigan State University Professor David Neumark found that higher minimum wages "have significant negative effects on the employment prospects of less-skilled teens, losses which are masked by their replacement in the work force by more highly skilled teens," and that minimum wage increases "are associated with an earlier age for leaving school."

As the Census Bureau notes, almost all low-wage workers move up the income ladder in about two years. However, if the first rung is removed due to the minimum wage, then low-skilled workers never get the work experience needed to eventually boost their earnings.

Battling global warming is another issue that at first glance might sound great to many people. After years of negotiating, in late 1997 in Kyoto, Japan, the Clinton Administration signed on to the United Nations treaty on global warming, which would oblige the United States to reduce so-called greenhouse gas emissions—mainly carbon-dioxide (CO2)—to 7% below 1990 levels by 2012. Developing nations, including behemoths like China and India, would be excluded from Kyoto dictates to reduce emissions. As this book went to press, President Clinton had not yet sent the Kyoto treaty to the U.S. Senate for ratification. Senate opposition was quite strong given the significant costs involved in meeting the Kyoto targets. Meanwhile, the very existence of global warming itself is, at best, highly questionable.

For example, according to ground-level measurements, the Earth's average temperature has increased by 0.5°C over the past 100 years, with most of that increase occurring before 1940. Meanwhile, satellite measurements indicate no warming trend over the past two decades.

There is little scientific agreement that global warming is happening largely due to mankind's activities. In the December 15, 1997 issue of *Insight* magazine, for example, reporter Jennifer Hickey noted the following:

- Only 13 percent of scientists polled by Greenpeace believe that there will be catastrophic consequences if consumption remains at present levels.
- A Gallup Poll of members of the American Geophysical Society and the Meteorological Society found that just 17% believe that greenhouse-gas emissions have been responsible for global warming.
- Citizens for a Sound Economy found that 89% of the scientists they polled agreed that "current science is unable to isolate and measure variations in global temperatures" caused by humans.
- The United Nations' Climate Change Bulletin surveyed 400 climate scientists and found they could not agree that "global warming is a process that is already under way."

S. Fred Singer, an atmospheric physicist and president of the Science & Environmental Policy Project, reported in the May 5, 1998 *Washington Times* ("Scientists Add to Heat Over Global Warming"):

> The Global Warming Treaty and its shaky science are under attack by the largest group of scientists ever. A petition, initiated by the Oregon Institute of Science and Medicine and endorsed by more than 15,000 scientists, urges President Clinton not to sign the Climate protocol negotiated in Kyoto, Japan, last December. . . . The 15,000-plus signers, about two-thirds of whom hold advanced academic degrees, question the uncertain science underlying the protocol, noting it does not agree with atmospheric data.

Singer goes on to also note how some top proponents of global warming—including the National Academy of Sciences—were warning in the 1970s of a drastic cooling of earth temperatures.

Writing in the *Wall Street Journal* on December 4, 1997, Arthur Robinson and Zachary Robinson, chemists at the Oregon Institute of Science and Medicine, simply declared:

> The global warming hypothesis . . . is no longer tenable. Scientists have been able to test it carefully, and it does not hold up. During the past 50 years, as atmospheric carbon dioxide levels have risen, scientists have made precise measurements of atmospheric temperature. These measurements have definitively shown that major atmospheric greenhouse warming of the atmosphere is not occurring and is unlikely ever to occur. The temperature of the atmosphere fluctuates over a wide range, the result of solar activity and other influences. During the past 3,000 years, there have been five extended periods when it was distinctly warmer than today. One of the two coldest periods, known as the Little Ice Age, occurred 300 years ago. Atmospheric temperatures have been rising from that low for the past 300 years, but remain below the 3,000-year average.

Despite many questions regarding the global warming theory, there are few doubts about the costs if the United States decides to meet the goals of Kyoto:

- WEFA (formerly Wharton Economic Forecasting Associates) analyzed the potential economic impact of reducing U.S. carbon emissions to 1990 levels by 2010. They found that lost GDP, just in the year 2010, would equal $227 billion (in 1992 dollars).

  Steep price increases would be felt by both consumers and businesses. For example, consumers would face price increases of 55% on home heating oil by 2010, and 79% by 2020; 50% on natural gas by 2010, and 79% by 2020; 48% on electricity by 2010, and 71% by 2020; 36% on motor gasoline by 2010, and 65% by 2020 (translating to an additional 44 cents per gallon by 2010, and 65 cents by 2020).

  Commercial establishments would see price hikes of 74% on distillate fuel oil by 2010, and 106% by 2020; 58% on natural gas by 2010, and 90% by 2020; 52% on electricity by 2010, and 77% by 2020. Industrial facilities would witness price increases of 139% on residual fuel oil by 2010, and 200% by 2020; 91% on natural gas by 2010, and 132% by 2020; and 73% on electricity by 2010, and 101% by 2020. Trucking and rail would see a 42% increase in the price of diesel by 2010, and 61% by 2020 (translating into 51 cents per gallon by 2010, and 76 cents by 2020).
- A May 1998 report by CONSAD Research Corporation ("The Kyoto Protocol: A Flawed Treaty Puts America at Risk") estimated that the Kyoto Protocol would devastate the U.S. economy. By 2010, employment losses would range between 1.6 million and 3.1 million. Lost output in 2010 would register between $178 billion and $316 billion (in 1995 dollars).
- In March 1998, the American Petroleum Institute (API) released a blunt and alarming report assessing the costs of reaching the Kyoto treaty's goal of reducing U.S. "greenhouse gas" emissions. API senior economist Ronald A. Sutherland noted in "Achieving the Kyoto Protocol: An Analysis of Policy Options," "If the U.S. were to achieve this target by the year 2010, carbon emission would have to decline by 2.32 percent per year from the year 2000, instead of increasing by 1.5 percent per year as in the [Energy Information Administration's] Reference Case projection."

  The author illustrated that altering the carbon/energy ratio or the development of new technologies will not come close to being enough to reduce carbon emissions. Indeed, continued economic growth and capital stock renewal will ensure that carbon levels continue rising. The author noted only two avenues that will allow the U.S. to meet its Kyoto goals: "A decline in GDP of about 4 percent per year would reduce the demand for energy and thereby carbon emissions sufficient to achieve the Kyoto target. Alternatively, an increase in the price of energy of about 12 percent per year for a ten year period also would achieve the Kyoto target."

- A DRI-McGraw Hill study by Dr. Lawrence Horowitz found that a $100 per ton carbon tax could lower emission levels close to 1990 levels by 2010 and would cost the economy $203 billion annually in lost output; while a $200 per ton carbon tax would be required to reduce emissions below 1990 levels, and would cost the economy $350 billion in lost products and services. Annual job losses from 1995 to 2010 under a $100 per ton carbon tax would hit 520,000, and would leap to 1.1 million annually under a $200 per ton carbon tax.

- The U.S. Department of Energy had the Argonne National Laboratory perform a study on the Kyoto treaty then under consideration. In February 1997, the study found that it would cause 20% to 30% of the basic chemical industry to move to developing countries within 15 or 20 years; all primary aluminum smelters to close by 2010; a 30% decline in the number of steel producers at a cost of 100,000 jobs; domestic paper production to be displaced by imports; a 20% reduction in the output of petroleum refiners; and the closing of between 23% and 35% of the cement industry, which is significant because many cement plants are major employers in small communities.

- Frederick H. Reuter noted in his study for the Center for the Study of American Business ("Framing a Coherent Climate Change Policy," October 1997) that "estimates from standard, multi-industry econometric models indicate that stabilizing annual CO_2 emissions at their 1990 levels by 2010 will reduce GDP by 0.2 to 0.7 percent and will decrease total employment by 900,000" by 2005. In addition, Reuter found: "Although the proposed economic incentive mechanisms would encourage firms to undertake pertinent technological research and development, they also would reduce firms' net revenues. The decline in net revenues would diminish firms' ability to fund research, development, and implementation of new technologies. Thus, on balance, the economic incentive mechanisms may impede crucial technological advancement instead of stimulating it."

- A 1997 study by Gary W. Yohe for the American Council for Capital Formation found that reducing CO_2 emissions to 1990 levels by 2010 would cause a 1% cut in the nation's annual rate of GDP growth rate; cut real annual wages and income by 5%; reduce fuel oil/coal consumption by 25% overall; cut electricity consumption by 20% overall; and reduce vehicle purchases by 3% overall.

- The American Farm Bureau reported that as a result of implementing Kyoto: "Total annual U.S. farm production expenses would rise over $10 billion under the low energy price scenario and more than $20 billion under the high energy price scenario. Given that U.S. net farm income has averaged $42.7 billion per year over the 1991 to 1995 period, this would represent a 24% and 48% decrease in the net farm income under the respective low/high energy price scenarios."

- In a report for the Center for the Study of American Business, Christopher Douglass and Murray Weidenbaum noted the following possible perverse effects from a global warming treaty that excludes developing nations ("The Quiet Reversal of U.S. Global Climate Change Policy," November 1996):

  Whichever means of curtailing carbon emissions is used, limiting emissions will degrade living standards. Moreover, if a carbon tax fell solely on industrialized nations and not on developing nations, as is currently the plan in every protocol before the Framework Convention, total worldwide greenhouse gas emissions would be likely to rise, not fall. If emission reduction standards become law in industrialized nations, total consumption of carbon-emitting goods will fall. Thus, the price of goods such as oil is likely to substantially decline on the world market. However, the lower prices of these goods would encourage poorer developing countries—with much less fuel efficient technology—to increase their use of fossil fuels, resulting in a net increase in greenhouse gas emissions.

Most other regulations present the same problem, i.e., the costs are quite real but often hidden, while the results range from dubious to dismal.

Monetary Policy

Since 1987, careers have been made and lost trying to figure out how exactly Alan Greenspan runs U.S. monetary policy. Over the years Greenspan has said so many different things regarding monetary policy that one is able to find anything one wants in his ruminations.

Greenspan is a supply-side, monetarist, Keynesian Fed chairman. For supply-siders, he has spoken at times of using the price of gold as a guide to monetary policy. On occasion, one hears traces of monetarism, and then there is the Keynesian Greenspan. "Keynesian Greenspan?" you ask. Indeed. Note some of his remarks in a speech in early May 1999:

> Subdued inflation, of course, has resulted, in part, from the sharp fall in oil prices from mid-1997 through early this year.

> The rapid increase in aggregate demand has generated growth of employment in excess of the growth in population, causing the number of potential workers to fall since the mid-1990s at a rate of a bit under one million annually. We cannot judge with precision how far this level can decline without sparking upward pressures on wages and prices.

> At some point, labor market conditions can become so tight that the rise in nominal wages will start increasingly outpacing the gains in labor productivity, and prices inevitably will then eventually begin to accelerate.

Such declarations illustrate some troubling weaknesses found in Keynesian economics:

1. Keynesians confuse changes in relative prices and changes in the general price level. Relative price changes, for example, in labor markets and energy markets, occur all the time. Only if the Fed responds to such changes by pushing money supply growth ahead of money demand can inflation, or a rise in the general price level, result. Greenspan's above declarations seemed to illustrate confusion on this fundamental economic point.
2. Keynesians confuse the causes and effects of monetary policy, i.e., they fail to grasp that excessive monetary policy boosts inflation expectations, which translate into increases in prices across the board. Greenspan's statements indicated that he may have tossed this equation out the window.

3. And of course, Keynesians have been completely co-opted by Phillips Curve thinking, i.e., that a trade-off exists between inflation and employment or economic growth. Greenspan seemed quite sympathetic to Phillips Curve thinking in these and, at times, other remarks.

4. Keynesians talk about macroeconomic "aggregate demand," while the rest of us understand that all economics is microeconomics (i.e., the study of decision-making at the individual and business firm levels). Coming from a Randian/Austrian economics background, Greenspan should know better.

Other Greenspan monetary statements seemed to carry half-truths, such as: "A pickup in the growth of labor productivity—beyond the effects of the business cycle—appears to have been an essential factor behind the slowing in inflation." No doubt, rising productivity makes the Fed's job far easier, but even rising productivity cannot completely negate inflationary monetary policy. Again, the Fed is the catalyst when it comes to changes in the general price level.

In this same speech, on the other hand, Greenspan occasionally reverted to near perfect monetary clarity, such as:

> The process of price containment has doubtless become, to some extent, self-reinforcing. Lower inflation in recent years has altered expectations. Workers no longer believe that large gains in nominal wages are needed to reap respectable increases in real wages.

> Over the long run, of course, the actions of the central bank determine the degree of over-all liquidity and, hence, the rate of inflation.

As always, a little bit for everybody.

Of course, some would like to argue that these particular Greenspan ruminations were in part a political ploy. A Greenspan pessimist might say that he was merely continuing the Fed's long-time policy of meticulously linking inflation with anything but Fed monetary policy, in order to place blame elsewhere when matters go awry.

In contrast, Greenspan optimists would say that the Fed Chairman was saying one thing for general consumption by subscribers to the still prevailing Keynesian monetary orthodoxy, but then actually carries out monetary policy in a more sound, supply-side method. If that were the case, however, one has to wonder what good the Fed Chairman was accomplishing with such a deception. After all, if he were really running a supply-side monetary policy purely driven by forward looking market signals, like the price of gold and long-term interest rates, then why not state that quite clearly, and with its commensurate success perhaps erase the Phillips Curve for good? Why run a stealth supply-side monetary policy?

Greenspan has made a fascinating journey from a Big Band musician to a free-market Randian to the consummate Washington political insider and the most successful Fed chairman in the post-gold era. His statements on non-monetary affairs are stated clearly and remain generally consistent with a free-market outlook (though faltering on occasion), such as his regular call to eliminate the capital gains tax. In fact, his description of recent leaps in the economy during this May 1999 speech verged on visionary, and is worth quoting extensively:

> The evident acceleration of the process of 'creative destruction,' which has accompanied these expanding opportunities and which has been reflected in the shifting of capital from

failing technologies into those technologies at the cutting edge, has been remarkable. Owing to advancing information capabilities and the resulting emergence of more accurate price signals and less costly price discovery, market participants have been able to detect and to respond to finely calibrated nuances in consumer demand. The process of capital reallocation has been assisted through a significant unbundling of risks made possible by the development of innovative financial products, not previously available. The proliferation of products of all different designs and qualities has opened up the potential for the satisfaction of consumer needs not evident even twenty years ago.

Unfortunately, the same cannot be said for his statements regarding monetary policy. Given his rather stellar monetary performance since the early 1990s, one would have hoped that he could be clearer as to exactly how the Fed has been running monetary policy recently, so that the post-Greenspan Fed may benefit accordingly. Alas, that has not happened, either because Greenspan sees some hidden benefits to being cryptic about Fed policy, or because he has largely been running monetary policy by feel, moving from one set of indicators to another as he personally deems appropriate. That is, either he won't or he can't provide clear monetary lessons—and either way that does not bode very well for the post-Greenspan era, whenever that may come.

In a May 1999 *New York Times* editorial, Floyd Norris wrote: "Much of the world is now quite happy to accept the idea that a greenback backed by Alan Greenspan is just as good as one backed by gold." He then went on to argue that monetary authorities no longer see any benefits of gold as a hedge against inflation. Of course, in the current low-inflation environment, it should not be all that surprising to witness such short-term thinking by government appointees. Norris concluded that the so-called "de-monetization" of gold would push gold prices lower, but then he sagely warned: "That could change if it turns out the central bankers are not the geniuses they are now deemed to be."

Looking ahead, Greenspan will hopefully continue his thus-far successful, if mystic, method of running monetary policy, and perhaps have time to pass on his sage ways to some monetary apprentices.

At the same time, let's all hope that the Keynesian Greenspan gives way to the supply-side Greenspan when it comes to actually making decisions about monetary policy in the coming months. Market signals in mid-to-late 1999 indicated that risks on the Fed front point to monetary policy being far too tight, not too loose.

Gold, of course, has always been unique in serving as the most sensitive signal of inflation expectations. Obviously, with gold on a steady, rather steep decline from early 1996 to late 1999 (as noted in the accompanying chart), inflation did not seem to be any kind of threat. Since the Fed runs monetary policy by setting short-term interest rates (e.g., the fed funds rate), it seems pretty clear that in early 1997, the Greenspan Fed broke with its gold price rule as the fed funds rate remained at lofty levels compared with where the price of gold and inflation expectations indicated it should be. Previously, from the very late 1980s to 1997, the Greenspan Fed seemed to follow gold quite closely.

The second chart shows the long decline since late 1987 in long-term interest rates. A comparison of long-term interest rates with the fed funds rate reinforces the idea that Fed policy is far too tight. Indeed, the latest increase in long-term rates on the chart could be attributed to monetary policy failing to meet monetary demand, not to rising inflation expectations.

Again, Greenspan's great failure has been his inability or unwillingness to leave a monetary policy legacy. No one knows why he does what he does. Indeed, at any moment, he might turn back to gold and get things back on track. But as this book went to press, it seemed that Greenspan was misguided and too tight.

The Greenspan mystery, and the rather pathetic performance by most previous Federal Reserve chairmen since the mid 1960s, support the idea that the dollar should be anchored once again to gold. A price target range for gold would probably work well.

The Greenspan Years 1987-1999:
Price of Gold vs. Fed Funds Rate

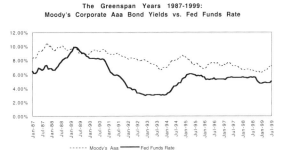

The Greenspan Years 1987-1999:
Moody's Corporate Aaa Bond Yields vs. Fed Funds Rate

In fact, in an increasingly integrated global economy, most nations would do well to link their currencies to gold, which would create a *de facto* world currency that would eliminate exchange rate and currency risks which can encumber international trade and business. After all, California, Oregon, and New York do not do business with different currencies, nor should the United States, Japan, and El Salvador in the coming century. Gold as the *de facto* world currency would allow individuals and businesses of all sizes to more easily do business around the globe, and obviously would squeeze inflation and devaluation risks out of global interest rates as well.

Trade

Throughout this book, a consistent theme is that the world is getting ever smaller, and individuals are increasingly able to buy and sell products and services around the world. Thus, understanding international trade and what trade policies work best is imperative.

Reducing trade barriers will help foster the expansion of markets, opportunity, and economic growth, while increasing choice and competition and reducing prices for consumers. Amazingly, few serious economists dispute the benefits of free trade. Politics, of course, is a different story, as it often does not take very much to push politicians into the protectionist camp.

Protectionists regularly hurl all sorts of unsubstantiated and just plain wrong accusations about trade into the policy arena. For example, they assert that free trade reduces wages and kills jobs in the United States. As mentioned earlier, trade deficits are considered inherently bad and it is suggested that they only result from free trade policies. Meanwhile, protectionists rarely address the fact that the policies they advocate, like higher tariffs and quotas, will raise costs and reduce choices for consumers, and kill export jobs as other nations retaliate. Again, the 1930s serve as a clear example of the dire ills of protectionism.

Interestingly, while perhaps diminished in total numbers in recent years, the protectionist camp has grown more diverse. Labor unions seem to have given up on the idea that their own membership can compete globally. They have been joined by environmentalists, who stand opposed to most measures that will help foster trade and commerce. Ross Perot and much of the Reform Party took up the protectionist cause, joined by former conservative commentator and now perpetual presidential candidate Pat Buchanan. It is no wonder that as this book went to press, Buchanan was seriously considering a run for the Reform Party presidential nod in 2000.

As laid out in his 1998 book, *The Great Betrayal*, Buchanan once was a proponent of free trade; but after hearing about and seeing some folks lose their jobs, he blamed it all on free trade and imports. Ever since, Buchanan has adopted the protectionist cause with the zeal of a convert. Unfortunately, while Buchanan is an entertaining commentator, he is not much of an economist.

It certainly is worth a moment to review the basic economics and benefits of free trade. Prior to the publication of Adam Smith's *An Inquiry into the Nature and Causes of the Wealth of Nations* in 1776, mercantilism reigned as the dominant school of thought on trade. Mercantilism essentially called for protectionist measures so that a nation could accrue large reserves of gold and silver, which was to be accomplished by encouraging exports and discouraging imports. The balance of trade was what mattered to mercantilists in the 18th century, as well as to today's mercantilists at the dawn of the 21st century.

Smith exposed and obliterated the myths of mercantilism. He wrote:

> Nothing, however, can be more absurd than this whole doctrine of the balance of trade, upon which, not only these restraints, but almost all other regulations of commerce are founded. When two places trade with one another, this doctrine supposes that if the balance be even neither of them either loses or gains; but if it leans in any degree to one side, that one of them loses, and the other gains in proportion to its declension from the exact equilibrium. Both suppositions are false . . . But that trade which, without force or constraint, is naturally and regularly carried on between any two places, is always advantageous, though not always equally so, to both.

Smith looked at the real world and saw the benefits of trade: "Every town and country . . . in proportion as they have opened their ports to all nations, instead of being ruined by this free trade, . . . have been enriched by it." Ultimately, Smith explained the benefits of trade through the concept of "absolute advantage":

> If a foreign country can supply us with a commodity cheaper than we ourselves can make it, better buy it from them with some part of the produce of our own industry, employed in a way in which we have some advantage.

However, early 19th century economist David Ricardo moved beyond "absolute advantage" to "comparative advantage." Some say the concept of comparative advantage is difficult to grasp, but it actually is quite simple. It merely shows that countries, businesses and individuals boost economic prosperity by producing the goods and services they are most efficient at producing, and then trading to acquire the other goods and services they need and want. Even if one holds an absolute advantage in a variety of areas, focusing on the endeavor where comparative advantage exists (i.e., where efficiency is maximized) and then trading with others, creates widespread prosperity. Economist Robert Eisner provided two current-day examples in the October 13, 1997 *Wall Street Journal:*

> Consider a couple of modern applications of Ricardo's wisdom: Michael Jordan may be able to mow a lawn faster than any gardener, but it is best for him to pass up lawn care and stick to basketball. Similarly, the U.S. may well be more productive than other countries in textiles as well as aircraft production, but it would do better to import those cheap shirts from China and ease the way for Boeing to export its planes all over the world.

In addition, when it comes to concerns regarding trade deficits, a simple economic truth espoused by another early 19th century classical economist, Jean-Baptiste Say, should be recalled. In his *Treatise on Political Economy,* Say observed that "products are always bought ultimately with products." Therefore, rising imports must mean rising production at home.

From these basic notions, it becomes clear that lower trade barriers mean more competition and rivalry, increased economic opportunity globally, and big benefits for consumers. Obviously, a more efficient allocation of resources, opening of new markets, increased competition, lower prices, and enhanced innovation and entrepreneurship resulting from free trade boost economic growth and job creation.

In the end, though, free trade is about freedom—allowing entrepreneurs and consumers to trade with whomever they choose and to pursue opportunities around the globe.

While trade's growing impact on the U.S. economy has already been touched upon, consider how much of U.S. economic growth from 1990 to 1998 can be accounted for by increased trade. In real 1992 dollars, U.S. GDP expanded from $6,136.3 billion in 1990 to $7,551.9 billion in 1998, an increase of $1,415.6 billion or 23%. Meanwhile, real U.S. exports rose from $564.4 billion in 1990 to $984.7 billion in 1998, an increase of $420.3 billion or 74%. Real imports jumped from $626.3 billion in 1990 to $1,222.9 billion in 1998, an increase of $596.6 billion or 95%.

Taking exports and imports together, a stunning 72% of U.S. economic growth from 1990 to 1998 was tied directly to international trade. Some would mistakenly argue that imports should not be included in this measurement, since, in calculating GDP, imports are subtracted out, and only net exports are counted. However, this is done only to avoid double counting. It is not that imports do not count or are a negative to the economy, it simply means imports are captured in other measures factoring into GDP.

In addition, businesses of all sizes are benefiting from expanded trade. The global marketplace is no longer the exclusive domain of large multinationals. For example, according to the U.S. Department of Commerce (August 1997), companies with fewer than 500 employees accounted for almost 30% of export value in 1992, and 96% of all exporters. Firms with fewer than 20 employees accounted for about one-third of exporting manufacturers, 75% of wholesalers, and 72% falling under the category "other companies." Meanwhile, *Investor's Business Daily* reported on February 26, 1997 that while 1 in 10 manufacturers with fewer than 100 employees exported in 1987, that number leaped to about 1 in 5 by 1992. Finally, the U.S. Small Business Administration has noted that 86% of U.S. businesses involved in international trade are wholesalers and other intermediaries, and those businesses are typically small.

With such enormous, widespread opportunities resulting from international trade, the most vision-ary step U.S. policy-makers could take would be unilateral reductions in U.S. trade barriers. Political reality, however, probably dictates something short of that, i.e., negotiating at every opportunity—with other nations, groups of nations, and international bodies—to lower trade barriers.

Granting the President of the United States fast-track trade negotiating authority is then critical. Fast track allows the President to negotiate trade accords, with Congress limiting itself to a "yes" or "no" vote in the end, thereby avoiding the big temptation to tack on changes or limitations at the behest of special interests. Narrowly focused special interests have long been the main obstacle to reap-ing the full benefits of free trade.

Education

Obviously, trade is not the only public policy issue touched upon by special interests. Education, unfortunately, is being smothered by the teachers' unions in the United States.

Of course, the public school education establishment stands united in opposition to all efforts to crack open and eventually topple their virtual monopoly on our children's education. Public schools and associated unions do not like the common sense idea of allowing parents to choose the schools their children attend, with the obvious effect of injecting competition into primary and secondary edu-cation, pushing forward quality improvements, and increasing student/parent satisfaction. Instead, the education establishment wants to protect their turf—no matter what the costs incurred by children.

Nonetheless, school choice is a mighty force, and is actually expanding. According to the Heritage Foundation's *School Choice 1999* publication, written by Nina Shokraii Rees and Sarah E. Youssef:

- Twenty-nine states have some degree of public school choice;
- Thirty-five states have some kind of charter school law in place—including 23 states classified as having medium to strong laws in favor of charters;
- Two cities have publicly sponsored full school choice program;
- Two states have publicly sponsored full school choice programs (now three states, with the addition of Florida);
- Three states have education tax deductions/credits.

As noted in the chapter on Ohio later in this book, a 1999 study performed by Harvard University's Program on Education Policy and Governance reported on a survey undertaken regarding Ohio's pilot school choice program in Cleveland. This survey showed that parents with children in choice schools were far more satisfied when it came to academic performance, school safety, and school discipline, when compared with public school parents.

The most exciting and radical idea on the choice front, though, is home schooling. In the July/August issue of the Heartland Institute's "Intellectual Ammunition," George Clows, editor of *School Reform News*, noted that:

- Twenty years ago home schooling was illegal in most places in the United States, and it was not until 1993 that home schooling became legal in all states;
- Home schoolers have become the fastest growing providers of the K–12 education instruction over the past decade, growing at 15% to 20% annually;
- An estimated 1.5 million children were being home schooled in 1999.

Home schooling parents are concerned about issues like teaching certain values, a safe environment, a closer family relationship, and academic performance.

In the aftermath of the Columbine High School shootings in April 1999, *The New York Times* reported (August 11, 1999) a pick-up in interest in home schooling. As reported in *Investor's Business Daily* on March 29, 1999, a study by Lawrence Rudner, a statistician at the University of Maryland, found that home schoolers in fact score much higher than the national average, and much higher than children in private schools on standardized tests.

Once again, the innovation and creativity of entrepreneurs are playing roles in spurring forward this revolution in education. Obviously, cheaper and more powerful computers, multiplying software programs, the ever expanding Internet, and telecommunications advancements are placing the home schooling option within the grasp of more and more parents concerned about the various failures of the public school monopoly.

Crime

An assessment of crime in the United States depends upon the time frame. In recent years, the trend has been dramatically positive. Looking at crime over a few decades, however, the picture gets darker.

As noted earlier, crime has been on a steady, rather steep decline since the early 1990s. But despite these indisputable trends, a continuous diet of extensive media coverage of high-profile criminal acts has obviously convinced many Americans that crime is increasing in the United States. Numerous media surveys and polls confirm this perception. When asked if there is more crime in the United States than there was a year ago, Americans in a late 1998 Gallup Poll found no less than 64% answering in the affirmative. It is easy to understand why so many Americans hold this opinion.

As reported by the Center for Media and Public Affairs in their January/February 1998 "Media Monitor," in 1997, a year when crime fell nationwide by 4% across the board, the number of network television news stories focusing on crime actually increased by 25% over the previous year. Indeed, 1,617 stories about crime were broadcast last year alone—almost twice the coverage devoted to any other topic. Stories about murders jumped 46%, while the actual number of murders fell by 9%.

Of course, the networks are only mirroring a national trend that crosses the boundaries of the medium. Cable networks, local radio and television stations, and the local and national print media have all contributed a disproportionate amount of news coverage to the issue of violence. So while the statisticians report that Americans are actually safer today than eight or ten years ago, many of us perceive the threat from violent crime to be greater than ever.

In contrast, however, the long-term trends give Americans good reason to continue their concern about crime. As noted earlier, from 1960 to 1998, total U.S. crime increased by 344%, violent crime by 307%, and property crime by 350%.

Not surprisingly, many U.S. citizens believe that the vast number of guns in our society is one of the underlying reasons for violent crime and that if America had more restrictive gun laws like Europe, crime would be reduced.

However, it is simply not true to state that "the U.S. has more guns available and far less restrictions than any other modern industrial nation," as is so often asserted. According to San Francisco-based criminologist, professor, and constitutional lawyer Don B. Kates writing in an October 1997 article for *The American Guardian*, that honor goes to Israel where the government even "loans" guns to its citizens, with Israelis routinely stopping by a police station to pick up an Uzi or a pistol when travelling to dangerous areas.

Kates goes on to point out that it is erroneous to believe that Europe is uniformly anti-gun, pointing out that while Luxembourg totally bans all guns from civilian ownership, France, Belgium and Germany allow citizens to own handguns. Every law-abiding citizen has a legal right to buy handguns in Austria, and in Switzerland. Every law-abiding, military-age Swiss male is issued a firearm and is expected to maintain it and be ready at a moment's notice to perform his mandatory militia obligations.

What then is the impact of guns on European societies? Kates' work shows that the homicide rate in handgun-banning Luxembourg is almost twice as high as Israel and Switzerland where guns are readily available. He argues that Western Europe has always had a low homicide rate in comparison to the United States. The comparative tables on homicides and suicides shown earlier in the book, clearly demonstrate that regardless of their gun laws, Western European nations have roughly comparable rates for violent crimes. Kates points out that in any society, truly violent people are only a small minority, and that criminals will neither obey gun bans or refrain from using other deadly instruments in their nefarious purposes, and concludes: "In sum, peaceful societies do not need gun bans and violent societies do not benefit from them."

University of Chicago professor, John R. Lott, Jr., who teaches criminal deterrence and law and economics, reported in his 1998 book, *More Guns Less Crime,* that, after an exhaustive 18-year review of the FBI's criminal statistics for all 3,054 U.S. counties, the "commonly held assumptions about gun control and its crime-fighting efficacy, are simply wrong." Lott concluded that waiting periods, gun buy-backs, and background checks yield little or no benefit to society in reducing crime. His controversial conclusion, substantiated by FBI statistics, was that the most dramatic decrease in gun-related crime occurred in U.S. states where law-abiding citizens are allowed to carry concealed handguns. Indeed, no less than 31 U.S. states now have concealed carry laws (called right-to-carry by pro-gun advocates).

What can and should be done to reduce crime in the United States? Enforcing tough, mandatory sentencing laws already on the books has proven to be the answer in cities like Richmond, Virginia. Under a program called Project Exile, developed by a single federal prosecutor acting on his own initiative, gun–related crime has been cut in half and other violent crimes have plummeted to their lowest levels in decades. Project Exile's success is based on zero tolerance and mandatory sentences. This program has been so successful that the Commonwealth of Virginia has crafted its own statewide version of the law. Under the Virginia Exile program, mandatory five-year sentences are imposed if a criminal is caught carrying a firearm on school property; if a criminal is caught possessing a firearm and drugs; or if a felon convicted of a violent crime is caught possessing a firearm. No probation is allowed under the new law and even felons convicted of non-violent crimes, who are caught with a gun, face a mandatory two-year sentence.

Time magazine reported in the August 16, 1999 issue, "The Richmond initiative is being adopted in Atlanta; Birmingham, AL; Fort Worth, Texas; New Orleans; Norfolk, VA; Philadelphia; Rochester, NY; and San Francisco."

The biggest success story has been New York City, which embraced the "broken windows" theory of fighting crime. James Q. Wilson and George L. Kelling are credited as the two who spelled out the "broken windows" idea, and described it as follows in the February 1989 issue of *The Atlantic:*

> If the first broken window in a building is not repaired, then people who like breaking
> windows will assume that no one cares about the building and more windows will be

broken. Soon the building will have no windows. Likewise, when disorderly behavior—say, rude remarks by loitering youths—is left unchallenged, the signal given is that no one cares. The disorder escalates, possibly to serious crime.

James Morrow further explained the Big Apple's strategy in *U.S. News & World Report* (January 11, 1999):

> The NYPD [New York Police Department] has thus cracked down on nuisance crimes like public urination and blaring boom boxes. The department has also revolutionized crime-fighting by holding precinct commanders personally responsible for crime reduction. A program called CompStat uses computer mapping to illuminate previously unseen crime trends, and the maps then serve as the basis for brainstorming sessions that hold commanders' feet to the fire.

Innovative programs carried out at the state and local levels show that prosecution is the best prevention in the war against crime.

Outlook

The "Entrepreneurial Revolution" is at hand. Individuals empowered by new ideas, services, products, and technologies promise to drive the United States on to new heights.

As explained above and in the following pages, public policy will need to be focused on lowering taxes, reducing the size of government, deregulating business, turning to market reforms in health care, shoring up the monetary foundation of our economy, and expanding choice in education. Of course, our society will require more than mere public policy changes and a robust economy to fully thrive.

Our popular culture, for example, needs to do more elevating and less degrading. The moral decay depicted in many movies and television shows is disturbing.

Along the same lines, our elected officials must do much more in terms of establishing standards for high character for the nation in general. We'll have to see, for example, what kind of impact recent unfortunate escapades in the Oval Office might have on our society in general. The public's response to recent lies and law-breaking was disturbingly complacent, however.

Meanwhile, though substantial gains in the fight against crime have been made in recent years, America is still a far less safe place to live than it was only 35 to 40 years ago. Cheap political points made at the expense of Second Amendment rights must give way to the hard work necessary to make the nation truly safer, like enforcing the laws on the books and toughening sentencing requirements for violent criminals.

However, crime is and should be treated as mainly a local issue. Federalization of crimes and police activities is not a desirable trend. Local officials generally better understand what is needed in terms of fighting crime.

A widening, apathetic acceptance of moral relativism must be replaced by a robust debate over moral absolutes. America's churches, for example, must get back to teaching right and wrong, and saving souls, rather than participating in a variety of unrelated social crusades and themselves often perpetuating moral relativism.

This breakdown of traditional morality has had and will continue to have devastating effects, such as broken families, the continuing tragedy of abortion, and illegitimacy. Indeed, the United States's continuing steep ascent in births to unmarried women will translate into the continuation and expansion of such societal ills as crime and welfare dependency.

In order for the "Entrepreneurial Revolution" to take full flight, in addition to low taxes, sound money and free trade, trust and a common understanding of right and wrong are required; a solid work ethic is needed; and the protection of life, limb, and property must stand strong. In the coming century, the "Entrepreneurial Revolution" will place the highest value on individual freedom and personal responsibility.

$\mathbf{A}$LABAMA

Alabama has one of the most conservative, free-market delegations in Congress. As noted below, five of Alabama's seven U.S. representatives are ranked very well by the American Conservative Union and the Small Business Survival Committee. Junior Senator Jeff Sessions also earns high conservative marks. And, of course, in 1994 conservative Democratic Senator Richard Shelby became a Republican after vociferously opposing President Clinton's tax increase in 1993.

Likewise, policy activity back home shows some strong conservative traits. The state imposes fairly low taxes, has shown some ability to keep government spending levels down compared with much of the rest of the nation, and carries a relatively light government debt burden. If such policies are continued, and even improved on, then Alabama will be positioned to excel in the entrepreneurial 21st century. Of note, the state has performed well in terms of disposable income growth, new business incorporations, reducing welfare rolls, and net domestic migration—all positive signs for the state's economy and fiscal well-being.

On the downside, though, Alabama ranks quite low in terms of households with computers and Internet access—somewhat of a worry as we move ever further toward an information-based economy. Again, however, if state and local taxes and regulations are kept low or reduced, the marketplace will respond, and entrepreneurs and businesses will redress this shortcoming through greater economic growth, more jobs and higher incomes.

Meanwhile, like other states, Alabama recently linked together two quite different policy issues—legalized gambling and educating children.

Even before Democrat Don Siegelman unseated incumbent Republican Governor Fob James by a healthy margin in November 1998, the debate over a state lottery was hot in Alabama. Siegelman was quoted in the *Wall Street Journal* on August 10, 1999 saying, "The people of Alabama voted for me, at least in part, to ensure their kids had a better chance in life . . . To me, there was a clear mandate to bring the lottery to Alabama." Interestingly, some in the state pointed out that, as lieutenant governor, Siegelman helped kill a similar measure in 1996, but dramatically reversed course for the 1998 gubernatorial campaign.

Siegelman put the same positive spin on a lottery as has been used elsewhere in the nation, namely, that the proceeds will be used for education—prekindergarten, computers in schools, and higher-education scholarships.

Meanwhile, a June 1999 report from the National Gambling Impact Study Commission confirmed what most of us already suspected, that is, that people earning less than $10,000 a year spend more on lottery tickets—almost $600 annually—than any other income group.

Perhaps the major problem with government-operated gambling is that it sends all the wrong signals. In effect, the government is telling people that there is a chance they can get ahead in life without hard work, without educating themselves, or without moral and economic self-improvement. (This might be the case for politicians, but not for the rest of us.)

As for linking gambling with education, three questions arise. First, one should ask if lottery money really makes a difference in education funding, or is it that other revenues are simply freed up to be spent on whatever politicians want? After all, money—especially taxpayer money—is quite fungible.

Second, and more fundamental, does it make sense to throw more money at public schools? After all, public schools in Alabama generally have not done a very good job with grades K through 12, so expanding the government's reach into pre-K is grossly ill-advised. Meanwhile, spending tax or lottery funds on bringing more computers into public schools has to be one of the all-time great government teacher union cons. It is not clear to us, not to mention many education researchers, how classroom computers and Internet access actually help children master reading, writing, mathematics, science, history, civics, and so on. It seems far more likely that classroom computer time only serves to take away from far more valuable teacher-student classroom time. The benefit of Internet access for schools mainly lies with teachers being able to gain access to new and expanded information, not with taking up more classroom time (which, after all, is limited) by placing kids in front of computer screens.

Lastly, a simple question: What kind of message is sent to children by using gambling to support education?

On October 12, 1999, Alabama voters answered by voting against a state lottery by a margin of 54.3% to 45.7%.

As evidenced by the education numbers below, Alabama state and local government spending on education generally trails the U.S. average; but it has been rising at a faster pace than the U.S. as a whole in recent decades.

Contrary to the hopes of many that increased education expenditures will raise the performance of Alabama students, as is evidenced by many big spending states and cities, more tax dollars spent on public schools accomplish little, if anything. To really improve the quality of education in the 21st century, Alabama should look to actually reduce, not increase, government's role. For example, private scholarship programs getting under way in Birmingham in order to expand school choice make sense.

Empowering students and parents with choice—such as through vouchers—will do far more to improve education in Alabama than hurling more money at public schools. Entrepreneurs in the education field will then have greater opportunities to serve education consumers, rather than being lost in the public education bureaucracy. As always, competition boosts quality across the board.

On this and other issues, it will be interesting to see how the state's Democratic governor and state legislature proceed in terms of policy making. Will they act like more traditional conservative southern Democrats, or will they veer more toward their party's big government brethren? One thing is for sure, pushing a new lottery, which would have taken hundreds of millions of dollars out of the private sector and hand it over to government, is cause for concern.

POLITICS

Registered Voters

No party registration

Federal Officials: Recent Election and Group Ratings

			ACU	ADA	SBSC
U.S. Senators:	Richard Shelby (R)		71	24	80
	1998 Shelby (R)	63%			
	Suddith (D)	37%			
	Jeff Sessions (D)		100	0	85
	1996 Sessions (R)	52%			
	Bedford (D)	45%			
U.S. Representatives:	Sonny Callahan (R-1)		94	3	95
	1998 Callahan (R)	NO			
	Terry Everett (R-2)		97	3	90
	1998 Everett (R)	69%			
	Fondren (D)	31%			
	Bob Riley (R-3)		98	3	90
	1998 Riley (R)	58%			
	Turnham (D)	42%			
	Robert Aderholt (R-4)		96	5	85
	1998 Aderholt (R)	56%			
	Bevill (D)	44%			
	Robert (Bud) Cramer (D-5)		45	47	40
	1998 Cramer (D)	70%			
	Aust (R)	30%			
	Spencer Bachus (R-6)		94	4	80
	1998 Bachus (R)	72%			
	Smalley (D)	28%			
	Earl Hilliard (D-7)		13	86	10
	1998 Hilliard (D)	NO			
Electoral Votes:	9				
1996 Presidential Results:	Clinton	50%			
	Dole	43%			
	Perot	6%			

State Officials

Governor 1998 Election:	Don Siegelman (D)	58%
	Fob James (R)	42%
Lt. Governor:	Steve Windom (R)	
Attorney General:	Bill Pryor (R)	

State Senate:	23 Democrats
	12 Republicans
State House:	69 Democrats
	36 Republicans

TAXES AND SPENDING

Total Revenues

Alabama's per capita state and local total revenues registered $4,591 in 1996, ranking 48th in the nation and trailing the U.S. average of $5,706 by 20%. From 1962 to 1996, real per capita state and local revenues increased by 336%, compared with an increase in the national average of 297%.

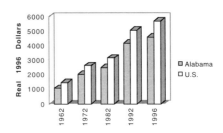

Real Per Capita State and Local Total Revenues: Alabama vs. U.S.

Taxes

Alabama's per capita state and local taxes registered $1,786 in 1996, ranking 51st in the nation and trailing the U.S. average of $2,597 by 31%. From 1962 to 1996, real per capita state and local taxes increased by 195%, compared with an increase in 152% in the U.S. average.

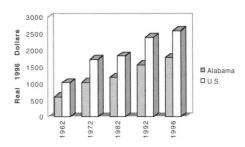

Real Per Capita State and Local Taxes: Alabama vs. U.S.

Property Taxes

Alabama's per capita state and local property taxes equaled $234 in 1996, ranking 51st in the nation and trailing the U.S. average of $789 by 70%. From 1962 to 1996, real per capita state and local property taxes increased by 89%, versus a 67% increase in the U.S. average.

Sales and Gross Receipts Taxes

Alabama's per capita state and local sales and gross receipts taxes came in at $914 in 1996, ranking 23d in the nation and trailing the U.S. average of $939 by 3%. From 1962 to 1996, real per capita state and local sales and gross receipts taxes increased by 197%, versus an increase of 214% in the U.S. average.

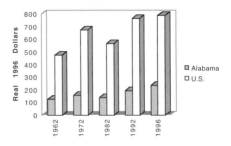

Real Per Capita State and Local Property Taxes: Alabama vs. U.S.

Income Taxes

Alabama's per capita state and local income (individual and corporate) taxes registered $436 in 1996, ranking 40th in the nation and trailing the U.S. average of $674 by 35%. From 1962 to 1996, real per capita state and local income taxes increased by 693%, versus a 567% increase in the U.S. average.

Personal Income Tax

A rate of 3.02%, ranking 12th in the nation (from lowest tax rate to highest), and comparing with the national average of 5.26%.

Capital Gains Tax

A rate of 4%, ranking 19th in the nation (from lowest tax rate to highest), and comparing with the national average of 4.68%.

Corporate Income Tax

A rate of 3.25%, ranking 6th in the nation (from lowest tax rate to highest), and comparing with the national average of 6.63%.

Total Expenditures

Alabama's per capita state and local total spending registered $4,517 in 1996, ranking 40th in the nation and trailing the U.S. average of $5,268 by 14%. From 1962 to 1996, real per capita state and local total spending increased by 303%, versus an increase of 254% in the U.S. average.

Welfare Expenditures

Alabama's per capita state and local public welfare spending registered $554 in 1996, ranking 41st in the nation and trailing the U.S. average of $729 by 24%. From 1962 to 1996, real per capita state and local public welfare spending increased by 301%, compared with a 488% increase in the U.S. average.

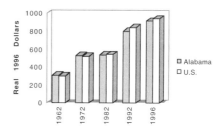

Real Per Capita State and Local Sales and Gross Receipts Taxes: Alabama vs. U.S.

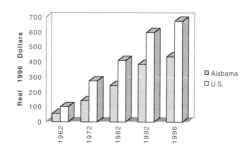

Real Per Capita State and Local Income Taxes: Alabama vs. U.S.

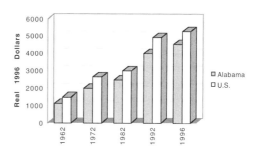

Real Per Capita State and Local Total Expenditures: Alabama vs. U.S.

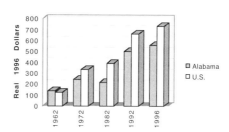

Real Per Capita State and Local Public Welfare Spending: Alabama vs. U.S.

Welfare Recipients (in thousands)

	1980	1989	3/99	Change 1989–99
Ala.	178	130	47	−64%
U.S.	10,923	10,987	7,335	−33%

Interest on General Debt

Alabama's per capita state and local interest on general debt registered $154 in 1996, ranking 36th in the nation and trailing the U.S. average of $222 by 31%. From 1962 to 1996, real per capita state and local interest on general debt increased by 316%, versus an increase of 335% in the U.S. average.

Total Debt Outstanding

Alabama's per capita state and local debt registered $2,718 in 1996, ranking 42d in the nation and trailing the U.S. average of $4,409 by 38%. From 1962 to 1996, real per capita state and local debt outstanding increased by 84%, versus an increase of 120% in the U.S. average.

Government Employees

Alabama's state and local government employees (full-time equivalent, or FTE) per 10,000 population registered 593.7 in 1997, ranking 11th in the nation and exceeding the U.S. average of 531.1 by 12%. From 1962 to 1996, state and local FTE employees per 10,000 population increased by 113%, compared with an increase in the U.S. average of 66%.

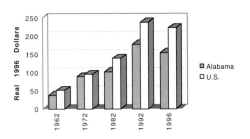

Real Per Capita State and Local Interest on General Debt: Alabama vs. U.S.

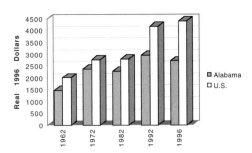

Real Per Capita State and Local Debt Outstanding: Alabama vs. U.S.

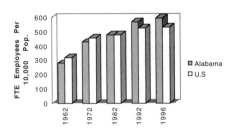

State and Local Government Employees (FTE) Per 10,000 Population: Alabama vs. U.S.

Per Capita Federal Government Expenditures, 1998

	1998	Ranking
Ala.	$5,813	17th
U.S.	$5,491	

Per capita federal spending in Alabama topped the national average by 6%.

EDUCATION

Total Education Spending

Alabama's per capita state and local education spending registered $1,357 in 1996, ranking 40th in the nation and trailing the U.S. average of $1,503 by 10%. From 1962 to 1996, real per capita total education spending increased by 232%, versus an increase in the U.S. average of 173%.

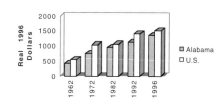

Real Per Capita State and Local Education Spending: Alabama vs. U.S.

Per Pupil Spending

Alabama's per pupil public school spending registered $4,499 in 1998, ranking 45th in the nation and trailing the U.S. average of $6,131 by 27%. From 1970 to 1998, Alabama's real per pupil public school spending increased by 137%, compared with a 120% increase in the U.S. average.

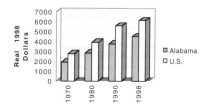

Real Per Pupil Public School Spending: Alabama vs. U.S.

Average Public School Teacher Salaries (in 1997–98 dollars)

	1970	1980	1990	1998	1998 Ranking
Ala.	29,193	27,209	31,626	32,818	40th
U.S.	36,934	33,272	39,956	39,385	

In 1998, the average public school teacher salary in Alabama trailed the U.S. average by 17%. From 1970 to 1998, the real average teacher salary in Alabama increased by 12%, versus an increase in the U.S. average of 7%.

Pupil/Teacher Ratio, Fall 1996

	Ratio	Rank
Ala.	16.6	26th
U.S.	17.1	

Teachers/Staff, Fall 1996

	Percent	Rank
Ala.	53.0	23d
U.S.	52.1	

Public School 4th-Grade Reading Proficiency, 1998

	Average	Rank (out of 40 states)
Ala.	211	28th
U.S.	215	

Public School 8th-Grade Reading Proficiency, 1998

	Average	Rank (out of 37 states)
Ala.	255	30th
U.S.	261	

Public School 4th-Grade Math Proficiency, 1996

	Average	Rank (out of 44 states)
Ala.	212	40th
U.S.	224	

Public School 8th-Grade Math Proficiency, 1996

	Average	Rank (out of 41 states)
Ala.	257	38th
U.S.	271	

Public School 8th-Grade Science Proficiency, 1996

	Average	Rank (out of 41 states)
Ala.	139	35th
U.S.	148	

Average Math SAT Scores

	1972	1982	1992	1998	Percentage Students Taking SAT in 1998
Ala.	466	523	539	558	8
U.S.	509	493	501	512	43

Average Verbal SAT Scores

	1972	1982	1992	1998	Percentage Students Taking SAT in 1998
Ala.	494	539	551	562	8
U.S.	530	504	500	505	43

Expenditures by Public Institutions of Higher Education Per Full-Time-Equivalent Student, 1996

	FTE Student Spending	Rank
Ala.	$12,129	27th
U.S.	$12,343	

Per-FTE-student spending in public institutions of higher education trailed the U.S. average by 2%.

Per Full-Time-Equivalent Student Revenues from Federal, State, and Local Governments for Public Institutions of Higher Education, 1996

	FTE Student Government Revenues	Rank
Ala.	$8,079	23d
U.S.	$8,101	

Per-FTE-student-government revenues in public institutions of higher education trailed the U.S. average by 0.3%.

Average Salary for Full-Time Professors at Public Universities, 1997

	Average	Rank
Ala.	$64,158	36th
U.S.	$72,599	

The average full-time public university professor salary trailed the U.S. average by 12%.

ECONOMY AND BUSINESS

Economic Growth

Over the period of 1977 to 1997, Alabama's real gross state product (GSP) grew by 68.3%—ranking 27th in the nation—as compared with real U.S. gross domestic product (GDP), expanding by 70.1%.

At $103.1 billion in 1997, Alabama's GSP ranked as 25th largest in the nation.

From 1993 to 1997, Alabama's annual real GSP growth averaged 3.13%—ranking 34th in the nation—as compared with annual real U.S. GDP growth, averaging 3.08%.

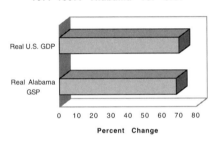

Real Economic Growth 1977-1997: Alabama vs. U.S.

Real U.S. GDP

Real Alabama GSP

0 10 20 30 40 50 60 70 80

Percent Change

Job Growth

	Growth in Employee Payrolls (Nonagricultural) 1962–98	Ranking
Ala.	140.7%	29th
U.S.	126.5%	

	Average Annual Growth in Employee Payrolls (Nonagricultural) 1993–98	Ranking
Ala.	2.62%	35th
U.S.	2.98%	

Per Capita Disposable Income, 1997

	1997	Ranking
Ala.	18,259	39th
U.S.	21,607	

Per capita disposable income trailed the U.S. average by 15%.

Real Growth 1962–97		Ranking
Ala.	161.7%	6th
U.S.	116.7%	

Average Annual Real Growth, 1993–97		Ranking
Ala.	1.66%	25th
U.S.	1.48%	

Number of Businesses

	1997	Percentage with Fewer than 500 Employees
Businesses with Employees	86,841	97.4
Self-employed Individuals	167,000	

New Business Incorporations

	1980	1986	1992	1997
Ala.	3,909	6,788	7,087	7,742

Percentage Change in Annual New Business Incorporations, 1980 vs. 1997

	Percent	Ranking
Ala.	98.1	10th
U.S.	49.7	

State Merchandise Exports to the World, 1998 (in millions of dollars)

	1998	Rank
Ala.	$4,560	27th

Small Business Survival Index, 1999

Alabama offered the 8th best policy environment for entrepreneurship.

Fortune 500 Headquarters in 1999

Total of 7 (ranked 20th), with Birmingham ranked 11th among U.S. cities with 6 headquarters.

Labor Union Membership, 1983 vs. 1997

| | Percentage of Workers | | |
	1983	1997	1997 Rank
Ala.	16.9	10.2	28th
U.S.	20.1	14.1	

Homeownership Rate, 1998

	Rate	Rank
Ala.	72.9	10th
U.S.	66.3	

CRIME

Crime Rates Per 100 Residents (ranking from best to worst crime rate)

Total Crime	1960	1970	1980	1990	1998	1998 Ranking
Ala.	0.79	1.87	4.93	4.92	4.60	28th
U.S.	1.04	2.74	5.90	5.82	4.62	

From 1960 to 1998, Alabama's crime rate increased by 482%, versus a U.S. increase of 344%. From 1990 to 1998, Alabama's crime rate dropped by 0.7%, versus a U.S. decrease of 21%.

Violent Crime	1960	1970	1980	1990	1998	1998 Ranking
Ala.	0.17	0.30	0.45	0.71	0.51	30th
U.S.	0.14	0.36	0.58	0.73	0.57	

From 1960 to 1998, Alabama's violent crime rate increased by 200%, versus a U.S. increase of 307%. From 1990 to 1998, Alabama's violent crime rate decreased by 28%, compared with a national decline of 22%.

Property Crime	1960	1970	1980	1990	1998	1998 Ranking
Ala.	0.79	1.57	4.49	4.21	4.09	29th
U.S.	0.90	2.38	5.32	5.09	4.05	

From 1960 to 1998, Alabama's property crime rate increased by 418%, versus a national increase of 350%. From 1990 to 1998, Alabama's property crime rate decreased by 3%, compared with a national decline of 20%.

Real Per Capita State and Local Police Protection Spending (in real 1996 dollars)

	1962	1972	1982	1992	1996	1996 Ranking
Ala.	28	52	76	104	118	39th
U.S.	51	95	114	148	168	

In 1996, per capita state and local police protection spending in Alabama trailed the U.S. average by 30%. From 1962 to 1996, real per capita state and local police protection spending increased by 321%, versus an increase of 229% in the U.S. average.

Prisoners in State and Federal Prisons Per 1,000 Population

	1980	1990	1996	1996 Ranking
Ala.	1.68	3.88	5.08	10th
U.S.	1.46	3.11	4.45	

From 1980 to 1996, prisoners per 1,000 population increased by 202%, versus a U.S. increase of 205%.

HEALTH CARE

Health-Care Spending

Alabama's per capita state and local health-care spending registered $174 in 1996, ranking 14th in the nation and exceeding the U.S. average of $151 by 15%. From 1962 to 1996, Alabama's real per capita state and local health-care spending increased by 1,143%, versus an increase of 739% in the U.S. average.

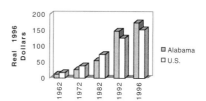

Real Per Capita State and Local Health Care Spending: Alabama vs. U.S.

Hospital Spending

Alabama's per capita state and local hospital spending registered $523 in 1996, ranking 2d in the nation and exceeding the U.S. average of $266 by 97%. From 1962 to 1996, Alabama's real per capita state and local hospital spending increased by 616%, as opposed to an increase of 189% in the U.S. average.

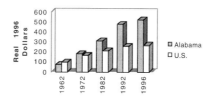

Real Per Capita State and Local Hospital Spending: Alabama vs. U.S.

Medicaid, 1997

	Spending Per Recipient	Ranking
Ala.	$2,877	41st
U.S.	$3,681	

Alabama's per recipient Medicaid spending trailed the U.S. average by 22%.

ENVIRONMENT

Parks and Recreation Spending

Alabama's per capita state and local parks and recreation spending registered $50 in 1996, ranking 35th in the nation and trailing the U.S. average of $72 by 31%. From 1962 to 1996, real per capita state and local parks and recreation spending increased by 456%, versus a 213% increase in the U.S. average.

Real Per Capita State and Local Parks and Recreation Spending: Alabama vs. U.S.

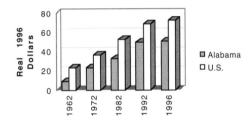

State and Local Natural Resources Spending, 1996

	Per Capita	Ranking
Ala.	$42	36th
U.S.	$60	

Per capita state and local natural resources spending in Alabama trailed the U.S. average by 30%.

State Parks Revenues as a Share of Operating Expenses, 1997

	Percent	Rank
Ala.	83	4th
U.S.	42	

Percentage of Land Owned by the Federal Government, 1996

	Percent	Rank
Ala.	3.3	32d
U.S.	24.8	

SOCIETY AND DEMOGRAPHICS

Population

Alabama's 1998 population of 4.352 million ranked 23d in the nation.

Alabama Population

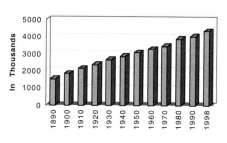

Population Growth, 1990–98

	Percentage Change in Population	Ranking
Ala.	7.72	23d
U.S.	8.66	

	Net International Migration	Ranking
Ala.	12,599	39th

	Net Domestic Migration	Ranking
Ala.	113,569	13th

Infant Mortality Rate, 1998

	Percent	Rank
Ala.	9.9	2d
U.S.	6.4	

Percentage of Births of Low Birthweight, 1997

	Percent	Rank
Ala.	9.2	4th
U.S.	7.5	

Percentage of Live Births to Unmarried Women, 1997

	Percent	Rank
Ala.	33.9	14th
U.S.	32.4	

Abortion Rate, Abortions Per 1,000 Women Ages 15–44, 1995

	Rate	Rank
Ala.	15.0	29th
U.S.	22.9	

LIFESTYLE

Percentage of Households with Computers, 1998

	Percent	Rank
Ala.	34.3	47th

Percentage of Households with Internet Access, 1998

	Percent	Rank
Ala.	21.6	40th

State Arts Agency Spending, 1999

	Per Capita	Rank
Ala.	$1.06	23d
U.S.	$1.35	

Per capita state arts spending in 1999 trailed the U.S. average by 21%.

Major League Sports Facilities

None

ALASKA

Alaskans like to refer to the contiguous states as the "lower 48." No matter what an Alaskan's financial or social standing, there is universal agreement that they are different. The state has a reputation for being a land of rugged individualism.

For many, the float plane has replaced the "family auto" as the typical means of transportation. Meanwhile, as a percentage of households, computer ownership and Internet access rank tops in the nation.

These go-it-alone types have a love-hate relationship with the federal government. Likewise, a major blow for individualism was struck in 1980 when the state's personal income tax was repealed. Alaska also imposes no general sales tax.

However, Alaska shows that even the most rugged of individualists can be tempted by the allure of revenues rolling into government coffers. With the discovery of oil in 1968 and the opening of the Alaska pipeline in 1977, oil leases, royalties, and taxes have turned "Seward's Folly" into "Seward's Gusher." While gushing oil revenues led to the repeal of the personal income tax, government spending exploded, as did borrowing.

Alaska's per capita state and local total expenditures and debt rank highest in the nation. Education expenditures are extremely lavish, and per capita welfare spending ranks third among the states. Alaska's welfare rolls actually increased by 47% between 1989 and March 1999, while the nation experienced a decline of 33%. State and local government employees as a share of population in Alaska ranks among the highest in the nation as well. For good measure, the state hands a check to each resident annually. In 1999 the check received was for $1,770.23.

But even oil money is not without limits. The state government has recently experienced financial shortfalls. To remedy the problem, an advisory vote was held on September 14, 1999, asking taxpayers for permission to use a billion dollars of their dividend fund earnings to balance the budget. Voters were outraged, and said "no" by a vote of 83% to 17%.

Governor Knowles's popularity took a nosedive as did that of many legislative leaders. Some Alaskans also were suspicious that the hidden sponsor of the legislation was none other than the oil industry itself. Understandably, the oil industry thinks the state needs a more stable tax base. But when the largest oil producer, ARCO, was taken over by foreign-owned British Petroleum, some xenophobia crept in as well.

Many Alaskans argue that the high cost of government in the state is not just a lack of will. With a population of 614,000 (roughly equivalent to the eastern half of Long Island) and a road system smaller than the state of Connecticut's spread over an area two-and-a-half times the size of Texas, it may be understandable that efficiency is a little hard to come by. In this often hostile environment, higher costs are just a way of life, inevitably prompting national retailers to add the phrase "prices slightly higher in Alaska." It should be clearly noted, however, that national retailers do not hike their prices by some 100 to 200 percent, which is how much Alaska's state and local government spending and revenues outdistance the U.S. average.

In a July 1994 analysis of taxes and spending in Alaska written for the Center for the Study of American Business (CSAB), Stephen L. Jackstadt, an economics professor at the University of Alaska, Anchorage, and Dwight R. Lee, an adjunct fellow at CSAB and economics professor at the University of Georgia, noted, "Since Alaskans pay only a small percentage of the taxes needed to finance government spending, there is little public opposition to government spending. It is easier for Alaskan politicians to increase taxes on the oil industry than to resist constituent demands for more spending. Taxes on the oil industry . . . increased eleven times [between 1955 and 1994]." Jackstadt and Lee reported that Alaska's tax rates on oil producers were the highest in the nation. The study's authors went on to itemize a long list of government waste and boondoggles, including subsidies to grow barley, to start a local dairy industry (it failed), and for a host of "renewable resources" projects (including a dog-powered washing machine), along with a wealth of pork projects like arts centers, convention centers, and sports arenas.

We have to wonder if, despite the absence of a state income tax, Alaska's wild and wooly spending ways are finally exacting a real cost. In recent years, the economic and disposable income growth have fallen far behind that of the nation as a whole, while new business incorporations also have languished badly. While Alaska's overall population growth from 1990 to 1998 outpaced that of the nation, thanks to births and international immigration (the state traditionally has considerable population turnover), net domestic migration—movements from state to state—revealed that Alaska exported people to the rest of the United States.

POLITICS

Registered Voters

17% Democrats
25% Republicans
58% Other

Federal Officials: Recent Election and Group Ratings

			ACU	ADA	SBSC
U.S. Senators:	Ted Stevens (R)		64	23	85
	1996 Stevens (R)	76%			
	Whittaker (G)	12%			
	Frank Murkowski (R)		79	10	90
	1998 Murkowski (R)	74%			
	Suddith (D)	20%			
U.S Representatives:	Don Young (R-1)		75	14	65
	1998 Young (R)	63%			
	Duncan (D)	35%			

Electoral Votes:	3	
1996 Presidential Results:	Clinton	33%
	Dole	51%
	Perot	11%

State Offices

Governor 1998 Election:	Tony Knowles (D)	51%
	Robin Taylor (R-Write-in)	20%
	John Lindauer (R)	18%
Lt. Governor:	Fran Ulmer (D)	
Attorney General:	Bruce M. Botelho (D)	
State Senate:	5 Democrats	
	15 Republicans	
State House:	16 Democrats	
	24 Republicans	

TAXES AND SPENDING

Total Revenues

Alaska's per capita state and local total revenues registered $16,477 in 1996, ranking highest in the nation and exceeding the U.S. average of $5,706 by 189%. From 1962 to 1996, real per capita state and local revenues increased by 539%, compared with an increase in the national average of 297%.

Taxes

Alaska's per capita state and local taxes registered $3,791 in 1996, ranking 4th in the nation and exceeding the U.S. average of $2,597 by 46%. From 1962 to 1996, real per capita state and local taxes increased by 280%, compared with an increase of 152% in the U.S. average.

Real Per Capita State and Local Total Revenues: Alaska vs. U.S.

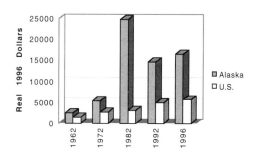

Real Per Capita State and Local Taxes: Alaska vs. U.S.

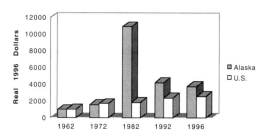

Property Taxes

Alaska's per capita state and local property taxes equaled $1,121 in 1996, ranking 8th in the nation and exceeding the U.S. average of $789 by 42%. From 1962 to 1996, real per capita state and local property taxes increased by 387%, versus a 67% increase in the U.S. average.

Sales and Gross Receipts Taxes

Alaska's per capita state and local sales and gross receipts taxes came in at $394 in 1996, ranking 47th in the nation and trailing the U.S. average of $939 by 58%. From 1962 to 1996, real per capita state and local sales and gross receipts taxes increased by 90%, versus a 214% increase in the U.S. average.

Income Taxes

Alaska's per capita state and local income (individual and corporate) taxes registered $538 in 1996, ranking 35th in the nation and trailing the U.S. average of $674 by 20%. From 1962 to 1996, real per capita state and local income taxes increased by 102%, versus a 567% increase in the U.S. average.

Personal Income Tax

A rate of 0%, ranking best in the nation (from lowest tax rate to highest), and comparing with the national average of 5.26%.

Capital Gains Tax

A rate of 0%, ranking best in the nation (from lowest tax rate to highest), and comparing with the national average of 4.68%.

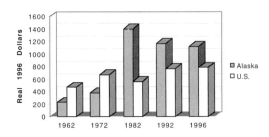

Real Per Capita State and Local Property Taxes: Alaska vs. U.S.

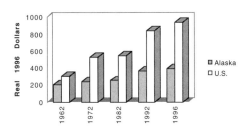

Real Per Capita State and Local Sales and Gross Receipts Taxes: Alaska vs. U.S.

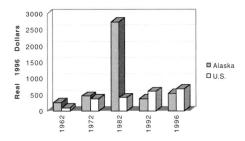

Real Per Capita State and Local Income Taxes: Alaska vs. U.S.

Corporate Income Tax

A rate of 9.4%, ranking 45th in the nation (from lowest tax rate to highest), and comparing to the U.S. average of 6.63%.

Total Expenditures

Alaska's per capita state and local total spending registered $11,866 in 1996, ranking highest in the nation and exceeding the U.S. average of $5,268 by 125%. From 1962 to 1996, real per capita state and local total spending increased by 366%, versus an increase of 254% in the U.S. average.

Welfare Expenditures

Alaska's per capita state and local public welfare spending registered $1,027 in 1996, ranking 3d highest in the nation and outpacing the U.S. average of $729 by 41%. From 1962 to 1996, real per capita state and local public welfare spending increased by 1,016%, compared with a 488% increase in the U.S. average.

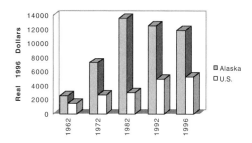

Real Per Capita State and Local Total Expenditures: Alaska vs. U.S.

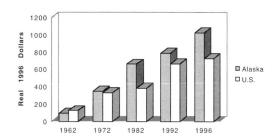

Real Per Capita State and Local Public Welfare Spending: Alaska vs. U.S.

Welfare Recipients (in thousands)

	1980	1989	3/99	Change 1989–99
Alaska	16	19	28	+47%
U.S.	10,923	10,987	7,335	−33%

Interest on General Debt

Alaska's per capita state and local interest on general debt registered $763 in 1996, ranking highest in the nation and exceeding the U.S. average of $222 by 244%. From 1962 to 1996, real per capita state and local interest on general debt increased by 1,092%, versus an increase of 335% in the U.S. average.

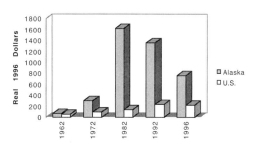

Real Per Capita State and Local Interest on General Debt: Alaska vs. U.S.

Total Debt Outstanding

Alaska's per capita state and local debt registered $11,201 in 1996, ranking highest in the nation and outrunning the U.S. average of $4,409 by 154%. From 1962 to 1996, real per capita state and local debt outstanding increased by 348%, versus an increase of 120% in the U.S. average. Amazingly, Alaska's per capita debt has actually declined from its stratospheric level of $26,563 (in 1996 dollars) in 1982.

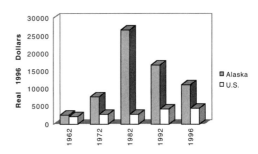

Real Per Capita State and Local Debt Outstanding: Alaska vs. U.S.

Government Employees

Alaska's state and local government employees (full-time equivalent, or FTE) per 10,000 population registered 747 in 1997, ranking 3d in the nation and exceeding the U.S. average of 531.1 by 41%. From 1962 to 1996, state and local FTE employees per 10,000 population increased by 115%, compared with an increase in the U.S. average of 66%.

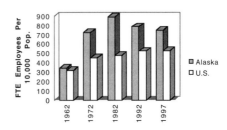

State and Local Government Employees (FTE) Per 10,000 Population: Alaska vs. U.S.

Per Capita Federal Government Expenditures, 1998

	1998	Ranking
Alaska	$7,763	4th
U.S.	$5,491	

Per capita federal spending in Alaska topped the national average by 41%.

EDUCATION

Total Education Spending

Alaska's per capita state and local education spending registered $2,554 in 1996, ranking highest in the nation and outpacing the U.S. average of $1,503 by 70%. From 1962 to 1996, real per capita total education spending increased by 220%, versus an increase in the U.S. average of 173%.

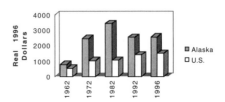

Real Per Capita State and Local Education Spending: Alaska vs. U.S.

Per Pupil Spending

Alaska's per pupil public school spending registered $8,458 in 1998, ranking 5th in the nation and exceeding the U.S. average of $6,131 by 38%. From 1970 to 1998, Alaska's real per pupil public school spending increased by 116%, compared with a 120% increase in the U.S. average.

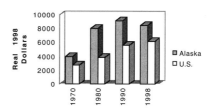

Real Per Pupil Public School Spending: Alaska vs. U.S.

Average Public School Teacher Salaries (in 1997–98 dollars)

	1970	1980	1990	1998	1998 Ranking
Alaska	45,215	56,690	54,969	51,738	1st
U.S.	36,934	33,272	39,956	39,385	

In 1998, the average public school teacher salary in Alaska outpaced the U.S. average by 31%. From 1970 to 1998, the real average teacher salary in Alaska increased by 14%, versus an increase in the U.S. average of 7%.

Pupil/Teacher Ratio, Fall 1996

	Ratio	Rank
Alaska	17.5	39th
U.S.	17.1	

Teachers/Staff, Fall 1996

	Percent	Rank
Alaska	50.2	44th
U.S.	52.1	

Public School 4th-Grade Math Proficiency, 1996

	Average	Rank (out of 44 states)
Alaska	224	20th
U.S.	224	

Public School 8th-Grade Math Proficiency, 1996

	Average	Rank (out of 41 states)
Alaska	278	10th
U.S.	271	

Public School 8th-Grade Science Proficiency, 1996

	Average	Rank (out of 41 states)
Alaska	153	15th
U.S.	148	

Average Math SAT Scores

	1972	1982	1992	1998	Percentage Students Taking SAT in 1998
Alaska	517	502	501	520	52
U.S.	509	493	501	512	43

Average Verbal SAT Scores

	1972	1982	1992	1998	Percentage Students Taking SAT in 1998
Alaska	550	523	509	521	52
U.S.	530	504	500	505	43

Expenditures by Public Institutions of Higher Education Per Full-Time-Equivalent Student, 1996

	FTE Student Spending	Rank
Alaska	$18,604	3d
U.S.	$12,343	

Per-FTE-student spending in public institutions of higher education exceeded the U.S. average by 51%.

Per Full-Time-Equivalent Student Revenues from Federal, State, and Local Governments for Public Institutions of Higher Education, 1996

	FTE Student Government Revenues	Rank
Alaska	$13,139	2d
U.S.	$8,101	

Per-FTE-student-government revenues in public institutions of higher education topped the U.S. average by 62%.

Average Salary for Full-Time Professors at Public Universities, 1997

	Average	Rank
Alaska	$64,801	35th
U.S.	$72,599	

The average full-time public university professor salary trailed the U.S. average by 11%.

ECONOMY AND BUSINESS

Economic Growth

Over the period of 1977 to 1997, Alaska's real gross state product (GSP) grew by 48.1%—ranking 41st in the nation—as compared with real U.S. gross domestic product (GDP) expanding by 70.1%.

At $24.5 billion in 1997, Alaska's GSP ranked as 46th largest in the nation.

From 1993 to 1997, Alaska's annual real GSP growth averaged −0.31%—ranking 50th in the nation—as compared with annual real U.S. GDP growth, averaging 3.08%.

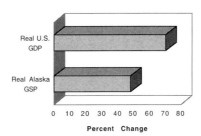

Real Economic Growth 1977-1997: Alaska vs. U.S.

Real U.S. GDP

Real Alaska GSP

0 10 20 30 40 50 60 70 80

Percent Change

Job Growth

	Growth in Employee Payrolls (Nonagricultural) 1962–98	Ranking
Alaska	367.6%	4th
U.S.	126.5%	

	Average Annual Growth in Employee Payrolls (Nonagricultural) 1993–98	Ranking
Alaska	2.18%	42d
U.S.	2.98%	

Per Capita Disposable Income, 1997

	1997	Ranking
Alaska	21,177	20th
U.S.	21,607	

Per capita disposable income trailed the U.S. average by 2%.

	Real Growth 1962–97	Ranking
Alaska	88.9%	45th
U.S.	116.7%	

	Average Annual Real Growth 1993–97	Ranking
Alaska	−0.31%	51st
U.S.	1.48%	

Number of Businesses

	1997	Percent with Fewer than 500 Employees
Businesses with Employees	15,788	91.7
Self-employed Individuals	35,000	

New Business Incorporations

	1980	1986	1992	1997
Alaska	1,691	1,722	1,461	1,163

Percentage Change in Annual New Business Incorporations, 1980 vs. 1997

	Percent	Ranking
Alaska	−31.2	50th
U.S.	49.7	

State Merchandise Exports to the World, 1998 (in millions of dollars)

	1998	Rank
Alaska	$758	46th

Small Business Survival Index, 1999

Alaska offered the 12th-best policy environment for entrepreneurship.

Fortune 500 Headquarters in 1999

None

Labor Union Membership, 1983 vs. 1997

	Percentage of Workers		
	1983	1997	1997 Rank
Alaska	24.9	20.0	6th
U.S.	20.1	14.1	

Homeownership Rate, 1998

	Rate	Rank
Alaska	66.3	38th
U.S.	66.3	

CRIME

Crime Rates Per 100 Residents (rankings from best to worst crime rate)

Total Crime	1960	1970	1980	1990	1998	1998 Ranking
Alaska	1.03	2.69	4.93	4.92	4.79	30th
U.S.	1.04	2.74	5.90	5.82	4.62	

From 1960 to 1998, Alaska's crime rate increased by 364%, versus a 344% U.S. increase. From 1990 to 1998, Alaska's crime rate dropped by 0.3%, versus a U.S. decrease of 21%.

Violent Crime	1960	1970	1980	1990	1998	1998 Ranking
Alaska	0.10	0.28	0.48	0.53	0.65	41st
U.S.	0.14	0.36	0.58	0.73	0.57	

From 1960 to 1998, Alaska's violent crime rate increased by 550%, versus a U.S. increase of 336%. From 1990 to 1998, Alaska's violent crime rate increased by 23%, compared with a national decline of 22%.

Property Crime	1960	1970	1980	1990	1998	1998 Ranking
Alaska	0.93	2.41	5.73	4.63	4.12	31st
U.S.	0.90	2.38	5.32	5.09	4.05	

From 1960 to 1998, Alaska's property crime rate increased by 343%, versus a national increase of 350%. From 1990 to 1998, Alaska's property crime rate decreased by 11%, compared with a national decline of 20%.

Real Per Capita Police Protection Spending (in real 1996 dollars)

	1962	1972	1982	1992	1996	1996 Ranking
Alaska	64	138	440	238	240	3d
U.S.	51	95	114	148	168	

In 1996, per capita state and local police protection spending in Alaska exceeded the U.S. average by 43%. From 1962 to 1996, real per capita state and local police protection spending increased by 275%, versus an increase of 229% in the U.S. average.

Prisoners in State and Federal Prisons Per 1,000 Population

	1980	1990	1996	1996 Ranking
Alaska	2.04	4.77	6.14	5th
U.S.	1.46	3.11	4.45	

From 1980 to 1996, prisoners per 1,000 population increased by 201%, just behind a U.S. increase of 205%.

HEALTH CARE

Health-Care Spending

Alaska's per capita state and local health-care spending registered $264 in 1996, ranking 3d in the nation and topping the U.S. average of $151 by 75%. From 1962 to 1996, Alaska's real per capita state and local health-care spending increased by 474%, versus an increase of 739% in the U.S. average.

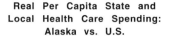

Real Per Capita State and Local Health Care Spending: Alaska vs. U.S.

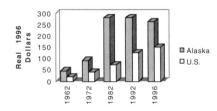

Hospital Spending

Alaska's per capita state and local hospital spending registered $138 in 1996, ranking 40th in the nation and trailing the U.S. average of $266 by 48%. From 1962 to 1996, Alaska's real per capita state and local hospital spending was flat—no increase—as opposed to an increase of 189% in the U.S. average.

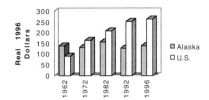

Real Per Capita State and Local Hospital Spending: Alaska vs. U.S.

Medicaid, 1997

	Spending Per Recipient	Ranking
Alaska	$4,397	16th
U.S.	$3,687	

Alaska's per-recipient Medicaid spending exceeded the U.S. average by 19%.

ENVIRONMENT

Parks and Recreation Spending

Alaska's per capita state and local parks and recreation spending registered $82 in 1996, ranking 18th in the nation and outpacing the U.S. average of $72 by 14%. From 1962 to 1996, real per capita state and local parks and recreation spending increased by 1,540%, versus a 213% increase in the U.S. average.

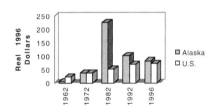

Real Per Capita State and Local Parks and Recreation Spending: Alaska vs. U.S.

State and Local Natural Resources Spending, 1996

	Per Capita	Ranking
Alaska	$442	1st
U.S.	$60	

Per capita state and local natural resources spending in Alaska exceeded the U.S. average by 637%.

State Parks Revenues as a Share of Operating Expenses, 1997

	Percent	Rank
Alaska	38	28th
U.S.	42	

Percentage of Land Owned by the Federal Government, 1996

	Percent	Rank
Alaska	47	6th
U.S.	24.8	

SOCIETY AND DEMOGRAPHICS

Population

Alaska's 1998 population of .614 million ranked 48th in the nation.

Population Growth, 1990–98

	Percentage Change in Population	Ranking
Alaska	11.64	14th
U.S.	8.66	

	Net International Migration	Ranking
Alaska	8,075	42d

	Net Domestic Migration	Ranking
Alaska	−21,302	36th

Infant Mortality Rate, 1998

	Percent	Rank
Alaska	4.6	50th
U.S.	6.4	

Percentage of Births of Low Birthweight, 1997

	Percent	Rank
Alaska	5.9	45th
U.S.	7.5	

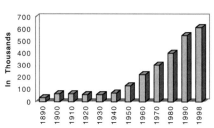

Alaska Population

Percentage of Live Births to Unmarried Women, 1997

	Percent	Rank
Alaska	30.3	30th
U.S.	32.4	

Abortion Rate—Abortions Per 1,000 Women Ages 15–44, 1995

	Rate	Rank
Alaska	14.2	32d
U.S.	22.9	

LIFESTYLE

Percentage of Households with Computers, 1998

	Percent	Rank
Alaska	62.4	1st

Percentage of Households with Internet Access, 1998

	Percent	Rank
Alaska	44.1	1st

State Arts Agency Spending, 1999

	Per Capita	Rank
Alaska	$0.75	29th
U.S.	$1.35	

Per capita state arts spending in 1999 trailed the U.S. average by 44%.

Major League Sports Facilities

None

Arizona

From the state of Arizona came one of the leading conservative politicians of the 20th century: former Republican U.S. Senator and 1964 presidential candidate Barry Goldwater. In a very real sense, Arizona can take a fair amount of credit for the growth of conservatism in U.S. politics, as well as for planting the seeds of the Reagan Revolution in the 1980s.

In a philosophical sense, it seems that Arizona has not changed all that much over the years, as today it claims a fairly conservative delegation to Congress, a Republican governor and a GOP-controlled state legislature. Interestingly, the state also brandishes a relatively strong libertarian streak, with Libertarian Party candidates sometimes garnering as much as 5% of the vote, or more, in key elections. For example, four congressional races in 1998 saw Libertarian candidates getting between 2% and 3% of the vote, while the Libertarian running for governor got 2.7% of the vote. In 1994, while Republican Jon Kyl won almost 54% of the vote to succeed Democratic U.S. Senator Dennis DeConcini, Libertarian Scott Grainger received almost 7% of the vote.

Obviously, much of Arizona still leans in favor of Goldwater-like libertarian/conservative thinking. This is illustrated in the charts below showing Arizona per capita state and local government spending consistently trailing the national average.

For a time, though, in terms of tax policy, Arizona wandered from its free-market roots. For example, in 1990 the state imposed a heavy income tax burden, with the top individual rate registering 8% and the corporate rate 10.5%. However, the 1990s marked a reversal of course, with the top personal rate now at 5.1% and the corporate rate sitting at 8%. While room certainly exists for further reductions in rates, the 1990s have shown some real progress in easing income tax burdens on Arizona's families, entrepreneurs and businesses. Ideally, despite his ongoing legal woes, former Governor Fife Symington's goal to eliminate the state personal income tax should be fulfilled. However, the state budget passed in 1999 led to charges by some that it was too long on spending increases and far too short on tax relief.

Meanwhile, the state's economy has performed quite well recently. Over the past two decades, Arizona's economy and employment levels have expanded at two to three times the national rates of growth. Arizona ranks high in terms of net domestic and international migration, as well as overall population growth. In recent years, disposable income growth has outpaced that of the nation, and during the same period, the state's economy has profited from a fairly unfavorable, antientrepreneur environment that emerged in neighboring California.

Robust economic growth, however, has presented Arizona with an unusual challenge over water. A dispute has been brewing between California, Arizona, and six other western states over one of the region's major sources of water, the Colorado River. Under a decades-old agreement, the amount of water each state can take from the river is regulated, with California having rights to any of the allotted but unused supply. But with increased population comes increased demands for water, and there are now accusations that California has grown overly reliant on the other states' surplus and is taking more than its fair share from the river. Federal authorities have stepped in to mediate the dispute, but regardless of the outcome, it is clear Arizona needs to find new sources of the valuable commodity if it is to continue growing in the desert.

In the June 30, 1999, *San Diego Union-Tribune* Elizabeth Fowler, a public policy fellow with the Pacific Research Institute, laid out the case for "water markets" to deal with this issue. Fowler reported that Interior Secretary Bruce Babbitt has expressed support, telling a conference in Boulder, Colorado, "There is sufficient developed water for today and for the future provided that we use it efficiently, and engage markets, modern science and conservation." Fowler argues for California purchasing or leasing Colorado River water from other states and decreasing agricultural water subsidies. She concludes, "If states and agencies engaged in the marketing of water, the perceived crisis over a shortage of Colorado River water would come to a close."

Arizona faces other problems too. Illegal immigration stirs up emotions, with the number of illegals apprehended by the Tucson sector of the Border Patrol in March 1999 hitting a record 60,500, according to the *Arizona Republic* (April 16, 1999). The total number of illegals apprehended just through March 1999 topped 200,000, according to another report.

"In the past, most of the immigrants came to America in search of a better life, and were generally looked upon positively by most Arizonans," says Mark Howell, a political consultant who has lived in Arizona for the past 12 years. "However, as Mexico has become a bigger player in the illegal drug trade, illegal immigrants are now being used to traffic marijuana and other drugs." Along with the drugs has come the emergence of Mexican gangs, whose members are increasingly violent and bold in their criminal undertakings. For instance, in 1998 members of the Mexican Mafia plotted to assassinate the state's prison chief, Terry Stewart, while he sat in a crowded restaurant. The plan failed only because, by sheer coincidence, several police officers were among the diners at the time. All of this feeds into concerns over Arizona's high crime rate.

Heightened enforcement at traditionally busy crossing points like San Diego and McAllen, Texas, reportedly have pushed much of the traffic to less regulated areas in Arizona, such as Douglas and Naco. While many Arizonans feel sympathy for those looking for a better life in the United States, the increased number of illegals has brought more feelings of resentment. Ranchers complain about stolen water and cut fences that allow cattle to escape, while others have become fed up with the garbage left behind by those crossing over. Some see their very livelihoods and safety being threatened. The Border Patrol has scrambled to stop the flood, but it appears to be fighting a losing battle at this point.

However, even with such problems, the broad numbers show that immigrants—legal and illegal—entering the United States do so at great risk and are seeking to work hard and create a better life. For example, on May 2, 1999, the *Arizona Republic* told the story of Carlos, a 22-year-old Mexican immigrant, who crossed the border illegally and who wanted "to do better to support his wife and two children." He works with other immigrants in a car wash, doing a job most natives will not. The *Republic* notes, "The car wash is usually full. Customers seem more concerned with the affordable price than with workers' immigration status."

A 1995 assessment of the economic and demographic facts surrounding immigration by the late Julian Simon for the Cato Institute, the National Immigration Forum, and 22 other organizations, found that immigrants, for example, do not increase the rate of unemployment among native-born Americans, that total per capita government spending on immigrants is much lower than on natives, that education levels of immigrants have been rising from decade to decade, and that natural resources and the environment are not at risk from immigration.

In addition, immigrants have a great penchant for entrepreneurship. George Gilder noted in his fine book, *Recapturing the Spirit of Enterprise*, "In nearly every nation, many of the most notable entrepreneurs are immigrants." In an earlier book, *The Economic Consequences of Immigration*, Simon reviewed the studies gauging entrepreneurship among immigrants and found, "Overall, and most important, immigrants clearly have a higher propensity for self-employment than do the native-born."

Clearly, Arizona's positives far outweigh its negatives, and it is fairly well positioned to succeed in the entrepreneurial 21st century.

POLITICS

Registered Voters

41% Democrats
45% Republicans
14% Other

Federal Officials: Recent Election and Group Ratings

			ACU	ADA	SBSC
U.S. Senators:	John McCain (R)		86	10	85
	1998 McCain (R)	69%			
	Ranger (D)	27%			
	Jon Kyl (R)		96	1	90
	1994 Kyl (R)	54%			
	Coppersmith (D)	40%			
U.S. Representatives:	Matt Salmon (R-1)		98	45	100
	1998 Salmon (R)	65%			
	Mendoza (D)	35%			
	Ed Pastor (D-2)		6	94	15
	1998 Pastor (D)	68%			
	Barron (R)	28%			
	Bob Stump (R-3)		96	1	90
	1998 Stump (R)	67%			
	Starky (D)	33%			
	John Shadegg (R-4)		99	3	100
	1998 Shadegg (R)	65%			
	Ehst (D)	31%			
	Jim Kolbe (R-5)		78	14	95
	1998 Kolbe (R)	52%			
	Volgy (D)	45%			

	ACU	ADA	SBSC
J.D. Hayworth (R-6)	99	1	100

1998	Hayworth (R)	53%
	Owens (D)	44%

Electoral Votes: 8

1996 Presidential Results:

Clinton	47%
Dole	44%
Perot	8%

State Officials

Governor 1998 Election:

Jane Hull (R)	61%
Paul Johnson (D)	36%

Attorney General: Janet Napolitano (D)

State Senate: 14 Democrats
16 Republicans

State House: 20 Democrats
40 Republicans

TAXES AND SPENDING

Total Revenues

Arizona's per capita state and local total revenues registered $4,694 in 1996, ranking 45th in the nation and trailing the U.S. average of $5,706 by 18%. From 1962 to 1996, real per capita state and local revenues increased by 209%, compared with an increase in the national average of 297%.

Taxes

Arizona's per capita state and local taxes registered $2,295 in 1996, ranking 30th in the nation and trailing the U.S. average of $2,597 by 12%. From 1962 to 1996, real per capita state and local taxes increased by 126%, compared with an increase of 152% in the U.S. average.

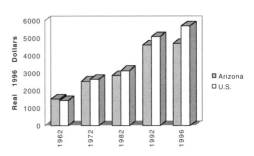

Real Per Capita State and Local Total Revenues: Arizona vs. U.S.

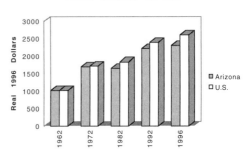

Real Per Capita State and Local Taxes: Arizona vs. U.S.

Property Taxes

Arizona's per capita state and local property taxes equaled $703 in 1996, ranking 31st in the nation and trailing the U.S. average of $789 by 11%. From 1962 to 1996, real per capita state and local property taxes increased by 46%, versus a 67% increase in the U.S. average.

Sales and Gross Receipts Taxes

Arizona's per capita state and local sales and gross receipts taxes came in at $1,025 in 1996, ranking 12th in the nation and exceeding the U.S. average of $939 by 9%. From 1962 to 1996, real per capita state and local sales and gross receipts taxes increased by 172%, versus an increase of 214% in the U.S. average.

Income Taxes

Arizona's per capita state and local income (individual and corporate) taxes registered $439 in 1996, ranking 39th in the nation and trailing the U.S. average of $674 by 35%. From 1962 to 1996, real per capita state and local income taxes increased by 586%, versus a 567% increase in the U.S. average.

Personal Income Tax

A rate of 5.1%, ranking 20th in the nation (from lowest tax rate to highest), and comparing with the national average of 5.26%.

Capital Gains Tax

A rate of 5.1%, ranking 26th in the nation (from lowest tax rate to highest), and comparing with the national average of 4.68%.

Corporate Income Tax

A rate of 8.0%, ranking 34th in the nation (from lowest tax rate to highest), and comparing with the national average of 6.63%.

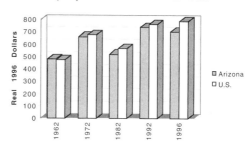

Real Per Capita State and Local Property Taxes: Arizona vs. U.S.

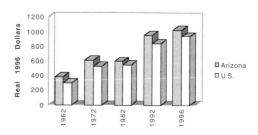

Real Per Capita State and Local Sales and Gross Receipts Taxes: Arizona vs. U.S.

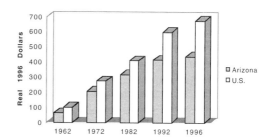

Real Per Capita State and Local Income Taxes: Arizona vs. U.S.

Total Expenditures

Arizona's per capita state and local total spending registered $4,523 in 1996, ranking 39th in the nation and trailing the U.S. average of $5,268 by 14%. From 1962 to 1996, real per capita state and local total spending increased by 177%, versus an increase of 254% in the U.S. average.

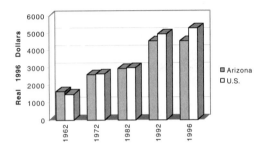

Real Per Capita State and Local Total Expenditures: Arizona vs. U.S.

Welfare Expenditures

Arizona's per capita state and local public welfare spending registered $593 in 1996, ranking 35th in the nation and trailing the U.S. average of $729 by 19%. From 1962 to 1996, real per capita state and local public welfare spending increased by 518%, compared with a 488% increase in the U.S. average.

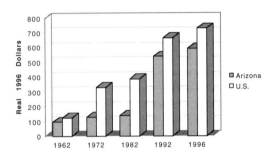

Real Per Capita State and Local Public Welfare Spending: Arizona vs. U.S.

Welfare Recipients (in thousands)

	1980	1989	3/99	Change 1989–99
Ariz.	60	117	92	−21%
U.S.	10,923	10,987	7,335	−33%

Interest on General Debt

Arizona's per capita state and local interest on general debt registered $198 in 1996, ranking 27th in the nation and trailing the U.S. average of $222 by 11%. From 1962 to 1996, real per capita state and local interest on general debt increased by 607%, versus an increase of 335% in the U.S. average.

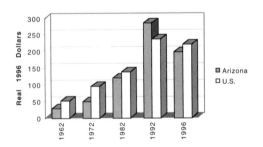

Real Per Capita State and Local Interest on General Debt: Arizona vs. U.S.

Total Debt Outstanding

Arizona's per capita state and local debt registered $4,338 in 1996, ranking 22d in the nation and trailing the U.S. average of $4,409 by 2%. From 1962 to 1996, real per capita state and local debt outstanding increased by 150%, versus an increase of 120% in the U.S. average.

Government Employees

Arizona's state and local government employees (full-time equivalent, or FTE) per 10,000 population registered 497.4 in 1997, ranking 44th in the nation and lagging behind the U.S. average of 531.1 by 6%. From 1962 to to 1996, state and local FTE employees per 10,000 population increased by 47%, compared with an increase in the U.S. average of 66%.

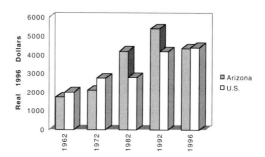

Real Per Capita State and Local Debt Outstanding: Arizona vs. U.S.

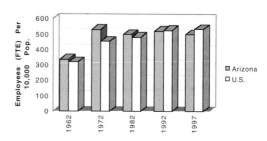

State and Local Government Employees (FTE) Per 10,000 Population: Arizona vs. U.S.

Per Capita Federal Government Expenditures, 1998

	1998	Ranking
Ariz.	$5,155	29th
U.S.	$5,491	

Per capita federal spending in Arizona trailed the national average by 5%.

EDUCATION

Total Education Spending

Arizona's per capita state and local education spending registered $1,389 in 1996, ranking 36th in the nation and trailing the U.S. average of $1,503 by 8%. From 1962 to 1996, real per capita total education spending increased by 96%, versus an increase in the U.S. average of 173%.

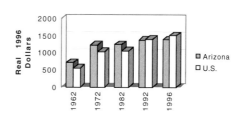

Real Per Capita State and Local Education Spending: Arizona vs. U.S.

Per Pupil Spending

Arizona's per pupil public school spending registered $4,579 in 1998, ranking 44th in the nation and trailing the U.S. average of $6,131 by 25%. From 1970 to 1998, Arizona's real per pupil public school spending increased by 83%, compared with a 120% increase in the U.S. average.

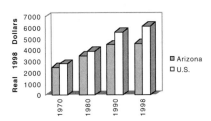

Real Per Pupil Public School Spending: Arizona vs. U.S.

Average Public School Teacher Salaries (in 1997–98 dollars)

	1970	1980	1990	1998	1998 Ranking
Ariz.	37,298	31,364	37,453	33,850	34th
U.S.	36,934	33,272	39,956	39,385	

In 1998, the average public school teacher salary in Arizona trailed the U.S. average by 14%. From 1970 to 1998, the real average teacher salary in Arizona decreased by 9%, versus an increase in the U.S. average of 7%.

Pupil/Teacher Ratio, Fall 1996

	Ratio	Rank
Ariz.	19.7	47th
U.S.	17.1	

Teachers/Staff, Fall 1996

	Percent	Rank
Ariz.	51.0	39th
U.S.	52.1	

Public School 4th-Grade Reading Proficiency, 1998

	Average	Rank (out of 40 states)
Ariz.	207	33d
U.S.	215	

Public School 8th-Grade Reading Proficiency, 1998

	Average	Rank (out of 36 states)
Ariz.	261	23d
U.S.	261	

Public School 4th-Grade Math Proficiency, 1996

	Average	Rank (out of 44 states)
Ariz.	218	31st
U.S.	224	

Public School 8th-Grade Math Proficiency, 1996

	Average	Rank (out of 41 states)
Ariz.	268	25th
U.S.	271	

Public School 8th-Grade Science Proficiency, 1996

	Average	Rank (out of 41 states)
Ariz.	145	26th
U.S.	148	

Average Math SAT Scores

	1972	1982	1992	1998	Percentage Taking SAT in 1998
Ariz.	552	532	517	528	32
U.S.	509	493	501	512	43

Average Verbal SAT Scores

	1972	1982	1992	1998	Percentage Taking SAT in 1998
Ariz.	582	547	516	525	32
U.S.	530	504	500	505	43

Expenditures by Public Institutions of Higher Education Per Full-Time-Equivalent Student, 1996

	FTE Student Spending	Rank
Ariz.	$10,882	44th
U.S.	$12,343	

Per-FTE-student spending in public institutions of higher education trailed the U.S. average by 12%.

Per Full-Time-Equivalent Student Revenues from Federal, State, and Local Governments for Public Institutions of Higher Education, 1996

	FTE Student Government Revenues	Rank
Ariz.	$7,654	29th
U.S.	$8,101	

Per-FTE-student-government revenues in public institutions of higher education trailed the U.S. average by 6%.

Average Salary for Full-Time Professors at Public Universities, 1997

	Average	Rank
Ariz.	$71,484	23d
U.S.	$72,599	

The average full-time public university professor salary trailed the U.S. average by 2%.

ECONOMY AND BUSINESS

Economic Growth

Over the period of 1977 to 1997, Arizona's real gross state product (GSP) grew by 166.2%—ranking 3d in the nation—as compared with real U.S. gross domestic product (GDP) expanding by 70.1%.

At $121.2 billion in 1997, Arizona's GSP ranked as 24th largest in the nation.

From 1993 to 1997, Arizona's annual real GSP growth averaged 7.14%—ranking 2d in the nation—as compared with annual real U.S. GDP growth averaging 3.08%.

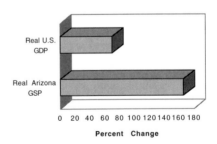

Real Economic Growth 1977-1997: Arizona vs. U.S.

Real U.S. GDP

Real Arizona GSP

0 20 40 60 80 100 120 140 160 180

Percent Change

Job Growth

	Growth in Employee Payrolls (Nonagricultural) 1962–98	Ranking
Ariz.	469.7%	2d
U.S.	126.5%	

	Average Annual Growth in Employee Payrolls (Nonagricultural) 1993–97	Ranking
Ariz.	6.47%	2d
U.S.	2.98%	

Per Capita Disposable Income, 1997

	1997	Ranking
Ariz.	$18,911	38th
U.S.	$21,607	

Per capita disposable income trailed the U.S. average by 12%.

	Real Growth 1962–97	Ranking
Ariz.	111.6%	33d
U.S.	116.7%	

	Average Annual Real Growth 1993–97	Ranking
Ariz.	1.70%	22d
U.S.	1.48%	

Number of Businesses

	1997	Percent with Fewer than 500 Employees
Businesses with Employees	97,009	97.3
Self-employed Individuals	164,000	

New Business Incorporations

	1980	1986	1992	1997
Ariz.	8,342	12,530	9,148	11,262

Percentage Change in Annual New Business Incorporations, 1980 vs. 1997

	Percent	Ranking
Ariz.	35.0	29th
U.S.	49.7	

State Merchandise Exports to the World, 1998 (in millions of dollars)

	1998	Rank
Ariz.	$10,753	18th

Small Business Survival Index, 1999

Arizona ranked 32d in terms of its policy environment for entrepreneurship.

Fortune 500 Headquarters in 1999

A total of 3 (ranked 28th)

Labor Union Membership, 1983 vs. 1997

	Percentage of Workers		
	1983	1997	1997 Rank
Ariz.	11.4	7.0	42d
U.S.	20.1	14.1	

Homeownership Rate, 1998

	Rate	Rank
Ariz.	64.3	41st
U.S.	66.3	

CRIME

Crime Rates Per 100 Residents (rankings from best to worst crime rate)

Total Crime	1960	1970	1980	1990	1998	1998 Ranking
Ariz.	1.63	3.45	8.17	7.89	6.58	48th
U.S.	1.04	2.74	5.90	5.82	4.62	

From 1960 to 1998, Arizona's crime rate increased by 304%, versus a U.S. increase of 344%. From 1990 to 1998, Arizona's crime rate dropped by 17%, versus a U.S. decrease of 21%.

Violent Crime	1960	1970	1980	1990	1998	1998 Ranking
Ariz.	0.20	0.37	0.65	0.65	0.58	35th
U.S.	0.14	0.36	0.58	0.73	0.57	

From 1960 to 1998, Arizona's violent crime rate increased by 190%, versus a U.S. increase of 307%. From 1990 to 1998, Arizona's violent crime rate decreased by 11%, compared with a national decline of 22%.

Property Crime	1960	1970	1980	1990	1998	1998 Ranking
Ariz.	1.44	3.07	7.52	7.24	6.00	50th
U.S.	0.90	2.38	5.32	5.09	4.05	

From 1960 to 1998, Arizona's property crime rate increased by 317%, versus a national increase of 350%. From 1990 to 1998, Arizona's property crime rate decreased by 17%, compared with national decline of 20%.

Real Per Capita Police Protection Spending (in real 1996 dollars)

	1962	1972	1982	1992	1996	1996 Ranking
Ariz.	51	108	164	172	175	12th
U.S.	51	95	114	148	168	

In 1996, per capita state and local police protection spending in Arizona exceeded the U.S. average by 4%. From 1962 to 1996, real per capita state and local police protection spending increased by 243%, versus an increase of 229% in the U.S. average.

Prisoners in State and Federal Prisons Per 1,000 Population

	1980	1990	1996	1996 Ranking
Ariz.	1.61	3.89	5.07	11th
U.S.	1.46	3.11	4.45	

From 1980 to 1996, prisoners per 1,000 population increased by 215%, versus a U.S. increase of 205%.

HEALTH CARE

Health-Care Spending

Arizona's per capita state and local health-care spending registered $117 in 1996, ranking 30th in the nation and lagging behind the U.S. average of $151 by 23%. From 1962 to 1996, Arizona's real per capita state and local health-care spending increased by 736%, versus an increase of 739% in the U.S. average.

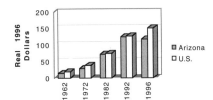

Real Per Capita State and Local Health Care Spending: Arizona vs. U.S.

Hospital Spending

Arizona's per capita state and local hospital spending registered $72 in 1996, ranking 47th in the nation and trailing the U.S. average of $266 by 73%. From 1962 to 1996, Arizona's real per capita state and local hospital spending increased by 57%, as opposed to an increase of 189% in the U.S. average.

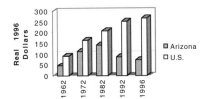

Real Per Capita State and Local Hospital Spending: Arizona vs. U.S.

Medicaid, 1997

	Spending Per Recipient	Ranking
Ariz.	$456	50th
U.S.	$3,681	

Arizona's per-recipient Medicaid spending trailed the U.S. average by 88%.

ENVIRONMENT

Parks and Recreation Spending

Arizona's per capita state and local parks and recreation spending registered $89 in 1996, ranking 15th in the nation and exceeding the U.S. average of $72 by 24%. From 1962 to 1996, real per capita state and local parks and recreation spending increased by 287%, versus a 213% increase in the U.S. average.

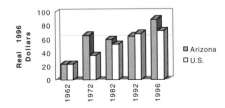

Real Per Capita State and Local Parks and Recreation Spending: Arizona vs. U.S.

State and Local Natural Resources Spending, 1996

	Per Capita	Ranking
Ariz.	87	20th
U.S.	60	

Per capita state and local natural resources spending in Arizona exceeded the U.S. average by 45%.

State Parks Revenues as a Share of Operating Expenses, 1997

	Percent	Rank
Ariz.	42	23d
U.S.	42	

Percentage of Land Owned by the Federal Government, 1996

	Percent	Rank
Ariz.	43.1	8th
U.S.	24.8	

SOCIETY AND DEMOGRAPHICS

Population

Arizona's 1998 population of 4.669 million ranked 21st in the nation.

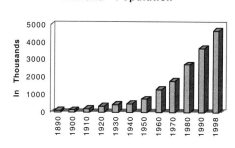

Arizona   Population

Population Growth, 1990–98

	Percentage Change in Population	Ranking
Ariz.	27.39	2d
U.S.	8.66	

	Net International Migration	Ranking
Ariz.	95,821	12th

	Net Domestic Migration	Ranking
Ariz.	518,820	4th

Infant Mortality Rate, 1998

	Percent	Rank
Ariz.	8.2	12th
U.S.	6.4	

Percentage of Births of Low Birthweight, 1997

	Percent	Rank
Ariz.	6.9	35th
U.S.	7.5	

Percentage of Live Births to Unmarried Women, 1997

	Percent	Rank
Ariz.	37.7	7th
U.S.	32.4	

Abortion Rate—Abortions Per 1,000 Women Ages 15–44, 1995

	Rate	Rank
Ariz.	19.1	24th
U.S.	22.9	

LIFESTYLE

Percentage of Households with Computers, 1998

	Percent	Rank
Ariz.	44.3	15th

Percentage of Households with Internet Access, 1998

	Percent	Rank
Ariz.	29.3	12th

State Arts Agency Spending, 1999

	Per Capita	Rank
Ariz.	$0.78	28th
U.S.	$1.35	

Per capita state arts spending in 1999 trailed the U.S. average by 42%.

Major League Sports Facilities

Year Opened/ Refurb.	Stadium/ Arena	Home Team	Millions of Nominal Dollars		Millions of Real 1997 Dollars	
			Estimated Total Cost	Estimated Taxpayer Cost	Estimated Total Cost	Estimated Taxpayer Cost
1958	Sun Devil Stadium	Cardinals (NFL) 1988–present	$1.0	$1.0	$5.6	$5.6
1988	Sun Devil Stadium (re)		$11.1	$8.7	$14.4	$11.3
1992	America West Arena	Suns (NBA) 1992–present Coyotes (NHL) 1996–present	$95.0	$45.0	$108.7	$51.5
1998	Bank One Ballpark	Diamondbacks (MLB)	$355.0	$238.0	$349.4	$234.3

ARKANSAS

In 1992, after Bill Clinton was elected president of the United States, it seemed that Arkansas might finally get some long-sought-after respect. Unfortunately for the fine folks of Arkansas, Clinton became the first elected U.S. president to be impeached. Rather than boosting Arkansas's reputation, Clinton's escapades in the White House only served to embarrass the residents of Arkansas, as well as many other Americans.

Fortunately, the burden of Bill Clinton will not hold Arkansas back. For example, in terms of the economy, real economic and disposable income growth, and job creation have run ahead of national averages in the post-Governor Clinton era in Arkansas. And over the past decade, Arkansas has reduced its welfare rolls at a far faster rate than the U.S. average. In addition, from 1990 to 1998, the state was a big net importer of people from other states.

Politically, Republicans have made formidable gains during Clinton's period in the White House. Tim Hutchinson (R) succeeded Democrat Senator David Pryor in 1996 (with brother Asa Hutchinson taking Tim's congressional seat), and after Democrat Governor Jim Guy Tucker was convicted on a charge related to a fraudulent loan and resigned, Republican Lieutenant Governor Mike Huckabee became governor and won election himself in 1998 by huge numbers.

At the same time, however, Democrats held onto the state's other U.S. Senate seat being vacated by Dale Bumpers in 1998, as Democrat Blanche Lambert Lincoln defeated Republican Fay Boozman by a handy margin. In addition, the state's four House seats are split, and the state legislature is solidly Democrat.

Meanwhile, per capita state and local government spending and debt come in below the national average, as do taxes in general. Property taxes are particularly low, while income tax rates are on the high side. On education, improvement is needed, as average math, reading, and science scores come in below the national average.

While crime comes in lower than the national rate, the increase in Arkansas was far more rapid than what has occurred nationally in recent decades. In addition, Arkansas's decrease in crime between 1990 and 1998 was far smaller than the nation's decline.

The state needs to set out in a new direction. Arkansas's bridge to the 21st century should be a distinctly anti-Clinton span. State officials should choose lower income taxes; school choice over cozying up to the education establishment; keeping government expenditures in check; cutting the number of state and local government employees, which ranks on the high side; and showing voters that politicians can be honorable and ethical as opposed to . . . well . . . being Clinton-esque.

POLITICS

Registered Voters

No party registration

Federal Officials: Recent Election and Group Ratings

				ACU	ADA	SBSC
U.S. Senators:	Tim Hutchinson (R)			100	3	90
	1996	Hutchinson (R)	52%			
		Bryant (D)	47%			
	Blanche Lambert Lincoln (D)			NA	NA	NA
	1998	Lincoln (D)	55%			
		Boozman (R)	42%			
U.S. Representatives:	Marion Berry (D-1)			36	73	30
	1998	Berry (D)	NO			
	Vic Snyder (D-2)			18	83	20
	1998	Snyder (D)	58%			
		Wyrick (R)	42%			
	Asa Hutchinson (R-3)			90	5	75
	1998	Hutchinson (R)	81%			
		Forbes (D)	19%			
	Jay Dickey (R-4)			94	3	95
	1998	Dickey (R)	58%			
		Smith (D)	42%			
Electoral Votes:	6					
1996 Presidential Results:	Clinton		54%			
	Dole		37%			
	Perot		8%			

State Officials

Governor 1998 Election:	Mike Huckabee (R)	60%
	Bill Bristow (D)	39%
Lt. Governor:	Winthrop Rockefeller (R)	
Attorney General:	Mark Pryor (D)	
State Senate:	29 Democrats	
	6 Republicans	
State House:	77 Democrats	
	23 Republicans	

TAXES AND SPENDING

Total Revenues

Arkansas's per capita state and local total revenues registered $4,540 in 1996, ranking 50th in the nation and trailing the U.S. average of $5,706 by 20%. From 1962 to 1996, real per capita state and local revenues increased by 334%, compared with an increase in the national average of 297%.

Taxes

Arkansas's per capita state and local taxes registered $1,933 in 1996, ranking 48th in the nation and trailing the U.S. average of $2,597 by 26%. From 1962 to 1996, real per capita state and local taxes increased by 205%, compared with an increase of 152% in the U.S. average.

Property Taxes

Arkansas's per capita state and local property taxes equaled $300 in 1996, ranking 49th in the nation and trailing the U.S. average of $789 by 62%. From 1962 to 1996, real per capita state and local property taxes increased by 68%, versus a 67% increase in the U.S. average.

Sales and Gross Receipts Taxes

Arkansas's per capita state and local sales and gross receipts taxes came in at $924 in 1996, ranking 21st in the nation and trailing the U.S. average of $939 by 2%. From 1962 to 1996, real per capita state and local sales and gross receipts taxes increased by 196%, versus an increase of 214% in the U.S. average.

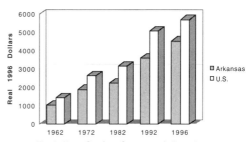

Real Per Capita State and Local Total Revenues: Arkansas vs. U.S.

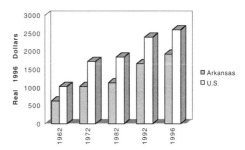

Real Per Capita State and Local Taxes: Arkansas vs. U.S.

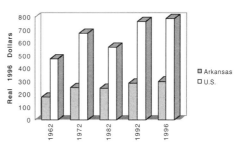

Real Per Capita State and Local Property Taxes: Arkansas vs. U.S.

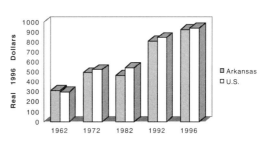

Real Per Capita State and Local Sales and Gross Receipts Taxes: Arkansas vs. U.S.

Income Taxes

Arkansas's per capita state and local income (individual and corporate) taxes registered $554 in 1996, ranking 32d in the nation and trailing the U.S. average of $674 by 18%. From 1962 to 1996, real per capita state and local income taxes increased by 907%, versus a 567% increase in the U.S. average.

Personal Income Tax

A rate of 7.0%, ranking 39th in the nation (from lowest tax rate to highest), and comparing with the national average of 5.26%.

Capital Gains Tax

A rate of 6.0%, ranking 30th in the nation (from lowest tax rate to highest), and comparing with the national average of 4.68%.

Corporate Income Tax

A rate of 6.5%, ranking 21st in the nation (from lowest tax rate to highest), and comparing with the national average of 6.63%.

Total Expenditures

Arkansas's per capita state and local total spending registered $3,849 in 1996, ranking 51st in the nation and trailing the U.S. average of $5,268 by 27%. From 1962 to 1996, real per capita state and local total spending increased by 281%, versus an increase of 254% in the U.S. average.

Welfare Expenditures

Arkansas's per capita state and local public welfare spending registered $632 in 1996, ranking 29th in the nation and trailing the U.S. average of $729 by 13%. From 1962 to 1996, real per capita state and local public welfare spending increased by 410%, compared with a 488% increase in the U.S. average.

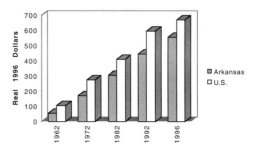

Real Per Capita State and Local Income Taxes: Arkansas vs. U.S.

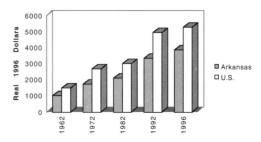

Real Per Capita State and Local Total Expenditures: Arkansas vs. U.S.

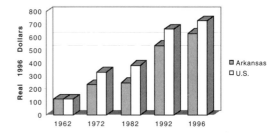

Real Per Capita State and Local Public Welfare Spending: Arkansas vs. U.S.

Welfare Recipients (in thousands)

	1980	1989	3/99	Change 1989–99
Ark.	85	71	29	−59%
U.S.	10,923	10,987	7,335	−33%

Interest on General Debt

Arkansas's per capita state and local interest on general debt registered $128 in 1996, ranking 46th in the nation and trailing the U.S. average of $222 by 42%. From 1962 to 1996, real per capita state and local interest on general debt increased by 457%, versus an increase of 335% in the U.S. average.

Total Debt Outstanding

Arkansas's per capita state and local debt registered $2,316 in 1996, ranking 48th in the nation and trailing the U.S. average of $4,409 by 47%. From 1962 to 1996, real per capita state and local debt outstanding increased by 147%, versus an increase of 120% in the U.S. average.

Government Employees

Arkansas's state and local government employees (full-time equivalent, or FTE) per 10,000 population registered 552.4 in 1997, ranking 23d in the nation and exceeding the U.S. average of 531.1 by 4%. From 1962 to 1996, state and local FTE employees per 10,000 population increased by 104%, compared with an increase in the U.S. average of 66%.

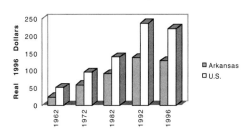

Real Per Capita State and Local Interest on General Debt: Arkansas vs. U.S.

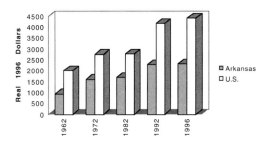

Real Per Capita State and Local Debt Outstanding: Arkansas vs. U.S.

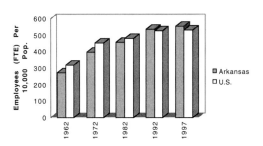

State and Local Government Employees (FTE) Per 10,000 Population: Arkansas vs. U.S.

Per Capita Federal Government Expenditures, 1998

	1998	Ranking
Ark.	$5,128	30th
U.S.	$5,491	

Per capita federal spending in Arkansas trailed the national average by 7%.

EDUCATION

Total Education Spending

Arkansas's per capita state and local education spending registered $1,261 in 1996, ranking 48th in the nation and trailing the U.S. average of $1,503 by 16%. From 1962 to 1996, real per capita total education spending increased by 244%, versus an increase in the U.S. average of 173%.

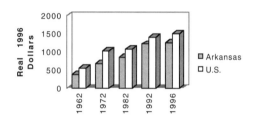

Real Per Capita State and Local Education Spending: Arkansas vs. U.S.

Per Pupil Spending

Arkansas's per pupil public school spending registered $4,078 in 1998, ranking 50th in the nation and trailing the U.S. average of $6,131 by 33%. From 1970 to 1998, Arkansas's real per pupil public school spending increased by 115%, compared with a 120% increase in the U.S. average.

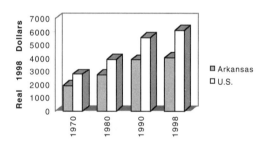

Real Per Pupil Public School Spending: Arkansas vs. U.S.

Average Public School Teacher Salaries (in 1997–98 dollars)

	1970	1980	1990	1998	1998 Ranking
Ark.	27,005	25,624	28,472	30,578	46th
U.S.	36,934	33,272	39,956	39,385	

In 1998, the average public school teacher salary in Arkansas trailed the U.S. average by 22%. From 1970 to 1998, the real average teacher salary in Arkansas increased by 13%, versus an increase in the U.S. average of 7%.

Pupil/Teacher Ratio, Fall 1996

	Ratio	Rank
Ark.	17.1	35th
U.S.	17.1	

Teachers/Staff, Fall 1996

	Percent	Rank
Ark.	52.3	31st
U.S.	52.1	

Public School 4th-Grade Reading Proficiency, 1998

	Average	Rank (out of 40 states)
Ark.	209	31st
U.S.	215	

Public School 8th-Grade Reading Proficiency, 1998

	Average	Rank (out of 37 states)
Ark.	256	28th
U.S.	261	

Public School 4th-Grade Math Proficiency, 1996

	Average	Rank (out of 44 states)
Ark.	216	33d
U.S.	224	

Public School 8th-Grade Math Proficiency, 1996

	Average	Rank (out of 41 states)
Ark.	262	33d
U.S.	271	

Public School 8th-Grade Science Proficiency, 1996

	Average	Rank (out of 41 states)
Ark.	144	29th
U.S.	148	

Average Math SAT Scores

	1972	1982	1992	1998	Percentage Taking SAT in 1998
Ark.	533	539	536	555	6
U.S.	509	493	501	512	43

Average Verbal SAT Scores

	1972	1982	1992	1998	Percentage Taking SAT in 1998
Ark.	562	556	549	568	6
U.S.	530	504	500	505	43

Expenditures by Public Institutions of Higher Education Per Full-Time-Equivalent Student, 1996

	FTE Student Spending	Rank
Ark.	$11,824	30th
U.S.	$12,343	

Per-FTE-student spending in public institutions of higher education trailed the U.S. average by 4%.

Per Full-Time-Equivalent Student Revenues from Federal, State, and Local Governments for Public Institutions of Higher Education, 1996

	FTE Student Government Revenues	Rank
Ark.	$8,519	16th
U.S.	$8,101	

Per-FTE-student-government revenues in public institutions of higher education exceeded the U.S. average by 5%.

Average Salary for Full-Time Professors at Public Universities, 1997

	Average	Rank
Ark.	$63,795	37th
U.S.	$72,599	

The average full-time public university professor salary trailed the U.S. average by 12%.

ECONOMY AND BUSINESS

Economic Growth

Over the period of 1977 to 1997, Arkansas' real gross state product (GSP) grew by 75.2%—ranking 24th in the nation—as compared with real U.S. gross domestic product (GDP) expanding by 70.1%.

At $58.5 billion in 1997, Arkansas' GSP ranked as 32d largest in the nation.

From 1993 to 1997, Arkansas' annual real GSP growth averaged 3.97%—ranking 19th in the nation—as compared with annual real U.S. GDP growth averaging 3.08%.

**Real Economic Growth
1977-1997: Arkansas vs. U.S.**

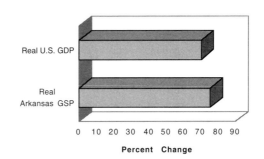

Percent Change

Job Growth

	Growth in Employee Payrolls (Nonagricultural) 1962–98	Ranking
Ark.	181.1%	17th
U.S.	126.5%	

	Average Annual Growth in Employee Payrolls (Nonagricultural) 1993–98	Ranking
Ark.	3.12%	23d
U.S.	2.98%	

Per Capita Disposable Income

	1997	Ranking
Ark.	$17,321	46th
U.S.	$21,607	

Per capita disposable income trailed the U.S. average by 20%.

	Real Growth 1962--7	Ranking
Ark.	159.2%	7th
U.S.	116.7%	

	Average Annual Real Growth 1993–97	Ranking
Ark.	1.80%	15th
U.S.	1.48%	

Number of Businesses

	1997	Percent with Fewer than 500 Employees
Businesses with Employees	58,526	97.3
Self-employed Individuals	115,000	

New Business Incorporations

	1980	1986	1992	1997
Ark.	3,924	5,829	6,078	6,994

Percentage Change in Annual New Business Incorporations, 1980 vs. 1997

	Percent	1997 Ranking
Ark.	78.2	14th
U.S.	49.7	

State Merchandise Exports to the World, 1998 (in millions of dollars)

	1998	Rank
Ark.	$1,934	38th

Small Business Survival Index, 1999

Arkansas ranked a shaky 35th in terms of its policy environment for entrepreneurship.

Fortune 500 Headquarters in 1999

A total of 4 (ranked 26th)

Labor Union Membership, 1983 vs. 1997

	Percentage of Workers		
	1983	1997	1997 Rank
Ark.	11.0	5.9	48th
U.S.	20.1	14.1	

Homeownership Rate, 1998

	Rate	Rank
Ark.	66.7	35th
U.S.	66.3	

CRIME

Crime Rates Per 100 Residents (rankings from best to worst crime rate)

Total Crime	1960	1970	1980	1990	1998	1998 Ranking
Ark.	0.58	1.60	3.81	4.87	4.28	22d
U.S.	1.04	2.74	5.90	5.82	4.62	

From 1960 to 1998, Arkansas's crime rate increased by 638%, versus a U.S. increase of 344%. From 1990 to 1998, Arkansas's crime rate dropped by 12%, versus a U.S. decrease of 21%.

Violent Crime	1960	1970	1980	1990	1998	1998 Ranking
Ark.	0.10	0.22	0.34	0.53	0.49	29th
U.S.	0.14	0.36	0.58	0.73	0.57	

From 1960 to 1998, Arkansas's violent crime rate increased by 390%, versus a U.S. increase of 307%. From 1990 to 1998, Arkansas's violent crime rate declined by 8%, compared with a national decline of 22%.

Property Crime	1960	1970	1980	1990	1998	1998 Ranking
Ark.	0.48	1.38	3.48	4.34	3.79	22d
U.S.	0.90	2.38	5.32	5.09	4.05	

From 1960 to 1998, Arkansas's property crime rate increased by 690%, versus a national increase of 350%. From 1990 to 1998, Arkansas's property crime rate decreased by 13% compared with a national decline of 20%.

Real Per Capita Police Protection Spending (in real 1996 dollars)

	1962	1972	1982	1992	1996	1996 Ranking
Ark.	23	39	58	77	101	48th
U.S.	51	95	114	148	168	

In 1996, per capita state and local police protection spending in Arkansas trailed the U.S. average by 40%. From 1962 to 1996, real per capita state and local police protection spending increased by 339%, versus an increase of 229% in the U.S. average.

Prisoners in State and Federal Prisons Per 1,000 Population

	1980	1990	1996	1996 Ranking
Ark.	1.27	3.11	3.75	23d
U.S.	1.46	3.11	4.45	

From 1980 to 1996, prisoners per 1,000 population increased by 195%, versus a U.S. increase of 205%.

HEALTH CARE

Health-Care Spending

Arkansas's per capita state and local health-care spending registered $111 in 1996, ranking 31st in the nation and trailing the U.S. average of $151 by 26%. From 1962 to 1996, Arkansas's real per capita state and local health-care spending increased by 1,133%, versus an increase of 739% in the U.S. average.

Real Per Capita State and Local Health Care Spending: Arkansas vs. U.S.

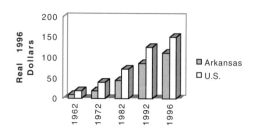

Hospital Spending

Arkansas's per capita state and local hospital spending registered $238 in 1996, ranking 24th in the nation and lagging behind the U.S. average of $266 by 11%. From 1962 to 1996, Arkansas's real per capita state and local hospital spending increased by 272%, as opposed to an increase of 189% in the U.S. average.

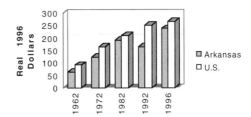

Real Per Capita State and Local Hospital Spending: Arkansas vs. U.S.

Medicaid, 1997

	Spending Per Recipient	Ranking
Ark.	$3,519	25th
U.S.	$3,681	

Arkansas's per-recipient Medicaid spending trailed the U.S. average by 4%.

ENVIRONMENT

Parks and Recreation Spending

Arkansas's per capita state and local parks and recreation spending registered $33 in 1996, ranking 49th in the nation and trailing the U.S. average of $72 by 54%. From 1962 to 1996, real per capita state and local parks and recreation spending increased by 560%, versus a 213% increase in the U.S. average.

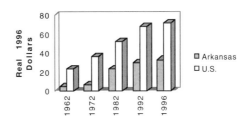

Real Per Capita State and Local Park and Recreation Spending: Arkansas vs. U.S.

State and Local Natural Resources Spending, 1996

	Per Capita	Ranking
Ark.	$56	31st
U.S.	$60	

Per capita state and local natural resources spending in Arkansas trailed the U.S. average by 7%.

State Parks Revenues as a Share of Operating Expenses, 1997

	Percent	Rank
Ark.	54	14th
U.S.	42	

Percentage of Land Owned by the Federal Government, 1996

	Percent	Rank
Ark.	8.2	18th
U.S.	24.8	

SOCIETY AND DEMOGRAPHICS

Population

Arkansas's 1998 population of 2.538 million ranked 33d in the nation.

Population Growth, 1990–98

	Percentage Change in Population	Ranking
Ark.	7.95	22d
U.S.	8.66	

	Net International Migration	Ranking
Ark.	9,376	40th

	Net Domestic Migration	Ranking
Ark.	105,616	14th

Infant Mortality Rate, 1998

	Percent	Rank
Ark.	7.6	17th
U.S.	6.4	

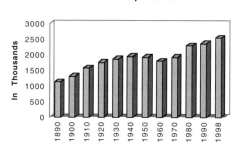

Arkansas Population

Percentage of Births of Low Birthweight, 1997

	Percent	Rank
Ark.	8.4	13th
U.S.	7.5	

Percentage of Live Births to Unmarried Women, 1997

	Percent	Rank
Ark.	34.2	12th
U.S.	32.4	

Abortion Rate—Abortions Per 1,000 Women Ages 15–44, 1995

	Rate	Rank
Ark.	11.1	39th
U.S.	22.9	

LIFESTYLE

Percentage of Households with Computers, 1998

	Percent	Rank
Ark.	29.8	49th

Percentage of Households with Internet Access, 1998

	Percent	Rank
Ark.	14.7	50th

State Arts Agency Spending, 1999

	Per Capita	Rank
Ark.	$0.52	43d
U.S.	$1.35	

Per capita state arts spending in 1999 trailed the U.S. average by 61%.

Major League Sports Facilities

None

CALIFORNIA

California not only claims the largest population among the states, but it also offers some of the biggest contrasts. Of course, there are famous geographic differences—from the beaches of southern California to Death Valley to the Redwoods up north—as well as regionalism—greater L.A. versus the rest of the state, as one wag told us.

But California's contrasts certainly do not stop there. With Hollywood being the world's movie capital, the Golden State has seen Frank Capra-directed films celebrating America and the average guy, as well as the cynical, conspiratorial, and often bizarre movies of Oliver Stone. Musically, could the Beach Boys' surfing tunes be much more different from the drug-laden music that emerged from San Francisco in the late 1960s and early 1970s? Even when it comes to baseball, the jewel that is Dodger Stadium outshines the wind-plagued 3Com (Candlestick) Park, which the Giants finally fled in April 2000.

Even when speaking of California Republicans who once sat in the Oval Office, the differences are dramatic. On the one hand, California gave us President Richard Nixon, arguably the most liberal GOP president ever. For example, Nixon oversaw the creation of the Occupational Safety and Health Administration and the Environmental Protection Agency, increased the capital gains tax, and officially detached the U.S. dollar from gold (therefore helping to push inflation skyward).

On the other hand, President Ronald Reagan, no doubt the most conservative Republican president since at least the 1920s, is a California resident and former state governor. Reagan slashed the top income tax rate from 70% to 28% and helped restore American confidence and prosperity. And nobody did more to win the cold war.

However, the glory days of Reagan Republicanism in California seem to be a distant memory, especially after former Governor Pete Wilson, a Republican, piled higher taxes on an already faltering state economy in the early 1990s. Again, the contrast today is stark, as state government—both legislative houses and the governor's office—completely shifted into Democratic hands in 1999 for the first time in 16 years.

In reaching agreement in June 1999 on the fiscal year 2000 state budget, Democratic Governor Gray Davis disappointed some of the most extreme left members of his party, but overall he toed the liberal line. Expenditure increases overwhelmed barely detectable tax cuts. School spending and teacher salaries were increased, while regulations on the state's more than 200 charter schools were tightened—all to the delight of education unions. In addition, an environmental lobbyist told the *Sacramento Bee* (June 30, 1999) that taxpayer funds to buy up land would more than double the previous year's level. State-subsidized health-care programs also were expanded, and a sum of $3 million was allocated to build a new governor's mansion in Sacramento.

Meanwhile, one of the major complaints from the minority Republicans related to government pork. Davis promised not to cut these projects if Republicans signed onto the budget. Republicans jumped on board, but Davis wound up vetoing a goodly amount of Republican pork anyway, along with a smaller portion of Democrat pork. Is making an issue out of lost pork projects the best path for Republicans looking to regain political clout in California?

Conscious of the national implications, Davis has made a clear decision to be the antigun governor, prodding the legislature and state bureaucrats to enact laws and regulations to make California one of the most hostile environments for private gun owners in the nation.

Meanwhile, California has struggled back from the economic depths of the early 1990s. However, real state economic growth, disposable income growth and job creation have still lagged behind that of the nation recently.

And while new business incorporations have picked up considerably, annual numbers still run far below levels exhibited in the early-to-mid 1980s. In fact, the Small Business Survival Committee ranks California's policy environment for entrepreneurship as being quite poor. Particularly burdensome are the state's extremely high corporate income, personal income and capital gains taxes, not to mention an additional income tax imposed on S-Corporations.

It also is quite telling that from 1990 to 1998 California ranked dead last in the nation in terms of net domestic migration—exporting more than two million people to elsewhere in the nation. Conversely, net international migration to California topped two million over the same period. Quite predictably, improving economic times have silenced much of the anti-immigration rhetoric that just recently flew around California's political circles. "Nobody cares about immigrations any more," according to Sacramento-based political strategist Wayne C. Johnson. "If you hear any complaints at all, it's typically 'why is everybody else rich, and I'm not?' And those who say that are probably tooling down Interstate 5 in their BMW convertibles." Joel Kotkin, a senior fellow at the Pacific Research Institute, has identified California's immigrant population as "one of the primary engines behind the Golden State's recent economic resurgence."

In so many ways—from a vibrant immigrant population, to being well positioned for trade on the Pacific Rim, to Silicon Valley, long the hottest computer technology spot on the planet—California seems to be ideally suited to experience entrepreneurial success in the 21st century. Unfortunately, these and other points in California's favor are substantially offset by a severe antigrowth tax system. Lift this tax burden and it is hard to imagine what will possibly hold the Golden State back.

POLITICS

Registered Voters

47% Democrats
36% Republicans
16% Other

Federal Officials: Recent Election and Group Ratings

				ACU	ADA	SBSC
U.S. Senators:	Dianne Feinstein (D)			10	87	15
	1994	Feinstein (D)	47%			
		Huffington (R)	45%			
	Barbara Boxter (D)			3	97	20
	1998	Boxer (D)	53%			
		Fong (R)	43%			
U.S. Representatives:	Mike Thompson (D-1)			NA	NA	NA
	1998	Thompson (D)	62%			
		Luce (R)	33%			
	Wally Herger (R-2)			98	4	95
	1998	Herger (R)	63%			
		Braden (D)	34%			
	Doug Ose (R-3)			NA	NA	NA
	1998	Ose (R)	52%			
		Dunn (D)	45%			
	John Doolittle (R-4)			99	4	90
	1998	Doolittle (R)	63%			
		Shapiro (D)	34%			
	Bob Matsui (D-5)			7	95	15
	1998	Matsui (D)	72%			
		Dinsmore (R)	26%			
	Lynn Woolsey (D-6)			3	99	10
	1998	Woolsey (D)	68%			
		McAuliffe (R)	30%			
	George Miller (D-7)			21	94	10
	1998	Miller (D)	77%			
		Reece (R)	23%			
	Nancy Pelosi (D-8)			2	94	10
	1998	Pelosi (D)	86%			
		Martz (R)	12%			
	Barbara Lee (D-9)			5	NA	0
	1998	Lee (D)	83%			
		Sanders (R)	13%			

			ACU	ADA	SBSC
Ellen Tauscher (D-10)			16	80	30
1998	Tauscher (D)	53%			
	Ball (R)	43%			
Richard Pombo (R-11)			98	22	85
1998	Pombo (R)	61%			
	Figueroa (D)	36%			
Tom Lantos (D-12)			8	98	10
1998	Lantos (D)	74%			
	Evans (R)	21%			
Fortney (Pete) Stark (D-13)			5	95	10
1998	Stark (D)	71%			
	Goetz (R)	27%			
Anna Eshoo (D-14)			5	90	15
1998	Eshoo (D)	69%			
	Haugen (R)	28%			
Tom Campbell (R-15)			59	38	65
1998	Campbell (R)	61%			
	Lane (D)	38%			
Zoe Lofgren (D-16)			6	93	15
1998	Lofgren (D)	73%			
	Thayn (R)	23%			
Sam Farr (D-17)			3	94	15
1998	Farr (D)	65%			
	McCampbell (R)	33%			
Gary Condit (D-18)			49	52	35
1998	Condit (D)	87%			
	Degroat (LBT)	13%			
George Radanovich (R-19)			98	0	80
1998	Radanovich (R)	79%			
	Richter (LBT)	21%			
Calvin Dooley (D-20)			10	66	25
1998	Dooley (D)	61%			
	Unruh (R)	39%			
William Thomas (R-21)			80	9	95
1998	Thomas (R)	79%			
	Evans (REF)	21%			

	ACU	ADA	SBSC
Lois Capps (D-22)	18	83	16
1998 Capps (D) 55%			
Bordonaro (R) 43%			
Elton Gallegly (R-23)	89	8	80
1998 Gallegly (R) 60%			
Gonzalez (D) 40%			
Bradley Sherman (D-24)	26	85	10
1998 Sherman (D) 57%			
Hoffman (R) 38%			
Howard McKeon (R-25)	95	1	95
1998 McKeon (R) 75%			
Acker (D) 25%			
Howard Berman (D-26)	6	89	10
1998 Berman (D) 82%			
Ros (LBT) 8%			
James Rogan (R-27)	96	0	95
1998 Rogan (R) 51%			
Gordon (D) 46%			
David Dreier (R-28)	94	3	90
1998 Dreier (R) 58%			
Nelson (D) 39%			
Henry Waxman (D-29)	5	95	15
1998 Waxman (D) 74%			
Gottlieb (R) 23%			
Xavier Becerra (D-30)	2	88	10
1998 Becerra (D) 81%			
Parker (R) 19%			
Matthew Martinez (D-31)	10	79	5
1998 Martinez (D) 70%			
Moreno (R) 23%			
Julian Dixon (D-32)	5	88	10
1998 Dixon (D) 87%			
Ardito (R) 11%			
Lucille Roybal-Allard (D-33) 3	95	5	
1998 Roybal-Allard (D) 87%			
Miller (R) 13%			

	ACU	ADA	SBS
Grace Flores Napolitano (D-34)	NA	NA	NA
1998 Napolitano (D) 68%			
Perez (R) 29%			
Maxine Waters (D-35)	4	93	0
1998 Waters (D) 89%			
Mego (AIP) 11%			
Steven Kuykendall (R-36)	21	NA	NA
1998 Kuykendall (R) 49%			
Hahn (D) 47%			
Juanita Millender-McDonald (D-37) 9	89	5	
1998 Millender-McDonald (D)85%			
Lankster (R) 15%			
Steve Horn (D-38)	56	34	60
1998 Horn (D) 53%			
Matthews (R) 44%			
Edward Royce (R-39)	99	8	60
1998 Royce (R) 63%			
Groom (D) 34%			
Jerry Lewis (R-40)	82	6	90
1998 Lewis (R) 65%			
Conaway (D) 32%			
Gary Miller (R-41)	NA	NA	NA
1998 Miller (R) 53%			
Ansari (D) 41%			
Joe Baca (D-42)	NA	NA	NA
1999(sp) Baca (D) 52%			
Pirozzo (R) 44%			
Ken Calvert (R-43)	91	0	95
1998 Calvert (R) 56%			
Rayburn (D) 38%			
Mary Bono (R-44)	95	0	92
1998 Bono (R) 60%			
Waite (D) 36%			
Dana Rohrabacher (R-45)	95	11	90
1998 Rohrabacher (R) 59%			
Neal (D) 37%			

			ACU	ADA	SBSC
Loretta Sanchez (D-46)			18	80	15
1998	Sanchez (D)	56%			
	Dorman (R)	39%			
Christopher Cox (R-47)			98	5	100
1998	Cox (R)	68%			
	Avalos (D)	30%			
Ron Packard (R-48)			93	3	95
1998	Packard (R)	77%			
	Miles (NL)	13%			
Brian Bilbray (R-49)			72	18	65
1998	Bilbray (R)	49%			
	Kehoe (D)	47%			
Bob Filmer (D-50)			5	91	5
1998	Filner (D)	NO			
Randy (Duke) Cunningham (R-51)		96	4	85	
1998	Cunningham (R)	61%			
	Kripke (D)	35%			
Duncan Hunter (R-52)			95	5	80
1998	Hunter (R)	76%			
	Badler (LBT)	14%			

Electoral Votes:	54	
1996 Presidential Results:	Clinton	51%
	Dole	38%
	Perot	7%

State Officials

Governor 1998 Election:	Gray Davis (D)	58%
	Dan Lungren (R)	38%
Lt. Governor:	Cruz M. Bustamante (D)	
Attorney General:	Bill Lockyer (D)	
State Senate:	25 Democrats	
	15 Republicans	
State General Assembly:	47 Democrats	
	32 Republicans	
	1 Green	

TAXES AND SPENDING

Total Revenues

California's per capita state and local total revenues registered $6,305 in 1996, ranking 12th in the nation and exceeding the U.S. average of $5,706 by 10%. From 1962 to 1996, real per capita state and local revenues increased by 228%, compared with an increase in the national average of 297%.

Taxes

California's per capita state and local taxes registered $2,705 in 1996, ranking 15th in the nation and exceeding the U.S. average of $2,597 by 4%. From 1962 to 1996, real per capita state and local taxes increased by 95%, compared with an increase of 152% in the U.S. average.

Property Taxes

California's per capita state and local property taxes equaled $715 in 1996, ranking 29th in the nation and trailing the U.S. average of $789 by 9%. From 1962 to 1996, real per capita state and local property taxes increased by 3%, versus a 67% increase in the U.S. average. With Proposition 13 passing in the late 1970s, per capita property taxes declined. So, from 1972 to 1996, California's real per capita property taxes dropped by 34% versus a national increase of 17%.

Sales and Gross Receipts Taxes

California's per capita state and local sales and gross receipts taxes came in at $968 in 1996, ranking 15th in the nation and topping the U.S. average of $939 by 3%. From 1962 to 1996, real per capita state and local sales and gross receipts taxes increased by 160%, versus an increase of 214% in the U.S. average.

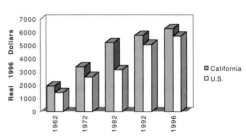

Real Per Capita State and Local Total Revenues: California vs. U.S.

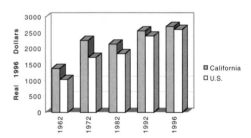

Real Per Capita State and Local Taxes: California vs. U.S.

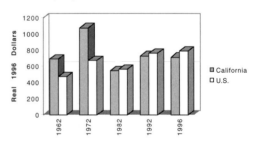

Real Per Capita State and Local Property Taxes: California vs. U.S.

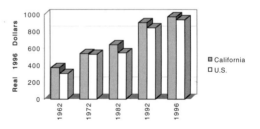

Real Per Capita State and Local Sales and Gross Receipts Taxes: California vs. U.S.

Income Taxes

California's per capita state and local income (individual and corporate) taxes registered $834 in 1996, ranking 13th in the nation and topping the U.S. average of $674 by 24%. From 1962 to 1996, real per capita state and local income taxes increased by 418%, versus a 567% increase in the U.S. average.

Personal Income Tax

A rate of 9.3%, ranking 48th in the nation (from lowest tax rate to highest), and comparing with the national average of 5.26%.

Capital Gains Tax

A rate of 9.3%, ranking 50th in the nation (from lowest tax rate to highest), and comparing with the national average of 4.68%.

Corporate Income Tax

A rate of 8.84%, ranking 39th in the nation (from lowest tax rate to highest), and comparing with the national average of 6.63%.

Total Expenditures

California's per capita state and local total spending registered $5,876 in 1996, ranking 11th in the nation and exceeding the U.S. average of $5,268 by 12%. From 1962 to 1996, real per capita state and local total spending increased by 193%, versus an increase of 254% in U.S. average.

Welfare Expenditures

California's per capita state and local public welfare spending registered $756 in 1996, ranking 16th in the nation and exceeding the U.S. average of $729 by 4%. From 1962 to 1996, real per capita state and local public welfare spending increased by 322%, compared with a 488% increase in the U.S. average.

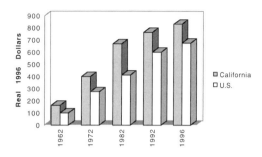

Real Per Capita State and Local Income Taxes: California vs. U.S.

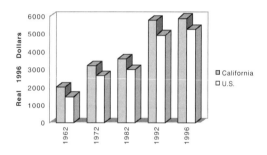

Real Per Capita State and Local Total Expenditures: California vs. U.S.

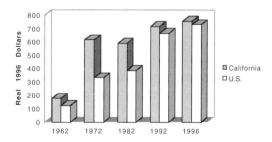

Real Per Capita State and Local Public Welfare Spending: California vs. U.S.

Welfare Recipients (in thousands)

	1980	1989	3/99	Change 1989–99
Calif.	1,498	1,833	1,818	−1%
U.S.	10,923	10,987	7,335	−33%

Interest on General Debt

California's per capita state and local interest on general debt registered $204 in 1996, ranking 26th in the nation and trailing the U.S. average of $222 by 8%. From 1962 to 1996, real per capita state and local interest on general debt increased by 271%, versus an increase of 335% in the U.S. average.

Total Debt Outstanding

California's per capita state and local debt registered $4,511 in 1996, ranking 19th in the nation and exceeding the U.S. average of $4,409 by 2%. From 1962 to 1996, real per capita state and local debt outstanding increased by 91%, versus an increase of 120% in the U.S. average.

Government Employees

California's state and local government employees (full-time equivalent, or FTE) per 10,000 population registered 474 in 1997, ranking 50th in the nation and trailing the U.S. average of 531.1 by 11%. From 1962 to 1996, state and local FTE employees per 10,000 population increased by 29%, compared with an increase in the U.S. average of 66%.

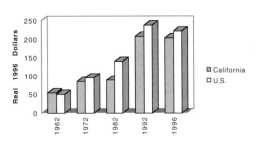

Real Per Capita State and Local Interest on General Debt: California vs. U.S.

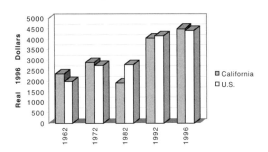

Real Per Capita State and Local Debt Outstanding: California vs. U.S.

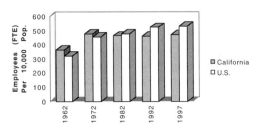

State and Local Government Employees (FTE) Per 10,000 Population: California vs. U.S.

Per Capita Federal Government Expenditures, 1998

	1998	Ranking
Calif.	$4,946	35th
U.S.	$5,491	

Per capita spending in California trailed the national average by 10%.

EDUCATION

Total Education Spending

California's per capita state and local education spending registered $1,374 in 1996, ranking 37th in the nation and trailing the U.S. average of $1,503 by 9%. From 1962 to 1996, real per capita total education spending increased by 75%, versus an increase in the U.S. average of 173%.

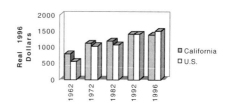

Real Per Capita State and Local Education Spending: California vs. U.S.

Per Pupil Spending

California's per pupil public school spending registered $5,789 in 1998, ranking 30th in the nation and trailing the U.S. average of $6,131 by 6%. From 1970 to 1998, California's real per pupil public school spending increased by 88%, compared with a 120% increase in the U.S. average.

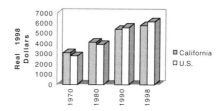

Real Per Pupil Public School Spending: California vs. U.S.

Average Public School Teacher Salaries (in 1997–98 dollars)

	1970	1980	1990	1998	1998 Ranking
Calif.	44,166	37,543	48,402	43,725	11th
U.S.	36,934	33,272	39,956	39,385	

In 1998, the average public school teacher salary in California exceeded the U.S. average by 11%. From 1970 to 1998, the real average teacher salary in California decreased by 1%, versus an increase in the U.S. average of 7%.

Pupil/Teacher Ratio, Fall 1996

	Ratio	Rank
Calif.	22.9	50th
U.S.	17.1	

Teacher/Staff, Fall 1996

	Percent	Rank
Calif.	53.1	21st
U.S.	52.1	

Public School 4th-Grade Reading Proficiency, 1998

	Average	Rank (out of 40 states)
Calif.	202	38th
U.S.	215	

Public School 8th-Grade Reading Proficiency, 1998

	Average	Rank (out of 37 states)
Calif.	253	32d
U.S.	261	

Public School 4th-Grade Math Proficiency, 1996

	Average	Rank (out of 44 states)
Calif.	209	41st
U.S.	224	

Public School 8th-Grade Math Proficiency, 1996

	Average	Rank (out of 41 states)
Calif.	263	31st
U.S.	271	

Public School 8th-Grade Science Proficiency, 1996

	Average	Rank (out of 41 states)
Calif.	138	37th
U.S.	148	

Average Math SAT Scores

	1972	1982	1992	1998	Percentage Taking SAT in 1998
Calif.	517	500	508	516	47
U.S.	509	493	501	512	43

Average Verbal SAT Scores

	1972	1982	1992	1998	Percentage Taking SAT in 1998
Calif.	541	503	492	497	47
U.S.	530	504	500	505	43

Expenditures by Public Institutions of Higher Education Per Full-Time-Equivalent Student, 1996

	FTE Student Spending	Rank
Calif.	$11,539	35th
U.S.	$12,343	

Per-FTE-student spending in public institutions of higher education trailed the U.S. average by 7%.

Per Full-Time-Equivalent Student Revenues from Federal, State, and Local Governments for Public Institutions of Higher Education, 1996

	FTE Student Government Revenues	Rank
Calif.	$8,228	21st
U.S.	$8,101	

Per-FTE-student-government revenues in public institutions of higher education exceeded the U.S. average by 2%.

Average Salary for Full-Time Professors at Public Universities, 1997

	Average	Rank
Calif.	$91,095	1st
U.S.	$72,599	

The average full-time public university professor salary topped the U.S. average by 25%.

ECONOMY AND BUSINESS

Economic Growth

Over the period of 1977 to 1997, California's real gross state product (GSP) grew by 88.2%—ranking 18th in the nation—as compared with real U.S. gross domestic product (GDP), expanding by 70.1%.

At $1.03 trillion in 1997, California's GSP ranked as the largest in the nation.

From 1993 to 1997, California's annual real GSP growth averaged 2.38%—ranking 44th in the nation—as compared with annual real U.S. GDP growth, averaging 3.08%.

Real Economic Growth
1977-1997: California vs. U.S.

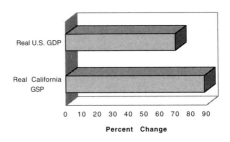

Job Growth

	Growth in Employee Payrolls (Nonagricultural) 1962–98	Ranking
Calif.	160.3%	21st
U.S.	126.5%	

	Average Annual Growth in Employee Payrolls (Nonagricultural) 1993–98	Ranking
Calif.	2.26%	40th
U.S.	2.98%	

Per Capita Disposable Income, 1997

	1997	Ranking
Calif.	$22,225	14th
U.S.	$21,607	

Per capita disposable income exceeded the U.S. average by 3%.

	Real Growth 1962–97	Ranking
Calif.	83.2%	48th
U.S.	116.7%	

	Average Annual Real Growth 1993–97	Ranking
Calif.	0.49%	49th
U.S.	1.48%	

Number of Businesses

	1997	Percent with Fewer than 500 Employees
Business with Employees	837,802	99.2
Self-employed Individuals	1,587,000	

New Business Incorporations

	1980	1986	1992	1997
Calif.	57,634	67,184	36,973	47,055

Percentage Change in Annual New Business Incorporation, 1980 vs. 1997

	Percent	Ranking
Calif.	−18.4	48th
U.S.	49.7	

State Merchandise Exports to the World, 1998 (in millions of dollars)

	1998	Rank
Calif.	$98,809	1st

Small Business Survival Index, 1999

California ranked a dismal 41st in terms of its policy environment for entrepreneurship.

Fortune 500 Headquarters in 1999

A total of 56 (ranked 2d), with San Francisco ranked 6th among U.S. cities with 9 headquarters, and Los Angeles ranked 11th with 6 headquarters

Labor Union Membership, 1983 vs. 1997

	1983	1997	1997 Rank
Calif.	21.9	16.0	16th
U.S.	20.1	14.1	

Homeownership Rate, 1998

	Rate	Rank
Calif.	56.0	48th
U.S.	66.3	

CRIME

Crime Rates Per 100 Residents (rankings from best to worst crime rates)

Total Crime	1960	1970	1980	1990	1998	1998 Ranking
Calif.	1.97	4.31	7.83	6.60	4.34	24th
U.S.	1.04	2.74	5.90	5.82	4.62	

From 1960 to 1998, California's crime rate increased by 120%, versus a U.S. increase of 344%. From 1990 to 1998, California's crime rate dropped by 34%, versus a U.S. decrease of 21%.

Violent Crime	1960	1970	1980	1990	1998	1998 Ranking
Calif.	0.24	0.47	0.89	1.05	0.70	42d
U.S.	0.14	0.36	0.58	0.73	0.57	

From 1960 to 1998, California's violent crime rate increased by 192%, versus a U.S. increase of 307%. From 1990 to 1998, California's violent crime rate declined by 33%, compared with a national decline of 22%.

Property Crime	1960	1970	1980	1990	1998	1998 Ranking
Calif.	1.73	3.83	6.94	5.56	3.64	19th
U.S.	0.90	2.38	5.32	5.09	4.05	

From 1960 to 1998, California's property crime rate increased by 110%, versus a national increase of 350%. From 1990 to 1998, California's property crime rate decreased by 35%, compared with a national decline of 20%.

Real Per Capita Police Protection Spending (in real 1996 dollars)

	1962	1972	1982	1992	1996	1996 Ranking
Calif.	73	135	158	209	226	4th
U.S.	51	95	114	148	168	

In 1996, per capita state and local police protection spending in California exceeded the U.S. average by 35%. From 1962 to 1996, real per capita state and local police protection spending increased by 210%, versus an increase of 229% in the U.S. average.

Prisoners in State and Federal Prisons Per 1,000 Population

	1980	1990	1996	1996 Ranking
Calif.	1.04	3.27	4.58	14th
U.S.	1.46	3.11	4.45	

From 1980 to 1996, prisoners per 1,000 population increased by 340%, versus a U.S. increase of 205%.

HEALTH CARE

Health-Care Spending

California's per capita state and local health-care spending registered $202 in 1996, ranking 10th in the nation and topping the U.S. average of $151 by 34%. From 1962 to 1996, California's real per capita state and local health-care spending increased by 778%, versus an increase of 739% in the U.S. average.

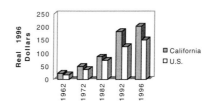

Real Per Capita State and Local Health Care Spending: California vs. U.S.

Hospital Spending

California's per capita state and local hospital spending registered $279 in 1996, ranking 17th in the nation and out-running the U.S. average of $266 by 5%. From 1962 to 1996, California's real per capita state and local hospital spending increased by 154%, as opposed to an increase of 189% in the U.S. average.

Real Per Capita State and Local Hospital Spending: California vs. U.S.

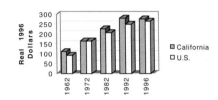

Medicaid, 1997

	Spending Per Recipient	Ranking
Calif.	$2,355	47th
U.S.	$3,681	

California's per-recipient Medicaid spending trailed the U.S. average by 37%.

ENVIRONMENT

Parks and Recreation Spending

California's per capita state and local parks and recreation spending registered $85 in 1996, ranking 17th in the nation and exceeding the U.S. average of $72 by 18%. From 1962 to 1996, real per capita state and local parks and recreation spending increased by 107%, versus a 213% increase in the U.S. average.

Real Per Capita State and Local Parks and Recreation Spending: California vs. U.S.

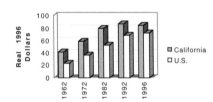

State and Local Natural Resources Spending, 1996

	Per Capita	Ranking
Calif.	$91	10th
U.S.	$60	

Per capita state and local natural resources spending in California exceeded the U.S. average by 52%.

State Parks Revenues as a Share of Operating Expenses, 1997

	Percent	Rank
Calif.	36	31st
U.S.	42	

Percentage of Land Owned by the Federal Government, 1996

	Percent	Rank
Calif.	44.7	7th
U.S.	24.8	

SOCIETY AND DEMOGRAPHICS

Population

California's 1998 population of 32.667 million ranked 1st in the nation.

Population Growth, 1990–98

California Population

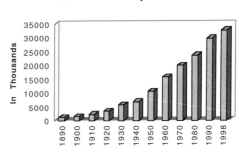

	Percentage Change in Population	Ranking
Calif.	9.67	20th
U.S.	8.66	

	Net International Migration	Ranking
Calif.	2,019,488	1st

	Net Domestic Migration	Ranking
Calif.	−2,081,928	51st

Infant Mortality Rate, 1998

	Percent	Rank
Calif.	5.8	39th
U.S.	6.4	

Percentage of Births of Low Birthweight, 1997

	Percent	Rank
Calif.	6.2	43d
U.S.	7.5	

Percentage of Live Births to Unmarried Women, 1997

	Percent	Rank
Calif.	32.8	21st
U.S.	32.4	

Abortion Rate—Abortions Per 1,000 Women Ages 15–44, 1995

	Rate	Rank
Calif.	33.4	6th
U.S.	22.9	

LIFESTYLE

Percentage of Households with Computers, 1998

	Percent	Rank
Calif.	47.5	11th

Percentage of Households with Internet Access, 1998

	Percent	Rank
Calif.	30.7	11th

State Arts Agency Spending, 1999

	Per Capita	Rank
Calif.	$1.38	16th
U.S.	$1.35	

Per capita state arts spending in 1999 exceeded the U.S. average by 2%.

Major League Sports Facilities

Year Opened/ Refurb.	Stadium/ Arena	Home Team	Millions of Nominal Dollars		Millions of Real 1997 Dollars	
			Estimated Total Cost	Estimated Taxpayer Cost	Estimated Total Cost	Estimated Taxpayer Cost
1923	Los Angeles Coliseum	Rams (NFL) 1946–79 Raiders (NFL) 1982–94 Dodgers (MLB) 1958–61	$1.0	$1.0	$9.0	$9.0
1931	L.A. Coliseum (re)	Lakers (NBA)	$1.0	$1.0	$10.0	$10.0
1959	Los Angeles Sports Arena	1960–67 Clippers (NBA) 1985–94	$5.9	$5.9	$32.6	$32.6
1960	3Com Park (Candlestick)	Giants (MLB) 1960–present 49ers (NFL) 1971–present Raiders (AFL) 1961	$32.0	$32.0	$173.9	$173.9
1971	3Com/Candlestick (re)		$24.0	$24.0	$95.2	$95.2
1986	3Com/Candlestick (re)		$30.0	$30.0	$43.9	$43.9
1962	Dodger Stadium	Dodgers (MLB) 1962–present Angels (MLB) 1962–65	$27.7	$4.7	$147.6	$25.2
1965	Oakland-Alameda Coliseum	A's (MLB) 1968–present Raiders (AFL/NFL) 1966–84, 1995–present	$25.0	$25.0	$127.6	$127.6
1996	Oakland Col. (re)		$225.0	$225.0	$230.1	$230.1

Year Opened/ Refurb.	Stadium/ Arena	Home Team	Millions of Nominal Dollars		Millions of Real 1997 Dollars	
			Estimated Total Cost	Estimated Taxpayer Cost	Estimated Total Cost	Estimated Taxpayer Cost
1966	Oakland Arena	Seals (NHL) 1967–76 Warriors (NBA) 1971–96, 1997–present	$25.5	$25.5	$126.2	$126.2
1997	Oakland Arena (re)		$130.0	$26.0	$130.0	$26.0
1966	Anaheim Stadium/ Edison Intl. Field	Angels (MLB) 1966–present Rams (NFL) 1980–94	$25.0	$24.0	$123.8	$118.8
1979	Anaheim/Edison (re)		$31.0	$31.0	$68.6	$68.6
1998	Anaheim/Edison (re)		$117.0	$30.0	$115.2	$29.5
1967	Qualcomm Stadium/ Jack Murphy Stadium	Padres (MLB) 1969–present Chargers (AFL/NFL) 1967–present	$27.8	$27.8	$133.4	$133.4
1983	Qualcomm/Murphy (re)		$11.0	$11.0	$17.7	$17.7
1997	Qualcomm/Murphy (re)		$78.00	$60.00	$78.0	$60.0
1967	Great Western Forum	Kings (NHL) 1967–99 Lakers (NBA) 1967–99	$20.0	$0.0	$96.2	$0.0
1988	ARCO Arena II	Kings (NBA) 1988–present	$40.0	$0.0	$54.3	$0.0
1993	San Jose Arena	Sharks (NHL) 1993–present Warriors (NBA) 1996–97	$168.0	$136.0	$186.7	$151.1

Year	Facility	Team(s)				
1993	Arrowhead Pond	Mighty Ducks 1993–present	$100.0	$100.0	$111.1	$111.1
1999	Staples Center	Lakers (NBA) 1999–present Clippers (NBA) 1999–present Kings (NHL) 1999–present	$350.0	$12.0	$337.8	$11.6
2000	Pac Bell Park 2000-present	Giants (MLB)	$345.0	$26.0	$325.8	$24.6

COLORADO

Although Colorado is a state of varying landscapes, the images most conjure up are its majestic mountains. These soaring peaks serve as just the right image for rising economic opportunity in Colorado.

In fact, the state has experienced some of the fastest economic, job, and disposable income growth in the nation recently. Overall population growth, net international migration, and net domestic migration have all ranked among the best in the country.

A one-time image of Colorado frequently conjured up was that of a state overrun by California. According to Rick Ridder of Denver, a Democratic political consultant and the current president of the International Association of Political Consultants, Coloradons still resent outsiders migrating to their state. "Twenty-five years ago you saw signs that read 'Don't Californicate Colorado.' Today, the signs are gone, but the resentment is still there." "People are a little testy and resistant to change," added Gurney Sloane, an advertising executive in Colorado Springs.

Messrs. Sloane and Ridder agree that the impact of Californians has diminished in recent years. "You're just as likely to see someone from Indiana or the mid-Atlantic as you are California," observed Sloane, who relocated to Colorado four years ago from Washington, D.C.

Meanwhile, per capita tax and spending levels generally have come in below the U.S. averages, though state and local debt levels run high. And on the education front, while per-pupil school spending comes in well below the U.S. average, student performance levels are fairly strong.

In 1999, Governor Bill Owens (R) and the state legislature decided not to rest on their laurels, but instead took some further progrowth policy steps. What has been reported as the largest tax relief package in state history became a reality. The centerpiece of the 20 tax cuts passed into law was a reduction in the state's personal income and capital gains tax rate from 5% to 4.75%. Further reductions in state taxes on capital gains, interest, dividends, and business property unfortunately are temporary, and they take effect when the state budget surplus hits certain levels.

Back in 1992, Colorado voters wisely approved the Taxpayer's Bill of Rights, which requires that state budget surpluses be returned to the people. To his credit, Governor Owens reportedly threatened to veto the state budget if the income tax cut was not made permanent. Obviously, making the reduction permanent takes money out of government hands and leaves it in the people's pockets over the long haul. It also solidifies the progrowth boost in incentives for locating, working, investing, and risk taking in the state.

In addition, businesses will get some relief from reforms in workers's compensation laws.

Looking ahead in terms of the economy, Colorado's future looks bright. If growth-minded politicians can keep government spending under control, the opportunity for further permanent tax reductions will present themselves, and opportunity will continue to soar to new levels in the Rockies.

POLITICS

Registered Voters

31% Democrats
36% Republicans
32% Other

Federal Officials: Recent Election and Group Ratings

			ACU	ADA	SBSC
U.S. Senators:	Ben Nighthorse Campbell (R)		40	43	80
	1998　Campbell (R)	62%			
	Lamm (D)	35%			
	Wayne Allard (R)		97	3	90
	1996　Allard (R)	52%			
	Bryant (D)	47%			
U.S. Representatives:	Diana Degette (D-1)		9	98	5
	1998　Degette (D)	67%			
	McClanahan (R)	30%			
	Mark Udall (D-2)		NA	NA	NA
	1998　Udall (D)	50%			
	Greenlee (R)	47%			
	Scott McInnis (R-3)		91	8	90
	1998　McInnis (R)	66%			
	Kelley (D)	31%			
	Bob Schaffer (R-4)		98	5	95
	1998　Schaffer (R)	59%			
	Kirkpatrick (D)	41%			
	Joel Hefley (R-5)		96	6	90
	1998　Hefley (R)	73%			
	Alfrod (D)	26%			
	Tom Tancredo (R-6)		NA	NA	NA
	1998　Tancredo (R)	56%			
	Strauss (D)	42%			
Electoral Votes:	8				
1996 Presidential Results:	Clinton	44%			
	Dole	46%			
	Perot	7%			

State Officials

Governor 1998 Election:	Bill Owens (R)	49%
	Gail Schoettler (D)	48%
Lt. Governor:	Joe Rogers (R)	
Attorney General:	Ken Salazar (D)	
State Senate:	15 Democrats	
	20 Republicans	
State House:	25 Democrats	
	40 Republicans	

TAXES AND SPENDING

Total Revenues

Colorado's per capita state and local total revenues registered $5,437 in 1996, ranking 21st in the nation and trailing the U.S. average of $5,706 by 5%. From 1962 to 1996, real per capita state and local revenues increased by 217%, compared with an increase in the national average of 297%.

Taxes

Colorado's per capita state and local taxes registered $2,418 in 1996, ranking 26th in the nation and trailing the U.S. average of $2,597 by 7%. From 1962 to 1996, real per capita state and local taxes increased by 110%, compared with an increase of 152% in the U.S. average.

Property Taxes

Colorado's per capita state and local property taxes equaled $743 in 1996, ranking 24th in the nation and trailing the U.S. average of $789 by 6%. From 1962 to 1996, real per capita state and local property taxes increased by 35%, versus a 67% increase in the U.S. average.

Real Per Capita State and Local Total Revenues: Colorado vs. U.S.

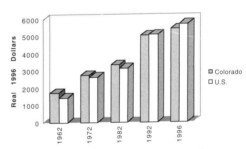

Real Per Capita State and Local Taxes: Colorado vs. U.S.

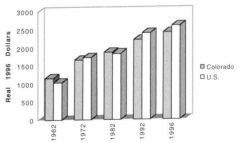

Real Per Capita State and Local Property Taxes: Colorado vs. U.S.

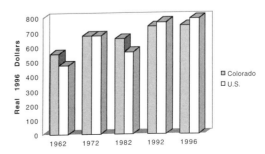

Sales and Gross Receipts Taxes

Colorado's per capita state and local sales and gross receipts taxes came in at $905 in 1996, ranking 25th in the nation and trailing the U.S. average of $939 by 4%. From 1962 to 1996, real per capita state and local sales and gross receipts taxes increased by 234%, versus an increase of 214% in the U.S. average.

Income Taxes

Colorado's per capita state and local income (individual and corporate) taxes registered $649 in 1996, ranking 24th in the nation and trailing the U.S. average of $674 by 4%. From 1962 to 1996, real per capita state and local income taxes increased by 245%, versus a 567% increase in the U.S. average.

Personal Income Tax

A rate of 4.75%, ranking 17th in the nation (from lowest tax rate to highest), and comparing with the national average of 5.26%.

Capital Gains Tax

A rate of 4.75%, ranking 22d in the nation (from lowest tax rate to highest), and comparing with the national average of 4.68%.

Corporate Income Tax

A rate of 5.0%, ranking 9th in the nation (from lowest tax rate to highest), and comparing with the national average of 6.63%.

Total Expenditures

Colorado's per capita state and local total spending registered $5,023 in 1996, ranking 19th in the nation and trailing the U.S. average of $5,268 by 5%. From 1962 to 1996, real per capita state and local total spending increased by 203%, versus an increase of 254% in the U.S. average.

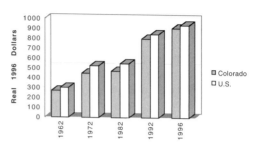

Real Per Capita State and Local Sales and Gross Receipts Taxes: Colorado vs. U.S.

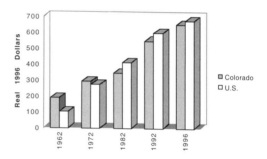

Real Per Capita State and Local Income Taxes: Colorado vs. U.S.

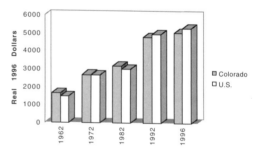

Real Per Capita State and Local Total Expenditures: Colorado vs. U.S.

Welfare Expenditures

Colorado's per capita state and local public welfare spending registered $561 in 1996, ranking 38th in the nation and trailing the U.S. average of $729 by 23%. From 1962 to 1996, real per capita state and local public welfare spending increased by 149%, compared with a 488% increase in the U.S. average.

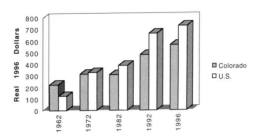

Real Per Capita State and Local Public Welfare Spending: Colorado vs. U.S.

Welfare Recipients (in thousands)

	1980	1989	3/99	Change 1989–99
Colo.	81	100	39	−61%
U.S.	10,923	10,987	7,335	−33%

Interest on General Debt

Colorado's per capita state and local interest on general debt registered $284 in 1996, ranking 13th in the nation and exceeding the U.S. average of $222 by 28%. From 1962 to 1996, real per capita state and local interest on general debt increased by 788%, versus an increase of 335% in the U.S. average.

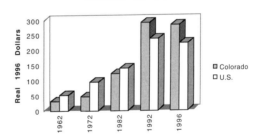

Real Per Capita State and Local Interest on General Debt: Colorado vs. U.S.

Total Debt Outstanding

Colorado's per capita state and local debt registered $5,036 in 1996, ranking 14th in the nation and topping the U.S. average of $4,409 by 14%. From 1962 to 1996, real per capita state and local debt outstanding increased by 196%, versus an increase of 120% in the U.S. average.

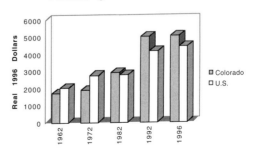

Real Per Capita State and Local Debt Outstanding: Colorado vs. U.S.

Government Employees

Colorado's state and local government employees (full-time equivalent, or FTE) per 10,000 population registered 546.1 in 1997, ranking 24th in the nation and exceeding the U.S. average of 531.1 by 3%. From 1962 to 1996, state and local FTE employees per 10,000 population increased by 47%, compared with an increase in the U.S. average of 66%.

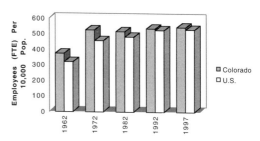

State and Local Government Employees (FTE) Per 10,000 Population: Colorado vs. U.S.

Per Capita Federal Government Expenditures, 1998

	1998	Ranking
Colo.	$5,291	26th
U.S.	$5,491	

Per capita federal spending in Colorado trailed the national average by 4%.

EDUCATION

Total Education Spending

Colorado's per capita state and local education spending registered $1,588 in 1996, ranking 18th in the nation and exceeding the U.S. average of $1,503 by 6%. From 1962 to 1996, real per capita total education spending increased by 126%, versus an increase in the U.S. average of 173%.

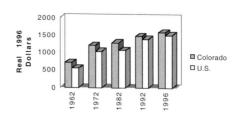

Real Per Capita State and Local Education Spending: Colorado vs. U.S.

Per Pupil Spending

Colorado's per pupil public school spending registered $4,946 in 1998, ranking 42d in the nation and trailing the U.S. average of $6,131 by 19%. From 1970 to 1998, Colorado's real per pupil public school spending increased by 95%, compared with a 120% increase in the U.S. average.

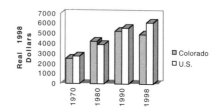

Real Per Pupil Public School Spending: Colorado vs. U.S.

Average Public School Teacher Salaries (in 1997–98 dollars)

	1970	1980	1990	1998	1998 Ranking
Colo.	33,230	33,762	39,180	37,052	23d
U.S.	36,934	33,272	39,956	39,385	

In 1998, the average public school teacher salary in Colorado trailed the U.S. average by 6%. From 1970 to 1998, the real average teacher salary in Colorado increased by 12%, versus an increase in the U.S. average of 7%.

Pupil/Teacher Ratio, Fall 1996

	Ratio	Rank
Colo.	18.5	42d
U.S.	17.1	

Teachers/Staff, Fall 1996

	Percent	Rank
Colo.	51.1	38th
U.S.	52.1	

Public School 4th-Grade Reading Proficiency, 1998

	Average	Rank (out of 40 states)
Colo.	222	8th
U.S.	215	

Public School 8th-Grade Reading Proficiency, 1998

	Average	Rank (out of 37 states)
Colo.	264	14th
U.S.	261	

Public School 4th-Grade Math Proficiency, 1996

	Average	Rank (out of 44 states)
Colo.	226	14th
U.S.	224	

Public School 8th-Grade Math Proficiency, 1996

	Average	Rank (out of 41 states)
Colo.	276	14th
U.S.	271	

Public School 8th-Grade Science Proficiency, 1996

	Average	Rank (out of 41 states)
Colo.	155	12th
U.S.	148	

Average Math SAT Scores

	1972	1982	1992	1998	Percentage Taking SAT in 1998
Colo.	542	536	528	542	31
U.S.	509	493	501	512	43

Average Verbal SAT Scores

	1972	1982	1992	1998	Percentage Taking SAT in 1998
Colo.	568	545	529	537	31
U.S.	530	504	500	505	43

Expenditures by Public Institutions of Higher Education Per Full-Time-Equivalent Student, 1996

	FTE Student Spending	Rank
Colo.	$11,767	32d
U.S.	$12,343	

Per-FTE-student spending in public institutions of higher education trailed the U.S. average by 5%.

Per Full-Time-Equivalent Student Revenues from Federal, State, and Local Governments for Public Institutions of Higher Education, 1996

	FTE Student Government Revenues	Rank
Colo.	$6,712	44th
U.S.	$8,101	

Per-FTE-student-government revenues in public institutions of higher education trailed the U.S. average by 17%.

Average Salary for Full-Time Professors at Public Universities, 1997

	Average	Rank
Colo.	$70,540	25th
U.S.	$72,599	

The average full-time public university professor salary trailed the U.S. average by 3%.

ECONOMY AND BUSINESS

Economic Growth

Over the period of 1977 to 1997, Colorado's real gross state product (GSP) grew by 108.4%—ranking 7th in the nation—as compared with real U.S. gross domestic product (GDP), expanding by 70.1%.

At $126.1 billion in 1997, Colorado's GSP ranked as 2nd largest in the nation.

From 1993 to 1997, Colorado's annual real GSP growth averaged 5.79%—ranking 8th in the nation—as compared with annual real U.S. GDP growth, averaging 3.08%.

Real Economic Growth 1977-1997: Colorado vs. U.S.

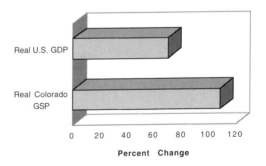

Job Growth

	Growth in Employee Payrolls (Nonagricultural) 1962–98	Ranking
Colo.	267.9%	5th
U.S.	126.5%	

Average Annual Growth in Employee Payrolls (Nonagricultural) 1993–98	Ranking
Colo.	5.11%	4th
U.S.	2.98%	

Per Capita Disposable Income, 1997

	1997	Ranking
Colo.	$22,787	11th
U.S.	$21,607	

Per capita disposable income topped the U.S. average by 5%.

	Real Growth 1962–97	Ranking
Colo.	126.0%	22d
U.S.	116.7%	

	Average Annual Real Growth 1993–97	Ranking
Colo.	2.40%	4th
U.S.	1.48%	

Number of Businesses

	1997	Percent with Fewer than 500 Employees
Businesses with Employees	120,898	97.6
Self-employed Individuals	184,000	

New Business Incorporations

	1980	1986	1992	1997
Colo.	10,234	15,861	14,876	15,670

Percentage Change in Annual New Business Incorporations, 1980 vs. 1997

	Percent	Ranking
Colo.	53.1	21st
U.S.	49.7	

State Merchandise Exports to the World, 1998 (in millions of dollars)

	1998	Rank
Colo.	$10,733	19th

Small Business Survival Index, 1999

Colorado ranked a solid 13th in terms of its policy environment for entrepreneurship.

Fortune 500 Headquarters in 1999

A total of 6 (ranked 23d)

Labor Union Membership, 1983 vs. 1997

	Percentage of Workers		
	1983	1997	1997 Rank
Colo.	13.6	9.6	30th
U.S.	20.1	14.1	

Homeownership Rate, 1998

	Rate	Rank
Colo.	65.2	39th
U.S.	66.3	

CRIME

Crime Rates Per 100 Residents (rankings from best to worst crime rate)

Total Crime	1960	1970	1980	1990	1998	1998 Ranking
Colo.	1.23	3.66	7.33	6.05	4.49	27th
U.S.	1.04	2.74	5.90	5.82	4.62	

From 1960 to 1998, Colorado's crime rate increased by 265%, versus a U.S. increase of 344%. From 1990 to 1998, Colorado's crime rate dropped by 26%, versus a U.S. decrease of 21%.

Violent Crime	1960	1970	1980	1990	1998	1998 Ranking
Colo.	0.14	0.36	0.53	0.53	0.36	20th
U.S.	0.14	0.36	0.58	0.73	0.57	

From 1960 to 1998, Colorado's violent crime rate increased by 171%, versus a U.S. increase of 307%. From 1990 to 1998, Colorado's violent crime rate declined by 28%, compared with a national decline of 22%.

Property Crime	1960	1970	1980	1990	1997	1997 Ranking
Colo.	1.10	3.31	6.80	5.53	4.29	30th
U.S.	0.09	2.38	5.32	5.09	4.31	

From 1960 to 1998, Colorado's property crime rate increased by 274%, versus a national increase of 350%. From 1990 to 1997, Colorado's property crime rate decreased by 26%, compared with a national decline of 20%.

Real Per Capita Police Protection Spending (in real 1996 dollars)

	1962	1972	1982	1992	1996	1996 Ranking
Colo.	51	79	123	146	157	19th
U.S.	51	95	114	148	168	

In 1996, per capita state and local police protection spending in Colorado trailed the U.S. average by 7%. From 1962 to 1996, real per capita state and local police protection spending increased by 208%, versus an increase of 229% in the U.S. average.

Prisoners in State and Federal Prisons Per 1,000 Population

	1980	1990	1996	1996 Ranking
Colo.	0.91	2.33	3.26	29th
U.S.	1.46	3.11	4.45	

From 1980 to 1996, prisoners per 1,000 population increased by 258%, versus a U.S. increase of 205%.

HEALTH CARE

Health-Care Spending

Colorado's per capita state and local health-care spending registered $86 in 1996, ranking 46th in the nation and trailing the U.S. average of $151 by 43%. From 1962 to 1996, Colorado's real per capita state and local health-care spending increased by 514%, versus an increase of 739% in the U.S. average.

Real Per Capita State and Local Health Care Spending: Colorado vs. U.S.

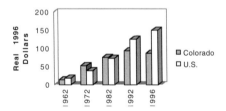

Hospital Spending

Colorado's per capita state and local hospital spending registered $195 in 1996, ranking 30th in the nation and lagging behind the U.S. average of $266 by 27%. From 1962 to 1996, Colorado's real per capita state and local hospital spending increased by 103%, as opposed to an increase of 189% in the U.S. average.

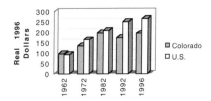

Real Per Capita State and Local Hospital Spending: Colorado vs. U.S.

Medicaid, 1996

	Spending Per Recipient	Ranking
Colo.	$4,478	15th
U.S.	$3,681	

Colorado's per-recipient Medicaid spending exceeded the U.S. average by 22%.

ENVIRONMENT

Parks and Recreation Spending

Colorado's per capita state and local parks and recreation spending registered $124 in 1996, ranking 4th in the nation and exceeding the U.S. average of $72 by 72%. From 1962 to 1996, real per capita state and local parks and recreation spending increased by 439%, versus a 213% increase in the U.S. average.

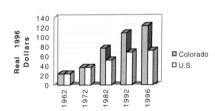

Real Per Capita State and Local Parks and Recreation Spending: Colorado vs. U.S.

State and Local Natural Resources Spending, 1996

	Per Capita	Ranking
Colo.	$49	33d
U.S.	$60	

Per capita state and local natural resources spending in Colorado trailed the U.S. average by 18%.

State Parks Revenues as a Share of Operating Expenses, 1997

	Percent	Rank
Colo.	57	13th
U.S.	42	

Percentage of Land Owned by the Federal Government, 1996

	Percent	Rank
Colo.	36.3	9th
U.S.	24.8	

SOCIETY AND DEMOGRAPHICS

Population

Colorado's 1998 population of 3.971 million ranked 24th in the nation.

Population Growth, 1990–98

	Percentage Change in Population	Ranking
Colo.	20.55	5th
U.S.	8.66	

	Net International Migration	Ranking
Colo.	57,861	17th

	Net Domestic Migration	Ranking
Colo.	359,054	8th

Infant Mortality Rate, 1998

	Percent	Rank
Colo.	6.8	28th
U.S.	6.4	

Percentage of Births of Low Birthweight, 1997

	Percent	Rank
Colo.	8.8	7th
U.S.	7.5	

Colorado   Population

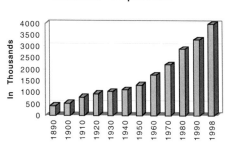

Percentage of Live Births to Unmarried Women, 1997

	Percent	Rank
Colo.	25.2	47th
U.S.	32.4	

Abortion Rate—Abortions Per 1,000 Women Ages 15–44, 1995

	Rate	Rank
Colo.	18.0	23d
U.S.	22.9	

LIFESTYLE

Percentage of Households with Computers, 1998

	Percent	Rank
Colo.	55.3	4th

Percentage of Households with Internet Access, 1998

	Percent	Rank
Colo.	34.5	5th

State Arts Agency Spending, 1999

	Per Capita	Rank
Colo.	$0.46	47th
U.S.	$1.35	

Per capita state arts spending in 1999 trailed the U.S. average by 66%.

Major League Sports Facilities

Year Opened/ Refurb.	Stadium/ Arena	Home Team	Millions of Nominal Dollars		Millions of Real 1997 Dollars	
			Estimated Total Cost	Estimated Taxpayer Cost	Estimated Total Cost	Estimated Taxpayer Cost
1948	Mile High Stadium	Broncos (AFL/NFL) 1960–present Rockies (MLB) 1993–94	$0.3	$0.0	$1.7	$0.0
1960	Mile High (re)		$0.8	$0.0	$4.1	$0.0
1977	Mile High (re)	Nuggets (NBA) 1975–99	$75.0	$75.0	$198.4	$198.4
1975	McNichols Arena	Rockies (NHL) 1976–82 Avalanche (NHL) 1995–99	$13.0	$13.0	$38.8	$38.8
1986	McNichols Arena (re)		$12.5	$12.5	$18.3	$18.3
1995	Coors Field	Rockies (MLB) 1995–present	$215.0	$200.0	$226.3	$210.5
1999	Pepsi Center	Nuggets (NBA) Avalanche (NHL)	$160.0	$0.0	$154.4	$0.0

CONNECTICUT

John Rowland squeaked by with a mere 36% of the vote to win the governorship of Connecticut in 1994.

Then-incumbent Governor Lowell Weicker decided not to run for reelection after feeling a nasty backlash against the imposition of a state personal income tax. Weicker has served as a Republican in the U.S. Senate before being unseated in 1988 by Democrat Joseph Lieberman, with the surprising assistance of leading conservative William F. Buckley Jr., who was determined to unseat the liberal Weicker. In 1990, Weicker won the race for governor as an independent, garnering 40% of the vote, with Republican Rowland running second.

Rowland ran in 1994 on a pledge to eliminate the newly imposed personal income tax and to cut an assortment of other taxes as well. Upon entering the State Capitol, Governor Rowland immediately gave up on his pledge to eliminate the personal income tax. Instead, he set his tax relief sights far lower, with a tiny cut in the personal income tax for very low incomes. But at least he was able to continue and extend efforts already under way to cut the state's draconian corporate income tax rate. Over several years, the corporate rate dropped from 11.5% to 7.5%. Given Rowland's original, ambitious proposals for tax relief, however, his tax-cut record has to be viewed as a major disappointment.

Nonetheless, as Connecticut's economy was dragged ahead largely by national economic trends, and given the inevitable improvement over his predecessor's dismal performance, Rowland won reelection in 1998, with a robust 63% of the vote.

Putting aside serious tax relief, Rowland's next big issue emerged just days after his November 1998 reelection. Rowland announced one of the biggest giveaways in the history of corporate welfare for professional sports teams—a proposal that would have tackled taxpayers for more than a half-billion dollars to build a new home in Hartford for the NFL's New England Patriots. Back in 1997, Rowland supported a new, rather lavishly subsidized arena to keep hockey's Whalers in Hartford, but the team wanted an even better deal and skated away to become the Carolina Hurricanes. Apparently, Rowland was not going to take any chances when it came to the Patriots. The Patriots were to get a new $375-million-plus stadium; revenues from most events at the facility; $15 million for a new practice facility; guaranteed income on premium seating, with taxpayers making up any shortfalls; taxpayers-funded insurance on the stadium; $200 million in stadium upgrades during the team's lease; some $100 million to move the business located on the stadium site; and tens of millions of dollars more for parking facilities.

The funny thing was that the NFL was none too pleased to see another major media market, that is, the Boston area, without a team. So after Rowland prostrated himself to the Patriots, team owner Robert Kraft walked away from the deal in late April 1999 and took a less lucrative—though still subsidized—offer to stay in Massachusetts.

After licking their football wounds, Rowland and state legislators passed a two-year budget in June 1999 that provided for annual spending increases of 4.8% and 4.7%—far outpacing inflation, which was expected to run to about 2%. Elected officials wound up spending $5 out of every $6 of Connecticut's 1999 state budget surplus, and the $1 left over was put into a sales tax rebate which will have no progrowth impact on a state economy that still desperately needs help. Rowland and legislators even came up with funding to build a new football stadium for the University of Connecticut.

As noted in the following pages, Connecticut's state and local spending and taxing levels outpace the U.S. average. Most egregiously, per capita state and local total, property, sales and gross receipts, and income taxes all rank among the very highest in the nation, as do total spending, public welfare expenditures and debt levels in Connecticut. And while public school students in Connecticut perform well versus the rest of the nation, per pupil spending and teacher salaries are far too high, ranking fourth and second highest, respectively, in the nation.

Meanwhile, recent economic trends—such as economic growth, job creation, and new businesses—lag behind the nation badly. Rates of job creation and new business incorporations have been particularly dismal.

Also, from 1990 to 1998, Connecticut was one of the very few states to lose population, with the state ranking as a major net exporter of people to other states.

On the positive side of the ledger, Connecticut claims a fairly low crime rate, and the state's reduction in crime from 1990 to 1998 outpaced that of the nation in percentage terms.

Overall, Governor Rowland and his predecessor, a majority of state legislators, along with a congressional delegation far too friendly to big government (they range from moderate Republicans to the most liberal of Democrats), have not positioned Connecticut well to succeed in the entrepreneurial 21st century.

POLITICS

Registered Voters

36% Democrats
25% Republicans
39% Other

Federal Officials: Recent Election and Group Ratings

			ACU	ADA	SBSC
U.S. Senators:	Christopher Dodd (D)		9	83	20
	1998 Dodd (D)	65%			
	Franks (R)	32%			
	Joseph Lieberman (D)		20	75	30
	1994 Lieberman (D)	67%			
	LaBriola (R)	31%			

	ACU	ADA	SBSC
U.S. Representatives: John Larson (D-1)	NA	NA	NA
1998 Larson (D) 58%			
O'Connor (R) 41%			
Sam Gejdenson (D-2)	5	93	10
1998 Gejdenson (D) 61%			
Koval (R) 35%			
Rosa DeLauro (D-3)	5	92	5
1998 DeLauro (D) 71%			
Reust (R) 27%			
Christopher Shays (R-4)	43	46	50
1998 Shays (R) 69%			
Kantrowitz (D) 30%			
James Maloney (D-5)	32	80	35
1998 Maloney (D) 50%			
Nielsen (R) 48%			
Nancy Johnson (R-6)	48	41	45
1998 Johnson (D) 58%			
Koskoff (R) 40%			

Electoral Votes: 8

1996 Presidential Results:

Clinton 53%

Dole 35%

Perot 10%

State Officials

State Senate: 19 Democrats
17 Republicans

State State House: 96 Democrats
55 Republicans

Governor 1998 Election: John Rowland (R) 63%
Barbara Kennelly (D) 35%

Lt. Governor: M. Jodi Rell (R)

Attorney General: Richard Blumenthal (D)

TAXES AND SPENDING

Total Revenues

Connecticut's per capita state and local total revenues registered $6,343 in 1996, ranking 11th in the nation and exceeding the U.S. average of $5,706 by 11%. From 1962 to 1996, real per capita state and local revenues increased by 307%, compared with an increase in the national average of 297%.

Taxes

Connecticut's per capita state and local total tax registered $3,831 in 1996, ranking 3d in the nation and topping the U.S. average of $2,597 by 48%. From 1962 to 1996, real per capita state and local taxes increased by 220%, compared with an increase of 152% in the U.S. average.

Property Taxes

Connecticut's per capita state and local property taxes equaled $1,422 in 1996, ranking 3d in the nation and exceeding the U.S. average of $789 by 80%. From 1962 to 1996, real per capita state and local property taxes increased by 121%, versus a 67% increase in the U.S. average.

Sales and Gross Receipts Taxes

Connecticut's per capita state and local sales and gross receipts taxes came in at $1,201 in 1996, ranking 7th in the nation and exceeding the U.S. average of $939 by 28%. From 1962 to 1996, real per capita state and local sales and gross receipts taxes increased by 200%, versus an increase of 214% in the U.S. average.

Real Per Capita State and Local Total Revenues: Connecticut vs. U.S.

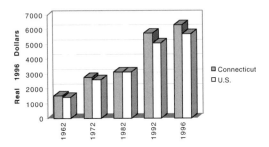

Real Per Capita State and Local Taxes: Connecticut vs. U.S.

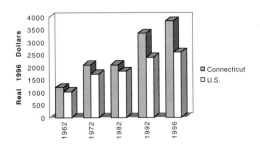

Real Per Capita State and Local Property Taxes: Connecticut vs. U.S.

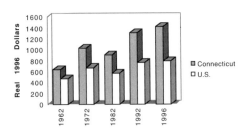

Real Per Capita State and Local Sales and Gross Receipts Taxes: Connecticut vs. U.S.

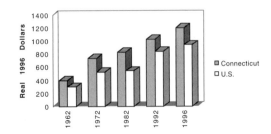

Income Taxes

Connecticut's per capita state and local income (individual and corporate) taxes registered $994 in 1996, ranking 7th in the nation and topping the U.S. average of $674 by 47%. From 1962 to 1996, real per capita state and local income taxes increased by 1,341%, versus a 567% increase in the U.S. average.

Personal Income Tax

A rate of 4.5%, ranking 16th in the nation (from lowest tax rate to highest), and comparing with the national average of 5.26%.

Capital Gains Tax

A rate of 4.5%, ranking 21st in the nation (from lowest tax rate to highest), and comparing with the national average of 4.68%.

Corporate Income Tax

A rate of 7.5%, ranking 29th in the nation (from lowest tax rate to highest), and comparing with the national average of 6.63%.

Total Expenditures

Connecticut's per capita state and local total spending registered $6,047 in 1996, ranking 8th in the nation and outpacing the U.S. average of $5,268 by 15%. From 1962 to 1996, real per capita state and local total spending increased by 265%, versus an increase of 254% in the U.S. average.

Welfare Expenditures

Connecticut's per capita state and local public welfare spending registered $860 in 1996, ranking 11th in the nation and topping the U.S. average of $729 by 18%. From 1962 to 1996, real per capita state and local public welfare spending increased by 623%, compared with a 488% increase in the U.S. average.

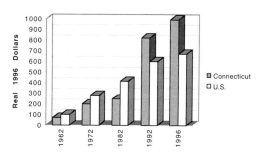

Real Per Capita State and Local Income Taxes: Connecticut vs. U.S.

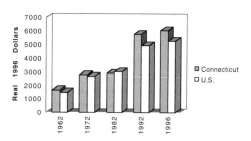

Real Per Capita State and Local Total Expenditures: Connecticut vs. U.S.

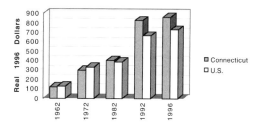

Real Per Capita State and Local Public Welfare Spending: Connecticut vs. U.S.

Welfare Recipients (in thousands)

	1980	1989	3/99	Change 1989–99
Conn.	140	117	91	−22%
U.S.	10,923	10,987	7,335	−33%

Interest on General Debt

Connecticut's per capita state and local interest on general debt registered $346 in 1996, ranking 8th in the nation and exceeding the U.S. average of $222 by 56%. From 1962 to 1996, real per capita state and local interest on general debt increased by 317%, versus an increase of 335% in the U.S. average.

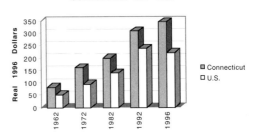

Real Per Capita State and Local Interest on General Debt: Connecticut vs. U.S.

Total Debt Outstanding

Connecticut's per capita state and local debt registered $7,810 in 1996, ranking 3d in the nation and outpacing the U.S. average of $4,409 by 77%. From 1962 to 1996, real per capita state and local debt outstanding increased by 127%, versus an increase of 120% in the U.S. average.

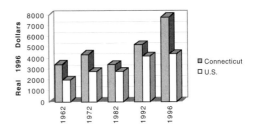

Real Per Capita State and Local Debt Outstanding: Connecticut vs. U.S.

Government Employees

Connecticut's state and local government employees (full-time equivalent, or FTE) per 10,000 population registered 501.9 in 1997, ranking 40th in the nation and trailing the U.S. average of 531.1 by 5%. From 1962 to 1996, state and local FTE employees per 10,000 population increased by 70%, compared with an increase in the U.S. average of 66%.

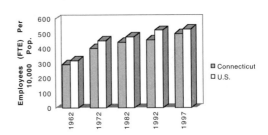

State and Local Government Employees (FTE) Per 10,000 Population: Connecticut vs. U.S.

Per Capita Federal Government Expenditures, 1998

	1998	Ranking
Conn.	$5,933	13th
U.S.	$5,491	

Per capita federal spending in Connecticut topped the national average by 8%.

EDUCATION

Total Education Spending

Connecticut's per capita state and local education spending registered $1,629 in 1996, ranking 16th in the nation and topping the U.S. average of $1,503 by 8%. From 1962 to 1996, real per capita total education spending increased by 186%, versus an increase in the U.S. average of 173%.

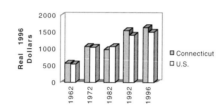

Real Per Capita State and Local Education Spending: Connecticut vs. U.S.

Per Pupil Spending

Connecticut's per pupil public school spending registered $8,701 in 1998, ranking 4th in the nation and exceeding the U.S. average of $6,131 by 42%. From 1970 to 1998, Connecticut's real per pupil public school spending increased by 158%, compared with a 120% increase in the U.S. average.

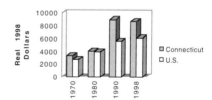

Real Per Pupil Public School Spending: Connecticut vs. U.S.

Average Public School Teacher Salaries (in 1997–98 dollars)

	1970	1980	1990	1998	1998 Ranking
Conn.	39,657	33,812	51,540	50,730	2d
U.S.	36,934	33,272	39,956	39,385	

In 1998, the average public school teacher salary in Connecticut exceeded the U.S. average by 29%. From 1970 to 1998, the real average teacher salary in Connecticut increased by 28%, versus an increase in the U.S. average of 7%.

Pupil/Teacher Ratio, Fall 1996

	Ratio	Rank
Conn.	14.4	5th
U.S.	17.1	

Teachers/Staff, Fall 1996

	Percent	Rank
Conn.	53.1	21st
U.S.	52.1	

Public School 4th-Grade Reading Proficiency, 1998

	Average	Rank (out of 40 states)
Conn.	232	1st
U.S.	215	

Public School 8th-Grade Reading Proficiency, 1998

	Average	Rank (out of 37 states)
Conn.	272	2d
U.S.	261	

Public School 4th-Grade Math Proficiency, 1996

	Average	Rank (out of 44 states)
Conn.	232	1st
U.S.	224	

Public School 8th-Grade Math Proficiency, 1996

	Average	Rank (out of 41 states)
Conn.	280	8th
U.S.	271	

Public School 8th-Grade Science Proficiency, 1996

	Average	Rank (out of 41 states)
Conn.	155	12th
U.S.	148	

Average Math SAT Scores

	1972	1982	1992	1998	Percentage Taking SAT in 1998
Conn.	509	491	496	509	80
U.S.	509	493	501	512	43

Average Verbal SAT Scores

	1972	1982	1992	1998	Percentage Taking SAT in 1998
Conn.	538	510	506	510	80
U.S.	530	504	500	505	43

Expenditures by Public Institutions of Higher Education Per Full-Time-Equivalent Student, 1996

	FTE Student Spending	Rank
Conn.	$14,407	8th
U.S.	$12,343	

Per-FTE-student spending in public institutions of higher education exceeded the U.S. average by 17%.

Per Full-Time-Equivalent Student Revenues from Federal, State, and Local Governments for Public Institutions of Higher Education, 1996

	FTE Student Government Revenues	Rank
Conn.	$8,951	8th
U.S.	$8,101	

Per-FTE-student-government revenues in public institutions of higher education topped the U.S. average by 10%.

Average Salary for Full-Time Professors at Public Universities, 1997

	Average	Rank
Conn.	$85,721	3d
U.S.	$72,599	

The average full-time public university professor salary exceeded the U.S. average by 18%.

ECONOMY AND BUSINESS

Economic Growth

Over the period of 1977 to 1997, Connecticut's real gross state product (GSP) grew by 87.1%—ranking 19th in the nation—as compared with real U.S. gross domestic product (GDP), expanding by 70.1%.

At $134.6 billion in 1997, Connecticut's GSP ranked as 21st largest in the nation.

From 1993 to 1997, Connecticut's annual real GSP growth averaged 2.85%—ranking 37th in the nation—as compared with annual real U.S. GDP growth, averaging 3.08%.

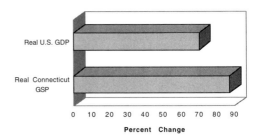

Real Economic Growth 1977-1997: Connecticut vs. U.S.

Real U.S. GDP

Real Connecticut GSP

0 10 20 30 40 50 60 70 80 90

Percent Change

Job Growth

	Growth in Employee Payrolls (Nonagricultural) 1962–98	Ranking
Conn.	73.2%	44th
U.S.	126.5%	

	Average Annual Growth in Employee Payrolls (Nonagricultural) 1993–98	Ranking
Conn.	1.51%	48th
U.S.	2.98%	

Per Capita Disposable Income, 1997

	1997	Ranking
Conn.	$29,311	2d
U.S.	$21,607	

Per capita disposable income exceeded the U.S. average by 36%.

	Real Growth 1962–97	Ranking
Conn.	129.0%	19th
U.S.	116.7%	

	Average Annual Real Growth 1993–97	Ranking
Conn.	1.88%	12th
U.S.	1.48%	

Number of Businesses

	1997	Percent with Fewer than 500 Employees
Businesses with Employees	94,289	97.6
Self-employed Individuals	108,000	

New Business Incorporations

	1980	1986	1992	1997
Conn.	7,513	12,451	7,339	3,375

Percentage Change in Annual New Business Incorporations, 1980 vs. 1997

	Percent	Ranking
Conn.	−55.1	51st
U.S.	49.7	

State Merchandise Exports to the World, 1998 (in millions of dollars)

	1998	Rank
Conn.	$12,140	15th

Small Business Survival Index, 1999

Connecticut ranked 29th in terms of its policy environment for entrepreneurship.

Fortune 500 Headquarters in 1999

A total of 16 (ranked 9th)

Labor Union Membership, 1983 vs. 1997

| | Percentage of Workers | | |
	1983	1997	1997 Rank
Conn.	22.7	16.9	15th
U.S.	20.1	14.1	

Homeownership Rate, 1998

	Rate	Rank
Conn.	69.3	27th
U.S.	66.3	

CRIME

Crime Rates Per 100 Residents (rankings from best to worst crime rate)

Total Crime	1960	1970	1980	1990	1998	1998 Ranking
Conn.	0.68	2.57	5.88	5.39	3.79	17th
U.S.	1.04	2.74	5.90	5.82	4.62	

From 1960 to 1998, Connecticut's crime rate increased by 457%, versus a U.S. increase of 344%. From 1990 to 1998, Connecticut's crime rate dropped by 30%, versus a U.S. decline of 21%.

Violent Crime	1960	1970	1980	1990	1998	1998 Ranking
Conn.	0.04	0.17	0.41	0.55	0.37	19th
U.S.	0.14	0.36	0.58	0.73	0.57	

From 1960 to 1998, Connecticut's violent crime rate increased by 825%, versus a U.S. increase of 307%. From 1990 to 1998, Connecticut's violent crime rate decreased by 33%, compared with a national decline of 22%.

Property Crime	1960	1970	1980	1990	1998	1998 Ranking
Conn.	0.64	2.40	5.47	4.83	3.42	16th
U.S.	0.90	2.38	5.32	5.09	4.05	

From 1960 to 1998, Connecticut's property crime rate increased by 437%, versus a national increase of 350%. From 1990 to 1997, Connecticut's property crime rate decreased by 29%, compared with a national decline of 20%.

Real Per Capita Police Protection Spending (in real 1996 dollars)

	1962	1972	1982	1992	1996	1996 Ranking
Conn.	60	95	105	156	171	13th
U.S.	51	95	114	148	168	

In 1996, per capita state and local police protection spending in Connecticut exceeded the U.S. average by 2%. From 1962 to 1996, real per capita state and local police protection spending increased by 185%, versus an increase of 229% in the U.S. average.

Prisoners in State and Federal Prisons Per 1,000 Population

	1980	1990	1996	1996 Ranking
Conn.	1.39	3.19	4.59	13th
U.S.	1.46	3.11	4.45	

From 1980 to 1996, prisoners per 1,000 population rose by 230%, versus a U.S. increase of 205%.

HEALTH CARE

Health-Care Spending

Connecticut's per capita state and local health-care spending registered $111 in 1996, ranking 31st in the nation and trailing the U.S. average of $151 by 26%. From 1962 to 1996, Connecticut's real per capita state and local health-care spending increased by 517%, versus an increase of 739% in the U.S. average.

Real Per Capita State and Local Health Care Spending: Connecticut vs. U.S.

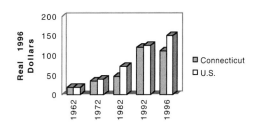

Hospital Spending

Connecticut's per capita state and local hospital spending registered $298 in 1996, ranking 15th in the nation and exceeding the U.S. average of $266 by 12%. From 1962 to 1996, Connecticut's real per capita state and local hospital spending increased by 259%, as opposed to an increase of 189% in the U.S. average.

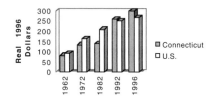

Real Per Capita State and Local Hospital Spending: Connecticut vs. U.S.

Medicaid, 1997

	Spending Per Recipient	Ranking
Conn.	$9,916	1st
U.S.	$3,681	

Connecticut's per-recipient Medicaid spending exceeded the U.S. average by 169%.

ENVIRONMENT

Parks and Recreation Spending

Connecticut's per capita state and local parks and recreation spending registered $59 in 1996, ranking 30th in the nation and trailing the U.S. average of $72 by 18%. From 1962 to 1996, real per capita state and local parks and recreation spending increased by 157%, versus a 213% increase in the U.S. average.

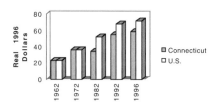

Real Per Capita State and Local Parks and Recreation Spending: Connecticut vs. U.S.

State and Local Natural Resources Spending, 1996

	Per Capita	Ranking
Conn.	$22	48th
U.S.	$60	

State Parks Revenues as a Share of Operating Expenses, 1997

	Percent	Rank
Conn.	40	27th
U.S.	42	

Percentage of Land Owned by the Federal Government, 1996

	Percent	Rank
Conn.	0.2	49th
U.S.	24.8	

SOCIETY AND DEMOGRAPHICS

Population

Connecticut's 1998 population of 3.971 million ranked 29th in the nation.

Population Growth, 1990–98

	Percentage Change in Population	Ranking
Conn.	−0.40	49th
U.S.	8.66	

	Net International Migration	Ranking
Conn.	68,059	15th

	Net Domestic Migration	Ranking
Conn.	−217,038	45th

Infant Mortality Rate, 1998

	Percent	Rank
Conn.	6.4	35th
U.S.	6.4	

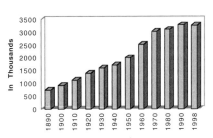

Connecticut Population

Percentage of Births of Low Birthweight, 1997

	Percent	Rank
Conn.	7.3	29th
U.S.	7.5	

Percentage of Live Births to Unmarried Women, 1997

	Percent	Rank
Conn.	32.4	23d
U.S.	32.4	

Abortion Rate—Abortions Per 1,000 Women Ages 15–44, 1995

	Rate	Rank
Conn.	23.0	13th
U.S.	22.9	

LIFESTYLE

Percentage of Households with Computers, 1998

	Percent	Rank
Conn.	43.8	17th

Percentage of Households with Internet Access, 1998

	Percent	Rank
Conn.	31.8	7th

State Arts Agency Spending, 1999

	Per Capita	Rank
Conn.	$1.44	13th
U.S.	$1.35	

Per capita state arts spending in 1999 topped the U.S. average by 7%.

Major League Sports Facilities

Year Opened/ Refurb.	Stadium/ Arena	Home Team	Millions of Nominal Dollars		Millions of Real 1997 Dollars	
			Estimated Total Cost	Estimated Taxpayer Cost	Estimated Total Cost	Estimated Taxpayer Cost
1979	Hartford Civic Center II	Whalers (NHL) 1979–97	$35	$35	$77.4	$77.4

DELAWARE

While sometimes called the Diamond State, politically speaking, Delaware is not exactly diamond-sharp. It is perhaps better defined by its contradictions than by its need to be to the point.

For example, the state senate is controlled by Democrats and the state house is in Republican hands. At-large Congressman Mike Castle is a classic moderate Republican, and in the U.S. Senate, Delaware claims one Republican and one Democrat. Even during the Civil War, Delaware was conflicted as a slave state that did not secede from the Union.

On taxes, per capita property and sales taxes are very low compared with the rest of the nation, while overall taxes and income tax burdens are fairly heavy.

Government spending levels generally rank high, and Delaware offers a classic case of spending rather lavishly on public schools, while getting little in return. Crime also runs just above the U.S. average.

Finally, state economic performance has settled right in the middle of the pack. Most notably, Delaware claims the most friendly incorporation laws in the nation, with reportedly about half of the Fortune 500 companies incorporated in Delaware.

Even beyond the political and economic, Delaware is rather remarkably middle of the road. Even the nickname for the University of Delaware's sports teams—the "Fightin' Blue Hens"—does not exactly stir that old college spirit.

However, Delaware stands out in terms of playing important roles in two revolutions that have forever changed history. Foremost, Delaware was the first state to ratify the U.S. Constitution, one of the most important documents for freedom and liberty the world has ever known. Now, that's an impressive historical note.

More recently, Delaware played a prominent role in the Reagan Revolution that brought about deep, progrowth tax cuts during the 1980s and spread elsewhere around the globe. In the late 1970s, Delaware Senator William Roth (R) joined forces with then-New York Congressman Jack Kemp (R) to propose a 30% across-the-board income tax reduction that became known as the Kemp-Roth tax cut. Kemp-Roth essentially was later adopted by President Ronald Reagan. Reagan-Kemp-Roth showed that Washington, D.C., *could* implement progrowth tax policies, and it helped spark an era of economic prosperity in this nation that has gone on almost unbroken for some 17-plus years.

Senators Roth's vision desperately needs to be replicated in Delaware itself at the dawn of the 21st century. For example, while recent income tax cuts have been welcome, much more remains to be done. Delaware needs to establish a proentrepreneur environment, so that businesses do more than just file incorporation papers in the state, they need to actually set up shop there to invent, innovate, create jobs, and spur the state's economy forward.

POLITICS

Registered Voters

42% Democrats
35% Republicans
22% Other

Federal Officials: Recent Election and Group Ratings

			ACU	ADA	SBSC
U.S. Senators:	William Roth Jr. (R)		69	22	70
	1994 Roth (R)	56%			
	Oberly (D)	42%			
	Joseph Biden Jr. (D)		13	76	20
	1998 Biden (D)	60%			
	Clatworthy (R)	38%			
U.S. Representatives:	Michael Castle (R)		59	28	60
	1998 Castle (R)	66%			
	Williams (D)	32%			
Electoral Votes:	3				
1996 Presidential Results:	Clinton	52%			
	Dole	37%			
	Perot	11%			

State Officials

Governor 1996 Election:	Thomas R. Carper (D)	69%
	Janet Rzewnicki (R)	31%
Lt. Governor:	Ruth Ann Minner (D)	
Attorney General:	M. Jane Brady (R)	
State Senate:	13 Democrats	
	8 Republicans	
State House:	15 Democrats	
	26 Republicans	

TAXES AND SPENDING

Total Revenues

Delaware's per capita state and local total revenues registered $6,113 in 1996, ranking 13th in the nation and exceeding the U.S. average of $5,706 by 7%. From 1962 to 1996, real per capita state and local revenues increased by 299%, compared with an increase in the national average of 297%.

Taxes

Delaware's per capita state and local taxes registered $2,822 in 1996, ranking 10th in the nation and exceeding the U.S. average of $2,597 by 9%. From 1962 to 1996, real per capita state and local taxes increased by 156%, compared with an increase of 152% in the U.S. average.

Property Taxes

Delaware's per capita state and local property taxes equaled $413 in 1996, ranking 44th in the nation and exceeding the U.S. average of $789 by 48%. From 1962 to 1996, real per capita state and local property taxes increased by 84%, versus a 67% increase in the U.S. average.

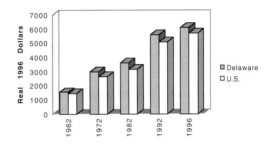

Real Per Capita State and Local Total Revenues: Delaware vs. U.S.

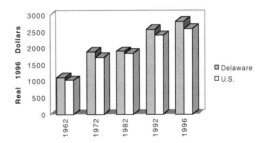

Real Per Capita State and Local Taxes: Delaware vs. U.S.

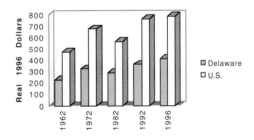

Real Per Capita State and Local Property Taxes: Delaware vs. U.S.

Sales and Gross Receipts Taxes

Delaware's per capita state and local sales and gross receipts taxes came in at $340 in 1996, ranking 49th in the nation and trailing the U.S. average of $939 by 64%. From 1962 to 1996, real per capita state and local sales and gross receipts taxes increased by 61%, versus an increase of 214% in the U.S. average.

Income Taxes

Delaware's per capita state and local income (individual and corporate) taxes registered $1,146 in 1996, ranking 4th in the nation and topping the U.S. average of $674 by 70%. From 1962 to 1996, real per capita state and local income taxes increased by 177%, versus a 567% increase in the U.S. average.

Personal Income Tax

A rate of 5.95%, ranking 25th in the nation (from lowest tax rate to highest), and comparing with the national average of 5.26%.

Capital Gains Tax

A rate of 5.95%, ranking 29th in the nation (from lowest tax rate to highest), and comparing with the national average of 4.68%.

Corporate Income Tax

A rate of 8.7%, ranking 38th in the nation (from lowest tax rate to highest), and comparing with the national average of 6.63%.

Total Expenditures

Delaware's per capita state and local total spending registered $5,818 in 1996, ranking 12th in the nation and exceeding the U.S. average of $5,268 by 10%. From 1962 to 1996, real per capita state and local total spending increased by 278%, versus an increase of 254% in the U.S. average.

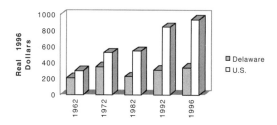

Real Per Capita State and Local Sales and Gross Receipts Taxes: Delaware vs. U.S.

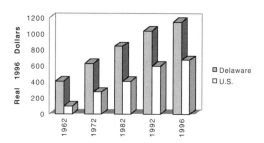

Real Per Capita State and Local Income Taxes: Delaware vs. U.S.

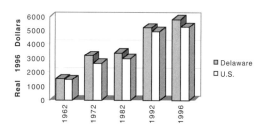

Real Per Capita State and Local Total Expenditures: Delaware vs. U.S.

Welfare Expenditures

Delaware's per capita state and local public welfare spending registered $639 in 1996, ranking 27th in the nation and trailing the U.S. average of $729 by 12%. From 1962 to 1996, real per capita state and local public welfare spending increased by 634%, compared with a 488% increase in the U.S. average.

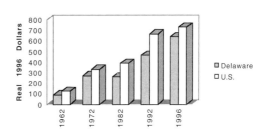

Public Welfare Spending: Delaware vs. U.S.

Welfare Recipients (in thousands)

	1980	1989	3/99	Change 1989–99
Del.	34	21	17	−19%
U.S.	10,923	10,987	7,335	−33%

Interest on General Debt

Delaware's per capita state and local interest on general debt registered $454 in 1996, ranking 3d in the nation and exceeding the U.S. average of $222 by 105%. From 1962 to 1996, real per capita state and local interest on general debt increased by 422%, versus an increase of 335% in the U.S. average.

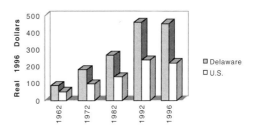

Real Per Capita State and Local Interest on General Debt: Delaware vs. U.S.

Total Debt Outstanding

Delaware's per capita state and local debt registered $7,597 in 1996, ranking 5th in the nation and topping the U.S. average of $4,409 by 72%. From 1962 to 1996, real per capita state and local debt outstanding increased by 123%, versus an increase of 120% in the U.S. average.

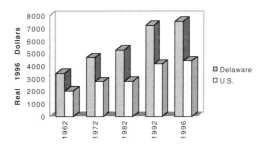

Real Per Capita State and Local Debt Outstanding: Delaware vs. U.S.

Government Employees

Delaware's state and local government employees (full-time equivalent, or FTE) per 10,000 population registered 556.6 in 1997, ranking 20th in the nation and exceeding the U.S. average of 531.1 by 5%. From 1962 to 1996, state and local FTE employees per 10,000 population increased by 67%, compared with an increase in the U.S. average of 66%.

State and Local Government Employees (FTE) Per 10,000 Population: Delaware vs. U.S.

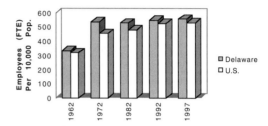

Per Capita Federal Government Expenditures, 1998

	1998	Ranking
Del.	$4,776	39th
U.S.	$5,491	

Per capita federal spending in Delaware trailed the national average by 13%.

EDUCATION

Total Education Spending

Delaware's per capita state and local education spending registered $1,878 in 1996, ranking 3d in the nation and exceeding the U.S. average of $1,503 by 25%. From 1962 to 1996, real per capita total education spending increased by 190%, versus an increase in the U.S. average of 173%.

Real Per Capita State and Local Education Spending: Delaware vs. U.S.

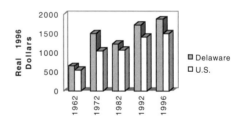

Per Pupil Spending

Delaware's per pupil public school spending registered $7,840 in 1998, ranking 6th in the nation and topping the U.S. average of $6,131 by 28%. From 1970 to 1998, Delaware's real per pupil public school spending increased by 154%, compared with a 120% increase in the U.S. average.

Real Per Pupil Public School Spending: Delaware vs. U.S.

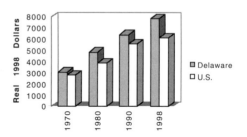

Average Public School Teacher Salaries (in 1997–98 dollars)

	1970	1980	1990	1998	1998 Ranking
Del.	38,600	33,643	42,516	42,439	12th
U.S.	36,934	33,272	39,956	39,385	

In 1998, the average public school teacher salary in Delaware outpaced the U.S. average by 8%. From 1970 to 1998, the real average teacher salary in Delaware increased by 10%, versus an increase in the U.S. average of 7%.

Pupil/Teacher Ratio, Fall 1996

	Ratio	Rank
Del.	16.6	26th
U.S.	17.1	

Teachers/Staff, Fall 1996

	Percent	Rank
Del.	54.4	12th
U.S.	52.1	

Public School 4th-Grade Reading Proficiency, 1998

	Average	Rank (out of 40 states)
Del.	212	26th
U.S.	215	

Public School 8th-Grade Reading Proficiency, 1998

	Average	Rank (out of 37 states)
Del.	256	28th
U.S.	261	

Public School 4th-Grade Math Proficiency, 1996

	Average	Rank (out of 44 states)
Del.	215	35th
U.S.	224	

Public School 8th-Grade Math Proficiency, 1996

	Average	Rank (out of 41 states)
Del.	267	27th
U.S.	271	

Public School 8th-Grade Science Proficiency, 1996

	Average	Rank (out of 41 states)
Del.	142	31st
U.S.	148	

Average Math SAT Scores

	1972	1982	1992	1998	Percentage Taking SAT in 1998
Del.	510	491	491	493	70
U.S.	509	493	501	512	43

Average Verbal SAT Scores

	1972	1982	1992	1998	Percentage Taking SAT in 1998
Del.	535	510	509	501	70
U.S.	530	504	500	505	43

Expenditures by Public Institutions of Higher Education Per Full-Time-Equivalent Student, 1996

	FTE Student Spending	Rank
Del.	$15,121	5th
U.S.	$12,343	

Per-FTE-student spending in public institutions of higher education topped the U.S. average by 23%.

Per Full-Time-Equivalent Student Revenues from Federal, State, and Local Governments, for Public Institutions of Higher Education, 1996

	FTE Student Government Revenues	Rank
Del.	$7,260	35th
U.S.	$8,101	

Per-FTE-student-government revenues in public institutions of higher education trailed the U.S. average by 10%.

Average Salary for Full-Time Professors at Public Universities, 1997

	Average	Rank
Del.	$82,337	4th
U.S.	$72,599	

The average full-time public university professor salary exceeded the U.S. average by 13%.

ECONOMY AND BUSINESS

Economic Growth

Over the period of 1977 to 1997, Delaware's real gross state product (GSP) grew by 96.6%—ranking 11th in the nation—as compared with real U.S. gross domestic product (GDP), expanding by 70.1%.

At $31.6 billion in 1997, Delaware's GSP ranked as 42d largest in the nation.

From 1993 to 1997, Delaware's annual real GSP growth averaged 3.14%—ranking 33d in the nation—as compared with annual real U.S. GDP growth, averaging 3.08%.

**Real Economic Growth
1977-1997: Delaware vs. U.S.**

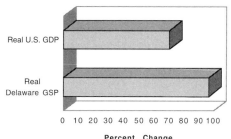

Percent Change

Job Growth

	Growth in Employee Payrolls (Nonagricultural) 1962–98	Ranking
Del.	155.4%	25th
U.S.	126.5%	

	Average Annual Growth in Employee Payrolls (Nonagricultural) 1993–98	Ranking
Del.	3.19%	20th
U.S.	2.98%	

Per Capita Disposable Income, 1997

	1997	Ranking
Del.	24,005	8th
U.S.	21,607	

Per capita disposable income topped the U.S. average by 11%.

	Real Growth 1962–97	Ranking
Del.	117.4%	26th
U.S.	116.7%	

	Average Annual Real Growth 1993–97	Ranking
Del.	1.63%	28th
U.S.	1.48%	

Number of Businesses

	1997	Percent with Fewer than 500 Employees
Businesses with Employees	24,116	94.0
Self-employed Individuals	19,000	

New Business Incorporations

	1980	1986	1992	1997
Del.	20,810	31,170	33,582	52,184

Percentage Change in Annual New Business Incorporations, 1980 vs. 1997

	Percent	Ranking
Del.	150.8	2d
U.S.	49.7	

State Merchandise Exports to the World, 1998 (in millions of dollars)

	1998	Rank
Del.	$4,969	26th

Small Business Survival Index, 1999

Delaware ranked 25th in terms of its policy environment for entrepreneurship.

Fortune 500 Headquarters in 1999

A total of 3 (ranked 28th)

Labor Union Membership, 1983 vs. 1997

Percentage of Workers	1983	1997	1997 Rank
Del.	20.1	11.7	27th
U.S.	20.1	14.1	

Homeownership Rate, 1998

	Rate	Rank
Del.	71.0	18th
U.S.	66.3	

CRIME

Crime Rates Per 100 Residents (rankings from best to worst crime rate)

Total Crime	1960	1970	1980	1990	1998	1998 Ranking
Del.	0.96	2.72	6.78	5.36	5.36	40th
U.S.	1.04	2.74	5.90	5.82	4.62	

From 1960 to 1998, Delaware's crime rate increased by 58%, versus a U.S. increase of 344%. From 1990 to 1998, Delaware's crime rate was unchanged, versus a U.S. decrease of 21%.

Violent Crime	1960	1970	1980	1990	1998	1998 Ranking
Del.	0.07	0.26	0.47	0.66	0.68	39th
U.S.	0.14	0.36	0.58	0.73	0.61	

From 1960 to 1998, Delaware's violent crime rate increased by 986%, versus a U.S. increase of 307%. From 1990 to 1998, Delaware's violent crime rate increased by 15%, compared with national decline of 22%.

Property Crime	1960	1970	1980	1990	1998	1998 Ranking
Del.	0.89	2.46	6.30	4.71	4.60	38th
U.S.	0.90	2.38	5.32	5.09	4.05	

From 1960 to 1998, Delaware's property crime rate increased by 401%, versus a national increase of 379%. From 1990 to 1998, Delaware's property crime rate decreased by 5%, compared with a national decline of 15%.

Real Per Capita Police Protection Spending (in real 1996 dollars)

	1962	1972	1982	1992	1996	1996 Ranking
Del.	41	92	123	156	176	10th
U.S.	51	95	114	148	168	

In 1996, per capita state and local police protection spending in Delaware exceeded the U.S. average by 5%. From 1962 to 1996, real per capita state and local police protection spending increased by 329%, versus an increase of 229% in the U.S. average.

Prisoners in State and Federal Prisons Per 1,000 Population

	1980	1990	1996	1996 Ranking
Del.	2.48	5.21	7.07	2d
U.S.	1.46	3.11	4.45	

From 1980 to 1996, prisoners per 1,000 population increased by 185%, versus a U.S. increase of 205%.

HEALTH CARE

Health-Care Spending

Delaware's per capita state and local health-care spending registered $205 in 1996, ranking 9th in the nation and exceeding the U.S. average of $151 by 36%. From 1962 to 1996, Delaware's real per capita state and local health-care spending increased by 1,039%, versus an increase of 739% in the U.S. average.

Real Per Capita State and Local Health Care Spending: Delaware vs. U.S.

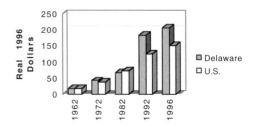

Hospital Spending

Delaware's per capita state and local hospital spending registered $81 in 1996, ranking 46th in the nation and lagging behind the U.S. average of $266 by 70%. From 1962 to 1996, Delaware's real per capita state and local hospital spending increased by 11%, as opposed to an increase of 189% in the U.S. average.

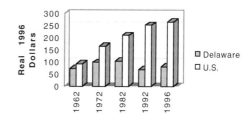

Real Per Capita State and Local Hospital Spending: Delaware vs. U.S.

Medicaid, 1997

	Spending Per Recipient	Ranking
Del.	$3,274	33d
U.S.	$3,681	

Delaware's per-recipient Medicaid spending trailed the U.S. average by 11%.

ENVIRONMENT

Parks and Recreation Spending

Delaware's per capita state and local parks and recreation spending registered $91 in 1996, ranking 14th in the nation and exceeding the U.S. average of $72 by 26%. From 1962 to 1996, real per capita state and local parks and recreation spending increased by 550%, versus a 213% increase in the U.S. average.

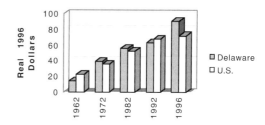

Real Per Capita State and Local Parks and Recreation Spending: Delaware vs. U.S.

State and Local Natural Resources, 1996

	Per Capita	Ranking
Del.	$70	23d
U.S.	$60	

Per capita state and local natural resources spending in Delaware topped the U.S. average by 17%.

State Parks Revenues as a Share of Operating Expenses, 1997

	Percent	Rank
Del.	44	21st
U.S.	42	

Percentage of Land Owned by the Federal Government, 1996

	Percent	Rank
Del.	0.2	49th
U.S.	24.8	

SOCIETY AND DEMOGRAPHICS

Population

Delaware's 1998 population of 744,000 ranked 45th in the nation.

Population Growth, 1990–98

	Percentage Change in Population	Ranking
Del.	11.71	13th
U.S.	8.66	

	Net International Migration	Ranking
Del.	8,307	41st

	Net Domestic Migration	Ranking
Del.	29,381	26th

Infant Mortality Rate, 1998

	Percent	Rank
Del.	9.9	2d
U.S.	6.4	

Percentage of Births of Low Birthweight, 1997

	Percent	Rank
Del.	8.7	12th
U.S.	7.5	

Delaware Population

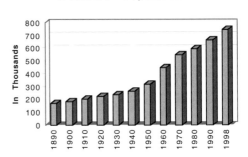

Percentage of Live Births to Unmarried Women, 1997

	Percent	Rank
Del.	38.0	5th
U.S.	32.4	

Abortion Rate—Abortions Per 1,000 Women Ages 15–44, 1995

	Rate	Rank
Del.	34.4	5th
U.S.	22.9	

LIFESTYLE

Percentage of Households with Computers, 1998

	Percent	Rank
Del.	40.5	36th

Percentage of Households with Internet Access, 1998

	Percent	Rank
Del.	25.1	28th

State Arts Agency Spending, 1999

	Per Capita	Rank
Del.	$2.04	8th
U.S.	$1.35	

Per capita state arts spending in 1999 topped the U.S. average by 51%.

Major League Sports Facilities

None

DISTRICT OF **C**OLUMBIA

Compared to the 50 states, the District of Columbia rates by far as the least prepared to enter the entrepreneurial 21st century.

Indeed, the District suffers under one-party political arrogance (that is, the Democrats); a welfare state run amok; a tax system hostile to economic growth and job creation; a heavy government debt burden; a bloated city payroll; a wasteful, failed public school system; and a government unable to fulfill its basic duties of protecting life, limb, and property. As a result, the District of Columbia has been plagued by a staggering loss in population, the most hostile environment in the nation for entrepreneurs or anyone else, and the country's slowest economic and job growth. In fact, the demise of Washington, D.C., although it serves as the seat of our federal government and receives massive amounts of federal largess, offers perhaps the clearest example in our nation's history that government in no way can guide or generate economic development.

For good measure, our nation's capital city is hampered by numerous social ills, including an illegitimate birth rate twice the U.S. average and an abortion rate almost seven times the national rate. The District not only suffers from deficits in terms of its economy and city budget, but also in terms of personal responsibility. Under a welfare-state regime that creates a disconnection between actions and outcomes, the personal responsibility shortfall should surprise no one.

One of the few bright spots for the District is that it claims the highest per capita disposable income in the nation.

Most District of Columbia elected officials wish to place blame for the city's long, dramatic decline on anyone but themselves. They would prefer to blame the lack of voting representation in Congress, a presumed need for more revenue from the federal government or from a commuter tax, or the amount of land owned in the District by the federal government. Reality tells a far different story.

For example, the percentage of land in the District owned by the federal government is actually less than in 12 states, and it is slightly less than the percentage of land owned by the federal government nationwide. In addition, the District's per capita government revenues show quite clearly that no shortage of funds exists; instead, the government is taking far too many resources out of the private sector already. As for voting representation in Congress, such a step would accomplish nothing in terms of improving the economy, fiscal well-being, or quality of life in the District. The U.S. Constitution, moreover, gives Congress authority over the seat of government.

Speaking of the District falling under federal authority, Congress and the White House have been long-time accomplices in the ongoing decay of Washington, D.C. Congress after Congress and a long line of individuals residing in the Oval Office have signed off on ever-more wasteful city government and increasingly onerous taxes.

Some hope emerged in early 1995, when Republicans took control of Congress. We were in the midst of this debate as our first book, *D.C. by the Numbers: A State of Failure,* was published that January. Our idea for answering the statehood cry of "no taxation without representation" was to make the District a federal tax-free zone. The idea received significant attention. And seeing Republicans like Jack Kemp and Newt Gingrich meet with then-Mayor Marion Barry, a Democrat, was fascinating and hopeful. However, particularly given the Clinton administration's aversion to tax relief, it wasn't all that long before positive measures like cutting taxes and seriously reducing the size of D.C. government gave way to a rather predictable federal government bailout and the institution of a financial control board.

The District's recent appearance of improved fiscal health is grossly deceptive. For example, from fiscal year 1993 to fiscal year 1998, total spending on city government jumped from $3.6 billion to $5.5 billion—a massive 53% increase. Meanwhile, federal funds flowing to the District of Columbia rose from $636 million to $1.138 billion—a leap of almost 80%. Therefore, the federal government actually rewarded the city for its waste and inefficiencies by "taking over" various city services, that is, in effect, handing city politicians more money.

However, in April 1999, a dramatic alternative was offered by city councilmen David Catania, a Republican, and Jack Evans, a Democrat. Catania and Evans proposed a three-year plan to cut property taxes and slash the city's onerous income taxes. The top personal income tax rate would fall from 9.5% to 6.5%—a better than 31 percent reduction—and the corporate rate would decline from 9.975% to 6.5%—a 35 percent cut. After years of suffering under a punitive tax system with hapless politicians crying out for more revenues, this was a stunning reversal. But this was not mere political posturing, because Catania and Evans cobbled together an overwhelming bipartisan, veto-proof majority in the city council to support the plan.

Unfortunately, Mayor Anthony Williams and financial control board chairwoman Alice Rivlin showed little interest. Williams's veto could have been overridden, but Rivlin presented a far more formidable obstacle—so much for the benefit of a financial control board. As a result, a far more tepid and precarious tax reduction plan was agreed on by the various parties. For example, the top personal income tax rate will only be reduced to 8.5%—a reduction of only 11 percent—phased in over a far lengthier five years. The corporate rate will be reduced to 8.5% in a two-step process in 2003 and 2004, though this far smaller, more remote reduction will only go ahead if the city meets rather lofty budget surplus and economic growth goals.

While the demeanor of officials like Williams and Rivlin is far different from that of the bombastic former-Mayor Marion Barry, their ideas for turning the city around are not all that different. Big government is still seen as a positive for the city's future. While he opposed substantive tax reduction, for example, Williams supported building a presumably tax-payer-subsidized ballpark in the District of Columbia and declared that "baseball would be an economic home run for the District." As is pointed out by most independent studies, taxpayer-funded ballparks accomplish nothing in terms of boosting economic growth, personal income, or job creation.[1] Meanwhile reductions in tax rates increase progrowth incentives for working, investing, and entrepreneurship.

In terms of education, with President Clinton leading the opposition to giving students and parents real choice (for example, through a voucher plan), countless children are being lost to a failed public school system.

---

1. For example, see Melvin L. Burstein and Arthur J. Rolnick, "Congress Should End the Economic War among the States," 1994 Annual Report Essay, Federal Reserve Bank of Minneapolis (March 1995), "Stadium Madness" editorial, *Investor's Business Daily*, December 30, 1997; Michael Walden, "Don't Play Ball," *Carolina Journal* (October/November 1997) Robert Baade, "Stadiums, Professional Sports, and Economic Development: Assessing the Reality," Hearthland Institute (March 28, 1994), and Robert Baade and Allen R. Sanderson, "The Employment Effect of Teams and Sports Facilities," in *Sports, Jobs, and Taxes*, ed. Roger G. Noll and Andrew Zimbalist (Washington: Brookings Institution Press, 1997), pp. 92–118.

The future of the District will be determined by a battle between the forces of the well-entrenched, near-ubiquitous welfare state versus some upstarts looking to get government off the backs of entrepreneurs, businesses, and families. The Catania-Evans tax relief measure offers hope in an otherwise desolate big government wasteland.

POLITICS

Federal Officials

U.S. House Delegate:	Eleanor Holmes Norton (D)	
	1998 Norton (D)	90%
	Wolterbeek (R)	6%
1996 Presidential Results:	Clinton	85%
	Dole	9%
	Perot	2%

City Officials

Mayoral 1998 Election:	Anthony Williams (D)	66%
	Carol Achwartz (R)	30%
City Council:	11 Democrats	
	2 Republicans	

TAXES AND SPENDING

Total Revenues

D.C.'s per capita state and local total revenues registered $10,451 in 1996, ranking 2d in the nation and exceeding the U.S. average of $5,706 by 83%. From 1962 to 1996, real per capita state and local revenues increased by 517%, compared with an increase in the national average of 297%.

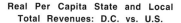

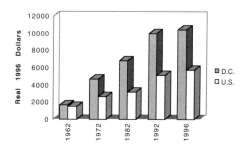

Real Per Capita State and Local Total Revenues: D.C. vs. U.S.

Taxes

D.C.'s per capita state and local taxes registered $4,569 in 1996, ranking highest in the nation and exceeding the U.S. average of $2,597 by 76%. From 1962 to 1996, real per capita state and local taxes increased by 329%, compared with an increase of 152% in the U.S. average.

Property Taxes

D.C.'s per capita state and local property taxes equaled $1,292, ranking 4th in the nation and exceeding the U.S. average of $789 by 64%. From 1962 to 1996, real per capita state and local property taxes increased by 227%, versus a 67% increase in the U.S. average.

Sales and Gross Receipts Taxes

D.C.'s per capita state and local sales and gross receipts taxes came in at $1,463 in 1996, ranking 4th in the nation and topping the U.S. average of $939 by 56%. From 1962 to 1996, real per capita state and local sales and gross receipts taxes increased by 309%, versus an increase of 214% in the U.S. average.

Income Taxes

D.C.'s per capita state and local income (individual and corporate) taxes registered $1,554 in 1996, ranking highest in the nation and topping the U.S. average of $674 by 131%. From 1962 to 1996, real per capita state and local income taxes increased by 606%, versus a 567% increase in the U.S. average.

Personal Income Tax

A rate of 9.5%, ranking 49th in the nation (from lowest tax rate to highest), and comparing with the national average of 5.26%.

Real Per Capita State and Local Taxes: D.C. vs. U.S.

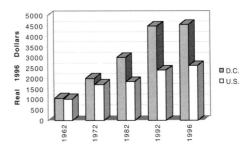

Real Per Capita State and Local Property Taxes: D.C. vs. U.S.

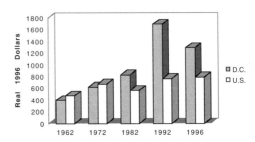

Real Per Capita State and Local Sales and Gross Receipts Taxes: D.C. vs. U.S.

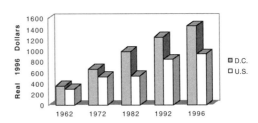

Real Per Capita State and Local Income Taxes: D.C. vs. U.S.

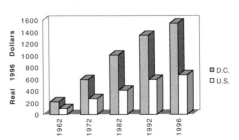

Capital Gains Tax

A rate of 9.5%, ranking last in the nation (from lowest tax rate to highest), and comparing with the national average of 4.68%.

Corporate Income Tax

A rate of 9.975%, ranking 50th in the nation (from lowest tax rate to highest), and comparing with the national average of 6.64%.

Total Expenditures

D.C.'s per capita state and local total spending registered $10,714 in 1996, ranking 2d in the nation and exceeding the U.S. average of $5,268 by 103%. From 1962 to 1996, real per capita state and local total spending increased by 457%, versus an increase of 254% in the U.S. average.

Welfare Expenditures

D.C.'s per capita state and local public welfare spending registered $2,158 in 1996, ranking highest in the nation and outpacing the U.S. average of $729 by 196%. From 1962 to 1996, real per capita state and local public welfare spending increased by 1,320%, compared with a 488% increase in the U.S. average.

Welfare Recipients (in thousands)

	1980	1989	3/99	Change 1989–99
D.C.	82	47	52	+11%
U.S.	10,923	10,987	7,335	−33%

Interest on General Debt

D.C.'s per capita state and local interest on general debt registered $577 in 1996, ranking 2d in the nation and exceeding the U.S. average of $222 by 160%. From 1962 to 1996, real per capita state and local interest on general debt increased by 2,409%, versus an increase of 335% in the U.S. average.

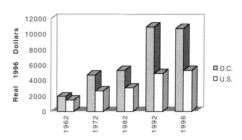

Real Per Capita State and Local Total Expenditures: D.C. vs. U.S.

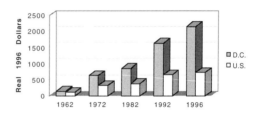

Real Per Capita State and Local Public Welfare Spending: D.C. vs. U.S.

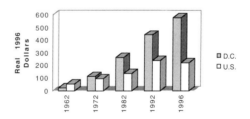

Real Per Capita State and Local Interest on General Debt: D.C. vs. U.S.

Total Debt Outstanding

D.C.'s per capita state and local debt registered $7,618 in 1996, ranking 4th in the nation and outrunning the U.S. average of $4,409 by 73%. From 1962 to 1996, real per capita local debt outstanding increased by 468%, versus an increase of 120% in the U.S. average.

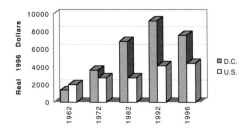

Real Per Capita State and Local Debt Outstanding: D.C. vs. U.S.

Government Employees

D.C.'s state and local government employees (full-time equivalent, or FTE) per 10,000 population registered 874.3 in 1997, ranking highest in the nation and exceeding the U.S. average of 531.1 by 65%. From 1962 to 1996, state and local FTE employees per 10,000 population increased by 151%, compared with an increase in the U.S. average of 66%.

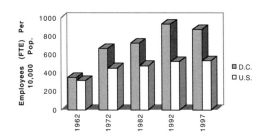

State and Local Government Employees (FTE) Per 10,000 Population: D.C. vs. U.S.

Per Capita Federal Government Expenditures, 1998

	1998	Ranking
D.C.	$45,946	1st
U.S.	$5,491	

Per capita federal spending in D.C. outpaced the national average by 737%.

EDUCATION

Total Education Spending

D.C.'s per capita state and local education spending registered $1,232 in 1996, ranking 50th in the nation and trailing the U.S. average of $1,503 by 18%. From 1962 to 1996, real per capita total education spending increased by 262%, versus an increase in the U.S. average of 173%.

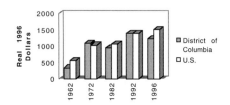

Real Per Capita State and Local Education Spending: District of Columbia vs. U.S.

Per Pupil Spending

D.C.'s per pupil public school spending registered $8,725 in 1998, ranking 3d in the nation and exceeding the U.S. average of $6,131 by 42%. From 1970 to 1998, D.C.'s real per pupil public school spending increased by 149%, compared with a 120% increase in the U.S. average.

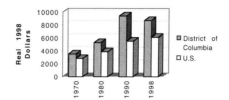

Real Per Pupil Public School Spending: District of Columbia vs. U.S.

Average Public School Teacher Salaries (in 1997–98 dollars)

	1970	1980	1990	1998	1998 Ranking
D.C.	44,037	46,231	48,917	46,350	7th
U.S.	36,934	33,272	39,956	39,385	

In 1998, the average public school teacher salary in D.C. exceeded the U.S. average by 18%. From 1970 to 1998, the real average teacher salary in the District increased by 5%, versus an increase in the U.S. average of 7%.

Pupil/Teacher Ratio, Fall 1996

	Ratio	Rank
D.C.	14.9	11th
U.S.	17.1	

Teachers/Staff, Fall 1996

	Percent	Rank
D.C.	56.8	5th
U.S.	52.1	

Public School 4th-Grade Reading Proficiency, 1998

	Average	Rank (out of 40 states)
D.C.	182	40th
U.S.	215	

Public School 8th-Grade Reading Proficiency, 1998

	Average	Rank (out of 37 states)
D.C.	236	37th
U.S.	261	

Public School 4th-Grade Math Proficiency, 1996

	Average	Rank (out of 44 states)
D.C.	187	44th
U.S.	224	

Public School 8th-Grade Math Proficiency, 1996

	Average	Rank (out of 41 states)
D.C.	233	41st
U.S.	271	

Public School 8th-Grade Science Proficiency, 1996

	Average	Rank (out of 41 states)
D.C.	113	41st
U.S.	148	

Average Math SAT Scores

	1972	1982	1992	1998	Percentage Taking SAT in 1998
D.C.	439	447	463	476	83
U.S.	509	493	501	512	43

Average Verbal SAT Scores

	1972	1982	1992	1998	Percentage Taking SAT in 1998
D.C.	468	472	478	488	83
U.S.	530	504	500	505	43

Expenditures by Public Institutions of Higher Education Per Full-Time-Equivalent Student, 1996

	FTE Student Spending	Rank
D.C.	$21,364	1st
U.S.	$12,343	

Per-FTE-student spending in public institutions of higher education exceeded the U.S. average by 73%.

Per Full-Time-Equivalent Student Revenues from Federal, State, and Local Governments for Public Institutions of Higher Education, 1996

	Government Revenues	FTE Student Rank
D.C.	$18,058	1st
U.S.	$8,101	

Per-FTE-student-government revenues in public institutions of higher education outpaced the U.S. average by 123%.

ECONOMY AND BUSINESS

Economic Growth

Over the period of 1977 to 1997, the District of Columbia's real gross state product (GSP) grew by 5.51%—ranking last in the nation—as compared with real U.S. gross domestic product (GDP), expanding by 70.1%.

At $52.4 billion in 1997, the District of Columbia's GSP ranked as 36th largest in the nation.

From 1993 to 1997, the District of Columbia's annual real GSP growth averaged −0.27%—ranking 49th in the nation—as compared with annual real U.S. GDP growth, averaging 3.08%.

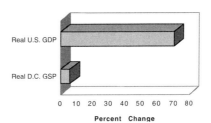

Real Economic Growth 1977-1997: District of Columbia vs. U.S.

Real U.S. GDP

Real D.C. GSP

0 10 20 30 40 50 60 70 80

Percent Change

Job Growth

	Growth in Employee Payrolls (Nonagricultural) 1962–98	Ranking
D.C.	16.7%	51st
U.S.	126.5%	

	Average Annual Growth in Employee Payrolls (Nonagricultural) 1993–98	Ranking
D.C.	−1.79%	51st
U.S.	2.98%	

Per Capita Disposable Income

	1997	Ranking
D.C.	$29,490	1st
U.S.	$21,607	

Per capita disposable income in 1997 exceeded the U.S. average by 36%.

	Real Growth 1962–97	Ranking
D.C.	144.7%	9th
U.S.	116.7%	

	Average Annual Real Growth 1993–97	Ranking
D.C.	1.41%	38th
U.S.	1.48%	

Number of Businesses

	1997	Percent with Fewer than 500 Employees
Businesses with Employees	23,050	94.1
Self-employed Individuals	14,000	

New Business Incorporations

	1980	1986	1992	1997
D.C.	1,316	2,252	2,256	1,462

Percentage Change in Annual New Business Incorporations, 1980 vs. 1997

	Percent	Ranking
D.C.	11.1	40th
U.S.	49.7	

State Merchandise Exports to the World, 1998 (in millions of dollars)

	1998	Rank
D.C.	$4,392	29th

Small Business Survival Index, 1999

The District of Columbia ranked dead last in terms of the policy environment for entrepreneurship.

Fortune 500 Headquarters in 1999

A total of 3 (ranked 28th)

Labor Union Membership, 1983 vs. 1997

	Percentage of Workers		
	1983	1997	1997 Rank
D.C.	19.5	13.6	23d
U.S.	20.1	14.1	

Homeownership Rate, 1998

	Rate	Rank
D.C.	40.3	51st
U.S.	66.3	

CRIME

Crime Rates Per 100 Residents (rankings from best to worst crime rate)

Total Crime	1970	1980	1990	1998	1998 Ranking
D.C.	7.84	10.24	10.77	8.84	51st
U.S.	2.74	5.90	5.82	4.62	

From 1970 to 1998, D.C.'s crime rate increased by 13%, versus a U.S. increase of 69%. From 1990 to 1998, D.C.'s crime rate dropped by 18%, versus a U.S. decrease of 21%.

Violent Crime	1970	1980	1990	1998	1998 Ranking
D.C.	2.17	2.08	2.46	1.72	51st
U.S.	0.36	0.58	0.73	0.57	

From 1970 to 1998, D.C.'s violent crime rate decreased by 21%, versus a U.S. increase of 58%. From 1990 to 1998, D.C.'s violent crime rate declined by 30%, compared with a national decline of 22%.

Property Crime	1970	1980	1990	1998	1998 Ranking
D.C.	8.73	8.15	8.32	7.12	51st
U.S.	2.38	5.32	5.09	4.05	

From 1970 to 1998, D.C.'s property crime rate decreased by 18% versus a national increase of 70%. From 1990 to 1998, D.C.'s property crime rate decreased by 14%, compared with a national decline of 20%.

Real Per Capita Police Protection Spending (in real 1996 dollars)

	1962	1972	1982	1992	1996	1996 Ranking
D.C.	124	334	306	510	458	1st
U.S.	51	95	114	148	168	

In 1996, per capita state and local police protection spending in D.C. topped the U.S. average by 173%. From 1962 to 1996, real per capita state and local police protection spending increased by 269%, versus an increase of 229% in the U.S. average.

Prisoners in State and Federal Prisons Per 1,000 Population

	1980	1990	1996	1996 Ranking
D.C.	4.93	16.39	17.40	1st
U.S.	1.46	3.11	4.45	

From 1980 to 1996, prisoners per 1,000 population increased by 253%, versus a U.S. increase of 205%.

HEALTH CARE

Health-Care Spending

D.C.'s per capita local health-care spending registered $303 in 1996, ranking highest in the nation and exceeding the U.S. average of $151 by 101%. From 1962 to 1996, D.C.'s real per capita local health-care spending increased by 719%, versus an increase of 739% in the U.S. average.

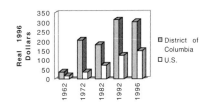

Real Per Capita State and Local Health Care Spending: District of Columbia vs. U.S.

Hospital Spending

D.C.'s per capita local hospital spending registered $493 in 1996, ranking 5th in the nation and exceeding the U.S. average of $266 by 85%. From 1962 to 1996, D.C.'s real per capita local hospital spending increased by 114%, as opposed to an increase of 189% in the U.S. average.

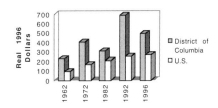

Real Per Capita State and Local Hospital Spending: District of Columbia vs. U.S.

Medicaid, 1997

	Spending Per Recipient	Ranking
D.C.	$5,438	8th
U.S.	$3,681	

The District of Columbia's per-recipient Medicaid spending in 1997 exceeded the U.S. average by 48%.

ENVIRONMENT

Parks and Recreation Spending

D.C.'s per capita state and local parks and recreation spending registered $110 in 1996, ranking 7th in the nation and outpacing the U.S. average of $72 by 53%. From 1962 to 1996, real per capita state and local parks and recreation spending increased by 4%, versus a 213% increase in the U.S. average.

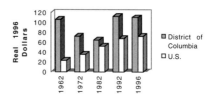

Real Per Capita State and Local Parks and Recreation Spending: District of Columbia vs. U.S.

State and Local Natural Resources Spending, 1996

	Per Capita	Ranking
D.C.	$0	51st
U.S.	$60	

Percentage of Land Owned by the Federal Government, 1996

	Percent	Rank
D.C.	23.4	13th
U.S.	24.8	

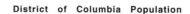

SOCIETY AND DEMOGRAPHICS

Population

D.C.'s 1998 population of 523,000 ranked 50th in the nation.

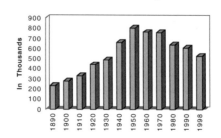

District of Columbia Population

Population Growth, 1990–98

	Percentage Change in Population	Ranking
D.C.	−13.84	51st
U.S.	8.66	

	Net International Migration	Ranking
D.C.	27,883	25th

	Net Domestic Migration	Ranking
D.C.	−139,048	42d

Infant Mortality Rate, 1998

	Percent	Rank
D.C.	9.7	5th
U.S.	6.4	

Percentage of Births of Low Birthweight, 1997

	Percent	Rank
D.C.	13.4	1st
U.S.	7.5	

Percentage of Live Births to Unmarried Women, 1997

	Percent	Rank
D.C.	63.6	1st
U.S.	32.4	

Abortion Rate—Abortions Per 1,000 Women Ages 15–44, 1995

	Rate	Rank
D.C.	151.7	1st
U.S.	22.9	

LIFESTYLE

Percentage of Households with Computers, 1998

	Percent	Rank
D.C.	41.4	31st

Percentage of Households with Internet Access, 1998

	Percent	Rank
D.C.	24.2	33d

State Arts Agency Spending, 1999

	Per Capita	Rank
D.C.	$3.35	2d
U.S.	$1.35	

Per capita state arts spending in 1999 topped the U.S. average by 148%.

Major League Sports Facilities

Year Opened/ Refurb.	Stadium/ Arena	Home Team	Millions of Nominal Dollars		Millions of Real 1997 Dollars	
			Estimated Total Cost	Estimated Taxpayer Cost	Estimated Total Cost	Estimated Taxpayer Cost
1903	Griffith Stadium	Senators I (MLB) 1903–60 Senators II (MLB) 1961	NA	$0.0	NA	$0.0
1962	RFK Stadium	Senators II (MLB) 1962–71 Redskins (NFL) 1961–97	$21.7	$21.7	$115.4	$115.4
1997	MCI Center	Capitals (NHL) 1997–present Wizards (NBA) 1997–present	$255.0	$70.0	$255.0	$70.0

FLORIDA

To many people, Florida conjures up images of senior citizens living out their golden years in a retirement community. While it remains a top relocation destination for retirees, Florida now stands out as one of the most economically dynamic states in the nation.

Florida, as noted in the following pages, claims one of the nation's largest and fastest-growing economies, an expanding population, sizeable exports, exploding new business incorporations, and robust job creation.

One of the keys to Florida's success is its state tax system. Most critically, Florida has become a magnet for labor and capital in part because the state imposes no individual income and capital gains taxes and effectively no death taxes.

In recent years, though, property taxes took a significant leap higher. For example, between 1972 and 1982, real per capita property taxes rose by just 6%, but from 1982 to 1992 they increased by 60% and continued to inch higher from 1992 to 1996.

In 1999 newly elected Governor Jeb Bush (R) and the state legislature implemented a tax relief package that featured a reduction in property taxes as well as a cut in the state's "intangibles tax," imposed annually on various assets. Future tax-cut efforts should focus on phasing out Florida's corporate income tax, which was imposed in 1971.

A more dynamic economy and younger citizenship seem to be creating a more conservative political environment, to the pleasure of Florida Republicans. In November 1998, Republicans not only won the governorship, but also majorities in both houses of the state legislature, giving them complete control for the first time in 122 years. The situation for the Democrats has deteriorated to the point that many experts now view the 2000 election for the seat of retiring Republican U.S. Senator Connie Mack as critical to the survival of the Democratic Party in the state. "The Democrats are going to go all out to win that seat," says political consultant Adam Goodman. "They're going to pour all their time and energy into that one race; and if the Republicans win, it will be a tremendous blow to the two-party system in Florida." While such analysis is no doubt hyperbolic—after all, Democrats do hold the other U.S. Senate seat and eight congressional seats and sat in the governor's chair for eight years in the 1990s—it does illustrate just how bad things have gotten for Florida Democrats.

The state's changing population has brought different issues to the forefront of public debate as well. In the days when empty nesters ruled Florida, education was not a high priority, giving way to health care and other social services. But as the school-age population has risen steadily, so has the demand for better schools. Historically, Florida has wallowed in the bottom tier of the 50 states when it comes to various education performance measures (see below)—a situation Governor Bush is addressing head on with a sweeping reform program entitled the "A+ Plan for Education," which features the nation's first statewide education choice program.

Under the Governor's plan, social promotion is ended, annual testing is implemented for grades 3 through 10, and the best-performing schools will be financially rewarded. Meanwhile, parents of students at the worst-performing schools are given vouchers to send their children to the public or private school of their choice.

In August 1999, 58 students participating in the state choice program began classes at four Roman Catholic schools and another private school, according to the *New York Times* (August 17, 1999). Bush asked a straightforward question: "Why should we trap kids in schools that aren't working?"

Not surprisingly, the defenders of failing or stagnant public schools complain that public education in general, and poor and minority students in particular, will be hurt. Of course, just the opposite is true. Public schools will be forced to improve, and poor and minority students who have long been failed by public schools will be given the opportunity for a better education. Indeed, choice supporters point to early signs that administrators of long-troubled schools have begun to take steps toward improvement in order to retain students.

Nina Shokrai Rees, a senior education analyst with the Heritage Foundation, captured the beauty of the Bush education program in an *Investor's Business Daily* (August 10, 1999) article: "In Florida, public schools are given a chance to prove they can teach; in exchange, they give up the right to hold a monopoly over education indefinitely." Unfortunately, as we went to press, school choice in Florida was under attack in the courts.

Florida officials also are moving to get tough on the state's long-time crime problem (as noted below, Florida's crime rates rank quite dismally compared with the rest of the nation.) A series of violent, high-profile attacks on foreign visitors and an unchecked drug trade had earned the state an unsavory reputation, which threatened the vital tourist industry and probably dissuaded some companies and individuals from putting down roots in the state. To their credit, the people and politicians of Florida pulled together to deal with the problem. Legislation was enacted that cracked down on criminals and gave law-abiding citizens the right to carry handguns for self-defense.

Governor Jeb Bush has been an ardent advocate of this approach, recently signing into law "10, 20, life" legislation, which provides stiff minimum penalties for anyone convicted of using a firearm in the commission of a crime. He also signed a "three strikes, you're out" law, which provides strict minimum sentences for violent repeat offenders.

"Some people are whining because they think '10, 20, life' is too tough," says Marion Hammer, head of Unified Sportsmen of Florida and a veteran state political operative. "They point to a group of teenagers who recently fired a gun while robbing a convenience store but didn't injure anyone. Because of '10, 20, life' they're facing 20 years minimum in prison."

"The liberals say that's not fair ... that they didn't know about the tough new penalties. What? They didn't know robbing a convenience store and shooting at someone was illegal? Come on," continues Hammer, echoing the prevailing attitude toward criminals among Floridians.

On the environment, however, there has been movement in a starkly opposite direction from the aforementioned free-market, conservative policies. In 1999, the legislature passed Governor Bush's "Florida Forever" initiative, which will provide $3 billion over the next 10 years to buy up and "protect" land. Bush also has continued the efforts of his Democratic predecessors to provide more land for the Everglades restoration project.

Overall, continued diversity and dynamism in population and the economic base, combined with continuing promarket policy reforms, will undoubtedly lead to increasing prosperity for all Floridians. The state appears to be on solid ground as it enters the 21st century.

POLITICS

Registered Voters

46% Democrats
41% Republicans
13% Other

Federal Officials: Recent Election and Group Ratings

			ACU	ADA	SBSC
U.S. Senators:	Bob Graham (D)		18	70	25
	1998 Graham (D)	62%			
	Crist (R)	38%			
	Connie Mack (R)		94	5	85
	1994 Mack (R)	71%			
	Rodham (D)	29%			
U.S. Representatives:	Joe Scarborough (R-1)		98	11	90
	1998 Scarborough (R) NO				
	F. Allen Boyd Jr. (D-2)	38	60	25	
	1998 Boyd (D)	NO			
	Corrine Brown (D-3)		10	89	5
	1998 Brown (D)	55%			
	Randall (R)	45%			
	Tillie Fowler (R-4)		87	9	80
	1998 Fowler (R)	NO			
	Karen Thurman (D-5)		18	76	15
	1998 Thurman (D)	66%			
	Gargan (REF)	34%			
	Clifford Stearns (R-6)		95	8	90
	1998 Stearns (R)	NO			
	John Mica (R-7)		96	4	90
	1998 Mica (R)	NO			
	Bill McCollum (R-8)		90	5	90
	1998 McCollum (R)	66%			
	Krulick (D)	34%			

			ACU	ADA	SBSC
Michael Bilirakis (R-9)			85	5	90
1998	Bilirakis (R)	NO			
C.W. (Bill) Young (R-10)			84	11	85
1998	Young (R)	NO			
Jim Davis (D-11)			16	80	30
1998	Davis (D)	65%			
	Chillura (R)	35%			
Charles Canady (R-12)			89	7	85
1998	Canady (R)	NO			
Dan Miller (R-13)			87	13	100
1998	Miller (R)	NO			
Porter Goss (R-14)			88	9	80
1998	Goss (R)	NO			
Dave Weldon (R-15)			94	1	95
1998	Weldon (R)	63%			
	Golding (D)	37%			
Mark Adam Foley (R-16)			84	18	80
1998	Foley (R)	NO			
Carrie Meek (D-17)			9	88	5
1998	Meek (D)	NO			
Ileana Ros-Lehtinen (R-18)			74	26	55
1998	Ros-Lehtinen (R)	NO			
Robert Wexler (D-19)			9	95	5
1998	Wexler (D)	NO			
Peter Deutsch (D-20)			18	80	10
1998	Deutsch (D)	NO			
Lincoln Diaz-Balart (R-21)			70	26	65
1998	Diaz-Balart (R)	75%			
	Cusack (D)	25%			
Clay Shaw Jr. (R-22)			84	12	95
1998	Shaw (R)	NO			
Alcee Hastings (D-23)			7	87	10
1998	Hastings (D)	NO			

Electoral Votes:	25	
1996 Presidential Results:	Clinton	48%
	Dole	42%
	Perot	9%

State Officials

Governor 1998 Election:	Jeb Bush (R)	55%
	Buddy McKay	45%
Lt. Governor:	Frank Brogan (R)	
Attorney General:	Bob Butterworth (D)	
State Senate:	15 Democrats	
	25 Republicans	
State House:	48 Democrats	
	72 Republicans	

TAXES AND SPENDING

Total Revenues

Florida's per capita state and local total revenues registered $5,153 in 1996, ranking 28th in the nation and trailing the U.S. average of $5,706 by 10%. From 1962 to 1996, real per capita state and local revenues increased by 301%, compared with an increase in the national average of 297%.

Taxes

Florida's per capita state and local taxes registered $2,330 in 1996, ranking 29th in the nation and trailing the U.S. average of $2,597 by 10%. From 1962 to 1996, real per capita state and local taxes increased by 160%, compared with an increase of 152% in the U.S. average.

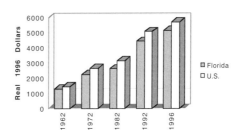

Real Per Capita State and Local Total Revenues: Florida vs. U.S.

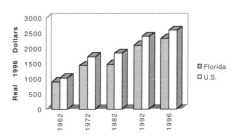

Real Per Capita State and Local Taxes: Florida vs. U.S.

Property Taxes

Florida's per capita state and local property taxes equaled $820 in 1996, ranking 19th in the nation and topping the U.S. average of $789 by 4%. From 1962 to 1996, real per capita state and local property taxes increased by 123%, versus a 67% increase in the U.S. average.

Sales and Gross Receipts Taxes

Florida's per capita state and local sales and gross receipts taxes came in at $1,221 in 1996, ranking 5th and exceeding the U.S. average of $939 by 30%. From 1962 to 1996, real per capita state and local sales and gross receipts taxes increased by 241%, versus an increase of 214% in the U.S. average.

Income Taxes

Florida's per capita state and local income (individual and corporate) taxes registered $70 in 1996, ranking 46th in the nation and trailing the U.S. average of $674 by 90%. Florida did not impose a corporate income tax until 1971.

Personal Income Tax

A rate of 0%, ranking best in the nation (from lowest tax rate to highest), and comparing with the national average of 5.26%.

Capital Gains Tax

A rate of 0%, ranking best in the nation (from lowest tax rate to highest), and comparing with the national average of 4.68%.

Corporate Income Tax

A rate of 5.5%, ranking 15th in the nation (from lowest tax rate to highest), and comparing with the national average of 6.63%.

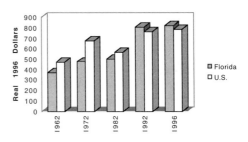

Real Per Capita State and Local Property Taxes: Florida vs. U.S.

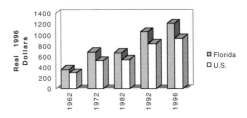

Real Per Capita State and Local Sales and Gross Receipts Taxes: Florida vs. U.S.

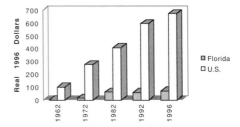

Real Per Capita State and Local Income Taxes: Florida vs. U.S.

Total Expenditures

Florida's per capita state and local total spending registered $4,763 in 1996, ranking 32d in the nation and trailing the U.S. average of $5,268 by 10%. From 1962 to 1996, real per capita state and local total spending increased by 264%, versus a 254% increase in the U.S. average.

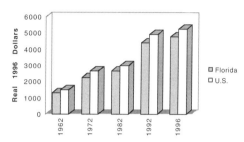

Real Per Capita State and Local Total Expenditures: Florida vs. U.S.

Welfare Expenditures

Florida's per capita state and local public welfare spending registered $513 in 1996, ranking 45th in the nation and trailing the U.S. average of $729 by 30%. From 1962 to 1996, real per capita state and local public welfare spending increased by 518%, compared with a 488% increase in the U.S. average.

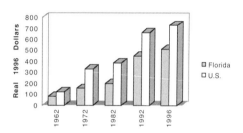

Real Per Capita State and Local Public Welfare Spending: Florida vs. U.S.

Welfare Recipients (in thousands)

	1980	1989	3/99	Change 1989–99
Fla.	279	356	198	−44%
U.S.	10,923	10,987	7,335	−33%

Interest on General Debt

Florida's per capita state and local interest on general debt registered $240 in 1996, ranking 19th in the nation and topping the U.S. average of $222 by 8%. From 1962 to 1996, real per capita state and local interest on general debt increased by 422%, versus an increase of 335% in the U.S. average.

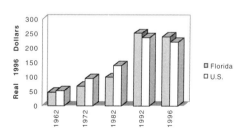

Real Per Capita State and Local Interest on General Debt: Florida vs. U.S.

Total Debt Outstanding

Florida's per capita state and local debt registered $4,525 in 1996, ranking 18th in the nation and outrunning the U.S. average of $4,409 by 3%. From 1962 to 1996, real per capita state and local debt outstanding increased by 165%, versus an increase of 120% in the U.S. average.

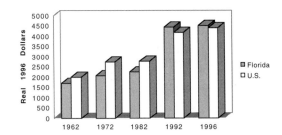

Real Per Capita State and Local Debt Outstanding: Florida vs. U.S.

Government Employees

Florida's state and local government employees (full-time equivalent, or FTE) per 10,000 population registered 498.8 in 1997, ranking 43d in the nation and trailing the U.S. average of 531.1 by 6%. From 1962 to 1996, state and local FTE employees per 10,000 population increased by 46%, compared with an increase in the U.S. average of 66%.

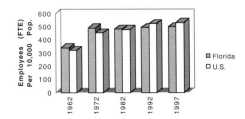

State and Local Government Employees (FTE) Per 10,000 Population: Florida vs. U.S.

Per Capita Federal Government Expenditures, 1998

	1998	Ranking
Fla.	$5,602	21st
U.S.	$5,491	

Per capita federal spending in Florida exceeded the national average by 2%.

EDUCATION

Total Education Spending

Florida's per capita state and local education spending registered $1,252 in 1996, ranking 49th in the nation and trailing the U.S. average of $1,503 by 17%. From 1962 to 1996, real per capita total education spending increased by 175%, versus an increase in the U.S. average of 173%.

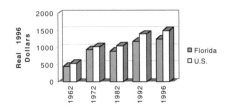

Real Per Capita State and Local Education Spending: Florida vs. U.S.

Per Pupil Spending

Florida's per pupil public school spending registered $5,483 in 1998, ranking 34th in the nation and trailing the U.S. average of $6,131 by 11%. From 1970 to 1998, Florida's real per pupil public school spending increased by 117%, compared with a 120% increase in the U.S. average.

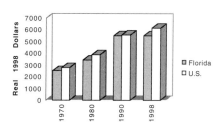

Real Per Pupil Public School Spending: Florida vs. U.S.

Average Public School Teacher Salaries (in 1997–98 dollars)

	1970	1980	1990	1998	1998 Ranking
Fla.	36,018	29,478	36,690	34,475	30th
U.S.	36,934	33,272	39,956	39,385	

In 1998, the average public school salary in Florida trailed the U.S. average by 12%. From 1970 to 1998, the real average teacher salary in Florida decreased by 4%, versus an increase in the U.S. average of 7%.

Pupil/Teacher Ratio, Fall 1996

	Ratio	Rank
Fla.	18.6	43d
U.S.	17.1	

Teachers/Staff, Fall 1996

	Percent	Rank
Fla.	48.4	47th
U.S.	52.1	

Public School 4th-Grade Reading Proficiency, 1998

	Average	Rank (out of 40 states)
Fla.	207	33d
U.S.	215	

Public School 8th-Grade Reading Proficiency, 1998

	Average	Rank (out of 37 states)
Fla.	253	32d
U.S.	261	

Public School 4th-Grade Math Proficiency, 1996

	Average	Rank (out of 44 states)
Fla.	216	33d
U.S.	224	

Public School 8th-Grade Math Proficiency, 1996

	Average	Rank (out of 41 states)
Fla.	264	30th
U.S.	271	

Public School 8th-Grade Science Proficiency, 1996

	Average	Rank (out of 41 states)
Fla.	142	31st
U.S.	148	

Average Math SAT Scores

	1972	1982	1992	1998	Percentage Taking SAT in 1998
Fla.	508	491	494	501	52
U.S.	509	493	501	512	43

Average Verbal SAT Scores

	1972	1982	1992	1998	Percentage Taking SAT in 1998
Fla.	535	504	493	500	52
U.S.	530	504	500	505	43

Expenditures by Public Institutions of Higher Education Per Full-Time-Equivalent Student, 1996

	FTE Student Spending	Rank
Fla.	$10,054	49th
U.S.	$12,343	

Per-FTE-student spending in public institutions of higher education trailed the U.S. average by 19%.

Per Full-Time-Equivalent Student Revenues from Federal, State, and Local Governments for Public Institutions of Higher Education, 1996

	FTE Student Government Revenues	Rank
Fla.	$7,110	36th
U.S.	$8,101	

Per-FTE-student-government revenues in public institutions of higher education trailed the U.S. average by 12%.

Average Salary for Full-Time Professors at Public Universities, 1997

	Average	Rank
Fla.	$68,784	28th
U.S.	$72,599	

The average full-time public university professor salary trailed the U.S. average by 5%.

ECONOMY AND BUSINESS

Economic Growth

Over the period of 1977 to 1997, Florida's real gross state product (GSP) grew by 132.9%—ranking 5th in the nation—as compared with real U.S. gross domestic product (GDP), expanding by 70.1%.

At $380.6 billion in 1997, Florida's GSP ranked as 5th largest in the nation.

From 1993 to 1997, Florida's annual real GSP growth averaged 3.83%—ranking 22d in the nation—as compared with annual real U.S. GDP growth, averaging 3.08%.

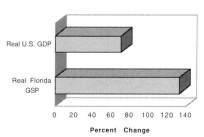

Real Economic Growth 1977-1997: Florida vs. U.S.

Real U.S. GDP

Real Florida GSP

0 20 40 60 80 100 120 140

Percent Change

Job Growth

	Growth in Employee Payrolls (Nonagricultural) 1962–98	Ranking
Fla.	381.1%	3d
U.S.	126.5%	

	Average Annual Growth in Employee Payrolls (Nonagricultural) 1993–98	Ranking
Fla.	4.48%	7th
U.S.	2.98%	

Per Capita Disposable Income, 1997

	1997	Ranking
Fla.	$21,370	19th
U.S.	$21,607	

Per capita disposable income trailed the U.S. average by 1%.

	Real Growth 1962–97	Ranking
Fla.	142.4%	12th
U.S.	116.7%	

	Average Annual Real Growth 1993–97	Ranking
Fla.	1.60%	30th
U.S.	1.48%	

Number of Businesses

	1997	Percent with Fewer than 500 Employees
Businesses with Employees	355,429	98.9
Self-employed Individuals	458,000	

New Business Incorporations

	1980	1986	1992	1997
Fla.	51,912	77,603	86,037	108,268

Percentage Change in Annual New Business Incorporations, 1980 vs. 1997

	Percent	Ranking
Fla.	108.6	7th
U.S.	49.7	

State Merchandise Exports to the World, 1998 (in millions of dollars)

	1998	Rank
Fla.	$23,173	8th

Small Business Survival Index, 1999

Florida ranked 7th best in terms of its policy environment for entrepreneurship.

Fortune 500 Headquarters in 1999

A total of 11 (ranked 15th)

Labor Union Membership, 1983 vs. 1997

	Percentage of Workers		
	1983	1997	1997 Rank
Fla.	10.2	6.8	45th
U.S.	20.1	14.1	

Homeownership Rate, 1998

	Rate	Rank
Fla.	66.9	34th
U.S.	66.3	

CRIME

Crime Rates Per 100 Residents (rankings from best to worst crime rate)

Total Crime	1960	1970	1980	1990	1998	1998 Ranking
Fla.	1.55	3.60	8.40	8.81	6.89	50th
U.S.	1.04	2.74	5.90	5.82	4.62	

From 1960 to 1998, Florida's crime rate increased by 345%, versus a U.S. increase of 344%. From 1990 to 1998, Florida's crime rate dropped by 22%, versus a U.S. decrease of 21%.

Violent Crime	1960	1970	1980	1990	1998	1998 Ranking
Fla.	0.21	0.50	0.98	1.24	0.94	49th
U.S.	0.14	0.36	0.58	0.73	0.57	

From 1960 to 1998, Florida's violent crime rate increased by 348%, versus a U.S. increase of 307%. From 1990 to 1998, Florida's violent crime rate decreased by 24%, compared with a national decline of 22%.

Property Crime	1960	1970	1980	1990	1998	1998 Ranking
Fla.	1.35	3.10	7.42	7.57	5.95	49th
U.S.	0.90	2.38	5.32	5.09	4.05	

From 1960 to 1998, Florida's property crime rate increased by 341%, versus a national increase of 350%. From 1990 to 1998, Florida's property crime rate decreased by 21%, compared with a national decline of 20%.

Real Per Capita Police Protection Spending (in real 1996 dollars)

	1962	1972	1982	1992	1996	1996 Ranking
Fla.	55	92	139	186	211	7th
U.S.	51	95	114	148	168	

In 1996, per capita state and local police protection spending in Florida exceeded the U.S. average by 26%. From 1962 to 1996, real per capita state and local police protection spending increased by 284%, versus an increase of 229% in the U.S. average.

Prisoners in State and Federal Prisons Per 1,000 Population

	1980	1990	1996	1996 Ranking
Fla.	2.13	3.43	4.42	15th
U.S.	1.46	3.11	4.45	

From 1980 to 1996, prisoners per 1,000 population increased by 108%, versus a U.S. increase of 205%.

HEALTH CARE

Health-Care Spending

Florida's per capita state and local health-care spending registered $165 in 1996, ranking 18th in the nation and topping the U.S. average of $151 by 9%. From 1962 to 1996, Florida's real per capita state and local health-care spending increased by 617%, versus an increase of 739% in the U.S. average.

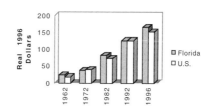

Real Per Capita State and Local Health Care Spending: Florida vs. U.S.

Hospital Spending

Florida's per capita state and local hospital spending registered $252 in 1996, ranking 22d in the nation and trailing the U.S. average of $266 by 5%. From 1962 to 1996, Florida's real per capita state and local hospital spending increased by 138%, as opposed to an increase of 189% in the U.S. average.

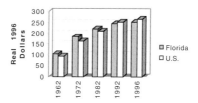

Real Per Capita State and Local Hospital Spending: Florida vs. U.S.

Medicaid, 1997

	Spending Per Recipient	Ranking
Fla.	$3,059	38th
U.S.	$3,681	

Florida's per-recipient Medicaid spending trailed the U.S. average by 17%.

ENVIRONMENT

Parks and Recreation Spending

Florida's per capita state and local parks and recreation spending registered $104 in 1996, ranking 9th in the nation and topping the U.S. average of $72 by 44%. From 1962 to 1996, real per capita state and local parks and recreation spending increased by 225%, versus a 213% increase in the U.S. average.

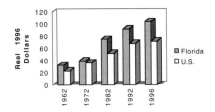

Real Per Capita State and Local Parks and Recreation Spending: Florida vs. U.S.

State and Local Natural Resources Spending, 1996

	Per Capita	Ranking
Fla.	$123	5th
U.S.	$60	

Per capita state and local natural resources spending in Florida exceeded the U.S. average by 105%.

State Parks Revenues as a Share of Operating Expenses, 1997

	Percent	Rank
Fla.	51	17th
U.S.	42	

Percentage of Land Owned by the Federal Government, 1996

	Percent	Rank
Fla.	7.6	20th
U.S.	24.8	

SOCIETY AND DEMOGRAPHICS

Population

Florida's 1998 population of 14.916 million ranked 4th in the nation.

Population Growth, 1980–98

	Percentage Change in Population	1997 Ranking
Fla.	15.29	10th
U.S.	8.66	

	Net International Migration	Ranking
Fla.	552,775	4th

	Net Domestic Migration	Ranking
Fla.	1,034,793	1st

Infant Mortality Rate, 1998

	Percent	Rank
Fla.	7.4	19th
U.S.	6.4	

Percentage of Births of Low Birthweight, 1997

	Percent	Rank
Fla.	8.0	15th
U.S.	7.5	

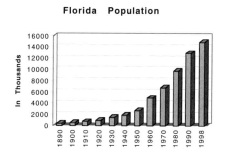

Florida   Population

Percentage of Live Births to Unmarried Women, 1997

	Percent	Rank
Fla.	36.0	8th
U.S.	32.4	

Abortion Rate—Abortions Per 1,000 Women Ages 15–44, 1995

	Rate	Rank
Fla.	30.0	7th
U.S.	22.9	

LIFESTYLE

Percentage of Households with Computers, 1998

	Percent	Rank
Fla.	39.5	38th

Percentage of Households with Internet Access, 1998

	Percent	Rank
Fla.	27.8	17th

State Arts Agency Spending, 1999

	Per Capita	Rank
Fla.	$2.33	6th
U.S.	$1.35	

Per capita state arts spending in 1999 topped the U.S. average by 73%.

Major League Sports Facilities

Year Opened/ Refurb.	Stadium/ Arena	Home Team	Millions of Nominal Dollars		Millions of Real 1997 Dollars	
			Estimated Total Cost	Estimated Taxpayer Cost	Estimated Total Cost	Estimated Taxpayer Cost
1967	Tampa Stadium	Buccaneers (NFL) 1976–97	$4.6	$4.6	$22.1	$22.1
1976	Tampa Stadium (re)		$10.5	$10.5	$29.6	$29.6
1987	Pro Player Stadium	Dolphins (NFL) 1987–present Marlins (MLB) 1993–present	$145.0	$30.0	$204.8	$42.4
1987	Miami Arena	Heat (NBA) 1988–99 Panthers (NHL) 1993–98	$52.0	$52.0	$73.4	$73.4
1988	Orlando Arena	Magic (NBA) 1989–present	$110.0	$110.0	$149.3	$149.3
1990	Tropicana Field	Devil Rays (MLB) 1998–present Lightning (NHL) 1993–96	$138.0	$138.0	$169.5	$169.5
1998	Tropicana Field (re)		$70.0	$62.0	$68.9	$61.0
1995	Gator Bowl/ ALLTEL Stadium (re)	Jaguars (NFL) 1995–present	$136.0	$136.0	$143.2	$143.2
1995	Ice Palace	Lightning (NHL) 1996–present	$161.8	$102.0	$170.3	$107.4
1998	National Car Rental Arena	Panthers (NHL) 1998–present	$185.0	$185.0	$182.1	$182.1
1998	Raymond James Stadium	Buccaneers (NFL) 1998–present	$168.0	$168.0	$165.3	$165.3
1999	American Airlines Arena	Heat (NBA) 1999–present	$228.0	$178.0	$220.1	$171.8

GEORGIA

In recent times, Georgia gave the United States two prominent politicians who offered quite different views of the world. But neither was able to hang around very long.

Democrat Jimmy Carter, of course, went from a little-known peanut farmer and governor to defeating incumbent Gerald Ford to become president of the United States in 1976. Carter's presidency proved a dismal failure both at home and internationally, though he is now viewed fondly by many for pitching in to build houses for low-income families after leaving the White House.

Republican Newt Gingrich journeyed from years as a back-bench bomb thrower in Congress to masterminding a historic Republican takeover of the House of Representatives in 1994 (with a little help from President Clinton, of course) and becoming Speaker of the House. But in 1998, Republicans suffered historic losses in the House elections, even as scandal swirled around Democrat Clinton. By 1999, Gingrich had stepped down as Speaker and had left Congress altogether. Time will tell whether or not Gingrich can repair his reputation as Carter has.

Indeed, the pinnacle of political success has not been kind to these Georgians. However, we suppose things could be worse. Consider Republican Guy Millner, who, in recent years, has lost two major contests—one for U.S. Senate and another for governor.

However, as is always the case in politics, if somebody is on the way down, someone else is on the way up. Some have pointed to Republican Senator Paul Coverdell as a pleasant surprise. Karen Kerrigan, chairman of the Small Business Survival Committee, told us: "Senator Coverdell has quietly emerged as the hero of those in the nation's capital who fight day in and day out for economic freedom. Unlike others who make up the Beltway political class, the battle to do what is right is much bigger than his ego. In other words, Senator Coverdell doesn't care who gets the credit, he just wants to get things done. And he does. Our economic liberties are more safely intact because of his leadership."

In terms of looking at what policy changes are needed in Georgia, it should first be noted that the state currently operates from a position of strength. For example, per capita state and local taxes for the most part come in below the U.S. average, as generally do government spending and debt levels. In particular, state and local per capita debt and interest paid on debt come in well below the national averages. However, the state's personal income and capital gains tax rates run a bit on the high side.

The state has been on a long-term tract of robust growth in terms of gross state product, disposable income, population, annual new business incorporations, and employment. In fact, Georgia ranks among the best in the nation in each of these categories.

However, the state's crime rate ranks among the worst in the nation.

Undertaking sound, progrowth, profamily reforms while generally sitting pretty, rather than waiting until matters decay, is a wise, but not widely followed, course of action. The Georgia Public Policy Foundation (GPPF) offers a wealth of sound ideas on numerous issues. For example, GPPF has spelled out the case for:

- expanding prison capacity and instituting "truth in sentencing" (that is, criminals serve the full time of their sentences) to help deal with the state's crime problem;
- privatization and competition to ensure the best possible mix of quality and cost in government;
- requiring cost/benefit studies for all proposed regulations, evaluating existing regulations and tossing out those no longer relevant, and affirming that regulations are firmly rooted in sound science;
- limiting the growth of government to the inflation rate plus the growth in population (GPPF estimated that taxpayers would have saved about $3 billion if this measure were in effect, for example, during the period of 1993 to 1997);
- and overhauling the state's tax system by eliminating corporate and individual income taxes and adopting a flat, broad-based sales tax.

Georgia's politicians would be wise to immerse themselves in the work and ideas produced by the Georgia Public Policy Foundation. After all, in the end, politicians maintaining sound policies and solid principles are the ones who stay on top.

POLITICS

Registered Voters

No party registration

Federal Officials: Recent Election and Group Ratings

			ACU	ADA	SBSC
U.S. Senators:	Paul Coverdell (R)		95	5	95
	1998 Coverdell (R)	52%			
	Coles (D)	45%			
	Max Cleland (D)		4	80	25
	1996 Cleland (D)	48%			
	Millner (R)	47%			
U.S. Representatives:	Jack Kingston (R-1)		99	4	90
	1998 Kingston (R)	NO			
	Sanford Bishop Jr. (D-2)		26	73	25
	1998 Bishop (D)	57%			
	McCormick (R)	43%			

			ACU	ADA	SBSC
Michael Collins (R-3)			95	3	95
1998	Collins (R)	NO			
Cynthia McKinney (D-4)			6	98	10
1998	McKinney (D)	61%			
	Warren (R)	39%			
John Lewis (D-5)			3	97	5
1998	Lewis (D)	79%			
	Lewis (R)	21%			
John Isakson (R-6)			NA	NA	NA
1999 (spec)	Isakson (R)	65%			
	Jeffrey (R)	25%			
Bob Barr (R-7)			97	4	85
1998	Barr (R)	55%			
	Williams (D)	45%			
Saxby Chambliss (R-8)			94	1	90
1998	Chambliss (R)	62%			
	Cain (D)	38%			
Nathan Deal (R-9)			81	8	80
1998	Deal (R)	NO			
Charlie Norwood (R-10)			99	1	85
1998	Norwood (R)	60%			
	Freeman (D)	40%			
John Linder (R-11)			95	1	100
1998	Linder (R)	69%			
	Littman (D)	31%			

Electoral Votes:	13	
1996 Presidential Results:	Clinton	46%
	Dole	47%
	Perot	6%

State Officials

Governor 1998 Election:	Roy Barnes (D)	53%
	Guy Millner (R)	44%
Lt. Governor:	Mark Taylor (D)	
Attorney General:	Thurbert Baker (D)	
State Senate:	33 Democrats	
	23 Republicans	
State House:	102 Democrats	
	78 Republicans	

TAXES AND SPENDING

Total Revenues

Georgia's per capita state and local total revenues registered $5,169 in 1996, ranking 27th in the nation and trailing the U.S. average of $5,706 by 9%. From 1962 to 1996, real per capita state and local revenues increased by 357%, compared with an increase in the national average of 297%.

Taxes

Georgia's per capita state and local taxes registered $2,354 in 1996, ranking 27th in the nation and trailing the U.S. average of $2,597 by 9%. From 1962 to 1996, real per capita state and local taxes increased by 233%, compared with an increase of 152% in the U.S. average.

Property Taxes

Georgia's per capita state and local property taxes equaled $652 in 1996, ranking 33d in the nation and trailing the U.S average of $789 by 17%. From 1962 to 1996, real per capita state and local property taxes increased by 190%, versus a 67% increase in the U.S. average.

Sales and Gross Receipts Taxes

Georgia's per capita state and local sales and gross receipts taxes came in at $928 in 1996, ranking 18th in the nation and trailing the U.S. average of $939 by 1%. From 1962 to 1996, real per capita state and local sales and gross receipts taxes increased by 173%, versus an increase of 214% in the U.S. average.

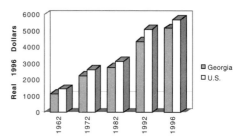

Real Per Capita State and Local Total Revenues: Georgia vs. U.S.

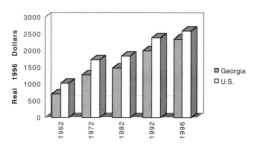

Real Per Capita State and Local Taxes: Georgia vs. U.S.

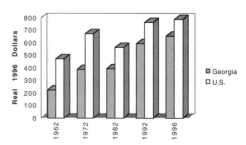

Real Per Capita State and Local Property Taxes: Georgia vs. U.S.

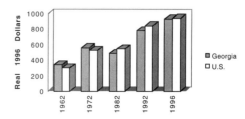

Real Per Capita State and Local Sales and Gross Receipts Taxes: Georgia vs. U.S.

Income Taxes

Georgia's per capita state and local income (individual and corporate) taxes registered $675 in 1996, ranking 21st in the nation and running just ahead of the U.S. average of $674. From 1962 to 1996, real per capita state and local income taxes increased by 765%, versus a 567% increase in the U.S. average.

Personal Income Tax

A rate of 6.0%, ranking 27th in the nation (from lowest tax rate to highest), and comparing with the national average of 5.26%.

Capital Gains Tax

A rate of 6.0%, ranking 30th in the nation (from lowest tax rate to highest), and comparing with the national average of 4.68%.

Corporate Income Tax

A rate of 6.0%, ranking 16th in the nation (from lowest tax rate to highest), and comparing with the national average of 6.63%.

Total Expenditures

Georgia's per capita state and local total spending registered $4,778 in 1996, ranking 30th in the nation and trailing the U.S. average of $5,268 by 15%. From 1962 to 1996, real per capita state and local total spending increased by 306%, versus an increase of 254% in the U.S. average.

Welfare Expenditures

Georgia's per capita state and local public welfare spending registered $638 in 1996, ranking 28th in the nation and trailing the U.S. average of $729 by 12%. From 1962 to 1996, real per capita state and local public welfare spending increased by 480%, compared with a 488% increase in the U.S. average.

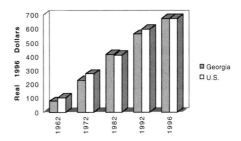

Real Per Capita State and Local Income Taxes: Georgia vs. U.S.

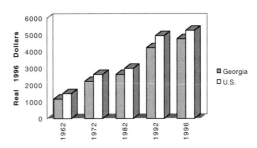

Real Per Capita State and Local Total Expenditures: Georgia vs. U.S.

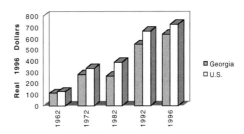

Real Per Capita State and Local Public Welfare Spending: Georgia vs. U.S.

Welfare Recipients (in thousands)

	1980	1989	3/99	Change 1989–99
Ga.	234	285	138	−52%
U.S.	10,923	10,987	7,335	−33%

Interest on General Debt

Georgia's per capita state and local interest on general debt registered $132 in 1996, ranking 42d in the nation and trailing the U.S. average of $222 by 41%. From 1962 to 1996, real per capita state and local interest on general debt increased by 257%, versus an increase of 335% in the U.S. average.

Total Debt Outstanding

Georgia's per capita state and local debt registered $3,223 in 1996, ranking 38th in the nation and trailing the U.S. average of $4,409 by 27%. From 1962 to 1996, real per capita state and local debt outstanding increased by 115%, versus an increase of 120% in the U.S. average.

Government Employees

Georgia's state and local government employees (full-time equivalent, or FTE) per 10,000 population registered 582.3 in 1997, ranking 14th in the nation and exceeding the U.S. average of 531.1 by 10%. From 1962 to 1996, state and local FTE employees per 10,000 population increased by 92%, compared with an increase in the U.S. average of 66%.

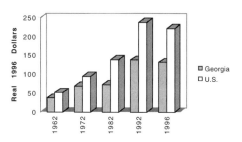

Real Per Capita State and Local Interest on General Debt: Georgia vs. U.S.

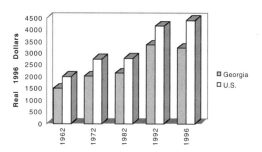

Real Per Capita State and Local Debt Outstanding: Georgia vs. U.S.

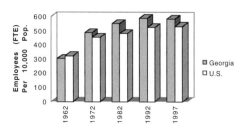

State and Local Government Employees (FTE) Per 10,000 Population: Georgia vs. U.S.

Per Capita Federal Government Expenditures, 1998

	1998	Ranking
Ga.	$4,861	37th
U.S.	$5,491	

Per capita federal spending in Georgia trailed the national average by 11%.

EDUCATION

Total Education Spending

Georgia's per capita state and local education spending registered $1,516 in 1996, ranking 24th in the nation and exceeding the U.S. average of $1,503 by 1%. From 1962 to 1996, real per capita total education spending increased by 275%, versus an increase in the U.S. average of 173%.

Real Per Capita State and Local Education Spending: Georgia vs. U.S.

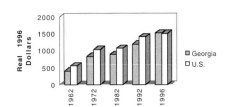

Per Pupil Spending

Georgia's per pupil public school spending registered $4,948 in 1998, ranking 41st in the nation and trailing the U.S. average of $6,131 by 19%. From 1970 to 1998, Georgia's real per pupil public school spending increased by 148%, compared with a 120% increase in the U.S. average.

Real Per Pupil Public School Spending: Georgia vs. U.S.

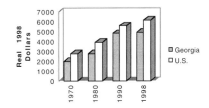

Average Public School Teacher Salaries (in 1997–98 dollars)

	1970	1980	1990	1998	1998 Ranking
Ga.	31,154	28,862	35,674	37,378	21st
U.S.	36,934	33,272	39,956	39,385	

In 1998, the average public school teacher salary in Georgia trailed the U.S. average by 5%. From 1970 to 1998, the real average teacher salary in Georgia increased by 20%, versus an increase in the U.S. average of 7%.

Pupil/Teacher Ratio, Fall 1996

	Ratio	Rank
Ga.	17.0	31st
U.S.	17.1	

Teachers/Staff, Fall 1996

	Percent	Rank
Ga.	53.3	18th
U.S.	52.1	

Public School 4th-Grade Reading Proficiency, 1998

	Average	Rank (out of 40 states)
Ga.	210	29th
U.S.	215	

Public School 8th-Grade Reading Proficiency, 1998

	Average	Rank (out of 37 states)
Ga.	257	26th
U.S.	261	

Public School 4th-Grade Math Proficiency, 1996

	Average	Rank (out of 44 states)
Ga.	215	35th
U.S.	224	

Public School 8th-Grade Math Proficiency, 1996

	Average	Rank (out of 41 states)
Ga.	262	33d
U.S.	271	

Public School 8th-Grade Science Proficiency, 1996

	Average	Rank (out of 41 states)
Ga.	142	31st
U.S.	148	

Average Math SAT Scores

	1972	1982	1992	1998	Percentage Taking SAT in 1998
Ga.	459	459	473	482	64
U.S.	509	493	501	512	43

Average Verbal SAT Scores

	1972	1982	1992	1998	Percentage Taking SAT in 1998
Ga.	483	472	475	486	64
U.S.	530	504	500	505	43

Expenditures by Public Institutions of Higher Education Per Full-Time-Equivalent Student, 1996

	FTE Student Spending	Rank
Ga.	$13,058	17th
U.S.	$12,343	

Per-FTE-student spending in public institutions of higher education exceeded the U.S. average by 6%.

Per Full-Time-Equivalent Student Revenues from Federal, State, and Local Governments for Public Institutions of Higher Education, 1996

	FTE Student Government Revenues	Rank
Ga.	$8,972	7th
U.S.	$8,101	

Per-FTE-student-government revenues in public institutions of higher education exceeded the U.S. average by 11%.

Average Salary for Full-Time Professors at Public Universities, 1997

	Average	Rank
Ga.	$73,791	14th
U.S.	$72,599	

The average full-time public university professor salary topped the U.S. average by 2%.

ECONOMY AND BUSINESS

Economic Growth

Over the period of 1977 to 1997, Georgia's real gross state product (GSP) grew by 137.4%—ranking 4th in the nation—as compared with real U.S. gross domestic product (GDP), expanding by 70.1%.

At $229.5 billion in 1997, Georgia's GSP ranked as 10th largest in the nation.

From 1993 to 1997, Georgia's annual real GSP growth averaged 5.29%—ranking 9th in the nation—as compared with annual real U.S. GDP growth, averaging 3.08%.

**Real Economic Growth
1977-1997: Georgia vs. U.S.**

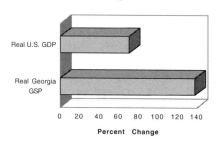

Job Growth

	Growth in Employee Payrolls (Nonagricultural) 1962–98	Ranking
Ga.	242.3%	7th
U.S.	126.5%	

	Average Annual Growth in Employee Payrolls (Nonagricultural) 1993–98	Ranking
Ga.	4.59%	6th
U.S.	2.98%	

Per Capita Disposable Income, 1997

	1997	Ranking
Ga.	$20,504	25th
U.S.	$21,607	

Per capita disposable income trailed the U.S. average by 5%.

	Real Growth 1962–97	Ranking
Ga.	167.1%	4th
U.S.	116.7%	

	Average Annual Real Growth 1993–97	Ranking
Ga.	1.98%	9th
U.S.	1.48%	

Number of Businesses

	1997	Percent with Fewer than 500 Employees
Businesses with Employees	176,643	97.6
Self-employed Individuals	241,000	

New Business Incorporations

	1980	1986	1992	1997
Ga.	12,343	17,551	21,046	29,321

Percentage Change in Annual New Business Incorporations, 1980 vs. 1997

	Percent	Ranking
Ga.	137.6	3d
U.S.	49.7	

State Merchandise Exports to the World, 1998 (in millions of dollars)

	1998	Rank
Ga.	$11,212	17th

Small Business Survival Index, 1999

Georgia ranked 27th in terms of its policy environment for entrepreneurship.

Fortune 500 Headquarters in 1999

A total of 15 (ranked 11th), with Atlanta ranked 4th among U.S. cities, with 11 headquarters

Labor Union Membership, 1983 vs. 1997

	Percentage of Workers		
	1983	1997	1997 Rank
Ga.	11.9	7.1	41st
U.S.	20.1	14.1	

Homeownership Rate, 1998

	Rate	Rank
Ga.	71.2	17th
U.S.	66.3	

CRIME

Crime Rates Per 100 Residents (rankings from best to worst crime rate)

Total Crime	1960	1970	1980	1990	1998	1998 Ranking
Ga.	0.86	2.21	5.60	6.76	5.46	42d
U.S.	1.04	2.74	5.90	5.82	4.62	

From 1960 to 1998, Georgia's crime rate increased by 535%, versus a U.S. increase of 344%. From 1990 to 1998, Georgia's crime rate dropped by 19%, versus a U.S. decrease of 21%.

Violent Crime	1960	1970	1980	1990	1998	1998 Ranking
Ga.	0.14	0.30	0.56	0.76	0.57	34th
U.S.	0.14	0.36	0.58	0.73	0.57	

From 1960 to 1998, Georgia's violent crime rate increased by 307%, equaling the U.S. increase. From 1990 to 1998, Georgia's violent crime rate declined by 25%, compared with a national decline of 22%.

Property Crime	1960	1970	1980	1990	1998	1998 Ranking
Ga.	0.71	1.90	5.05	6.01	4.89	42d
U.S.	0.90	2.38	5.32	5.09	4.05	

From 1960 to 1998, Georgia's property crime rate increased by 589%, versus a national increase of 350%. From 1990 to 1998, Georgia's property crime rate decreased by 19%, compared with a national decline of 20%.

Real Per Capita Police Protection Spending (in real 1996 dollars)

	1962	1972	1982	1992	1996	1996 Ranking
Ga.	32	59	86	115	137	28th
U.S.	51	95	114	148	168	

In 1996, per capita state and local police protection spending in Georgia trailed the U.S. average by 18%. From 1962 to 1996, real per capita state and local police protection spending increased by 328%, versus an increase of 229% in the U.S. average.

Prisoners in State and Federal Prisons Per 1,000 Population

	1980	1990	1996	1996 Ranking
Ga.	2.23	3.46	4.79	12th
U.S.	1.46	3.11	4.45	

From 1980 to 1996, prisoners per 1,000 population increased by 115%, versus a U.S. increase of 205%.

HEALTH CARE

Health-Care Spending

Georgia's per capita state and local health-care spending registered $77 in 1996, ranking 48th in the nation and trailing the U.S. average of $151 by 49%. From 1962 to 1996, Georgia's real per capita state and local health-care spending increased by 328%, versus an increase of 739% in the U.S. average.

Real Per Capita State and Local Health Care Spending: Georgia vs. U.S.

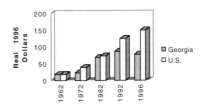

Hospital Spending

Georgia's per capita state and local hospital spending registered $439 in 1996, ranking 8th in the nation and topping the U.S. average of $266 by 65%. From 1962 to 1996, Georgia's real per capita state and local hospital spending increased by 282%, as opposed to an increase of 189% in the U.S. average.

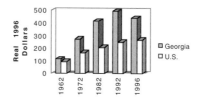

Real Per Capita State and Local Hospital Spending: Georgia vs. U.S.

Medicaid, 1997

	Spending Per Recipient	Ranking
Ga.	$2,558	46th
U.S.	$3,681	

Georgia's per-recipient Medicaid spending trailed the U.S. average by 31%.

ENVIRONMENT

Parks and Recreation Spending

Georgia's per capita state and local parks and recreation spending registered $63 in 1996, ranking 24th in the nation and trailing the U.S. average of $72 by 13%. From 1962 to 1996, real per capita state and local parks and recreation spending increased by 600%, versus a 213% increase in the U.S. average.

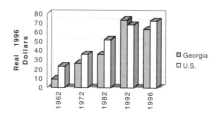

Real Per Capita State and Local Parks and Recreation Spending: Georgia vs. U.S.

State and Local Natural Resources Spending, 1996

	Per Capita	Ranking
Ga.	$51	32d
U.S.	$60	

Per capita state and local natural resources spending in Georgia trailed the U.S. average by 15%.

State Parks Revenues as a Share of Operating Expenses, 1997

	Percent	Rank
Ga.	33	34th
U.S.	42	

Percentage of Land Owned by the Federal Government, 1996

	Percent	Rank
Ga.	3.9	30th
U.S.	24.8	

SOCIETY AND DEMOGRAPHICS

Population

Georgia's 1998 population of 7.642 million ranked 10th in the nation.

Population Growth, 1990–98

	Percentage Change in Population	Ranking
Ga.	17.97	6th
U.S.	8.66	

	Net International Migration	Ranking
Ga.	90,291	13th

	Net Domestic Migration	Ranking
Ga.	597,916	2d

Infant Mortality Rate, 1998

	Percent	Rank
Ga.	8.3	11th
U.S.	6.4	

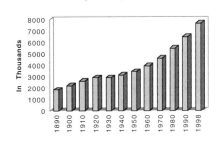

Georgia Population

Percentage of Births of Low Birthweight, 1997

	Percent	Rank
Ga.	8.8	7th
U.S.	7.5	

Percentage of Live Births to Unmarried Women, 1997

	Percent	Rank
Ga.	35.4	10th
U.S.	32.4	

Abortion Rate—Abortions Per 1,000 Women Ages 15–44, 1995

	Rate	Rank
Ga.	21.2	16th
U.S.	22.9	

LIFESTYLE

Percentage of Households with Computers, 1998

	Percent	Rank
Ga.	35.8	44th

Percentage of Households with Internet Access, 1998

	Percent	Rank
Ga.	23.9	34th

State Arts Agency Spending, 1999

	Per Capita	Rank
Ga.	$0.61	38th
U.S.	$1.35	

Per capita state arts spending in 1999 trailed the U.S. average by 55%.

Major League Sports Facilities

Year Opened/ Refurb.	Stadium/ Arena	Home Team	Millions of Nominal Dollars		Millions of Real 1997 Dollars	
			Estimated Total Cost	Estimated Taxpayer Cost	Estimated Total Cost	Estimated Taxpayer Cost
1964	Atlanta-Fulton County Stadium	Braves (MLB) 1966–96 Falcons (NFL) 1966–91	$18.5	$18.5	$95.9	$95.9
1975	Atlanta-Fulton (re)		$1.5	$1.5	$4.5	$4.5
1977	Atlanta-Fulton (re)		$44.1	$44.1	$116.7	$116.7
1986	Atlanta-Fulton (re)		$14.0	$14.0	$20.5	$20.5
1972	The Omni	Hawks (NBA) 1972–96 Flames (NHL) 1972–80	$17.0	$17.0	$65.4	$65.4
1992	Georgia Dome	Falcons (NFL) 1992–present Hawks (NBA) 1997–99	$210.0	$210.0	$240.3	$240.3
1996	Turner Field	Braves (MLB) 1996–present	$232.0	$0.0	$232.0	$0.0
1999	Philips Arena	Hawks (NBA) 1999–present Thrashers (NHL) 1999–present	$213.0	$140.0	$205.6	$135.1

HAWAII

Mention Hawaii, and many of us think of beaches, surfing, Don Ho, "book 'em Danno," a massive tome by James Michener, and *Magnum, P.I.* Let's throw on a Hawaiian shirt, hop in the Ferrari, listen to the Beach Boys and have fun, fun, fun!

However, economic reality has been far less sunny in the Hawaiian isles of late. Liberal politicians, who seem to have been out in the sun too long, have established a dismal environment for entreprenuership and economic growth.

In fact, only Washington, D.C.'s policy climate ranks as more inhospitable in the Small Business Survival Committee's ratings. Likewise, the May 31, 1999, issue of *Forbes* magazine rated Honolulu 160th out of 162 metropolitan areas for high-technology business development.

The resulting economic toll has been severe. In fact, as measured by growth in jobs, disposable income, and gross state product, the state's economy seems to have been in near-perpetual recession in recent years. Welfare rolls actually rose over the decade of 1989 to 1999, while declining significantly in the country overall; net domestic migration shows a significant outflow of people to elsewhere in the nation; and new business incorporations generally lag. As a result of recent Asian economic woes, Hawaii's merchandise exports dropped by more than 30% in 1998.

There finally seems to be some recognition of late that Hawaii needs to improve its public policies—in particular, a need to redress what amounts to one of the most destructive tax systems in the nation. Recent legislation will provide some small relief from high income taxes, while cutting the state's oppressive consumption taxes. However, these are but small steps in the right direction. In particular, far deeper cuts in income taxes are required, and they need to be implemented immediately, not phased in over time.

Commensurately, politicians have to roll back government spending. A combination of progrowth tax cuts and reductions in state and local government expenditures would mean a dramatic, positive shift in resources away from government, with its inherent incentives for waste, to the private sector, where incentives point to serving consumers and boosting efficiency.

Meanwhile, crime is a surprising issue in Hawaii. While violent crime is relatively controlled compared with much of the rest of America, property crime stands out as a problem. Where is Steve McGarret when you need him?

Politically, Hawaii can only benefit by breaking away from its current one-party strangle hold. In 1998, many thought that Governor Ben Cayetano, though not exactly a typical hard-left Hawaiian Democrat, might be unseated by Republican Linda Lingle, who played up the state's economic mess. In the end, though, Cayetano held on for victory.

In terms of its geography and beautiful climate, Hawaii could easily be a Pacific outpost of growth and entrepreneurship in the 21st century. But that will in no way happen under the current policy regime. Minor tinkering will not get the job done. An entirely new Hawaiian way of thinking about the relationship between government, taxpayers, entrepreneurs, consumers, and the economy is needed. The temptation to dip further into the waters of government programs that try to guide or foster economic development must be resisted. Only broad-based tax and regulatory relief, coupled with smaller government overall, can unleash the entrepreneurial spirit in Hawaii.

POLITICS

Registered Voters

No party registration

Federal Officials: Recent Elections and Group Ratings

			ACU	ADA	SBSC
U.S. Senators:	Daniel Inouye (D)		7	72	15
	1998 Inouye (D)	79%			
	Young (R)	18%			
	Daniel Akaka (D)		2	92	15
	1998 Akaka (D)	72%			
	Hustace (R)	24%			
U.S. Representatives:	Neil Abercrombie (D-1)		5	96	5
	1998 Abercrombie (D)	62%			
	Ward (R)	36%			
	Patsy Mink (D-2)		4	98	5
	1998 Mink (D)	69%			
	Douglass (R)	24%			
Electoral Votes:	4				
1996 Presidential Results:	Clinton	57%			
	Dole	32%			
	Perot	8%			

State Officials

Governor 1998 Election:	Benjamin Cayetano (D)	50%
	Linda Lingle (R)	48%
Lt. Governor:	Mazie Hirono (D)	
Attorney General:	Margery Bronster (D)	
State Senate:	23 Democrats	
	2 Republicans	
State House:	39 Democrats	
	12 Republicans	

TAXES AND SPENDING

Total Revenues

Hawaii's per capita state and local total revenues registered $6,605 in 1996, ranking 9th in the nation and exceeding the U.S. average of $5,706 by 16%. From 1962 to 1996, real per capita state and local revenues increased by 268%, compared with an increase in the national average of 297%.

Taxes

Hawaii's per capita state and local taxes registered $3,245 in 1996, ranking 6th in the nation and exceeding the U.S. average of $2,597 by 25%. From 1962 to 1996, real per capita state and local taxes increased by 181%, compared with an increase of 152% in the U.S. average.

Property Taxes

Hawaii's per capita state and local property taxes equaled $517 in 1996, ranking 38th in the nation and trailing the U.S. average of $789 by 34%. From 1962 to 1996, real per capita state and local property taxes increased by 181%, versus a 67% increase in the U.S. average.

Sales and Gross Receipts Taxes

Hawaii's per capita state and local sales and gross receipts taxes came in at $1,683 in 1996, ranking 3d in the nation and outpacing the U.S. average of $939 by 79%. From 1962 to 1996, real per capita state and local sales and gross receipts taxes increased by 178%, versus an increase of 214% in the U.S. average.

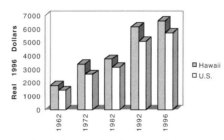

Real Per Capita State and Local Total Revenues: Hawaii vs. U.S.

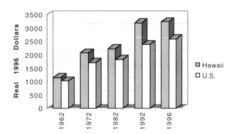

Real Per Capita State and Local Taxes: Hawaii vs. U.S.

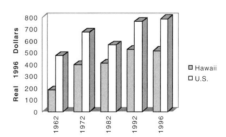

Real Per Capita State and Local Property Taxes: Hawaii vs. U.S.

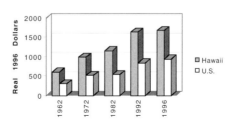

Real Per Capita State and Local Sales and Gross Receipts Taxes: Hawaii vs. U.S.

Income Taxes

Hawaii's per capita state and local income (individual and corporate) taxes registered $900 in 1996, ranking 10th in the nation and topping the U.S. average of $674 by 34%. From 1962 to 1996, real per capita state and local income taxes increased by 263%, versus a 567% increase in the U.S. average.

Personal Income Tax

A rate of 8.75%, ranking 46th in the nation (from lowest tax rate to highest), and comparing with the national average of 5.26%.

Capital Gains Tax

A rate of 8.75%, ranking 47th in the nation (from lowest tax rate to highest), and comparing with the national average of 4.68%.

Corporate Income Tax

A rate of 6.4%, ranking 20th in the nation (from lowest tax rate to highest), and comparing to the U.S. average of 6.63%.

Total Expenditures

Hawaii's per capita state and local total spending registered $6,393 in 1996, ranking 4th in the nation and exceeding the U.S. average of $5,268 by 21%. From 1962 to 1996, real per capita state and local total spending increased by 226%, versus an increase of 254% in the U.S. average.

Welfare Expenditures

Hawaii's per capita state and local public welfare spending registered $772 in 1996, ranking 14th in the nation and outpacing U.S. average of $729 by 6%. From 1962 to 1996, real per capita state and local public welfare spending increased by 1,106%, compared with a 488% increase in the U.S. average.

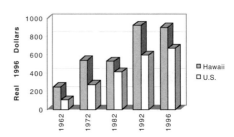

Real Per Capita State and Local Income Taxes: Hawaii vs. U.S.

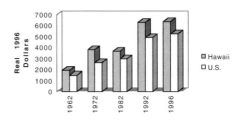

Real Per Capita State and Local Total Expenditures: Hawaii vs. U.S.

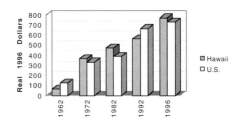

Real Per Capita State and Local Public Welfare Spending: Hawaii vs. U.S.

Welfare Recipients (in thousands)

	1980	1989	3/99	Change 1989–99
Hawaii	61	44	46	+5%
U.S.	10,923	10,987	7,335	−33%

Interest on General Debt

Hawaii's per capita state and local interest on general debt registered $398 in 1996, ranking 4th in the nation and exceeding the U.S. average of $222 by 79%. From 1962 to 1996, real per capita state and local interest on general debt increased by 445%, versus an increase of 335% in the U.S. average.

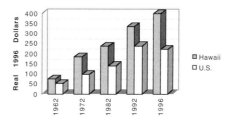

Real Per Capita State and Local Interest on General Debt: Hawaii vs. U.S.

Total Debt Outstanding

Hawaii's per capita state and local debt registered $6,086 in 1996, ranking 8th in the nation and outrunning the U.S. average of $4,409 by 38%. From 1962 to 1996, real per capita state and local debt outstanding increased by 151%, versus an increase of 120% in the U.S. average.

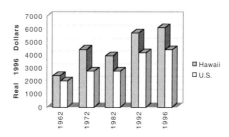

Real Per Capita State and Local Debt Outstanding: Hawaii vs. U.S.

Government Employees

Hawaii's state and local government employees (full-time equivalent, or FTE) per 10,000 population registered 556 in 1997, ranking 21st in the nation and exceeding the U.S. average of 531.1 by 5%. From 1962 to 1996, state and local FTE employees per 10,000 population increased by 71%, compared with an increase in the U.S. average of 66%.

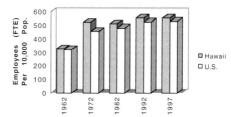

State and Local Government Employees (FTE) Per 10,000 Population: Hawaii vs. U.S.

Per Capita Federal Government Expenditures, 1998

	1998	Ranking
Hawaii	$7,076	6th
U.S.	$5,491	

Per capita federal spending in Hawaii exceeded the national average by 29%.

EDUCATION

Total Education Spending

Hawaii's per capita state and local education spending registered $1,308 in 1996, ranking 44th in the nation and trailing the U.S. average of $1,503 by 13%. From 1962 to 1996, real per capita total education spending increased by 116%, versus an increase in the U.S. average of 173%.

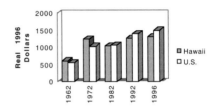

Real Per Capita State and Local Education Spending: Hawaii vs. U.S.

Per Pupil Spending

Hawaii's per pupil public school spending registered $5,384 in 1998, ranking 35th in the nation and lagging behind the U.S. average of $6,131 by 12%. From 1970 to 1998, Hawaii's real per pupil public school spending increased by 84%, compared with a 120% increase in the U.S. average.

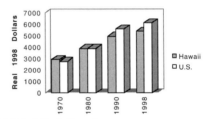

Real Per Pupil Public School Spending: Hawaii vs. U.S.

Average Public School Teacher Salaries (in 1997–98 dollars)

	1970	1980	1990	1998	1998 Ranking
Hawaii	40,475	41,502	40,822	38,377	20th
U.S.	36,934	33,272	39,956	39,385	

In 1998, the average public school teacher salary in Hawaii trailed the U.S. average by 3%. From 1970 to 1998, the real average teacher salary in Hawaii decreased by 5%, versus an increase in the U.S. average of 7%.

Pupil/Teacher Ratio, Fall 1996

	Ratio	Rank
Hawaii	17.7	41st
U.S.	17.1	

Teachers/Staff, Fall 1996

	Percent	Rank
Hawaii	62.7	2d
U.S.	52.1	

Public School 4th-Grade Reading Proficiency, 1998

	Average	Rank (out of 40 states)
Hawaii	200	39th
U.S.	215	

Public School 8th-Grade Reading Proficiency, 1998

	Average	Rank (out of 37 states)
Hawaii	250	36th
U.S.	261	

Public School 4th-Grade Math Proficiency, 1996

	Average	Rank (out of 44 states)
Hawaii	215	35th
U.S.	224	

Public School 8th-Grade Math Proficiency, 1996

	Average	Rank (out of 41 states)
Hawaii	262	33d
U.S.	271	

Public School 8th-Grade Science Proficiency, 1996

	Average	Rank (out of 41 states)
Hawaii	135	38th
U.S.	148	

Average Math SAT Scores

	1972	1982	1992	1998	Percentage Taking SAT in 1998
Hawaii	513	491	502	513	55
U.S.	509	493	501	512	43

Average Verbal SAT Scores

	1972	1982	1992	1998	Percentage Taking SAT in 1998
Hawaii	511	470	477	483	55
U.S.	530	504	500	505	43

Expenditures by Public Institutions of Higher Education Per Full-Time-Equivalent Student, 1996

	FTE Student Spending	Rank
Hawaii	$16,979	4th
U.S.	$12,343	

Per-FTE-student spending in public institutions of higher education exceeded the U.S. average by 38%.

Per Full-Time-Equivalent Student Revenues from Federal, State, and Local Governments for Public Institutions of Higher Education, 1996

	FTE Student Government Revenues	Rank
Hawaii	$12,092	3d
U.S.	$8,101	

Per-FTE-student-government revenues in public institutions of higher education outpaced the U.S. average by 49%.

Average Salary for Full-Time Professors at Public Universities, 1997

	Average	Rank
Hawaii	$73,539	15th
U.S.	$72,599	

The average full-time public university professor salary exceeded the U.S. average by 1%.

ECONOMY AND BUSINESS

Economic Growth

Over the period of 1977 to 1997, Hawaii's real gross state product (GSP) grew by 53.0%—ranking 37th in the nation—as compared with real U.S. gross domestic product (GDP), expanding by 70.1%.

At $38.0 billion in 1997, Hawaii's GSP ranked as 41st largest in the nation.

From 1993 to 1997, Hawaii's annual real GSP growth averaged −0.84%—ranking 51st in the nation—as compared with annual real U.S. GDP growth, averaging 3.08%.

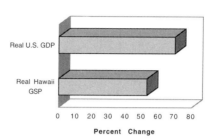

Real Economic Growth 1977-1997: Hawaii vs. U.S.

Real U.S. GDP

Real Hawaii GSP

0 10 20 30 40 50 60 70 80

Percent Change

Job Growth

	Growth in Employee Payrolls (Nonagricultural) 1962–98	Ranking
Hawaii	171.5%	19th
U.S.	126.5%	

	Average Annual Growth in Employee Payrolls (Nonagricultural) 1993–98	Ranking
Hawaii	−0.48%	50th
U.S.	2.98%	

Per Capita Disposable Income, 1997

	1997	Ranking
Hawaii	$22,217	15th
U.S.	$21,607	

Per capita disposable income exceeded the U.S. average by 3%.

	Real Growth 1962–97	Ranking
Hawaii	111.2%	34th
U.S.	116.7%	

	Average Annual Real Growth 1993–97	Ranking
Hawaii	0.15%	50th
U.S.	1.48%	

Number of Businesses

	1997	Percent with Fewer than 500 Employees
Businesses with Employees	26,881	97.1
Self-employed Individuals	59,000	

New Business Incorporations

	1980	1986	1992	1997
Hawaii	3,270	2,871	3,792	3,792

Percentage Change in Annual New Business Incorporations, 1980 vs. 1997

	Percent	Ranking
Hawaii	16.0	38th
U.S.	49.7	

State Merchandise Exports to the World, 1998 (in millions of dollars)

	1998	Rank
Hawaii	$211	50th

Small Business Survival Index, 1999

Hawaii ranked worst among the 50 states, with only the District of Columbia rating worse, in terms of its policy environment for entrepreneurs.

Fortune 500 Headquarters in 1999

None

Labor Union Membership, 1983 vs. 1997

	Percentage of Workers		
	1983	1997	1997 Rank
Hawaii	29.2	26.3	1st
U.S.	20.1	14.1	

Homeownership Rate, 1998

	Rate	Rank
Hawaii	52.8	49th
U.S.	66.3	

CRIME

Crimes Rates Per 100 Residents (rankings from best to worst crime rate)

Total Crime	1960	1970	1980	1990	1998	1998 Ranking
Hawaii	1.10	3.40	7.48	6.12	5.33	39th
U.S.	1.04	2.74	5.90	5.82	4.62	

From 1960 to 1998, Hawaii's crime rate increased by 385%, versus a U.S. increase of 344%. From 1990 to 1998, Hawaii's crime rate dropped by 13%, versus a 21% U.S. decline.

Violent Crime	1960	1970	1980	1990	1998	1998 Ranking
Hawaii	0.02	0.12	0.30	0.28	0.25	7th
U.S.	0.14	0.36	0.58	0.73	0.57	

From 1960 to 1998, Hawaii's violent crime rate increased by 1,150%, versus a U.S. increase of 307%. From 1990 to 1998, Hawaii's violent crime rate fell by 11%, compared with a national decline of 22%.

Property Crime	1960	1970	1980	1990	1998	1998 Ranking
Hawaii	1.08	3.27	7.18	5.83	5.09	43d
U.S.	0.90	2.38	5.32	5.09	4.05	

From 1960 to 1998, Hawaii's property crime rate increased by 371%, versus a national increase of 350%. From 1990 to 1998, Hawaii's property crime rate decreased by 13%, compared with a national decline to 20%.

Real Per Capita Police Protection Spending (in real 1996 dollars)

	1962	1972	1982	1992	1996	1996 Ranking
Hawaii	60	128	117	157	153	22d
U.S.	51	95	114	148	168	

In 1996, per capita state and local police protection spending in Hawaii trailed the U.S. average by 9%. From 1962 to 1996, real per capita state and local police protection spending increased by 155%, versus an increase of 299% in the U.S. average.

Prisoners in State and Federal Prisons Per 1,000 Population

	1980	1990	1996	1996 Ranking
Hawaii	1.02	2.29	3.39	25th
U.S.	1.46	3.11	4.45	

From 1980 to 1996, prisoners per 1,000 population increased by 232%, versus a U.S. increase of 205%.

HEALTH CARE

Health-Care Spending

Hawaii's per capita state and local health-care spending registered $262 in 1996, ranking 4th in the nation and exceeding the U.S. average of $151 by 74%. From 1962 to 1996, Hawaii's real per capita state and local health-care spending increased by 719%, versus an increase of 739% in the U.S. average.

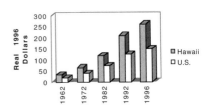

Real Per Capita State and Local Health Care Spending: Hawaii vs. U.S.

Hospital Spending

Hawaii's per capita state and local hospital spending registered $153 in 1996, ranking 33d in the nation and trailing the U.S. average of $266 by 42%. From 1962 to 1996, Hawaii's real per capita state and local hospital spending increased by 33%, as opposed to an increase of 189% in the U.S. average.

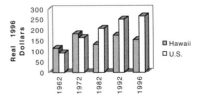

Real Per Capita State and Local Hospital Spending: Hawaii vs. U.S.

Medicaid (1996)

	Spending Per Recipient	Ranking
Hawaii	$6,488	2d
U.S.	$3,466	

Hawaii's per-recipient Medicaid spending exceeded the U.S. average by 87%.

ENVIRONMENT

Parks and Recreation Spending

Hawaii's per capita state and local parks and recreation spending registered $189 in 1996, ranking highest in the nation and outpacing the U.S. average of $72 by 163%. From 1962 to 1996, real per capita state and local parks and recreation spending increased by 361%, versus a 213% increase in the U.S. average.

Real Per Capita State and Local Parks and Recreation Spending: Hawaii vs. U.S.

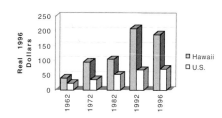

State and Local Natural Resources Spending, 1996

	Per Capita	Ranking
Hawaii	$70	23d
U.S.	$60	

Per capita state and local natural resources spending in Hawaii exceeded the U.S. average by 17%.

State Parks Revenues as a Share of Operating Expenses, 1997

	Percent	Rank
Hawaii	5	50th
U.S.	42	

Percentage of Land Owned by the Federal Government, 1996

	Percent	Rank
Hawaii	8.5	17th
U.S.	24.8	

SOCIETY AND DEMOGRAPHICS

Population

Hawaii's 1998 population of 1.193 million ranked 41st in the nation.

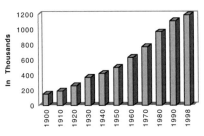

Hawaii   Population

Population Growth, 1990–98

	Percentage Change in Population	Ranking
Hawaii	7.67	24th
U.S.	8.66	

	Net International Migration	Ranking
Hawaii	51,460	18th

	Net Domestic Migration	Ranking
Hawaii	−80,263	40th

Infant Mortality Rate, 1998

	Percent	Rank
Hawaii	6.7	30th
U.S.	6.4	

Percentage of Births of Low Birthweight, 1997

	Percent	Rank
Hawaii	7.2	32d
U.S.	7.5	

Percentage of Live Births to Unmarried Women, 1997

	Percent	Rank
Hawaii	29.8	31st
U.S.	32.4	

Abortion Rate—Abortions Per 1,000 Women Ages 15–44, 1995

	Rate	Rank
Hawaii	29.3	8th
U.S.	22.9	

LIFESTYLE

Percentage of Households with Computers, 1998

	Percent	Rank
Hawaii	42.3	25th

Percentage of Households with Internet Access, 1998

	Percent	Rank
Hawaii	27.9	16th

State Arts Agency Spending, 1999

	Per Capita	Rank
Hawaii	$6.20	1st
U.S.	$1.35	

Per capita state arts spending in 1999 topped the U.S. average by 359%.

Major League Sports Facilities

None

IDAHO

Mention Idaho to most people and they think of potatoes. That's justified, since most estimates peg Idaho-processed potato production at two-thirds of U.S. totals.

However, there are reasons to think of Idaho in ways beyond mashed, baked, or french fried.

For example, to say that Idaho leans a bit Republican is like saying that Bill Clinton shades the truth just a little. Idaho's governor, lieutenant governor, attorney general, two U.S. senators, and two members of the House of Representatives are all GOPers. In 1996, Bob Dole lapped up a whopping 52% of the vote as opposed to Clinton's lowly 34%. For good measure, the two houses of the state legislature are completely dominated by Republicans.

Refreshingly, in terms of public policy, one pretty much gets what people say you are supposed to get when Republicans are in charge. In the following pages, of the 21 government spending, employment, and taxing indicators, 16 of Idaho's come in below the U.S. average. Over the long haul, from 1962 to 1996, real per capita state and local government spending also rose at a much slower rate than the U.S. average. It seems that Idaho Republicans are on the relatively frugal side compared with much of the rest of the nation.

Meanwhile, as for the state's economy, real growth was particularly robust in the mid-to-late 1990s, as was growth in payrolls and real disposable income. Levels of entrepreneurship also have shown fairly steady growth. A recent cut in the state's capital gains tax will boost incentives for economically critical investing and risk taking.

The GOP reputation for being tough on crime seems evident in Idaho too, as the state's crime rates are quite low compared to national rates.

Not surprisingly, Idaho has managed to attract people and businesses from elsewhere in the nation, with former Californians apparently being a fairly sizeable import in recent years. Overall population and net domestic migration numbers in Idaho were quite healthy from 1990 to 1998.

While Idaho is on the right track, there is always room for improvement. On the tax front, for example, Idaho would do well to roll back its very high personal and corporate income tax rates. Indeed, these two levies are the most daunting governmental obstacles to Idaho's continued prosperity. When it comes to potatoes and beyond, Idaho is pretty well positioned to compete in the 21st century.

POLITICS

Registered Voters

No party registration

Federal Officials: Recent Election and Group Ratings

			ACU	ADA	SBSC
U.S. Senators:	Larry Craig (R)		94	3	95
	1996 Craig (R)	57%			
	Minnick (D)	39%			
	Michael Crapo (R)		NA	NA	NA
	1998 Crapo (R)	70%			
	Mauk (D)	28%			
U.S. Representatives:	Helen Chenoweth (R-1)		94	9	80
	1998 Chenoweth (R)	55%			
	Williams (D)	45%			
	Michael Simpson (R-2)		NA	NA	NA
	1998 Simpson (R)	53%			
	Stallings (D)	45%			
Electoral Votes:	4				
1996 Presidential Results:	Clinton	34%			
	Dole	52%			
	Perot	13%			

State Officials

Governor 1998 Election:	Dirk Kempthorne (R)	68%
	Robert Huntley (D)	29%
Lt. Governor:	C.L. "Butch" Otter (R)	
Attorney General:	Alan Lance (R)	
State Senate:	4 Democrats	
	31 Republicans	
State House:	12 Democrats	
	58 Republicans	

TAXES AND SPENDING

Total Revenues

Idaho's per capita state and local total revenues registered $4,989 in 1996, ranking 34th in the nation and trailing the U.S. average of $5,706 by 13%. From 1962 to 1996, real per capita state and local revenues increased by 250%, compared with an increase in the national average of 297%.

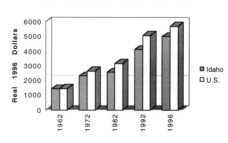

Real Per Capita State and Local
Total Revenues: Idaho vs. U.S.

Taxes

Idaho's per capita state and local taxes registered $2,138 in 1996, ranking 40th in the nation and lagging behind the U.S. average of $2,597 by 18%. From 1962 to 1996, real per capita state and local taxes increased by 139%, compared with an increase of 152% in the U.S. average.

Property Taxes

Idaho's per capita state and local property taxes equaled $548 in 1996, ranking 36th in the nation and trailing the U.S. average of $789 by 31%. From 1962 to 1996, real per capita state and local property taxes increased by 26%, versus a 67% increase in the U.S. average.

Sales and Gross Receipts Taxes

Idaho's per capita state and local sales and gross receipts taxes came in at $724 in 1996, ranking 43d in the nation and trailing the U.S. average of $939 by 23%. From 1962 to 1996, real per capita state and local sales and gross receipts taxes increased by 364%, versus an increase of 214% in the U.S. average.

Income Taxes

Idaho's per capita state and local income (individual and corporate) taxes registered $679 in 1996, ranking 20th in the nation and topping the U.S. average of $674 by 1%. From 1962 to 1996, real per capita state and local income taxes increased by 288%, versus a 567% increase in the U.S. average.

Personal Income Tax

A rate of 8.2%, ranking 43d in the nation (from lowest tax rate to highest), and comparing with the national average of 5.26%.

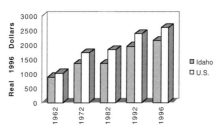

Real Per Capita State and Local Taxes: Idaho vs. U.S.

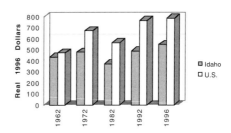

Real Per Capita State and Local Property Taxes: Idaho vs. U.S.

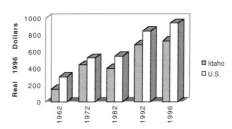

Real Per Capita State and Local Sales and Gross Receipts Taxes: Idaho vs. U.S.

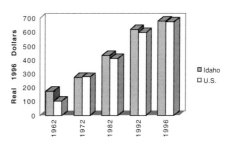

Real Per Capita State and Local Income Taxes: Idaho vs. U.S.

Capital Gains Tax

A rate of 3.28%, ranking 16th in the nation (from lowest tax rate to highest), and comparing with the national average of 4.68%.

Corporate Income Tax

A rate of 8.0%, ranking 34th in the nation (from lowest tax rate to highest), and comparing with the national average of 6.63%.

Total Expenditures

Idaho's per capita state and local total spending registered $4,267 in 1996, ranking 46th in the nation and trailing the U.S. average of $5,268 by 19%. From 1962 to 1996, real per capita state and local total spending increased by 193%, versus an increase of 254% in the U.S. average.

Welfare Expenditures

Idaho's per capita state and local public welfare spending registered $471 in 1996, ranking 49th in the nation and trailing the U.S. average of $729 by 35%. From 1962 to 1996, real per capita state and local public welfare spending increased by 344%, compared with a 488% increase in the U.S. average.

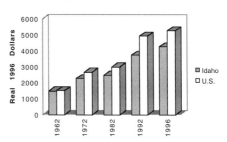

Real Per Capita State and Local Total Expenditures: Idaho vs. U.S.

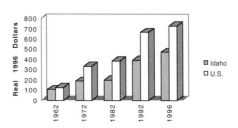

Real Per Capita State and Local Public Welfare Spending: Idaho vs. U.S.

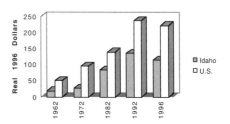

Real Per Capita State and Local Interest on General Debt: Idaho vs. U.S.

Welfare Recipients (in thousands)

	1980	1989	3/99	Change 1989–99
Idaho	20	16	3	−81%
U.S.	10,923	10,987	7,335	−33%

Interest on General Debt

Idaho's per capita state and local interest on general debt registered $114 in 1996, ranking 50th in the nation and trailing the U.S. average of $222 by 49%. From 1962 to 1996, real per capita state and local interest on general debt increased by 533%, versus an increase of 335% in the U.S. average.

Total Debt Outstanding

Idaho's per capita state and local debt registered $1,954 in 1996, ranking 51st in the nation and trailing the U.S. average of $4,409 by 56%. From 1962 to 1996, real per capita state and local debt outstanding increased by 129%, versus an increase of 120% in the U.S. average.

Government Employees

Idaho's state and local government employees (full-time equivalent, or FTE) per 10,000 population registered 566.7 in 1997, ranking 18th in the nation and exceeding the U.S. average of 531.1 by 7%. From 1962 to 1996, state and local FTE employees per 10,000 population increased by 64%, compared with an increase in the U.S. average of 66%.

Real Per Capita State and Local Debt Outstanding: Idaho vs. U.S.

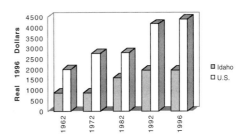

State and Local Government Employees (FTE) Per 10,000 Population: Idaho vs. U.S.

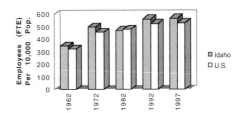

Per Capita Federal Government Expenditures, 1998

	1998	Ranking
Idaho	$4,850	38th
U.S.	$5,491	

Per capita federal spending in Idaho trailed the national average by 12%.

EDUCATION

Total Education Spending

Idaho's per capita state and local education spending registered $1,522 in 1996, ranking 23d in the nation and exceeding the U.S. average of $1,503 by 1%. From 1962 to 1996, real per capita total education spending increased by 207%, versus an increase in the U.S. average of 173%.

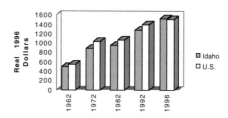

Real Per Capita State and Local Education Spending: Idaho vs. U.S.

Per Pupil Spending

Idaho's per pupil public school spending registered $5,966 in 1998, ranking 26th in the nation and lagging behind the U.S. average of $6,131 by 3%. From 1970 to 1998, Idaho's real per pupil public school spending increased by 181%, compared with a 120% increase in the U.S. average.

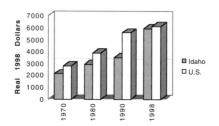

Real Per Pupil Public School Spending: Idaho vs. U.S.

Average Public School Teacher Salaries (in 1997–98 dollars)

	1970	1980	1990	1998	1998 Ranking
Idaho	29,501	28,357	30,394	32,775	41st
U.S.	36,934	33,272	39,956	39,385	

In 1998, the average public school teacher salary in Idaho trailed the U.S. average by 17%. From 1970 to 1998, the real average teacher salary in Idaho increased by 11%, versus an increase in the U.S. average of 7%.

Pupil/Teacher Ratio, Fall 1996

	Ratio	Rank
Idaho	18.8	44th
U.S.	17.1	

Teachers/Staff, Fall 1996

	Percent	Rank
Idaho	57.8	4th
U.S.	52.1	

Average Math SAT Scores

	1972	1982	1992	1998	Percentage Taking SAT in 1998
Idaho	537	534	526	544	16
U.S.	509	493	501	512	43

Average Verbal SAT Scores

	1972	1982	1992	1998	Percentage Taking SAT in 1998
Idaho	570	558	537	545	16
U.S.	530	504	500	505	43

Expenditures by Public Institutions of Higher Education Per Full-Time-Equivalent Student, 1996

	FTE Student Spending	Rank
Idaho	$11,053	42d
U.S.	$12,343	

Per-FTE-student spending in public institutions of higher education trailed the U.S. average by 10%.

Per Full-Time-Equivalent Student Revenues from Federal, State, and Local Governments for Public Institutions of Higher Education, 1996

	FTE Student Government Revenues	Rank
Idaho	$8,521	15th
U.S.	$8,101	

Per-FTE-student-government revenues in public institutions of higher education exceeded the U.S. average by 5%.

Average Salary for Full-Time Professors at Public Universities, 1997

	Average	Rank
Idaho	$58,137	47th
U.S.	$72,599	

The average full-time public university professor salary trailed the U.S. average by 20%.

ECONOMY AND BUSINESS

Economic Growth

Over the period of 1977 to 1997, Idaho's real gross state product (GSP) grew by 95.9%—ranking 12th in the nation—as compared with real U.S. gross domestic product (GDP), expanding by 70.1%

At $29.1 billion in 1997, Idaho's GSP ranked as 44th largest in the nation.

From 1993 to 1997, Idaho's annual real GSP growth averaged 6.38%—ranking 6th in the nation—as compared with annual real U.S. GDP growth, averaging 3.08%.

**Real Economic Growth
1977-1997: Idaho vs. U.S.**

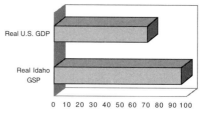

Percent Change

Job Growth

	Growth in Employee Payrolls (Nonagricultural) 1962–98	Ranking
Idaho	217.2%	9th
U.S.	126.5%	

	Average Annual Growth in Employee Payrolls (Nonagricultural) 1993–98	Ranking
Idaho	4.62%	5th
U.S.	2.98%	

Per Capita Disposable Income, 1997

	1997	Ranking
Idaho	$17,663	44th
U.S.	$21,607	

Per capita disposable income lagged behind the U.S. average by 18%.

	Real Growth 1962–97	Ranking
Idaho	101.4%	42d
U.S.	116.7%	

	Average Annual Real Growth 1993–97	Ranking
Idaho	1.74%	18th
U.S.	1.48%	

Number of Businesses

	1997	Percent with Fewer than 500 Employees
Businesses with Employees	36,003	97.3
Self-employed Individuals	68,000	

New Business Incorporations

	1980	1986	1992	1997
Idaho	1,813	1,765	2,127	2,489

Percentage Change in Annual New Business Incorporations, 1980 vs. 1997

	Percent	Ranking
Idaho	37.3	28th
U.S.	49.7	

State Merchandise Exports to the World, 1998 (in millions of dollars)

	1998	Rank
Idaho	$1,460	41st

Small Business Survival Index, 1999

Idaho ranks 28th in terms of its policy environment for entrepreneurs.

Fortune 500 Headquarters, 1999

A total of 3 (ranked 28th)

Labor Union Membership, 1983 vs. 1997

| | Percentage of Workers | | |
	1983	1997	1997 Rank
Idaho	12.5	8.5	35th
U.S.	20.1	14.1	

Homeownership Rate, 1998

	Rate	Rank
Idaho	72.6	11th
U.S.	66.3	

CRIME

Crime Rates Per 100 Residents (rankings from best to worst crime rate)

Total Crime	1960	1970	1980	1990	1998	1998 Ranking
Idaho	0.70	1.79	4.78	4.06	3.71	16th
U.S.	1.04	2.74	5.90	5.82	4.62	

From 1960 to 1998, Idaho's crime rate increased by 430%, versus a U.S. increase of 344%. From 1990 to 1998, Idaho's crime rate dropped by 9%, versus a U.S. decrease of 21%.

Violent Crime	1960	1970	1980	1990	1998	1998 Ranking
Idaho	0.04	0.12	0.31	0.28	0.28	11th
U.S.	0.14	0.36	0.58	0.73	0.57	

From 1960 to 1998, Idaho's violent crime rate increased by 600%, versus a U.S. increase of 307%. From 1990 to 1998, Idaho's violent crime rate was steady, compared with a national decline of 22%.

Property Crime	1960	1970	1980	1990	1998	1998 Ranking
Idaho	0.67	1.66	4.47	3.78	3.43	17th
U.S.	0.90	2.38	5.32	5.09	4.05	

From 1960 to 1998, Idaho's property crime rate increased by 412%, versus a national increase of 350%. From 1990 to 1998, Idaho's property crime rate decreased by 9%, compared with a national decline of 20%.

Real Per Capita Police Protection Spending (in real 1996 dollars)

	1962	1972	1982	1992	1996	1996 Ranking
Idaho	41	66	83	115	130	34th
U.S.	51	95	114	148	168	

In 1996, per capita state and local police protection spending in Idaho trailed the U.S. average by 23%. From 1962 to 1996, real per capita state and local police protection spending increased by 217%, versus an increase of 229% in the U.S. average.

Prisoners in State and Federal Prisons Per 1,000 Population

	1980	1990	1996	1996 Ranking
Idaho	0.87	1.95	3.23	30th
U.S.	1.46	3.11	4.45	

From 1980 to 1996, prisoners per 1,000 population increased by 271%, versus a U.S. increase of 205%.

HEALTH CARE

Health-Care Spending

Idaho's per capita state and local health-care spending registered $88 in 1996, ranking 45th in the nation and trailing the U.S. average of $151 by 42%. From 1962 to 1996, Idaho's real per capita state and local health-care spending increased by 389%, versus an increase of 739% in the U.S. average.

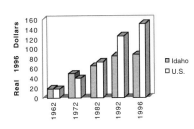

Real Per Capita Health Care Spending: Idaho vs. U.S.

Hospital Spending

Idaho's per capita state and local hospital spending registered $250 in 1996, ranking 23d in the nation and lagging behind the U.S. average of $266 by 6%. From 1962 to 1996, Idaho's real per capita state and local hospital spending increased by 242%, as opposed to an increase of 189% in the U.S. average.

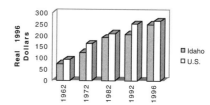

Real Per Capita State and Local Hospital Spending: Idaho vs. U.S.

Medicaid, 1997

	Spending Per Recipient	Ranking
Idaho	$3,757	22d
U.S.	$3,681	

Idaho's per-recipient Medicaid spending exceeded the U.S. average by 2%.

ENVIRONMENT

Parks and Recreation Spending

Idaho's per capita state and local parks and recreation spending registered $48 in 1996, ranking 37th in the nation and trailing the U.S. average of $72 by 33%. From 1962 to 1996, real per capita state and local parks and recreation spending increased by 243%, versus a 213% increase in the U.S. average.

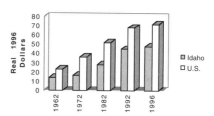

Real Per Capita State and Local Parks and Recreation Spending: Idaho vs. U.S.

State and Local Natural Resources Spending, 1996

	Per Capita	Ranking
Idaho	$118	6th
U.S.	$60	

Per capita state and local natural resources spending in Idaho topped the U.S. average by 97%.

State Parks Revenues as a Share of Operating Expenses, 1997

	Percent	Rank
Idaho	46	20th
U.S.	42	

Percentage of Land Owned by the Federal Government, 1996

	Percent	Rank
Idaho	62.3	3d
U.S.	24.8	

SOCIETY AND DEMOGRAPHICS

Population

Idaho's 1998 population of 1.229 million ranked 40th in the nation.

Population Growth, 1990–98

	Percentage Change in Population	Ranking
Idaho	22.05	3d
U.S.	8.66	

	Net International Migration	Ranking
Idaho	15,286	36th

	Net Domestic Migration	Ranking
Idaho	128,531	11th

Idaho Population

Infant Mortality Rate, 1998

	Percent	Rank
Idaho	6.4	35th
U.S.	6.4	

Percentage of Births of Low Birthweight, 1997

	Percent	Rank
Idaho	6.3	40th
U.S.	7.5	

Percentage of Live Births to Unmarried Women, 1997

	Percent	Rank
Idaho	20.7	50th
U.S.	32.4	

Abortion Rate—Abortions Per 1,000 Women Ages 15–44, 1995

	Rate	Rank
Idaho	5.8	49th
U.S.	22.9	

LIFESTYLE

Percentage of Households with Computers, 1998

	Percent	Rank
Idaho	50.0	7th

Percentage of Households with Internet Access, 1998

	Percent	Rank
Idaho	27.4	18th

State Arts Agency Spending, 1999

	Per Capita	Rank
Idaho	$0.71	33d
U.S.	$1.35	

Per capita state arts spending in 1999 trailed the U.S. average by 47%.

Major League Sports Facilities

None

ILLINOIS

Illinois-native Hillary Clinton understands that if you are a Chicago Cubs fan, you cannot be a White Sox fan as well. (Of course, a Cubs fan cannot really be a Yankees fan either, but that apparently is an issue for New Yorkers to deal with now.) The Cubs and slugger Sammy Sosa are on the north side in the privately built Wrigley Field, and the Chisox and Frank Thomas are on the south side in the government-funded Comiskey Park, and never the twain shall meet—except during that mild atrocity known as interleague play.

Illinois politics sometimes seem to play along similarly stark lines. For example, Senator Richard Durbin is a liberal Democrat, while Peter Fitzgerald (R) had a conservative reputation upon entering the Senate after defeating Carol Moseley-Braun (D). Over in the House, one finds major-league liberals like Bobby Rush, Jesse Jackson Jr., Luis Gutierrez, Danny Davis, and Lane Evans. At the same time, some of the House's leading conservatives hail from Illinois, including Henry Hyde and Phil Crane. Oh yes, and GOP House Speaker Dennis Hastert represents the state's 14th congressional district.

However, actual results in politics are rarely ever as cleanly divided as Cubs versus White Sox, or even liberal Democrats versus conservative Republicans. What you usually get after the pulling and tugging, the to and fro of representative democracy, is a rather muddy middle with occasional moments of philosophical clarity.

This is seen in Illinois' government numbers below. For example, per capita total government revenues, taxes, spending and debt hover around the U.S. average. However, property taxes run well ahead of the nation, but per capita income taxes come in below the mean. In terms of rates, personal income and capital gains taxes are relatively low, while the corporate rate runs high. According to the Small Business Survival Committee's "Small Business Survival Index," Illinois's policy environment for entrepreneurship comes in just a bit better than average.

To no one's surprise then, while Illinois's economic performance has not been disastrous, it has not exactly been as exciting as a Sosa roundtripper deposited into the bleachers at Wrigley Field. On the positive side, Illinois claims the fourth largest state economy; ninth highest per capita disposable income; the third most Fortune 500 companies (including Chicago, ranking second among U.S. cities); business incorporations that have consistently crept higher (but not at explosive rates); and after long lagging behind the nation, real gross state product and job growth that recently have edged ahead of the U.S. rates.

As for some prominent negatives, the crime rate runs ahead of the national average with violent crime particularly high; overall population growth from 1990 to 1998 ranked poorly among the states; and in terms of net domestic migration, Illinois was the third largest net exporter of people to the rest of the nation.

It is no coincidence that Illinois experienced strong, steady growth in population until the welfare state tightened its grip around 1970. Government was vastly expanded during this era, with emphasis placed on taking earnings from society's most productive individuals—for example, Illinois imposed income taxes in 1969—and handing those dollars over, in one form or another, to the least productive.

Whether intended or not, the quite predictable result was to punish hard work and risk taking and to reward those deciding to do little or nothing. Illinois' per capita public welfare spending runs ahead of the quite-lavish U.S. average. Ever since, Illinois has been relatively stagnant.

Moving into the entrepreneurial 21st century, Illinois needs to recognize that government—controlled by politics and manipulated by special interests—is a muddy endeavor, while the private sector—guided by consumers, ingenuity, prices, profits, and losses—offers true clarity. All Illinois requires is that rare moment from a majority of voters and politicians in which the oppressive spotlight of government and taxes are dimmed and the liberating fires of entrepreneurship are ignited.

POLITICS

Registered Voters

No party registration

Federal Officials: Recent Election and Group Ratings

			ACU	ADA	SBSC
U.S. Senators:	Richard Durbin (D)		1	98	20
	1996 Durbin (D)	56%			
	Salvi (R)	40%			
	Peter Fitzgerald (R)		NA	NA	NA
	1998 Fitzgerald (R)	50%			
	Moseley-Braun (D)	47%			
U.S. Representatives:	Bobby Rush (D-1)		3	95	10
	1998 Rush (D)	87%			
	Ahimaz (R)	11%			
	Jesse Jackson Jr. (D-2)		4	100	5
	1998 Jackson (D)	89%			
	Gordon (R)	10%			
	William Lipinski (D-3)		39	49	20
	1998 Lipinski (D)	72%			
	Marshall (R)	28%			
	Luis Gutierrez (D-4)		9	95	10
	1998 Gutierrez (D)	82%			
	Birch (R)	16%			
	Rod Blagojevich (D-5)		12	95	15
	1998 Blagojevich (D)	74%			
	Spitz (R)	26%			
	Henry Hyde (R-6)		86	10	95
	1998 Hyde (R)	67%			
	Cramer (D)	30%			

			ACU	ADA	SBSC
Danny Davis (D-7)			8	98	5
1998	Davis (D)	93%			
	Van Cleave (LBT)	7%			
Philip Crane (R-8)			99	4	100
1998	Crane (R)	69%			
	Rothman (D)	31%			
Janice Schakowsky (D-9)			NA	NA	NA
1998	Schakowsky (D)	75%			
	Sohn (R)	23%			
John Edward Porter (R-10)			62	28	70
1998	Porter (R)	NO			
Jerry Welle (R-11)			87	6	75
1998	Weller (R)	59%			
	Muller (D)	41%			
Jerry Costello (D-12)			30	68	25
1998	Costello (D)	60%			
	Price (R)	40%			
Judy Biggert (R-13)			NA	NA	NA
1998	Biggert (R)	61%			
	Hynes (D)	39%			
Dennis Hastert (R-14)			91	4	95
1998	Hastert (R)	70%			
	Cozzi (D)	30%			
Thomas Ewing (R-15)			94	8	85
1998	Ewing (R)	62%			
	Prussing (D)	38%			
Don Manzullo (R-16)			98	3	100
1998	Manzullo (R)	NO			
Lane Evans (D-17)			6	98	10
1998	Evans (D)	52%			
	Baker (R)	48%			
Ray LaHood (R-18)			68	15	60
1998	LaHood (R)	NO			
David Phelps (D-19)			NA	NA	NA
1998	Phelps (D)	58%			
	Winters (R)	42%			

	ACU	ADA	SBSC
John Shimkus (R-20)	88	10	85

1998	Shimkus (R)	61%
	Verticchio (D)	39%

Electoral Votes:	22	
1996 Presidential Results:	Clinton	54%
	Dole	37%
	Perot	8%

State Officials

Governor 1998 Election:	George Ryan (R)	51%
	Glenn Poshard (D)	47%
Lt. Governor:	Corinne Wood (R)	
Attorney General:	Jim Ryan (R)	
State Senate:	27 Democrats	
	32 Republicans	
State General Assembly:	62 Democrats	
	56 Republicans	

TAXES AND SPENDING

Total Revenues

Illinois's per capita state and local total revenues registered $5,394 in 1996, ranking 23d in the nation and trailing the U.S. average of $5,706 by 5%. From 1962 to 1996, real per capita state and local revenues increased by 271%, compared with an increase in the national average of 297%.

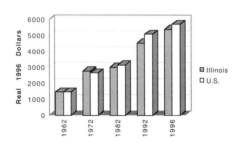

Real Per Capita State and Local Total Revenues: Illinois vs. U.S.

Taxes

Illinois's per capita state and local taxes registered $2,757 in 1996, ranking 13th in the nation and exceeding the U.S. average of $2,597 by 6%. From 1962 to 1996, real per capita state and local taxes increased by 146%, compared with an increase of 152% in the U.S. average.

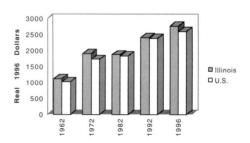

Real Per Capita State and Local Taxes: Illinois vs. U.S.

Property Taxes

Illinois's per capita state and local property taxes equaled $1,056 in 1996, ranking 11th in the nation and topping the U.S. average of $789

by 34%. From 1962 to 1996, real per capita state
and local property taxes increased by 77%,
versus a 67% increase in the U.S. average.

Sales and Gross Receipts Taxes

Illinois's per capita state and local sales and
gross receipts taxes came in at $926 in 1996,
ranking 19th in the nation and trailing the
U.S. average of $939 by 1%. From 1962 to
1996, real per capita state and local sales and
gross receipts taxes increased by 149%, versus
an increase of 214% in the U.S. average.

Income Taxes

Illinois's per capita state and local income
(individual and corporate) taxes registered $625
in 1996, ranking 29th in the nation and trailing
the U.S. average of $674 by 7%. Illinois did not
impose any income taxes until 1969.

Personal Income Tax

A rate of 3.0%, ranking 11th in the nation
(from lowest tax rate to highest), and
comparing with the national average of 5.26%.

Capital Gains Tax

A rate of 3.0%, ranking 15th in the nation
(from lowest tax rate to highest), and
comparing with the national average of 4.68%.

Corporate Income Tax

A rate of 7.3%, ranking 28th in the nation
(from lowest tax rate to highest), and
comparing with the national average of 6.63%.

Total Expenditures

Illinois's per capita state and local total
spending registered $5,044 in 1996, ranking
18th in the nation and trailing the U.S. average
of $5,268 by 4%. From 1962 to 1996, real per
capita state and local total spending increased
by 241%, versus an increase of 254% in the
U.S. average.

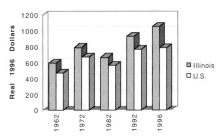

Real Per Capita State and Local
Property Taxes: Illinois vs. U.S.

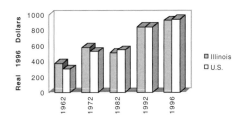

Sales and Gross Receipts Taxes:
Illinois vs. U.S.

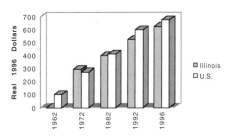

Real Per Capita State and Local
Income Taxes: Illinois vs. U.S.

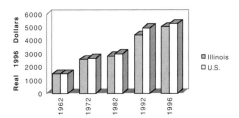

Real Per Capita State and Local
Total Expenditures:
Illinois vs. U.S.

Welfare Expenditures

Illinois's per capita state and local public welfare spending registered $745 in 1996, ranking 17th in the nation and topping the U.S. average of $729 by 2%. From 1962 to 1996, real per capita state and local public welfare spending increased by 425%, compared with a 488% increase in the U.S. average.

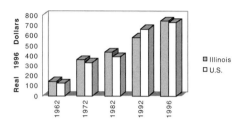

Real Per Capita State and Local Public Welfare Spending: Illinois vs. U.S.

Welfare Recipients (in thousands)

	1980	1989	3/99	Change 1989–99
Ill.	691	623	383	−39%
U.S.	10,923	10,987	7,335	−33%

Interest on General Debt

Illinois's per capita state and local interest on general debt registered $260 in 1996, ranking 17th in the nation and exceeding the U.S. average of $222 by 17%. From 1962 to 1996, real per capita state and local interest on general debt increased by 373%, versus an increase of 335% in the U.S. average.

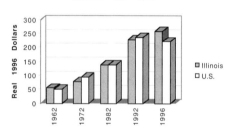

Real Per Capita State and Local Interest on General Debt: Illinois vs. U.S.

Total Debt Outstanding

Illinois's per capita state and local debt registered $4,425 in 1996, ranking 20th in the nation and topping the U.S. average of $4,409 by 0.4%. From 1962 to 1996, real per capita state and local debt outstanding increased by 108%, versus an increase of 120% in the U.S. average.

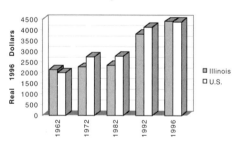

Real Per Capita State and Local Debt Outstanding: Illinois vs. U.S.

Government Employees

Illinois's state and local government employees (full-time equivalent, or FTE) per 10,000 population registered 505.1 in 1997, ranking 39th in the nation and lagging behind the U.S. average of 531.1 by 5%. From 1962 to 1996, state and local FTE employees per 10,000 population increased by 68%, compared with an increase in the U.S. average of 66%.

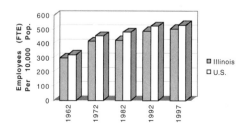

State and Local Government Employees (FTE) Per 10,000 Population: Illinois vs. U.S.

Per Capita Federal Government Expenditures, 1998

	1998	Ranking
Ill.	$4,605	44th
U.S.	$5,491	

Per capita federal spending in Illinois trailed the national average by 16%.

EDUCATION

Total Education Spending

Illinois's per capita state and local education spending registered $1,436 in 1996, ranking 32d in the nation and trailing the U.S. average of $1,503 by 4%. From 1962 to 1996, real per capita total education spending increased by 165%, versus an increase in the U.S. average of 173%.

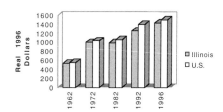

Real Per Capita State and Local Education Spending: Illinois vs. U.S.

Per Pupil Spending

Illinois's per pupil public school spending registered $6,460 in 1998, ranking 14th in the nation and exceeding the U.S. average of $6,131 by 5%. From 1970 to 1998, Illinois's real per pupil public school spending increased by 114%, compared with a 120% increase in the U.S. average.

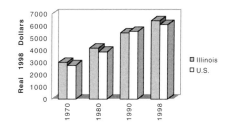

Real Per Pupil Public School Spending: Illinois vs. U.S.

Average Public School Teacher Salaries (in 1997–98 dollars)

	1970	1980	1990	1998	1998 Ranking
Ill.	40,972	36,670	41,773	43,873	10th
U.S.	36,934	33,272	39,956	39,385	

In 1998, the average public school teacher salary in Illinois exceeded the U.S. average by 11%. From 1970 to 1998, the real average teacher salary in Illinois increased by 7%, equal to the increase in the U.S. average.

Pupil/Teacher Ratio, Fall 1996

	Ratio	Rank
Ill.	17.0	31st
U.S.	17.1	

Teachers/Staff, Fall 1996

	Percent	Rank
Ill.	52.5	30th
U.S.	52.1	

Average Math SAT Scores

	1972	1982	1992	1998	Percentage Taking SAT in 1998
Ill.	529	536	555	581	13
U.S.	509	493	501	512	43

Average Verbal SAT Scores

	1972	1982	1992	1998	Percentage Taking SAT in 1998
Ill.	551	539	549	564	13
U.S.	530	504	500	505	43

Expenditures by Public Institutions of Higher Education Per Full-Time-Equivalent Student, 1996

	FTE Student Spending	Rank
Ill.	$11,008	43d
U.S.	$12,343	

Per-FTE-student spending in public institutions of higher education trailed the U.S. average by 11%.

Per Full-Time-Equivalent Student Revenues from Federal, State, and Local Governments for Public Institutions of Higher Education, 1996

	FTE Student Government Revenues	Rank
Ill.	$7,085	37th
U.S.	$8,101	

Per-FTE-student-government revenues in public institutions of higher education behind lagged the U.S. average by 13%.

Average Salary for Full-Time Professors at Public Universities, 1997

	Average	Rank
Ill.	$73,121	16th
U.S.	$72,599	

The average full-time public university professor salary topped the U.S. average by 1%.

ECONOMY AND BUSINESS

Economic Growth

Over the period of 1977 to 1997, Illinois's real gross state product (GSP) grew by 50.3%—ranking 38th in the nation—as compared with real U.S. gross domestic product (GDP), expanding by 70.1%.

At $393.5 billion in 1997, Illinois's GSP ranked as 4th largest in the nation.

From 1993 to 1997, Illinois's annual real GSP growth averaged 3.71%—ranking 25th in the nation—as compared with annual real U.S. GDP growth, averaging 3.08%.

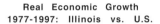

**Real Economic Growth
1977-1997: Illinois vs. U.S.**

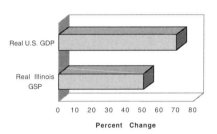

Job Growth

	Growth in Employee Payrolls (Nonagricultural) 1962–98	Ranking
Ill.	65.0%	45th
U.S.	126.5%	

	Average Annual Growth in Employee Payrolls (Nonagricultural) 1993–98	Ranking
Ill.	2.40%	38th
U.S.	2.98%	

Per Capita Disposable Income, 1997

	1997	Ranking
Ill.	$23,584	9th
U.S.	$21,607	

Per capita disposable income topped the U.S. average by 9%.

	Real Growth 1962–97	Ranking
Ill.	99.9%	43d
U.S.	116.7%	

	Average Annual Real Growth 1993–97	Ranking
Ill.	1.73%	19th
U.S.	1.48%	

Number of Businesses

	1997	Percent with Fewer than 500 Employees
Businesses with Employees	270,471	98.4
Self-employed Individuals	383,000	

New Business Incorporations

	1980	1986	1992	1997
Ill.	24,804	26,955	30,298	36,090

Percentage Change in Annual New Business Incorporations, 1980 vs. 1997

	Percent	Ranking
Ill.	45.5	25th
U.S.	49.7	

State Merchandise Exports to the World, 1998 (in millions of dollars)

	1998	Rank
Ill.	$33,838	6th

Small Business Survival Index, 1999

Illinois ranks 20th in terms of it policy environment for entrepreneurship.

Fortune 500 Headquarters in 1999

A total of 39 (ranked 3d), with Chicago placing second among U.S. cities, with 14 headquarters

Labor Union Membership, 1983 vs. 1997

| | Percentage of Workers | | |
	1983	1997	1997 Rank
Ill.	24.2	18.5	12th
U.S.	20.1	14.1	

Homeownership Rate, 1998

	Rate	Rank
Ill.	68.0	31st
U.S.	66.3	

CRIME

Crime Rates Per 100 Residents (rankings from best to worst crime rate)

Total Crime	1960	1970	1980	1990	1998	1998 Ranking
Ill.	1.67	2.35	5.28	5.94	4.87	33d
U.S.	1.04	2.74	5.90	5.82	4.62	

From 1960 to 1998, Illinois's crime rate increased by 192%, versus a U.S. increase of 344%. From 1990 to 1998, Illinois's crime rate dropped by 18%, versus a U.S. decrease of 21%.

Violent Crime	1960	1970	1980	1990	1998	1998 Ranking
Ill.	0.36	0.47	0.49	0.97	0.81	47th
U.S.	0.14	0.36	0.58	0.73	0.57	

From 1960 to 1998, Illinois's violent crime rate increased by 125%, versus a U.S. increase of 307%. From 1990 to 1998, Illinois's violent crime rate decreased by 16%, compared with a national decline of 22%.

Property Crime	1960	1970	1980	1990	1998	1998 Ranking
Ill.	1.32	1.88	4.78	4.97	4.07	29th
U.S.	0.90	2.38	5.32	5.09	4.05	

From 1960 to 1998, Illinois's property crime rate increased by 208%, versus a national increase of 350%. From 1990 to 1998, Illinois's property crime rate decreased by 18%, compared with a national decline of 20%.

Real Per Capita Police Protection Spending (in real 1996 dollars)

	1962	1972	1982	1992	1996	1996 Ranking
Ill.	69	118	131	162	192	8th
U.S.	51	95	114	148	168	

In 1996, per capita state and local police protection spending in Illinois topped the U.S. average by 14%. From 1962 to 1996, real per capita state and local police protection spending increased by 178%, versus an increase of 229% in the U.S. average.

Prisoners in State and Federal Prisons Per 1,000 Population

	1980	1990	1996	1996 Ranking
Ill.	1.04	2.41	3.28	28th
U.S.	1.46	3.11	4.45	

From 1980 to 1996, prisoners per 1,000 population increased by 215%, versus a U.S. increase of 205%.

HEALTH CARE

Health-Care Spending

Illinois's per capita state and local health-care spending registered $154 in 1996, ranking 19th in the nation and topping the U.S. average of $151 by 2%. From 1962 to 1996, Illinois's real per capita state and local health-care spending increased by 1,000%, versus an increase of 739% in the U.S. average.

Real Per Capita State and Local Health Care Spending: Illinois vs. U.S.

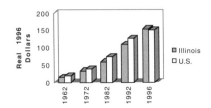

Hospital Spending

Illinois's per capita state and local hospital spending registered $153 in 1996, ranking 33d in the nation and lagging behind the U.S. average of $266 by 42%. From 1962 to 1996, Illinois's real per capita state and local hospital spending increased by 110%, as opposed to an increase of 189% in the U.S. average.

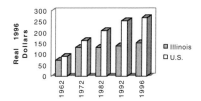

Real Per Capita State and Local Hospital Spending: Illinois vs. U.S.

Medicaid, 1997

	Spending Per Recipient	Ranking
Ill.	$4,131	19th
U.S.	$3,681	

Illinois's per-recipient Medicaid spending topped the U.S. average by 12%.

ENVIRONMENT

Parks and Recreation Spending

Illinois's per capita state and local parks and recreation spending registered $141 in 1996, ranking 3d in the nation and exceeding the U.S. average of $72 by 96%. From 1962 to 1996, real per capita state and local parks and recreation spending increased by 281%, versus a 213% increase in the U.S. average.

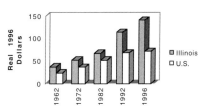

Real Per Capita State and Local Parks and Recreation Spending: Illinois vs. U.S.

State and Local Natural Resources Spending, 1996

	Per Capita	Ranking
Ill.	$25	46th
U.S.	$60	

Per capita state and local natural resources spending in Illinois trailed the U.S. average by 58%.

State Parks Revenues as a Share of Operating Expenses, 1997

	Percent	Rank
Ill.	14	47th
U.S.	42	

Percentage of Land Owned by the Federal Government, 1996

	Percent	Rank
Ill.	1.1	41st
U.S.	24.8	

SOCIETY AND DEMOGRAPHICS

Population

Illinois's 1998 population of 12.045 million ranked 5th in the nation.

Population Growth, 1990–98

	Percentage Change in Population	Ranking
Ill.	5.37	38th
U.S.	8.66	

	Net International Migration	Ranking
Ill.	336,841	6th

	Net Domestic Migration	Ranking
Ill.	−516,424	49th

Infant Mortality Rate, 1998

	Percent	Rank
Ill.	8.2	12th
U.S.	6.4	

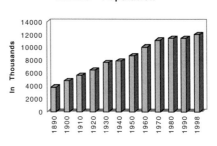

Illinois Population

Percentage of Births of Low Birthweight, 1997

	Percent	Rank
Ill.	7.9	16th
U.S.	7.5	

Percentage of Live Births to Unmarried Women, 1997

	Percent	Rank
Ill.	33.4	17th
U.S.	32.4	

Abortion Rate—Abortions Per 1,000 Women Ages 15–44, 1995

	Rate	Rank
Ill.	25.6	10th
U.S.	22.9	

LIFESTYLE

Percentage of Households with Computers, 1998

	Percent	Rank
Ill.	42.7	24th

Percentage of Households with Internet Access, 1998

	Percent	Rank
Ill.	26.5	20th

State Arts Agency Spending, 1999

	Per Capita	Rank
Ill.	$1.40	14th
U.S.	$1.35	

Per capita state arts spending in 1999 exceeded the U.S. average by 4%.

Major League Sports Facilities

Year Opened/ Refurb.	Stadium/ Arena	Home Team	Millions of Nominal Dollars		Millions of Real 1997 Dollars	
			Estimated Total Cost	Estimated Taxpayer Cost	Estimated Total Cost	Estimated Taxpayer Cost
1910	Comiskey Park	White Sox (MLB) 1910–90 Cardinals (NFL) 1922–25, 1929–59	$0.7	$0.0	$12.1	$0.0
1914	Wrigley Field	Cubs (MLB) 1914–present Bears (NFL) 1921–70	$0.3		$4.0	$0.0
1929	Soldier Field	Bears (NFL) 1971–present	$7.9	$7.9	$73.8	$73.8
1980	Soldier Field (renovation)		$30.0	$30.0	$58.5	$58.5
1929	Chicago Stadium	Blackhawks (NHL) 1929–94 Bulls (NBA) 1967–94	$7.0	$0.0	$65.4	$0.0
1991	Comiskey Park II	White Sox (MLB) 1991–present	$150.0	$150.0	$176.7	$176.7
1994	United Center	Blackhawks (NHL) 1994–present Bulls (NBA) 1994–present	$175.0	$10.0	$189.6	$10.8

INDIANA

During the closing months of the 20th century, newspapers, media outlets, and a host of others provided their "best" or "top" lists. For example, the American Film Institute listed the best films of the century, and ESPN served up the top athletes.

Meanwhile, the *Indianapolis Star* offered its "Top 10 Indiana Sports Stories of All Time." Of course, topping the list was the inspirational story that served as the basis for the greatest basketball movie ever made—"Hoosiers" (1986). In 1954, as the *Star* reported almost a half-century ago, Milan High School became the smallest school, with total enrollment of 162 (73 boys), since 1915 to win Indiana's high school basketball championship, as Bobby Plump's jump shot hit nothing but net with three seconds left on the clock. Since that night at Butler Fieldhouse, when David slew Goliath on the hardwood, no one doubts that basketball is "Indiana's Game."

If one were to list the best of Indiana's crop of politicians at the turn of the century, names like former Vice President Dan Quayle (R), Governor Frank O'Bannon (D), or Senator Richard Lugar (R) might come to mind. U.S. Representative Dan Burton (R), who heads up the House Government Reform Committee, might make the list as well. But at the top of our Indiana list of politicians to watch are Democrat Senator Evan Bayh, who is at the top of most lists, and Republican Congressman David McIntosh.

After eight successful years as governor, the somewhat moderate Bayh cruised to his Senate victory in 1998, succeeding Republican Dan Coats, while grabbing about 30 percent of the GOP vote. Previously, in his 1992 reelection campaign for governor, he reportedly grabbed 40% of the Republican vote. In fact, in his last two statewide races, Bayh has garnered no less than 62% in this traditionally Republican state.

It obviously helped that Bayh, according to the *Indianapolis Star*, made a point of avoiding the word "Democrat" during the campaign and emphasized fiscal conservatism—quite a contrast to his more liberal father Senator Birch Bayh, who was defeated by Dan Quayle in 1980. It is not unusual to hear Evan Bayh mentioned as a possible name on a Democratic national ticket in the near future. It certainly would not surprise us.

Meanwhile, it is amazing how little oddities can help spark a congressional career. In David McIntosh's case, his leading opponent in the 1994 Republican primary actually never got into the race because she failed to file the necessary paperwork on time. McIntosh scraped by in the primary and was later elected to Congress. His subsequent margins of victory expanded to the point that he garnered 61% of the vote in 1998.

McIntosh has combined conservative principles—he is often labeled a "true believer"—with some smart politics. While quickly rising in the House Republican ranks and with a future Speakership not out of the question, McIntosh decided in 1999 instead to run for governor in 2000 against in incumbent O'Bannon.

O'Bannon will likely continue to talk about the Bayh-O'Bannon years to capitalize on the popular senator, while attacking McIntosh as a right-wing extremist. However, McIntosh seems too smooth and knowledgeable for that to stick. The biggest hurdle for McIntosh to clear may simply be facing an incumbent during good economic times, assuming they continue.

Seeing a Governor McIntosh emerge on election night 2000 would not reach the magnitude of Milan's win in 1954, but it could be seen by many as an upset. But we would not bet against this David.

Beyond election politics, as noted in the following pages, Indiana offers a promising, but mixed outlook for the next century. In recent years, real state economic growth has edged above national growth and new business incorporations have shown a steady climb. Job creation, though, has lagged behind national growth and real per capita disposable income growth hovers around the average.

As for state and local per capita measures of government spending, taxing, and debt, Indiana tends to come in below the national averages. In fact, per capita state and local total revenues rank lowest in the nation, and total expenditures come in at 48th among the states and Washington, D.C. Debt burdens—state and local per capita debt outstanding and interest paid—also rank among the lowest in the nation.

State and local per capita total income taxes run ahead of the U.S. average, however. Individual income and capital gains tax rates are on the low side, while the corporate income tax rate is a bit high.

And when it comes to crime and education numbers, Indiana is remarkably average on most accounts.

If elected officials keep government spending and debt under control and move to reduce the tax burden, Indiana should be well positioned for the new century.

POLITICS

Registered Voters

No party registration

Federal Officials: Recent Election and Group Ratings

			ACU	ADA	SBSC
U.S. Senators:	Richard Lugar (R)		81	10	80
	1994 Lugar (R)	67%			
	Jontz (D)	31%			
	Evan Bayh (D)		NA	8	NA
	1998 Bayh (D)	64%			
	Helmke (R)	35%			
U.S. Representatives:	Peter Visclosky (D-1)		10	82	15
	1998 Visclosky (D)	73%			
	Petyo (R)	26%			

			ACU	ADA	SBSC
David McIntosh (R-2)			100	4	95
1998	McIntosh (R)	61%			
	Boles (D)	38%			
Tim Roemer (D-3)			20	59	40
1998	Roemer (D)	58%			
	Holtz (R)	42%			
Mark Souder (R-4)			95	9	75
1998	Souder (R)	63%			
	Wehrle (D)	37%			
Steve Buyer (R-5)			92	3	90
1998	Buyer (R)	63%			
	Steele (D)	36%			
Dan Burton (R-6)			97	6	80
1998	Burton (R)	72%			
	Kern (D)	17%			
Edward Pease (R-7)			98	8	85
1998	Pease (R)	69%			
	Hillenburg (D)	28%			
John Hostettler (R-8)			90	10	80
1998	Hostettler (R)	52%			
	Riecken (D)	46%			
Baron Hill (D-9)			NA	NA	NA
1998	Hill (D)	51%			
	Leising (R)	48%			
Julia Carson (D-10)			5	93	10
1998	Carson (D)	58%			
	Hofmeister (R)	39%			

Electoral Votes:	12	
1996 Presidential Results:	Clinton	42%
	Dole	47%
	Perot	11%

State Officials

Governor 1996 Election:	Frank O'Bannon (D)	52%
	Stephen Goldsmith (R)	47%
Lt. Governor:	Joseph Kernan (D)	
Attorney General:	Jeff Modisett (D)	
State Senate:	19 Democrats	
	31 Republicans	
State House:	53 Democrats	
	47 Republicans	

TAXES AND SPENDING

Total Revenues

Indiana's per capita state and local total revenues registered $4,416 in 1996, ranking 51st in the nation and trailing the U.S. average of $5,706 by 23%. From 1962 to 1996, real per capita state and local revenues increased by 240%, compared with an increase in the national average of 297%.

Taxes

Indiana's per capita state and local taxes registered $2,222 in 1996, ranking 36th in the nation and trailing the U.S. average of $2,597 by 14%. From 1962 to 1996, real per capita state and local taxes increased by 137%, compared with an increase of 152% in the U.S. average.

Property Taxes

Indiana's per capita state and local property taxes equaled $690 in 1996, ranking 32d in the nation and trailing the U.S. average of $789 by 13%. From 1962 to 1996, real per capita state and local property taxes increased by 31%, versus a 67% increase in the U.S. average.

Sale and Gross Receipts Taxes

Indiana's per capita state and local sales and gross receipts taxes came in at $651 in 1996, ranking 45th in the nation and trailing the U.S. average of $939 by 31%. From 1962 to 1996, real per capita state and local sales and gross receipts taxes rose by 89%, versus an increase of 214% in the U.S. average.

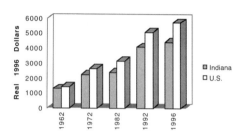

Real Per Capita State and Local Total Revenues: Indiana vs. U.S.

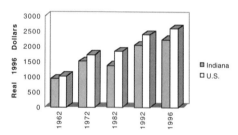

Real Per Capita State and Local Taxes: Indiana vs. U.S.

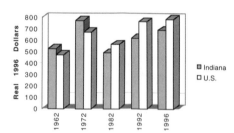

Real Per Capita State and Local Property Taxes: Indiana vs. U.S.

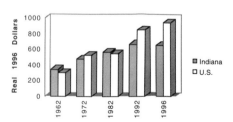

Real Per Capita State and Local Sales and Gross Receipts Taxes: Indiana vs. U.S.

Income Taxes

Indiana's per capita state and local income (individual and corporate) taxes registered $821 in 1996, ranking 14th in the nation and topping the U.S. average of $674 by 22%. Indiana imposed no income taxes until 1963, while the U.S. average increased by 567% between 1962 and 1996. From 1972 to 1996, Indiana's real per capita income taxes rose by 346%, versus a U.S. increase of 145%.

Personal Income Tax

A rate of 3.4%, ranking 13th in the nation (from lowest tax rate to highest), and comparing with the national average of 5.26%.

Capital Gains Tax

A rate of 3.4%, ranking 17th in the nation(from lowest tax rate to highest), and comparing with the national average of 4.68%.

Corporate Income Tax

A rate of 7.9%, ranking 32d in the nation (from lowest tax rate to highest), and comparing with the national average of 6.63%.

Total Expenditures

Indiana's per capita state and local total spending registered $4,155 in 1996, ranking 48th in the nation and trailing the U.S. average of $5,268 by 21%. From 1962 to 1996, real per capita state and local total spending increased by 206%, versus an increase of 254% in the U.S. average.

Welfare Expenditures

Indiana's per capita state and local public welfare spending registered $555 in 1996, ranking 40th in the nation and trailing the U.S. average of $729 by 24%. From 1962 to 1996, real per capita state and local public welfare spending increased by 767%, compared with a 488% increase in the U.S. average.

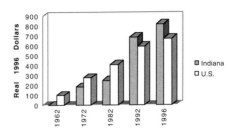

Real Per Capita State and Local Income Taxes: Indiana vs. U.S.

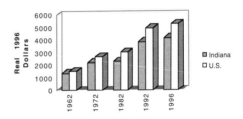

Real Per Capita State and Local Total Expenditures: Indiana vs. U.S.

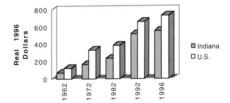

Real Per Capita State and Local Public Welfare Spending: Indiana vs. U.S.

Welfare Recipients (in thousands)

	1980	1989	3/99	Change 1989–99
Ind.	170	149	110	−26%
U.S.	10,923	10,987	7,335	−33%

Interest on General Debt

Indiana's per capita state and local interest on general debt registered $132 in 1996, ranking 42d in the nation and trailing the U.S. average of $222 by 41%. From 1962 to 1996, real per capita state and local interest on general debt increased by 257%, versus an increase of 335% in the U.S. average.

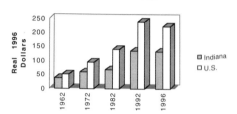

Real Per Capita State and Local Interest on General Debt: Indiana vs. U.S.

Total Debt Outstanding

Indiana's per capita state and local debt registered $2,635 in 1996, ranking 45th in the nation and trailing the U.S. average of $4,409 by 40%. From 1962 to 1996, real per capita state and local debt outstanding increased by 99%, versus an increase of 120% in the U.S. average.

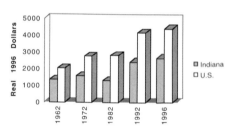

Real Per Capita State and Local Debt Outstanding: Indiana vs. U.S.

Government Employees

Indiana's state and local government employees (full-time equivalent, or FTE) per 10,000 population registered 524.2 in 1997, ranking 32d in the nation and trailing the U.S. average of 531.1 by 1%. From 1962 to 1996, state and local FTE employees per 10,000 population increased by 66%, same as the U.S. average of 66%.

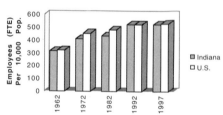

State and Local Government Employees (FTE) Per 10,000 Population: Indiana vs. U.S.

Per Capita Federal Government Expenditures, 1998

	1998	Ranking
Ind.	$4,424	46th
U.S.	$5,491	

Per capita federal spending in Indiana trailed the national average by 19%.

EDUCATION

Total Education Spending

Indiana's per capita state and local education spending registered $1,577 in 1996, ranking 20th in the nation and exceeding the U.S. average of $1,503 by 5%. From 1962 to 1996, real per capita total education spending increased by 145%, versus an increase in the U.S. average of 173%.

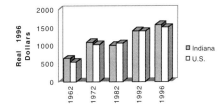

Real Per Capita State and Local Education Spending: Indiana vs. U.S.

Per Pupil Spending

Indiana's per pupil public school spending registered $6,114 in 1998, ranking 21st in the nation and trailing the U.S. average of $6,131 by 0.3%. From 1970 to 1998, Indiana's real per pupil public school spending increased by 150%, compared with a 120% increase in the U.S. average.

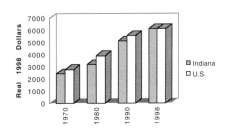

Real Per Pupil Public School Spending: Indiana vs. U.S.

Average Public School Teacher Salaries (in 1997–98 dollars)

	1970	1980	1990	1998	1998 Ranking
Ind.	37,820	32,499	39,363	39,682	16th
U.S.	36,934	33,272	39,956	39,385	

In 1998, the average public school teacher salary in Indiana exceeded the U.S. average by 1%. From 1970 to 1998, the real average teacher salary in Indiana increased by 5%, versus an increase in the U.S. average of 7%.

Pupil/Teacher Ratio, Fall 1996

	Ratio	Rank
Ind.	17.3	38th
U.S.	17.1	

Teachers/Staff, Fall 1996

	Percent	Rank
Ind.	47.3	49th
U.S.	52.1	

Public School 4th-Grade Math Proficiency, 1996

	Average	Rank (out of 44 states)
Ind.	229	6th
U.S.	224	

Public School 8th-Grade Match Proficiency, 1996

	Average	Rank (out of 41 states)
Ind.	276	14th
U.S.	271	

Public School 8th-Grade Science Proficiency, 1996

	Average	Rank (out of 41 states)
Ind.	153	15th
U.S.	148	

Average Math SAT Scores

	1972	1982	1992	1998	Percentage Taking SAT in 1998
Ind.	498	481	487	500	59
U.S.	509	493	501	512	43

Average Verbal SAT Scores

	1972	1982	1992	1998	Percentage Taking SAT in 1998
Ind.	513	486	486	497	59
U.S.	530	504	500	505	43

Expenditures by Public Institutions of Higher Education Per Full-Time-Equivalent Student, 1996

	FTE Student Spending	Rank
Ind.	$13,587	14th
U.S.	$12,343	

Per-FTE-student spending in public institutions of higher education exceeded the U.S. average by 10%.

Per Full-Time-Equivalent Student Revenues from Federal, State, and Local Governments for Public Institutions of Higher Education, 1996

	FTE Student Government Revenues	Rank
Ind.	$7,618	31st
U.S.	$8,101	

Per-FTE-student-government revenues in public institutions of higher education trailed the U.S. average by 6%.

Average Salary for Full-Time Professors at Public Universities, 1997

	Average	Rank
Ind.	$70,174	26th
U.S.	$72,599	

The average full-time public university professor salary trailed the U.S. average by 3%.

ECONOMY AND BUSINESS

Economic Growth

Over the period of 1977 to 1997, Indiana's real gross state product (GSP) grew by 54.7%—ranking 34th in the nation—as compared with real U.S. gross domestic product (GDP), expanding by 70.1%.

At $161.7 billion in 1997, Indiana's GSP ranked as 15th largest in the nation.

From 1993 to 1997, Indiana's annual real GSP growth averaged 3.94%—ranking 20th in the nation—as compared with annual real U.S. GDP growth, averaging 3.08%.

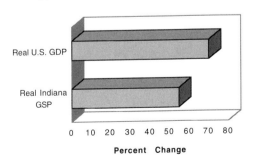

Real Economic Growth 1977-1997: Indiana vs. U.S.

Real U.S. GDP

Real Indiana GSP

0 10 20 30 40 50 60 70 80

Percent Change

Job Growth

	Growth in Employee Payrolls (Nonagricultural) 1962–98	Ranking
Ind.	99.7%	39th
U.S.	126.5%	

	Average Annual Growth in Employee Payrolls (Nonagricultural) 1993–98	Ranking
Ind.	2.70%	33d
U.S.	2.98%	

Per Capita Disposable Income, 1997

	1997	Ranking
Ind.	$19,830	34th
U.S.	$21,607	

Per capita disposable income trailed the U.S. average by 8%.

	Real Growth 1962–97	Ranking
Ind.	99.9%	44th
U.S.	116.7%	

	Average Annual Real Growth 1993–97	Ranking
Ind.	1.52%	32d
U.S.	1.48%	

Number of Businesses

	1997	Percent with Fewer than 500 Employees
Businesses with Employees	123,555	97.7
Self-employed Individuals	183,000	

New Business Incorporations

	1980	1986	1992	1997
Ind.	8,009	10,656	11,119	12,734

Percentage Change in Annual New Business Incorporations, 1980 vs. 1997

	Percent	Ranking
Ind.	59.0	19th
U.S.	49.7	

State Merchandise Exports to the World, 1998 (in millions of dollars)

	1998	Rank
Ind.	$13,949	12th

Small Business Survival Index, 1999

Indiana ranked 16th in terms of its policy environment for entrepreneurship.

Fortune 500 Headquarters in 1999

A total of 7 (ranked 20th)

Labor Union Membership, 1983 vs. 1997

| | Percentage of Workers | | |
	1983	1997	1997 Rank
Ind.	24.9	14.6	20th
U.S.	20.1	14.1	

Homeownership Rate, 1998

	Rate	Rank
Ind.	72.6	11th
U.S.	66.3	

CRIME

Crime Rates Per 100 Residents (rankings from best to worst crime rate)

Total Crime	1960	1970	1980	1990	1998	1998 Ranking
Ind.	0.85	2.27	4.93	4.68	4.17	21st
U.S.	1.04	2.74	5.90	5.82	4.62	

From 1960 to 1998, Indiana's crime rate increased by 391%, versus a U.S. increase of 344%. From 1990 to 1998, Indiana's crime rate dropped by 11%, versus a U.S. decrease of 21%.

Violent Crime	1960	1970	1980	1990	1998	1998 Ranking
Ind.	0.08	0.23	0.38	0.47	0.43	25th
U.S.	0.14	0.36	0.58	0.73	0.57	

From 1960 to 1998, Indiana's violent crime rate increased by 438%, versus a U.S. increase of 307%. From 1990 to 1998, Indiana's violent crime rate decreased by 9%, compared with a national decline of 22%.

Property Crime	1960	1970	1980	1990	1998	1998 Ranking
Ind.	0.77	2.05	4.55	4.21	3.74	20th
U.S.	0.90	2.38	5.32	5.09	4.05	

From 1960 to 1998, Indiana's property crime rate increased by 386%, versus a national increase of 350%. From 1990 to 1998, Indiana's property crime rate decreased by 11%, compared with a national decline of 20%.

Real Per Capita Police Protection Spending (in real 1996 dollars)

	1962	1972	1982	1992	1996	1996 Ranking
Ind.	41	59	69	83	106	45th
U.S.	51	95	114	148	168	

In 1996, per capita state and local police protection spending in Indiana trailed the U.S. average by 37%. From 1962 to 1996, real per capita state and local police protection spending increased by 159%, versus an increase of 229% in the U.S. average.

Prisoners in State and Federal Prisons Per 1,000 Population

	1980	1990	1996	1996 Ranking
Ind.	1.22	2.30	2.91	34th
U.S.	1.46	3.11	4.45	

From 1980 to 1996, prisoners per 1,000 population increased by 139%, versus a U.S. increase of 205%.

HEALTH CARE

Health-Care Spending

Indiana's per capita state and local health-care spending registered $78 in 1996, ranking 47th in the nation and trailing the U.S. average of $151 by 48%. From 1962 to 1996, Indiana's real per capita state and local health-care spending increased by 767%, versus an increase of 739% in the U.S. average.

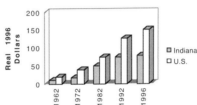

Real Per Capita State and Local Health Care Spending: Indiana vs. U.S.

Hospital Spending

Indiana's per capita state and local hospital spending registered $273 in 1996, ranking 20th in the nation and exceeding the U.S. average of $266 by 3%. From 1962 to 1996, Indiana's real per capita state and local hospital spending increased by 214%, as opposed to an increase of 189% in the U.S. average.

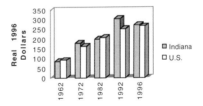

Real Per Capita State and Local Hospital Spending: Indiana vs. U.S.

Medicaid, 1997

	Spending Per Recipient	Ranking
Ind.	$4,625	13th
U.S.	$3,681	

Indiana's per-recipient Medicaid spending topped the U.S. average by 26%.

ENVIRONMENT

Parks and Recreation Spending

Indiana's per capita state and local parks and recreation spending registered $48 in 1996, ranking 37th in the nation and trailing the U.S average of $72 by 33%. From 1962 to 1996, real per capita state and local parks and recreation spending increased by 243%, versus a 213% increase in the U.S. average.

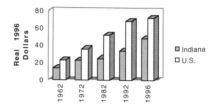

Real Per Capita State and Local Parks and Recreation Spending: Indiana vs. U.S.

State and Local Natural Resources Spending, 1996

	Per Capita	Ranking
Ind.	$34	42d
U.S.	$60	

Per capita state and local natural resources spending in Indiana trailed the U.S. average by 43%.

State Parks Revenues as a Share of Operating Expenses, 1997

	Percent	Rank
Ind.	62	11th
U.S.	42	

Percentage of Land Owned by the Federal Government, 1996

	Percent	Rank
Ind.	1.7	38th
U.S.	24.8	

SOCIETY AND DEMOGRAPHICS

Population

Indiana's 1998 population of 5.899 million ranked 14th in the nation.

Indiana Population

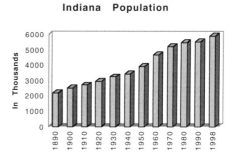

Population Growth, 1990–98

	Percentage Change in Population	Ranking
Ind.	6.40	30th
U.S.	8.66	

	Net International Migration	Ranking
Ind.	24,974	29th

	Net Domestic Migration	Ranking
Ind.	75,868	19th

Infant Mortality Rate, 1998

	Percent	Rank
Ind.	5.3	46th
U.S.	6.4	

Percentage of Births of Low Birthweight, 1997

	Percent	Rank
Ind.	7.7	21st
U.S.	7.5	

Percentage of Live Births to Unmarried Women, 1997

	Percent	Rank
Ind.	32.2	25th
U.S.	32.4	

Abortion Rate—Abortions Per 1,000 Women Ages 15–44, 1995

	Rate	Rank
Ind.	10.6	40th
U.S.	22.9	

LIFESTYLE

Percentage of Households with Computers, 1998

	Percent	Rank
Ind.	43.5	19th

Percentage of Households with Internet Access, 1998

	Percent	Rank
Ind.	26.1	22d

State Arts Agency Spending, 1999

	Per Capita	Rank
Ind.	$0.52	42d
U.S.	$1.35	

Per capita state arts spending in 1999 trailed the U.S. average by 61%.

Major League Sports Facilities

Year Opened/ Refurb.	Stadium/ Arena	Home Team	Millions of Nominal Dollars		Millions of Real 1997 Dollars	
			Estimated Total Cost	Estimated Taxpayer Cost	Estimated Total Cost	Estimated Taxpayer Cost
1974	Market Square	Pacers (NBA) 1974–99	$16.0	$16.0	$52.1	$52.1
1984	RCA/Hoosierdome	Colts (NFL) 1984–present	$78.0	$48.0	$120.6	$74.2
1999	Conseco Fieldhouse	Pacers (NBA) 1999–present	$175.0	$71.0	$168.9	$68.5

IOWA

In 1996, Congress passed the Freedom to Farm Act, designed to steer farming away from government subsidies and regulation and toward free markets. Three years later, in 1999, Democrats and Republicans were competing with each other to provide an additional $20 billion in emergency aide and other subsidies to farmers in Iowa and across the nation.

Why the 180-degree turn? A number of converging circumstances prodded legislators to backpedal. Shrinking crop demand because of economic slowdowns elsewhere in the world, record production, trade disputes with Canada and Europe, and some fears of genetically engineered corn and other commodities in Japan and Europe combined to give farmers a tough time not only in Iowa but in other parts of the United States as well.

A Republican state party official lamented, "Here come Bill Clinton and the Democrats with big handouts and we [Republicans] counter their cash with theoretical discussions of free markets and how they are better for farmers in the long run. Then we seem surprised when they don't buy it, so we turn around and compete with the Democrats to increase the handouts."

The inclination of elected officials to use government funds as a political weapon is not limited to farm subsidies. "The Iowa Legislature has what it calls a surplus, and it has gotten easier and easier for Democrats and Republicans alike to promise something for everyone," remarked the GOP party official, who requested anonymity.

Republicans, who lost the governorship to popular Democrat Tom Vilsack in 1998, fear that their traditional farm base is vulnerable to erosion in the 2000 presidential elections.

In the end, despite the perceived romance and very real politics of farming, it is a business, just like any other business. Efficiencies throughout the 20th century have boosted production, while slashing the number of people working on farms, to the benefit of all. And as is the case with any kind of government welfare program, those receiving farm aid are none too pleased to have it taken away. When things take a bad turn, they predictably seek a government bailout, and politicians predictably give in and tax the rest of us for such a bailout. Make no mistake, a free-market effort to get farmers off the dole, liberate them from government regulations, and cut their taxes (for example, death and capital gains taxes) is meant to foster a change in farming so that the inefficient are forced to improve or fail; the efficient thrive; and consumers benefit from lower prices and better products. That is how it works for other businesses, and that is how it should work for farming.

Meanwhile, small towns in Iowa have more to worry about than their tether to the farm economy. Crime is a major concern. Iowa ranks a positive 11th in the total crime rate in the United States, but the rate of increase over the past three-plus decades has far outstripped the national increase. Many small towns, which once considered themselves immune to such problems, are facing a starkly different reality. "Almost all of rural crime is government created," declares Kayne Robinson, recently retired chief of police for Des Moines.

"Talk to the cops in virtually any small town in the state and ask to see where their crime is coming from and everyone of them will take you to the same place. The new government financed public housing," explained Chief Robinson. Ironically, the very same concept of public housing that has been discredited in places like Chicago and New York is the federal government's newest welfare tool in small-town Iowa. Concentrating people in government housing has created a negative synergy and brought crimes traditionally associated with urban areas to communities ill equipped to deal with them. In the end, law-abiding citizens both inside and outside such housing projects suffer.

Education is one of the state's bright spots. No doubt it has played a factor in the economy. A number of high-tech employers and the insurance industry have provided Des Moines and other cities a degree of diversity that insulates them against the plight of the farmers. Iowa's public schools' math-, reading-, and science-proficiency scores rank among the best in the nation.

Few would be surprised that Iowa has lagged behind the nation in population growth, ranking 42d, and that it has actually experienced a net domestic migration loss of over 13,000 from 1990 to 1998. Annual new business incorporations dropped through the floor in recent years as well. But economic woes may not be the only reason Iowans leave.

"This state is boring. People would stay if there were things to do," observes Robinson. However, there are no statistics available to rate the boring ratio of U.S. states. And we are not so sure. After all, that baseball diamond carved out of a cornfield for the movie "Field of Dreams" is in Iowa. Not only is that pretty darn exciting for baseball fans, but it is an intriguing alternative to farm subsidies.

POLITICS

Registered Voters

33% Democrats
34% Republicans
33% Other

Federal Officials: Recent Election and Group Ratings

			ACU	ADA	SBSC
U.S. Senators:	Charles Grassley (R)		80	16	80
	1998 Grassley (R)	68%			
	Osterberg (D)	30%			
	Tom Harkin (D)		9	93	5
	1996 Harkin (D)	51%			
	Lightfoot (R)	46%			

			ACU	ADA	SBSC
U.S. Representatives:	James Leach (R-1)		41	52	55
	1998 Leach (R)	57%			
	Rush (D)	42%			
	Jim Nussle (R-2)		84	14	90
	1998 Nussle (R)	55%			
	Tully (D)	44%			
	Leonard Boswell (D-3)		32	65	45
	1998 Boswell (D)	57%			
	McKibben (R)	41%			
	Greg Ganske (R-4)		74	14	65
	1998 Ganske (R)	65%			
	Dvorak (D)	34%			
	Tom Latham (R-5)		85	4	95
	1998 Latham (R)	NO			

Electoral Votes:	7	
1996 Presidential Results:	Clinton	50%
	Dole	40%
	Perot	9%

State Officials

Governor 1998 Election:	Tom Vilsack (D)	52%
	Jim Lightfoot (R)	47%
Lt. Governor:	Sally Pederson (D)	
Attorney General:	Tom Miller (D)	
State Senate:	20 Democrats	
	30 Republicans	
State House:	44 Democrats	
	56 Republicans	

TAXES AND SPENDING

Total Revenues

Iowa's per capita state and local total revenues registered $5,021 in 1996, ranking 32d in the nation and trailing the U.S. average of $5,706 by 12%. From 1962 to 1996, real per capita state and local revenues increased by 246%, compared with an increase in the national average of 297%.

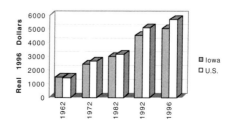

Real Per Capita State and Local Total Revenues: Iowa vs. U.S.

Taxes

Iowa's per capita state and local taxes registered $2,448 in 1996, ranking 24th in the nation and trailing the U.S. average of $2,597 by 6%. From 1962 to 1996, real per capita state and local taxes increased by 132%, compared with an increase of 152% in the U.S. average.

Property Taxes

Iowa's per capita state and local property taxes equaled $836 in 1996, ranking 32d in the nation and topping the U.S. average of $789 by 6%. From 1962 to 1996, real per capita state and local property taxes increased by 40%, versus a 67% increase in the U.S. average.

Sales and Gross Receipts Taxes

Iowa's per capita state and local sales and gross receipts taxes came in at $786 in 1996, ranking 36th in the nation and trailing the U.S. average of $939 by 16%. From 1962 to 1996, real per capita state and local sales and gross receipts taxes rose by 185%, versus an increase of 214% in the U.S. average.

Income Taxes

Iowa's per capita state and local income (individual and corporate) taxes registered $637 in 1996, ranking 26th in the nation and trailing the U.S. average of $674 by 5%. From 1962 to 1996, real per capita state and local income taxes increased by 717%, versus a 567% increase in the U.S. average.

Personal Income Tax

A rate of 5.42%, ranking 21st in the nation (from lowest tax rate to highest), and comparing with the national average of 5.26%.

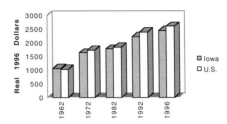

Real Per Capita State and Local Taxes: Iowa vs. U.S.

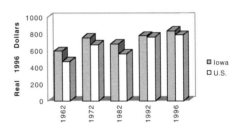

Real Per Capita State and Local Property Taxes: Iowa vs. U.S.

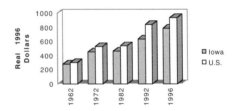

Real Per Capita State and Local Sales and Gross Receipts Taxes: Iowa vs. U.S.

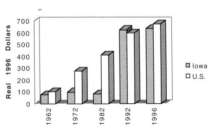

Real Per Capita State and Local Income Taxes: Iowa vs. US.

Capital Gains Tax

A rate of 7.184%, ranking 42d in the nation (from lowest tax rate to highest), and comparing with the national average of 4.68%.

Corporate Income Tax

A rate of 9.9%, ranking 49th in the nation (from lowest tax rate to highest), and comparing with the national average of 6.63%.

Total Expenditures

Iowa's per capita state and local total spending registered $4,722 in 1996, ranking 35th in the nation and trailing the U.S. average of $5,268 by 10%. From 1962 to 1996, real per capita state and local total spending increased by 220%, versus an increase of 254% in the U.S. average.

Welfare Expenditures

Iowa's per capita state and local public welfare spending registered $627 in 1996, ranking 30th in the nation and trailing the U.S. average of $729 by 14%. From 1962 to 1996, real per capita state and local public welfare spending increased by 406%, compared with a 488% increase in the U.S. average.

Welfare Recipients (in thousands)

	1980	1989	3/99	Change 1989–99
Iowa	111	97	60	−38%
U.S.	10,923	10,987	7,335	−33%

Interest on General Debt

Iowa's per capita state and local interest on general debt registered $119 in 1996, ranking 49th in the nation and trailing the U.S. average of $222 by 46%. From 1962 to 1996, real per capita state and local interest on general debt increased by 417%, versus an increase of 335% in the U.S. average.

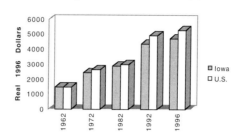

Real Per Capita State and Local Total Expenditures: Iowa vs. U.S.

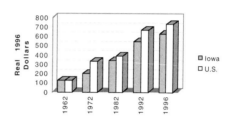

Real Per Capita State and Local Public Welfare Spending: Iowa vs. U.S.

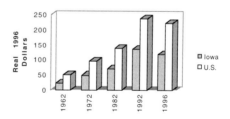

Real Per Capita State and Local Interest on General Debt: Iowa vs. U.S.

Total Debt Outstanding

Iowa's per capita state and local debt registered $2,228 in 1996, ranking 50th in the nation and trailing the U.S. average of $4,409 by 49%. From 1962 to 1996, real per capita state and local debt outstanding increased by 161%, versus an increase of 120% in the U.S. average.

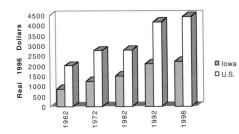

Real Per Capita State and Local Debt Outstanding: Iowa vs. U.S.

Government Employees

Iowa's state and local government employees (full-time equivalent, or FTE) per 10,000 population registered 590.9 in 1997, ranking 12th in the nation and exceeding the U.S. average of 531.1 by 11%. From 1962 to 1996, state and local FTE employees per 10,000 population increased by 76%, exceeding the U.S. average of 66%.

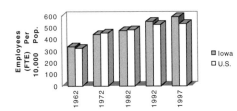

State and Local Government Employees (FTE) Per 10,000 Population: Iowa vs. U.S.

Per Capita Federal Government Expenditures, 1998

	1998	Ranking
Iowa	$5,079	32d
U.S.	$5,491	

Per capita federal spending in Iowa trailed the national average by 8%.

EDUCATION

Total Education Spending

Iowa's per capita state and local education spending registered $1,624 in 1996, ranking 17th in the nation and exceeding the U.S. average of $1,503 by 8%. From 1962 to 1996, real per capita total education spending increased by 168%, versus an increase in the U.S. average of 173%.

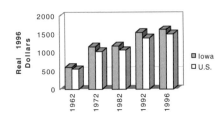

Real Per Capita State and Local Education Spending: Iowa vs. U.S.

Per Pupil Spending

Iowa's per pupil public school spending registered $5,989 in 1998, ranking 25th in the nation and trailing the U.S. average of $6,131 by 2%. From 1970 to 1998, Iowa's real per pupil public school spending increased by 103%, compared with a 120% increase in the U.S. average.

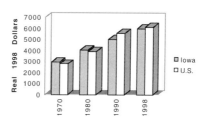

Real Per Pupil Public School Spending: Iowa vs. U.S.

Average Public School Teacher Salaries (in 1997–98 dollars)

	1970	1980	1990	1998	1998 Ranking
Iowa	35,774	31,674	34,071	34,040	32d
U.S.	36,934	33,272	39,956	39,385	

In 1998, the average public school teacher salary in Iowa trailed the U.S. average by 14%. From 1970 to 1998, the real average teacher salary in Iowa decreased by 5%, versus an increase in the U.S. average of 7%.

Pupil/Teacher Ratio, Fall 1996

	Ratio	Rank
Iowa	15.4	16th
U.S.	17.1	

Teachers/Staff, Fall 1996

	Percent	Rank
Iowa	51.7	36th
U.S.	52.1	

Public School 4th-Grade Reading Proficiency, 1998

	Average	Rank (out of 40 states)
Iowa	223	7th
U.S.	215	

Public School 4th-Grade Math Proficiency, 1996

	Average	Rank (out of 44 states)
Iowa	229	6th
U.S.	224	

Public School 8th-Grade Math Proficiency, 1996

	Average	Rank (out of 41 states)
Iowa	284	1st
U.S.	271	

Public School 8th-Grade Science Proficiency, 1996

	Average	Rank (out of 41 states)
Iowa	158	6th
U.S.	148	

Average Math SAT Scores

	1972	1982	1992	1998	Percentage Taking SAT in 1998
Iowa	579	586	595	601	5
U.S.	509	493	501	512	43

Average Verbal SAT Scores

	1972	1982	1992	1998	Percentage Taking SAT in 1998
Iowa	600	590	585	593	5
U.S.	530	504	500	505	43

Expenditures by Public Institutions of Higher Education Per Full-Time-Equivalent Student, 1996

	FTE Student Spending	Rank
Iowa	$14,626	6th
U.S.	$12,343	

Per-FTE-student spending in public institutions of higher education exceeded the U.S. average by 18%.

Per Full-Time-Equivalent Student Revenues from Federal, State, and Local Governments for Public Institutions of Higher Education, 1996

	FTE Student Government Revenues	Rank
Iowa	$10,024	5th
U.S.	$8,101	

Per-FTE-student-government revenues in public institutions of higher education exceeded the U.S. average by 24%.

Average Salary for Full-Time Professors at Public Universities, 1997

	Average	Rank
Iowa	$75,140	11th
U.S.	$72,599	

The average full-time public university professor salary topped the U.S. average by 4%.

ECONOMY AND BUSINESS

Economic Growth

Over the period of 1977 to 1997, Iowa's real gross state product (GSP) grew by 48.0%—ranking 42d in the nation—as compared with real U.S. gross domestic product (GDP), expanding by 70.1%.

At $80.5 billion in 1997, Iowa's GSP ranked as 29th largest in the nation.

From 1993 to 1997, Iowa's annual real GSP growth averaged 4.42%—ranking 12th in the nation—as compared with annual real U.S. GDP growth, averaging 3.08.%.

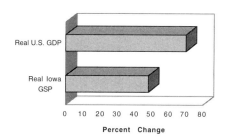

Real Economic Growth 1977-1997: Iowa vs. U.S.

Real U.S. GDP

Real Iowa GSP

0 10 20 30 40 50 60 70 80

Percent Change

Job Growth

	Growth in Employee Payrolls (Nonagricultural) 1962–98	Ranking
Iowa	111.1%	37th
U.S.	126.5%	

Average Annual Growth in Employee Payrolls (Nonagricultural) 1993–98	Ranking
Iowa	2.91%	28th
U.S.	2.98%	

Per Capita Disposable Income, 1997

	1997	Ranking
Iowa	$20,113	31st
U.S.	$21,607	

Per capita disposable income trailed the U.S. average by 7%.

	Real Growth 1962–97	Ranking
Iowa	110.5%	35th
U.S.	116.7%	

	Average Annual Real Growth 1993–97	Ranking
Iowa	2.36%	5th
U.S.	1.48%	

Number of Businesses

	1997	Percent with Fewer than 500 Employees
Businesses with Employees	67,453	97.8
Self-employed Individuals	173,000	

New Business Incorporations

	1980	1986	1992	1997
Iowa	5,120	4,196	4,918	4,695

Percentage Change in Annual New Business Incorporations, 1980 vs. 1997

	Percent	Ranking
Iowa	−8.3	47th
U.S.	49.7	

State Merchandise Exports to the World, 1998 (in millions of dollars)

	1998	Rank
Iowa	$3,412	32d

Small Business Survival Index, 1999

Iowa ranked a fairly poor 36th in terms of its environment for entrepreneurship.

Fortune 500 Headquarters in 1999

A total of 2 (ranked 34th)

Labor Union Membership, 1983 vs. 1997

	Percentage of Workers		
	1983	1997	1997 Rank
Iowa	17.2	13.2	25th
U.S.	20.1	14.1	

Homeownership Rate, 1998

	Rate	Rank
Iowa	72.1	13th
U.S.	66.3	

CRIME

Crime Rates Per 100 Residents (rankings from best to worst crime rate)

Total Crime	1960	1970	1980	1990	1998	1998 Ranking
Iowa	0.51	1.44	4.75	4.10	3.50	10th
U.S.	1.04	2.74	5.90	5.82	4.62	

From 1960 to 1998, Iowa's crime rate increased by 586%, versus a U.S. increase of 344%. From 1990 to 1998, Iowa's crime rate dropped by 15%, versus a U.S. decrease of 21%.

Violent Crime	1960	1970	1980	1990	1998	1998 Ranking
Iowa	0.02	0.08	0.20	0.30	0.31	13th
U.S.	0.14	0.36	0.58	0.73	0.57	

From 1960 to 1998, Iowa's violent crime rate increased by 1,450%, versus a U.S. increase of 307%. From 1990 to 1998, Iowa's violent crime rate increased by 3%, compared with a national decline of 22%.

Property Crime	1960	1970	1980	1990	1998	1998 Ranking
Iowa	0.49	1.36	4.55	3.80	3.19	11th
U.S.	0.90	2.38	5.32	5.09	4.05	

From 1960 to 1998, Iowa's property crime rate increased by 551%, versus a national increase of 350%. From 1990 to 1998, Iowa's property crime rate decreased by 16%, compared with a national decline of 20%.

Real Per Capita Police Protection Spending (in real 1996 dollars)

	1962	1972	1982	1992	1996	1996 Ranking
Iowa	37	59	78	102	117	40th
U.S.	51	95	114	148	168	

In 1996, per capita state and local police protection spending in Iowa trailed the U.S. average by 30%. From 1962 to 1996, real per capita state and local police protection spending increased by 216%, versus an increase of 229% in the U.S. average.

Prisoners in State and Federal Prisons Per 1,000 Population

	1980	1990	1996	1996 Ranking
Iowa	0.85	1.43	2.23	42d
U.S.	1.46	3.11	4.45	

From 1980 to 1996, prisoners per 1,000 population increased by 162%, versus a U.S. increase of 205%.

HEALTH CARE

Health-Care Spending

Iowa's per capita state and local health-care spending registered $104 in 1996, ranking 34th in the nation and trailing the U.S. average of $151 by 31%. From 1962 to 1996, Iowa's real per capita state and local health-care spending increased by 1,056%, versus an increase of 739% in the U.S. average.

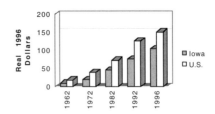

Real Per Capita State and Local Health Care Spending: Iowa vs. U.S.

Hospital Spending

Iowa's per capita state and local hospital spending registered $365 in 1996, ranking 10th in the nation and exceeding the U.S. average of $266 by 37%. From 1962 to 1996, Iowa's real per capita state and local hospital spending increased by 368%, as opposed to an increase of 189% in the U.S. average.

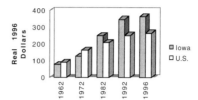

Real Per Capita State and Local Hospital Spending: Iowa vs. U.S.

Medicaid, 1997

	Spending Per Recipient	Ranking
Iowa	$3,684	24th
U.S.	$3,681	

Iowa's per-recipient Medicaid spending topped the U.S. average by 0.1%.

ENVIRONMENT

Parks and Recreation Spending

Iowa's per capita state and local parks and recreation spending registered $61 in 1996, ranking 26th in the nation and trailing the U.S. average of $72 by 15%. From 1962 to 1996, real per capita state and local parks and recreation spending increased by 239%, versus a 213% increase in the U.S. average.

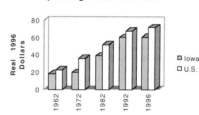

Real Per Capita State and Local Parks and Recreation Spending: Iowa vs. U.S.

State and Local Natural Resources Spending, 1996

	Per Capita	Ranking
Iowa	$75	18th
U.S.	$60	

Per capita state and local natural resources spending in Iowa topped the U.S. average by 25%.

State Parks Revenues as a Share of Operating Expenses, 1997

	Percent	Rank
Iowa	32	36th
U.S.	42	

Percentage of Land Owned by the Federal Government, 1996

	Percent	Rank
Iowa	0.1	51st
U.S.	24.8	

SOCIETY AND DEMOGRAPHICS

Population

Iowa's 1998 population of 2.862 million ranked 30th in the nation.

Population Growth, 1990–98

	Percentage Change in Population	Ranking
Iowa	3.06	42d
U.S.	8.66	

	Net International Migration	Ranking
Iowa	18,954	33d

	Net Domestic Migration	Ranking
Iowa	−13,030	34th

Iowa   Population

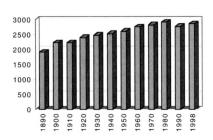

Infant Mortality Rate, 1998

	Percent	Rank
Iowa	6.5	32d
U.S.	6.4	

Percentage of Births of Low Birthweight, 1997

	Percent	Rank
Iowa	6.4	38th
U.S.	7.5	

Percentage of Live Births to Unmarried Women, 1997

	Percent	Rank
Iowa	26.2	43d
U.S.	32.4	

Abortion Rate—Abortions Per 1,000 Women Ages 15–44, 1995

	Rate	Rank
Iowa	9.8	41st
U.S.	22.9	

LIFESTYLE

Percentage of Households with Computers, 1998

	Percent	Rank
Iowa	41.4	30th

Percentage of Households with Internet Access, 1998

	Percent	Rank
Iowa	21.8	39th

State Arts Agency Spending, 1999

	Per Capita	Rank
Iowa	$0.59	39th
U.S.	$1.35	

Per capita state arts spending in 1999 trailed the U.S. average by 56%.

Major League Sports Facilities

None

KANSAS

In August 1999, the Kansas State Board of Education voted not to include the Darwinian theory of "macro-evolution"—that is, that one species is developed from another—in its suggested high school standards. The resulting firestorm was quite predictable.

Of course, the debate over how to teach evolution and creationism, not to mention economics, history, civics, and many other subjects, was long raged and will continue to rage on while primary and secondary education stands as a virtual government monopoly. School choice is an obvious solution, allowing parents to select the schools they think are best for their children. Unfortunately, Kansas has made no headway in moving to private or public school choice.

Beyond education, Kansas has lagged behind in terms of positive reforms in other areas as well. In fact, when it comes to where it ranks for state and local spending and taxes, the state's economy, and crime, Kansas is an amazingly average state. It is in the middle of the pack in most areas.

Of course, middle of the pack will not cut it in the robust, entrepreneurial competition of the 21st century. The state needs to get out front on competition in education, privatization of government services and assets, reducing the reach of government, and lowering taxes. For example, Erin Rooney of the Kansas Public Policy Institute has pointed out that had state general spending merely accelerated at the national rate of inflation since 1991, in fiscal year 2000, the state would have spent $1.3 billion less than planned. Rooney asserts that the state overspent more than $5.1 billion—or about $2,000 for every man, woman, and child in the state—between 1991 and 2000.

Bob Corkins, president of the Kansas Public Policy Institute, had a good idea when he called for limiting government spending growth to the pace of personal income growth and for devoting excess revenues to lowering income tax rates until the income tax was eliminated in about a decade.

From education to income taxes, the main thrust for the 21st century needs to be a shift in power away from government and into the hands of individuals. Kansas must awaken quickly to this reality. If Kansas can think outside the box on evolution, then they can do so on other critical issues as well.

POLITICS

Registered Voters

30% Democrats
45% Republicans
25% Other

Federal Officials: Recent Election and Group Ratings

			ACU	ADA	SBSC
U.S. Senators:	Sam Brownback (R)		97	0	95
	1998 Brownback (R)	65%			
	Feleciano (D)	32%			
	Pat Roberts (R)		87	8	80
	1996 Roberts (R)	62%			
	Thompson (D)	34%			
U.S. Representatives:	Jerry Moran (R-1)		94	NA	95
	1998 Moran (R)	81%			
	Phillips (D)	19%			
	Jim Ryun (R-2)		67	NA	95
	1998 Ryun (R)	61%			
	Clark (D)	39%			
	Dennis Moore (D-3)		NA	NA	NA
	1998 Moore (D)	52%			
	Snowbarger (R)	48%			
	Todd Tiahrt (R-4)		100	3	95
	1998 Tiahrt (R)	58%			
	Lawing (D)	39%			
Electoral Votes:	6				
1996 Presidential Results:	Clinton	36%			
	Dole	54%			
	Perot	9%			

State Officials

Governor 1998 Election:	Bill Graves (R)	73%
	Tom Sawyer (D)	23%
Lt. Governor:	Gary Sherrer (R)	
Attorney General:	Carla Stovall (R)	
State Senate:	13 Democrats	
	27 Republicans	
State House:	48 Democrats	
	77 Republicans	

TAXES AND SPENDING

Total Revenues

Kansas's per capita state and local total revenues registered $5,005 in 1996, ranking 33d in the nation and trailing the U.S. average of $5,706 by 12%. From 1962 to 1996, real per capita state and local revenues increased by 234%, compared with an increase in the national average of 297%.

Taxes

Kansas's per capita state and local taxes registered $2,478 in 1996, ranking 23d in the nation and trailing the U.S. average of $2,597 by 4%. From 1962 to 1996, real per capita state and local taxes increased by 131%, compared with an increase of 152% in the U.S. average.

Property Taxes

Kansas's per capita state and local property taxes equaled $772 in 1996, ranking 21st in the nation and trailing the U.S. average of $789 by 2%. From 1962 to 1996, real per capita state and local property taxes increased by 28%, versus a 67% increase in the U.S. average.

Sales and Gross Receipts Taxes

Kansas's per capita state and local sales and gross receipts taxes came in at $904 in 1996, ranking 26th in the nation and trailing the U.S. average of $939 by 4%. From 1962 to 1996, real per capita state and local sales and gross receipts taxes increased by 202%, versus an increase of 214% in the U.S. average.

Real Per Capita State and Local Total Revenues: Kansas vs. U.S.

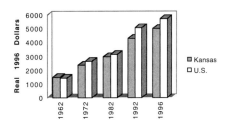

Real Per Capita State and Local Taxes: Kansas vs. U.S.

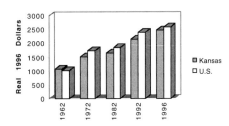

Real Per Capita State and Local Property Taxes: Kansas vs. U.S.

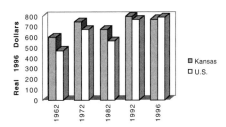

Real Per Capita State and Local Sales and Gross Receipts Taxes: Kansas vs. U.S.

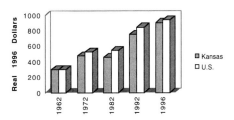

Income Taxes

Kansas's per capita state and local income (individual and corporate) taxes registered $635 in 1996, ranking 27th in the nation and trailing the U.S. average of $674 by 6%. From 1962 to 1996, real per capita state and local income taxes increased by 770%, versus a 567% increase in the U.S. average.

Personal Income Tax

A rate of 6.45%, ranking 31st in the nation (from lowest tax rate to highest), and comparing with the national average of 5.26%.

Capital Gains Tax

A rate of 6.45%, ranking 36th in the nation (from lowest tax rate to highest), and comparing with the national average of 4.68%.

Corporate Income Tax

A rate of 4.134%, ranking 7th in the nation (from lowest tax rate to highest), and comparing with the national average of 6.63%.

Total Expenditures

Kansas's per capita state and local total spending registered $4,749 in 1996, ranking 34th in the nation and trailing the U.S. average of $5,268 by 10%. From 1962 to 1996, real per capita state and local total spending increased by 217%, versus an increase of 254% in the U.S. average.

Welfare Expenditures

Kansas's per capita state and local public welfare spending registered $440 in 1996, ranking 50th in the nation and trailing the U.S. average of $729 by 24%. From 1962 to 1996, real per capita state and local public welfare spending increased by 270%, compared with a 488% increase in the U.S. average.

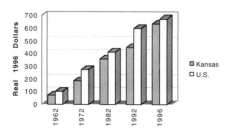

Real Per Capita State and Local Income Taxes: Kansas vs. U.S.

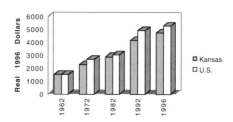

Real Per Capita State and Local Total Expenditures: Kansas vs. U.S.

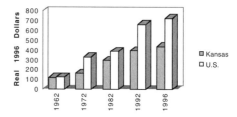

Real Per Capita State and Local Public Welfare Spending: Kansas vs. U.S.

Welfare Recipients (in thousands)

	1980	1989	3/99	Change 1989–99
Kans.	72	77	33	−57%
U.S.	10,923	10,987	7,335	−33%

Interest on General Debt

Kansas's per capita state and local interest on general debt registered $178 in 1996, ranking 33d in the nation and trailing the U.S. average of $222 by 20%. From 1962 to 1996, real per capita state and local interest on general debt increased by 287%, versus an increase of 335% in the U.S. average.

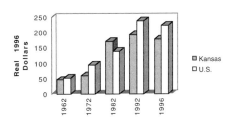

Real Per Capita State and Local Interest on General Debt: Kansas vs. U.S.

Total Debt Outstanding

Kansas's per capita state and local debt registered $3,130 in 1996, ranking 40th in the nation and trailing the U.S. average of $4,409 by 29%. From 1962 to 1996, real per capita state and local debt outstanding increased by 75%, versus an increase of 120% in the U.S. average.

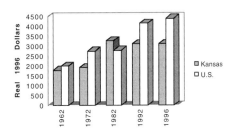

Real Per Capita State and Local Debt Outstanding: Kansas vs. U.S.

Government Employees

Kansas's state and local government employees (full-time equivalent, or FTE) per 10,000 population registered 627.3 in 1997, ranking 7th in the nation and exceeding the U.S. average of 531.1 by 18%. From 1962 to 1996, state and local FTE employees per 10,000 population increased by 75%, compared with an increase in the U.S. average of 66%.

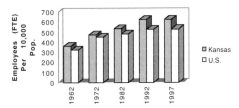

State and Local Government Employees (FTE) Per 10,000 Population: Kansas vs. U.S.

Per Capita Federal Government Expenditures, 1998

	1998	Ranking
Kans.	$5,107	31st
U.S.	$5,491	

Per capita federal spending in Kansas trailed the national average by 7%.

EDUCATION

Total Education Spending

Kansas's per capita state and local education spending registered $1,651 in 1996, ranking 15th in the nation and topping the U.S. average of $1,503 by 10%. From 1962 to 1996, real per capita total education spending increased by 172%, versus an increase in the U.S. average of 173%.

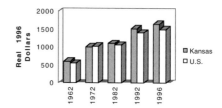

Real Per Capita State and Local Education Spending: Kansas vs. U.S.

Per Pupil Spending

Kansas's per pupil public school spending registered $5,669 in 1998, ranking 31st in the nation and trailing the U.S. average of $6,131 by 8%. From 1970 to 1998, Kansas's real per pupil public school spending increased by 119%, compared with a 120% increase in the U.S. average

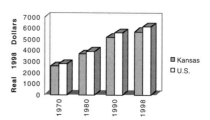

Real Per Pupil Public Schools Spending: Kansas vs. U.S.

Average Public School Teacher Salaries (in 1997–98 dollars)

	1970	1980	1990	1998	1998 Ranking
Kans.	32,592	28,522	36,614	36,811	24th
U.S.	36,934	33,272	39,956	39,385	

In 1998, the average public school teacher salary in Kansas trailed the U.S. average by 7%. From 1970 to 1998, the real average teacher salary in Kansas increased by 13%, versus an increase in the U.S. average of 7%.

Pupil/Teacher Ratio, Fall 1996

	Ratio	Rank
Kans.	15.1	13th
U.S.	17.1	

Teachers/Staff, Fall 1996

	Percent	Rank
Kans.	53.2	19th
U.S.	52.1	

Public School 4th-Grade Reading Proficiency, 1998

	Average	Rank (out of 40 states)
Kans.	222	8th
U.S.	215	

Public School 8th-Grade Reading Proficiency, 1998

	Average	Rank (out of 37 states)
Kans.	268	5th
U.S.	261	

Average Math SAT Scores

	1972	1982	1992	1998	Percentage Taking SAT in 1998
Kans.	560	562	562	585	9
U.S.	509	493	501	512	43

Average Verbal SAT Scores

	1972	1982	1992	1998	Percentage Taking SAT in 1998
Kans.	582	575	562	582	9
U.S.	530	504	500	505	43

Expenditures by Public Institutions of Higher Education Per Full-Time-Equivalent Student, 1996

	FTE Student Spending	Rank
Kans.	$11,364	39th
U.S.	$12,343	

Per-FTE-student spending in public institutions of higher education trailed the U.S. average by 8%.

Per Full-Time-Equivalent Student Revenues from Federal, State, and Local Governments for Public Institutions of Higher Education, 1996

	FTE Student Government Revenues	Rank
Kans.	$7,635	30th
U.S.	$8,101	

Per-FTE-student-government revenues in public institutions of higher education trailed the U.S. average by 6%.

Average Salary for Full-Time Professors at Public Universities, 1997

	Average	Rank
Kans.	$62,199	41st
U.S.	$72,599	

The average full-time public university professor salary trailed the U.S. average by 14%.

ECONOMY AND BUSINESS

Economic Growth

Over the period of 1977 to 1997, Kansas's real gross state product (GSP) grew by 50.1%—ranking 39th in the nation—as compared with real U.S. gross domestic product (GDP), expanding by 70.1%

At $71.7 billion in 1997, Kansas's GSP ranked as 31st largest in the nation.

From 1993 to 1997, Kansas's annual real GSP growth averaged 2.94%—ranking 36th in the nation—as compared with annual real U.S. GDP growth, averaging 3.08%.

**Real Economic Growth
1977-1997: Kansas vs. U.S.**

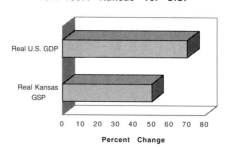

Job Growth

	Growth in Employee Payrolls (Nonagricultural) 1962–98	Ranking
Kans.	128.8%	33d
U.S.	126.5%	

	Average Annual Growth in Employee Payrolls (Nonagricultural) 1993–98	Ranking
Kans.	3.30%	16th
U.S.	2.98%	

Per Capita Disposable Income, 1997

	1997	Ranking
Kans.	$20,594	24th
U.S.	$21,607	

Per capita disposable income trailed the U.S. average by 5%.

	Real Growth 1962–97	Ranking
Kans.	115.1%	28th
U.S.	116.7%	

	Average Annual Real Growth 1993–97	Ranking
Kans.	1.50%	34th
U.S.	1.48%	

Number of Businesses

	1997	Percent with Fewer than 500 Employees
Businesses with Employees	65,155	97.2
Self-employed Individuals	134,000	

New Business Incorporations

	1980	1986	1992	1997
Kans.	4,827	4,350	4,305	4,847

Percentage Change in Annual New Business Incorporations, 1980 vs. 1997

	Percent	Ranking
Kans.	0.4	44th
U.S.	49.7	

State Merchandise Exports to the World, 1998 (in millions of dollars)

	1998	Rank
Kans.	$4,402	28th

Small Business Survival Index, 1999

Kansas ranked a rather dismal 40th in terms of its policy environment for entrepreneurship.

Fortune 500 Headquarters in 1999

A total of 2 (ranked 34th)

Labor Union Membership, 1983 vs. 1997

	Percentage of Workers		
	1983	1997	1997 Rank
Kans.	13.7	7.8	40th
U.S.	20.1	14.1	

Homeownership Rate, 1998

	Rate	Rank
Kans.	66.7	35th
U.S.	66.3	

CRIME

Crime Rates Per 100 Residents (rankings from best to worst crime rate)

Total Crime	1960	1970	1980	1990	1998	1998 Ranking
Kans.	0.66	2.14	5.38	5.19	4.86	32d
U.S.	1.04	2.74	5.90	5.82	4.62	

From 1960 to 1998, Kansas's crime rate increased by 636%, versus a U.S. increase of 344%. From 1990 to 1998, Kansas's crime rate dropped by 6%, versus a U.S. decrease of 21%.

Violent Crime	1960	1970	1980	1990	1998	1998 Ranking
Kans.	0.06	0.20	0.39	0.45	0.40	21st
U.S.	0.14	0.36	0.58	0.73	0.57	

From 1960 to 1998, Kansas's violent crime rate increased by 567%, versus a U.S. increase of 344%. From 1990 to 1998, Kansas's violent crime rate decreased by 11%, compared with a national decline of 22%.

Property Crime	1960	1970	1980	1990	1998	1998 Ranking
Kans.	0.61	1.94	4.99	4.75	4.46	34th
U.S.	0.90	2.38	5.32	5.09	4.05	

From 1960 to 1998, Kansas's property crime rate increased by 631%, versus a national increase of 350%. From 1990 to 1998, Kansas's property crime rate decreased by 6%, compared with a national decline of 20%.

Real Per Capita Police Protection Spending (in real 1996 dollars)

	1962	1972	1982	1992	1996	1996 Ranking
Kans.	32	56	83	117	142	26th
U.S.	51	95	114	148	168	

In 1996, per capita state and local police protection spending in Kansas trailed the U.S. average by 15%. From 1962 to 1996, real per capita state and local police protection spending increased by 344%, versus an increase of 229% in the U.S. average.

Prisoners in State and Federal Prisons Per 1,000 Population

	1980	1990	1996	1996 Ranking
Kans.	1.05	2.33	3.01	32d
U.S.	1.46	3.11	4.45	

From 1980 to 1996, prisoners per 1,000 population increased by 187%, versus a U.S. increase of 205%.

HEALTH CARE

Health-Care Spending

Kansas's per capita state and local health-care spending registered $131 in 1996, ranking 27th in the nation and lagging behind the U.S. average of $151 by 13%. From 1962 to 1996, Kansas's real per capita state and local health-care spending increased by 836%, versus an increase of 739% in the U.S. average.

Real Per Capita State and Local Health Care Spending: Kansas vs. U.S.

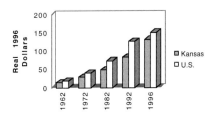

Hospital Spending

Kansas's per capita state and local hospital spending registered $257 in 1996, ranking 21st in the nation and trailing the U.S. average of $266 by 3%. From 1962 to 1996, Kansas's real per capita state and local hospital spending increased by 179%, as opposed to an increase of 189% in the U.S. average.

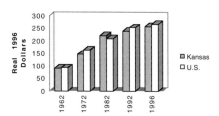

Real Per Capita State and Local Hospital Spending: Kansas vs. U.S.

Medicaid, 1997

	Spending Per Recipient	Ranking
Kans.	$3,944	20th
U.S.	$3,681	

Kansas's per-recipient Medicaid spending exceeded the U.S. average by 7%.

ENVIRONMENT

Parks and Recreation Spending

Kansas's per capita state and local parks and recreation spending registered $53 in 1996, ranking 33d in the nation and trailing the U.S. average of $72 by 26%. From 1962 to 1996, real per capita state and local parks and recreation spending increased by 489%, versus a 213% increase in the U.S. average.

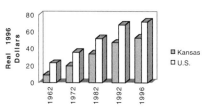

Real Per Capita State and Local Parks and Recreation Spending: Kansas vs. U.S.

State and Local Natural Resources Spending, 1996

	Per Capita	Ranking
Kans.	$73	20th
U.S.	$60	

Per capita state and local natural resources spending in Kansas exceeded the U.S. average by 22%.

State Parks Revenues as a Share of Operating Expenses, 1997

	Percent	Rank
Kans.	52	16th
U.S.	42	

Percentage of Land Owned by the Federal Government, 1996

	Percent	Rank
Kans.	0.7	46th
U.S.	24.8	

SOCIETY AND DEMOGRAPHICS

Population

Kansas's 1998 population of 2.629 million ranked 32d in the nation.

Population Growth, 1990–98

	Percentage Change in Population	Ranking
Kans.	6.75	33d
U.S.	8.66	

	Net International Migration	Ranking
Kans.	24,830	31st

	Net Domestic Migration	Ranking
Kans.	−12,804	33d

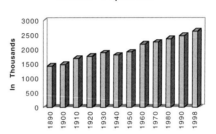

Kansas Population

Infant Mortality Rate, 1998

	Percent	Rank
Kans.	7.3	22d
U.S.	6.4	

Percentage of Births of Low Birthweight, 1997

	Percent	Rank
Kans.	6.9	35th
U.S.	7.5	

Percentage of Live Births to Unmarried Women, 1997

	Percent	Rank
Kans.	27.6	39th
U.S.	32.4	

Abortion Rate—Abortions Per 1,000 Women Ages 15–44, 1995

	Rate	Rank
Kans.	18.3	22d
U.S.	22.9	

LIFESTYLE

Percentage of Households with Computers, 1998

	Percent	Rank
Kans.	43.7	18th

Percentage of Households with Internet Access, 1998

	Percent	Rank
Kans.	25.7	25th

State Arts Agency Spending, 1999

	Per Capita	Rank
Kans.	$0.56	41st
U.S.	$1.35	

Per capita state arts spending in 1999 trailed the U.S. average by 59%.

Major League Sports Facilities

Year Opened/ Refurb.	Stadium/ Arena	Home Team	Millions of Nominal Dollars		Millions of Real 1997 Dollars	
			Estimated Total Cost	Estimated Taxpayer Cost	Estimated Total Cost	Estimated Taxpayer Cost
1975	Kemper Arena	Kings (NBA) 1975–85	$22.0	$22.0	$65.7	$65.7

KENTUCKY

In his 17-year Hall-of-Fame career as a major league baseball pitcher, it is hard to imagine that Jim Bunning (R) faced a tougher contest than his razor-thin victory in 1998 to become a U.S. senator. Well, then again, let us not get carried away. After all, Bunning did pitch a no-hitter in 1958, and then a perfect game in 1964.

Bunning's tough win over Scotty Baesler (himself a former college basketball star at the University of Kentucky) was just the latest victory for surging Kentucky Republicans. The GOP now holds five of Kentucky's six seats in the U.S. House of Representatives and both Senate seats. Kentucky Republicans also have boosted their state senate numbers from 8 in 1990 to 20 in 1999. In July and August of 1999, two Democratic state senators switched to the Republicans, creating a GOP majority. According to news reports, Republicans only held a state legislative majority in Kentucky once—in the state house in 1920.

However, the GOP also inexplicably stumbled in 1999, when the party and leading GOPer Senator Mitch McConnell failed to come up with a respectable challenger to Democrat Governor Paul Patton, who had won by a less than breathtaking margin of 51%–49% in 1995. It just goes to show, no matter what the recent trends, few political parties can afford to get lazy or cocky—or both.

As for how state politicians have actually performed, government spending is on the low side compared with the national average. Major taxes also compare favorably, except for income levies. Unfortunately, if you are going to have one particular tax running on the high side, you do not want it to be income taxes, because they directly affect critical economic decisions regarding work, investment, and entrepreneurship.

Meanwhile, per capita state and local debt in Kentucky took a big leap between 1982 and 1992, leaving the state with one of the highest debt burdens in the nation. Kentucky politicians will have to be quite frugal to ensure that this borrowing binge does not translate into higher taxes down the road.

Other indicators point to the state being rather people friendly. Kentucky seems to be relatively proficient in protecting life, limb, and property, as crime rates are very low. And while the state's overall population growth has lagged behind that of the nation, Kentucky is a rather large net importer of people from other states. In addition, recent economic performance has generally been just above average.

If it can reduce those antigrowth income taxes, even with ongoing government threats looming around tobacco (the top state agricultural product), Kentucky's future in the 21st century should be bright.

POLITICS

Registered Voters

62% Democrats
31% Republicans
7% Other

Federal Officials: Recent Election and Group Ratings

			ACU	ADA	SBSC
U.S. Senators:	Mitch McConnell Jr. (R)		89	6	90
	1996 McConnell (R)	55%			
	Beshear (D)	42%			
	Jim Bunning (R)		NA	NA	NA
	1998 Bunning (R)	50%			
	Baesler (D)	49%			
U.S. Representatives:	Ed Whitfield (R-1)		93	5	75
	1998 Whitfield (R)	55%			
	Barlow (D)	45%			
	Ron Lewis (R-2)		97	1	95
	1998 Lewis (R)	64%			
	Evans (D)	35%			
	Anne Meagher Northup (R-3)	88	3	90	
	1998 Northup (R)	52%			
	Gorman (D)	48%			
	Kenneth Lucas (D-4)		NA	NA	NA
	1998 Lucas (D)	53%			
	Williams (R)	47%			
	Harold Rogers (R-5)		84	11	85
	1998 Rogers (R)	78%			
	Bailey-Bamer (D)	22%			
	Ernest Fletcher (R-6)		NA	NA	NA
	1998 Fletcher (R)	53%			
	Scorsone (D)	46%			
Electoral Votes:	8				
1996 Presidential Results:	Clinton	46%			
	Dole	45%			
	Perot	9%			

State Officials

Governor 1999 Election:	Paul Patton (D)	62%
	Peppy Martin (R)	24%
Lt. Governor:	Steve Henry (D)	
Attorney General:	Ben Chandler (D)	
State Senate:	18 Democrats	
	20 Republicans	
State House:	66 Democrats	
	34 Republicans	

TAXES AND SPENDING

Total Revenues

Kentucky's per capita state and local total revenues registered $4,767 in 1996, ranking 42d in the nation and trailing the U.S. average of $5,706 by 16%. From 1962 to 1996, real per capita state and local revenues increased by 340%, compared with an increase in the national average of 297%.

Taxes

Kentucky's per capita state and local taxes registered $2,166 in 1996, ranking 38th in the nation and trailing the U.S. average of $2,597 by 17%. From 1962 to 1996, real per capita state and local taxes increased by 212%, compared with an increase of 152% in the U.S. average.

Property Taxes

Kentucky's per capita state and local property taxes equaled $363 in 1996, ranking 46th in the nation and trailing the U.S. average of $789 by 54%. From 1962 to 1996, real per capita state and local property taxes increased by 72%, versus a 67% increase in the U.S. average.

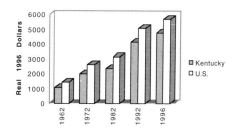

Real Per Capita State and Local Total Revenues: Kentucky vs. U.S.

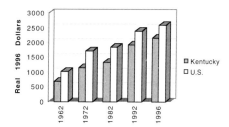

Real Per Capita State and Local Taxes: Kentucky vs. U.S.

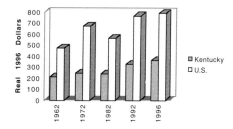

Real Per Capita State and Local Property Taxes: Kentucky vs. U.S.

Sales and Gross Receipts Taxes

Kentucky's per capita state and local sales and gross receipts taxes came in at $827 in 1996, ranking 32d in the nation and trailing the U.S. average of $939 by 12%. From 1962 to 1996, real per capita state and local sales and gross receipts taxes rose by 169%, versus an increase of 214% in the U.S. average.

Income Taxes

Kentucky's per capita state and local income (individual and corporate) taxes registered $730 in 1996, ranking 18th in the nation and topping the U.S. average of $674 by 8%. From 1962 to 1996, real per capita state and local income taxes increased by 739%, versus a 567% increase in the U.S. average.

Personal Income Tax

A rate of 6.0%, ranking 27th in the nation (from lowest tax rate to highest), and comparing with the national average of 5.26%.

Capital Gains Tax

A rate of 6.0%, ranking 30th in the nation (from lowest tax rate to highest), and comparing with the national average of 4.68%.

Corporate Income Tax

A rate of 8.25%, ranking 36th in the nation (from lowest tax rate to highest), and comparing with the national average of 6.63%.

Total Expenditures

Kentucky's per capita state and local total spending registered $4,288 in 1996, ranking 45th in the nation and trailing the U.S. average of $5,268 by 19%. From 1962 to 1996, real per capita state and local total spending increased by 220%, versus an increase of 254% in the U.S. average.

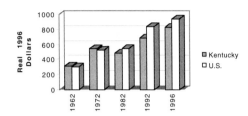

Real Per Capita State and Local Sales and Gross Receipts Taxes: Kentucky vs. U.S.

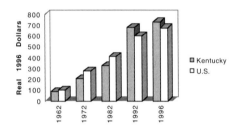

Real Per Capita State and Local Income Taxes: Kentucky vs. U.S.

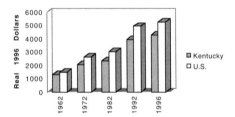

Real Per Capita State and Local Total Expenditures: Kentucky vs. U.S.

Welfare Expenditures

Kentucky's per capita state and local public welfare spending registered $718 in 1996, ranking 18th in the nation and trailing the U.S. average of $729 by 2%. From 1962 to 1996, real per capita state and local public welfare spending increased by 503%, compared with a 488% increase in the U.S. average.

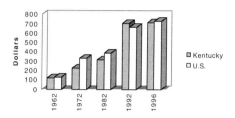

Real Per Capita State and Local Public Welfare Spending: Kentucky vs. U.S.

Welfare Recipients (in thousands)

	1980	1989	3/99	Change 1989–99
Ky.	175	171	100	−42%
U.S.	10,923	10,987	7,335	−33%

Interest on General Debt

Kentucky's per capita state and local interest on general debt registered $296 in 1996, ranking 10th in the nation and exceeding the U.S. average of $222 by 33%. From 1962 to 1996, real per capita state and local interest on general debt increased by 480%, versus an increase of 335% in the U.S. average.

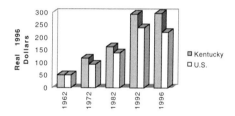

Real Per Capita State and Local Interest on General Debt: Kentucky vs. U.S.

Total Debt Outstanding

Kentucky's per capita state and local debt registered $4,995 in 1996, ranking 15th in the nation and outpacing the U.S. average of $4,409 by 13%. From 1962 to 1996, real per capita state and local debt outstanding increased by 191%, versus an increase of 120% in the U.S. average.

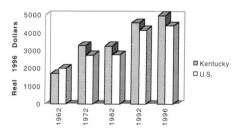

Real Per Capita State and Local Debt Outstanding: Kentucky vs. U.S.

Government Employees

Kentucky's state and local government employees (full-time equivalent, or FTE) per 10,000 population registered 528 in 1997, ranking 31st in the nation and trailing the U.S. average of 531.1 by 1%. From 1962 to 1996, state and local FTE employees per 10,000 population increased by 99%, versus the U.S. average of 66%.

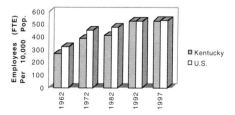

State and Local Government Employees (FTE) Per 10,000 Population: Kentucky vs. U.S.

Per Capita Federal Government Expenditures, 1998

	1998	Ranking
Ky.	$5,884	15th
U.S.	$5,491	

Per capita federal spending in Kentucky exceeded the national average by 7%.

EDUCATION

Total Education Spending

Kentucky's per capita state and local education spending registered $1,372 in 1996, ranking 38th in the nation and lagging behind the U.S. average of $1,503 by 9%. From 1962 to 1996, real per capita total education spending increased by 211%, versus an increase in the U.S. average of 173%.

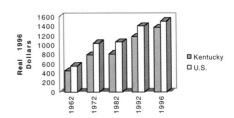

Real Per Capita State and Local Education Spending: Kentucky vs. U.S.

Per Pupil Spending

Kentucky's per pupil public school spending registered $4,442 in 1998, ranking 47th in the nation and trailing the U.S. average of $6,131 by 28%. From 1970 to 1998, Kentucky's real per pupil public school spending increased by 139%, compared with a 120% increase in the U.S. average.

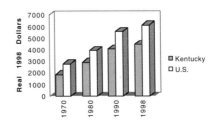

Real Per Pupil Public School Spending: Kentucky vs. U.S.

Average Public School Teacher Salaries (in 1997–98 dollars)

	1970	1980	1990	1998	1998 Ranking
Ky.	29,771	30,251	33,491	34,525	29th
U.S.	36,934	33,272	39,956	39,385	

In 1998, the average public school teacher salary in Kentucky trailed the U.S. average by 12%. From 1970 to 1998, the real average teacher salary in Kentucky increased by 16%, versus an increase in the U.S. average of 7%.

Pupil/Teacher Ratio, Fall 1996

	Ratio	Rank
Ky.	16.7	29th
U.S.	17.1	

Teachers/Staff, Fall 1996

	Percent	Rank
Ky.	52.4	31st
U.S.	52.1	

Public School 4th-Grade Reading Proficiency, 1998

	Average	Rank (out of 40 states)
Ky.	218	13th
U.S.	215	

Public School 8th-Grade Reading Proficiency, 1998

	Average	Rank (out of 37 states)
Ky.	262	17th
U.S.	261	

Public School 4th-Grade Math Proficiency, 1996

	Average	Rank (out of 44 states)
Ky.	220	28th
U.S.	224	

Public School 8th-Grade Math Proficiency, 1996

	Average	Rank (out of 41 states)
Ky.	267	27th
U.S.	271	

Public School 8th-Grade Science Proficiency, 1996

	Average	Rank (out of 41 states)
Ky.	147	22d
U.S.	148	

Average Math SAT Scores

	1972	1982	1992	1998	Percentage Taking SAT in 1998
Ky.	531	532	538	550	13
U.S.	509	493	501	512	43

Average Verbal SAT Scores

	1972	1982	1992	1998	Percentage Taking SAT in 1998
Ky.	553	551	545	547	13
U.S.	530	504	500	505	43

Expenditures by Public Institutions of Higher Education Per Full-Time-Equivalent Student, 1996

	FTE Student Spending	Rank
Ky.	$12,408	24th
U.S.	$12,343	

Per-FTE-student spending in public institutions of higher education exceeded the U.S. average by 1%.

Per Full-Time-Equivalent Student Revenues from Federal, State, and Local Governments for Public Institutions of Higher Education, 1996

	FTE Student Government Revenues	Rank
Ky.	$7,713	27th
U.S.	$8,101	

Per-FTE-student-government revenues in public institutions of higher education trailed the U.S. average by 5%.

Average Salary for Full-Time Professors at Public Universities, 1997

	Average	Rank
Ky.	$68,359	30th
U.S.	$72,599	

The average full-time public university professor salary trailed the U.S. average by 6%.

ECONOMY AND BUSINESS

Economic Growth

Over the period of 1977 to 1997, Kentucky's real gross state product (GSP) grew by 61.9%—ranking 31st in the nation—as compared with real U.S. gross domestic product (GDP), expanding by 70.1%.

At $100.1 billion in 1997, Kentucky's GSP ranked as 26th largest in the nation.

From 1993 to 1997, Kentucky's annual real GSP growth averaged 4.16%—ranking 14th in the nation—as compared with annual real U.S. GDP growth, averaging 3.08%.

**Real Economic Growth
1977-1997: Kentucky vs. U.S.**

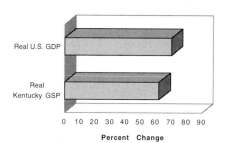

Job Growth

	Growth in Employee Payrolls (Nonagricultural) 1962–98	Ranking
Ky.	160.2%	22d
U.S.	126.5%	

	Average Annual Growth in Employee Payrolls (Nonagricultural) 1993–98	Ranking
Ky.	3.04%	26th
U.S.	2.98%	

Per Capita Disposable Income

	1997	Ranking
Ky.	$17,864	43d
U.S.	$21,607	

Per capita disposable income trailed the U.S. average by 17%.

	Real Growth 1962–97	Ranking
Ky.	136.4%	14th
U.S.	116.7%	

	Average Annual Real Growth 1993–97	Ranking
Ky.	1.67%	24th
U.S.	1.48%	

Number of Businesses

	1997	Percent with Fewer than 500 Employees
Businesses with Employees	78,958	97.2
Self-employed Individuals	136,000	

New Business Incorporations

	1980	1986	1992	1997
Ky.	5,223	7,747	7,155	8,397

Percentage Change in Annual New Business Incorporations, 1980 vs. 1997

	Percent	Ranking
Ky.	60.8	17th
U.S.	49.7	

State Merchandise Exports to the World, 1998 (in millions of dollars)

	1998	Rank
Ky.	$7,440	23d

Small Business Survival Index, 1999

Kentucky ranked 22d in terms of its policy environment for entrepreneurship.

Fortune 500 Headquarters in 1999

A total of 6 (ranked 23d)

Labor Union Membership, 1983 vs. 1997

| | Percentage of Workers | | |
	1983	1997	1997 Rank
Ky.	17.9	12.2	26th
U.S.	20.1	14.1	

Homeownership Rate, 1998

	Rate	Rank
Ky.	75.1	3d
U.S.	66.3	

CRIME

Crime Rates Per 100 Residents (rankings from best to worst crime rate)

Total Crime	1960	1970	1980	1990	1998	1998 Ranking
Ky.	0.80	1.92	3.43	3.30	2.89	5th
U.S.	1.04	2.74	5.90	5.82	4.62	

From 1960 to 1998, Kentucky's crime rate increased by 261%, versus a U.S. increase of 344%. From 1990 to 1998, Kentucky's crime rate dropped by 12%, versus a U.S. decrease of 21%.

Violent Crime	1960	1970	1980	1990	1998	1998 Ranking
Ky.	0.10	0.22	0.27	0.39	0.28	11th
U.S.	0.14	0.36	0.58	0.73	0.57	

From 1960 to 1998, Kentucky's violent crime rate increased by 180%, versus a U.S. increase of 307%. From 1990 to 1998, Kentucky's violent crime rate decreased by 28%, compared with a national decline of 22%.

Property Crime	1960	1970	1980	1990	1998	1998 Ranking
Ky.	0.70	1.70	3.17	2.91	2.61	5th
U.S.	0.90	2.38	5.32	5.09	4.05	

From 1960 to 1998, Kentucky's property crime rate increased by 273%, versus a national increase of 350%. From 1990 to 1998, Kentucky's property crime rate decreased by 10%, compared with a national decline of 20%.

Real Per Capita Police Protection Spending (in real 1996 dollars)

	1962	1972	1982	1992	1996	1996 Ranking
Ky.	32	52	73	88	96	49th
U.S.	51	95	114	148	168	

In 1996, per capita state and local police protection spending in Kentucky trailed the U.S. average by 43%. From 1962 to 1996, real per capita state and local police protection spending increased by 200%, versus an increase of 229% in the U.S. average.

Prisoners in State and Federal Prisons Per 1,000 Population

	1980	1990	1996	1996 Ranking
Ky.	0.98	2.45	3.33	26th
U.S.	1.46	3.11	4.45	

From 1980 to 1996, prisoners per 1,000 population increased by 240%, versus a U.S. increase of 205%.

HEALTH CARE

Health-Care Spending

Kentucky's per capita state and local health-care spending registered $100 in 1996, ranking 35th in the nation and trailing the U.S. average of $151 by 34%. From 1962 to 1996, Kentucky's real per capita state and local health-care spending increased by 614%, versus an increase of 739% in the U.S. average.

Real Per Capita State and Local Health Care Spending: Kentucky vs. U.S.

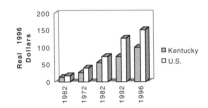

Hospital Spending

Kentucky's per capita state and local hospital spending registered $147 in 1996, ranking 37th in the nation and trailing the U.S. average of $266 by 45%. From 1962 to 1996, Kentucky's real per capita state and local hospital spending increased by 188%, similar to an increase of 189% in the U.S. average.

Real Per Capita State and Local Hospital Spending: Kentucky vs. U.S.

Medicaid, 1997

	Spending Per Recipient	Ranking
Ky.	$3,417	29th
U.S.	$3,681	

Kentucky's per-recipient Medicaid spending trailed the U.S. average by 7%.

ENVIRONMENT

Parks and Recreation Spending

Kentucky's per capita state and local parks and recreation spending registered $41 in 1996, ranking 42d in the nation and trailing the U.S. average of $72 by 43%. From 1962 to 1996, real per capita state and local parks and recreation spending increased by 720%, versus as 213% increase in the U.S. average.

Real Per Capita State and Local Parks and Recreation Spending: Kentucky vs. U.S.

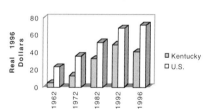

State and Local Natural Resources Spending, 1996

	Per Capita	Ranking
Ky.	$74	19th
U.S.	$60	

Per capita state and local natural resources spending in Kentucky topped the U.S. average by 23%.

State Parks Revenues as a Share of Operating Expenses, 1997

	Percent	Rank
Ky.	65	10th
U.S.	42	

Percentage of Land Owned by the Federal Government, 1996

	Percent	Rank
Ky.	4.2	28th
U.S.	24.8	

SOCIETY AND DEMOGRAPHICS

Population

Kentucky's 1998 population of 3.936 million ranked 25th in the nation.

Population Growth 1990–98

	Percentage Change in Population	Ranking
Ky.	6.75	29th
U.S.	8.66	

	Net International Migration	Ranking
Ky.	13,803	38th

	Net Domestic Migration	Ranking
Ky.	90,068	16th

Kentucky Population

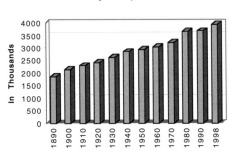

Infant Mortality Rate, 1998

	Percent	Rank
Ky.	7.7	15th
U.S.	6.4	

Percentage of Births of Low Birthweight, 1997

	Percent	Rank
Ky.	7.8	18th
U.S.	7.5	

Percentage of Live Births to Unmarried Women, 1997

	Percent	Rank
Ky.	29.5	33d
U.S.	32.4	

Abortion Rate—Abortions Per 1,000 Women Ages 15–44, 1995

	Rate	Rank
Ky.	8.8	45th
U.S.	22.9	

LIFESTYLE

Percentage of Households with Computers, 1998

	Percent	Rank
Ky.	35.9	43d

Percentage of Households with Internet Access, 1998

	Percent	Rank
Ky.	21.1	44th

State Arts Agency Spending, 1999

	Per Capita	Rank
Ky.	$1.01	24th
U.S.	$1.35	

Per capita state arts spending in 1999 trailed the U.S. average by 25%.

Major League Sports Facilities

None

LOUISIANA

In the 1989 movie *Blaze*, Paul Newman, portraying former Louisiana Governor Earl Long, declares that his political entourage is "the finest bunch of yes-men ever assembled." One gets the feeling that such a statement neatly summarizes much of the political scene in Louisiana today.

Earl Long had a good teacher, his older brother Huey, who also was governor from 1928 to 1931, before being elected to the United States Senate. Huey Long's egalitarian "share the wealth" programs were seen as a threat by Franklin Roosevelt and many believe were instrumental in forcing the four-term democratic president to embrace liberal programs such as Social Security.

Louisiana has long been a study in contrast. Blacks versus whites, Cajuns versus Baptists, and New Orleans versus the rest of the state. LSU Professor David Pearlmutter observed, "Until Huey Long built roads in the 1930s, people in New Orleans didn't even know there were other parts of the state, nor did they care." The only things the citizens of the state seemed to have in common was their poverty and acceptance of rogue politicians.

One of us attended a meeting of policy wonks in New Orleans in the early 1990s, and the Louisiana folks declared you do not know what political corruption is until you have seen Louisiana. So comfortable are Louisianans with their misery that many even seem to object to the premise that things could or should be better. When Baton Rouge Congressman Henson Moore ran against John Breaux in 1986, he asserted that things were picking up under Reagonomics. Breaux responded with a classic radio commercial featuring a poor Louisianan with a thick Cajun accent, "Things are pickin' up alright. First they pick up my pickup truck, then they take my Evenrude. I'm afraid to go home; that might be gone too."

Though outspent two to one, Breaux defeated Moore.

In the 1995 gubernatorial election, Democrat Cleo Fields remarked, "I'm tired of Louisiana being last in everything good and first in everything bad." Fields was defeated by Republican Mike Foster. Your other humble coauthor had a chance to chat with Governor Foster. When asked about crime and corruption in the state—Louisiana has a very high crime rate and lots of people in jail—Foster admitted it might takes years to fix things.

Make no mistake, given the controversial and scandal-plagued former Governor Edwin Edwards (D), former Ku Klux Klan leader David Duke periodically popping up on the political scene, and a long line of other rogues in Louisiana politics over the years, Governor Foster (R) seemed to be a welcome change, if not so much for what he is, as for what he is not.

It should be noted that even with Foster as governor and two prominent Democrats becoming Republicans in recent years—former Governor Buddy Roemer and U.S. Representative Billy Tauzin—Louisiana remains a fairly friendly place to Democrats in the increasingly Republican South. For example, despite the fact that between 1993 and 1999 Republicans picked up one Louisiana congressional seat (thanks to Tauzin's switch), Louisiana's two U.S. Senate seats and both state legislative houses stayed in Democratic hands.

As for the size and burden of government, taxes and spending generally rank low or very low relative to the rest of the nation. As one might expect, however, given the state's political history, patronage is big. State and local government employees as a share of population rate among the most lavish in the United States.

Meanwhile, according to various measures, education performance in the state has been dismal. While Louisiana has a small charter school program, as noted in the Heritage Foundation's *School Choice 1999*, a visionary bill proposed by Republican State Senator Tom Greene to phase in the use of school vouchers over a dozen years was defeated in 1997.

As for the economy, as laid out in the charts and numbers below, Louisiana offers a mixed record. For example, a long-term perspective on real economic growth shows Louisiana badly lagging behind the nation (ranking 50th in the nation over the period of 1977 to 1997), but more recent data reveals an upward trend. Disposable income growth has been very good, and job creation runs above average. However, population growth in recent years (actually since at least 1980) has been quite sluggish, annual new business incorporations have been flat, and Louisiana is a big net exporter of people to other states.

The primary struggle that faces Louisiana in its efforts to excel in the 21st century is the exact same struggle it has fought over the past seven decades: To leave behind pandering populism and fully embrace a pro-opportunity, promarket governing philosophy. Government patronage must give way to the private sector.

POLITICS

Registered Voters

65% Democrats
21% Republicans
14% Other

Federal Officials: Recent Election and Group Ratings

			ACU	ADA	SBSC
U.S. Senators:	John Breaux (D)		46	53	15
	1998 Breaux (D)	64%			
	Donelon (R)	32%			
	Mary Landrieu (D)		12	80	20
	1996 Landrieu (D)	50%			
	Jenkins (R)	49%			
U.S. Representatives:	David Vitter (R-1)		NA	NA	NA
	1999 (spec.) Vitter (R)	51%			
	Treen (R)	49%			

			ACU	ADA	SBSC
William Jefferson (D-2)			8	83	0
1998	Jefferson (D)	86%			
	Reed (D)	9%			
Billy Tauzin (R-3)			73	18	90
1998	Tauzin (R)	NO			
Jim McCrery (R-4)			NA	7	90
1998	McCrery (R)	NO			
John Cooksey (R-5)			94	5	80
1998	Cooksey (R)	NO			
Richard Baker (R-6)			93	1	95
1998	Baker (R)	51%			
	McKeithen (D)	49%			
Chris John (D-7)			55	45	35
1998	John (D)	NO			

Electoral Votes: 9
1996 Presidential Results:

Clinton	52%
Dole	40%
Perot	7%

State Officials

Governor 1999 Election:	Murphy J. "Mike" Foster (R)	62%
	William Jefferson (D)	30%
Lt. Governor:	Kathleen Babineaux Blanco (D)	
Attorney General:	Richard Ieyoub (D)	
State Senate:	25 Democrats	
	14 Republicans	
State House:	78 Democrats	
	27 Republicans	

TAXES AND SPENDING

Total Revenues

Louisiana's per capita state and local total revenues registered $4,932 in 1996, ranking 37th in the nation and trailing the U.S. average of $5,706 by 14%. From 1962 to 1996, real per capita state and local revenues increased by 237%, compared with an increase in the national average of 297%.

Real Per Capita State and Local Total Revenues: Louisiana vs. U.S.

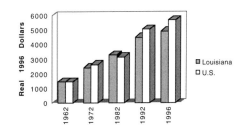

Taxes

Louisiana's per capita state and local taxes registered $1,946 in 1996, ranking 47th in the nation and trailing the U.S. average of $2,597 by 25%. From 1962 to 1996, real per capita state and local taxes increased by 118%, compared with an increase of 152% in the U.S. average.

Property Taxes

Louisiana's per capita state and local property taxes equaled $312 in 1996, ranking 47th in the nation and trailing the U.S. average of $789 by 60%. From 1962 to 1996, real per capita state and local property taxes increased by 54%, versus a 67% increase in the U.S. average.

Sales and Gross Receipts Taxes

Louisiana's per capita state and local sales and gross receipts taxes came in at $1,067 in 1996, ranking 10th in the nation and topping the U.S. average of $939 by 14%. From 1962 to 1996, real per capita state and local sales and gross receipts taxes rose by 242%, versus an increase of 214% in the U.S. average.

Income Taxes

Louisiana's per capita state and local income (individual and corporate) taxes registered $342 in 1996, ranking 43d in the nation and trailing the U.S. average of $674 by 49%. From 1962 to 1996, real per capita state and local income taxes increased by 470%, versus a 567% increase in the U.S. average.

Personal Income Tax

A rate of 3.624%, ranking 14th in the nation (from lowest tax rate to highest), and comparing with the national average of 5.26%.

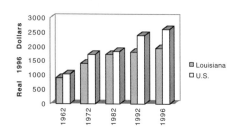

Real Per Capita State and Local Taxes: Louisiana vs. U.S.

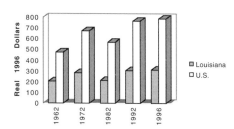

Real Per Capita State and Local Property Taxes: Louisiana vs. U.S.

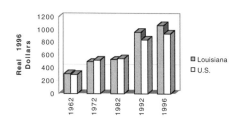

Real Per Capita State and Local Sales and Gross Receipts Taxes: Louisiana vs. U.S.

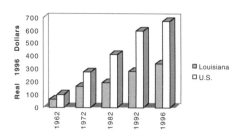

Real Per Capita State and Local Income Taxes: Louisiana vs. U.S.

Capital Gains Tax

A rate of 4.8%, ranking 23d in the nation (from lowest tax rate to highest), and comparing with the national average of 4.68%.

Corporate Income Tax

A rate of 5.2%, ranking 14th in the nation (from lowest tax rate to highest), and comparing with the national average of 6.63%.

Total Expenditures

Louisiana's per capita state and local total spending registered $4,753 in 1996, ranking 33d in the nation and trailing the U.S. average of $5,268 by 10%. From 1962 to 1996, real per capita state and local total spending increased by 207%, versus an increase of 254% in the U.S. average.

Welfare Expenditures

Louisiana's per capita state and local public welfare spending registered $684 in 1996, ranking 24th in the nation and trailing the U.S. average of $729 by 6%. From 1962 to 1996, real per capita state and local public welfare spending increased by 181%, compared with a 488% increase in the U.S. average.

Welfare Recipients (in thousands)

	1980	1989	3/99	Change 1989–99
La.	219	281	111	−60%
U.S.	10,923	10,987	7,335	−33%

Interest on General Debt

Louisiana's per capita state and local interest on general debt registered $289 in 1996, ranking 11th in the nation and exceeding the U.S. average of $222 by 30%. From 1962 to 1996, real per capita state and local interest on general debt increased by 207%, versus an increase of 335% in the U.S. average.

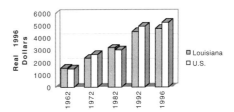

Real Per Capita State and Local Total Expenditures: Louisiana vs. U.S.

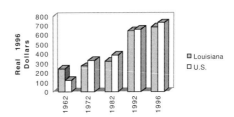

Real Per Capita State and Local Public Welfare Spending: Louisiana vs. U.S.

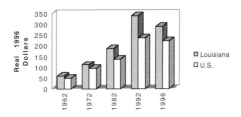

Real Per Capita State and Local Interest on General Debt: Louisiana vs. U.S.

Total Debt Outstanding

Louisiana's per capita state and local debt registered $3,752 in 1996, ranking 31st in the nation and lagging behind the U.S. average of $4,409 by 15%. From 1962 to 1996, real per capita state and local debt outstanding increased by 78%, versus an increase of 120% in the U.S. average.

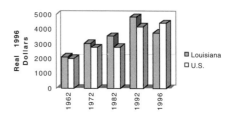

Real Per Capita State and Local Debt Outstanding: Louisiana vs. U.S.

Government Employees

Louisiana's state and local government employees (full-time equivalent, or FTE) per 10,000 population registered 607.7 in 1997, ranking 9th in the nation and topping the U.S. average of 531.1 by 14%. From 1962 to 1996, state and local FTE employees per 10,000 population increased by 71%, topping the U.S. average of 66%.

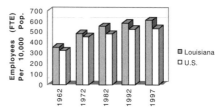

State and Local Government Employees (FTE) Per 10,000 Population: Louisiana vs. U.S.

Per Capita Federal Government Expenditures, 1998

	1998	Ranking
La.	$5,242	27th
U.S.	$5,491	

Per capita federal spending in Louisiana trailed the national average by 5%.

EDUCATION

Total Education Spending

Louisiana's per capita state and local education spending registered $1,299 in 1996, ranking 45th in the nation and lagging behind the U.S. average of $1,503 by 14%. From 1962 to 1996, real per capita total education spending increased by 162%, versus an increase in the U.S. average of 173%.

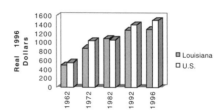

Real Per Capita State and Local Education Spending: Louisiana vs. U.S.

Per Pupil Spending

Louisiana's per pupil public school spending registered $4,483 in 1998, ranking 46th in the nation and trailing the U.S. average of $6,131 by 27%. From 1970 to 1998, Louisiana's real per pupil public school spending increased by 163%, compared with a 120% increase in the U.S. average.

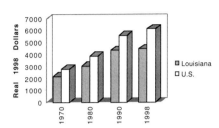

Real Per Pupil Public School Spending: Louisiana vs. U.S.

Average Public School Teacher Salaries (in 1997–98 dollars)

	1970	1980	1990	1998	1998 Ranking
La.	30,092	28,668	30,954	29,650	48th
U.S.	36,934	33,272	39,956	39,385	

In 1998, the average public school teacher salary in Louisiana trailed the U.S. average by 25%. From 1970 to 1998, the real average teacher salary in Louisiana decreased by 1%, versus an increase in the U.S. average of 7%.

Pupil/Teacher Ratio, Fall 1996

	Ratio	Rank
La.	16.6	26th
U.S.	17.1	

Teachers/Staff, Fall 1996

	Percent	Rank
La.	50.3	43d
U.S.	52.1	

Public School 4th-Grade Reading Proficiency, 1998

	Average	Rank (out of 40 states)
La.	204	36th
U.S.	215	

Public School 8th-Grade Reading Proficiency, 1998

	Average	Rank (out of 37 states)
La.	252	34th
U.S.	261	

Public School 4th-Grade Math Proficiency, 1996

	Average	Rank (out of 44 states)
La.	209	41st
U.S.	224	

Public School 8th-Grade Math Proficiency, 1996

	Average	Rank (out of 41 states)
La.	252	39th
U.S.	271	

Public School 8th-Grade Science Proficiency, 1996

	Average	Rank (out of 41 states)
La.	132	40th
U.S.	148	

Average Math SAT Scores

	1972	1982	1992	1998	Percentage Taking SAT in 1998
La.	508	527	540	558	8
U.S.	509	493	501	512	43

Average Verbal SAT Scores

	1972	1982	1992	1998	Percentage Taking SAT in 1998
La.	532	546	547	562	8
U.S.	530	504	500	505	43

Expenditures by Public Institutions of Higher Education Per Full-Time-Equivalent Student, 1996

	FTE Student Spending	Rank
La.	$10,584	47th
U.S.	$12,343	

Per-FTE-student spending in public institutions of higher education trailed the U.S. average by 14%.

Per Full-Time-Equivalent Student Revenues from Federal, State, and Local Governments for Public Institutions of Higher Education, 1996

	FTE Student Government Revenues	Rank
La.	$6,430	47th
U.S.	$8,101	

Per-FTE-student-government revenues in public institutions of higher education trailed the U.S. average by 21%.

Average Salary for Full-Time Professors at Public Universities, 1997

	Average	Rank
La.	$70,607	24th
U.S.	$72,599	

The average full-time public university professor salary trailed the U.S. average by 3%.

ECONOMY AND BUSINESS

Economic Growth

Over the period of 1977 to 1997, Louisiana's real gross state product (GSP) grew by 28.8%—ranking 50th in the nation—as compared with real U.S. gross domestic product (GDP), expanding by 70.1%

At $124.4 billion in 1997, Louisiana's GSP ranked as 23d largest in the nation.

From 1993 to 1997, Louisiana's annual real GSP growth averaged 4.17%—ranking 13th in the nation—as compared with annual real U.S. GDP growth, averaging 3.08%.

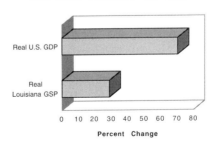

Real Economic Growth 1977-1997: Louisiana vs. U.S.

Real U.S. GDP

Real Louisiana GSP

0 10 20 30 40 50 60 70 80

Percent Change

Job Growth

	Growth in Employee Payrolls (Nonagricultural) 1962–98	Ranking
La.	140.1%	30th
U.S.	126.5%	

	Average Annual Growth in Employee Payrolls (Nonagricultural) 1993–98	Ranking
La.	3.11%	24th
U.S.	2.98%	

Per Capita Disposable Income, 1997

	1997	Ranking
La.	$18,138	40th
U.S.	$21,607	

Per capita disposable income trailed the U.S. average by 16%.

	Real Growth 1962–97	Ranking
La.	138.7%	13th
U.S.	116.7%	

	Average Annual Real Growth 1993–97	Ranking
La.	1.85%	13th
U.S.	1.48%	

Number of Businesses

	1997	Percent with Fewer than 500 Employees
Businesses with Employees	90,539	97.6
Self-employed Individuals	149,000	

New Business Incorporations

	1980	1986	1992	1997
La.	11,308	11,741	10,839	11,152

Percentage Change in Annual New Business Incorporations, 1980 vs. 1997

	Percent	Ranking
La.	−1.4	45th
U.S.	49.7	

State Merchandise Exports to the World, 1998 (in millions of dollars)

	1998	Rank
La.	$4,392	30th

Small Business Survival Index, 1999

Louisiana ranked 19th in terms of its policy environment for entrepreneurship.

Fortune 500 Headquarters in 1999

A total of 1 (ranked 38th)

Labor Union Membership, 1983 vs. 1997

	Percentage of Workers		
	1983	1997	1997 Rank
La.	13.8	7.0	42d
U.S.	20.1	14.1	

Homeownership Rate, 1998

	Rate	Rank
La.	66.6	37th
U.S.	66.3	

CRIME

Crime Rates Per 100 Residents (rankings from best to worst crime rate)

Total Crime	1960	1970	1980	1990	1998	1998 Ranking
La.	0.95	2.40	5.45	6.49	6.10	47th
U.S.	1.04	2.74	5.90	5.82	4.62	

From 1960 to 1998, Louisiana's crime rate increased by 542%, versus a U.S. increase of 344%. From 1990 to 1998, Louisiana's crime rate dropped by 6%, versus a U.S. decrease of 21%.

Violent Crime	1960	1970	1980	1990	1998	1998 Ranking
La.	0.14	0.41	0.67	0.90	0.78	45th
U.S.	0.14	0.36	0.58	0.73	0.57	

From 1960 to 1998, Louisiana's violent crime rate increased by 457%, versus a U.S. increase of 307%. From 1990 to 1998, Louisiana's violent crime rate decreased by 13%, compared with a national decline of 22%.

Property Crime	1960	1970	1980	1990	1998	1998 Ranking
La.	0.80	1.99	4.79	5.59	5.32	46th
U.S.	0.90	2.38	5.32	5.09	4.05	

From 1960 to 1998, Louisiana's property crime rate increased by 565%, versus a national increase of 350%. From 1990 to 1998, Louisiana's property crime rate declined by 5%, compared with a national decline of 20%.

Real Per Capita Police Protection Spending (in real 1996 dollars)

	1962	1972	1982	1992	1996	1996 Ranking
La.	46	72	114	139	157	19th
U.S.	51	95	114	148	168	

In 1996, per capita state and local police protection spending in Louisiana trailed the U.S. average by 7%. From 1962 to 1996, real per capita state and local police protection spending increased by 241%, versus an increase of 229% in the U.S. average.

Prisoners in State and Federal Prisons Per 1,000 Population

	1980	1990	1996	1996 Ranking
La.	2.11	4.41	6.17	4th
U.S.	1.46	3.11	4.45	

From 1980 to 1996, prisoners per 1,000 population increased by 192%, versus a U.S. increase of 205%.

HEALTH CARE

Health-Care Spending

Louisiana's per capita state and local health-care spending registered $106 in 1996, ranking 33d in the nation and trailing the U.S. average of $151 by 30%. From 1962 to 1996, Louisiana's real per capita state and local health-care spending increased by 657%, versus an increase of 739% in the U.S. average.

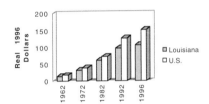

Real Per Capita State and Local Health Care Spending: Louisiana vs. U.S.

Hospital Spending

Louisiana's per capita state and local hospital spending registered $506 in 1996, ranking 4th in the nation and exceeding the U.S. average of $266 by 90%. From 1962 to 1996, Louisiana's real per capita state and local hospital spending increased by 510%, outpacing an increase of 189% in the U.S. average.

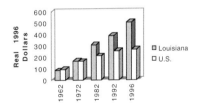

Real Per Capita State and Local Hospital Spending: Louisiana vs. U.S.

Medicaid, 1992

	Spending Per Recipient	Ranking
La.	$3,131	35th
U.S.	$3,681	

Louisiana's per-recipient Medicaid spending trailed the U.S. average by 15%.

ENVIRONMENT

Parks and Recreation Spending

Louisiana's per capita state and local parks and recreation spending registered $60 in 1996, ranking 27th in the nation and trailing the U.S. average of $72 by 17%. From 1962 to 1996, real per capita state and local parks and recreation spending increased by 329%, versus a 213% increase in the U.S. average.

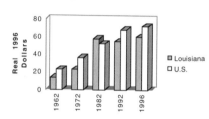

Real Per Capita State and Local Parks and Recreation Spending: Louisiana vs. U.S.

State and Local Natural Resources Spending, 1996

	Per Capita	Ranking
La.	$86	12th
U.S.	$60	

Per capita state and local natural resources spending in Louisiana topped the U.S. average by 43%.

State Parks Revenues as a Share of Operating Expenses, 1997

	Percent	Rank
La.	23	42d
U.S.	42	

Percentage of Land Owned by the Federal Government, 1996

	Percent	Rank
La.	2.6	34th
U.S.	24.8	

SOCIETY AND DEMOGRAPHICS

Population

Louisiana's 1998 population of 4.369 million ranked 22d in the nation.

Population Growth, 1990–98

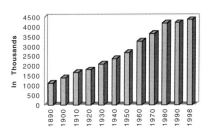

Louisiana   Population

	Percentage Change in Population	Ranking
La.	3.48	40th
U.S.	8.66	

	Net International Migration	Ranking
La.	24,889	30th

	Net Domestic Migration	Ranking
La.	−117,459	41st

Infant Mortality Rate, 1998

	Percent	Rank
La.	9.8	4th
U.S.	6.4	

Percentage of Births of Low Birthweight, 1997

	Percent	Rank
La.	10.2	2d
U.S.	7.5	

Percentage of Live Births to Unmarried Women, 1997

	Percent	Rank
La.	43.9	3d
U.S.	32.4	

Abortion Rate—Abortions Per 1,000 Women Ages 15–44, 1995

	Rate	Rank
La.	14.7	30th
U.S.	22.9	

LIFESTYLE

Percentage of Households with Computers, 1998

	Percent	Rank
La.	31.1	48th

Percentage of Households with Internet Access, 1998

	Percent	Rank
La.	17.8	48th

State Arts Agency Spending, 1999

	Per Capita	Rank
La.	$1.15	21st
U.S.	$1.35	

Per capita state arts spending in 1999 trailed the U.S. average by 15%.

Major League Sports Facilities

Year Opened/ Refurb.	Stadium/ Arena	Home Team	Millions of Nominal Dollars		Millions of Real 1997 Dollars	
			Estimated Total Cost	Estimated Taxpayer Cost	Estimated Total Cost	Estimated Taxpayer Cost
1975	Superdome	Saints (NFL) 1975–present Jazz (NBA) 1975–79	$168.0	$168.0	$501.5	$501.5

MAINE

While a handful of cities—most prominently Milwaukee—have struggled to provide relief for parents and children from an often-moribund public school monopoly through the establishment of school choice programs, Maine took a major step in the opposite direction in the 1980s. Maine officials decided to move away from a more than 200-year-old tradition of allowing parents and children in towns without public schools to choose the private, religious, or public school that best fit their needs and desires.

The Institute for Justice, a legal organization that often helps to advance school choice in the courts, reports that during colonial years, and throughout the 18th and 19th centuries, many towns in Maine provided for their residents' education by paying tuition to private schools—many of them being religious. In 1903, the Maine legislature passed a law guaranteeing a high-school education and required that towns not operating secondary schools pay tuition for residents to attend private or public schools elsewhere, with the state reimbursing half the cost. However, in 1980 Maine's Attorney General Joseph Brennan declared that "tuitioning" students who attend religious schools violated the establishment clause of the U.S. Constitution. The state legislature then passed a law excluding religious schools from the tuitioning system.

In July 1997, the Institute for Justice joined with five families to file a lawsuit—*Bagley, et al. v. Raymond School Department, et al.*—alleging that the Maine law excluding religious schools from its tuitioning system violates the U.S. Constitution's guarantee of equal protection and free exercise of religion. In early 1999, Maine's highest court backed up the current law; and in October 1999, the U.S. Supreme Court decided not to review the case. Nonetheless, the alteration of Maine's tuitioning law in the early 1980s clearly was discriminatory against religion, religious institutions, and people of faith. In addition, the discriminatory provision rests on the increasingly accepted, though grossly mistaken assumption that when the First Amendment states that "Congress shall make no law respecting an establishment of religion," the intent was to completely separate religion and government. In reality, of course, this was meant to prevent the establishment of an official state church, as was the case in England.

As the Institute for Justice points out, most recent court decisions have run counter to the Maine decision. For example, the Wisconsin Supreme Court supported the inclusion of religious schools in Milwaukee's educational choice program. The U.S Supreme Court has prohibited the University of Virginia from barring funding for a student religious publication while funding nonreligious publications, and it invalidated a Tennessee law barring the clergy from public office.

Allowing parents and children at all income levels to choose their schools ultimately is about choice and freedom. Unfortunately, choice and freedom in Maine are not only restrained when it comes to choosing a religious school, but are also restrained in terms of taxes. Maine imposes a heavy property tax burden and inflicts some of the most onerous income tax rates in the nation. No doubt, high taxes limit choice and freedom. On the flip side, government handouts give "freedom" a bad name by fostering a disconnect between actions and responsibility. In Maine, both public welfare and Medicaid spending, for example, far exceed the U.S. averages.

As for the economy, Maine's rates of growth in terms of real gross state product, population, jobs, and real per capita disposable income have badly lagged behind the rest of the nation in recent years. The state also offers a rather poor climate for small business and entrepreneurs—the necessary backbone of any strong economy.

However, it must be acknowledged that freedom is given a big boost in Maine because of the state's very low rate of crime. Government's duty to protect individuals, families, and businesses from the ravages of crime is fundamental to the well-being of a free society. Maine not only fulfills this duty far better than most other states, but for good measure, it is accomplished at a relative bargain price, as both per capita police spending and prisoners as a share of population rank quite low compared to the rest of the nation. That is a tribute not only to law enforcement and the justice system, but also to the people of Maine themselves.

POLITICS

Registered Voters

32% Democrats
29% Republicans
39% Other

Elected Officials: Recent Election and Group Ratings

			ACU	ADA	SBSC
U.S. Senators:	Olympia Snowe (R)		50	41	60
	1994　Snowe (R)	60%			
	Andrews (D)	36%			
	Susan Collins (R)		42	43	70
	1996　Collins (R)	49%			
	Brennan (D)	43%			
U.S. Representatives:	Thomas Allen (D-1)		4	98	10
	1998　Allen (D)	60%			
	Connelly (R)	36%			
	John Baldacci (D-2)		10	90	15
	1998　Baldacci (D)	76%			
	Reisman (R)	24%			
Electoral Votes:	4				
1996 Presidential Results:	Clinton	52%			
	Dole	31%			
	Perot	14%			

State Officials

Governor 1998 Election:	Angus King Jr. (I)	59%
	James Longley (R)	19%
	Thomas Connolly (D)	12%
Attorney General:	Andrew Ketterer (D)	
State Senate:	20 Democrats	
	14 Republicans	
	1 Independent	
State General Assembly:	79 Democrats	
	71 Republicans	
	1 Independent	

TAXES AND SPENDING

Total Revenues

Maine's per capita state and local total revenues registered $4,943 in 1996, ranking 36th in the nation and trailing the U.S. average of $5,706 by 13%. From 1962 to 1996, real per capita state and local revenues increased by 294%, compared with an increase in the national average of 297%.

Taxes

Maine's per capita state and local taxes registered $2,600 in 1996, ranking 17th in the nation and exceeding the U.S. average of $2,597 by 0.1%. From 1962 to 1996, real per capita state and local taxes increased by 180%, compared with an increase of 152% in the U.S. average.

Property Taxes

Maine's per capita state and local property taxes equaled $1,088 in 1996, ranking 9th in the nation and exceeding the U.S. average of $789 by 38%. From 1962 to 1996, real per capita state and local property taxes increased by 121%, versus a 67% increase in the U.S. average.

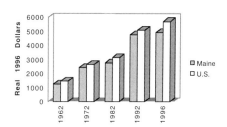

Real Per Capita State and Local Total Revenues: Maine vs. U.S.

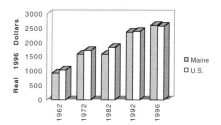

Real Per Capita State and Local Taxes: Maine vs. U.S.

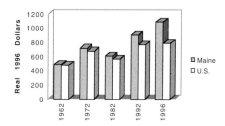

Real Per Capita State and Local Property Taxes: Maine vs. U.S.

Sales and Gross Receipts Taxes

Maine's per capita state and local sales and gross receipts taxes came in at $754 in 1996, ranking 38th in the nation and trailing the U.S. average of $939 by 20%. From 1962 to 1996, real per capita state and local sales and gross receipts taxes increased by 122%, versus an increase of 214% in the U.S. average.

Income Taxes

Maine's per capita state and local income (individual and corporate) taxes registered $628 in 1996, ranking 28th in the nation and trailing the U.S. average of $674 by 7%. Maine imposed no income taxes until both personal and corporate income taxes were imposed in 1969.

Personal Income Tax

A rate of 8.5%, ranking 45th in the nation (from lowest tax rate to highest), and comparing with the national average of 5.26%.

Capital Gains Tax

A rate of 8.5%, ranking 46th in the nation (from lowest tax rate to highest), and comparing with the national average of 4.68%.

Corporate Income Tax

A rate of 8.93%, ranking 40th in the nation (from lowest tax rate to highest), and comparing to the U.S. average of 6.63%.

Total Expenditures

Maine's per capita state and local total spending registered $4,832 in 1996, ranking 28th in the nation and lagging behind the U.S. average of $5,268 by 8%. From 1962 to 1996, real per capita state and local total spending increased by 261%, versus an increase of 254% in the U.S. average.

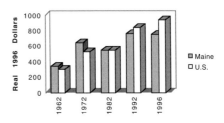

Real Per Capita State and Local Sales and Gross Receipts Taxes: Maine vs. U.S.

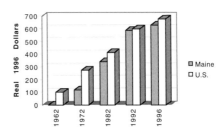

Real Per Capita State and Local Income Taxes: Maine vs. U.S.

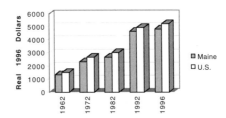

Real Per Capita State and Local Total Expenditures: Maine vs. U.S.

Welfare Expenditures

Maine's per capita state and local public welfare spending registered $1,026 in 1996, ranking 4th in the nation and outpacing the U.S. average of $729 by 41%. From 1962 to 1996, real per capita state and local public welfare spending increased by 727%, compared with a 488% increase in the U.S. average.

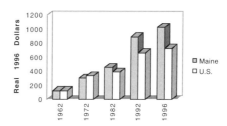

Real Per Capita State and Local Public Welfare Spending: Maine vs. U.S.

Welfare Recipients (in thousands)

	1980	1989	3/99	Change 1989–99
Maine	58	53	34	−36%
U.S.	10,923	10,987	7,335	−33%

Interest on General Debt

Maine's per capita state and local interest on general debt registered $206 in 1996, ranking 24th in the nation and trailing the U.S. average of $222 by 7%. From 1962 to 1996, real per capita state and local interest on general debt increased by 544%, versus an increase of 335% in the U.S. average.

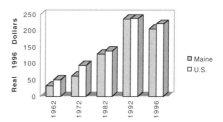

Real Per Capita State and Local Interest on General Debt: Maine vs. U.S.

Total Debt Outstanding

Maine's per capita state and local debt registered $3,766 in 1996, ranking 29th in the nation and trailing the U.S. average of $4,409 by 15%. From 1962 to 1996, real per capita state and local debt outstanding increased by 205%, versus an increase of 120% in the U.S. average.

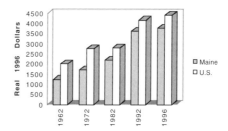

Real Per Capita State and Local Debt Outstanding: Maine vs. U.S.

Government Employees

Maine's state and local government employees (full-time equivalent, or FTE) per 10,000 population registered 534.5 in 1997, ranking 27th in the nation and exceeding the U.S. average of 531.1 by 0.6%. From 1962 to 1996, state and local FTE employees per 10,000 population increased by 77%, compared with an increase in the U.S. average of 66%.

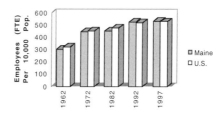

State and Local Government Employees (FTE) Per 10,000 Population: Maine vs. U.S.

Per Capita Federal Government Expenditures, 1998

	1998	Ranking
Maine	$5,999	12th
U.S.	$5,491	

Per capita federal spending in Maine exceeded the national average by 9%.

EDUCATION

Total Education Spending

Maine's per capita state and local education spending registered $1,483 in 1996, ranking 29th in the nation and trailing the U.S. average of $1,503 by 1%. From 1962 to 1996, real per capita total education spending increased by 205%, versus an increase in the U.S. average of 173%.

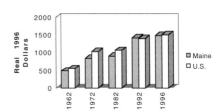

Real Per Capita State and Local Education Spending: Maine vs. U.S.

Per Pupil Spending

Maine's per pupil public school spending registered $6,327 in 1998, ranking 19th in the nation and exceeding the U.S. average of $6,131 by 3%. From 1970 to 1998, Maine's real per pupil public school spending increased by 163%, compared with a 120% increase in the U.S. average.

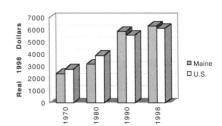

Real Per Pupil Public School Spending: Maine vs. U.S.

Average Public School Teacher Salaries (in 1997–98 dollars)

	1970	1980	1990	1998	1998 Ranking
Maine	32,421	27,232	34,241	34,349	31st
U.S.	36,934	33,272	39,956	39,385	

In 1998, the average public school teacher salary in Maine trailed the U.S. average by 13%. From 1970 to 1998, the real average teacher salary in Maine increased by 6%, versus an increase in the U.S. average of 7%.

Pupil/Teacher Ratio, Fall 1996

	Ratio	Rank
Maine	13.7	2d
U.S.	17.1	

Teachers/Staff, Fall 1996

	Percent	Rank
Maine	51.9	33d
U.S.	52.1	

Public School 4th-Grade Reading Proficiency, 1998

	Average	Rank (out of 40 states)
Maine	225	4th
U.S.	215	

Public School 8th-Grade Reading Proficiency, 1998

	Average	Rank (out of 37 states)
Maine	273	1st
U.S.	261	

Public School 4th-Grade Math Proficiency, 1996

	Average	Rank (out of 44 states)
Maine	232	1st
U.S.	224	

Public School 8th-Grade Math Proficiency, 1996

	Average	Rank (out of 41 states)
Maine	284	1st
U.S.	271	

Public School 8th-Grade Science Proficiency, 1996

	Average	Rank (out of 41 states)
Maine	163	1st
U.S.	148	

Average Math SAT Scores

	1972	1982	1992	1998	Percentage Taking SAT in 1998
Maine	506	491	488	501	68
U.S.	509	493	501	512	43

Average Verbal SAT Scores

	1972	1982	1992	1998	Percentage Taking SAT in 1998
Maine	529	506	500	504	68
U.S.	530	504	500	505	43

Expenditures by Public Institutions of Higher Education Per Full-Time-Equivalent Student, 1996

	FTE Student Spending	Rank
Maine	$13,202	16th
U.S.	$12,343	

Per-FTE-student spending in public institutions of higher education topped the U.S. average by 7%.

Per Full-Time-Equivalent Student Revenues From Federal, State, and Local Governments for Public Institutions of Higher Education, 1996

	FTE Student Government Revenues	Rank
Maine	$7,968	25th
U.S.	$8,101	

Per-FTE-student-government revenues in public institutions of higher education lagged behind the U.S. average by 2%.

Average Salary for Full-Time Professors at Public Universities, 1997

	Average	Rank
Maine	$60,026	44th
U.S.	$72,599	

The average full-time public university professor salary trailed the U.S. average by 17%.

ECONOMY AND BUSINESS

Economic Growth

Over the period of 1977 to 1997, Maine's real gross state product (GSP) grew by 62.9%—ranking 30th in the nation—as compared with real U.S. gross domestic product (GDP), expanding by 70.1%.

At $30.2 billion in 1997, Maine's GSP ranked as 43d largest in the nation.

From 1993 to 1997, Maine's annual real GSP growth averaged 2.20%—ranking 46th in the nation—as compared with annual real U.S. GDP growth averaging 3.08%.

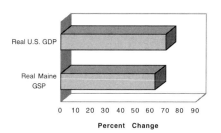

Real Economic Growth 1977-1997: Maine vs. U.S.

Real U.S. GDP

Real Maine GSP

0 10 20 30 40 50 60 70 80 90

Percent Change

Job Growth

	Growth in Employee Payrolls (Nonagricultural) 1962–98	Ranking
Maine	103.8%	38th
U.S.	126.5%	

	Average Annual Growth in Employee Payrolls (Nonagricultural) 1993–98	Ranking
Maine	2.16%	43d
U.S.	2.98%	

Per Capita Disposable Income, 1997

	1997	Ranking
Maine	$19,053	37th
U.S.	$21,607	

Per capita disposable income trailed the U.S. average by 12%.

	Real Growth 1962–97	Ranking
Maine	131.6%	16th
U.S.	116.7%	

	Average Annual Real Growth 1993–97	Ranking
Maine	1.39%	40th
U.S.	1.48%	

Number of Businesses

	1997	Percent with Fewer than 500 Employees
Businesses with Employees	36,660	97.6
Self-employed Individuals	71,000	

New Business Incorporations

	1980	1986	1992	1997
Maine	1,698	3,036	2,431	2,823

Percentage Change in Annual New Business Incorporations, 1980 vs. 1997

	Percent	Ranking
Maine	66.3	16th
U.S.	49.7	

State Merchandise Exports to the World, 1998 (in millions of dollars)

	1998	Rank
Maine	$1,664	40th

Small Business Survival Index, 1999

Maine ranks a very poor 42d in terms of its policy environment for entrepreneurship.

Fortune 500 Headquarters in 1999

A total of 2 (ranked 34th)

Labor Union Membership, 1983 vs. 1997

| | Percentage of Workers | | |
	1983	1997	1997 Rank
Maine	21.0	13.5	24th
U.S.	20.1	14.1	

Homeownership Rate, 1998

	Rate	Rank
Maine	74.6	6th
U.S.	66.3	

CRIME

Crime Rates Per 100 Residents (rankings from best to worst crime rate)

Total Crime	1960	1970	1980	1990	1998	1998 Ranking
Maine	0.54	1.14	4.37	3.70	3.04	6th
U.S.	1.04	2.74	5.90	5.82	4.62	

From 1960 to 1998, Maine's crime rate increased by 463%, versus a U.S. increase of 344%. From 1990 to 1998, Maine's crime rate dropped by 18%, versus a 21% U.S. decline.

Violent Crime	1960	1970	1980	1990	1998	1998 Ranking
Maine	0.03	0.08	0.19	0.14	0.13	4th
U.S.	0.14	0.36	0.58	0.73	0.57	

From 1960 to 1998, Maine's violent crime rate increased by 333%, versus a U.S. increase of 307%. From 1990 to 1998, Maine's violent crime rate decreased by 7%, compared with a national decline of 22%.

Property Crime	1960	1970	1980	1990	1998	1998 Ranking
Maine	0.51	1.06	4.17	3.56	2.91	8th
U.S.	0.90	2.38	5.32	5.09	4.05	

From 1960 to 1998, Maine's property crime rate increased by 471%, versus a national increase of 350%. From 1990 to 1998, Maine's property crime rate decreased by 18%, compared with a national decline of 20%.

Real Per Capita Police Protection Spending (in real 1996 dollars)

	1962	1972	1982	1992	1996	1996 Ranking
Maine	32	56	70	88	104	47th
U.S.	51	96	114	148	168	

In 1996, per capita state and local police protection spending in Maine trailed the U.S. average by 38%. From 1962 to 1996, real per capita state and local police protection spending increased by 225%, versus an increase of 229% in the U.S. average.

Prisoners in State and Federal Prisons Per 1,000 Population

	1980	1990	1996	1996 Ranking
Maine	0.72	1.24	1.15	49th
U.S.	1.46	3.11	4.45	

From 1980 to 1996, prisoners per 1,000 population increased by 60%, versus a U.S. increase of 205%.

HEALTH CARE

Health-Care Spending

Maine's per capita state and local health-care spending registered $151 in 1996, ranking 20th in the nation and equaling the U.S. average of $151. From 1962 to 1996, Maine's real per capita state and local health-care spending increased by 979%, versus an increase of 739% in the U.S. average.

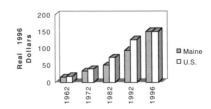

Real Per Capita State and Local Health Care Spending: Maine vs. U.S.

Hospital Spending

Maine's per capita state and local hospital spending registered $84 in 1996, ranking 45th in the nation and trailing the U.S. average of $266 by 68%. From 1962 to 1996, Maine's real per capita state and local hospital spending increased by 40%, as opposed to an increase of 189% in the U.S. average.

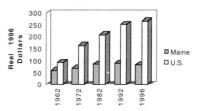

Real Per Capita State and Local Hospital Spending: Maine vs. U.S.

Medicaid, 1997

	Spending Per Recipient	Ranking
Maine	$4,671	12th
U.S.	$3,681	

Maine's per-recipient Medicaid spending exceeded the U.S. average by 27%.

ENVIRONMENT

Parks and Recreation Spending

Maine's per capita state and local parks and recreation spending registered $32 in 1996, ranking 50th in the nation and lagging behind the U.S. average of $72 by 56%. From 1962 to 1996, real per capita state and local parks and recreation spending increased by 540%, versus a 213% increase in the U.S. average.

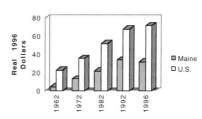

Real Per Capita State and Local Parks and Recreation Spending: Maine vs. U.S.

State and Local Natural Resources Spending, 1996

	Per Capita	Ranking
Maine	$85	14th
U.S.	$60	

Per capita state and local natural resources spending in Maine exceeded the U.S. average by 42%.

State Parks Revenues as a Share of Operating Expenses, 1997

	Percent	Rank
Maine	25	39th
U.S.	42	

Percentage of Land Owned by the Federal Government, 1996

	Percent	Rank
Maine	1.0	44th
U.S.	24.8	

SOCIETY AND DEMOGRAPHICS

Population

Maine's 1998 population of 1.244 million ranked 39th in the nation.

Population Growth, 1990–98

	Percentage Change in Population	Ranking
Maine	1.30	44th
U.S.	8.66	

	Net International Migration	Ranking
Maine	3,484	48th

	Net Domestic Migration	Ranking
Maine	−14,808	35th

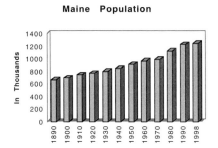

Maine Population

Infant Mortality Rate, 1998

	Percent	Rank
Maine	5.4	44th
U.S.	6.4	

Percentage of Births of Low Birthweight, 1997

	Percent	Rank
Maine	5.9	45th
U.S.	7.5	

Percentage of Live Births to Unmarried Women, 1997

	Percent	Rank
Maine	29.7	32d
U.S.	32.4	

Abortion Rate—Abortions Per 1,000 Women Ages 15–44, 1995

	Rate	Rank
Maine	9.6	42d
U.S.	22.9	

LIFESTYLE

Percentage of Households with Computers, 1998

	Percent	Rank
Maine	43.4	20th

Percentage of Households with Internet Access, 1998

	Percent	Rank
Maine	26.0	23d

State Arts Agency Spending, 1999

	Per Capita	Rank
Maine	$0.61	36th
U.S.	$1.35	

Per capita state arts spending in 1999 trailed the U.S. average by 55%.

Major League Sports Facilities

None

MARYLAND

Apparently hundreds of millions of taxpayer dollars spent in Maryland on new baseball and football stadiums in recent years are not enough. A 1999 study performed for the city of Baltimore recommended that a new $200 million arena be built. (Since the city has no NBA or NHL teams, no doubt, state and city taxpayers would be burdened with a big portion of the bill to acquire such a team.)

In 1984, when the Colts bolted to Indianapolis in the middle of the night, Baltimore was seen as a victim in the stadiums game. In reality, Baltimore and the state of Maryland have long been notorious players when it comes to pilfering taxpayer funds for major league sports facilities. Baltimore, in fact, was guilty long ago of helping to spark the sports subsidies fire, and has thrown more fuel on the conflagration in recent years.

Before the early 1950s, the general rule was that major league teams built their own facilities. In baseball, for example, only the Cleveland Indians played in a government ballpark. However, in 1953, the Boston Braves picked up and moved to Milwaukee's new taxpayer-funded County Stadium, and anticipating the arrival of a major league baseball team, Baltimore rebuilt Memorial Stadium at a cost of $7.5 million (the equivalent of about $46 million in 1997 dollars). In 1954, the lowly St. Louis Browns were transformed into the Baltimore Orioles.

Almost four decades later, in 1992, the Orioles moved into the $210-million, government-funded Camden Yards. Camden Yards set the new standard for ballparks and got team owners and politicians across the nation salivating anew for old-time ballparks with modern amenities and funded by taxpayers.

Naturally, football was not left out, as taxpayers coughed up $75 million towards a $255-million stadium for the Redskins and $200 million of the $220 million cost for a new home for the former Cleveland Browns, now the Baltimore Ravens. Some officials apparently believe that basketball and hockey merely stand next in line for handouts.

Politicians and team owners justify sports welfare mainly on the assertion that these facilities provide a major boost to the region's economy. Those advocating a new arena in Baltimore magically assert that even though government may be picking up part of all of the tab, it will not really cost taxpayers anything. Supporters argue that jobs and the local economy will receive such a boost that the resulting new tax revenues will cover most of the public costs. If you happen to catch a ball game at Camden Yards and see all the hustle and bustle and the buying and selling, you actually might buy into such fantasies.

However, economic reality is far different. First, very few people outside of the general area attend sporting events. Therefore, most of the money spent at the ballpark or arena is merely being shifted around from other forms of entertainment. After all, at any given time, a family only has so many leisure dollars to spend. As for the few out-of-towners who take in a game, most of them do not remain in the area, and for the tiny numbers who are in the city for a few days, most of them did not come to the city specifically for baseball or basketball. More likely, they have come here on business and happen to take in a game as well.

Economist Roger Noll has revealed the dubious assumptions underlying studies reporting that tax-payer-funded stadiums are an economic plus: "For most teams, five to 10 percent of the people who attend the game don't actually live in that area. So what you do then is assume that these people came to town for the purpose of seeing the game and staying the average duration of a tourist visit. Then you multiply those days by the total expenditures that people spend on vacation. That means one person buying at $25 ticket to a game causes you to add $1,000 to the economic impact of the team."[1]

Contrary to the economic guesswork provided by supporters of stadium subsidies, legitimate economic analysis assesses actual changes in regional economies resulting from the presence of stadiums, arenas, and sports teams, and all of these studies show no positive impact resulting from stadium and arena subsidies.[2] In Maryland, for example, even with the state's stadium frenzy, led by Democratic Governor Parris Glendering, real economic growth, population growth, real disposable income growth, and job creation have lagged behind the nation. In addition, from 1990 to 1998, Maryland was a net exporter of people to other states. Baltimore's population declined during the 1990s as well.

Baltimore and the state of Maryland would be foolish to waste more taxpayer dollars on pro sports. Instead, politicians should concentrate on policies that will truly spur the economy forward, like downsizing government, deregulation, and cutting taxes, including the elimination of Baltimore's antientrepreneur, antigrowth income tax. Recent small steps to cut the state's personal income tax make sense, but more is necessary considering that Maryland's state and local levies run ahead of the U.S. average.

It is hard to muster much confidence that most of the state's leading politicians will clearly see what the state needs. For example, Maryland's two U.S. senators rank among the nation's most liberal, as do the state's four House Democrats. The state houses are firmly in Democratic hands as well, and Governor Glendening's record is not exactly inspiring.

Meanwhile, Representative Constance Morella resides among the most left-leaning of the Republican members in Congress. In fact, it is really quite difficult to find many true conservatives in the state of Maryland. GOP 1994 and 1998 gubernatorial candidate Ellen Sauerbrey (R) and Congressman Roscoe Bartlett (R) come to mind, but after that, it is pretty slim pickings.

One of the most remarkable things about Marylanders is how different their political philosophy is from that of their southern neighbors in Virginia. Although the states share a long border, their attitudes about social and economic issues are diametrically opposed. In Maryland, government is seen as the answer, while in Virginia, government is viewed more as a necessary evil—best kept small and out of the way. Maryland severely restricts and taxes tobacco; has some of the toughest gun control laws in the nation; and is debating the so-called "living wage." Virginia has done little in the way of smoking regulations; is the home of the National Rifle Association; and its attitude toward government welfare was perhaps best summed up by one of its most well-known political icons, Harry Byrd, who said he did not "want to take the taxes from the wage earners of America and give those, in the form of welfare checks, to able-bodied men who refuse to work."

---

1. Quoted by Tom Farrey, "Getting Your Money's Worth," <http:www.espn.go.com>, accessed September 18, 1998.
2. For example, see Melvin L. Burstein and Arthur J. Rolnick, "Congress Should End the Economic War among the States," 1994 Annual Report Essay (Federal Reserve Bank of Minneapolis, March 1995), "Stadium Madness," editorial, *Investor's Business Daily*, December 30, 1997; Michael Walden, "Don't Play Ball," *Carolina Journal* (October/November 1997), Robert Baade, "Stadiums, Professional Sports, and Economic Development: Assessing the Reality," Heartland Institute, March 28, 1994; and Robert Baade and Allen R. Sanderson, "The Employment Effect of Teams and Sports Facilities," in *Sports, Jobs and Taxes*, ed. Roger G. Noll and Andrew Zimbalist (Washington, D.C.: Brookings Institution Press, 1997), pp. 92–118.

It is no coincidence that when Democratic politicians and staffers come to the area to work in Washington, they tend to move to the Maryland side of the Potomac, while Republicans clearly favor the Virginia side.

As we enter the 21st century, the success and prosperity of Maryland is a real question mark. It is time to give up on false idols like government-subsidized stadiums and arenas and more federal revenues. (Maryland ranks very high in terms of federal spending in the state.) Instead, state officials should concentrate on policy reforms that liberate and protect (the crime rate is high in Maryland) the private sector to truly turn the state's economy around. Dare we say that Maryland could learn something from Virginia?

POLITICS

Registered Voters

59% Democrats
30% Republicans
11% Other

Federal Officials: Recent Election and Group Ratings

			ACU	ADA	SBSC
U.S. Senators:	Paul Sarbanes (D)		6	93	15
	1994 Sarbanes (D)	59%			
	Brock (R)	41%			
	Barbara Mikulski (D)		5	92	20
	1998 Mikulski (D)	70%			
	Pierpont (R)	30%			
U.S. Representatives:	Wayne Gilchrest (R-1)		64	27	65
	1998 Gilchrest (R)	69%			
	Pinder (D)	31%			
	Robert Ehrlich Jr. (R-2)		81	9	95
	1998 Ehrlich (R)	69%			
	Bosley (D)	31%			
	Benjamin Cardin (D-3)		7	86	10
	1998 Cardin (D)	78%			
	Harby (R)	22%			
	Albert Wynn (D-4)		4	95	10
	1998 Wynn (D)	86%			
	Kimble (R)	14%			

		ACU	ADA	SBSC
Steny Hoyer (D-5)		8	82	10
1998 Hoyer (D)	65%			
Ostrom (R)	35%			
Roscoe Bartlett (R-6)		100	3	90
1998 Bartlett (R)	63%			
McCown (D)	37%			
Elijah Cummings (D-7)		4	97	5
Cummings (D)	86%			
Kondner (R)	14%			
Constance Morella (R-8)		24	66	40
1998 Morella (R)	60%			
Neas (D)	40%			

Electoral Votes: 10
1996 Presidential Results: Clinton   54%
                             Dole   38%
                             Perot   7%

State Officials

Governor 1998 Election: Parris Glendering (D)   55%
                             Ellen Sauerbrey (R)   45%
Lt. Governor: Kathleen Kennedy Townsend (D)
Attorney General: J. Joseph Curran Jr. (D)
State Senate: 32 Democrats
                               15 Republicans
State House of Delegates: 106 Democrats
                               35 Republicans

TAXES AND SPENDING

Total Revenues

Maryland's per capita state and local total revenues registered $5,095 in 1996, ranking 31st in the nation and trailing the U.S. average of $5,706 by 11%. From 1962 to 1996, real per capita state and local revenues increased by 266%, compared with an increase in the national average of 297%.

Real Per Capita State and Local Total Revenues: Maryland vs. U.S.

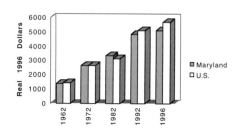

Taxes

Maryland's per capita state and local taxes registered $2,786 in 1996, ranking 12th in the nation and exceeding the U.S. average of $2,597 by 7%. From 1962 to 1996, real per capita state and local taxes increased by 174%, compared with an increase of 152% in the U.S. average.

Property Taxes

Maryland's per capita state and local property taxes equaled $748 in 1996, ranking 23d in the nation and lagging behind the U.S. average of $789 by 5%. From 1962 to 1996, real per capita state and local property taxes increased by 77%, versus a 67% increase in the U.S. average.

Sales and Gross Receipts Taxes

Maryland's per capita state and local sales and gross receipts taxes came in at $742 in 1996, ranking 40th in the nation and trailing the U.S. average of $939 by 21%. From 1962 to 1996, real per capita state and local sales and gross receipts taxes increased by 130%, versus an increase of 214% in the U.S. average.

Income Taxes

Maryland's per capita state and local income (individual and corporate) taxes registered $1,108 in 1996, ranking 5th in the nation and topping the U.S. average of $674 by 64%. From 1962 to 1996, real per capita state and local income taxes increased by 552%, versus a 567% increase in the U.S. average.

Personal Income Tax

A rate of 4.85%, ranking 18th in the nation (from lowest tax rate to highest), and comparing with the national average of 5.26%.

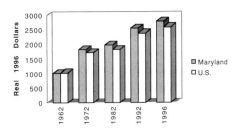

Real Per Capita State and Local Taxes: Maryland vs. U.S.

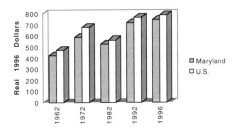

Real Per Capita State and Local Property Taxes: Maryland vs. U.S.

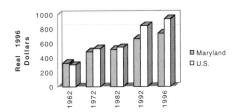

Real Per Capita State and Local Sales and Gross Receipts Taxes: Maryland vs. U.S.

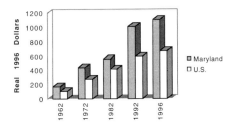

Real Per Capita State and Local Income Taxes: Maryland vs. U.S.

Capital Gains Tax

A rate of 4.85%, ranking 24th in the nation (from lowest tax rate to highest), and comparing with the national average of 4.68%.

Corporate Income Tax

A rate of 7.0%, ranking 26th in the nation (from lowest tax rate to highest), and comparing with the national average of 6.63%.

Total Expenditures

Maryland's per capita state and local total spending registered $4,872 in 1996, ranking 26th in the nation and trailing the U.S. average of $5,268 by 8%. From 1962 to 1996, real per capita state and local total spending increased by 230%, versus an increase of 254% in the U.S. average.

Welfare Expenditures

Maryland's per capita state and local public welfare spending registered $584 in 1996, ranking 37th in the nation and trailing the U.S. average of $729 by 20%. From 1962 to 1996, real per capita state and local public welfare spending increased by 746%, compared with a 488% increase in the U.S. average.

Welfare Recipients (in thousands)

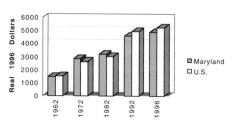

Real Per Capita State and Local Total Expenditures: Maryland vs. U.S.

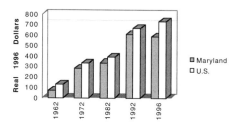

Real Per Capita State and Local Public Welfare Spending: Maryland vs. U.S.

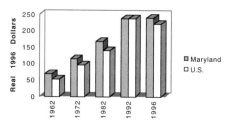

Real Per Capita State and Local Interest on General Debt: Maryland vs. U.S.

	1980	1989	3/99	Change 1989–99
Md.	220	181	89	−51%
U.S.	10,923	10,987	7,335	−33%

Interest on General Debt

Maryland's per capita state and local interest on general debt registered $240 in 1996, ranking 20th in the nation and exceeding the U.S. average of $222 by 8%. From 1962 to 1996, real per capita state and local interest on general debt increased by 248%, versus an increase of 335% in the U.S. average.

Total Debt Outstanding

Maryland's per capita state and local debt registered $4,387 in 1996, ranking 21st in the nation and trailing the U.S. average of $4,409 by 0.5%. From 1962 to 1996, real per capita state and local debt outstanding increased by 59%, versus an increase of 120% in the U.S. average.

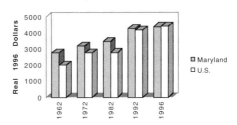

Real Per Capita State and Local Debt Outstanding: Maryland vs. U.S.

Government Employees

Maryland's state and local government employees (full-time equivalent, or FTE) per 10,000 population registered 494.1 in 1997, ranking 46th in the nation and trailing the U.S. average of 531.1 by 7%. From 1962 to 1996, state and local FTE employees per 10,000 population increased by 56%, compared with an increase in the U.S. average of 66%.

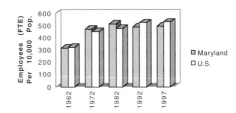

State and Local Government Employees (FTE) Per 10,000 Population: Maryland vs. U.S.

Per Capita Federal Government Expenditures, 1998

	1998	Ranking
Md.	$8,094	3d
U.S.	$5,491	

Per capita federal spending in Maryland outpaced the national average by 47%.

EDUCATION

Total Education Spending

Maryland's per capita state and local education spending registered $1,523 in 1996, ranking 22d in the nation and topping the U.S. average of $1,503 by 1%. From 1962 to 1996, real per capita total education spending increased by 172%, versus an increase in the U.S. average of 173%.

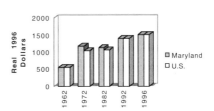

Real Per Capita State and Local Education Spending: Maryland vs. U.S.

Per Pupil Spending

Maryland's per pupil public school spending registered $6,021 in 1998, ranking 22d in the nation and lagging behind the U.S. average of $6,131 by 2%. From 1970 to 1998, Maryland's real per pupil public school spending increased by 101%, compared with a 120% increase in the U.S. average.

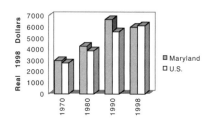

Real Per Pupil Public School Spending: Maryland vs. U.S.

Average Public School Teacher Salaries (in 1997–98 dollars)

	1970	1980	1990	1998	1998 Ranking
Md.	40,175	36,581	46,263	41,739	14th
U.S.	36,934	33,272	39,956	39,385	

In 1998, the average public school teacher salary in Maryland outpaced the U.S. average by 6%. From 1970 to 1998, the real average teacher salary in Maryland increased by 4%, versus an increase in the U.S. average of 7%.

Pupil/Teacher Ratio, Fall 1996

	Ratio	Rank
Md.	17.1	35th
U.S.	17.1	

Teachers/Staff, Fall 1996

	Percent	Rank
Md.	56.1	6th
U.S.	52.1	

Public School 4th-Grade Reading Proficiency, 1998

	Average	Rank (out of 40 states)
Md.	215	23d
U.S.	215	

Public School 8th-Grade Reading Proficiency, 1998

	Average	Rank (out of 37 states)
Md.	262	17th
U.S.	261	

Public School 4th-Grade Math Proficiency, 1996

	Average	Rank (out of 44 states)
Md.	221	27th
U.S.	224	

Public School 8th-Grade Math Proficiency, 1996

	Average	Rank (out of 41 states)
Md.	270	20th
U.S.	271	

Public School 8th-Grade Science Proficiency, 1996

	Average	Rank (out of 41 states)
Md.	145	26th
U.S.	148	

Average Math SAT Scores

	1972	1982	1992	1998	Percentage Taking SAT in 1998
Md.	507	490	501	508	65
U.S.	509	493	501	512	43

Average Verbal SAT Scores

	1972	1982	1992	1998	Percentage Taking SAT in 1998
Md.	531	503	507	506	65
U.S.	530	504	500	505	43

Expenditures by Public Institutions of Higher Education Per Full-Time-Equivalent Student, 1996

	FTE Student Spending	Rank
Md.	$13,017	20th
U.S.	$12,343	

Per-FTE-student spending in public institutions of higher education exceeded the U.S. average by 5%.

Per Full-Time-Equivalent Student Revenues from Federal, State, and Local Governments for Public Institutions of Higher Education, 1996

	FTE Student Government Revenues	Rank
Md.	$8,289	20th
U.S.	$8,101	

Per-FTE-student-government revenues in public institutions of higher education topped the U.S. average by 2%.

Average Salary for Full-Time Professors at Public Universities, 1997

	Average	Rank
Md.	$76,329	9th
U.S.	$72,599	

The average full-time public university professor salary exceeded the U.S. average by 5%.

ECONOMY AND BUSINESS

Economic Growth

Over the period of 1977 to 1997, Maryland's real gross state product (GSP) grew by 69.2%—ranking 26th in the nation—as compared with real U.S. gross domestic product (GDP), expanding by 70.1%.

At $153.8 billion in 1997, Maryland's GSP ranked as 16th largest in the nation.

From 1993 to 1997, Maryland's annual real GSP growth averaged 2.61%—ranking 41st in the nation—as compared with annual real U.S. GDP growth, averaging 3.08%.

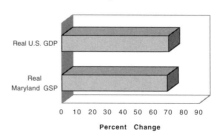

Real Economic Growth 1977-1997: Maryland vs. U.S.

Real U.S. GDP

Real Maryland GSP

0 10 20 30 40 50 60 70 80 90

Percent Change

Job Growth

	Growth in Employee Payrolls (Nonagricultural) 1962–98	Ranking
Md.	145.5%	26th
U.S.	126.5%	

	Average Annual Growth in Employee Payrolls (Nonagricultural) 1993–98	Ranking
Md.	2.23%	41st
U.S.	2.98%	

Per Capita Disposable Income, 1997

	1997	Ranking
Md.	$24,028	7th
U.S.	$21,607	

Per capita disposable income exceeded the U.S. average by 11%.

	Real Growth 1962–97	Ranking
Md.	129.8%	18th
U.S.	116.7%	

	Average Annual Real Growth 1993–97	Ranking
Md.	1.23%	44th
U.S.	1.48%	

Number of Businesses

	1997	Percent with Fewer than 500 Employees
Businesses with Employees	125,755	97.7
Self-employed Individuals	190,000	

New Business Incorporations

	1980	1986	1992	1997
Md.	8,548	16,035	17,201	18,066

Percentage Change in Annual New Business Incorporations, 1980 vs. 1997

	Percent	Ranking
Md.	111.3	6th
U.S.	49.7	

State Merchandise Exports to the World, 1998 (in millions of dollars)

	1998	Rank
Md.	$4,014	31st

Small Business Survival Index, 1999

Maryland ranked 24th in terms of its policy environment for entrepreneurship.

Fortune 500 Headquarters in 1999

A total of 10 (ranked 16th)

Labor Union Membership, 1983 vs. 1997

	Percentage of Workers		Rank
	1983	1997	
Md.	18.5	14.9	19th
U.S.	20.1	14.1	

Homeownership Rate, 1998

	Rate	Rank
Md.	68.7	29th
U.S.	66.3	

CRIME

Crime Rates Per 100 Residents (rankings from best to worst crime rate)

Total Crime	1960	1970	1980	1990	1998	1998 Ranking
Md.	0.93	3.35	6.63	5.83	5.37	41st
U.S.	1.04	2.74	5.90	5.82	4.62	

From 1960 to 1998, Maryland's crime rate increased by 477%, versus a U.S. increase of 344%. From 1990 to 1998, Maryland's crime rate dropped by 8%, versus a U.S. decrease of 21%.

Violent Crime	1960	1970	1980	1990	1998	1998 Ranking
Md.	0.14	0.62	0.85	0.92	0.80	46th
U.S.	0.14	0.36	0.58	0.73	0.57	

From 1960 to 1998, Maryland's violent crime rate increased by 471%, versus a U.S. increase of 307%. From 1990 to 1998, Maryland's violent crime rate decreased by 13%, compared with a national decline of 22%.

Property Crime	1960	1970	1980	1990	1998	1998 Ranking
Md.	0.79	2.72	5.78	4.91	4.57	37th
U.S.	0.90	2.38	5.32	5.09	4.05	

From 1960 to 1998, Maryland's property crime rate increased by 478%, versus a national increase of 350%. From 1990 to 1998, Maryland's property crime rate decreased by 7%, compared with a national decline of 20%.

Real Per Capita Police Protection Spending (in real 1996 dollars)

	1962	1972	1982	1992	1996	1996 Ranking
Md.	64	111	125	158	176	10th
U.S.	51	95	114	148	168	

In 1996, per capita state and local police protection spending in Maryland exceeded the U.S. average by 5%. From 1962 to 1996, real per capita state and local police protection spending increased by 175%, versus an increase of 229% in the U.S. average.

Prisoners in State and Federal Prisons Per 1,000 Population

	1980	1990	1996	1996 Ranking
Md.	1.83	3.73	4.36	16th
U.S.	1.46	3.11	4.45	

From 1980 to 1996, prisoners per 1,000 population increased by 138%, versus a U.S. increase of 205%.

HEALTH CARE

Health-Care Spending

Maryland's per capita state and local health-care spending registered $142 in 1996, ranking 23d in the nation and trailing the U.S. average of $151 by 6%. From 1962 to 1996, Maryland's real per capita state and local health-care spending increased by 407%, versus an increase of 739% in the U.S. average.

Real Per Capita State and Local Health Care Spending: Maryland vs. U.S.

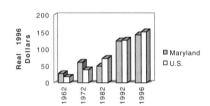

Hospital Spending

Maryland's per capita state and local hospital spending registered $62 in 1996, ranking 49th in the nation and lagging behind the U.S. average of $266 by 77%. From 1962 to 1996, Maryland's real per capita state and local hospital spending decreased by 35%, as opposed to an increase of 189% in the U.S. average.

Real Per Capita State and Local Hospital Spending: Maryland vs. U.S.

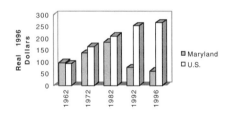

Medicaid, 1997

	Spending Per Recipient	Ranking
Md.	$5,475	7th
U.S.	$3,681	

Maryland's per-recipient Medicaid spending exceeded the U.S. average by 49%.

ENVIRONMENT

Parks and Recreation Spending

Maryland's per capita state and local parks and recreation spending registered $95 in 1996, ranking 11th in the nation and exceeding the U.S. average of $72 by 32%. From 1962 to 1996, real per capita state and local parks and recreation spending increased by 197%, versus a 213% increase in the U.S. average.

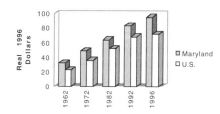

Real Per Capita State and Local Parks and Recreation Spending: Maryland vs. U.S.

State and Local Natural Resources Spending, 1996

	Per Capita	Ranking
Md.	$60	29th
U.S.	$60	

Per capita state and local natural resources spending in Maryland equaled the U.S. average.

State Parks Revenues as a Share of Operating Expenses, 1997

	Percent	Rank
Md.	33	34th
U.S.	42	

Percentage of Land Owned by the Federal Government, 1996

	Percent	Rank
Md.	2.5	35th
U.S.	24.8	

SOCIETY AND DEMOGRAPHICS

Population

Maryland's 1998 population of 5.135 million ranked 19th in the nation.

Population Growth

	Percentage Change in Population	Ranking
Md.	7.40	25th
U.S.	8.66	

	Net International Migration	Ranking
Md.	117,813	10th

	Net Domestic Migration	Ranking
Md.	−49,150	38th

Infant Mortality Rate, 1998

	Percent	Rank
Md.	8.5	8th
U.S.	6.4	

Percentage of Births of Low Birthweight, 1997

	Percent	Rank
Md.	8.8	7th
U.S.	7.5	

Maryland Population

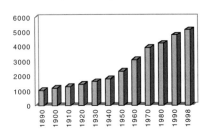

Percentage of Live Births to Unmarried Women, 1997

	Percent	Rank
Md.	33.5	16th
U.S.	32.4	

Abortion Rate—Abortions Per 1,000 Women Ages 15–44, 1995

	Rate	Rank
Md.	25.6	10th
U.S.	22.9	

LIFESTYLE

Percentage of Households with Computers, 1998

	Percent	Rank
Md.	46.3	13th

Percentage of Households with Internet Access, 1998

	Percent	Rank
Md.	31.0	10th

State Arts Agency Spending, 1999

	Per Capita	Rank
Md.	$1.67	11th
U.S.	$1.35	

Per capita state arts spending in 1999 topped the U.S. average by 24%.

Major League Sports Facilities

Year Opened/ Refurb.	Stadium/ Arena	Home Team	Millions of Nominal Dollars		Millions of Real 1997 Dollars	
			Estimated Total Cost	Estimated Taxpayer Cost	Estimated Total Cost	Estimated Taxpayer Cost
1953	Memorial Stadium	Orioles (MLB) 1954–91 Colts (NFL) 1953–83	$7.5	$7.5	$45.7	$45.7
1973	USAir Arena	Capitals (NHL) 1974–97 Wizards (NBA) 1973–97	$18.0	$0.0	$65.0	$0.0
1992	Camden Yards	Orioles (MLB) 1992–present	$210.0	$210.0	$240.3	$240.3
1997	Jack Kent Cooke Stadium	Redskins (NFL) 1997–present	$255.0	$75.0	$255.0	$75.0
1998	Ravens' Stadium	Ravens (NFL) 1998–present	$220.0	$200.0	$216.5	$196.9

MASSACHUSETTS

Massachusetts's unfailing ability to send Ted Kennedy back to the U.S. Senate not only is a source of pride for liberals in the New England state, but also is a secret delight for many Republicans and conservatives elsewhere in the nation. After all, Kennedy serves as the perfect foil on most issues of concern to conservatives, including lavish government spending, socialized medicine, high taxes, abortion, family values, and so on.

Beyond the state's political absorption with the Kennedy family in general, there are no Republicans in the Massachusetts congressional delegation, and the state's congressional Democrats are of the hard-left variety. The state legislature also is overwhelmingly Democratic.

Meanwhile, Massachusetts' most famous and successful Republican in recent years—William Weld—won the governorship in 1990 by a small margin, gained reelection in 1994 with an astounding 71% of the vote, and then quit his job in July 1997 in a rather quixotic pursuit to be President Clinton's ambassador to Mexico. Ironically, the appointment was killed by conservative Republicans (mainly, North Carolina Senator Jesse Helms) because of his position on drug legalization. Republican Paul Cellucci took office upon Weld's resignation and won election himself in November 1998. (Incidentally, Weld has since moved to New York, with some speculation that he would like to become the Empire State's governor one day.)

During his tenure, Weld managed to get the state legislature to eliminate the tax on long-term capital gains, as well as death taxes, but made no headway in cutting either Massachusetts's personal income tax rate (which was increased by his predecessor Michael Dukakis [D]), or the state's very high corporate income tax.

Even more scarce on the political front than a typical Republican in Massachusetts is a social conservative. Indeed, both Weld and Cellucci are social liberals.

Given the state's liberal leanings, Massachusetts's state and local government spending, taxing, and borrowing categories outdistance the U.S. averages, but for a few exceptions. Meanwhile, the economic story is far more mixed. For example, while real gross state product and disposable income growth have run ahead of national trends, job creation, population growth, and new business incorporations in Massachusetts have lagged behind. Also, the state ranked quite poorly in terms of net domestic migration from 1990 to 1998, claiming a net loss of more than 235,000 people to other parts of the nation.

Massachusetts promises continued uneven performance in coming years unless it moves in a far more promarket, proentrepreneur direction. Rather than looking to the big government philosophy of a Dukakis or Ted Kennedy, Massachusetts would do well to look back earlier in this century to two other Massachusetts's politicians—former Massachusetts Governor (1919–21), U.S. Vice President (1921–23), and U.S. President (1923–29) Calvin Coolidge, and former U.S. Representative (1947–53), U.S. Senator (1953–61), and U.S. President (1961–63) John F. Kennedy. Interestingly, of the three serious efforts to cut taxes at the federal level during the 20th century, two were led by U.S. presidents who were politicians from Massachusetts.

The policies promoted and implemented by Coolidge and his predecessor, President Warren G. Harding, are worth serious consideration at the start of the 21st century. For example, federal government expenditures actually fell from $5.06 billion in 1921 to $3.13 billion in 1923 and $3.12 billion in 1929. Coolidge also halted government activism, perhaps most prominent being the McNary-Haugen bill, which would have had the federal government buy up farm surpluses to sell abroad and hike prices domestically for U.S. consumers.

Under Coolidge, tax rates also were slashed. For example, the top personal income tax rate eventually dropped from 73% to 25%, and the capital gains tax from 73% to 12.5%. Coolidge and his Treasury secretary, Andrew Mellon, got Congress to eliminate the recently imposed gift tax and to reduce the estate tax. The corporate income tax also was cut under Coolidge.

The impact of these policies was quite positive. For example, real annual economic growth averaged 6.2% from 1922 to 1929 (the first tax cut came in November 1921), and consumer prices actually fell. Large federal budget surpluses resulted, and the outstanding federal debt fell by 30% between 1921 and 1929.

Coolidge offers Massachusetts (not to mention his birth state of Vermont) a proud legacy—his character was unimpeachable—and solid public policy lessons for smaller government and dramatically lower taxes.

Similarly, Kennedy pushed for big reductions in the wartime income tax rates that were still in effect in the early 1960s. After his death, Kennedy's tax plan was passed, featuring a cut in the top federal income tax rate from 91% to 70%.

However, it remains a long shot that the liberal Massachusetts of the early 21st century will act according to the principles of, arguably, the most conservative U.S. president of the 20th century in Coolidge, and the last Democratic president with some conservative inclinations in JFK—whether they were from the Bay State or not.

Picking Ted Kennedy over Calvin Coolidge or even Ted's brother, JFK, will only hurt Massachusetts in the long run.

POLITICS

Registered Voters

38% Democrats
14% Republicans
48% Other

Federal Officials: Recent Election and Group Ratings

			ACU	ADA	SBSC
U.S. Senators:	Edward Kennedy (D)		3	89	20
	1994 Kennedy (D)	58%			
	Romney (R)	41%			

				ACU	ADA	SBSC
John Kerry (D)				5	93	25
	1996	Kerry (D)	52%			
		Weld (R)	44%			

U.S. Representatives:

				ACU	ADA	SBSC
John Olver (D-1)				2	98	10
	1998	Olver (D)	72%			
		Morgan (R)	28%			
Richard Neal (D-2)				11	87	20
	1998	Neal (D)	NO			
James McGovern (D-3)				4	100	10
	1998	McGovern (D)	57%			
		Amorello (R)	41%			
Barney Frank (D-4)				4	98	15
	1998	Frank (D)	NO			
Martin Meehan (D-5)				13	88	15
	1998	Meehan (D)	71%			
		Coleman (R)	29%			
John Tierney (D-6)				8	100	15
	1998	Tierney (D)	55%			
		Torkildsen (R)	42%			
Edward Markey (D-7)				4	93	10
	1998	Markey (D)	71%			
		Long (R)	29%			
Michael Capuano (D-8)				NA	NA	NA
	1998	Capuano (D)	82%			
		Hyde (R)	12%			
Joseph Moakley (D-9)				7	80	5
	1998	Moakley (D)	NO			
William Delahunt (D-10)				4	100	10
	1998	Delahunt (D)	70%			
		Bleicken (R)	30%			

Electoral Votes: 12

1996 Presidential Results:

Clinton	61%
Dole	28%
Perot	9%

State Officials

Governor 1998 Election:

Paul Cellucci (R)	50%
Scott Harshbarger (D)	47%

Lt. Governor: Jane Swift (R)

Attorney General: Thomas F. Reilly (D)

State Senate: 33 Democrats
7 Republicans

State House: 131 Democrats
28 Republicans
1 Independent

TAXES AND SPENDING

Total Revenues

Massachusetts's per capita state and local total revenues registered $6,078 in 1996, ranking 14th in the nation and exceeding the U.S. average of $5,706 by 7%. From 1962 to 1996, real per capita state and local revenues increased by 280%, compared with an increase in the national average of 297%.

Taxes

Massachusetts's per capita state and local taxes registered $3,139 in 1996, ranking 7th in the nation and exceeding the U.S. average of $2,597 by 21%. From 1962 to 1996, real per capita state and local taxes increased by 149%, compared with an increase of 152% in the U.S. average.

Property Taxes

Massachusetts's per capita state and local property taxes equaled $1,063 in 1996, ranking 10th in the nation and exceeding the U.S. average of $789 by 35%. From 1962 to 1996, real per capita state and local property taxes increased by 39%, versus a 67% increase in the U.S. average.

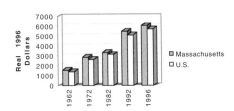

Real Per Capita State and Local Total Revenues: Massachusetts vs. U.S.

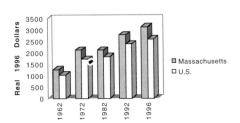

Real Per Capita State and Local Income Taxes: Massachusetts vs. U.S.

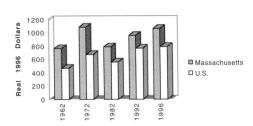

Real Per Capita State and Local Property Taxes: Massachusetts vs. U.S.

Sales and Gross Receipts Taxes

Massachusetts's per capita state and local sales and gross receipts taxes came in at $649 in 1996, ranking 46th in the nation and trailing the U.S. average of $939 by 31%. From 1962 to 1996, real per capita state and local sales and gross receipts taxes increased by 282%, versus an increase of 214% in the U.S. average.

Income Taxes

Massachusetts's per capita state and local income (individual and corporate) taxes registered $1,302 in 1996, ranking 3d in the nation and topping the U.S. average of $674 by 93%. From 1962 to 1996, real per capita state and local income taxes increased by 593%, versus a 567% increase in the U.S. average.

Personal Income Tax

A rate of 5.95%, ranking 26th in the nation (from lowest tax rate to highest), and comparing with the national average of 5.26%.

Capital Gains Tax

A rate of 0% (on long-term gains), ranking best in the nation (from lowest tax rate to highest), and comparing with the national average of 4.68%.

Corporate Income Tax

A rate of 9.5%, ranking 46th in the nation (from lowest tax rate to highest), and comparing with the national average of 6.63%.

Total Expenditures

Massachusetts's per capita state and local total spending registered $6,014 in 1996, ranking 9th in the nation and exceeding the U.S. average of $5,268 by 14%. From 1962 to 1996, real per capita state and local total spending increased by 281%, versus an increase of 254% in the U.S. average.

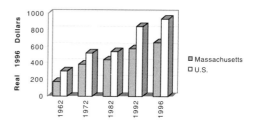

Real Per Capita State and Local Sales and Gross Receipts Taxes: Massachusetts vs. U.S.

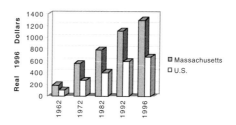

Real Per Capita State and Local Income Taxes: Massachusetts vs. U.S.

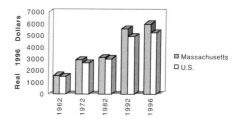

Real Per Capita State and Local Total Expenditures: Massachusetts vs. U.S.

Welfare Expenditures

Massachusetts's per capita state and local public welfare spending registered $949 in 1996, ranking 6th in the nation and outpacing the U.S. average of $729 by 30%. From 1962 to 1996, real per capita state and local public welfare spending increased by 430%, compared with a 488% increase in the U.S. average.

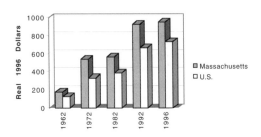

Real Per Capita State and Local Public Welfare Spending: Massachusetts vs. U.S.

Welfare Recipients (in thousands)

	1980	1989	3/99	Change 1989–99
Mass.	348	256	152	−41%
U.S.	10,923	10,987	7,335	−33%

Interest on General Debt

Massachusetts's per capita state and local interest on general debt registered $327 in 1996, ranking 9th in the nation and exceeding the U.S. average of $222 by 47%. From 1962 to 1996, real per capita state and local interest on general debt increased by 445%, versus an increase of 335% in the U.S. average.

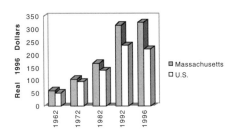

Real Per Capita State and Local Interest on General Debt: Massachusetts vs. U.S.

Total Debt Outstanding

Massachusetts's per capita state and local debt registered $6,670 in 1996, ranking 6th in the nation and outrunning the U.S. average of $4,409 by 51%. From 1962 to 1996, real per capita state and local debt outstanding increased by 158%, versus an increase of 120% in the U.S. average.

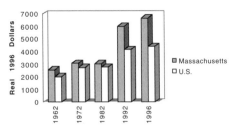

Real Per Capita State and Local Debt Outstanding: Massachusetts vs. U.S.

Government Employees

Massachusetts's state and local government employees (full-time equivalent, or FTE) per 10,000 population registered 496.3 in 1997, ranking 45th in the nation and trailing the U.S. average of 531.1 by 7%. From 1962 to 1996, state and local FTE employees per 10,000 population increased by 46%, compared with an increase in the U.S. average of 66%.

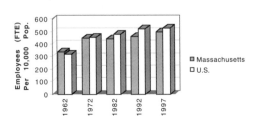

State and Local Government Employees (FTE) Per 10,000 Population: Massachusetts vs. U.S.

Per Capita Federal Government Expenditures, 1998

	1998	Ranking
Mass.	$6,047	10th
U.S.	$5,491	

Per capita federal spending in Massachusetts outpaced the national average by 10%.

EDUCATION

Total Education Spending

Massachusetts's per capita state and local education spending registered $1,322 in 1996, ranking 43d in the nation and trailing the U.S. average of $1,503 by 12%. From 1962 to 1996, real per capita total education spending increased by 182%, versus an increase in the U.S. average of 173%.

Real Per Capita State and Local Education Spending: Massachusetts vs. U.S.

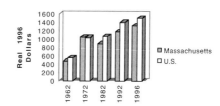

Per Pupil Spending

Massachusetts's per pupil public school spending registered $7,506 in 1998, ranking 8th in the nation and exceeding the U.S. average of $6,131 by 22%. From 1970 to 1998, Massachusetts's real per pupil public school spending increased by 156%, compared with a 120% increase in the U.S. average.

Real Per Pupil Public School Spending: Massachusetts vs. U.S.

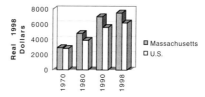

Average Public School Teacher Salaries (in 1997–98 dollars)

	1970	1980	1990	1998	1998 Ranking
Mass.	37,525	35,945	44,216	43,930	9th
U.S.	36,934	33,272	39,956	39,385	

In 1998, the average public school teacher salary in Massachusetts outpaced the U.S. average by 12%. From 1970 to 1998, the real average teacher salary in Massachusetts increased by 17%, versus an increase in the U.S. average of 7%.

Pupil/Teacher Ratio, Fall 1996

	Ratio	Rank
Mass.	14.5	6th
U.S.	17.1	

Teachers/Staff, Fall 1996

	Percent	Rank
Mass.	55.3	8th
U.S.	52.1	

Public School 4th-Grade Reading Proficiency, 1998

	Average	Rank (out of 40 states)
Mass.	225	4th
U.S.	215	

Public School 8th-Grade Reading Proficiency, 1998

	Average	Rank (out of 37 states)
Mass.	269	4th
U.S.	261	

Public School 4th-Grade Math Proficiency, 1996

	Average	Rank (out of 44 states)
Mass.	229	6th
U.S.	224	

Public School 8th-Grade Math Proficiency, 1996

	Average	Rank (out of 41 states)
Mass.	278	10th
U.S.	271	

Public School 8th-Grade Science Proficiency, 1996

	Average	Rank (out of 41 states)
Mass.	157	8th
U.S.	148	

Average Math SAT Scores

	1972	1982	1992	1998	Percentage Taking SAT in 1998
Mass.	506	490	499	508	77
U.S.	509	493	501	512	43

Average Verbal SAT Scores

	1972	1982	1992	1998	Percentage Taking SAT in 1998
Mass.	530	503	503	508	77
U.S.	530	504	500	505	43

Expenditures by Public Institutions of Higher Education Per Full-Time-Equivalent Student, 1996

	FTE Student Spending	Rank
Mass.	$12,126	28th
U.S.	$12,343	

Per-FTE-student spending in public institutions of higher education trailed the U.S. average by 2%.

Per Full-Time-Equivalent Student Revenues from Federal, State, and Local Governments for Public Institutions of Higher Education, 1996

	FTE Student Government Revenues	Rank
Mass.	$7,328	34th
U.S.	$8,101	

Per-FTE-student-government revenues in public institutions of higher education lagged behind the U.S. average by 10%.

Average Salary for Full-Time Professors at Public Universities, 1997

	Average	Rank
Mass.	$75,034	12th
U.S.	$72,599	

The average full-time public university professor salary exceeded the U.S. average by 3%.

ECONOMY AND BUSINESS

Economic Growth

Over the period of 1977 to 1997, Massachusetts's real gross state product (GSP) grew by 86.7%—ranking 20th in the nation—as compared with real U.S. gross domestic product (GDP), expanding by 70.1%.

At $221 billion in 1997, Massachusetts's GSP ranked as 11th largest in the nation.

From 1993 to 1997, Massachusetts's annual real GSP growth averaged 3.66%—ranking 26th in the nation—as compared with annual real U.S. GDP growth, averaging 3.08%.

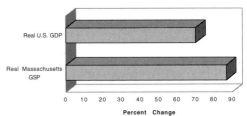

Real Economic Growth 1977-1997: Massachusetts vs. U.S.

Job Growth

	Growth in Employee Payrolls (Nonagricultural) 1962–98	Ranking
Mass.	63.5%	46th
U.S.	126.5%	

	Average Annual Growth in Employee Payrolls (Nonagricultural) 1993–98	Ranking
Mass.	2.59%	36th
U.S.	2.98%	

Per Capita Disposable Income, 1997

	1997	Ranking
Mass.	$25,711	4th
U.S.	$21,607	

Per capita disposable income exceeded the U.S. average by 19%.

	Real Growth 1962–97	Ranking
Mass.	132.9%	15th
U.S.	116.7%	

	Average Annual Real Growth 1993–97	Ranking
Mass.	1.89%	11th
U.S.	1.48%	

Number of Businesses

	1997	Percent with Fewer than 500 Employees
Businesses with Employees	162,792	98.1
Self-employed Individuals	221,000	

New Business Incorporations

	1980	1986	1992	1997
Mass.	11,291	17,321	12,197	12,437

Percentage Change in Annual New Business Incorporations, 1980 vs. 1997

	Percent	Ranking
Mass.	10.1	41st
U.S.	49.7	

State Merchandise Exports to the World, 1998 (in millions of dollars)

	1998	Rank
Mass.	$16,467	11th

Small Business Survival Index, 1999

Massachusetts ranked 30th in terms of its policy environment for entrepreneurship.

Fortune 500 Headquarters in 1999

A total of 16 (ranked 9th), with Boston ranking 11th among U.S. cities, with 6 headquarters

Labor Union Membership, 1983 vs. 1997

	Percentage of Workers		
	1983	1997	1997 Rank
Mass.	23.7	15.1	18th
U.S.	20.1	14.1	

Homeownership Rate, 1998

	Rate	Rank
Mass.	61.3	46th
U.S.	66.3	

CRIME

Crime Rates Per 100 Residents (rankings from best to worst crime rate)

Total Crime	1960	1970	1980	1990	1998	1998 Ranking
Mass.	0.75	3.00	6.08	5.30	3.44	9th
U.S.	1.04	2.74	5.90	5.82	4.62	

From 1960 to 1998, Massachusetts's crime rate increased by 359%, versus a U.S. increase of 344%. From 1990 to 1998, Massachusetts's crime rate dropped by 35%, versus a U.S. decrease of 21%.

Violent Crime	1960	1970	1980	1990	1998	1998 Ranking
Mass.	0.05	0.20	0.60	0.74	0.62	37th
U.S.	0.14	0.36	0.58	0.73	0.57	

From 1960 to 1998, Massachusetts's violent crime rate increased by 1,140%, versus a U.S. increase of 307%. From 1990 to 1997, Massachusetts's violent crime rate decreased by 16%, compared with a national decline of 22%.

Property Crime	1960	1970	1980	1990	1998	1998 Ranking
Mass.	0.70	2.80	5.48	4.56	2.81	6th
U.S.	0.90	2.38	5.32	5.09	4.05	

From 1960 to 1998, Massachusetts's property crime rate increased by 301%, versus a national increase of 350%. From 1990 to 1998, Massachusetts's property crime rate decreased by 38%, compared with a national decline of 20%.

Real Per Capita Police Protection Spending (in real 1996 dollars)

	1962	1972	1982	1992	1996	1996 Ranking
Mass.	64	105	106	143	183	9th
U.S.	51	95	114	148	168	

In 1996, per capita state and local police protection spending in Massachusetts exceeded the U.S. average by 9%. From 1962 to 1996, real per capita state and local police protection spending increased by 186%, versus an increase of 229% in the U.S. average.

Prisoners in State and Federal Prisons Per 1,000 Population

	1980	1990	1996	1996 Ranking
Mass.	0.56	1.39	1.94	45th
U.S.	1.46	3.11	4.45	

From 1980 to 1996, prisoners per 1,000 population increased by 246%, versus a U.S. increase of 205%.

HEALTH CARE

Health-Care Spending

Massachusetts's per capita state and local health-care spending registered $224 in 1996, ranking 5th in the nation and exceeding the U.S. average of $151 by 48%. From 1962 to 1996, Massachusetts's real per capita state and local health-care spending increased by 1,144%, versus an increase of 739% in the U.S. average.

Real Per Capita State and Local Health Care Spending: Massachusetts vs. U.S.

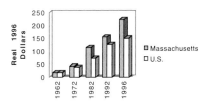

Hospital Spending

Massachusetts's per capita state and local hospital spending registered $238 in 1996, ranking 24th in the nation and lagging behind the U.S. average of $266 by 11%. From 1962 to 1996, Massachusetts's real per capita state and local hospital spending increased by 84%, as opposed to an increase of 189% in the U.S. average.

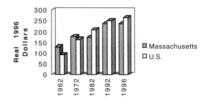

Real Per Capita State and Local Hospital Spending: Massachusetts vs. U.S.

Medicaid, 1997

	Spending Per Recipient	Ranking
Mass.	$5,332	10th
U.S.	$3,681	

Massachusetts's per-recipient Medicaid spending exceeded the U.S. average by 45%.

ENVIRONMENT

Parks and Recreation Spending

Massachusetts's per capita state and local parks and recreation spending registered $34 in 1996, ranking 48th in the nation and trailing the U.S. average of $72 by 53%. From 1962 to 1996, real per capita state and local parks and recreation spending increased by 89%, versus a 213% increase in the U.S. average.

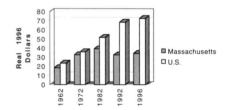

Real Per Capita State and Local Parks and Recreation Spending: Massachusetts vs. U.S.

State and Local Natural Resources Spending, 1996

	Per Capita	Ranking
Mass.	$33	43d
U.S.	$60	

Per capita state and local natural resources spending in Massachusetts trailed the U.S. average by 45%.

State Parks Revenues as a Share of Operating Expenses, 1997

	Percent	Rank
Mass.	11	49th
U.S.	42	

Percentage of Land Owned by the Federal Government, 1996

	Percent	Rank
Mass.	1.0	44th
U.S.	24.8	

SOCIETY AND DEMOGRAPHICS

Population

Massachusetts's 1998 population of 6.147 million ranked 13th in the nation.

Population Growth, 1990–98

	Percentage Change in Population	Ranking
Mass.	2.18	43d
U.S.	8.66	

	Net International Migration	Ranking
Mass.	135,103	7th

	Net Domestic Migration	Ranking
Mass.	−236,697	47th

Infant Mortality Rate, 1998

	Percent	Rank
Mass.	4.8	49th
U.S.	6.4	

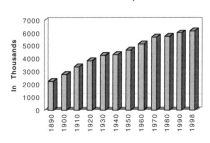

Massachusetts   Population

Percentage of Births of Low Birthweight, 1997

	Percent	Rank
Mass.	7.0	33d
U.S.	7.5	

Percentage of Live Births to Unmarried Women, 1997

	Percent	Rank
Mass.	26.0	44th
U.S.	32.4	

Abortion Rate—Abortions Per 1,000 Women Ages 15–44, 1995

	Rate	Rank
Mass.	29.2	9th
U.S.	22.9	

LIFESTYLE

Percentage of Households with Computers, 1998

	Percent	Rank
Mass.	43.4	21st

Percentage of Households with Internet Access, 1998

	Percent	Rank
Mass.	28.1	14th

State Arts Agency Spending, 1999

	Per Capita	Rank
Mass.	$2.82	3d
U.S.	$1.35	

Per capita state arts spending in 1999 topped the U.S. average by 109%.

Major League Sports Facilities

Year Opened/ Refurb.	Stadium/ Arena	Home Team	Millions of Nominal Dollars		Millions of Real 1997 Dollars	
			Estimated Total Cost	Estimated Taxpayer Cost	Estimated Total Cost	Estimated Taxpayer Cost
1912	Fenway Park	Red Sox (MLB) 1912–present Patriots (AFL/NFL) 1963–68	$0.4	$0.0	$6.1	$0.0
1915	Braves Field	Braves (MLB) 1915–52	NA	NA	NA	NA
1928	Boston Garden	Bruins (NHL) 1928–95 Celtics (NBA) 1946–95	$10.0	$0.0	$93.5	$0.0
1971	Foxboro Stadium	Patriots (NFL) 1971–present	$6.7	$0.0	$26.6	$0.0
1995	Fleet Center	Bruins (NHL) 1995–present Celtics (NBA) 1995–present	$275.0	$115.0	$289.5	$121.1

Michigan

On Election Day 1998, while Republicans suffered big setbacks nationally, Michigan voters handed the Republicans control of both houses of the legislature, giving the GOP complete control of state government for the first time in 70 years. Interestingly, GOP gains in Michigan were not surprising. Under Republican Governor John Engler's years as governor, Michigan seems to have been transformed from a rust belt has-been to a state at the cutting edge of reform. The economy certainly has picked up in recent years, as evidenced by the state's economic growth, rate of job creation, disposable income growth, and new business incorporations.

During the Engler years, Michigan has made major headlines on the welfare, education, and tax fronts. As for welfare, the general assistance program for able-bodied, childless adults was terminated in October 1991; white work, school, or community service requirements were established. The results have been positive, as illustrated by the fact that Michigan witnessed a 59% decline in welfare recipients between 1989 and March 1999, versus a national decline of 33%. As with recent declarations of welfare-reform miracles elsewhere in the nation, the true story will be told during the next recession. Engler also has been a leader in calling for state and local control over welfare, which undergirded recent welfare reform measures at the federal level.

Meanwhile on the education front, charter school legislation was passed in December 1994. As Nina Shokraii Rees and Sarah E. Youssef report in the Heritage Foundation's publication *School Choice 1999*, Michigan registered 139 charter schools in 1998–99; these schools targeted a diverse set of students, from at-risk Hispanic students to those with learning disabilities, to those excelling in math and science.

As for taxes, the big reform, which occurred in 1993–94, focused on school financing. In effect, property taxes were reduced and sales taxes were increased. As noted in charts below, between 1992 and 1996, real (1996 dollars) per capita property taxes fell from $1,041 to $740, while real per capita sales and gross receipts revenues increased from $584 to $873. Since property taxes tend to be more damaging to the economy—because of their effects on investments in homes and businesses—than sales taxes, this was a generally positive reform.

In terms of the income tax, Engler has pushed through small but positive measures. The top personal income tax rate fell from 4.6% in 1990 to 4.2% in 2000 and is scheduled to decline to 3.9% by 2003. The corporate tax rate declined from 2.4% to 2.3%.

Unfortunately, while doing much to roll back welfare for individuals, Engler actually has expanded welfare for corporations. For example, in 1995 the state created MEGA—the Michigan Economic Growth Authority (a government "Growth Authority" sounds rather Soviet-like)—to issue tax credits and other incentives to companies expanding in or moving to Michigan. MEGA is part of the Michigan Jobs Commission's larger corporate welfare efforts, whose appropriations have ballooned by better than 50% since 1994. In a July 1999 analysis for the Mackinac Center for Public Policy, Michigan's leading think tank, Michael LaFaive found that of the reported 3,007 new or expanded corporate facilities in Michigan in 1997 and 1998, only 29 of those firms "acknowledged that their decision to locate or expand in Michigan was related to MEGA incentives." The companies were required to make such acknowledgments in order to get their tax credits. Of the "estimated 338,000 new jobs. . . created in the four years since MEGA began," only 0.7 percent can be somehow linked to MEGA. LaFaive notes, however, "Even these job claims may be inflated because MEGA officials cannot prove that the companies involved would not have expanded or moved to Michigan *without* MEGA assistance."

Engler and state legislators would do well to follow the advice laid out in the Mackinac Center's "Keeping Michigan on Track" agenda, which, among other things, calls for increasing privatization efforts; expanding upon the 2,000 rules and regulations already rolled back under the Engler Administration; continuing with welfare reform by setting time limits and promoting marriage and responsibility; requiring drug testing and imposing tougher work requirements for those receiving government assistance; establishing a "family cap" to discourage welfare recipients from having more children; expanding the number of and lifting regulations on charter schools; ending corporate welfare programs; and pushing ahead with broad-based income tax reduction.

Implementing such an agenda would make Michigan an entrepreneurial leader in the 21st century.

POLITICS

Registered Voters

No party registration

Federal Officials: Recent Election and Group Ratings

			ACU	ADA	SBSC
U.S. Senators:	Carl Levin (D)		7	91	15
	1996　Levin (D)	58%			
	Romney (R)	39%			
	Spencer Abraham (R)		82	1	100
	1994　Abraham (R)	52%			
	Carr (D)	43%			
U.S. Representatives:	Bart Stupak (D-1)		21	77	10
	1998　Stupak (D)	59%			
	McManus (R)	40%			
	Peter Hoekstra (R-2)		90	13	95
	1998　Hoekstra (R)	69%			
	Schrauger (D)	30%			

		ACU	ADA	SBSC
Vernon Ehlers (R-3)		71	20	75
1998 Ehlers (R)	73%			
Ferguson (D)	25%			
Dave Camp (R-4)		88	10	85
1998 Camp (R)	91%			
Marsh (LBT)	6%			
James Barcia (D-5)		49	62	30
1998 Barcia (D)	71%			
Brewster (R)	27%			
Fred Upton (R-6)		71	24	70
1998 Upton (R)	70%			
Annen (D)	28%			
Nick Smith (R-7)		90	12	80
1998 Smith (R)	57%			
Berryman (D)	40%			
Debbie Stabenow (D-8)		11	98	20
1998 Stabenow (D)	57%			
Munsell (R)	39%			
Dale Kildee (D-9)		10	89	5
1998 Kildee (D)	56%			
McMillan (R)	42%			
David Bonior (D-10)		5	93	5
1998 Bonior (D)	52%			
Palmer (R)	45%			
Joseph Knollenberg (R-11)		91	3	90
1998 Knollenberg (R)	64%			
Reeds (D)	34%			
Sander Levin (D-12)		3	93	10
1998 Levin (D)	56%			
Touma (R)	42%			
Lynn Rivers (D-13)		12	98	10
1998 Rivers (D)	58%			
Hickey (R)	40%			
John Conyers Jr. (D-14)		5	89	5
1998 Conyers (D)	87%			
Collins (R)	11%			

			ACU	ADA	SBSC
Carolyn Kilpatrick (D-15)			6	95	5
1998	Kilpatrick (D)	87%			
	Boyd-Fields (R)	10%			
John Dingell (D-16)			9	74	5
1998	Dingell (D)	67%			
	Morse (R)	31%			

Electoral Votes: 18

1996 Presidential Results:

Clinton 52%
Dole 39%
Perot 9%

State Officials

Governor 1998 Election: John Engler (R)   62%
                             Geoffrey Fieger (D)   38%

Lt. Governor: Dick Posthumus (R)
Attorney General: Jennifer Granholm (D)
State Senate: 15 Democrats
                   23 Republicans
State General Assembly: 52 Democrats
                             58 Republicans

TAXES AND SPENDING

Total Revenues

Michigan's per capita state and local total revenues registered $5,481 in 1996, ranking 20th in the nation and trailing the U.S. average of $5,706 by 4%. From 1962 to 1996, real per capita state and local revenues increased by 271%, compared with an increase in the national average of 297%.

Taxes

Michigan's per capita state and local taxes registered $2,588 in 1996, ranking 18th in the nation and trailing the U.S. average of $2,597 by 0.3%. From 1962 to 1996, real per capita state and local taxes increased by 139%, compared with an increase of 152% in the U.S. average.

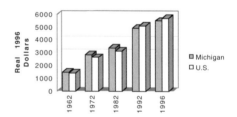

Real Per Capita State and Local
Total Revenues:
Michigan vs. U.S.

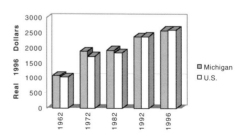

Real Per Capita State and Local
Taxes: Michigan vs. U.S.

Property Taxes

Michigan's per capita state and local property taxes equaled $740 in 1996, ranking 25th in the nation and lagging behind the U.S. average of $789 by 6%. From 1962 to 1996, real per capita state and local property taxes increased by 39%, versus a 67% increase in the U.S. average.

Sales and Gross Receipts Taxes

Michigan's per capita state and local sales and gross receipts taxes came in at $873 in 1996, ranking 28th in the nation and trailing the U.S. average of $939 by 7%. From 1962 to 1996, real per capita state and local sales and gross receipts taxes increased by 116%, versus an increase of 214% in the U.S. average.

Income Taxes

Michigan's per capita state and local income (individual and corporate) taxes registered $842 in 1996, ranking 12th in the nation and topping the U.S. average of $674 by 25%. Michigan did not impose income taxes until 1967, while real per capita income taxes across the U.S. increased by 567% between 1962 and 1996.

Personal Income Tax

A rate 4.2%, ranking 15th in the nation (from lowest tax rate to highest), and comparing with the national average of 5.26%.

Capital Gains Tax

A rate of 4.2%, ranking 20th in the nation (from lowest tax rate to highest), and comparing with the national average of 4.68%.

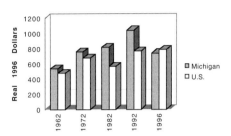

Real Per Capita State and Local Property Taxes: Michigan vs. U.S.

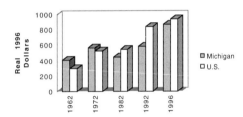

Real Per Capita State and Local Sales and Gross Receipts Taxes: Michigan vs. U.S.

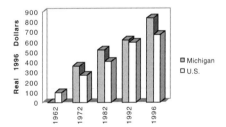

Real Per Capita State and Local Income Taxes: Michigan vs. U.S.

Corporate Income Tax

A rate of 2.3%, ranking 5th in the nation (from lowest tax rate to highest), and comparing with the national average of 6.63%. It should be noted that Michigan applies a 2.3% business tax on partnerships and individuals in business on top of the personal income tax.

Total Expenditures

Michigan's per capita state and local total spending registered $5,115 in 1996, ranking 17th in the nation and trailing the U.S. average of $5,268 by 3%. From 1962 to 1996, real per capita state and local total spending increased by 222%, versus an increase of 254% in the U.S. average.

Welfare Expenditures

Michigan's per capita state and local public welfare spending registered $705 in 1996, ranking 21st in the nation and trailing the U.S. average of $729 by 3%. From 1962 to 1996, real per capita state and local public welfare spending increased by 541%, compared with a 488% increase in the U.S. average.

Welfare Recipients (in thousands)

	1980	1989	3/99	Change 1989–99
Mich.	753	641	264	−59%
U.S.	10,923	10,987	7,335	−33%

Interest on General Debt

Michigan's per capita state and local interest on general debt registered $171 in 1996, ranking 34th in the nation and trailing the U.S. average of $222 by 23%. From 1962 to 1996, real per capita state and local interest on general debt increased by 235%, versus an increase of 335% in the U.S. average.

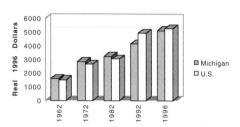

Real Per Capita State and Local Total Expenditures: Michigan vs. U.S.

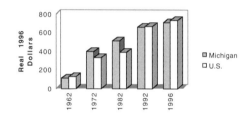

Real Per Capita State and Local Public Welfare Spending: Michigan vs. U.S.

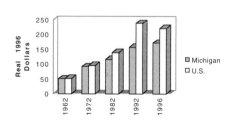

Real Per Capita State and Local Interest on General Debt: Michigan vs. U.S.

Total Debt Outstanding

Michigan's per capita state and local debt registered $3,295 in 1996, ranking 35th in the nation and trailing the U.S. average of $4,409 by 25%. From 1962 to 1996, real per capita state and local debt outstanding increased by 88%, versus an increase of 120% in the U.S. average.

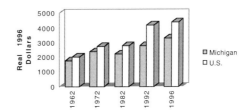

Real Per Capita State and Local Debt Outstanding: Michigan vs. U.S.

Government Employees

Michigan's state and local government employees (full-time equivalent, or FTE) per 10,000 population registered 481.5 in 1997, ranking 47th in the nation and trailing the U.S. average of 531.1 by 9%. From 1962 to 1996, state and local FTE employees per 10,000 population increased by 50%, compared with an increase in the U.S. average of 66%.

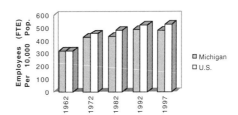

State and Local Government Employees (FTE) Per 10,000 Population: Michigan vs. U.S.

Per Capita Federal Government Expenditures, 1998

	1998	Ranking
Mich.	$4,270	49th
U.S.	$5,491	

Per capita federal spending in Michigan trailed the national average by 22%.

EDUCATION

Total Education Spending

Michigan's per capita state and local education spending registered $1,797 in 1996, ranking 6th in the nation and topping the U.S. average of $1,503 by 20%. From 1962 to 1996, real per capita total education spending increased by 182%, versus an increase in the U.S. average of 173%.

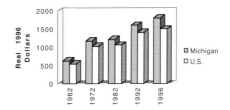

Real Per Capita State and Local Education Spending: Michigan vs. U.S.

Per Pupil Spending

Michigan's per pupil public school spending registered $6,800 in 1998, ranking 11th in the nation and exceeding the U.S. average of $6,131 by 11%. From 1970 to 1998, Michigan's real per pupil public school spending increased by 118%, compared with a 120% increase in the U.S. average.

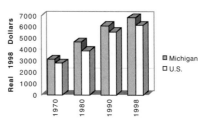

Real Per Pupil Public School Spending: Michigan vs. U.S.

Average Public School Teacher Salaries (in 1997–98 dollars)

	1970	1980	1990	1998	1998 Ranking
Mich.	42,072	40,966	47,223	49,277	4th
U.S.	36,934	33,272	39,956	39,385	

In 1998, the average public school teacher salary in Michigan exceeded the U.S. average by 25%. From 1970 to 1998, the real average teacher salary in Michigan increased by 17%, versus an increase in the U.S. average of 7%.

Pupil/Teacher Ratio, Fall 1996

	Ratio	Rank
Mich.	19.1	45th
U.S.	17.1	

Teachers/Staff, Fall 1996

	Percent	Rank
Mich.	45.2	51st
U.S.	52.1	

Public School 4th-Grade Reading Proficiency, 1998

	Average	Rank (out of 40 states)
Mich.	217	16th
U.S.	215	

Public School 4th-Grade Math Proficiency, 1996

	Average	Rank (out of 44 states)
Mich.	226	14th
U.S.	224	

Public School 8th-Grade Math Proficiency, 1996

	Average	Rank (out of 41 states)
Mich.	277	12th
U.S.	271	

Public School 8th-Grade Science Proficiency, 1996

	Average	Rank (out of 41 states)
Mich.	153	17th
U.S.	148	

Average Math SAT Scores

	1972	1982	1992	1998	Percentage Taking SAT in 1998
Mich.	517	535	542	569	11
U.S.	509	493	501	512	43

Average Verbal SAT Scores

	1972	1982	1992	1998	Percentage Taking SAT in 1998
Mich.	535	536	540	558	11
U.S.	530	504	500	505	43

Expenditures by Public Institutions of Higher Education Per Full-Time-Equivalent Student, 1996

	FTE Student Spending	Rank
Mich.	$13,893	10th
U.S.	$12,343	

Per-FTE-student spending in public institutions of higher education exceeded the U.S. average by 13%.

Per Full-Time-Equivalent Student Revenues from Federal, State, and Local Governments for Public Institutions of Higher Education, 1996

	FTE Student Government Revenues	Rank
Mich.	$8,084	22d
U.S.	$8,101	

Per-FTE-student-government revenues in public institutions of higher education trailed the U.S. average by 0.2%.

Average Salary for Full-Time Professors at Public Universities, 1997

	Average	Rank
Mich.	$79,054	7th
U.S.	$72,599	

The average full-time public university professor salary exceeded the U.S. average by 9%.

ECONOMY AND BUSINESS

Economic Growth

Over the period of 1977 to 1997, Michigan's real gross state product (GSP) grew by 34.9%—ranking 47th in the nation—as compared with real U.S. gross domestic product (GDP), expanding by 70.1%.

At $272.6 billion in 1997, Michigan's GSP ranked as 9th largest in the nation.

From 1993 to 1997, Michigan's annual real GSP growth averaged 4.12%—ranking 15th in the nation—as compared with annual real U.S. GDP growth, averaging 3.08%.

**Real Economic Growth
1977-1997: Michigan vs. U.S.**

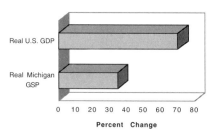

Job Growth

	Growth in Employee Payrolls (Nonagricultural) 1962–98	Ranking
Mich.	93.3%	41st
U.S.	126.5%	

Average Annual Growth in Employee Payrolls (Nonagricultural) 1993–98	Ranking
Mich.	2.82%	31st
U.S.	2.98%	

Per Capita Disposable Income

	1997	Ranking
Mich.	$21,165	21st
U.S.	$21,607	

Per capita disposable income trailed the U.S. average by 2%.

	Real Growth 1962–97	Ranking
Mich.	103.3%	38th
U.S.	116.7%	

	Average Annual Real Growth 1993–97	Ranking
Mich.	1.79%	16th
U.S.	1.48%	

Number of Businesses

	1997	Percent with Fewer than 500 Employees
Businesses with Employees	208,598	98.5
Self-employed Individuals	287,000	

New Business Incorporations

	1980	1986	1992	1997
Mich.	16,660	22,910	24,726	31,280

Percentage Change in Annual New Business Incorporations, 1980 vs. 1997

	Percent	Ranking
Mich.	87.8	12th
U.S.	49.7	

State Merchandise Exports to the World, 1998 (in millions of dollars)

	1998	Rank
Mich.	$39,269	4th

Small Business Survival Index, 1999

Michigan ranked 21st in terms of the policy environment for entrepreneurship.

Fortune 500 Headquarters in 1999

A total of 14 (ranked 13th)

Labor Union Membership, 1983 vs. 1997

	Percentage of Workers		
	1983	1997	1997 Rank
Mich.	30.4	23.1	3d
U.S.	20.1	14.1	

Homeownership Rate, 1998

	Rate	Rank
Mich.	74.4	7th
U.S.	66.3	

CRIME

Crime Rates Per 100 Residents (rankings from best to worst crime rate)

Total Crime	1960	1970	1980	1990	1998	1998 Ranking
Mich.	1.22	3.66	6.68	6.00	4.68	29th
U.S.	1.04	2.74	5.90	5.82	4.62	

From 1960 to 1998, Michigan's crime rate increased by 284%, versus a U.S. increase of 344%. From 1990 to 1998, Michigan's crime rate dropped by 22%, versus a U.S. decrease of 21%.

Violent Crime	1960	1970	1980	1990	1998	1998 Ranking
Mich.	0.18	0.56	0.64	0.79	0.62	37th
U.S.	0.14	0.36	0.58	0.73	0.57	

From 1960 to 1998, Michigan's violent crime rate increased by 244%, versus a U.S. increase of 307%. From 1990 to 1998, Michigan's violent crime rate decreased by 22%, equal to a national decline of 22%.

Property Crime	1960	1970	1980	1990	1998	1998 Ranking
Mich.	1.04	3.10	6.04	5.20	4.06	27th
U.S.	0.90	2.38	5.32	5.09	4.05	

From 1960 to 1998, Michigan's property crime rate increased by 290%, versus a national increase of 350%. From 1990 to 1998, Michigan's property crime rate decreased by 22%, compared with a national decline of 20%.

Real Per Capita Police Protection Spending (in real 1996 dollars)

	1962	1972	1982	1992	1996	1996 Ranking
Mich.	55	102	128	147	152	23d
U.S.	51	95	114	148	168	

In 1996, per capita state and local police protection spending in Michigan trailed the U.S. average by 10%. From 1962 to 1996, real per capita state and local police protection spending increased by 176%, versus an increase of 229% in the U.S. average.

Prisoners in State and Federal Prisons Per 1,000 Population

	1980	1990	1996	1996 Ranking
Mich.	1.63	3.69	4.35	17th
U.S.	1.46	3.11	4.45	

From 1980 to 1996, prisoners per 1,000 population increased by 167%, versus a U.S. increase of 205%.

HEALTH CARE

Health-Care Spending

Michigan's per capita state and local health-care spending registered $216 in 1996, ranking 7th in the nation and exceeding the U.S. average of $151 by 43%. From 1962 to 1996, Michigan's real per capita state and local health-care spending increased by 1,100%, versus an increase of 739% in the U.S. average.

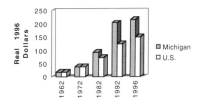

Real Per Capita State and Local Health Care Spending: Michigan vs. U.S.

Hospital Spending

Michigan's per capita state and local hospital spending registered $215 in 1996, ranking 28th in the nation and trailing the U.S. average of $266 by 19%. From 1962 to 1996, Michigan's real per capita state and local hospital spending increased by 81%, as opposed to an increase of 189% in the U.S. average.

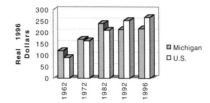

Real Per Capita State and Local Hospital Spending: Michigan vs. U.S.

Medicaid, 1997

	Spending Per Recipient	Ranking
Mich.	$3,169	34th
U.S.	$3,681	

Michigan's per-recipient Medicaid spending trailed the U.S. average by 14%.

ENVIRONMENT

Parks and Recreation Spending

Michigan's per capita state and local parks and recreation spending registered $42 in 1996, ranking 41st in the nation and trailing the U.S. average of $72 by 42%. From 1962 to 1996, real per capita state and local parks and recreation spending increased by 83%, versus a 213% increase in the U.S. average.

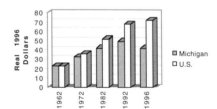

Real Per Capita State and Local Parks and Recreation Spending: Michigan vs. U.S.

State and Local Natural Resources Spending, 1996

	Per Capita	Ranking
Mich.	$65	27th
U.S.	$60	

Per capita state and local natural resources spending in Michigan exceeded the U.S. average by 8%.

State Parks Revenues as a Share of Operating Expenses, 1997

	Percent	Rank
Mich.	71	7th
U.S.	42	

Percentage of Land Owned by the Federal Government, 1996

	Percent	Rank
Mich.	10.9	15th
U.S.	24.8	

SOCIETY AND DEMOGRAPHICS

Population

Michigan's 1998 population of 9.817 million ranked 8th in the nation.

Population Growth, 1990–98

	Percent Change in Population	Ranking
Mich.	5.62	36th
U.S.	8.66	

	Net International Migration	Ranking
Mich.	87,333	14th

	Net Domestic Migration	Ranking
Mich.	−190,363	44th

Infant Mortality Rate, 1998

	Percent	Rank
Mich.	8.1	14th
U.S.	6.4	

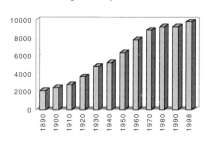

Michigan Population

Percentage of Births of Low Birthweight, 1997

	Percent	Rank
Mich.	7.7	21st
U.S.	7.5	

Percentage of Live Births to Unmarried Women, 1997

	Percent	Rank
Mich.	33.3	18th
U.S.	32.4	

Abortion Rate—Abortions Per 1,000 Women Ages 15–44, 1995

	Rate	Rank
Mich.	22.6	14th
U.S.	22.9	

LIFESTYLE

Percentage of Households with Computers, 1998

	Percent	Rank
Mich.	44.0	16th

Percentage of Households with Internet Access, 1998

	Percent	Rank
Mich.	25.4	26th

State Arts Agency Spending, 1999

	Per Capita	Rank
Mich.	$2.21	7th
U.S.	$1.35	

Per capita state arts spending in 1999 topped the U.S. average by 64%.

Major League Sports Facilities

Year Opened/ Refurb.	Stadium/ Arena	Home Team	Millions of Nominal Dollars		Millions of Real 1997 Dollars	
			Estimated Total Cost	Estimated Taxpayer Cost	Estimated Total Cost	Estimated Taxpayer Cost
1912	Tiger Stadium	Tigers (MLB) 1912–99 Lions (NFL) 1938–74	$0.5	$0.0	$8.3	$0.0
1978	Tiger Stadium (re)		$13.5	$13.5	$35.7	$35.7
1982	Tiger Stadium (re)		$3.6	$3.6	$6.0	$6.0
1927	Olympia Stadium	Red Wings (NHL) 1927–79	$2.5	$0.0	$23.1	$0.0
1975	Silverdome	Lions (NFL) 1975–present Pistons (NBA) 1978–88	$56.0	$56.0	$167.2	$167.2
1977	Palace of Auburn Hills	Pistons (NBA) 1988–present	$70.0	$0.0	$185.2	$0.0
1979	Joe Louis Arena	Red Wings (NHL) 1979–present	$27.0	$27.0	$59.7	$59.7
2000	Comerica Park	Tigers (MLB) 2000–present	$300.0	$100.0	$283.3	$94.4

MINNESOTA

With the election of Jesse "The Body" Ventura as governor in 1998, Minnesota was thrust from the shadows of American politics into the national limelight. A former professional wrestler whose only previous political experience was a four-year stint as mayor of Brooklyn Park, Ventura scored a stunning upset over Republican Norm Coleman and Democrat Hubert "Skip" Humphrey. Ventura became the first candidate of the fledgling Reform Party to capture a statewide office.

The circus-like atmosphere surrounding his candidacy helped Ventura attract many young and formerly disinterested voters to the polls. However, while the media focused on his flair for the eccentric, Ventura seemed to offer Minnesota voters an appealing platform of more limited government and lower taxes. His primary purpose was to return the state's budget surplus to the taxpayers.

After his inauguration, Ventura took some protaxpayer stances, such as opposing efforts to subsidize major league sports teams, like the Twins, with taxpayer-funded stadiums. However, many of Governor Ventura's positions on issues have been at odds with the positions once taken by candidate Ventura. His effort to return the full budget surplus evaporated rather quickly. For example, the budget he proposed in 1999 included a rather hapless tax rebate—tax rebates accomplish nothing in terms of boosting progrowth incentives for working and risk taking—and a tiny income tax cut. On day care, candidate Ventura said it was not the government's responsibility, but Governor Ventura signed legislation providing massive state funding for child care. His support for large increases in spending for public education does not exactly coincide with a belief in limited government. Indeed, his first budget proposal was generally more about increased government spending than serious tax reduction. However, to the credit of Ventura and Republicans in the state legislature, the final budget passed in 1999 included a small personal income tax cut.

Like the Reform Party itself, though, Ventura often seems rather confused in terms of what he believes. First he said he was a libertarian, but then after talking to libertarians, he said he wasn't a libertarian. After talking up the need to cut taxes, in mid-1999 he spoke favorably of former U.S. Senator and once-governor of Connecticut Lowell Weicker as a possible Reform Party presidential candidate in 2000. Weicker, of course, was the guy who imposed a personal income tax in Connecticut.

Noted Minnesota radio storyteller Garrison Keillor may not be the only one growing weary of Ventura's antics. In August 1999, for example, Ventura returned to the wrestling world to referee a match during the World Wrestling Federation's "Summer Slam" event. "When people can separate the personality from the job, there doesn't seem to be too much question that he's been effective and that he's doing a good job," counters Bill Hillsman, who served as Ventura's media consultant during the campaign. Hillsman says that "people aren't concerned about a wrestler running the state government." Ventura eventually fled the Reform Party, which he painted as dysfunctional.

Ventura was sure to face opposition during the following session of the legislature, when he reportedly would lead a fight to scrap the traditional bicameral legislative body and replace it with a single-house legislature. Moving to a unicameral system supposedly would reduce the number of legislators, and make representatives more accountable. Minnesota has more state lawmakers (201) than even California (120). It remains a mystery to us, however, how his proposed reform would hold legislators more accountable. More important, a single-house legislature is a bad idea because it makes passing new laws far too easy. New laws, more often than not, mean more government spending, more regulating, and more taxing. In addition, separate legislative houses often act as checks on each other.

A unicameral legislature will prove a hard sell to state legislators who might lose their jobs. Before voters have the opportunity to vote on the constitutional amendment necessary to make the switch, the state senate and house must first agree to put the measure on the ballot—a long shot, to say the least.

As for the economy, Minnesota's performance generally has been in the middle of the pack when compared with the other states. The state recently launched a "Come Home to Minnesota" campaign to encourage ex-Minnesotans to return to the state. While Minnesota's chilly climate—the average winter temperature is 13 degrees—might hamper government and business efforts to draw skilled workers to the area, a much bigger obstacle is big government. Minnesota's total, property, sales, and income taxes all rank among the most burdensome in the nation, and state and local government spending tops the U.S. average pretty much across the board. Also, as pointed out in the Small Business Survival Committee's annual "Small Business Survival Index," the public policy environment in the state is downright frigid to entrepreneurs.

It remains to be seen just how much success Ventura will be able to achieve as a third-party governor. In order to succeed in the 21st century, it is clear that the state will need to undergo a public policy revolution—turning Minnesota away from its long-time infatuation with government action and working to establish an environment far more friendly to private-sector investment and entrepreneurship. That might seem unlikely, given Minnesota's history and its rather liberal (with two notable exceptions) congressional delegation. However, reforms on the education front over the years show that Minnesota is capable of real, positive change. For example, leading the nation in terms of statewide public school open enrollment, establishing charter schools, as well as offering tax deductions and credits for nontuition education expenditures for students in public, private, and parochial schools. However, despite all the glitz and hype, as a politician, Ventura seems rather conventional thus far.

One thing, however, is certain—with the colorful Jesse "The Body" Ventura now a fixture on the national stage, there is little doubt Minnesota will remain in the spotlight for at least the next few years.

POLITICS

Registered Voters

No party registration

Federal Officials: Recent Election and Group Ratings

			ACU	ADA	SBSC
U.S. Senators:	Paul Wellstone (D)		4	99	20
	1996 Wellstone (D)	50%			
	Boschwitz (R)	41%			
	Rod Grams (R)		97	1	90
	1994 Grams (R)	49%			
	Wynia (D)	44%			
U.S. Representatives:	Gil Gutknecht (R-1)		94	6	90
	1998 Gutknecht (R)	55%			
	Beckman (D)	45%			
	David Minge (D-2)		22	73	25
	1998 Minge (D)	57%			
	Duehring (R)	38%			
	Jim Ramstad (R-3)		68	30	75
	1998 Ramstad (R)	72%			
	Leino (D)	23%			
	Bruce Vento (D-4)		3	95	15
	1998 Vento (D)	54%			
	Newinski (R)	40%			
	Martin Olav Sabo (D-5)		3	96	15
	1998 Sabo (D)	67%			
	Taylor (R)	28%			
	William Luther (D-6)		15	85	20
	1998 Luther (D)	50%			
	Kline (R)	46%			
	Collin Peterson (D-7)		44	58	30
	1998 Peterson (D)	72%			
	Edin (R)	28%			
	James Oberstar (D-8)		9	88	10
	1998 Oberstar (D)	66%			
	Shuster (R)	26%			
Electoral Votes:	10				
1996 Presidential Results:	Clinton	51%			
	Dole	35%			
	Perot	12%			

State Officials

Governor 1998 Election:	Jesse Ventura (Reform)	37%
	Norm Coleman (IR)	34%
	Skip Humphrey (DFL)	28%
Lt. Governor:	Mae Schunk (Reform)	
Attorney General:	Mike Hatch (D)	
State Senate:	40 Democrats	
	26 Republicans	
	1 Independent	
State House:	63 Democrats	
	71 Republicans	

TAXES AND SPENDING

Total Revenues

Minnesota's per capita state and local total revenues registered $6,611 in 1996, ranking 8th in the nation and exceeding the U.S. average of $5,706 by 16%. From 1962 to 1996, real per capita state and local revenues increased by 309%, compared with an increase in the national average of 297%.

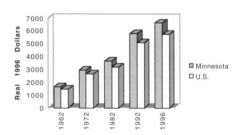

Real Per Capita State and Local Total Revenues: Minnesota vs. U.S.

Taxes

Minnesota's per capita state and local taxes registered $3,128 in 1996, ranking 8th in the nation and exceeding the U.S. average of $2,597 by 20%. From 1962 to 1996, real per capita state and local taxes increased by 171%, compared with an increase of 152% in the U.S. average.

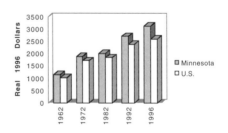

Real Per Capita State and Local Taxes: Minnesota vs. U.S.

Property Taxes

Minnesota's per capita state and local property taxes equaled $884 in 1996, ranking 15th in the nation and exceeding the U.S. average of $789 by 12%. From 1962 to 1996, real per capita state and local property taxes increased by 39%, versus a 67% increase in the U.S. average.

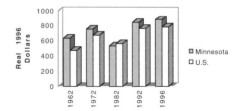

Real Per Capita State and Local Property Taxes: Minnesota vs. U.S.

Sales and Gross Receipts Taxes

Minnesota's per capita state and local sales and gross receipts taxes came in at $990 in 1996, ranking 13th in the nation and topping the U.S. average of $939 by 5%. From 1962 to 1996, real per capita state and local sales and gross receipts taxes increased by 438%, versus an increase of 214% in the U.S. average.

Income Taxes

Minnesota's per capita state and local income (individual and corporate) taxes registered $1,039 in 1996, ranking 6th in the nation and topping the U.S. average of $674 by 54%. From 1962 to 1996, real per capita state and local income taxes increased by 392%, versus a 567% increase in the U.S. average.

Personal Income Tax

A rate of 8.0%, ranking 42d in the nation (from lowest tax rate to highest), and comparing with the national average of 5.26%.

Capital Gains Tax

A rate of 8.0%, ranking 44th in the nation (from lowest tax rate to highest), and comparing with the national average of 4.68%.

Corporate Income Tax

A rate of 9.8%, ranking 48th in the nation (from lowest tax rate to highest), and comparing with the national average of 6.63%.

Total Expenditures

Minnesota's per capita state and local total spending registered $5,988 in 1996, ranking 10th in the nation and exceeding the U.S. average of $5,268 by 14%. From 1962 to 1996, real per capita state and local total spending increased by 258%, versus an increase of 254% in the U.S. average.

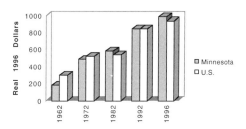

Real Per Capita State and Local Sales and Gross Receipts Taxes: Minnesota vs. U.S.

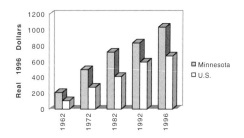

Real Per Capita State and Local Income Taxes: Minnesota vs. U.S.

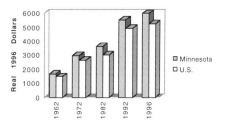

Real Per Capita State and Local Total Expenditures: Minnesota vs. U.S.

Welfare Expenditures

Minnesota's per capita state and local public welfare spending registered $1,003 in 1996, ranking 5th in the nation and outpacing the U.S. average of $729 by 38%. From 1962 to 1996, real per capita state and local public welfare spending increased by 560%, compared with a 488% increase in the U.S. average.

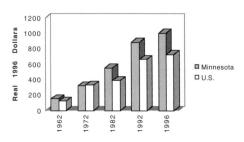

Real Per Capita State and Local Property Taxes: Minnesota vs. U.S.

Welfare Recipients (in thousands)

	1980	1989	3/99	Change 1989–99
Minn.	146	164	140	−15%
U.S.	10,923	10,987	7,335	−33%

Interest on General Debt

Minnesota's per capita state and local interest on general debt registered $262 in 1996, ranking 16th in the nation and exceeding the U.S. average of $222 by 18%. From 1962 to 1996, real per capita state and local interest on general debt increased by 414%, versus an increase of 335% in the U.S. average.

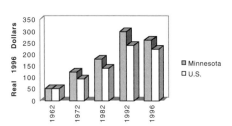

Real Per Capita State and Local Interest on General Debt: Minnesota vs. U.S.

Total Debt Outstanding

Minnesota's per capita state and local debt registered $4,737 in 1996, ranking 17th in the nation and outrunning the U.S. average of $4,409 by 7%. From 1962 to 1996, real per capita state and local debt outstanding increased by 136%, versus an increase of 120% in the U.S. average.

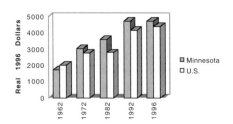

Real Per Capita State and Local Debt Outstanding: Minnesota vs. U.S.

Government Employees

Minnesota's state and local government employees (full-time equivalent, or FTE) per 10,000 population registered 555.4 in 1997, ranking 22d in the nation and exceeding the U.S. average of 531.1 by 5%. From 1962 to 1996, state and local FTE employees per 10,000 population increased by 71%, compared with an increase in the U.S. average of 66%.

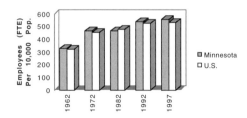

State and Local Government Employees (FTE) Per 10,000 Population: Minnesota vs. U.S.

Per Capita Federal Government Expenditures, 1998

	1998	Ranking
Minn.	$4,317	48th
U.S.	$5,491	

Per capita federal spending in Minnesota trailed the national average by 21%.

EDUCATION

Total Education Spending

Minnesota's per capita state and local education spending registered $1,772 in 1996, ranking 8th in the nation and topping the U.S. average of $1,503 by 18%. From 1962 to 1996, real per capita total education spending increased by 164%, versus an increase in the U.S. average of 173%.

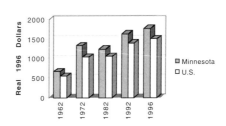

Real Per Capita State and Local Education Spending: Minnesota vs. U.S.

Per Pupil Spending

Minnesota's per pupil public school spending registered $6,292 in 1998, ranking 20th in the nation and exceeding the U.S. average of $6,131 by 3%. From 1970 to 1998, Minnesota's real per pupil public school spending increased by 99%, compared with a 120% increase in the U.S. average.

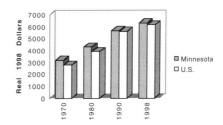

Real Per Pupil Public School Spending: Minnesota vs. U.S.

Average Public School Teacher Salaries (in 1997–98 dollars)

	1970	1980	1990	1998	1998 Ranking
Minn.	37,071	33,151	41,004	39,106	17th
U.S.	36,934	33,272	39,956	39,385	

In 1998, the average public school teacher salary in Minnesota trailed the U.S. average by 1%. From 1970 to 1998, the real average teacher salary in Minnesota increased by 5%, versus an increase in the U.S. average of 7%.

Pupil/Teacher Ratio, Fall 1996

	Ratio	Rank
Minn.	17.6	40th
U.S.	17.1	

Teacher/Staff, Fall 1996

	Percent	Rank
Minn.	55.5	7th
U.S.	52.1	

Public School 4th-Grade Reading Proficiency, 1998

	Average	Rank (out of 40 states)
Minn.	222	8th
U.S.	215	

Public School 8th-Grade Reading Proficiency, 1998

	Average	Rank (out of 37 states)
Minn.	267	6th
U.S.	261	

Public School 4th-Grade Math Proficiency, 1996

	Average	Rank (out of 44 states)
Minn.	232	1st
U.S.	224	

Public School 8th-Grade Math Proficiency, 1996

	Average	Rank (out of 41 states)
Minn.	284	1st
U.S.	271	

Public School 8th-Grade Science Proficiency, 1996

	Average	Rank (out of 41 states)
Minn.	159	5th
U.S.	148	

Average Math SAT Scores

	1972	1982	1992	1998	Percentage Taking SAT in 1998
Minn.	563	560	575	598	9
U.S.	509	493	501	512	43

Average Verbal SAT Scores

	1972	1982	1992	1998	Percentage Taking SAT in 1998
Minn.	584	561	567	585	9
U.S.	530	504	500	505	43

Expenditures by Public Institutions of Higher Education Per Full-Time-Equivalent Student, 1996

	FTE Student Spending	Rank
Minn.	$13,651	13th
U.S.	$12,343	

Per-FTE-student spending in public institutions of higher education exceeded the U.S. average by 11%.

Per Full-Time-Equivalent Student Revenues from Federal, State, and Local Governments for Public Institutions of Higher Education, 1996

	FTE Student Government Revenues	Rank
Minn.	$8,477	17th
U.S.	$8,101	

Per-FTE-student-government revenues in public institutions of higher education outpaced the U.S. average by 5%.

Average Salary for Full-Time Professors at Public Universities, 1997

	Average	Rank
Minn.	$76,087	10th
U.S.	$72,599	

The average full-time public university professor salary exceeded the U.S. average by 5%.

ECONOMY AND BUSINESS

Economic Growth

Over the period of 1977 to 1997, Minnesota's real gross state product (GSP) grew by 85.4%—ranking 22d in the nation—as compared with real U.S. gross domestic product (GDP), expanding by 70.1%.

At $149.4 billion in 1997, Minnesota's GSP ranked as 18th largest in the nation.

From 1993 to 1997, Minnesota's annual real GSP growth averaged 3.89%—ranking 21st in the nation—as compared with annual real U.S. GDP growth, averaging 3.08%.

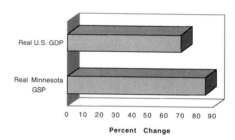

**Real Economic Growth
1977-1997: Minnesota vs. U.S.**

Job Growth

	Growth in Employee Payrolls (Nonagricultural) 1962–98	Ranking
Minn.	160.1%	23d
U.S.	126.5%	

Average Annual Growth in Employee Payrolls (Nonagricultural) 1993–98	Ranking
Minn.	3.21%	18th
U.S.	2.98%	

Per Capita Disposable Income

	1997	Ranking
Minn.	$21,697	18th
U.S.	$21,607	

Per capita disposable income exceeded the U.S. average by 0.4%.

	Real Growth 1962–97	Ranking
Minn.	128.0%	20th
U.S.	116.7%	

	Average Annual Real Growth 1993–97	Ranking
Minn.	1.46%	35th
U.S.	1.48%	

Number of Businesses

	1997	Percent with Fewer than 500 Employees
Businesses with Employees	121,688	97.9
Self-employed Individuals	265,000	

New Business Incorporations

	1980	1986	1992	1997
Minn.	6,998	9,691	10,002	12,655

Percentage Change in Annual New Business Incorporations, 1980 vs. 1997

	Percent	Ranking
Minn.	80.8	13th
U.S.	49.7	

State Merchandise Exports to the World, 1998 (in millions of dollars)

	1998	Rank
Minn.	$13,499	13th

Small Business Survival Index, 1999

Minnesota ranked an extremely poor 44th in terms of its policy environment for entrepreneurship.

Fortune 500 Headquarters in 1999

A total of 13 (ranked 14th), with Minneapolis ranked 11th among U.S. cities, with 6 headquarters

Labor Union Membership, 1983 vs. 1997

	Percentage of Workers		
	1983	1997	1997 Rank
Minn.	23.2	19.9	7th
U.S.	20.1	14.1	

Homeownership Rate, 1998

	Rate	Rank
Minn.	75.4	2d
U.S.	66.3	

CRIME

Crime Rates Per 100 Residents (rankings from best to worst crime rate)

Total Crime	1960	1970	1980	1990	1998	1998 Ranking
Minn.	0.74	2.10	4.80	4.54	4.05	19th
U.S.	1.04	2.74	5.90	5.82	4.62	

From 1960 to 1998, Minnesota's crime rate increased by 447%, versus a U.S. increase of 344%. From 1990 to 1998, Minnesota's crime rate dropped by 11%, versus a U.S. decrease of 21%.

Violent Crime	1960	1970	1980	1990	1998	1998 Ranking
Minn.	0.04	0.15	0.23	0.31	0.31	13th
U.S.	0.14	0.36	0.58	0.73	0.57	

From 1960 to 1998, Minnesota's violent crime rate increased by 675%, versus a U.S. increase of 307%. From 1990 to 1998, Minnesota's violent crime rate remained steady, compared with a national decline of 22%.

Property Crime	1960	1970	1980	1990	1998	1998 Ranking
Minn.	0.70	1.95	4.57	4.23	3.74	20th
U.S.	0.90	2.38	5.32	5.09	4.05	

From 1960 to 1998, Minnesota's property crime rate increased by 434%, versus a national increase of 350%. From 1990 to 1998, Minnesota's property crime rate decreased by 12%, compared with a national decline of 20%.

Real Per Capita Police Protection Spending (in real 1996 dollars)

	1962	1972	1982	1992	1996	1996 Ranking
Minn.	41	62	98	125	140	27th
U.S.	51	95	114	148	168	

In 1996, per capita state and local police protection spending in Minnesota trailed the U.S. average by 17%. From 1962 to 1996, real per capita state and local police protection spending increased by 241%, versus an increase of 229% in the U.S. average.

Prisoners in State and Federal Prisons Per 1,000 Population

	1980	1990	1996	1996 Ranking
Minn.	0.49	0.73	1.11	51st
U.S.	1.46	3.11	4.45	

From 1980 to 1996, prisoners per 1,000 population increased by 127%, versus a U.S. increase of 205%.

HEALTH CARE

Health-Care Spending

Minnesota's per capita state and local health-care spending registered $148 in 1996, ranking 22d in the nation and trailing the U.S. average of $151 by 2%. From 1962 to 1996, Minnesota's real per capita state and local health-care spending increased by 457%, versus an increase of 739% in the U.S. average.

Real Per Capita State and Local Health Care Spending: Minnesota vs. U.S.

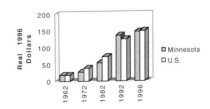

Hospital Spending

Minnesota's per capita state and local hospital spending registered $336 in 1996, ranking 12th in the nation and exceeding the U.S. average of $266 by 26%. From 1962 to 1996, Minnesota's real per capita state and local hospital spending increased by 250%, as opposed to an increase of 189% in the U.S. average.

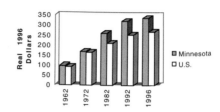

Real Per Capita State and Local Hospital Spending: Minnesota vs. U.S.

Medicaid, 1997

	Spending Per Recipient	Ranking
Minn.	$6,358	4th
U.S.	$3,681	

Minnesota's per-recipient Medicaid spending exceeded the U.S. average by 73%.

ENVIRONMENT

Parks and Recreation Spending

Minnesota's per capita state and local parks and recreation spending registered $104 in 1996, ranking 9th in the nation and outpacing the U.S. average of $72 by 44%. From 1962 to 1996, real per capita state and local parks and recreation spending increased by 352%, versus a 213% increase in the U.S. average.

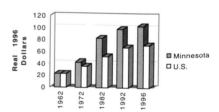

Real Per Capita State and Local Parks and Recreation Spending: Minnesota vs. U.S.

State and Local Natural Resources Spending, 1996

	Per Capita	Ranking
Minn.	$78	17th
U.S.	$60	

Per capita state and local natural resources spending in Minnesota exceeded the U.S. average by 30%.

State Parks Revenues as a Share of Operating Expenses, 1997

	Percent	Rank
Minn.	48	19th
U.S.	42	

Percentage of Land Owned by the Federal Government, 1996

	Percent	Rank
Minn.	7.9	19th
U.S.	24.8	

SOCIETY AND DEMOGRAPHICS

Population

Minnesota's 1998 population of 4.725 million ranked 20th in the nation.

Population Growth, 1990–98

	Percent Change in Population	Ranking
Minn.	7.98	21st
U.S.	8.66	

	Net International Migration	Ranking
Minn.	46,905	21st

	Net Domestic Migration	Ranking
Minn.	71,242	20th

Infant Mortality Rate, 1998

	Percent	Rank
Minn.	5.1	48th
U.S.	6.4	

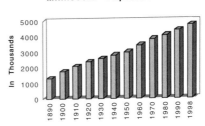

Minnesota Population

Percentage of Births of Low Birthweight, 1997

	Percent	Rank
Minn.	5.9	45th
U.S.	7.5	

Percentage of Live Births to Unmarried Women, 1997

	Percent	Rank
Minn.	24.7	48th
U.S.	32.4	

Abortion Rate—Abortions Per 1,000 Women Ages 15–44, 1995

	Rate	Rank
Minn.	14.2	32d
U.S.	22.9	

LIFESTYLE

Percentage of Households with Computers, 1998

	Percent	Rank
Minn.	47.6	10th

Percentage of Households with Internet Access, 1998

	Percent	Rank
Minn.	29.0	13th

State Arts Agency Spending, 1999

	Per Capita	Rank
Minn.	$2.76	4th
U.S.	$1.35	

Per capita state arts spending in 1999 topped the U.S. average by 104%.

Major League Sports Facilities

Year Opened/ Refurb.	Stadium/ Arena	Home Team	Millions of Nominal Dollars		Millions of Real 1997 Dollars	
			Estimated Total Cost	Estimated Taxpayer Cost	Estimated Total Cost	Estimated Taxpayer Cost
1956	Metropolitan Stadium	Vikings (NFL) 1961–81 Twins (MLB) 1960–81	$4.5	$4.5	$26.6	$26.6
1967	Met Center	North Stars (NHL) 1967–93	$6.0	$6.0	$28.8	$28.8
1982	Metrodome	Vikings (NFL) 1982–present Twins (MLB) 1982–present Timberwolves (NBA) 1989–90	$75.0	$68.0	$124.8	$124.8
1990	Target Center	Timberwolves (NBA) 1990–present	$104.2	$66.0	$128.0	$81.1

MISSISSIPPI

Looking at the numbers for Mississippi, two different stories stand out: the economy and education.

Mississippi's economic performance has been stellar in recent years. Real rates of economic growth and job creation have outpaced the U.S. averages, while inflation-adjusted disposable income growth ranks among the most robust in the country. Such income growth will help remedy Mississippi's dubious position of claiming the smallest shares of households with computers and access to the Internet among the states.

In addition, Mississippi's recent performance on the welfare front has been admirable. Per capita welfare spending comes in well below the U.S. average, and welfare rolls plummeted by 79% between 1989 and March 1999, far outdistancing the U.S. decline of 33%. Other societal measures are disturbing, though, such as ranking highest in terms of infant mortality and second highest in illegitimacy.

Many business owners obviously find the fact that labor union membership ranks among the lowest in the country quite appealing. A high percentage of union membership in a state's workforce not only translates into higher labor costs, but it also tends to result in more regulatory and tax costs as labor unions rank among the most vocal lobbyists in favor of expanding the reach of government.

Indeed, a key contribution to Mississippi's economic well-being has been the state's ability, thus far, to keep expenditures and taxes low relative to the rest of the nation. Per capita state and local government spending, revenues, total taxes, property taxes, and income taxes register among the lowest in the states. Mississippi also carries the third lowest per capita government debt burden in the nation—a positive signal for future levels of taxation.

Meanwhile, education performance has been dismal. For example, Mississippi ranks below average in terms of math, science, and reading proficiency.

Mississippi's per pupil public school spending in 1998 ranked 49th in the nation, as did the average teacher salary. Whenever confronted with poor performing public schools, the education establishment quickly calls for more government spending to remedy these ills.

However, more government spending on education will accomplish nothing in terms of boosting school performance. A government monopoly, like public schools, possesses every incentive to waste additional resources, as no relationship exists between funding and performance. In fact, government tends to reward failure with more money. That is exactly what supporters of more tax dollars for failed public schools in Mississippi are arguing. Many Mississippi schools do not work well, so let us reward them with more money. That is a perverse system.

To the contrary, it is clear that Mississippi should be implementing policies that reunite performance and rewards, like tuition tax credits or vouchers. Providing parents with the ability to pull their children out of failing public schools and choose the school they deem most appropriate for their children would have a powerful impact in boosting overall education quality in the state. Private school innovation and expansion would be stimulated, while public schools would become more focused on the consumer (that is, parents and students) rather than on the bureaucracy (that is, teachers and administrators).

In many ways, Mississippi is set to do well in the 21st century, but its most glaring failure—education—desperately needs the tonic of choice, competition, and entrepreneurship.

POLITICS

Registered Voters

No party registration

Federal Officials: Recent Election and Group Ratings

			ACU	ADA	SBSC
U.S. Senators:	Thad Cochrane (R)		81	8	80
	1996 Cochrane (R)	71%			
	Hunt (D)	27%			
	Trent Lott (R)		93	4	90
	1994 Lott (R)	69%			
	Harper (D)	31%			
U.S. Representatives:	Roger Wicker (R-1)		88	0	95
	1998 Wicker (R)	67%			
	Weathers (D)	31%			
	Bennie Thompson (D-2)		12	89	10
	1998 Thompson (D)	71%			
	Chipman (LBT)	29%			
	Charles Pickering (R-3)		96	0	90
	1998 Pickering (R)	85%			
	Scarborough (LBT)	15%			
	Ronnie Shows (D-4)		NA	NA	NA
	1998 Shows (D)	53%			
	Hosemann (R)	45%			
	Gene Taylor (D-5)		78	25	65
	1998 Taylor (D)	78%			
	McDonnell (R)	19%			
Electoral Votes:	7				
1996 Presidential Results:	Clinton	44%			
	Dole	49%			
	Perot	6%			

State Officials

Governor 1999 Election: Ronnie Musgrove (D)   50%
                           Mike Parker (R)   49%
Lt. Governor: Amy Tuck (D)
Attorney General: Mike Moore (D)
State Senate: 34 Democrats
                           18 Republicans
State House: 86 Democrats
                           33 Republicans
                            3 Independents

TAXES AND SPENDING

Total Revenues

Mississippi's per capita state and local total revenues registered $4,608 in 1996, ranking 47th in the nation and trailing the U.S. average of $5,706 by 19%. From 1962 to 1996, real per capita state and local revenues increased by 344%, compared with an increase in the national average of 297%.

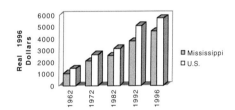

Real Per Capita State and Local Total Revenues: Mississippi vs. U.S.

Taxes

Mississippi's per capita state and local taxes registered $1,894 in 1996, ranking 49th in the nation and trailing the U.S. average of $2,597 by 27%. From 1962 to 1996, real per capita state and local taxes increased by 195%, compared with an increase of 152% in the U.S. average.

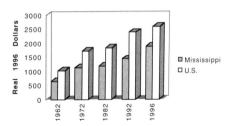

Real Per Capita State and Local Taxes: Mississippi vs. U.S.

Property Taxes

Mississippi's per capita state and local property taxes equaled $445 in 1996, ranking 42d in the nation and trailing the U.S. average of $789 by 44%. From 1962 to 1996, real per capita state and local property taxes increased by 131%, versus a 67% increase in the U.S. average.

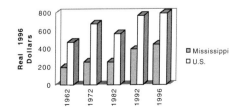

Real Per Capita State and Local Property Taxes: Mississippi vs. U.S.

Sales and Gross Receipts Taxes

Mississippi's per capita state and local sales and gross receipts taxes came in at $979 in 1996, ranking 14th in the nation and exceeding the U.S. average of $939 by 4%. From 1962 to 1996, real per capita state and local sales and gross receipts taxes increased by 223%, versus an increase of 214% in the U.S. average.

Income Taxes

Mississippi's per capita state and local income (individual and corporate) taxes registered $348 in 1996, ranking 42d in the nation and trailing the U.S. average of $674 by 48%. From 1962 to 1996, real per capita state and local income taxes increased by 749%, versus a 567% increase in the U.S. average.

Personal Income Tax

A rate of 5.0%, ranking 19th in the nation (from lowest tax rate to highest), and comparing with the national average of 5.26%.

Capital Gains Tax

A rate of 0%, ranking best in the nation (from lowest tax rate to highest), and comparing with the national average of 4.68%.

Corporate Income Tax

A rate of 5.0%, ranking 9th in the nation (from lowest tax rate to highest), and comparing with the national average of 6.63%.

Total Expenditures

Mississippi's per capita state and local total spending registered $4,312 in 1996, ranking 44th in the nation and trailing the U.S. average of $5,268 by 18%. From 1962 to 1996, real per capita state and local total spending increased by 272%, versus an increase of 254% in the U.S. average.

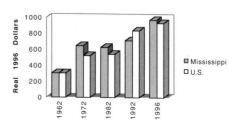

Real Per Capita State and Local Sales and Gross Receipts Taxes: Mississippi vs. U.S.

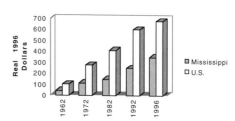

Real Per Capita State and Local Income Taxes: Mississippi vs. U.S.

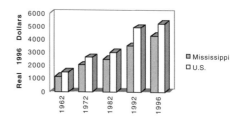

Real Per Capita State and Local Total Expenditures: Mississippi vs. U.S.

Welfare Expenditures

Mississippi's per capita state and local public welfare spending registered $592 in 1996, ranking 36th in the nation and trailing the U.S. average of $729 by 19%. From 1962 to 1996, real per capita state and local public welfare spending increased by 377%, compared with a 488% increase in the U.S. average.

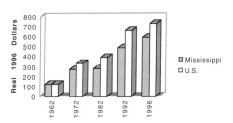

Real Per Capita State and Local Public Welfare Spending: Mississippi vs. U.S.

Welfare Recipients (in thousands)

	1980	1989	3/99	Change 1989–99
Miss.	176	178	38	−79%
U.S.	10,923	10,987	7,335	−33%

Interest on General Debt

Mississippi's per capita state and local interest on general debt registered $132 in 1996, ranking 42d in the nation and trailing the U.S. average of $222 by 41%. From 1962 to 1996, real per capita state and local interest on general debt increased by 257%, versus an increase of 335% in the U.S. average.

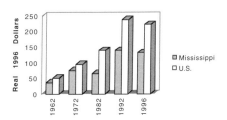

Real Per Capita State and Local Interest on General Debt: Mississippi vs. U.S.

Total Debt Outstanding

Mississippi's per capita state and local debt registered $2,264 in 1996, ranking 49th in the nation and trailing the U.S. average of $4,409 by 49%. From 1962 to 1996, real per capita state and local debt outstanding increased by 70%, versus an increase of 120% in the U.S. average.

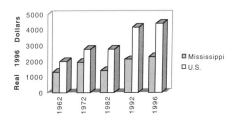

Real Per Capita State and Local Debt Outstanding: Mississippi vs. U.S.

Government Employees

Mississippi's state and local government employees (full-time equivalent, or FTE) per 10,000 population registered 635.6 in 1997, ranking 11th in the nation and exceeding the U.S. average of 531.1 by 20%. From 1962 to 1996, state and local FTE employees per 10,000 population increased by 118%, compared with an increase in the U.S. average of 66%.

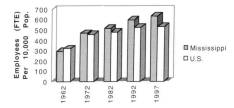

State and Local Government Employees (FTE) Per 10,000 Population: Mississippi vs. U.S.

Per Capita Federal Government Expenditures, 1998

	1998	Ranking
Miss.	$5,565	22d
U.S.	$5,491	

Per capita federal spending in Mississippi topped the national average by 1%.

EDUCATION

Total Education Spending

Mississippi's per capita state and local education spending registered $1,344 in 1996, ranking 41st in the nation and trailing the U.S. average of $1,503 by 11%. From 1962 to 1996, real per capita total education spending increased by 229%, versus an increase in the U.S. average of 173%.

Real Per Capita State and Local Education Spending: Mississippi vs. U.S.

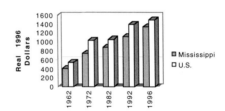

Per Pupil Spending

Mississippi's per pupil public school spending registered $4,231 in 1998, ranking 49th in the nation and trailing the U.S. average of $6,131 by 31%. From 1970 to 1998, Mississippi's real per pupil public school spending increased by 150%, compared with a 120% increase in the U.S. average.

Real Per Pupil Public Spending: Mississippi vs. U.S.

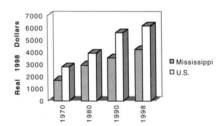

Average Public School Teacher Salaries (in 1997–98 dollars)

	1970	1980	1990	1998	1998 Ranking
Miss.	24,825	24,689	30,943	29,547	49th
U.S.	36,934	33,272	39,956	39,385	

In 1998, the average public school teacher salary in Mississippi trailed the U.S. average by 25%. From 1970 to 1998, the real average teacher salary in Mississippi increased by 19%, versus an increase in the U.S. average of 7%.

Pupil/Teacher Ratio, Fall 1996

	Ratio	Rank
Miss.	17.2	37th
U.S.	17.1	

Teachers/Staff, Fall 1996

	Percent	Rank
Miss.	47.9	48th
U.S.	52.1	

Public School 4th-Grade Reading Proficiency, 1998

	Average	Rank (out of 40 states)
Miss.	204	36th
U.S.	215	

Public School 8th-Grade Reading Proficiency, 1998

	Average	Rank (out of 37 states)
Miss.	251	35th
U.S.	261	

Public School 4th-Grade Math Proficiency, 1996

	Average	Rank (out of 44 states)
Miss.	208	43d
U.S.	224	

Public School 8th-Grade Math Proficiency, 1996

	Average	Rank (out of 41 states)
Miss.	250	40th
U.S.	271	

Public School 8th-Grade Science Proficiency, 1996

	Average	Rank (out of 41 states)
Miss.	133	39th
U.S.	148	

Average Math SAT Scores

	1972	1982	1992	1998	Percentage Taking SAT in 1998
Miss.	461	531	545	549	4
U.S.	509	493	501	512	43

Average Verbal SAT Scores

	1972	1982	1992	1998	Percentage Taking SAT in 1998
Miss.	487	555	552	562	4
U.S.	530	504	500	505	43

Expenditures by Public Institutions of Higher Education Per Full-Time-Equivalent Student, 1996

	FTE Student Spending	Rank
Miss.	$11,473	39th
U.S.	$12,343	

Per-FTE-student spending in public institutions of higher education trailed the U.S. average by 7%.

Per Full-Time-Equivalent Student Revenues from Federal, State, and Local Governments for Public Institutions of Higher Education, 1996

	FTE Student Government Revenues	Rank
Miss.	$8,548	13th
U.S.	$8,101	

Per-FTE-student-government revenues in public institutions of higher education topped the U.S. average by 6%.

Average Salary for Full-Time Professors at Public Universities, 1997

	Average	Rank
Miss.	$59,110	45th
U.S.	$72,599	

The average full-time public university professor salary trailed the U.S. average by 19%.

ECONOMY AND BUSINESS

Economic Growth

Over the period of 1977 to 1997, Mississippi's real gross state product (GSP) grew by 61.2%—ranking 32d in the nation—as compared with real U.S. gross domestic product (GDP), expanding by 70.1%.

At $58.3 billion in 1997, Mississippi's GSP ranked as 33d largest in the nation.

From 1993 to 1997, Mississippi's annual real GSP growth averaged 4.09%—ranking 16th in the nation—as compared with annual real U.S. GDP growth, averaging 3.08%.

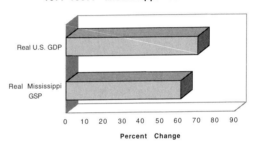

Real Economic Growth 1977-1997: Mississippi vs. U.S.

Real U.S. GDP

Real Mississippi GSP

0 10 20 30 40 50 60 70 80 90

Percent Change

Job Growth

	Growth in Employee Payrolls (Nonagricultural) 1962–98	Ranking
Miss.	165.8%	20th
U.S.	126.5%	

	Average Annual Growth in Employee Payrolls (Nonagricultural) 1993–98	Ranking
Miss.	3.34%	14th
U.S.	2.98%	

Per Capita Disposable Income, 1997

	1997	Ranking
Miss.	$16,351	51st
U.S.	$21,607	

Per capita disposable income trailed the U.S. average by 24%.

	Real Growth 1962–97	Ranking
Miss.	180.2%	1st
U.S.	116.7%	

	Average Annual Real Growth 1993–97	Ranking
Miss.	2.41%	3d
U.S.	1.48%	

Number of Businesses

	1997	Percent with Fewer than 500 Employees
Businesses with Employees	50,852	97.0
Self-employed Individuals	91,000	

New Business Incorporations

	1980	1986	1992	1997
Miss.	4,852	3,098	3,758	4,910

Percentage Change in Annual New Business Incorporations, 1980 vs. 1997

	Percent	Ranking
Miss.	1.2	43d
U.S.	49.7	

State Merchandise Exports to the World, 1998 (in millions of dollars)

	1998	Rank
Miss.	$1,414	42d

Small Business Survival Index, 1999

Mississippi ranks 10th best in terms of its policy environment for entrepreneurship.

Fortune 500 Headquarters in 1999

A total of 1 (ranked 38th)

Labor Union Membership, 1983 vs. 1997

| | Percent of Workers | | |
	1983	1997	1997 Rank
Miss.	9.9	5.4	49th
U.S.	20.1	14.1	

Homeownership Rate, 1998

	Rate	Rank
Miss.	75.1	3d
U.S.	66.3	

CRIME

Crime Rates Per 100 Residents (rankings from best to worst crime rate)

Total Crime	1960	1970	1980	1990	1998	1998 Ranking
Miss.	0.44	0.86	3.42	3.87	4.38	25th
U.S.	1.04	2.74	5.90	5.82	4.62	

From 1960 to 1998, Mississippi's crime rate increased by 895%, versus a U.S. increase of 344%. From 1990 to 1998, Mississippi's crime rate increased by 13%, versus a U.S. decrease of 21%.

Violent Crime	1960	1970	1980	1990	1998	1998 Ranking
Miss.	0.10	0.18	0.34	0.34	0.41	22d
U.S.	0.14	0.36	0.58	0.73	0.57	

From 1960 to 1998, Mississippi's violent crime rate increased by 310%, versus a U.S. increase of 301%. From 1990 to 1998, Mississippi's violent crime rate increased by 21%, compared with a national decline of 22%.

Property Crime	1960	1970	1980	1990	1998	1998 Ranking
Miss.	0.34	0.68	3.08	3.53	3.97	25th
U.S.	0.90	2.38	5.32	5.09	4.05	

From 1960 to 1998, Mississippi's property crime rate increased by 1,068%, versus a national increase of 350%. From 1990 to 1998, Mississippi's property crime rate increased by 12%, compared with a nation decline of 20%.

Real Per Capita Police Protection Spending (in real 1996 dollars)

	1962	1972	1982	1992	1996	1996 Ranking
Miss.	23	43	66	79	106	45th
U.S.	51	95	114	148	168	

In 1996, per capita state and local police protection spending in Mississippi trailed the U.S. average by 37%. From 1962 to 1996, real per capita state and local police protection spending increased by 361%, versus an increase of 229% in the U.S. average.

Prisoners in State and Federal Prisons Per 1,000 population

	1980	1990	1996	1996 Ranking
Miss.	1.55	3.25	5.11	9th
U.S.	1.46	3.11	4.45	

From 1980 to 1996, prisoners per 1,000 population increased by 230%, versus a U.S. increase of 205%.

HEALTH CARE

Health Care Spending

Mississippi's per capita state and local health-care spending registered $98 in 1996, ranking 36th in the nation and lagging behind the U.S. average of $151 by 35%. From 1962 to 1996, Mississippi's real per capita state and local health-care spending increased by 600%, versus an increase of 739% in the U.S. average.

Real Per Capita State and Local Health Care Spending: Mississippi vs. U.S.

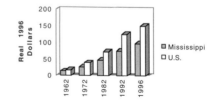

Hospital Spending

Mississippi's per capita state and local hospital spending registered $488 in 1996, ranking 6th in the nation and exceeding the U.S. average of $266 by 83%. From 1962 to 1996, Alabama's real per capita state and local hospital spending increased by 526%, as opposed to an increase of 189% in the U.S. average.

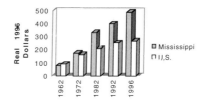

Real Per Capita State and Local Hospital Spending: Mississippi vs. U.S.

Medicaid, 1997

	Spending Per Recipient	Ranking
Miss.	$2,825	43d
U.S.	$3,681	

Mississippi's per-recipient Medicaid spending trailed the U.S. average by 23%.

ENVIRONMENT

Parks and Recreation Spending

Mississippi's per capita state and local parks and recreation spending registered $32 in 1996, ranking 50th in the nation and trailing the U.S. average of $72 by 56%. From 1962 to 1996, real per capita state and local parks and recreation spending increased by 540%, versus a 213% increase in the U.S. average.

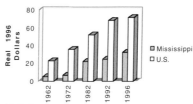

Real Per Capita State and Local Parks and Recreation Spending: Mississippi vs. U.S.

State and Local Natural Resources Spending, 1996

	Per Capita	Ranking
Miss.	$67	25th
U.S.	$60	

Per capita state and local natural resources spending in Mississippi topped the U.S. average by 12%.

State Parks Revenues as a Share of Operating Expenses, 1997

	Percent	Rank
Miss.	44	21st
U.S.	42	

Percentage of Land Owned by the Federal Government, 1996

	Percent	Rank
Miss.	4.2	28th
U.S.	24.8	

SOCIETY AND DEMOGRAPHICS

Population

Mississippi's 1998 population of 2.752 million ranked 31st in the nation.

Population Growth, 1990–98

	Percentage Change in Population	Ranking
Miss.	6.87	26th
U.S.	8.66	

	Net International Migration	Ranking
Miss.	6,499	43d

	Net Domestic Migration	Ranking
Miss.	42,748	25th

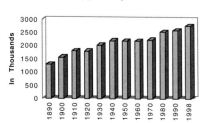

Mississippi Population

Infant Mortality Rate, 1998

	Percent	Rank
Miss.	10.4	1st
U.S.	6.4	

Percentage of Births of Low Birthweight, 1997

	Percent	Rank
Miss.	10.1	3d
U.S.	7.5	

Percentage of Live Births to Unmarried Women, 1997

	Percent	Rank
Miss.	45.5	2d
U.S.	32.4	

Abortion Rate—Abortions Per 1,000 Women Ages 15–44, 1995

	Rate	Rank
Miss.	5.5	50th
U.S.	22.9	

LIFESTYLE

Percentage of Households with Computers, 1998

	Percent	Rank
Miss.	25.7	51st

Percentage of Households with Internet Access, 1998

	Percent	Rank
Miss.	13.6	51st

State Arts Agency Spending, 1999

	Per Capita	Rank
Miss.	$0.77	30th
U.S.	$1.35	

Per capita state arts spending in 1999 trailed the U.S. average by 43%.

Major League Sports Facilities

None

MISSOURI

Slugger Mark McGwire came to St. Louis, Missouri, during the 1997 baseball season. Of course, in 1998, McGwire achieve what many thought was impossible—not only breaking Roger Maris's single season home-run record of 61 but "going yard" 70 times by the end of the year. In 1999, he passed the magic career home run mark of 500. No doubt, after McGwire eventually retires from the game, his next stop will be Cooperstown and the Baseball Hall of Fame, joining fellow St. Louis Cardinals like Stan Musial, Lou Brock, and Dizzy Dean.

Meanwhile, Missouri also claims a host of natives who belong in their professions' respective "halls of fame," like writer Mark Twain, General Omar Bradley, poet T. S. Eliot, news man Walter Cronkite, and hoofer and actress Ginger Rogers.

Of course, there also is Harry S. Truman, 33d U.S. president. Truman is worshiped by many for his straightforward talk and oversight of the end of World War II. His policies offered much for liberals and conservatives to discuss, agree to, or argue about, including the Korean War, the Truman Doctrine, the creation of the United Nations, the recognition of Israel, the attempted nationalization of the steel industry, the opposition to the Taft-Hartley Act, and his so-called "Fair Deal" that called for a vast expansion of federal programs and powers. Truman, in the end, was a true New Dealer—opposing the Nazis, becoming a Cold Warrior, and fully embracing bigger government at home.

Today in Missouri, two names come to mind when one thinks of political players with national stature. On the Democratic side is U.S. Representative Richard Gephardt. Gephardt is the current minority leader in the U.S. House of Representatives. He ran for the Democratic presidential nod in 1988 but failed, and he seemed to ponder a challenge to Vice President Al Gore in the 2000 race. However, he gave up a long-shot run for the White House to try to become House Speaker if Democrats can grab just a handful of seats away from Republicans in 2000.

Meanwhile, on the GOP side, U.S. Senator John Ashcroft also pondered a run for president in 2000, but he opted out and decided to seek reelection for the Senate against Democratic Governor Mel Carnahan. While Gephardt over the years has drifted from being a more middle-of-the-road Democrat to being a quite liberal one, Ashcroft ranks as one of the Senate's most conservative members.

However, looking into the future, we think the person to watch from Missouri is U.S. Representative Jim Talent. Talent was elected to Congress in 1992 with 50% of the vote, which climbed to 70% by 1998. Talent is a man who clearly enjoys analyzing, discussing, and debating the issues, and he stands out on Capitol Hill for his knowledge. Testifying before the House Small Business Committee, of which he is chairman, is a rare treat; more often than not, the atmosphere turns out to resemble a policy roundtable. While Talent stakes out strong promarket, conservative positions, he is fair and possesses masterful political skills that engage people on the other side of the aisle.

Talent has decided to run for governor of Missouri in 2000. If he wins and establishes a strong pro-growth, conservative record, we would watch for an eventual presidential run by Jim Talent, perhaps in 2008 or 2012.

In the meantime, whoever wins the gubernatorial election in 2000 will take the reins of a state that has been relatively frugal in terms of state and local per capita government spending in most major expenditure categories. Per capita taxes come in on the low side as well, though individual income and capital gains tax rates are a bit high and certainly leave room for reductions. In fact, such cuts would do some economic good, as the record on economic growth, job creation, disposable income, and population have been mixed—ahead of the nation in some areas, lagging behind in others.

The state's crime rate leaves room for improvement, as well.

Given the increasing importance of entrepreneurship in the 21st century, significant tax relief and government reforms will be needed to allow Missouri to break out of mediocrity and have a "hall of fame" future.

POLITICS

Registered Voters

No party registration

Federal Officials: Recent Election and Group Ratings

			ACU	ADA	SBSC
U.S. Senators:	Kit Bond (R)		81	13	75
	1998 Bond (R)	53%			
	Nixon (D)	44%			
	John Ashcroft (R)		99	3	95
	1998 Ashcroft (R)	60%			
	Wheat (D)	36%			
U.S. Representatives:	William Clay (D-1)		4	88	5
	1998 Clay (D)	73%			
	Soluade (R)	25%			
	James Talent (R-2)		97	6	95
	1998 Talent (R)	70%			
	Ross (D)	28%			
	Richard Gephardt (D-3)		11	71	10
	1998 Gephardt (D)	56%			
	Federer (R)	42%			
	Ike Skelton (D-4)		51	24	25
	1998 Skelton (D)	71%			
	Noland (R)	27%			

			ACU	ADA	SBSC
Karen McCarthy (D-5)			12	85	10
1998	McCarthy (D)	66%			
	Bennett (R)	31%			
Pat Danner (D-6)			37	61	35
1998	Danner (D)	71%			
	Bailey (R)	27%			
Roy Blunt (R-7)			90	5	90
1998	Blunt (R)	73%			
	Perkel (D)	24%			
Jo Ann Emerson (R-8)			89	7	90
1998	Emerson (R)	63%			
	Heckemeyer (D)	36%			
Kenny Hulshof (R-9)			90	15	90
1998	Hulshof (R)	62%			
	Vogt (D)	36%			

Electoral Votes: 11

1996 Presidential Results:

Clinton	48%
Dole	41%
Perot	10%

State Officials

Governor 1996 Election:	Mel Carnahan (D)	57%
	Margaret Kelly (R)	40%
Lt. Governor:	Roger Wilson (D)	
Attorney General:	Jay Nixon (D)	
State Senate:	17 Democrats	
	16 Republicans	
	1 vacancy	
State House:	86 Democrats	
	76 Republicans	
	1 Independent	

TAXES AND SPENDING

Total Revenues

Missouri's per capita state and local total revenues registered $4,786 in 1996, ranking 41st in the nation and trailing the U.S. average of $5,706 by 16%. From 1962 to 1996, real per capita state and local revenues increased by 283%, compared with an increase in the national average of 297%.

Real Per Capita State and Local Total Revenues: Missouri vs. U.S.

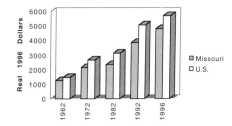

Taxes

Missouri's per capita state and local taxes registered $2,181 in 1996, ranking 37th in the nation and trailing the U.S. average of $2,597 by 16%. From 1962 to 1996, real per capita state and local taxes increased by 150%, compared with an increase of 152% in the U.S. average.

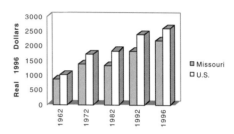

Real Per Capita State and Local Taxes: Missouri vs. U.S.

Property Taxes

Missouri's per capita state and local property taxes equaled $488 in 1996, ranking 40th in the nation and trailing the U.S. average of $789 by 38%. From 1962 to 1996, real per capita state and local property taxes increased by 31%, versus a 67% increase in the U.S. average.

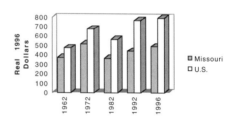

Real Per Capita State and Local Property Taxes: Missouri vs. U.S.

Sales and Gross Receipts Taxes

Missouri's per capita state and local sales and gross receipts taxes came in at $909 in 1996, ranking 24th in the nation and trailing the U.S. average of $939 by 3%. From 1962 to 1996, real per capita state and local sales and gross receipts taxes increased by 259%, versus an increase of 214% in the U.S. average.

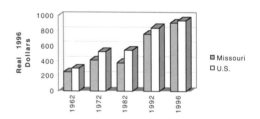

Real Per Capita State and Local Sales and Gross Receipts Taxes: Missouri vs. U.S.

Income Taxes

Missouri's per capita state and local income (individual and corporate) taxes registered $638 in 1996, ranking 25th in the nation and trailing the U.S. average of $674 by 5%. From 1962 to 1996, real per capita state and local income taxes increased by 633%, versus a 567% increase in the U.S. average.

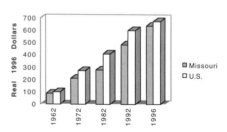

Real Per Capita State and Local Income Taxes: Missouri vs. U.S.

Personal Income Tax

A rate of 6.0%, ranking 27th in the nation (from lowest tax rate to highest), and comparing with the national average of 5.26%.

Capital Gains Tax

A rate of 6.0%, ranking 30th in the nation (from lowest tax rate to highest), and comparing with the national average of 4.68%.

Corporate Income Tax

A rate of 5.16%, ranking 13th in the nation (from lowest tax rate to highest), and comparing with the national average of 6.63%.

Total Expenditures

Missouri's per capita state and local spending registered $4,033 in 1996, ranking 50th in the nation and lagging behind the U.S. average of $5,268 by 23%. From 1962 to 1996, real per capita state and local total spending increased by 225%, versus an increase of 254% in the U.S. average.

Welfare Expenditures

Missouri's per capita state and local public welfare spending registered $550 in 1996, ranking 42d in the nation and trailing the U.S. average of $729 by 25%. From 1962 to 1996, real per capita state and local public welfare spending increased by 253%, compared with a 488% increase in the U.S. average.

Welfare Recipients (in thousands)

	1980	1989	3/99	Change 1989–99
Mo.	216	207	135	−35%
U.S.	10,923	10,987	7,335	−33%

Interest on General Debt

Missouri's per capita state and local interest on general debt registered $141 in 1996, ranking 40th in the nation and lagging behind the U.S. average of $222 by 36%. From 1962 to 1996, real per capita state and local interest on general debt increased by 404%, versus an increase of 335% in the U.S. average.

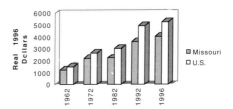

Real Per Capita State and Local Total Expenditures: Missouri vs. U.S.

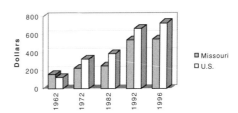

Real Per Capita State and Local Public Welfare Spending: Missouri vs. U.S.

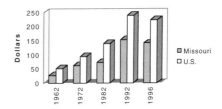

Real Per Capita State and Local Interest on General Debt: Missouri vs. U.S.

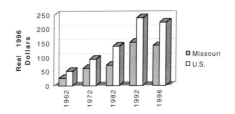

Real Per Capita State and Local Interest on General Debt: Missouri vs. U.S.

Total Debt Outstanding

Missouri's per capita state and local debt registered $2,589 in 1996, ranking 47th in the nation and trailing the U.S. average of $4,409 by 41%. From 1962 to 1996, real per capita state and local debt outstanding increased by 113%, versus an increase of 120% in the U.S. average.

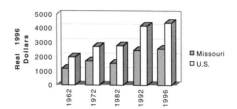

Real Per Capita State and Local Debt Outstanding: Missouri vs. U.S.

Government Employees

Missouri's state and local government employees (full-time equivalent, or FTE) per 10,000 population registered 537.7 in 1997, ranking 26th in the nation and topping the U.S. average of 531.1 by 1%. From 1962 to 1996, state and local FTE employees per 10,000 population increased by 88%, compared with an increase in the U.S. average of 66%.

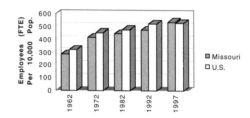

State and Local Government Employees (FTE) Per 10,000 Population: Missouri vs. U.S.

Per Capita Federal Government Expenditures, 1998

	1998	Ranking
Mo.	$6,009	11th
U.S.	$5,491	

Per capita federal spending in Missouri outpaced the national average by 9%.

EDUCATION

Total Education Spending

Missouri's per capita state and local education spending registered $1,331 in 1996, ranking 42d in the nation and trailing the U.S. average of $1,503 by 11%. From 1962 to 1996, real per capita total education spending increased by 196%, versus an increase in the U.S. average of 173%.

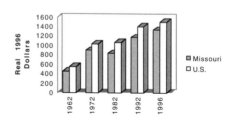

Real Per Capita State and Local Education Spending: Missouri vs. U.S.

Per Pupil Spending

Missouri's per pupil public school spending registered $5,075 in 1998, ranking 38th in the nation and lagging behind the U.S. average of $6,131 by 17%. From 1970 to 1998, Missouri's real per pupil public school spending increased by 130%, compared with a 120% increase in the U.S. average.

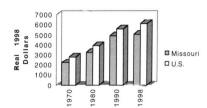

Real Per Pupil Public School Spending: Missouri vs. U.S.

Average Public School Teacher Salaries (in 1997–98 dollars)

	1970	1980	1990	1998	1998 Ranking
Mo.	33,393	28,505	34,513	33,975	33d
U.S.	36,934	33,272	39,956	39,385	

In 1998, the average public school teacher salary in Missouri trailed the U.S. average by 14%. From 1970 to 1998, the real average teacher salary in Missouri increased by 2%, versus an increase in the U.S. average of 7%.

Pupil/Teacher Ratio, Fall 1996

	Ratio	Rank
Mo.	15.1	13th
U.S.	17.1	

Teachers/Staff, Fall 1996

	Percent	Rank
Mo.	52.9	26th
U.S.	52.1	

Public School 4th-Grade Reading Proficiency, 1998

	Average	Rank (out of 40 states)
Mo.	216	20th
U.S.	215	

Public School 8th-Grade Reading Proficiency, 1998

	Average	Rank (out of 37 states)
Mo.	263	16th
U.S.	261	

Public School 4th-Grade Math Proficiency, 1996

	Average	Rank (out of 44 states)
Mo.	225	17th
U.S.	224	

Public School 8th-Grade Math Proficiency, 1996

	Average	Rank (out of 41 states)
Mo.	273	19th
U.S.	271	

Public School 8th-Grade Science Proficiency, 1996

	Average	Rank (out of 41 states)
Mo.	151	18th
U.S.	148	

Average Math SAT Scores

	1972	1982	1992	1998	Percentage Taking SAT in 1998
Mo.	533	531	547	573	8
U.S.	509	493	501	512	43

Average Verbal SAT Scores

	1972	1982	1992	1998	Percentage Taking SAT in 1998
Mo.	559	542	550	570	8
U.S.	530	504	500	505	43

Expenditures by Public Institutions of Higher Education Per Full-Time-Equivalent Student, 1996

	FTE Student Spending	Rank
Mo.	$11,504	37th
U.S.	$12,343	

Per-FTE-student spending in public institutions of higher education trailed the U.S. average by 7%.

Per Full-Time-Equivalent Student Revenues from Federal, State, and Local Governments for Public Institutions of Higher Education, 1996

	FTE Student Government Revenues	Rank
Mo.	$6,801	41st
U.S.	$8,101	

Per-FTE-student-government revenues in public institutions of higher education lagged behind the U.S. average by 16%.

Average Salary for Full-Time Professors at Public Universities, 1997

	Average	Rank
Mo.	$72,974	19th
U.S.	$72,599	

The average full-time public university professor salary exceeded the U.S. average by 0.5%.

ECONOMY AND BUSINESS

Economic Growth

Over the period of 1977 to 1997, Missouri's real gross state product (GSP) grew by 54.3%—ranking 35th in the nation—as compared with real U.S. gross domestic product (GDP), expanding by 70.1%.

At $152.1 billion in 1997, Missouri's GSP ranked as 17th largest in the nation.

From 1993 to 1997, Missouri's annual real GSP growth averaged 3.62%—ranking 27th in the nation—as compared with annual real U.S. GDP growth, averaging 3.08%

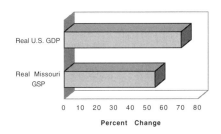

Real Economic Growth
1977-1997: Missouri vs. U.S.

Real U.S. GDP

Real Missouri GSP

0 10 20 30 40 50 60 70 80

Percent Change

Job Growth

	Growth in Employee Payrolls (Nonagricultural) 1962–98	Ranking
Mo.	98.0%	40th
U.S.	126.5%	

	Average Annual Growth in Employee Payrolls (Nonagricultural) 1993–98	Ranking
Mo.	2.85%	29th
U.S.	2.98%	

Per Capita Disposable Income, 1997

	1997	Ranking
Mo.	$20,485	26th
U.S.	$21,607	

Per capita disposable income trailed the U.S. average by 5%.

	Real Growth 1962–97	Ranking
Mo.	116.1%	27th
U.S.	116.7%	

	Average Annual Real Growth 1993–97	Ranking
Mo.	1.71%	21st
U.S.	1.48%	

Number of Businesses

	1997	Percent with Fewer than 500 Employees
Businesses with Employees	125,833	97.8%
Self-employed individuals	246,000	

New Business Incorporations

	1980	1986	1992	1997
Mo.	8,612	11,242	10,020	10,273

Percentage Change in Annual New Business Incorporations, 1980 vs. 1997

	Percent	Ranking
Mo.	19.3	35th
U.S.	49.7	

State Merchandise Exports to the World, 1998 (in millions of dollars)

	1998	Rank
Mo.	$6,832	24th

Small Business Survival Index, 1999

Missouri ranked a solid 15th in terms of its policy environment for entrepreneurship.

Fortune 500 Headquarters in 1999

A total of 15 (ranked 11th), with St. Louis ranked 4th among U.S. cities, with 11 headquarters

Labor Union Membership, 1983 vs. 1997

	Percentage of Workers		
	1983	1997	1997 Rank
Mo.	20.8	14.6	20th
U.S.	20.1	14.1	

Homeownership Rate, 1998

	Rate	Rank
Mo.	70.7	19th
U.S.	66.3	

CRIME

Crime Rates Per 100 Residents (rankings from best to worst crime rate)

Total Crime	1960	1970	1980	1990	1998	1998 Ranking
Mo.	1.22	2.77	5.43	5.12	4.83	31st
U.S.	1.04	2.74	5.90	5.82	4.62	

From 1960 to 1998, Missouri's crime rate increased by 296%, versus a U.S. increase of 344%. From 1990 to 1998, Missouri's crime rate dropped by 6%, versus a U.S. decrease of 21%.

Violent Crime	1960	1970	1980	1990	1998	1998 Ranking
Mo.	0.17	0.41	0.55	0.72	0.56	32d
U.S.	0.14	0.36	0.58	0.73	0.57	

From 1960 to 1998, Missouri's violent crime rate increased by 229%, versus a U.S. increase of 307%. From 1990 to 1998, Missouri's violent crime rate decreased by 22%, matching a national decline of 22%.

Property Crime	1960	1970	1980	1990	1998	1998 Ranking
Mo.	1.05	2.36	4.88	4.41	4.27	32d
U.S.	0.90	2.38	5.32	5.09	4.05	

From 1960 to 1998, Missouri's property crime rate increased by 307%, versus a national increase of 350%. From 1990 to 1998, Missouri's property crime rate decreased by 3%, compared with a national decline of 20%.

Real Per Capita Police Protection Spending (in real 1996 dollars)

	1962	1972	1982	1992	1996	1996 Ranking
Mo.	51	82	100	112	134	32d
U.S.	51	95	114	148	168	

In 1996, per capita state and local police protection spending in Missouri trailed the U.S. average by 20%. From 1962 to 1996, real per capita state and local police protection spending increased by 163%, versus an increase of 229% in the U.S. average.

Prisoners in State and Federal Prisons Per 1,000 Population

	1980	1990	1996	1996 Ranking
Mo.	1.16	2.92	4.10	21st
U.S.	1.46	3.11	4.45	

From 1980 to 1996, prisoners per 1,000 population increased by 253%, versus a U.S. increase of 205%.

HEALTH CARE

Health-Care Spending

Missouri's per capita state and local health-care spending registered $133 in 1996, ranking 25th in the nation and trailing the U.S. average of $151 by 12%. From 1962 to 1996, Missouri's real per capita state and local health-care spending increased by 850%, versus an increase of 739% in the U.S. average.

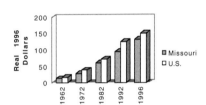

Real Per Capita State and Local Health Care Spending: Missouri vs. U.S.

Hospital Spending

Missouri's per capita state and local hospital spending registered $192 in 1996, ranking 29th in the nation and lagging behind the U.S. average of $266 by 28%. From 1962 to 1996, Missouri's real per capita state and local hospital spending increased by 146%, as opposed to an increase of 189% in the U.S. average.

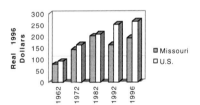

Real Per Capita State and Local Hospital Spending: Missouri vs. U.S.

Medicaid, 1997

	Spending Per Recipient	Ranking
Mo.	$3,883	21st
U.S.	$3,681	

Missouri's per-recipient Medicaid spending topped the U.S. average by 5%.

ENVIRONMENT

Parks and Recreation Spending

Missouri's per capita state and local parks and recreation spending registered $75 in 1996, ranking 21st in the nation and exceeding the U.S. average of $72 by 4%. From 1962 to 1996, real per capita state and local parks and recreation spending increased by 226%, versus a 213% increase in the U.S. average.

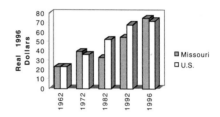

Real Per Capita State and Local Parks and Recreation Spending: Missouri vs. U.S.

State and Local Natural Resources Spending, 1996

	Per Capita	Ranking
Mo.	$42	36th
U.S.	$60	

Per capita state and local natural resources spending in Missouri trailed the U.S. average by 30%.

State Parks Revenues as a Share of Operating Expenses, 1997

	Percent	Rank
Mo.	24	41st
U.S.	42	

Percentage of Land Owned by the Federal Government, 1996

	Percent	Rank
Mo.	3.7	31st
U.S.	24.8	

SOCIETY AND DEMOGRAPHICS

Population

Missouri's 1998 population of 5.439 million ranked 16th in the nation.

Population Growth, 1990–98

	Percentage Change in Population	Ranking
Mo.	6.29	32d
U.S.	8.66	

	Net International Migration	Ranking
Mo.	33,521	24th

	Net Domestic Migration	Ranking
Mo.	94,299	15th

Infant Mortality Rate, 1998

	Percent	Rank
Mo.	7.7	15th
U.S.	6.4	

Percentage of Births of Low Birthweight, 1997

	Percent	Rank
Mo.	7.7	21st
U.S.	7.5	

Missouri   Population

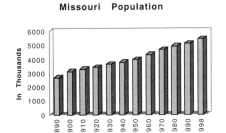

Percentage of Live Births to Unmarried Women, 1997

	Percent	Rank
Mo.	33.1	19th
U.S.	32.4	

Abortion Rate—Abortions Per 1,000 Women Ages 15–44, 1995

	Rate	Rank
Mo.	8.9	44th
U.S.	22.9	

LIFESTYLE

Percentage of Households with Computers, 1998

	Percent	Rank
Mo.	41.8	27th

Percentage of Households with Internet Access, 1998

	Percent	Rank
Mo.	24.3	32d

State Arts Agency Spending, 1999

	Per Capita	Rank
Mo.	$1.89	10th
U.S.	$1.35	

Per capita state arts spending in 1999 topped the U.S. average by 40%.

Major League Sports Facilities

Year Opened/ Refurb.	Stadium/ Arena	Home Team	Millions of Nominal Dollars		Millions of Real 1997 Dollars	
			Estimated Total Cost	Estimated Taxpayer Cost	Estimated Total Cost	Estimated Taxpayer Cost
1925	Sportsman's Park	Cardinals (MLB) 1920–66 Browns (MLB) 1902–53	$0.5	$0.0	$4.6	$0.0
1922	Municipal Stadium	Royals (MLB) 1969–72 Chiefs (AFL/NFL) 1963–71	$0.4	$0.0	$3.8	$0.0
1955	Municipal Stadium (re)		$7.5	$7.5	$45.7	$45.7
1929	St. Louis Arena	Blues (NHL) 1967–94	$2.0	$0.0	$18.7	$0.0
1966	Busch Memorial	Cardinals (MLB) 1966–present Cardinals (NFL) 1966–87	$24.0	$19.0	$118.8	$94.1
1972	Arrowhead Stadium	Chiefs (NFL) 1972–present	$53.0	$53.0	$203.8	$203.8
1973	Kauffman Stadium	Royals (MLB) 1973–present	$50.5	$47.0	$182.1	$169.7
1994	Kiel Center	Blues (NHL) 1994–present	$171.5	$36.5	$185.8	$39.5
1995	Trans World Dome	Rams (NFL) 1995–present	$290.0	$290.0	$305.3	$305.3

Montana

When President Bill Clinton brags about the nation's economic prosperity, many Montanans are at a loss to understand what he is talking about. "Montana is always six to eight years behind the rest of the nation, with one foot planted firmly in the past and the other on an uncertain future," observes Cy Jamison, lifetime resident and 1994 Republican congressional candidate.

The state's governor, Marc Racicot, is fond of saying, "Montana is what America used to be," but "Big Sky" country is changing too. Until 1992, the state had two congressional districts that almost perfectly mirrored its political and geographic makeup. In the conservative flat farm country of the east, Republicans ruled. In the mountainous resort area of the west, liberals felt secure in their stronghold. However, a loss in population of only 15,000 forced the state back to one congressional seat.

Change is apparent on the landscape as well. Twenty years ago, Montanans started seeing affluent second homes popping up along the ridges. In subsequent years, the pace has quickened as more and more "view" ranches spread from west to east across the state. With the influx of name-brand "weekend warriors" such as Tom Brokaw, Ted Turner, Meryl Streep, Hank Williams Jr., and Mel Gibson, Republicans feared that Montana would go the same way as many other western states.

Celebrities aside, the new residents have proven to be nontraditional liberals. "No doubt they're liberal on environmental issues, but they're unquestionably fiscal and social conservatives," remarks Cindy Marlenee, a lobbyist who splits her time between the state and Washington, D.C. The new residents also have had an unexpected impact. Republican dominance in Flathead and Ravalli counties has marginalized Democrats in the western part of the state.

As for the economy, many of the numbers in the following pages confirm what some folks in the state say about poor economic performance. For example, real economic growth, job creation, and real disposable income growth trail the U.S. average. While per capita government spending and taxing levels hover around or below the U.S. averages, the state's tax system is biased in an antigrowth direction—heavy on income and property taxes, which effectively tax the returns on working, saving, investing, and entrepreneurship, and light on consumption taxes. Studies, such as work done by economist Richard Vedder, consistently show that consumption-based tax systems are more favorable to economic growth than are systems that tax production. Increasing business incorporations and a recent pickup in population provide a couple of positives on which Montana can build.

Anecdotes paint a mixed picture of the economy and lifestyle. As is the case everywhere, farm population is heading down. Meanwhile, retirees are moving into little towns. A well-respected public school system graduates young adults who move to Billings or out of state to begin their adulthood.

Meanwhile, Montana's love-hate relationship with the federal government is slowly becoming more hate than love. Biologists have replaced traditional Park Rangers in Yellowstone. The Forest Service is closing more and more land to public access, making hunting and fishing more difficult for native Montanans. What perhaps most angers residents in small-town Montana is the site of Bureau of Land Management (BLM) personnel. "They drive around in their brand new pickup trucks, when the best the locals can afford is 10 years old; being paid $68,000 a year with taxpayer dollars, more than the bank president and all the time micromanaging everyone's lives," laments Cy Jamison.

Montana has a longer border with Canada than any other state in the United States. In some respects, the traffic across that border, known as the "high line," is the continuous silent commentary on the differences between the United States and Canada.

For example, during the U.S. health-care debates in 1993, Canada's socialized medicine was portrayed as superior to the U.S. health-care system. The parking lots of Montana hospitals, however, tell a different story. Canadian license plates rank only second to those of in-state vehicles. Many Canadians who cannot or will not wait for free health care in their country rent a post office box in the United States, buy a health insurance policy, and head to Montana's regionally renowned hospitals and doctors. Incidentally, according to the U.S. Census Bureau, Montana ranks 10th in the nation in terms of physicians per 100,000 population.

Is Montana poised for the 21st century? Well, since some say the state is years behind the rest of the nation, Montanans may not have to deal with that question for another few years.

POLITICS

Registered Voters

No party registration

Federal Officials: Recent Election and Group Ratings

			ACU	ADA	SBSC
U.S. Senators:	Max Baucus (D)		11	77	30
	1996 Baucus (D)	49%			
	Rehberg (R)	44%			
	Conrad Burns (R)		89	6	95
	1994 Burns (R)	62%			
	Mudd (D)	38%			
U.S. Representatives:	Rick Hill (R)		86	5	85
	1998 Hill (R)	53%			
	Deschamps (D)	44%			
Electoral Votes:	3				
1996 Presidential Results:	Clinton	41%			
	Dole	44%			
	Perot	14%			

State Officials

Governor 1996 Election:	Marc Racicot (R)	81%
	Judy Jacobson (D)	19%
Lt. Governor:	Judy Martz (R)	
Attorney General:	Joseph Mazurek (D)	
State Senate:	18 Democrats	
	32 Republicans	
State House:	41 Democrats	
	59 Republicans	

TAXES AND SPENDING

Total Revenues

Montana's per capita state and local total revenues registered $5,125 in 1996, ranking 29th in the nation and trailing the U.S. average of $5,706 by 10%. From 1962 to 1996, real per capita state and local revenues increased by 207%, compared with an increase in the national average of 297%.

Taxes

Montana's per capita state and local taxes registered $2,027 in 1996, ranking 42d in the nation and trailing the U.S. average of $2,597 by 22%. From 1962 to 1996, real per capita state and local taxes increased by 89%, compared with an increase of 152% in the U.S. average.

Property Taxes

Montana's per capita state and local property taxes equaled $883 in 1996, ranking 16th in the nation and topping the U.S. average of $789 by 12%. From 1962 to 1996, real per capita state and local property taxes increased by 46%, versus a 67% increase in the U.S. average.

Real Per Capita State and Local Total Revenues: Montana vs. U.S.

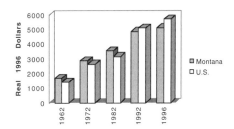

Real Per Capita State and Local Taxes: Montana vs. U.S.

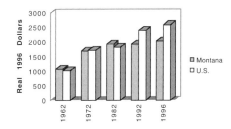

Real Per Capita State and Local Property Taxes: Montana vs. U.S.

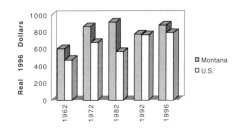

Sales and Gross Receipts Taxes

Montana's per capita state and local sales and gross receipts taxes came in at $307 in 1996, ranking 50th in the nation and trailing the U.S. average of $939 by 67%. From 1962 to 1996, real per capita state and local sales and gross receipts taxes increased by 45%, versus an increase of 214% in the U.S. average.

Income Taxes

Montana's per capita state and local income (individual and corporate) taxes registered $522 in 1996, ranking 36th in the nation and trailing the U.S. average of $674 by 23%. From 1962 to 1996, real per capita state and local income taxes increased by 1,531%, versus a 567% increase in the U.S. average.

Personal Income Tax

A rate of 6.64%, ranking 33d in the nation (from lowest tax rate to highest), and comparing with the national average of 5.26%.

Capital Gains Tax

A rate of 8.8%, ranking 44th in the nation (from lowest tax rate to highest), and comparing with the national average of 4.68%.

Corporate Income Tax

A rate 6.75%, ranking 23d in the nation (from lowest tax rate to highest), and comparing with the national average of 6.63%.

Total Expenditures

Montana's per capita state and local total spending registered $4,777 in 1996, ranking 31st in the nation and trailing the U.S. average of $5,268 by 9%. From 1962 to 1996, real per capita state and local total spending increased by 195%, versus an increase of 254% in the U.S. average.

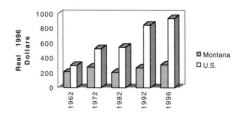

Real Per Capita State and Local Sales and Gross Receipts Taxes: Montana vs. U.S.

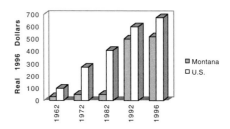

Real Per Capita State and Local Income Taxes: Montana vs. U.S.

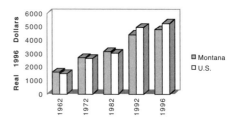

Real Per Capita State and Local Total Expenditures: Montana vs. U.S.

Welfare Expenditures

Montana's per capita state and local public welfare spending registered $597 in 1996, ranking 34th in the nation and trailing the U.S. average of $729 by 18%. From 1962 to 1996, real per capita state and local public welfare spending increased by 491%, compared with a 488% increase in the U.S. average.

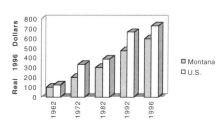

Real Per Capita State and Local
Public Welfare Spending:
Montana vs. U.S.

Welfare Recipients (in thousands)

	1980	1989	3/99	Change 1989–99
Mont.	20	32	16	−50%
U.S.	10,923	10,987	7,335	−33%

Interest on General Debt

Montana's per capita state and local interest on general debt registered $197 in 1996, ranking 28th in the nation and trailing the U.S. average of $222 by 11%. From 1962 to 1996, real per capita state and local interest on general debt increased by 432%, versus an increase of 335% in the U.S. average.

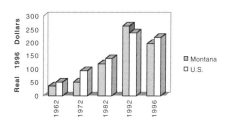

Real Per Capita State and Local
Interest on General Debt:
Montana vs. U.S.

Total Debt Outstanding

Montana's per capita state and local debt registered $3,331 in 1996, ranking 34th in the nation and trailing the U.S. average of $4,409 by 24%. From 1962 to 1996, real per capita state and local debt outstanding increased by 169%, versus an increase of 120% in the U.S. average.

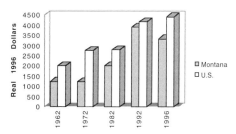

Real Per Capita State and Local
Debt Outstanding: Montana vs. U.S.

Government Employees

Montana's state and local government employees (full-time equivalent, or FTE) per 10,000 population registered 579.3 in 1997, ranking 15th in the nation and topping the U.S. average of 531.1 by 9%. From 1962 to 1996, state and local FTE employees per 10,000 population increased by 62%, compared with an increase in the U.S. average of 66%.

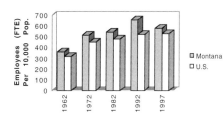

State and Local Government
Employees (FTE) Per 10,000
Population: Montana vs. U.S.

Per Capita Federal Government Expenditures, 1998

	1998	Ranking
Mont.	$6,210	8th
U.S.	$5,491	

Per capita federal spending in Montana topped the national average by 13%.

EDUCATION

Total Education Spending

Montana's per capita state and local education spending registered $1,671 in 1996, ranking 13th in the nation and topping the U.S. average of $1,503 by 11%. From 1962 to 1996, real per capita total education spending increased by 176%, versus an increase in the U.S. average of 173%.

Per Pupil Spending

Montana's per pupil public school spending registered $5,994 in 1998, ranking 24th in the nation and trailing the U.S. average of $6,131 by 2%. From 1970 to 1998, Montana's real per pupil public school spending increased by 122%, compared with a 120% increase in the U.S. average.

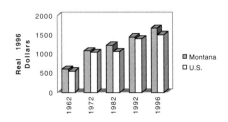

Real Per Capita State and Local Education Spending: Montana vs. U.S.

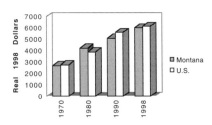

Real Per Pupil Public School Spending: Montana vs. U.S.

Average Public School Teacher Salaries (in 1997–98 dollars)

	1970	1980	1990	1998	1998 Ranking
Mont.	32,567	30,287	31,948	30,617	44th
U.S.	36,934	33,272	39,956	39,385	

In 1998, the average public school teacher salary in Montana trailed the U.S. average by 22%. From 1970 to 1998, the real average teacher salary in Montana decreased by 6%, versus an increase in the U.S. average of 7%.

Pupil/Teacher Ratio, Fall 1996

	Ratio	Rank
Mont.	16.0	22d
U.S.	17.1	

Teachers/Staff, Fall 1996

	Percent	Rank
Mont.	54.4	12th
U.S.	52.1	

Public School 4th-Grade Reading Proficiency, 1998

	Average	Rank (out of 40 states)
Mont.	226	2d
U.S.	215	

Public School 8th-Grade Reading Proficiency, 1998

	Average	Rank (out of 37 states)
Mont.	270	3d
U.S.	261	

Public School 4th-Grade Math Proficiency, 1996

	Average	Rank (out of 44 states)
Mont.	228	10th
U.S.	224	

Public School 8th-Grade Math Proficiency, 1996

	Average	Rank (out of 41 states)
Mont.	283	5th
U.S.	271	

Public School 8th-Grade Science Proficiency, 1996

	Average	Rank (out of 41 states)
Mont.	162	2d
U.S.	148	

Average Math SAT Scores

	1972	1982	1992	1998	Percentage Taking SAT in 1998
Mont.	565	563	542	546	24
U.S.	509	493	501	512	43

Average Verbal SAT Scores

	1972	1982	1992	1998	Percentage Taking SAT in 1998
Mont.	586	563	541	543	24
U.S.	530	504	500	505	43

Expenditures by Public Institutions of Higher Education Per Full-Time-Equivalent Student, 1996

	FTE Student Spending	Rank
Mont.	$10,722	46th
U.S.	$12,343	

Per-FTE-student spending in public institutions of higher education trailed the U.S. average by 13%.

Per Full-Time-Equivalent Student Revenues from Federal, State, and Local Governments for Public Institutions of Higher Education, 1996

	FTE Student Government Revenues	Rank
Mont.	$6,370	46th
U.S.	$8,101	

Per-FTE-student-government revenues in public institutions of higher education trailed the U.S. average by 21%.

Average Salary for Full-Time Professors at Public Universities, 1997

	Average	Rank
Mont.	$54,288	48th
U.S.	$72,599	

The average full-time public university professor salary trailed the U.S. average by 25%.

ECONOMY AND BUSINESS

Economic Growth

Over the period of 1977 to 1997, Montana's real gross state product (GSP) grew by 32.0%—ranking 48th in the nation—as compared with real U.S. gross domestic product (GDP), expanding by 70.1%.

At $19.2 billion in 1997, Montana's GSP ranked as 48th largest in the nation.

From 1993 to 1997, Montana's annual real GSP growth averaged 2.85%—ranking 38th in the nation—as compared with annual real U.S. GDP growth, averaging 3.08%.

**Real Economic Growth
1977-1997: Montana vs. U.S.**

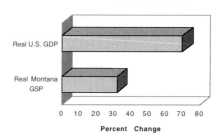

Job Growth

	Growth in Employee Payrolls (Nonagricultural) 1962–98	Ranking
Mont.	119.7%	36th
U.S.	126.5%	

	Average Annual Growth in Employee Payrolls (Nonagricultural) 1993–98	Ranking
Mont.	3.32%	15th
U.S.	2.98%	

Per Capita Disposable Income, 1997

	1997	Ranking
Mont.	$17,186	48th
U.S.	$21,607	

Per capita disposable income trailed the U.S. average by 20%.

	Real Growth 1962–97	Ranking
Mont.	73.5%	51st
U.S.	116.7%	

	Average Annual Real Growth 1993–97	Ranking
Mont.	1.24%	43d
U.S.	1.48%	

Number of Businesses

	1997	Percent with Fewer than 500 Employees
Businesses with Employees	29,259	97.8
Self-employed Individuals	67,000	

New Business Incorporations

	1980	1986	1992	1997
Mont.	1,487	1,572	1,948	3,219

Percentage Change in Annual New Business Incorporations, 1980 vs. 1997

	Percent	Ranking
Mont.	116.5	5th
U.S.	49.7	

State Merchandise Exports to the World, 1998 (in millions of dollars)

	1998	Rank
Mont.	$390	48th

Small Business Survival Index, 1999

Montana ranks a poor 37th in terms of its policy environment for entrepreneurship.

Fortune 500 Headquarters in 1999

None

Labor Union Membership, 1983 vs. 1997

	Percentage of Workers		
	1983	1997	1997 Rank
Mont.	18.3	13.8	22d
U.S.	20.1	14.1	

Homeownership Rate, 1998

	Rate	Rank
Mont.	68.6	30th
U.S.	66.3	

CRIME

Crime Rates Per 100 Residents (rankings from best to worst crime rate)

Total Crime	1960	1970	1980	1990	1998	1998 Ranking
Mont.	0.97	1.64	5.02	4.50	4.07	20th
U.S.	1.04	2.74	5.90	5.82	4.62	

From 1960 to 1998, Montana's crime rate increased by 320%, versus a U.S. increase of 344%. From 1990 to 1998, Montana's crime rate dropped by 10%, versus a U.S. decrease of 21%.

Violent Crime	1960	1970	1980	1990	1998	1998 Ranking
Mont.	0.06	0.11	0.22	0.16	0.14	5th
U.S.	0.14	0.36	0.58	0.73	0.57	

From 1960 to 1998, Montana's violent crime rate increased by 133%, versus a U.S. increase of 307%. From 1990 to 1998, Montana's violent crime rate decreased by 13%, compared with a national decline of 22%.

Property Crime	1960	1970	1980	1990	1998	1998 Ranking
Mont.	0.91	1.53	4.80	4.34	3.93	23d
U.S.	0.90	2.38	5.32	5.09	4.05	

From 1960 to 1998, Montana's property crime rate increased by 332%, versus a national increase of 350%. From 1990 to 1998, Montana's property crime rate decreased by 9%, compared with a national decline of 20%.

Real Per Capita Police Protection Spending (in real 1996 dollars)

	1962	1972	1982	1992	1996	1996 Ranking
Mont.	37	59	92	97	116	41st
U.S.	51	95	114	148	168	

In 1996, per capita state and local police protection spending in Montana trailed the U.S. average by 31%. From 1962 to 1996, real per capita state and local police protection spending increased by 214%, versus an increase of 229% in the U.S. average.

Prisoners in State and Federal Prisons Per 1,000 Population

	1980	1990	1996	1996 Ranking
Mont.	0.94	1.78	2.61	39th
U.S.	1.46	3.11	4.45	

From 1980 to 1996, prisoners per 1,000 population increased by 178%, versus a U.S. increase of 205%.

HEALTH CARE

Health-Care Spending

Montana's per capita state and local health-care spending registered $166 in 1996, ranking 17th in the nation and exceeding the U.S. average of $151 by 10%. From 1962 to 1996, Montana's real per capita state and local health-care spending increased by 1,086%, versus an increase of 739% in the U.S. average.

Real Per Capita State and Local Health Care Spending: Montana vs. U.S.

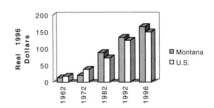

Hospital Spending

Montana's per capita state and local hospital spending registered $86 in 1996, ranking 44th in the nation and trailing the U.S. average of $266 by 68%. From 1962 to 1996, Montana's real per capita state and local hospital spending increased by 56%, as opposed to an increase of 189% in the U.S. average.

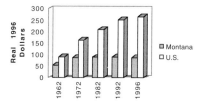

Real Per Capita State and Local Hospital Spending: Montana vs. U.S.

Medicaid, 1997

	Spending Per Recipient	Ranking
Mont.	$3,312	31st
U.S.	$3,681	

Montana's per-recipient Medicaid spending trailed the U.S. average by 10%.

ENVIRONMENT

Parks and Recreation Spending

Montana's per capita state and local parks and recreation spending registered $39 in 1996, ranking 45th in the nation and trailing the U.S. average of $72 by 46%. From 1962 to 1996, real per capita state and local parks and recreation spending increased by 333%, versus a 213% increase in the U.S. average.

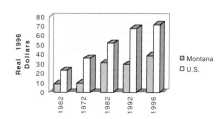

Real Per Capita State and Local Parks and Recreation Spending: Montana vs. U.S.

State and Local Natural Resources Spending, 1996

	Per Capita	Ranking
Mont.	$142	4th
U.S.	$60	

Per capita state and local natural resources spending in Montana exceeded the U.S. average by 137%.

State Parks Revenues as a Share of Operating Expenses, 1997

	Percent	Rank
Mont.	23	42d
U.S.	42	

Percentage of Land Owned by the Federal Government, 1996

	Percent	Rank
Mont.	27.3	12th
U.S.	24.8	

SOCIETY AND DEMOGRAPHICS

Population

Montana's 1998 population of .880 million ranked 44th in the nation.

Population Growth, 1990–98

	Percentage Change in Population	Ranking
Mont.	10.14	17th
U.S.	8.66	

	Net International Migration	Ranking
Mont.	2,689	50th

	Net Domestic Migration	Ranking
Mont.	48,006	23d

Infant Mortality Rate, 1998

	Percent	Rank
Mont.	7.0	24th
U.S.	6.4	

Montana Population

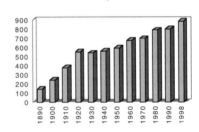

Percentage of Births of Low Birthweight, 1997

	Percent	Rank
Mont.	6.3	40th
U.S.	7.5	

Percentage of Live Births to Unmarried Women, 1997

	Percent	Rank
Mont.	26.8	42d
U.S.	32.4	

Abortion Rate—Abortions Per 1,000 Women Ages 15–44, 1995

	Rate	Rank
Mont.	16.2	25th
U.S.	22.9	

LIFESTYLE

Percentage of Households with Computers, 1998

	Percent	Rank
Mont.	40.9	33d

Percentage of Households with Internet Access, 1998

	Percent	Rank
Mont.	21.5	41st

State Arts Agency Spending, 1999

	Per Capita	Rank
Mont.	$0.28	50th
U.S.	$1.35	

Per capita state arts spending in 1999 trailed the U.S average by 79%.

Major League Sports Facilities

None

NEBRASKA

Even if they do not like corn or Cornhuskers football, liberals should love Nebraska. Oh sure, the state is largely Republican today, but the Left can look fondly on one of the most prominent politicians Nebraska gave the United States—William Jennings Bryan.

Bryan was not a native Nebraskan, but he did serve two terms (1891–95) as a U.S. congressman from the state and was editor in chief of the *Omaha World-Herald* for a couple of years. Of course, Bryan led the Nebraska delegation to the Democratic convention in 1896, made his famous "Cross of Gold" speech, and walked away with the party's presidential nomination. Bryan favored imposing an income tax, moving off the gold standard, and making the federal government bigger and more activist. He wound up being the Democrats' nominee for president in 1896, 1900, and 1908—and lost each race. However, Bryan laid the groundwork for the ascendency of 20th-century Leftism and the expansion of government.

Though you do not hear much in liberal circles today about Bryan, he really is the Democratic version of Barry Goldwater—he lost, but set the philosophical stage for those coming after him. Before Woodrow Wilson, Franklin Delano Roosevelt, and Lyndon B. Johnson, there was William Jennings Bryan.

Judging by the people elected recently, one might think that Nebraskans are trying to forget their liberal roots. All three Nebraska members of the U.S. House of Representatives are Republicans, as is one senator (Chuck Hagel), with the other senator (Bob Kerrey) sometimes considered a more moderate Democrat. Governor Michael Johanns is a Republican as well, while the state legislature is officially nonpartisan.

However, the tax and budget record is rather mixed, with per capita state and local government revenues, property taxes, and expenditures running on the high side. Nebraska also claims a very large number of government employees as a share of population. The state's income tax rates are quite lofty as well (Bryan would be proud). In contrast, though, per capita state and local interest paid on general debt registers as the lowest in the nation, and state and local debt has been declining since 1982.

The state's economy has not exactly been red hot. In most measures, Nebraska's economy tends to fall in the middle of the pack. The state also lags behind the nation in terms of population growth. However, new business incorporations have been rising at an excellent rate.

So, maybe this very Republican state is still somehow haunted by the ghost of William Jennings Bryan. What would be a sure-fire exorcism? Kill the state's income taxes.

POLITICS

Registered Voters

38% Democrats
50% Republicans
13% Other

Federal Officials: Recent Election and Group Ratings

			ACU	ADA	SBSC
U.S. Senators:	Robert Kerrey (D)		8	82	10
	1994 Kerrey (D)	55%			
	Stoney (R)	45%			
	Chuck Hagel (R)		76	3	85
	1996 Hagel (R)	56%			
	Nelson (D)	41%			
U.S. Representatives:	Douglas Bereuter (R-1)		69	20	80
	1998 Bereuter (R)	73%			
	Eret (D)	26%			
	Lee Terry (R-2)		NA	NA	NA
	1998 Terry (R)	66%			
	Scott (D)	34%			
	Bill Barrett (R-3)		87	5	85
	1998 Barrett (R)	84%			
	Hickman (LBT) 15%				
Electoral Votes:	5				
1996 Presidential Results:	Clinton	35%			
	Dole	54%			
	Perot	11%			

State Officials

Governor 1998 Election:	Michael Johanns (R)	54%
	Bill Hoppner (D)	46%
Lt. Governor:	Dave Maurstad (R)	
Attorney General:	Don Stenberg (R)	
Unicameral State Legislature:	49 senators, officially nonpartisan	

TAXES AND SPENDING

Total Revenues

Nebraska's per capita state and local total revenues registered $5,992 in 1996, ranking 15th in the nation and topping the U.S. average of $5,706 by 5%. From 1962 to 1996, real per capita state and local revenues increased by 359%, compared with an increase in the national average of 297%.

Taxes

Nebraska's per capita state and local taxes registered $2,531 in 1996, ranking 20th in the nation and trailing the U.S. average of $2,597 by 3%. From 1962 to 1996, real per capita state and local taxes increased by 195%, compared with an increase of 152% in the U.S. average.

Property Taxes

Nebraska's per capita state and local property taxes equaled $956 in 1996, ranking 13th in the nation and topping the U.S. average of $789 by 21%. From 1962 to 1996, real per capita state and local property taxes increased by 58%, versus a 67% increase in the U.S. average.

Sales and Gross Receipts Taxes

Nebraska's per capita state and local sales and gross receipts taxes came in at $848 in 1996, ranking 29th in the nation and trailing the U.S. average of $939 by 10%. From 1962 to 1996, real per capita state and local sales and gross receipts taxes increased by 414%, versus an increase of 214% in the U.S. average.

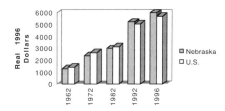

Real Per Capita State and Local Total Revenues: Nebraska vs. U.S.

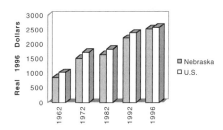

Real Per Capita State and Local Taxes: Nebraska vs. U.S.

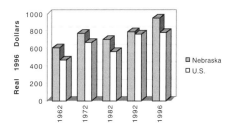

Real Per Capita State and Local Property Taxes: Nebraska vs. U.S.

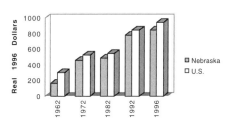

Real Per Capita State and Local Sales and Gross Receipts Taxes: Nebraska vs. U.S.

Income Taxes

Nebraska's per capita state and local income (individual and corporate) taxes registered $585 in 1996, ranking 30th in the nation and trailing the U.S. average of $674 by 13%. Nebraska did not impose income taxes until 1967, while between 1962 and 1996 the U.S. average increased by 567%.

Personal Income Tax

A rate of 6.68%, ranking 34th in the nation (from lowest tax rate to highest), and comparing with the national average of 5.26%.

Capital Gains Tax

A rate of 6.68%, ranking 38th in the nation (from lowest tax rate to highest), and comparing with the national average of 4.68%.

Corporate Income Tax

A rate of 7.81% ranking 31st in the nation (from lowest tax rate to highest), and comparing with the national average of 6.63%.

Total Expenditures

Nebraska's per capita state and local total spending registered $5,440 in 1996, ranking 15th in the nation and topping the U.S. average of $5,268 by 3%. From 1962 to 1996, real per capita state and local total spending increased by 310%, versus an increase of 254% in the U.S. average.

Welfare Expenditures

Nebraska's per capita state and local public welfare spending registered $616 in 1996, ranking 32d in the nation and trailing the U.S. average of $729 by 16%. From 1962 to 1996, real per capita state and local public welfare spending increased by 642%, compared with a 488% increase in the U.S. average.

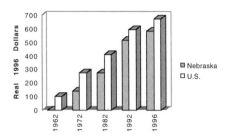

Real Per Capita State and Local Income Taxes: Nebraska vs. U.S.

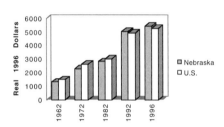

Real Per Capita State and Local Total Expenditures: Nebraska vs. U.S.

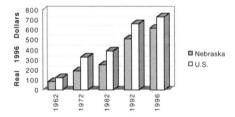

Real Per Capita State and Local Public Welfare Spending: Nebraska vs. U.S.

Welfare Recipients (in thousands)

	1980	1989	3/99	Change 1989–99
Nebr.	38	41	35	−15%
U.S.	10,923	10,987	7,335	−33%

Interest on General Debt

Nebraska's per capita state and local interest on general debt registered $106 in 1996, ranking 51st in the nation and trailing the U.S. average of $222 by 52%. From 1962 to 1996, real per capita state and local interest on general debt increased by 489%, versus an increase of 335% in the U.S. average.

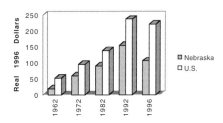

Real Per Capita State and Local Interest on General Debt: Nebraska vs. U.S.

Total Debt Outstanding

Nebraska's per capita state and local debt registered $3,766 in 1996, ranking 30th in the nation and trailing the U.S. average of $4,409 by 15%. From 1962 to 1996, real per capita state and local debt outstanding increased by 83%, versus an increase of 120% in the U.S. average. It is worth noting that Nebraska's per capita debt declined by 27% from 1982 to 1996, versus a U.S. increase of 58%.

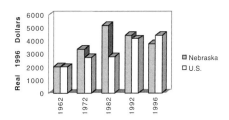

Real Per Capita State and Local Debt Outstanding: Nebraska vs. U.S.

Government Employees

Nebraska's state and local government employees (full-time equivalent, or FTE) per 10,000 population registered 634.3 in 1997, ranking 6th in the nation and exceeding the U.S. average of 531.1 by 19%. From 1962 to 1996, state and local FTE employees per 10,000 population increased by 76%, compared with an increase in the U.S. average of 66%.

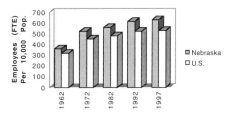

State and Local Government Employees (FTE) Per 10,000 Population: Nebraska vs. U.S.

Per Capita Federal Government Expenditures, 1998

	1998	Ranking
Nebr.	$4,963	34th
U.S.	$5,491	

Per capita federal spending in Nebraska trailed the national average by 10%.

EDUCATION

Total Education Spending

Nebraska's per capita state and local education spending registered $1,711 in 1996, ranking 11th in the nation and outpacing the U.S. average of $1,503 by 14%. From 1962 to 1996, real per capita total education spending increased by 245%, versus an increase in the U.S. average of 173%.

Per Pupil Spending

Nebraska's per pupil public school spending registered $5,949 in 1998, ranking 27th in the nation and trailing the U.S. average of $6,131 by 3%. From 1970 to 1998, Nebraska's real per pupil public school spending increased by 129%, compared with 120% increase in the U.S. average.

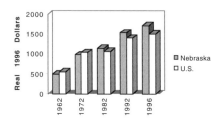

Real Per Capita State and Local Education Spending: Nebraska vs. U.S.

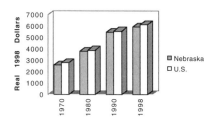

Real Per Pupil Public School Spending: Nebraska vs. U.S.

Average Public School Teacher Salaries (in 1997–98 dollars)

	1970	1980	1990	1998	1998 Ranking
Nebr.	31,578	28,159	32,510	32,668	42d
U.S.	36,934	33,272	39,956	39,385	

In 1998, the average public school teacher salary in Nebraska trailed the U.S. average by 17%. From 1970 to 1998, the real average teacher salary in Nebraska increased by 3%, versus an increase in the U.S. average of 7%.

Pupil/Teacher Ratio, Fall 1996

	Ratio	Rank
Nebr.	14.5	6th
U.S.	17.1	

Teacher/Staff, Fall 1996

	Percent	Rank
Nebr.	53.0	23d
U.S.	52.1	

Public School 4th-Grade Math Proficiency, 1996

	Average	Rank (out of 44 states)
Nebr.	228	10th
U.S.	224	

Public School 8th-Grade Math Proficiency, 1996

	Average	Rank (out of 41 states)
Nebr.	283	5th
U.S.	271	

Public School 8th-Grade Science Proficiency, 1996

	Average	Rank (out of 41 states)
Nebr.	157	8th
U.S.	148	

Average Math SAT Scores

	1972	1982	1992	1998	Percentage Taking SAT in 1998
Nebr.	525	568	557	571	8
U.S.	509	493	501	512	43

Average Verbal SAT Scores

	1972	1982	1992	1998	Percentage Taking SAT in 1998
Nebr.	532	569	553	565	8
U.S.	530	504	500	505	43

Expenditures by Public Institutions of Higher Education Per Full-Time-Equivalent Student, 1996

	FTE Student Spending	Rank
Nebr.	$10,815	45th
U.S.	$12,343	

Per-FTE-student spending in public institutions of higher education trailed the U.S. average by 12%.

Per Full-Time-Equivalent Student Revenues from Federal, State, and Local Governments for Public Institutions of Higher Education, 1996

	FTE Student Government Revenues	Rank
Nebr.	$8,401	19th
U.S.	$8,101	

Per-FTE-student-government revenues in public institutions of higher education topped the U.S. average by 4%.

Average Salary for Full-Time Professors at Public Universities, 1997

	Average	Rank
Nebr.	$73,016	18th
U.S.	$72,599	

The average full-time public university professor salary exceeded the U.S. average by 1%.

ECONOMY AND BUSINESS

Economic Growth

Over the period of 1977 to 1997, Nebraska's real gross state product (GSP) grew by 66.3%—ranking 29th in the nation—as compared with real U.S. gross domestic product (GDP), expanding by 70.1%.

At $48.8 billion in 1997, Nebraska's GSP ranked as 37th largest in the nation.

From 1993 to 1997, Nebraska's annual real GSP growth averaged 3.56%—ranking 29th in the nation—as compared with annual real U.S. GDP growth, averaging 3.08%.

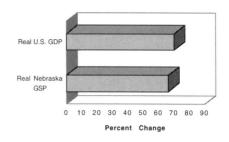

Real Economic Growth 1977-1997: Nebraska vs. U.S.

Real U.S. GDP

Real Nebraska GSP

0 10 20 30 40 50 60 70 80 90

Percent Change

Job Growth

	Growth in Employee Payrolls (Nonagricultural) 1962–98	Ranking
Nebr.	120.3%	35th
U.S.	126.5%	

	Average Annual Growth in Employee Payrolls (Nonagricultural) 1993–98	Ranking
Nebr.	3.08%	25th
U.S.	2.98%	

Per Capita Disposable Income, 1997

	1997	Ranking
Nebr.	$20,452	27th
U.S.	$21,607	

Per capita disposable income trailed the U.S. average by 5%.

	Real Growth 1962–97	Ranking
Nebr.	113.1%	30th
U.S.	116.7%	

	Average Annual Real Growth 1993–97	Ranking
Nebr.	1.63%	26th
U.S.	1.48%	

Number of Businesses

	1997	Percent with Fewer than 500 Employees
Businesses with Employees	43,344	97.1
Self-employed Individuals	109,000	

New Business Incorporations

	1980	1986	1992	1997
Nebr.	2,889	2,616	3,302	3,523

Percentage Change in Annual New Business Incorporations, 1980 vs. 1997

	Percent	Ranking
Nebr.	116.6	5th
U.S.	49.7	

State Merchandise Exports to the World, 1998 (in millions of dollars)

	1998	Rank
Nebr.	$2,472	36th

Small Business Survival Index, 1999

Nebraska ranks 33d in terms of its policy environment for entrepreneurship.

Fortune 500 Headquarters in 1999

A total of 6 (ranked 23d)

Labor Union Membership, 1983 vs. 1997

	Percentage of Workers		
	1983	1997	1997 Rank
Nebr.	13.6	9.3	31st
U.S.	20.1	14.1	

Homeownership Rate, 1998

	Rate	Rank
Nebr.	69.9	23d
U.S.	66.3	

CRIME

Crime Rates Per 100 Residents (rankings from best to worst crime rate)

Total Crime	1960	1970	1980	1990	1998	1998 Ranking
Nebr.	0.52	1.52	4.31	4.21	4.41	26th
U.S.	1.04	2.74	5.90	5.82	4.62	

From 1960 to 1998, Nebraska's crime rate increased by 748%, versus a U.S. increase of 344%. From 1990 to 1998, Nebraska's crime rate increased by 5%, versus a U.S. decrease of 21%.

Violent Crime	1960	1970	1980	1990	1998	1998 Ranking
Nebr.	0.04	0.18	0.22	0.33	0.45	28th
U.S.	0.14	0.36	0.58	0.73	0.57	

From 1960 to 1998, Nebraska's violent crime rate increased by 1,025%, versus a U.S. increase 307%. From 1990 to 1998, Nebraska's violent crime rate increased by 36%, compared with a national decline of 22%.

Property Crime	1960	1970	1980	1990	1998	1998 Ranking
Nebr.	0.48	1.33	4.08	3.88	3.95	24th
U.S.	0.90	2.38	5.32	5.09	4.05	

From 1960 to 1998, Nebraska's property crime rate increased by 723%, versus a national increase of 350%. From 1990 to 1998, Nebraska's property crime rate increased by 2%, compared with a national decline of 20%.

Real Per Capita Police Protection Spending (in real 1996 dollars)

	1962	1972	1982	1992	1996	1996 Ranking
Nebr.	32	62	78	96	107	44th
U.S.	51	95	114	148	168	

In 1996, per capita state and local police protection spending in Nebraska trailed the U.S. average by 36%. From 1962 to 1996, real per capita state and local police protection spending increased by 234%, versus an increase of 229% in the U.S. average.

Prisoners in State and Federal Prisons Per 1,000 Population

	1980	1990	1996	1996 Ranking
Nebr.	0.92	1.52	1.99	43d
U.S.	1.46	3.11	4.45	

From 1980 to 1996, prisoners per 1,000 population increased by 116%, versus a U.S. increase of 205%.

HEALTH CARE

Health-Care Spending

Nebraska's per capita state and local health-care spending registered $70 in 1996, ranking 50th in the nation and lagging behind the U.S. average of $151 by 67%. From 1962 to 1996, Nebraska's real per capita state and local health-care spending increased by 678%, versus an increase of 739% in the U.S. average.

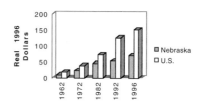

Real Per Capita State and Local Health Care Spending: Nebraska vs. U.S.

Hospital Spending

Nebraska's per capita state and local hospital spending registered $306 in 1996, ranking 14th in the nation and exceeding the U.S. average of $266 by 15%. From 1962 to 1996, Nebraska's real per capita state and local hospital spending increased by 343%, as opposed to an increase of 189% in the U.S. average.

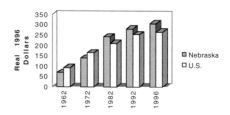

Real Per Capita State and Local Hospital Spending: Nebraska vs. U.S.

Medicaid, 1997

	Spending Per Recipient	Ranking
Nebr.	$3,429	28th
U.S.	$3,681	

Nebraska's per-recipient Medicaid spending trailed the U.S. average by 7%.

ENVIRONMENT

Parks and Recreation Spending

Nebraska's per capita state and local parks and recreation spending registered $56 in 1996, ranking 32d in the nation and trailing the U.S. average of $72 by 22%. From 1962 to 1996, real per capita state and local parks and recreation spending increased by 211%, versus a 213% increase in the U.S. average.

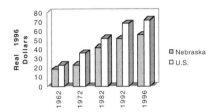

Real Per Capita State and Local Parks and Recreation Spending: Nebraska vs. U.S.

State and Local Natural Resources Spending, 1996

	Per Capita	Ranking
Nebr.	$91	10th
U.S.	$60	

Per capita state and local natural resources spending in Nebraska topped the U.S. average by 52%.

State Parks Revenues as a Share of Operating Expenses, 1997

	Percent	Rank
Nebr.	73	6th
U.S.	42	

Percentage of Land Owned by the Federal Government, 1996

	Percent	Rank
Nebr.	1.1	41st
U.S.	24.8	

SOCIETY AND DEMOGRAPHICS

Population

Nebraska's 1998 population of 1.663 million ranked 38th in the nation.

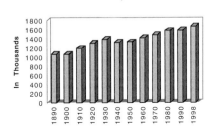

Nebraska Population

Population Growth, 1990–98

	Percentage Change in Population	Ranking
Nebr.	5.39	37th
U.S.	8.66	

	Net International Migration	Ranking
Nebr.	14,034	37th

	Net Domestic Migration	Ranking
Nebr.	1,519	31st

Infant Mortality Rate, 1998

	Percent	Rank
Nebr.	6.9	27th
U.S.	6.4	

Percentage of Births of Low Birthweight, 1997

	Percent	Rank
Nebr.	7.0	33d
U.S.	7.5	

Percentage of Live Births to Unmarried Women, 1997

	Percent	Rank
Nebr.	25.8	46th
U.S.	32.4	

Abortion Rate—Abortions Per 1,000 Women Ages 15–44, 1995

	Rate	Rank
Nebr.	12.1	36th
U.S.	22.9	

LIFESTYLE

Percentage of Households with Computers, 1998

	Percent	Rank
Nebr.	42.9	23d

Percentage of Households with Internet Access, 1998

	Percent	Rank
Nebr.	22.9	37th

State Arts Agency Spending, 1999

	Per Capita	Rank
Nebr.	$0.85	27th
U.S.	$1.35	

Per capita state arts spending in 1999 trailed the U.S. average by 37%.

Major League Sports Facilities

None

NEVADA

Gambling, drinks, tunes, antics, and beautiful women—from the 1950s into the mid-1960s, the Rat Pack epitomized "cool" for a generation. Indeed, watching Frank Sinatra, Dean Martin, Sammy Davis Jr., Peter Lawford, Joey Bishop, and others, in old clips or in the movie "Oceans 11" leaves the impression that everybody in Las Vegas was having a damn good time for themselves.

Actually, the good times have continued to roll along for Nevada in general—though, for most, they have been good times of a different kind than the Rat Packers experienced. Nevada has combined a relatively frugal government sector with one of the best tax systems in the nation, and as a result, can claim the most vibrant economy among the states.

The numbers are breathtaking. In most state and local government spending categories, Nevada trails the national average. Meanwhile, the number of state and local government employees (per 10,000 population) declined steadily from 1972 to 1997.

As for minimizing the most economically destructive taxes imposed by government, Nevada shines. Property taxes are quite low, and the state imposes no personal income, capital gains, or corporate income taxes.

This policy environment has provided a sound foundation on which an economy can grow, and, oh boy, has Nevada's economy grown. From 1977 to 1997, Nevada's real gross state product expanded at three times the rate of the U.S. economy. In recent years, real annual economic growth has averaged better than twice the U.S. average.

Similarly, Nevada ranked tops in terms of population growth between 1990 and 1998. Over the long haul (1962 to 1997), Nevada's payrolls grew at a rate 400% higher than the national rate, and annual job creation in recent years has outdistanced that of the United States by better than 185%. New business incorporations have skyrocketed, with the Small Business Survival Committee ranking Nevada among the very best climates for entrepreneurship in the nation.

Meanwhile, back in Vegas, the city has undergone a major change, from a place with distinct roots in organized crime to a city with corporations running casinos and undertaking efforts to become far more family friendly. However, some old ways die hard, as Democrat and reputed mob lawyer Oscar Goodman won the June 1999 contest to become mayor of Las Vegas with a formidable 64% of the vote. In a fascinating look at Goodman and his race for mayor in the *New Yorker* magazine (August 16, 1999), Connie Bruck writes that Goodman "is said to have tried out a line that he would use repeatedly as his campaign progressed: 'I'm running for mayor, I need your financial support. And if you don't give it to me'—he breaks into a squinty-eyed grin—I'll have you whacked!'" Ah, a little bit of the old Vegas lives on.

In her article, Bruck makes it clear that Goodman had long hated government. Unfortunately, defending mobsters means that Goodman tended to dislike the good guys in government, that is, the police (though he also may carry some justified distaste for the Internal Revenue Service). It will be interesting to see if his many battles with law enforcement officials can be transformed into a more healthy skepticism of activist government reaching beyond core duties like, well, fighting crime.

In fact, one of the big troubles in Nevada is crime, ranking among the worst in the nation. The state's violent crime rate actually increased from 1990 to 1997, while violent crime dropped rather dramatically nationwide. So, every roll of the dice in Nevada does not turn up "seven."

In addition, Nevada faces some political inconsistencies. For example, while establishing a state environment seemingly drawn up by a bunch of free-market, libertarian types—low taxes, smaller government, gambling, and prostitution—voters have seen fit to send some real liberals to Congress. However, Senator Harry Reid won reelection by the slimmest of margins (by less than 500 votes) in 1998. One of the reasons Reid won was that he grabbled 70% of the Hispanic vote.

Former U.S. Representative John Ensign (R), who lost to Reid, seems poised to take a good run at retiring Senator Richard Bryan's (D) seat in 2000. Indeed, one should not be surprised to see the state of Nevada generally follow Frank Sinatra's own political path from Democrat to Republican in coming years.

While labor unions, who always favor bigger government, claim some serious turf in the Las Vegas area, Nevada for the most part is well positioned to extend its entrepreneurial success story well into the 21st century. Other states would do well to replicate Nevada's progrowth tax system.

POLITICS

Registered Voters

42% Democrats
42% Republicans
16% Other

Federal Officials: Recent Election and Group Ratings

			ACU	ADA	SBSC
U.S. Senators:	Richard Bryan (D)		19	75	20
	1994 Bryan (D)	51%			
	Furman (R)	41%			
	Harry Reid (D)		22	74	30
	1998 Reid (D)	48%			
	Ensign (R)	48%			
U.S. Representatives:	Shelley Berkley (D-1)		NA	NA	NA
	1998 Berkley (D)	49%			
	Chairez (R)	46%			
	James Gibbons (R-2)		92	10	85
	1998 Gibbons (R)	81%			
	Horne (IAP)	8%			

Electoral Votes:	4	
1996 Presidential Results:	Clinton	51%
	Dole	37%
	Perot	9%

State Officials

Governor 1998 Election:	Kenny Guinn (R)	53%
	Jan Jones (D)	41%
Lt. Governor:	Lorraine Hunt (R)	
Attorney General:	Frankie Sue Del Papa (D)	
State Senate:	9 Democrats	
	12 Republicans	
State Assembly:	28 Democrats	
	14 Republicans	

TAXES AND SPENDING

Total Revenues

Nevada's per capita state and local total revenues registered $5,692 in 1996, ranking 19th in the nation and trailing the U.S. average of $5,706 by 0.2%. From 1962 to 1996, real per capita state and local revenues increased by 183%, compared with an increase in the national average of 297%.

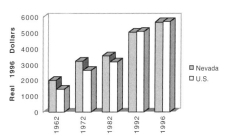

Real Per Capita State and Local Total Revenues: Nevada vs. U.S.

Taxes

Nevada's per capita state and local taxes registered $2,661 in 1996, ranking 16th in the nation and topping the U.S. average of $2,597 by 2%. From 1962 to 1996, real per capita state and local taxes increased by 113%, compared with an increase of 152% in the U.S. average.

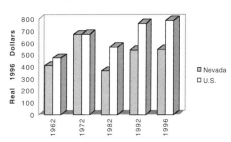

Real Per Capita State and Local Property Taxes: Nevada vs. U.S.

Property Taxes

Nevada's per capita state and local property taxes equaled $548 in 1996, ranking 36th in the nation and trailing the U.S. average of $789 by 31%. From 1962 to 1996, real per capita state and local property taxes increased by 34%, versus a 67% increase in the U.S. average.

Sales and Gross Receipts Taxes

Nevada's per capita state and local sales and gross receipts taxes came in at $1,733 in 1996, ranking highest in the nation and outpacing the U.S. average of $939 by 85%. From 1962 to 1996, real per capita state and local sales and gross receipts taxes increased by 207%, versus an increase of 214% in the U.S. average.

Income Taxes

Nevada's per capita state and local income (individual and corporate) taxes registered $0 in 1996, ranking lowest in the nation and comparing quite well to the U.S. average of $674. Nevada imposes no income taxes.

Personal Income Tax

A rate of 0%, ranking best in the nation (from lowest tax rate o highest), and comparing with the national average of 5.26%.

Capital Gains Tax

A rate of 0%, ranking best in the nation (from lowest tax rate to highest), and comparing with the national average of 4.68%.

Corporate Income Tax

A rate 0%, ranking best in the nation (from lowest tax rate to highest), and comparing with the national average of 6.63%.

Real Per Capita State and Local Taxes: Nevada vs. U.S.

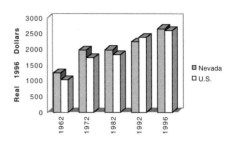

Real Per Capita State and Local Sales and Gross Receipts Taxes: Nevada vs. U.S.

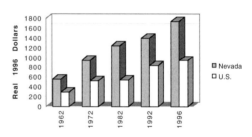

Real Per Capita State and Local Income Taxes: Nevada vs. U.S.

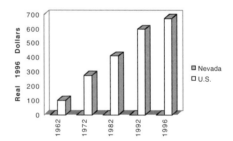

Total Expenditures

Nevada's per capita state and local total spending registered $4,960 in 1996, ranking 22d in the nation and trailing the U.S. average of $5,268 by 6%. From 1962 to 1996, real per capita state and local total spending increased by 125%, versus an increase of 254% in the U.S. average.

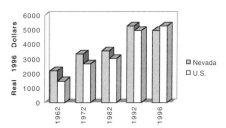

Real Per Capita State and Local Total Expenditures: Nevada vs. U.S.

Welfare Expenditures

Nevada's per capita state and local public welfare spending registered $436 in 1996, ranking 51st in the nation and trailing the U.S. average of $729 by 40%. From 1962 to 1996, real per capita state and local public welfare spending actually decreased by 3%, compared with a 488% increase in the U.S. average.

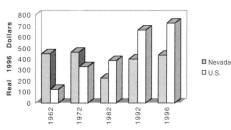

Real Per Capita State and Local Public Welfare Spending: Nevada vs. U.S.

Welfare Recipients (in thousands)

	1980	1989	3/99	Change 1989–99
Nev.	14	23	20	−13%
U.S.	10,923	10,987	7,335	−33%

Interest on General Debt

Nevada's per capita state and local interest on general debt registered $267 in 1996, ranking 15th in the nation and exceeding the U.S. average of $222 by 20%. From 1962 to 1996, real per capita state and local interest on general debt increased by 385%, versus an increase of 335% in the U.S. average.

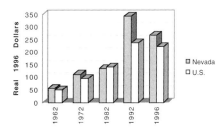

Real Per Capita State and Local Interest on General Debt: Nevada vs. U.S.

Total Debt Outstanding

Nevada's per capita state and local debt registered $5,094 in 1996, ranking 13th in the nation and topping the U.S. average of $4,409 by 16%. From 1962 to 1996, real per capita state and local debt outstanding increased by 200%, versus an increase of 120% in the U.S. average.

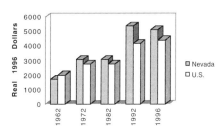

Real Per Capita State and Local Debt Outstanding: Nevada vs. U.S.

Government Employees

Nevada's state and local government employees (full-time equivalent, or FTE) per 10,000 population registered 474.5 in 1997, ranking 49th in the nation and trailing the U.S. average of 531.1 by 11%. From 1962 to 1996, state and local FTE employees per 10,000 population increased by 24%, compared with an increase in the U.S. average of 66%.

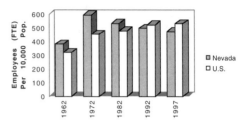

State and Local Government Employees (FTE) Per 10,000 Population: Nevada vs. U.S.

Per Capita Federal Government Expenditures, 1998

	1998	Ranking
Nev.	$4,331	47th
U.S.	$5,491	

Per capita federal spending in Nevada trailed the national average by 21%.

EDUCATION

Total Education Spending

Nevada's per capita state and local education spending registered $1,270 in 1996, ranking 47th in the nation and trailing the U.S. average of $1,503 by 16%. From 1962 to 1996, real per capita total education spending increased by 84%, versus an increase in the U.S. average of 173%.

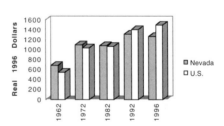

Real Per Capita State and Local Education Spending: Nevada vs. U.S.

Per Pupil Spending

Nevada's per pupil public school spending registered $5,917 in 1998, ranking 28th in the nation and trailing the U.S. average of $6,131 by 3%. From 1970 to 1998, Nevada's real per pupil public school spending increased by 126%, compared with a 120% increase in the U.S. average.

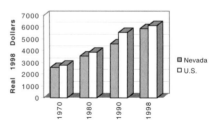

Real Per Pupil Public School Spending: Nevada vs. U.S.

Average Public School Teacher Salaries (in 1997–98 dollars)

	1970	1980	1990	1998	1998 Ranking
Nev.	39,456	33,949	38,966	37,093	22d
U.S.	36,934	33,272	39,956	39,385	

In 1998, the average public school teacher salary in Nevada trailed the U.S. average by 6%. From 1970 to 1998, the real average teacher salary in Nevada decreased by 6%, versus an increase in the U.S. average of 7%.

Pupil/Teacher Ratio, Fall 1996

	Ratio	Rank
Nev.	19.1	45th
U.S.	17.1	

Teachers/Staff, Fall 1996

	Percent	Rank
Nev.	58.1	3d
U.S.	52.1	

Public School 4th-Grade Reading Proficiency, 1998

	Average	Rank (out of 40 states)
Nev.	208	32d
U.S.	215	

Public School 8th-Grade Reading Proficiency, 1998

	Average	Rank (out of 37 states)
Nev.	257	26th
U.S.	261	

Public School 4th-Grade Math Proficiency, 1996

	Average	Rank (out of 44 states)
Nev.	218	31st
U.S.	224	

Average Math SAT Scores

	1972	1982	1992	1998	Percentage Taking SAT in 1998
Nev.	532	507	512	513	33
U.S.	509	493	501	512	43

Average Verbal SAT Scores

	1972	1982	1992	1998	Percentage Taking SAT in 1998
Nev.	561	514	511	510	33
U.S.	530	504	500	505	43

Expenditures by Public Institutions of Higher Education Per Full-Time-Equivalent Student, 1996

	FTE Student Spending	Rank
Nev.	$11,511	36th
U.S.	$12,343	

Per-FTE-student spending in public institutions of higher education trailed the U.S. average by 7%.

Per Full-Time-Equivalent Student Revenues from Federal, State, and Local Governments for Public Institutions of Higher Education, 1996

	FTE Student Government Revenues	Rank
Nev.	$7,672	28th
U.S.	$8,101	

Per-FTE-student-government revenues in public institutions of higher education lagged behind the U.S. average by 5%.

Average Salary for Full-Time Professors at Public Universities, 1997

	Average	Rank
Nev.	$74,895	13th
U.S.	$72,599	

The average full-time public university professor salary exceeded the U.S. average by 3%.

ECONOMY AND BUSINESS

Economic Growth

Over the period of 1977 to 1997, Nevada's real gross state product (GSP) grew by 201.4%—ranking best in the nation—as compared with real U.S. gross domestic product (GDP), expanding by 70.1%.

At $57.4 billion in 1997, Nevada's GSP ranked as 34th largest in the nation.

From 1993 to 1997, Nevada's annual real GSP growth averaged 6.88%—ranking 4th in the nation—as compared with annual real U.S. GDP growth, averaging 3.08%.

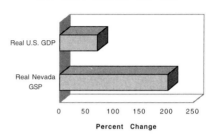

Real Economic Growth
1977-1997: Nevada vs. U.S.

Real U.S. GDP

Real Nevada GSP

0   50   100   150   200   250

Percent Change

Job Growth

	Growth in Employee Payrolls (Nonagricultural) 1962–98	Ranking
Nev.	628.5%	1st
U.S.	126.5%	

	Average Annual Growth in Employee Payrolls (Nonagricultural) 1993–1998	Ranking
Nev.	7.65%	1st
U.S.	2.98%	

Per Capita Disposable Income, 1997

	1997	Ranking
Nev.	$22,465	12th
U.S.	$21,607	

Per capita disposable income topped the U.S. average by 4%.

	Real Growth 1962–97	Ranking
Nev.	75.9%	50th
U.S.	116.7%	

	Average Annual Real Growth 1993–97	Ranking
Nev.	1.28%	42d
U.S.	1.48%	

Number of Businesses

	1997	Percent with Fewer than 500 Employees
Businesses with Employees	39,518	95.8
Self-employed Individuals	192,000	

New Business Incorporations

	1980	1986	1992	1997
Nev.	6,000	9,528	12,610	26,999

Percentage Change in Annual New Business Incorporations, 1980 vs. 1997

	Percent	Ranking
Nev.	350.0	1st
U.S.	49.7	

State Merchandise Exports to the World, 1998 (in millions of dollars)

	1998	Rank
Nev.	$764.8	45th

Small Business Survival Index, 1999

Nevada ranks third best in terms of its policy environment for entrepreneurship.

Fortune 500 Headquarters in 1999

None

Labor Union Membership, 1983 vs. 1997

	Percentage of Workers		
	1983	1997	1997 Rank
Nev.	22.4	19.1	8th
U.S.	20.1	14.1	

Homeownership Rate, 1998

	Rate	Rank
Nev.	61.4	45th
U.S.	66.3	

CRIME

Crime Rates Per 100 Residents (rankings from best to worst crime rate)

Total Crime	1960	1970	1980	1990	1998	1998 Ranking
Nev.	1.99	4.00	8.85	6.06	5.28	37th
U.S.	1.04	2.74	5.90	5.82	4.62	

From 1960 to 1998, Nevada's crime rate increased by 165%, versus a U.S. increase of 344%. From 1990 to 1998, Nevada's crime rate dropped by 13%, versus a U.S. decrease of 21%.

Violent Crime	1960	1970	1980	1990	1998	1998 Ranking
Nev.	0.15	0.40	0.91	0.60	0.64	39th
U.S.	0.14	0.36	0.58	0.73	0.57	

From 1960 to 1998, Nevada's violent crime rate increased by 327%, versus a U.S. increase of 307%. From 1990 to 1998, Nevada's violent crime rate increased by 7%, compared with a national decline of 22%.

Property Crime	1960	1970	1980	1990	1998	1998 Ranking
Nev.	1.85	3.60	7.94	5.46	4.64	39th
U.S.	0.90	2.38	5.32	5.09	4.05	

From 1960 to 1998, Nevada's property crime rate increased by 151%, versus a national increase of 350%. From 1990 to 1998, Nevada's property crime rate decreased by 15%, compared with a national decline of 20%.

Real Per Capita Police Protection Spending (in real 1996 dollars)

	1962	1972	1982	1992	1996	1996 Ranking
Nev.	83	174	150	209	213	6th
U.S.	51	95	114	148	168	

In 1996, per capita state and local police protection spending in Nevada exceeded the U.S. average by 27%. From 1962 to 1996, real per capita state and local police protection spending increased by 157%, versus an increase of 229% in the U.S. average.

Prisoners in State and Federal Prisons Per 1,000 Population

	1980	1990	1996	1996 Ranking
Nev.	2.30	4.43	5.27	43d
U.S.	1.46	3.11	4.45	

From 1980 to 1996, prisoners per 1,000 population increased by 129%, versus a U.S. increase of 205%.

HEALTH CARE

Health-Care Spending

Nevada's per capita state and local health-care spending registered $89 in 1996, ranking 44th in the nation and trailing the U.S. average of $151 by 41%. From 1962 to 1996, Nevada's real per capita state and local health-care spending increased by 287%, versus an increase of 739% in the U.S. average.

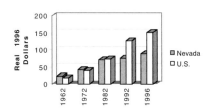

Real Per Capita State and Local Health Care Spending: Nevada vs. U.S.

Hospital Spending

Nevada's per capita state and local hospital spending registered $277 in 1996, ranking 18th in the nation and exceeding the U.S. average of $266 by 4%. From 1962 to 1996, Nevada's real per capita state and local hospital spending increased by 101%, as opposed to an increase of 189% in the U.S. average.

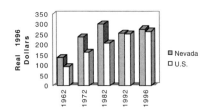

Real Per Capita State and Local Hospital Spending: Nevada vs. U.S.

Medicaid, 1997

	Spending Per Recipient	Ranking
Nev.	$3,519	26th
U.S.	$3,681	

Nevada's per-recipient Medicaid spending trailed the U.S. average by 4%.

ENVIRONMENT

Parks and Recreation Spending

Nevada's per capita state and local parks and recreation spending registered $155 in 1996, ranking 2d in the nation and exceeding the U.S. average of $72 by 115%. From 1962 to 1996, real per capita state and local parks and recreation spending increased by 384%, versus a 213% increase in the U.S. average.

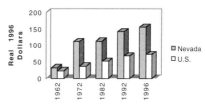

Real Per Capita State and Local Parks and Recreation Spending: Nevada vs. U.S.

State and Local Natural Resources Spending, 1996

	Per Capita	Ranking
Nev.	$60	29th
U.S.	$60	

Per capita state and local natural resources spending in Nevada equaled the U.S. average.

State Parks Revenues as a Share of Operating Expenses, 1997

	Percent	Rank
Nev.	23	42d
U.S.	42	

Percentage of Land Owned by the Federal Government, 1996

	Percent	Rank
Nev.	79.8	1st
U.S.	24.8	

SOCIETY AND DEMOGRAPHICS

Population

Nevada's 1998 population of 1.747 million ranked 36th in the nation.

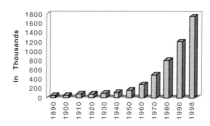

Nevada Population

Population Growth, 1990–98

	Percentage Change in Population	Ranking
Nev.	45.34	1st
U.S.	8.66	

	Net International Migration	Ranking
Nev.	45,369	22nd

	Net Domestic Migration	Ranking
Nev.	396,647	6th

Infant Mortality Rate, 1998

	Percent	Rank
Nev.	7.3	22d
U.S.	6.4	

Percentage of Births of Low Birthweight, 1997

	Percent	Rank
Nev.	7.6	26th
U.S.	7.5	

Percentage of Live Births to Unmarried Women, 1997

	Percent	Rank
Nev.	35.5	9th
U.S.	32.4	

Abortion Rate—Abortions Per 1,000 Women Ages 15–44, 1995

	Rate	Rank
Nev.	46.7	2d
U.S.	22.9	

LIFESTYLE

Percentage of Households with Computers, 1998

	Percent	Rank
Nev.	41.6	28th

Percentage of Households with Internet Access, 1998

	Percent	Rank
Nev.	26.5	21st

State Arts Agency Spending, 1999

	Per Capita	Rank
Nev.	$0.67	34th
U.S.	$1.35	

Per capita state arts spending in 1999 trailed the U.S. average by 50%.

Major League Sports Facilities

None

NEW HAMPSHIRE

New Hampshire has long served as a beacon of economic sanity in the often fiscally crazy northeast. While neighbors were taxing and spending with abandon, with their economies suffering accordingly, the Granite State seemed immovable in its commitment to maintaining a low-tax, entrepreneur-friendly environment.

It has been called the "New Hampshire Advantage." The *Manchester Union Leader* (August 16, 1999 editorial) defines it as "a great four-season New England climate, mixed with friendly small towns and cities, and no income or sales taxes equals a fine quality of life and place to do business." Certainly sounds good to us—and apparently to others as well.

New Hampshire's economy has responded accordingly. Real economic growth in New Hampshire has long been running at more than twice the national rate. Job creation has out-stripped the U.S. average by a good margin, as has growth in real disposable income. Though not yet recovering to mid-1980s heights, annual new business incorporations have climbed nicely, too.

Of course, an enduring constant in the world is the ability for politicians and judges to screw up good things. Since late 1997, the state's activist supreme court and elected officials from both political parties have placed the "New Hampshire Advantage" at grave risk.

In a not-unusual attempt to grab more taxpayer dollars, five school districts in New Hampshire decided to sue the state in 1991 for allegedly not providing an adequate education under the local property-tax-based system for funding schools. In December 1997, the state supreme court struck down the system and ordered that a new one be created by April 1, 1999.

Of course, the undergirding idea that more money means better schooling is contradicted by the fact that, for years, rising public education spending levels have been tied to falling or stagnant performance nationwide. This is in contrast to much lower rates of per pupil spending by many private schools and often with far better performance results. In addition, that the courts see fit to dictate how schools should be funded and to what degree is a dangerous case of judicial activism.

The most appropriate response to the supreme court's overreach, as suggested by some state legislators, was to send the voters a constitutional amendment rolling back the court's decision. Governor Jeanne Shaheen (D) and various Democratic and Republican legislative leaders killed that measure, choosing instead to start playing a risky game of tax increases.

Those looking to impose a general personal income tax—the state already imposes a 5% tax on interest and dividends and a 7% corporate income tax—were actually led by Republican State Representative Elizabeth Hager. Others proposed a seemingly endless stream of other tax hikes, including a statewide property tax, a cigarette tax increase, a sales tax on cars and boats, a poll tax, an entertainment tax, a capital gains tax, increases in the business income tax, boosting the real-estate transfer tax, and so on. Thankfully, the income tax idea faltered, at least temporarily, but a statewide property tax was imposed, along with a new car rental tax, and increases in various business, cigarette, and property sales taxes. By the way, New Hampshire already claimed the second highest per capita property taxes in all the land.

However, state spending is rocketing skyward. According to the *Union Leader*, Shaheen proposed a 12% spending increase in 1999, and Republican and Democrat state legislators boosted outlays even higher. The state is still on the prowl, ready to pounce on more taxpayer dollars to fill expected budget gaps. The lawsuit crowd is back, looking for the courts to boost education spending even higher.

With New Hampshire Republicans in philosophical disarray and Democrats more than willing to spend and tax more, the Granite State was in a perilous position toward the end of 1999. In late August, Shaheen, who had promised not to impose an income tax, toyed with the idea of imposing a capital gains tax, and others were still trying to revive a general income tax.

Shaheen has been rather cavalierly toying with New Hampshire's economic future, and it seems that Republicans are in too much chaos to offer a serious response.

Just a couple of years ago, we would have confidently labeled New Hampshire as being the state best positioned in the northeast to prosper in the 21st century. Now, we have serious doubts. New Hampshire could stay on the growth track, but that would require a return to the economic and fiscal sanity for which the Granite State had been so well known over the years. It is not too late.

POLITICS

Registered Voters

30% Democrats
39% Republicans
32% Other

Federal Officials: Recent Election and Group Ratings

			ACU	ADA	SBSC
U.S. Senators:	Bob Smith (I)		96	6	95
	1996 Smith(R)	49%			
	Swett (D)	46%			
	Judd Gregg (R)		80	8	85
	1998 Gregg (R)	68%			
	Condodemetraky (D)	28%			
U.S. Representatives:	John Sununu (R)		92	3	95
	1998 Sununu (R)	67%			
	Flood (D)	33%			
	Charles Bass (R-2)		78	10	75
	1998 Bass (R)	53%			
	Rauh (D)	45%			

Electoral Votes:	4	
1996 Presidential Results:	Clinton	49%
	Dole	39%
	Perot	10%

State Officials

Governor 1998 Election:	Jeanne Shaheen (D)	66%
	Jay Lucas (R)	31%
State Senate:	13 Democrats	
	11 Republicans	
State General Assembly:	153 Democrats	
	246 Republicans	
	1 Independent	

TAXES AND SPENDING

Total Revenues

New Hampshire's per capita state and local total revenues registered $4,810 in 1996, ranking 39th in the nation and trailing the U.S. average of $5,706 by 16%. From 1962 to 1996, real per capita state and local revenues increased by 261%, compared with an increase in the national average of 297%.

Taxes

New Hampshire's per capita state and local taxes registered $2,254 in 1996, ranking 33d in the nation and trailing the U.S. average of $2,597 by 13%. From 1962 to 1996, real per capita state and local taxes increased by 143%, compared with an increase of 152% in the U.S. average.

Real Per Capita State and Local Total Revenues: New Hampshire vs. U.S.

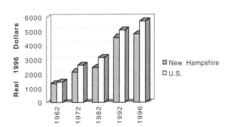

Real Per Capita State and Local Taxes: New Hampshire vs. U.S.

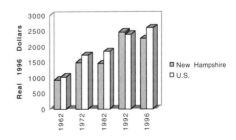

Property Taxes

New Hampshire's per capita state and local property taxes equaled $1,520 in 1996, ranking 2d in the nation and topping the U.S. average of $789 by 93%. From 1962 to 1996, real per capita state and local property taxes increased by 159%, versus a 67% increase in the U.S. average.

Sales and Gross Receipts Taxes

New Hampshire's per capita state and local sales and gross receipts taxes came in at $369 in 1996, ranking 48th in the nation and trailing the U.S. average of $939 by 61%. From 1962 to 1996, real per capita state and local sales and gross receipts taxes increased by 75%, versus an increase in 214% in the U.S. average.

Income Taxes

New Hampshire's per capita state and local income (individual and corporate) taxes registered $199 in 1996, ranking 44th in the nation and trailing the U.S. average of $674 by 70%. From 1962 to 1996, real per capita state and local income taxes increased by 1,321%, versus a 567% increase in the U.S. average.

Personal Income Tax

A rate of 0%, ranking best in the nation (from lowest tax rate to highest), and comparing with the national average of 5.26%.

Capital Gains Tax

A rate of 0%, ranking best in the nation (from lowest tax rate to highest), and comparing with the national average of 4.68%.

Corporate Income Tax

A rate of 7.0%, ranking 26th in the nation (from lowest tax rate to highest), and comparing with the national average of 6.63%.

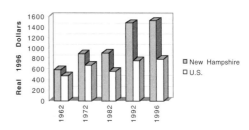

Real Per Capita State and Local Property Taxes: New Hampshire vs. U.S.

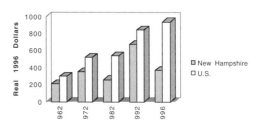

Real Per Capita State and Local Sales and Gross Receipts Taxes: New Hampshire vs. U.S.

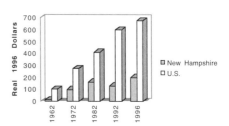

Real Per Capita State and Local Income Taxes: New Hampshire vs. U.S.

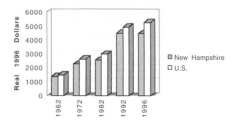

Real Per Capita State and Local Total Expenditures: New Hampshire vs. U.S.

Total Expenditures

New Hampshire's per capita state and local total spending registered $4,468 in 1996, ranking 41st in the nation and trailing the U.S. average of $5,268 by 15%. From 1962 to 1996, real per capita state and local total spending increased by 222%, versus a 254% increase in the U.S. average.

Welfare Expenditures

New Hampshire's per capita state and local public welfare spending registered $886 in 1996, ranking 8th in the nation and topping the U.S. average of $729 by 22%. From 1962 to 1996, real per capita state and local public welfare spending increased by 777%, compared with a 488% increase in the U.S. average.

Welfare Recipients (in thousands)

	1980	1989	3/99	Change 1989–99
N.H.	24	15	16	+ 7%
U.S.	10,923	10,987	7,335	− 33%

Interest on General Debt

New Hampshire's per capita state and local interest on general debt registered $368 in 1996, ranking 6th in the nation and exceeding the U.S. average of $222 by 66%. From 1962 to 1996, real per capita state and local interest on general debt increased by 1,050%, versus an increase of 335% in the U.S. average.

Total Debt Outstanding

New Hampshire's per capita state and local debt registered $5,970 in 1996, ranking 9th in the nation and exceeding the U.S. average of $4,409 by 35%. From 1962 to 1996, real per capita state and local debt outstanding increased by 336%, versus an increase of 120% in the U.S. average.

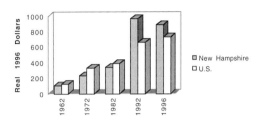

Real Per Capita State and Local Public Welfare Spending: New Hampshire vs. U.S.

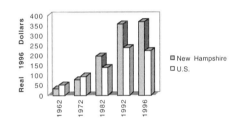

Real Per Capita State and Local Interest on General Debt: New Hampshire vs. U.S.

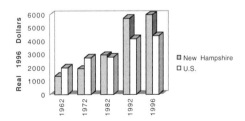

Real Per Capita State and Local Debt Outstanding: New Hampshire vs. U.S.

Government Employees

New Hampshire's state and local government employees (full-time equivalent, or FTE) per 10,000 population registered 476.2 in 1997, ranking 48th in the nation and trailing the U.S. average of 531.1 by 10%. From 1962 to 1996, state and local FTE employees per 10,000 population increased by 61%, compared with an increase in the U.S. average of 66%.

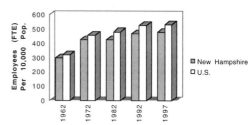

State and Local Government Employees (FTE) Per 10,000 Population: New Hampshire vs. U.S.

Per Capita Federal Government Expenditures, 1998

	1998	Ranking
N.H.	$4,449	45th
U.S.	$5,491	

Per capita federal spending in New Hampshire trailed the national average by 19%.

EDUCATION

Total Education Spending

New Hampshire's per capita state and local education spending registered $1,399 in 1996, ranking 34th in the nation and trailing the U.S. average of $1,503 by 7%. From 1962 to 1996, real per capita total education spending increased by 211%, versus an increase in the U.S. average of 173%.

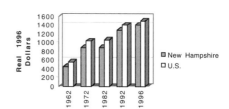

Real Per Capita State and Local Education Spending: New Hampshire vs. U.S.

Per Pupil Spending

New Hampshire's per pupil public school spending registered $6,549 in 1998, ranking 13th in the nation and exceeding the U.S. average of $6,131 by 7%. From 1970 to 1998, New Hampshire's real per pupil public school spending increased by 165%, compared with a 120% increase in the U.S. average.

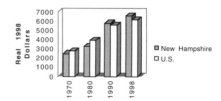

Real Per Pupil Public School Spending: New Hampshire vs. U.S.

Average Public School Teacher Salaries (in 1997–98 dollars)

	1970	1980	1990	1998	1998 Ranking
N.H.	33,273	27,120	36,923	36,640	26th
U.S.	36,934	33,272	39,956	39,385	

In 1998, the average public school teacher salary in New Hampshire trailed the U.S. average by 7%. From 1970 to 1998, the real average teacher salary in New Hampshire increased by 10%, versus an increase in the U.S. average of 7%.

Pupil/Teacher Ratio, Fall 1996

	Ratio	Rank
N.H.	15.6	19th
U.S.	17.1	

Teachers/Staff, Fall 1996

	Percent	Rank
N.H.	53.0	23d
U.S.	52.1	

Public School 4th-Grade Reading Proficiency, 1998

	Average	Rank (out of 40 states)
N.H.	226	2d
U.S.	215	

Average Math SAT Scores

	1972	1982	1992	1998	Percentage Taking SAT in 1998
N.H.	526	507	508	520	74
U.S.	509	493	501	512	43

Average Verbal SAT Scores

	1972	1982	1992	1998	Percentage Taking SAT in 1998
N.H.	546	521	517	523	74
U.S.	530	504	500	505	43

Expenditures by Public Institutions of Higher Education Per Full-Time-Equivalent Student, 1996

	FTE Student Spending	Rank
N.H.	$11,731	33d
U.S.	$12,343	

Per-FTE-student spending in public institutions of higher education trailed the U.S. average by 5%.

Per Full-Time-Equivalent Student Revenues from Federal, State, and Local Governments for Public Institutions of Higher Education, 1996

	FTE Student Government Revenues	Rank
N.H.	$4,764	51st
U.S.	$8,101	

Per-FTE-student-government revenues in public institutions of higher education lagged behind the U.S. average by 41%.

Average Salary for Full-Time Professors at Public Universities, 1997

	Average	Rank
N.H.	$63,794	38th
U.S.	$72,599	

The average full-time public university professor salary trailed the U.S. average by 12%.

ECONOMY AND BUSINESS

Economic Growth

Over the period of 1977 to 1997, New Hampshire's real gross state product (GSP) grew by 170.9%—ranking 2d in the nation—as compared with real U.S. gross domestic product (GDP), expanding by 70.1%.

At $38.1 billion in 1997, New Hampshire's GSP ranked as 40th largest in the nation.

From 1993 to 1997, New Hampshire's annual real GSP growth averaged 6.24%—ranking 7th in the nation—as compared with annual real U.S. GDP growth, averaging 3.08%.

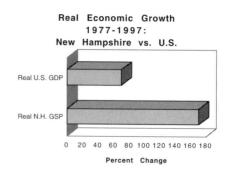

Real Economic Growth
1977-1997:
New Hampshire vs. U.S.

Real U.S. GDP

Real N.H. GSP

0 20 40 60 80 100 120 140 160 180

Percent Change

Job Growth

	Growth in Employee Payrolls (Nonagricultural) 1962–98	Ranking
N.H.	182.6%	16th
U.S.	126.5%	

	Average Annual Growth in Employee Payrolls (Nonagricultural) 1993–98	Ranking
N.H.	3.81%	11th
U.S.	2.98%	

Per Capita Disposable Income, 1997

	1997	Ranking
N.H.	$24,146	6th
U.S.	$21,607	

Per capita disposable income outdistanced the U.S. average by 12%.

	Real Growth 1962–97	Ranking
N.H.	143.7%	10th
U.S.	116.7%	

	Average Annual Real Growth 1993–97	Ranking
N.H.	1.76%	17th
U.S.	1.48%	

Number of Businesses

	1997	Percent with Fewer than 500 Employees
Businesses with Employees	36,622	96.9
Self-employed Individuals	61,000	

New Business Incorporations

	1980	1986	1992	1997
N.H.	1,373	3,859	2,577	2,791

Percentage Change in Annual New Business Incorporations, 1980 vs. 1997

	Percent	Ranking
N.H.	103.3	8th
U.S.	49.7	

State Merchandise Exports to the World, 1998 (in millions of dollars)

	1998	Rank
N.H.	$1,987	37th

Small Business Survival Index, 1999

New Hampshire ranks 4th best in the nation in terms of its policy environment for entrepreneurship.

Fortune 500 Headquarters in 1999

None

Labor Union Membership, 1983 vs. 1997

	Percentage of Workers		
	1983	1997	1997 Rank
N.H.	11.5	10.2	28th
U.S.	20.1	14.1	

Homeownership Rate, 1998

	Rate	Rank
N.H.	69.6	25th
U.S.	66.3	

CRIME

Crime Rates Per 100 Residents (rankings from best to worst crime rate)

Total Crime	1960	1970	1980	1990	1998	1998 Ranking
N.H.	0.34	1.19	4.68	3.65	2.42	1st
U.S.	1.04	2.74	5.90	5.82	4.62	

From 1960 to 1998, New Hampshire's crime rate increased by 612%, versus a U.S. increase of 344%. From 1990 to 1998, New Hampshire's crime rate dropped by 34%, versus a U.S. decrease of 21%.

Violent Crime	1960	1970	1980	1990	1998	1998 Ranking
N.H.	0.01	0.06	0.18	0.13	0.11	2d
U.S.	0.14	0.36	0.58	0.73	0.57	

From 1960 to 1998, New Hampshire's violent crime rate increased by 1,000%, versus a U.S. increase of 307%. From 1990 to 1998, New Hampshire's violent crime rate decreased by 15%, compared with a national decline of 22%.

Property Crime	1960	1970	1980	1990	1998	1998 Ranking
N.H.	0.33	1.14	4.50	3.51	2.31	2d
U.S.	0.90	2.38	5.32	5.09	4.05	

From 1960 to 1998, New Hampshire's property crime rate increased by 600%, versus a national increase of 350%. From 1990 to 1998, New Hampshire's property crime rate decreased by 34%, compared with a national decline of 20%.

Real Per Capita Police Protection Spending (in real 1996 dollars)

	1962	1972	1982	1992	1996	1996 Ranking
N.H.	37	62	87	125	126	35th
U.S.	51	95	114	148	168	

In 1996, per capita state and local police protection spending in New Hampshire trailed the U.S. average by 25%. From 1962 to 1996, real per capita state and local police protection spending increased by 241%, versus an increase of 229% in the U.S average.

Prisoners in State and Federal Prisons Per 1,000 Population

	1980	1990	1996	1996 Ranking
N.H.	0.35	1.21	1.78	47th
U.S.	1.46	3.11	4.45	

From 1980 to 1996, prisoners per 1,000 population increased by 409%, versus a U.S. increase of 205%.

HEALTH CARE

Health-Care Spending

New Hampshire's per capita state and local health-care spending registered $76 in 1996, ranking 49th in the nation and lagging behind the U.S. average of $151 by 50%. From 1962 to 1996, New Hampshire's real per capita state and local health-care spending increased by 322%, versus an increase of 739% in the U.S. average.

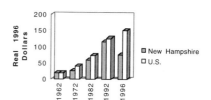

Real Per Capita State and Local Health Care Spending: New Hampshire vs. U.S.

Hospital Spending

New Hampshire's per capita state and local hospital spending registered $34 in 1996, ranking 50th in the nation and trailing the U.S. average of $266 by 87%. From 1962 to 1996, New Hampshire's real per capita state and local hospital spending decreased by 53%, as opposed to an increase of 189% in the U.S. average.

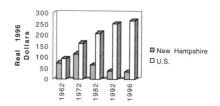

Real Per Capita State and Local Hospital Spending: New Hampshire vs. U.S.

Medicaid, 1997

	Spending Per Recipient	Ranking
N.H.	$5,832	6th
U.S.	$3,681	

New Hampshire's per-recipient Medicaid spending exceeded the U.S. average by 58%.

ENVIRONMENT

Parks and Recreation Spending

New Hampshire's per capita state and local parks and recreation spending registered $38 in 1996, ranking 46th in the nation and trailing the U.S. average of $72 by 47%. From 1962 to 1996, real per capita state and local parks and recreation spending increased by 171%, versus a 213% increase in the U.S. average.

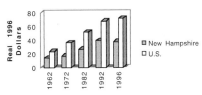

Real Per Capita State and Local Parks and Recreation Spending: New Hampshire vs. U.S.

State and Local Natural Resources Spending, 1996

	Per Capita	Ranking
N.H.	$35	41st
U.S.	$60	

Per capita state and local natural resources spending in New Hampshire trailed the U.S. average by 42%.

State Parks Revenues as a Share of Operating Expenses, 1997

	Percent	Rank
N.H.	104	1st
U.S.	42	

Percentage of Land Owned by the Federal Government, 1996

	Percent	Rank
N.H.	12.7	14th
U.S.	24.8	

SOCIETY AND DEMOGRAPHICS

Population

New Hampshire's 1998 population of 1.185 million ranked 42d in the nation.

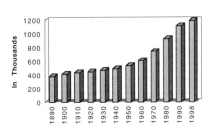

New Hampshire Population

Population Growth, 1990–98

	Percentage Change in Population	Ranking
N.H.	6.86	27th
U.S.	8.66	

	Net International Migration	Ranking
N.H.	6,189	44th

	Net Domestic Migration	Ranking
N.H.	18,536	27th

Infant Mortality Rate, 1998

	Percent	Rank
N.H.	5.6	42d
U.S.	6.4	

Percentage of Births of Low Birthweight, 1997

	Percent	Rank
N.H.	5.8	48th
U.S.	7.5	

Percentage of Live Births to Unmarried Women, 1997

	Percent	Rank
N.H.	23.8	49th
U.S.	32.4	

Abortion Rate—Abortions Per 1,000 Women Ages 15–44, 1995

	Rate	Rank
N.H.	12.0	38th
U.S.	22.9	

LIFESTYLE

Percentage of Households with Computers, 1998

	Percent	Rank
N.H.	54.2	5th

Percentage of Households with Internet Access, 1998

	Percent	Rank
N.H.	37.1	2d

State Arts Agency Spending, 1999

	Per Capita	Rank
N.H.	$0.48	46th
U.S.	$1.35	

Per capita state arts spending in 1999 lagged behind the U.S. average by 81%.

Major League Sports Facilities

None

NEW JERSEY

It was almost inevitable. As New York City's neighbor to the west, New Jersey eventually became infected by the "New York disease," an illness brought on by an expansive welfare state and burdensome taxes.

Make no mistake, fiscal and economic sanity valiantly tried to hold out in the Garden State. After all, New Jersey did not impose a state personal income tax until 1976, versus 1919 in New York. Nonetheless, the virus was spreading. In the early 1990s, the disease may have reached its apex when then-Governor Jim Florio (D) doubled the personal income tax rate from 3.5% to 7%.

In his 1993 reelection bid, Florio faced Christine Todd Whitman, the unknown Republican who in 1990, though outspent 15 to 1, almost unseated former basketball star Bill Bradley (D) from his U.S. Senate seat. Whitman ran a rather lackluster campaign for governor until she took sage advice from the supply-side economics team of magazine publisher Steve Forbes and economist Larry Kudlow to cut income taxes as a means of boosting the state's economy while offering a clear contrast to the tax-hiking Florio. Whitman managed a 49%–48% upset.

As governor, Whitman cut the personal income tax and did it ahead of schedule. She also said "no" to a plan to build a new arena to lure the NBA's 76ers from Philadelphia to Camden. Whitman immediately became a rising GOP star on the national stage.

However, the star soon faded. Rather than being a first step in reducing taxes and perhaps even cutting the size of government in New Jersey, Whitman's first tax cut seemed to be her final serious effort at tax reduction. The top individual income tax rate only declined from 7% to 6.37% under Whitman's plan—still far above the pre-Florio rate of 3.5%. In addition, Whitman's early support for school choice disappeared rather quickly.

In 1997, Whitman gained reelection with a smaller percentage of the vote—winning 47%–46%—than she had received four years earlier. Contrary to downsizing government, Whitman has proven to be a big spender. In 1998, she advocated and aggressively pushed for voter approval of a large debt issue for environmental spending. The state budget approved in June 1999 provided for a massive spending increase of more than 7%—running about four times the inflation rate. So, despite the fact that Republicans control both state houses and the governor's office, New Jersey's big government ways show no signs of ebbing soon.

That does not bode well for a state already suffering from some of the highest taxes (especially property taxes), spending (like welfare and education expenditures), and debt levels in the nation, as well as a state recently lagging behind badly in terms of growth in the economy, population, jobs, and disposable income. According to the Small Business Survival Committee's "Small Business Survival Index," New Jersey offers one of the bleakest policy climates for entrepreneurship in the nation.

Unfortunately, it is difficult to see where much-needed policy changes are likely to come from in the near term.

New Jersey is a state that has long struggled to create an identity independent from its neighbor New York. Nevertheless, the Garden State remains plagued by "New York disease."

POLITICS

Registered Voters

> 26% Democrats
> 20% Republicans
> 55% Other

Federal Officials: Recent Election and Group Ratings

				ACU	ADA	SBSC
U.S. Senators:	Frank Lautenberg (D)			6	93	25
	1994	Lautenberg (D)	50%			
		Haytaian (R)	47%			
	Robert Torricelli (D)			2	83	30
	1996	Torricelli (D)	52%			
		Zimmer (R)	42%			
U.S. Representatives:	Robert Andrews (D-1)			25	69	25
	1998	Andrews (D)	73%			
		Richards (R)	23%			
	Frank LoBiondo (R-2)			71	29	65
	1998	LoBiondo (R)	66%			
		Hunsberger (D)	31%			
	Jim Saxton (R-3)			77	20	70
	1998	Saxton (R)	62%			
		Polansky (D)	35%			
	Christopher Smith (R-4)			56	42	55
	1998	Smith (R)	62%			
		Schneider (D)	35%			
	Marge Roukema (R-5)			50	38	70
	1998	Roukema (R)	64%			
		Schneider (D)	33%			
	Frank Pallone (D-6)			19	88	15
	1998	Pallone (D)	57%			
		Ferguson (R)	40%			

			ACU	ADA	SBSC
Robert Franks (R-7)			61	41	65
1998	Franks (R)	53%			
	Connelly (D)	44%			
William Pascrell (D-8)			26	83	15
1998	Pascrell (D)	62%			
	Kirnan (R)	35%			
Steven Rothman (D-9)			11	95	10
1998	Rothman (D)	65%			
	Lonegan (R)	34%			
Donald Payne (D-10)			5	93	0
1998	Payne (D)	84%			
	Wnuck (R)	11%			
Rodney Frelinghuysen (R-11)			58	24	75
1998	Frelinghuysen (R)	68%			
	Scollo (D)	30%			
Rush Holt (D-12)			90	NA	NA
1998	Holt (D)	50%			
	Pappas (R)	47%			
Robert Menendez (D-12)			10	90	10
1998	Menendez (D)	80%			
	de Leon (R)	17%			

Electoral Votes:	15	
1996 Presidential Results:	Clinton	54%
	Dole	36%
	Perot	9%

State Officials

Governor 1997 Election:	Christie Whitman (R)	47%
	James McGreevey (D)	46%
Attorney General:	Peter Verniera (R)	
State Senate:	16 Democrats	
	24 Republicans	
State Assembly:	35 Democrats	
	45 Republicans	

TAXES AND SPENDING

Total Revenues

New Jersey's per capita state and local total revenues registered $6,718 in 1996, ranking 7th in the nation and exceeding the U.S. average of $5,706 by 18%. From 1962 to 1996, real per capita state and local revenues increased by 380%, compared with an increase in the national average of 297%.

Taxes

New Jersey's per capita state and local taxes registered $3,436 in 1996, ranking 5th in the nation and exceeding the U.S. average of $2,597 by 32%. From 1962 to 1996, real per capita state and local taxes increased by 216%, compared with an increase of 152% in the U.S. average.

Property Taxes

New Jersey's per capita state and local property taxes equaled $1,604 in 1996, ranking highest in the nation and exceeding the U.S. average of $789 by 103%. From 1962 to 1996, real per capita state and local property taxes increased by 128%, versus a 67% increase in the U.S. average.

Sales and Gross Receipts Taxes

New Jersey's per capita state and local sales and gross receipts taxes came in at $926 in 1996, ranking 20th in the nation and lagging behind the U.S. average of $939 by 1%. From 1962 to 1996, real per capita state and local sales and gross receipts taxes increased by 403%, versus an increase of 214% in the U.S. average.

Real Per Capita State and Local Total Revenues: New Jersey vs. U.S.

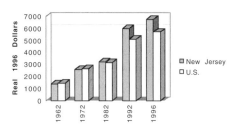

Real Per Capita State and Local Total Taxes: New Jersey vs. U.S.

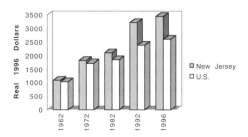

Real Per Capita State and Local Property Taxes: New Jersey vs. U.S.

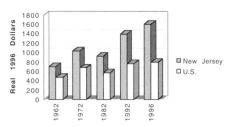

Real Per Capita State and Local Sales and Gross Receipts Taxes: New Jersey vs. U.S.

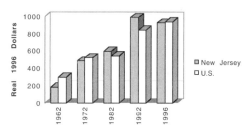

Income Taxes

New Jersey's per capita state and local income (individual and corporate) taxes registered $740 in 1996, ranking 16th in the nation and topping the U.S. average of $674 by 10%. From 1962 to 1996, real per capita state and local income taxes increased by 3,117%, versus a 567% increase in the U.S. average.

Personal Income Tax

A rate of 6.37%, ranking 30th in the nation (from lowest tax rate to highest), and comparing with the national average of 5.26%.

Capital Gains Tax

A rate of 6.37%, ranking 35th in the nation (from lowest tax rate to highest), and comparing with the national average of 4.68%.

Corporate Income Tax

A rate of 9%, ranking 41st in the nation (from lowest tax rate to highest), and comparing to the U.S. average of 6.63%.

Total Expenditures

New Jersey's per capita state and local total spending registered $6,138 in 1996, ranking 7th in the nation and exceeding the U.S. average of $5,268 by 17%. From 1962 to 1996, real per capita state and local total spending increased by 331%, versus an increase of 254% in the U.S. average.

Welfare Expenditures

New Jersey's per capita state and local public welfare spending registered $888 in 1996, ranking 7th in the nation and outpacing the U.S. average of $729 by 22%. From 1962 to 1996, real per capita state and local public welfare spending increased by 1,116%, compared with a 488% increase in the U.S. average.

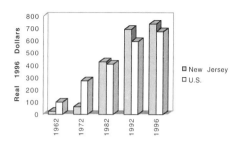

Real Per Capita State and Local Income Taxes: New Jersey vs. U.S.

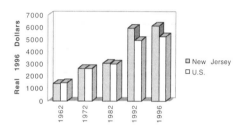

Real Per Capita State and Local Total Expenditures: New Jersey vs. U.S.

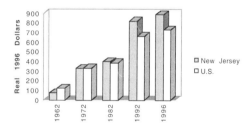

Real Per Capita State and Local Public Welfare Spending: New Jersey vs. U.S.

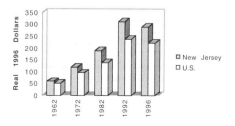

Real Per Capita State and Local Interest on General Debt: New Jersey vs. U.S.

Welfare Recipients (in thousands)

	1980	1989	3/99	Change 89–99
N.J.	469	308	175	−43%
U.S.	10,923	10,987	7,335	−33%

Interest on General Debt

New Jersey's per capita state and local interest on general debt registered $289 in 1996, ranking 12th in the nation and exceeding the U.S. average of $222 by 30%. From 1962 to 1996, real per capita state and local interest on general debt increased by 382%, versus an increase of 335% in the U.S. average.

Total Debt Outstanding

New Jersey's per capita state and local debt registered $5,212 in 1996, ranking 12th in the nation and outrunning the U.S. average of $4,409 by 18%. From 1962 to 1996, real per capita state and local debt outstanding increased by 150%, versus an increase of 120% in the U.S. average.

Government Employees

New Jersey's state and local government employees (full-time equivalent, or FTE) per 10,000 population registered 523.1 in 1997, ranking 33d in the nation and trailing the U.S. average of 531.1 by 2%. From 1962 to 1996, state and local FTE employees per 10,000 population increased by 79%, compared with an increase in the U.S. average of 66%.

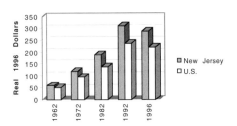

Real Per Capita State and Local Interest on General Debt: New Jersey vs. U.S.

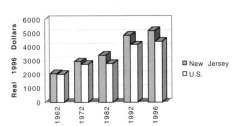

Real Per Capita State and Local Debt Outstanding: New Jersey vs. U.S.

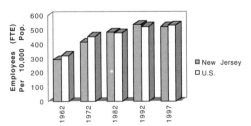

State and Local Government Employees (FTE) Per 10,000 Population: New Jersey vs. U.S.

Per Capita Federal Government Expenditures, 1998

	1998	Ranking
N.J.	$4,975	33d
U.S.	$5,491	

Per capita federal spending in New Jersey trailed the national average by 9%.

EDUCATION

Total Education Spending

New Jersey's per capita state and local education spending registered $1,825 in 1996, ranking 4th in the nation and outpacing the U.S. average of $1,503 by 21%. From 1962 to 1996, real per capita total education spending increased by 248%, versus an increase in the U.S. average of 173%.

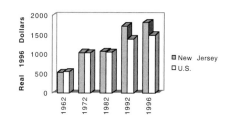

Real Per Capita State and Local Education Spending: New Jersey vs. U.S.

Per Pupil Spending

New Jersey's per pupil public school spending registered $9,576 in 1998, ranking highest in the nation and exceeding the U.S. average of $6,131 by 56%. From 1970 to 1998, New Jersey's real per pupil public school spending increased by 180%, compared with a 120% increase in the U.S. average.

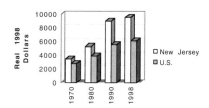

Real Per Pupil Public School Spending: New Jersey vs. U.S.

Average Public School Teacher Salaries (in 1997–98 dollars)

	1970	1980	1990	1998	1998 Ranking
N.J.	39,092	35,754	45,444	50,442	3d
U.S.	36,934	33,272	39,956	39,385	

In 1998, the average public school teacher salary in New Jersey outpaced the U.S. average by 28%. From 1970 to 1998, the real average teacher salary in New Jersey increased by 29%, versus an increase in the U.S. average of 7%.

Pupil/Teacher Ratio, Fall 1996

	Ratio	Rank
N.J.	13.6	1st
U.S.	17.1	

Teachers/Staff, Fall 1996

	Percent	Rank
N.J.	52.8	28th
U.S.	52.1	

Public School 4th-Grade Math Proficiency, 1996

	Average	Rank (out of 44 states)
N.J.	227	12th
U.S.	224	

Average Math SAT Scores

	1972	1982	1992	1998	Percentage Taking SAT in 1998
N.J.	497	481	497	508	79
U.S.	509	493	501	512	43

Average Verbal SAT Scores

	1972	1982	1992	1998	Percentage Taking SAT in 1998
N.J.	523	494	497	497	79
U.S.	530	504	500	505	43

Expenditures by Public Institutions of Higher Education Per Full-Time-Equivalent Student, 1996

	FTE Student Spending	Rank
N.J.	$13,435	15th
U.S.	$12,343	

Per-FTE-student spending in public institutions of higher education exceeded the U.S. average by 9%.

Per Full-Time-Equivalent Student Revenues from Federal, State, and Local Governments for Public Institutions of Higher Education, 1996

	FTE Student Government Revenues	Rank
N.J.	$8,590	12th
U.S.	$8,101	

Per-FTE-student-government revenues in public institutions of higher education outpaced the U.S. average by 6%.

Average Salary for Full-Time Professors at Public Universities, 1997

	Average	Rank
N.J.	$91,007	2d
U.S.	$72,599	

The average full-time public university professor salary exceeded the U.S. average by 25%.

ECONOMY AND BUSINESS

Economic Growth

Over the period of 1977 to 1997, New Jersey's real gross state product (GSP) grew by 82.2%—ranking 23d in the nation—as compared with real U.S. gross domestic product (GDP), expanding by 70.1%.

At $294.1 billion in 1997, New Jersey's GSP ranked as 8th largest in the nation.

From 1993 to 1997, New Jersey's annual real GSP growth averaged 2.30%—ranking 45th in the nation—as compared with annual real U.S. GDP growth, averaging 3.08%.

**Real Economic Growth
1977-1997: New Jersey vs. U.S.**

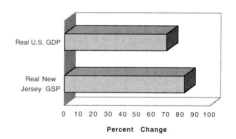

Percent Change

Job Growth

	Growth in Employee Payrolls (Nonagricultural) 1962–98	Ranking
N.J.	81.3%	42d
U.S.	126.5%	

	Average Annual Growth in Employee Payrolls (Nonagricultural) 1993–98	Ranking
N.J.	1.91%	45th
U.S.	2.98%	

Per Capita Disposable Income

	1997	Ranking
N.J.	$27,160	3d
U.S.	$21,607	

Per capita disposable income exceeded the U.S. average by 26%.

	Real Growth 1962–97	Ranking
N.J.	122.3%	23d
U.S.	116.7%	

	Average Annual Real Growth 1993–97	Ranking
N.J.	1.04%	47th
U.S.	1.48%	

Number of Businesses

	1997	Percent with Fewer than 500 Employees
Businesses with Employees	212,820	98.5
Self-employed Individuals	192,000	

New Business Incorporations

	1980	1986	1992	1997
N.J.	21,484	33,130	29,983	34,349

Percentage Change in Annual New Business Incorporations, 1980 vs. 1997

	Percent	Ranking
N.J.	59.9	18th
U.S.	49.7	

State Merchandise Exports to the World, 1998 (in millions of dollars)

	1998	Rank
N.J.	$20,033	9th

Small Business Survival Index, 1999

New Jersey ranks a pathetic 45th in terms of its policy environment for entrepreneurship.

Fortune 500 Headquarters in 1999

A total of 24 (ranked 7th)

Labor Union Membership, 1983 vs. 1997

	Percentage of Workers		Rank
	1983	1997	
N.J.	26.9	22.0	4th
U.S.	20.1	14.1	

Homeownership Rate, 1998

	Rate	Rank
N.J.	63.1	43d
U.S.	66.3	

CRIME

Crime Rates Per 100 Residents (rankings from best to worst crime rate)

Total Crime	1960	1970	1980	1990	1998	1998 Ranking
N.J.	0.96	2.74	6.40	5.45	3.65	14th
U.S.	1.04	2.74	5.90	5.82	4.62	

From 1960 to 1998, New Jersey's crime rate increased by 280%, versus a U.S. increase of 344%. From 1990 to 1998, New Jersey's crime rate dropped by 37%, versus a 21% U.S. decline.

Violent Crime	1960	1970	1980	1990	1998	1998 Ranking
N.J.	0.11	0.29	0.60	0.65	0.44	27th
U.S.	0.14	0.36	0.58	0.73	0.57	

From 1960 to 1998, New Jersey's violent crime rate increased by 300%, versus a U.S. increase of 307%. From 1990 to 1998, New Jersey's violent crime rate decreased by 32%, compared with a national decline of 22%.

Property Crime	1960	1970	1980	1990	1998	1998 Ranking
N.J.	0.85	2.46	5.80	4.80	3.21	12th
U.S.	0.90	2.38	5.32	5.09	4.05	

From 1960 to 1998, New Jersey's property crime rate increased by 278%, versus a national increase of 350%. From 1990 to 1998, New Jersey's property crime rate decreased by 33%, compared with a national decline of 20%.

Real Per Capita Police Protection Spending (in real 1996 dollars)

	1962	1972	1982	1992	1996	1996 Ranking
N.J.	78	121	133	186	225	5th
U.S.	51	95	114	148	168	

In 1996, per capita state and local police protection spending in New Jersey exceeded the U.S. average by 34%. From 1962 to 1996, real per capita state and local police protection spending increased by 188%, versus an increase of 229% in the U.S. average.

Prisoners in State and Federal Prisons Per 1,000 Population

	1980	1990	1996	1996 Ranking
N.J.	0.80	2.73	3.44	24th
U.S.	1.46	3.11	4.45	

From 1980 to 1996, prisoners per 1,000 population increased by 330%, versus a U.S. increase of 205%.

HEALTH CARE

Health-Care Spending

New Jersey's per capita state and local health-care spending registered $98 in 1996, ranking 36th in the nation and trailing the U.S. average of $151 by 35%. From 1962 to 1996, New Jersey's real per capita state and local health-care spending increased by 600%, versus an increase of 739% in the U.S. average.

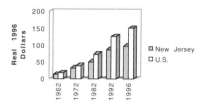

Real Per Capita State and Local Health Care Spending: New Jersey vs. U.S.

Hospital Spending

New Jersey's per capita state and local hospital spending registered $155 in 1996, ranking 32d in the nation and trailing the U.S. average of $266 by 42%. From 1962 to 1996, New Jersey's real per capita state and local hospital spending increased by 87%, as opposed to an increase of 189% in the U.S. average.

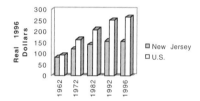

Real Per Capita State and Local Hospital Spending: New Jersey vs. U.S.

Medicaid, 1997

	Spending Per Recipient	Ranking
N.J.	$6,634	3d
U.S.	$3,681	

New Jersey's per-recipient Medicaid spending exceeded the U.S. average by 80%.

ENVIRONMENT

Parks and Recreation Spending

New Jersey's per capita state and local parks and recreation spending registered $88 in 1996, ranking 16th in the nation and outpacing the U.S. average of $72 by 22%. From 1962 to 1996, real per capita state and local parks and recreation spending increased by 214%, versus a 213% increase in the U.S. average.

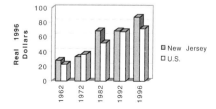

Real Per Capita State and Local Parks and Recreation Spending: New Jersey vs. U.S.

State and Local Natural Resources Spending, 1996

	Per Capita	Ranking
N.J.	$17	50th
U.S.	$60	

Per capita state and local natural resources spending in New Jersey trailed the U.S. average by 72%.

State Parks Revenues as a Share of Operating Expenses, 1997

	Percent	Rank
N.J.	27	37th
U.S.	42	

Percentage of Land Owned by the Federal Government, 1996

	Percent	Rank
N.J.	2.1	37th
U.S.	24.8	

SOCIETY AND DEMOGRAPHICS

Population

New Jersey's 1998 population of 8.115 million ranked 9th in the nation.

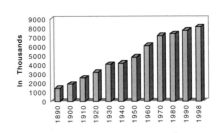

New Jersey Population

Population Growth, 1990–98

	Percentage Change in Population	Ranking
N.J.	4.74	40th
U.S.	8.66	

	Net International Migration	Ranking
N.J.	359,843	5th

	Net Domestic Migration	Ranking
N.J.	−349,617	48th

Infant Mortality Rate, 1998

	Percent	Rank
N.J.	5.5	43d
U.S.	6.4	

Percentage of Births of Low Birthweight, 1997

	Percent	Rank
N.J.	7.9	16th
U.S.	7.5	

Percentage of Live Births to Unmarried Women, 1997

	Percent	Rank
N.J.	27.8	38th
U.S.	32.4	

Abortion Rate—Abortions Per 1,000 Women Ages 15–44, 1995

	Rate	Rank
N.J.	34.5	4th
U.S.	22.9	

LIFESTYLE

Percentage of Households with Computers, 1998

	Percent	Rank
N.J.	48.1	9th

Percentage of Households with Internet Access, 1998

	Percent	Rank
N.J.	31.3	9th

State Arts Agency Spending, 1999

	Per Capita	Rank
N.J.	$1.95	9th
U.S.	$1.35	

Per capita state arts spending in 1999 topped the U.S. average by 44%.

Major League Sports Facilities

Year Opened/ Refurb.	Stadium/ Arena	Home Team	Millions of Nominal Dollars		Millions of Real 1997 Dollars	
			Estimated Total Cost	Estimated Taxpayer Cost	Estimated Total Cost	Estimated Taxpayer Cost
1976	Giants Stadium	Giants (NFL) 1976–present Jets (NFL) 1984–present	$68.0	$68.0	$191.5	$191.5
1981	Byrne Meadowlands/ Continental Airlines Arena	Nets (NBA) 1981–present Devils (NHL) 1982–present	$85.0	$85.0	$150.2	$150.2

NEW MEXICO

Libertarian advocates of legalizing drugs added a rather mainstream Republican to their ranks in 1999—New Mexico Republican Governor Gary Johnson.

On August 13, 1999, the Associated Press quoted Johnson admitting, "Right now, I'm out on my own. Some day we'll address this, and maybe this is one of the first dominoes that gets the whole thing moving." He added, "I'm not trying to be a wacko."

Indeed, the free market case for drug legalization carries a significant degree of common sense. Legalize drugs; the price will fall; related criminal activity will drop dramatically; and government will save all kinds of money currently spent fighting the illegal drug trade, which thrives because prices are so high. For some, it is worth the risk to break the law in order to get the big pay day. Besides, the argument goes, drugs should not be made illegal because they do not really hurt anybody, or they just hurt the individual using them.

Johnson told the *New York Times* (August 22, 1999): "As an extension of everything I've done in office, I made a cost-benefit analysis, and this one really stinks." He asserted that drugs could be regulated and people held accountable for their misdeeds while under the influence.

Sounds rather neat and tidy, unless one questions the assertion that drugs do not hurt users, their families and friends, and others. If drugs like LSD, heroine, cocaine, crack, and even marijuana do considerable harm, and legalization lowers the price and expands access, then the drug legalization argument runs into serious trouble. Naturally, both sides have their studies and analyses supporting their respective positions, but it seems to us that the woes of drug use reach well beyond only the violence specifically related to its illegality—like addiction, violence resulting from drug use, broken families, lost economic output, and death, to name a few.

Those seeking legalization, of course, respond that alcohol has similar effects, and it is legal. However, alcohol has long been accepted in society, while drug use has not. In addition, it is highly debatable that alcohol and hard drugs carry the same impact.

Whatever one's position on the issue, on a certain level you have to give Johnson some credit for raising this issue in a state where drug trafficking is a major problem. (New Mexico carries one of the worst crime rates in the nation.) At the same time, though, Johnson reportedly does not plan to run again for political office after his term as governor expires, which makes his drug legalization position easier to stake out.

There is more to discuss, however, on the policy front in New Mexico than drugs. While state and local spending and taxing levels generally run around the U.S. average, a few vary considerably. For example, a big positive is the state's extremely low property taxes (ranking second lowest in the nation on a per capita basis).

As for the negatives, while welfare rolls nationwide declined by 33% between 1989 and March 1999, New Mexico's actually increased by 35%. The state also carries one of the heaviest state and local government employee burdens in the nation. Per capita parks and recreation spending took an enormous leap between 1992 and 1996, with the state now ranking among the most lavish in the nation. Worst of all, though, is the fact that New Mexico's income tax rates rank among the most burdensome.

New Mexico's economic performance has been generally fine, but it is not without its problems. While real economic growth, job creation, and population growth have been good, real disposable income growth and new business incorporations have lagged behind a bit.

In the 21st century, New Mexico's politicians should worry far more about the costs of sky-high income tax rates than about the costs of the drug war. Eliminating the state income tax, for example, would help to unleash the very best in mankind—creativity, innovation, and hard work. Eliminating laws against drug use might only serve to tap into the dark side of human nature.

POLITICS

Registered Voters

55% Democrats
34% Republicans
12% Other

Federal Officials: Recent Election and Group Ratings

			ACU	ADA	SBSC
U.S. Senators:	Pete Domenici (R)		69	14	80
	1998 Domenici (R)	64%			
	Trujillo (D)	29%			
	Jeff Bingaman (D)		11	76	20
	1994 Bingaman (D)	54%			
	McMillan (R)	46%			
U.S. Representatives:	Heather Wilson (R-1)		83	NA	88
	1998 Wilson (R)	48%			
	Maloof (D)	42%			
	Joe Skeen (R-2)		84	0	95
	1998 Skeen (R)	58%			
	Baca (D)	42%			
	Tom Udall (D-3)		92	NA	NA
	1998 Udall (D)	53%			
	Redmond (R)	43%			
Electoral Votes:	5				
1996 Presidential Results:	Clinton	49%			
	Dole	42%			
	Perot	6%			

State Officials

Governor 1998 Election:	Gary Johnson (R)	55%
	Martin Chavez (D)	45%
Lt. Governor:	Walter Bradley (R)	
Attorney General:	Patricia Madrid (D)	
State Senate:	25 Democrats	
	17 Republicans	
State House:	40 Democrats	
	30 Republicans	

TAXES AND SPENDING

Total Revenues

New Mexico's per capita state and local total revenues registered $5,923 in 1996, ranking 16th in the nation and topping the U.S. average of $5,706 by 4%. From 1962 to 1996, real per capita state and local revenues increased by 273%, compared with an increase in the national average of 297%.

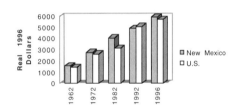

Real Per Capita State and Local Total Revenues: New Mexico vs. U.S.

Taxes

New Mexico's per capita state and local taxes registered $2,263 in 1996, ranking 31st in the nation and trailing the U.S. average of $2,597 by 13%. From 1962 to 1996, real per capita state and local taxes increased by 162%, compared with an increase of 152% in the U.S. average.

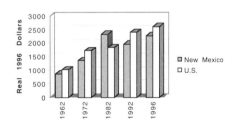

Real Per Capita State and Local Taxes: New Mexico vs. U.S.

Property Taxes

New Mexico's per capita state and local property taxes equaled $276 in 1996, ranking 50th in the nation and trailing the U.S. average of $789 by 65%. From 1962 to 1996, real per capita state and local property taxes increased by 28%, versus a 67% increase in the U.S. average.

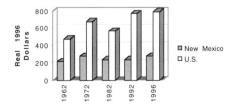

Real Per Capita State and Local Property Taxes: New Mexico vs. U.S.

Sales and Gross Receipts Taxes

New Mexico's per capita state and local sales and gross receipts taxes came in at $1,216 in 1996, ranking 6th in the nation and exceeding the U.S. average of $939 by 29%. From 1962 to 1996, real per capita state and local sales and gross receipts taxes increased by 248%, versus an increase of 214% in the U.S. average.

Income Taxes

New Mexico's per capita state and local income (individual and corporate) taxes registered $471 in 1996, ranking 38th in the nation and trailing the U.S. average of $674 by 30%. From 1962 to 1996, real per capita state and local income taxes increased by 685%, versus a 567% increase in the U.S. average.

Personal Income Tax

A rate of 8.2%, ranking 44th in the nation (from lowest tax rate to highest), and comparing with the national average of 5.26%.

Capital Gains Tax

A rate of 8.2%, ranking 45th in the nation (from lowest tax rate to highest), and comparing with the national average of 4.68%.

Corporate Income Tax

A rate of 9.8%, ranking 48th in the nation (from lowest tax rate to highest), and comparing with the national average of 6.63%.

Total Expenditures

New Mexico's per capita state and local total spending registered $5,019 in 1996, ranking 20th in the nation and trailing the U.S. average of $5,268 by 5%. From 1962 to 1996, real per capita state and local total spending increased by 237%, versus an increase of 254% in the U.S. average.

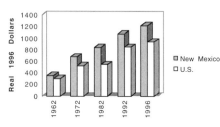

Real Per Capita State and Local Sales and Gross Receipts Tax: New Mexico vs. U.S.

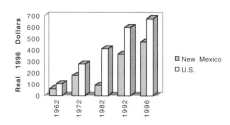

Real Per Capita State and Local Income Taxes: New Mexico vs. U.S.

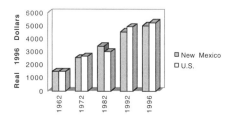

Real Per Capita State and Local Total Expenditures: New Mexico vs. U.S.

Welfare Expenditures

New Mexico's per capita state and local public welfare spending registered $683 in 1996, ranking 25th in the nation and trailing the U.S. average of $729 by 6%. From 1962 to 1996, real per capita state and local public welfare spending increased by 429%, compared with a 488% increase in the U.S. average.

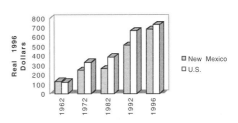

Real Per Capita State and Local Public Welfare Spending: New Mexico vs. U.S.

Welfare Recipients (in thousands)

	1980	1989	3/99	Change 1989–99
N. Mex.	56	60	81	+ 35%
U.S.	10,923	10,987	7,335	− 33%

Interest on General Debt

New Mexico's per capita state and local interest on general debt registered $150 in 1996, ranking 37th in the nation and trailing the U.S. average of $222 by 32%. From 1962 to 1996, real per capita state and local interest on general debt increased by 552%, versus an increase of 335% in the U.S. average.

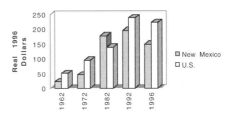

Real Per Capita State and Local Interest on General Debt: New Mexico vs. U.S.

Total Debt Outstanding

New Mexico's per capita state and local debt registered $3,168 in 1996, ranking 39th in the nation and trailing the U.S. average of $4,409 by 28%. From 1962 to 1996, real per capita state and local debt outstanding increased by 151%, versus an increase of 120% in the U.S. average.

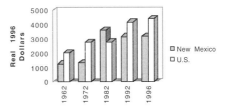

Real Per Capita State and Local Debt Outstanding: New Mexico vs. U.S.

Government Employees

New Mexico's state and local government employees (full-time equivalent, or FTE) per 10,000 population registered 641.5 in 1997, ranking 4th in the nation and exceeding the U.S. average of 531.1 by 21%. From 1962 to 1996, state and local FTE employees per 10,000 population increased by 95%, compared with an increase in the U.S. average of 66%.

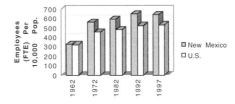

State and Local Government Employees (FTE) Per 10,000 Population: New Mexico vs. U.S.

Per Capita Federal Government Expenditures, 1998

	1998	Ranking
N. Mex.	$7,446	5th
U.S.	$5,491	

Per capita federal spending in New Mexico exceeded the national average by 36%.

EDUCATION

Total Education Spending

New Mexico's per capita state and local education spending registered $1,526 in 1996, ranking 21st in the nation and topping the U.S. average of $1,503 by 2%. From 1962 to 1996, real per capita total education spending increased by 120%, versus an increase in the U.S. average of 173%.

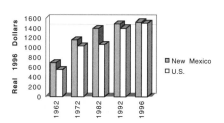

Real Per Capita State and Local Education Spending: New Mexico vs. U.S.

Per Pupil Spending

New Mexico's per pupil public school spending registered $5,486 in 1998, ranking 33d in the nation and trailing the U.S. average of $6,131 by 11%. From 1970 to 1998, New Mexico's real per pupil public school spending increased by 123%, compared with a 120% increase in the U.S. average.

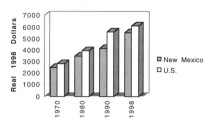

Real Per Pupil Public School Spending: New Mexico vs. U.S.

Average Public School Teacher Salaries (in 1997–98 dollars)

	1970	1980	1990	1998	1998 Ranking
N. Mex.	33,380	31,016	31,534	30,152	47th
U.S.	36,934	33,272	39,956	39,385	

In 1998, the average public school teacher salary in New Mexico trailed the U.S. average by 23%. From 1970 to 1998, the real average teacher salary in New Mexico decreased by 10%, versus an increase in the U.S. average of 7%.

Pupil/Teacher Ratio, Fall 1996

	Ratio	Rank
N. Mex.	16.7	29th
U.S.	17.1	

Teachers/Staff, Fall 1996

	Percent	Rank
N. Mex.	49.0	46th
U.S.	52.1	

Public School 4th-Grade Reading Proficiency, 1998

	Average	Rank (out of 40 states)
N. Mex.	206	35th
U.S.	215	

Public School 8th-Grade Reading Proficiency, 1998

	Average	Rank (out of 37 states)
N. Mex.	258	25th
U.S.	261	

Public School 4th-Grade Math Proficiency, 1996

	Average	Rank (out of 44 states)
N. Mex.	214	38th
U.S.	224	

Public School 8th-Grade Math Proficiency, 1996

	Average	Rank (out of 41 states)
N. Mex.	262	33d
U.S.	271	

Public School 8th-Grade Science Proficiency, 1996

	Average	Rank (out of 41 states)
N. Mex.	141	34th
U.S.	148	

Average Math SAT Scores

	1972	1982	1992	1998	Percentage taking SAT in 1998
N. Mex.	543	538	541	551	12
U.S.	509	493	501	512	43

Average Verbal SAT Scores

	1972	1982	1992	1998	Percentage taking SAT in 1998
N. Mex.	567	556	550	554	12
U.S.	530	504	500	505	43

Expenditures by Public Institutions of Higher Education Per Full-Time-Equivalent Student, 1996

	FTE Student Spending	Rank
N. Mex.	$14,552	7th
U.S.	$12,343	

Per-FTE-student spending in public institutions of higher education exceeded the U.S. average by 18%.

Per Full-Time-Equivalent Student Revenues from Federal, State, and Local Governments for Public Institutions of Higher Education, 1996

	FTE Student Government Revenues	Rank
N. Mex.	$11,786	4th
U.S.	$8,101	

Per-FTE-student-government revenues in public institutions of higher education topped the U.S. average by 45%.

Average Salary for Full-Time Professors at Public Universities, 1997

	Average	Rank
N. Mex.	$63,004	40th
U.S.	$72,599	

The average full-time public university professor salary trailed the U.S. average by 13%.

ECONOMY AND BUSINESS

Economic Growth

Over the period of 1977 to 1997, New Mexico's real gross state product (GSP) grew by 88.3%—ranking 17th in the nation—as compared with real U.S. gross domestic product (GDP), expanding by 70.1%.

At $45.2 billion in 1997, New Mexico's GSP ranked as 38th largest in the nation.

From 1993 to 1997, New Mexico's annual real GSP growth averaged 6.48%—ranking 5th in the nation—as compared with annual real U.S. GDP growth, averaging 3.08%.

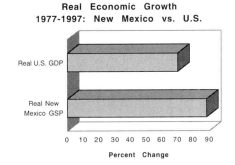

Real Economic Growth 1977-1997: New Mexico vs. U.S.

Job Growth

	Growth in Employee Payrolls (Nonagricultural) 1962–98	Ranking
N. Mex.	197.2%	13th
U.S.	126.5%	

	Average Annual Growth in Employee Payrolls (Nonagricultural) 1993–98	Ranking
N. Mex.	3.69%	12th
U.S.	2.98%	

Per Capita Disposable Income, 1997

	1997	Ranking
N. Mex.	$16,959	49th
U.S.	$21,607	

Per capita disposable income trailed the U.S. average by 22%.

	Real Growth 1962–97	Ranking
N. Mex.	103.1%	39th
U.S.	116.7%	

	Average Annual Real Growth 1993–97	Ranking
N. Mex.	1.51%	33d
U.S.	1.48%	

Number of Businesses

	1997	Percent with Fewer than 500 Employees
Businesses with Employees	40,462	96.5
Self-employed Individuals	86,000	

New Business Incorporations

	1980	1986	1992	1997
N. Mex.	2,450	2,495	2,843	2,919

Percentage Change in Annual New Business Incorporations, 1980 vs. 1997

	Percent	Ranking
N. Mex.	19.1	36th
U.S.	49.7	

State Merchandise Exports to the World, 1998 (in millions of dollars)

	1998	Rank
N. Mex.	$1,896	39th

Small Business Survival Index, 1999

New Mexico ranks a dire 48th in the nation in terms of its policy environment for entrepreneurship.

Fortune 500 Headquarters in 1999

A total of 1 (ranked 38th)

Labor Union Membership, 1983 vs. 1997

	Percentage of Workers		
	1983	1997	1997 Rank
N. Mex.	11.8	8.4	37th
U.S.	20.1	14.1	

Homeownership Rate, 1998

	Rate	Rank
N. Mex.	71.3	14th
U.S.	66.3	

CRIME

Crime Rates Per 100 Residents (rankings from best to worst crime rate)

Total Crime	1960	1970	1980	1990	1998	1998 Ranking
N. Mex.	1.22	2.87	5.98	6.68	6.72	49th
U.S.	1.04	2.74	5.90	5.82	4.62	

From 1960 to 1998, New Mexico's crime rate increased by 451%, versus a U.S. increase of 344%. From 1990 to 1998, New Mexico's crime rate increased by 1%, versus a U.S. decrease of 21%.

Violent Crime	1960	1970	1980	1990	1998	1998 Ranking
N. Mex.	0.15	0.29	0.62	0.78	0.96	50th
U.S.	0.14	0.36	0.58	0.73	0.57	

From 1960 to 1998, New Mexico's violent crime rate increased by 540%, versus a U.S. increase of 307%. From 1990 to 1998, New Mexico's violent crime rate increased by 23%, compared with a national decline of 22%.

Property Crime	1960	1970	1980	1990	1998	1998 Ranking
N. Mex.	1.07	2.57	5.36	5.90	5.76	48th
U.S.	0.90	2.38	5.32	5.09	4.05	

From 1960 to 1998, New Mexico's property crime rate increased by 438%, versus a national increase of 350%. From 1990 to 1998, New Mexico's property crime rate decreased by 2%, compared with a national decline of 20%.

Real Per Capita Police Protection Spending (in real 1996 dollars)

	1962	1972	1982	1992	1996	1996 Ranking
N. Mex.	41	79	117	148	165	17th
U.S.	51	95	114	148	168	

In 1996, per capita state and local police protection spending in New Mexico trailed the U.S. average by 2%. From 1962 to 1996, real per capita state and local police protection spending increased by 302%, versus an increase of 229% in the U.S. average.

Prisoners in State and Federal Prisons Per 1,000 Population

	1980	1990	1996	1996 Ranking
N. Mex.	0.98	2.10	2.76	37th
U.S.	1.46	3.11	4.45	

From 1980 to 1996, prisoners per 1,000 population increased by 182%, versus a U.S. increase of 205%.

HEALTH CARE

Health-Care Spending

New Mexico's per capita state and local health-care spending registered $171 in 1996, ranking 15th in the nation and topping the U.S. average of $151 by 13%. From 1962 to 1996, New Mexico's real per capita state and local health-care spending increased by 1,121%, versus an increase of 739% in the U.S. average.

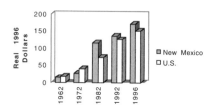

Real Per Capita State and Local Health Care Spending: New Mexico vs. U.S.

Hospital Spending

New Mexico's per capita state and local hospital spending registered $292 in 1996, ranking 16th in the nation and topping the U.S. average of $266 by 10%. From 1962 to 1996, New Mexico's real per capita state and local hospital spending increased by 431%, as opposed to an increase of 189% in the U.S. average.

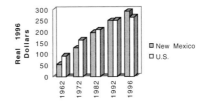

Real Per Capita State and Local Hospital Spending: New Mexico vs. U.S.

Medicaid, 1997

	Spending Per Recipient	Ranking
N. Mex.	$2,569	45th
U.S.	$3,681	

New Mexico's per-recipient Medicaid spending trailed the U.S. average by 30%.

ENVIRONMENT

Parks and Recreation Spending

New Mexico's per capita state and local parks and recreation spending registered $120 in 1996, ranking 5th in the nation and exceeding the U.S. average of $72 by 67%. From 1962 to 1996, real per capita state and local parks and recreation spending increased by 757%, versus a 213% increase in the U.S. average.

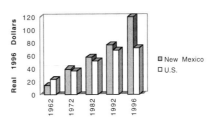

Real Per Capita State and Local Parks and Recreation Spending: New Mexico vs. U.S.

State and Local Natural Resources Spending, 1996

	Per Capita	Ranking
N. Mex.	$66	26th
U.S.	$60	

Per capita state and local natural resources spending in New Mexico exceeded the U.S. average by 10%.

State Parks Revenues as a Share of Operating Expenses, 1997

	Percent	Rank
N. Mex.	25	39th
U.S.	42	

Percentage of Land Owned by the Federal Government, 1996

	Percent	Rank
N. Mex.	33.7	10th
U.S.	24.8	

SOCIETY AND DEMOGRAPHICS

Population

New Mexico's 1998 population of 1.737 million ranked 37th in the nation.

Population Growth, 1990–98

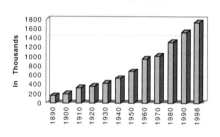

New Mexico Population

	Percentage Change in Population	Ranking
N. Mex.	14.65	11th
U.S.	8.66	

	Net International Migration	Ranking
N. Mex.	35,854	23d

	Net Domestic Migration	Ranking
N. Mex.	55,264	22d

Infant Mortality Rate, 1998

	Percent	Rank
N. Mex.	6.5	32d
U.S.	6.4	

Percentage of Births of Low Birthweight, 1997

	Percent	Rank
N. Mex.	7.8	18th
U.S.	7.5	

Percentage of Live Births to Unmarried Women, 1997

	Percent	Rank
N. Mex.	43.5	4th
U.S.	32.4	

Abortion Rate—Abortions Per 1,000 Women Ages 15–44, 1995

	Rate	Rank
N. Mex.	14.4	31st
U.S.	22.9	

LIFESTYLE

Percentage of Households with Computers, 1998

	Percent	Rank
N. Mex.	42.2	26th

Percentage of Households with Internet Access, 1998

	Percent	Rank
N. Mex.	25.8	24th

State Arts Agency Spending, 1999

	Per Capita	Rank
N. Mex.	$1.60	11th
U.S.	$1.35	

Per capita state arts spending in 1999 exceeded the U.S. average by 19%.

Major League Sports Facilities

None

NEW YORK

If it were not for Wall Street, New York would be in far worse shape. After all, upstate New York (that is, north of Westchester County) remains in the economic doldrums, while downstate suburbs and New York City have been doing little more than riding a recent robust stock market.

For example, a July 1999 report from the Federal Reserve Bank of New York reveals that the securities industry accounted for 18.8% of total earnings in New York City in 1998, versus 4.5% in 1969. New York City's 18.8% compared with just 2% nationwide. Extending the analysis to encompass finance, banking, insurance, and real estate (FIRE), these earnings registered 31.3% of total New York City earnings, compared with 14.1% in 1969. Across the nation in 1998, FIRE accounted for 9% of total earnings. As the market goes, so goes much of New York.

Quite ominously, however, the ongoing, vast leaps being witnessed in computer and telecommunications technologies have lessened and will continue to diminish the necessity of locating the financial community actually on or around Wall Street. When information and capital can increasingly travel at the speed of light around the globe, they are more and more able and likely to seek out less-taxing and less-regulatory climates. Unfortunately, almost none of New York's politicians seem to recognize this economic reality.

Especially since the late 1950s, but even as far back as the early 1930s, both New York State and New York City have established environments hostile to entrepreneurship and business. Interestingly, it was Republicans who did the most damage. Under the Republican governorship of Nelson Rockefeller from the late 1950s into the early 1970s, and the Big Apple GOP mayoralty of John Lindsay from the mid-1960s into the early 1970s, government spending exploded, existing tax levies were increased, and a host of new taxes were imposed. At least Lindsay had the decency to become a Democrat, while Rockefeller tried to reshape the entire Republican Party in his own liberal image. Rockefeller did exactly that in New York, and the jury is still out as to whether or not he succeeded nationally.

Of course, Democrats did their part as well, led by Governor Mario Cuomo from 1982 to 1994. However, it should be pointed out that Democratic Governor Hugh Carey managed to actually get rid of the state's onerous, antientrepreneur unincorporated business income tax during his reign in the governor's mansion from 1974 to 1982, while also signing off on reductions in the state's personal income and capital gains tax rates. By the mid-1970s, New York's top individual income tax rate actually reached beyond 15%, and the capital gains rate topped 9%. Both rates today register 6.85%—which still exceed the U.S. averages.

In recent years, Governor George Pataki and New York City Mayor Rudy Giuliani, both Republicans, have received an enormous amount of credit for cutting taxes and doing much to turn New York around. Reality is not so simple.

Pataki has offered small- to medium-sized tax cuts, which were quite welcome after several years of broken tax-cut promises and various tax hikes served up by former Governor Cuomo. With revenues pouring into state coffers, however, Pataki has shown an unnerving penchant for increased spending over more serious tax relief. For example, increases in the last three state budgets have far exceeded the rate of inflation. He also has advocated big jumps in environmental spending, not to mention local school aid and corporate welfare expenditures.

In addition, Pataki has signed off on several tax increases in the form of extending taxes that were due to expire and granting state approval for local tax increases. Pataki also pushed through a property tax plan that is more gimmick than tax reduction. Essentially, the plan calls for local school property tax reductions, with the loss of school revenues made up by the state. Of course, without any caps on state or local spending or on local property taxes, in the long run Pataki's property tax cut will become a mere illusion.

As for Giuliani, his own tax cuts actually measure smaller in estimated revenues than the temporary taxes he extended that were due to expire. Indeed, 1998 witnessed the rather bizarre scenario of Republican mayor Giuliani fighting against Democratic efforts in the city council to allow one of the city's personal income tax surcharges to expire. Thankfully, though, in the end Giuliani reluctantly agreed to let the surcharge expire. In 1999, Giuliani likewise opposed state Republican efforts to eliminate the city's commuter income tax. To the taxpayers' delight, he lost that battle. Giuliani also has accomplished nothing in terms of downsizing the city's bloated budget.

In fact, one of Giuliani's leading issues is taxpayer handouts to professional sports teams. At various times during his mayoralty, Giuliani has advocated new homes for the Mets, Yankees, Jets, Knicks, Rangers, and two minor league baseball teams. If Giuliani gets his way, the sports pork tally in New York City could easily total more than $4 billion, with taxpayers picking up most of the tab. (The nearby Islanders on Long Island, and New Jersey's Nets and Devils also are looking for new sports palaces. The New York City metropolitan area easily ranks as the busiest region in the nation in terms of sports teams looking for the taxpayers to pad their bottom lines.)

On the positive side, Giuliani periodically acted as a voice for school choice in New York City. Though the effort has not gotten very far as yet, Giuliani deserves enormous credit for getting choice injected into the city's education debate. If the positives of choice, competition, and parent/student empowerment were needed anywhere, it would be in New York City where the public school bureaucracy is infamous for its size and incompetence.

Of course, Giuliani also deserves at least partial credit for the dramatic reduction in crime in New York City since he was elected in 1993. For example, between 1993 and 1998, the city's crime rate plummeted by 46% from 8.17 to 4.39. Interestingly, over this same period, Gotham accounted for an astounding 17% of the decline in crime across the entire nation, not to mention 77% of the decline in crime in the state of New York.

It is worth noting that the Big Apple's decline in crime began before Giuliani took office. For example, the crime rate fell from 9.67 in 1989 to 8.17 in 1993—a 16% decline. The rate of improvement, though, has been far more dramatic during the Giuliani years.

Meanwhile, New York City's suburbs, such as Westchester, Nassau, and Suffolk Counties, still stand out as both bastions of Republicanism (though the mighty Nassau County GOP machine suffered a major defeat on Election Day 1999), as well as some of the highest taxed counties in the entire nation. Spending remains lavish in school districts, counties, towns, and assorted other local government entities.

Across the state, rising public school per pupil spending and teacher salaries have firmly entrenched New York as one of the big-spending education states, but student performance measures such as SAT scores either have stagnated or declined.

New York State and New York City led this nation in entrepreneurship and economic growth from the late 18th century through the 1920s. New York's dominance leveled off in subsequent years, and since the early 1960s the Empire State and the Big Apple have been in relative decline. As is evidenced by the tax, spending, economic, and education numbers below, the outlook is not all that positive for New York to take a leadership role in the 21st century.

New York can no longer assume it is the economic capital of the world. It has been dethroned by a combination of bad public policies and liberating technological advancements. However, the decline of the state and the city is anything but inevitable. New York still has one of the nation's largest economies—a formidable base on which to build—and if progrowth policies are implemented, then entrepreneurial dynamism can be reignited.

However, this will require clear political and economic vision. When you think of the big names in New York politics today—Giuliani, Pataki, U.S. Senator Chuck Schumer, and Hillary Clinton—one gets cloudiness at best, or a warped vision in favor of more government control. In fact, among New York's 31 members of the U.S. House of Representatives and two U.S. senators, only one seems to see matters clearly.

The relatively unknown Staten Island Congressman Vito Fossella (R-13) recently led a charge in Congress for a 30%, across-the-board personal income tax cut, and he claims the most proentrepreneur, profree-market, conservative voting record among the Empire State's House delegation. One against at least 30—talk about a long shot. However, if New York is to help lead our nation in the 21st century, even more dramatic action than Fossella's proposed income tax cut will be needed at the federal, state, and local levels. For example, New York City will have to eliminate its city-imposed personal income, capital gains, unincorporated business income, and corporate income taxes, which are imposed in addition to state income taxes.

In fact, all of New York began the 20th century unburdened by any income taxes at all. Reestablishing New York as an income-tax-free state would be the surest path to higher growth, entrepreneurial diversification, and the reinstatement of the Empire State as the world's global economic leader.

POLITICS

Registered Voters

47% Democrats
30% Republicans
24% Other

Federal Officials: Recent Election and Group Ratings

			ACU	ADA	SBSC
U.S. Senators:	Daniel Patrick Moynihan (D)		6	83	20
	1994 Moynihan (D)	55%			
	Castro (R)	42%			
	Charles Schumer (D)		NA	NA	NA
	1998 Schumer (D)	55%			
	D'Amato (R)	44%			
U.S. Representatives:	Michael Forbes (D-1)		69	31	40
	1998 Forbes (R)	64%			
	Holst (D)	36%			
	Rick Lazio (R-2)		65	28	60
	1998 Lazio (R)	66%			
	Bace (D)	30%			
	Peter King (R-3)		75	13	85
	1998 King (R)	64%			
	Langberg (D)	35%			
	Carolyn McCarthy (D-4)		20	85	25
	1998 McCarthy (D)	53%			
	Becker (R)	47%			
	Gary Ackerman (D-5)		4	90	10
	1998 Ackerman (D)	65%			
	Pinzon (R)	33%			
	Gregory Meeks (D-6)		5	NA	5
	1998 Meeks (D)	NO			
	Joseph Crowley (D-7)		NA	NA	NA
	1998 Crowley (D)	69%			
	Dillon (R)	26%			
	Jerrold Nadler (D-8)		5	99	15
	1998 Nadler (D)	86%			
	Howard (R)	14%			
	Anthony David Weiner (D-9)		NA	NA	NA
	1998 Weiner (D)	66%			
	Telano (R)	23%			
	Edolphus Towns (D-10)		4	93	5
	1998 Towns (D)	92%			
	Brown (R)	6%			

			ACU	ADA	SBSC
Major Owens (D-11)			3	90	5
1998	Owens (D)	90%			
	Greene (R)	9%			
Nydia Velazquez (D-12)			4	98	5
1998	Velazquez (D)	84%			
	Markgraf (R)	12%			
Vito Fossella (R-13)			98	0	100
1998	Fossella (R)	65%			
	Prisco (D)	34%			
Carolyn Maloney (D-14)			4	93	10
1998	Maloney (D)	77%			
	Kupferman (R)	23%			
Charles Rangel (D-15)			6	91	0
1998	Rangel (D)	93%			
	Cunningham (R)	6%			
Jose Serrano (D-16)			3	96	5
1998	Serrano (D)	95%			
	Bayley (R)	3%			
Eliot Engel (D-17)			6	97	5
1998	Engel (D)	88%			
	Fiumefreddo (R)	12%			
Nita Lowey (D-18)			6	92	15
1998	Lowey (D)	83%			
	McMahon (C)	11%			
Sue Kelly (R-19)			61	31	55
1998	Kelly (R)	62%			
	Collins (D)	34%			
Benjamin Gilman (R-20)			45	45	45
1998	Gilman (R)	58%			
	Feiner (D)	39%			
Michael McNulty (D-21)			26	80	15
1998	McNulty (D)	74%			
	Ayers (R)	26%			
John Sweeney (R-22)			NA	NA	NA
1998	Sweeney (R)	55%			
	Bordewich (D)	42%			

			ACU	ADA	SBSC
Sherwood Boehlert (R-23)			34	53	40
1998	Boehlert (R)	81%			
	Vickers (C-RTL)	19%			
John McHugh (R-24)			NA	16	75
1998	McHugh (R)	79%			
	Tallon (D)	21%			
James Walsh (R-25)			66	29	50
1998	Walsh (R)	69%			
	Rothenberg (D)	31%			
Maurice Hinchey (D-26)			6	96	5
1998	Hinchey (D)	62%			
	Walker (R)	31%			
Thomas Reynolds (R-27)			NA	NA	NA
1998	Reynolds (R)	57%			
	Cook (D)	43%			
Louise Slaughter (D-28)			7	NA	10
1998	Slaughter (D)	65%			
	Kaplan (R)	31%			
John LaFalce (D-29)			14	80	10
1998	LaFalce (D)	57%			
	Collins (R)	41%			
Jack Quinn (R-30)			59	29	55
1998	Quinn (R)	68%			
	Peoples (D)	32%			
Amory Houghton (R-31)			54	28	45
1998	Houghton (R)	68%			
	Rossiter (D)	25%			

Electoral Votes:	33	
1996 Presidential Results:	Clinton	59%
	Dole	31%
	Perot	8%

State Officials

Governor 1998 Election:	George Pataki (R)	52%
	Peter Vallone (D)	31%
Lt. Governor:	Mary Donohue (R)	
Attorney General:	Eliot Spitzer (D)	
State Senate:	26 Democrats	
	35 Republicans	
State Assembly:	98 Democrats	
	52 Republicans	

TAXES AND SPENDING

Total Revenues

New York's per capita state and local total revenues registered $8,492 in 1996, ranking 3d in the nation and exceeding the U.S. average of $5,706 by 49%. From 1962 to 1996, real per capita state and local revenues increased by 369%, compared with an increase in the national average of 297%.

Taxes

New York's per capita state and local taxes registered $3,985 in 1996, ranking 2d in the nation (only trailing Washington, D.C.) and exceeding the U.S. average of $2,597 by 53%. From 1962 to 1996, real per capita state and local taxes increased by 178%, compared with an increase of 152% in the U.S. average.

Property Taxes

New York's per capita state and local property taxes equaled $1,279 in 1996, ranking 5th in the nation and exceeding the U.S. average of $789 by 62%. From 1962 to 1996, real per capita state and local property taxes increased by 102%, versus a 67% increase in the U.S. average.

Sales and Gross Receipts Taxes

New York's per capita state and local sales and gross receipts taxes came in at $1,067 in 1996, ranking 11th in the nation and topping the U.S. average of $939 by 14%. From 1962 to 1996, real per capita state and local sales and gross receipts taxes increased by 510%, versus a 214% increase in the U.S. average.

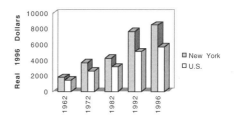

Real Per Capita State and Local Total Revenues: New York vs. U.S.

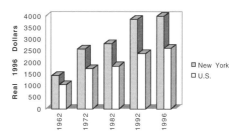

Real Per Capita State and Local Total Taxes: New York vs. U.S.

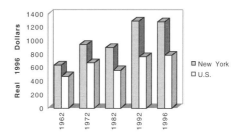

Real Per Capita State and Local Property Taxes: New York vs. U.S.

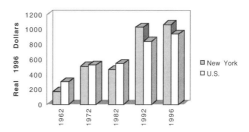

Real Per Capita State and Local Sales and Gross Receipts Taxes: New York vs. U.S.

Income Taxes

New York's per capita state and local income (individual and corporate) taxes registered $1,466 in 1996, ranking 2d highest in the nation (trailing only Washington, D.C.) and topping the U.S. average of $674 by 118%. From 1962 to 1996, real per capita state and local income taxes increased by 331%, versus a 567% increase in the U.S. average.

Personal Income Tax

A rate of 6.85%, ranking 38th in the nation (from lowest tax rate to highest), and comparing with the national average of 5.26%.

Capital Gains Tax

A rate of 6.85%, ranking 41st in the nation (from lowest tax rate to highest), and comparing with the national average of 4.68%.

Corporate Income Tax

A rate of 9.36% (8% statewide plus a 17-percent surcharge in the New York City region), ranking 44th in the nation (from lowest tax rate to highest), and comparing to the U.S. average of 6.63%.

Total Expenditures

New York's per capita state and local total spending registered $7,990 in 1996, ranking 3d in the nation and exceeding the U.S. average of $5,268 by 52%. From 1962 to 1996, real per capita state and local total spending increased by 332%, versus an increase of 254% in the U.S. average.

Welfare Expenditures

New York's per capita state and local public welfare spending registered $1,377 in 1996, ranking 2d highest in the nation (only behind Washington, D.C.) and outpacing the U.S.

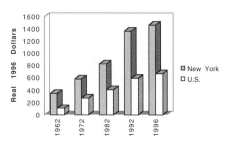

Real Per Capita State and Local Income Taxes: New York vs. U.S.

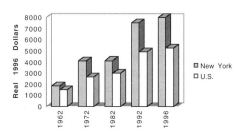

Real Per Capita State and Local Total Expenditures: New York vs. U.S.

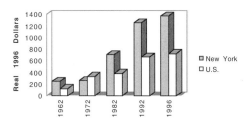

Real Per Capita State and Local Public Welfare Spending: New York vs. U.S.

average of $729 by 89%. From 1962 to 1996, real per capita state and local public welfare spending increased by 467%, compared with a 488% increase in the U.S. average.

Welfare Recipients (in thousands)

	1980	1989	3/99	Change 1989–99
N.Y.	1,110	964	828	−14%
U.S.	10,923	10,987	7,335	−33%

Interest on General Debt

New York's per capita state and local interest on general debt registered $396 in 1996, ranking 5th in the nation and exceeding the U.S. average of $222 by 78%. From 1962 to 1996, real per capita state and local interest on general debt increased by 355%, versus an increase of 335% in the U.S. average.

Total Debt Outstanding

New York's per capita state and local debt registered $8,232 in 1996, ranking 2d in the nation and outrunning the U.S. average of $4,409 by 87%. From 1962 to 1996, real per capita state and local debt outstanding increased by 125%, versus an increase of 120% in the U.S. average.

Government Employees

New York's state and local government employees (full-time equivalent, or FTE) per 10,000 population registered 612.1 in 1997, ranking 8th in the nation and exceeding the U.S. average of 531.1 by 15%. From 1962 to 1996, state and local FTE employees per 10,000 population increased by 64%, compared with an increase in the U.S. average of 66%.

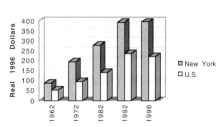

Real Per Capita State and Local Interest on General Debt: New York vs. U.S.

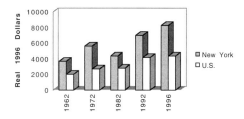

Real Per Capita State and Local Debt Outstanding: New York vs. U.S.

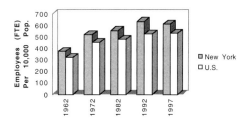

State and Local Government Employees (FTE) Per 10,000 Population: New York vs. U.S.

Per Capita Federal Government Expenditures, 1998

	1998	Ranking
N.Y.	$5,489	23d
U.S.	$5,491	

Per capita federal spending in New York trailed the national average by 0.03%.

EDUCATION

Total Education Spending

New York's per capita state and local education spending registered $1,812 in 1996, ranking 5th in the nation and outpacing the U.S. average of $1,503 by 21%. From 1962 to 1996, real per capita total education spending increased by 221%, versus an increase in the U.S. average of 173%.

Per Pupil Spending

New York's per pupil public school spending registered $8,898 in 1998, ranking 2d in the nation and exceeding the U.S. average of $6,131 by 45%. From 1970 to 1998, New York's real per pupil public school spending increased by 101%, compared with a 120% increase in the U.S. average.

Real Per Capita State and Local Education Spending: New York vs. U.S.

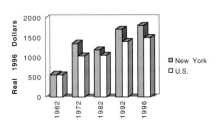

Real Per Pupil Public School Spending: New York vs. U.S.

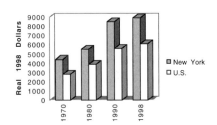

Average Public School Teacher Salaries (in 1997–98 dollars)

	1970	1980	1990	1998	1998 Ranking
N.Y.	44,256	41,277	49,583	49,034	5th
U.S.	36,934	33,272	39,956	39,385	

In 1998, the average public school teacher salary in New York outpaced the U.S. average by 24%. From 1970 to 1998, the real average teacher salary in New York increased by 11%, versus an increase in the U.S. average of 7%.

Pupil/Teacher Ratio, Fall 1996

	Ratio	Rank
N.Y.	15.4	16th
U.S.	17.1	

Teachers/Staff, Fall 1996

	Percent	Rank
N.Y.	50.9	41st
U.S.	52.1	

Public School 4th-Grade Reading Proficiency, 1998

	Average	Rank (out of 40 states)
N.Y.	216	20th
U.S.	215	

Public School 8th-Grade Reading Proficiency, 1998

	Average	Rank (out of 37 states)
N.Y.	266	7th
U.S.	261	

Public School 4th-Grade Math Proficiency, 1996

	Average	Rank (out of 44 states)
N.Y.	223	22d
U.S.	224	

Public School 8th-Grade Math Proficiency, 1996

	Average	Rank (out of 41 states)
N.Y.	270	20th
U.S.	271	

Public School 8th-Grade Science Proficiency, 1996

	Average	Rank (out of 41 states)
N.Y.	146	25th
U.S.	148	

Average Math SAT Scores

	1972	1982	1992	1998	Percentage Taking SAT in 1998
N.Y.	519	494	492	503	76
U.S.	509	493	501	512	43

Average Verbal SAT Scores

	1972	1982	1992	1998	Percentage Taking SAT in 1998
N.Y.	537	507	493	495	76
U.S.	530	504	500	505	43

Expenditures by Public Institutions of Higher Education Per Full-Time-Equivalent Student, 1996

	FTE Student Spending	Rank
N.Y.	$13,026	19th
U.S.	$12,343	

Per-FTE-student spending in public institutions of higher education exceeded the U.S. average by 6%.

Per Full-Time-Equivalent Student Revenues from Federal, State, and Local Governments for Public Institutions of Higher Education, 1996

	FTE Student Government Revenues	Rank
N.Y.	$5,954	49th
U.S.	$8,101	

Per-FTE-student-government revenues in public institutions of higher education lagged behind the U.S. average by 27%.

Average Salary for Full-Time Professors at Public Universities, 1997

	Average	Rank
N.Y.	$78,429	8th
U.S.	$72,599	

The average full-time public university professor salary exceeded the U.S. average by 8%.

ECONOMY AND BUSINESS

Economic Growth

Over the period of 1977 to 1997, New York's real gross state product (GSP) grew by 49.6%—ranking 40th in the nation—as compared with real U.S. gross domestic product (GDP), expanding by 70.1%.

At $651.7 billion in 1997, New York's GSP ranked as 2d largest in the nation.

From 1993 to 1997, New York's annual real GSP growth averaged 1.96%—ranking 48th in the nation—as compared with annual real U.S. GDP growth, averaging 3.08%.

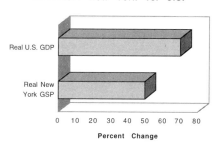

Real Economic Growth 1977-1997: New York vs. U.S.

Real U.S. GDP
Real New York GSP

0 10 20 30 40 50 60 70 80

Percent Change

Job Growth

	Growth in Employee Payrolls (Nonagricultural) 1962–98	Ranking
N.Y.	31.4%	50th
U.S.	126.5%	

	Average Annual Growth in Employee Payrolls (Nonagricultural) 1993–98	Ranking
N.Y.	1.26%	49th
U.S.	2.98%	

Per Capita Disposable Income, 1997

	1997	Ranking
N.Y.	$25,206	5th
U.S.	$21,607	

Per capita disposable income exceeded the U.S. average by 17%.

	Real Growth 1962–97	Ranking
N.Y.	114.2%	29th
U.S.	116.7%	

	Average Annual Real Growth 1993–97	Ranking
N.Y.	1.30%	41st
U.S.	1.48%	

Number of Businesses

	1997	Percent with Fewer than 500 Employees
Businesses with Employees	446,048	99.0
Self-employed Individuals	521,000	

New Business Incorporations

	1980	1986	1992	1997
N.Y.	56,489	76,890	67,503	74,397

Percentage Change in Annual New Business Incorporations, 1980 vs. 1997

	Percent	Ranking
N.Y.	31.7	30th
U.S.	49.7	

State Merchandise Exports to the World, 1998 (in millions of dollars)

	1998	Rank
N.Y.	$45,564	3d

Small Business Survival Index, 1999

New York ranks an extremely dismal 47th in terms of its policy environment for entrepreneurship.

Fortune 500 Headquarters in 1999

A total of 59 (ranked 1st), with New York City ranking tops among U.S. cities with 46 headquarters

Labor Union Membership, 1983 vs. 1997

| | Percentage of Workers | | |
	1983	1997	1997 Rank
N.Y.	32.5	26.3	1st
U.S.	20.1	14.1	

Homeownership Rate, 1998

	Rate	Rank
N.Y.	52.8	49th
U.S.	66.3	

CRIME

Crime Rates Per 100 Residents (rankings from best to worst crime rate)

Total Crime	1960	1970	1980	1990	1998	1998 Ranking
N.Y.	1.04	3.92	6.91	6.36	3.59	13th
U.S.	1.04	2.74	5.90	5.82	4.62	

From 1960 to 1998, New York's crime rate increased by 245%, versus a U.S. increase of 344%. From 1990 to 1998, New York's crime rate dropped by 44%, versus a U.S. decrease of 21%.

Violent Crime	1960	1970	1980	1990	1998	1998 Ranking
N.Y.	0.13	0.68	1.03	1.18	0.64	40th
U.S.	0.14	0.36	0.58	0.73	0.57	

From 1960 to 1998, New York's violent crime rate increased by 392%, versus a U.S. increase of 307%. From 1990 to 1998, New York's violent crime rate decreased by 46%, compared with a national decline of 22%.

Property Crime	1960	1970	1980	1990	1998	1998 Ranking
N.Y.	0.92	3.25	5.88	5.18	2.95	9th
U.S.	0.90	2.38	5.32	5.09	4.05	

From 1960 to 1998, New York's property crime rate increased by 221%, versus a national increase of 350%. From 1990 to 1998, New York's property crime rate decreased by 38%, compared with a national decline of 20%

Real Per Capita Police Protection Spending (in real 1996 dollars)

	1962	1972	1982	1992	1996	1996 Ranking
N.Y.	87	174	158	225	254	2d
U.S.	51	95	114	148	168	

In 1996, per capita state and local police protection spending in New York exceeded the U.S. average by 51%. From 1962 to 1996, real per capita state and local police protection spending increased by 192%, versus an increase of 229% in the U.S. average.

Prisoners in State and Federal Prisons Per 1,000 Population

	1980	1990	1996	1996 Results
N.Y.	1.24	3.05	3.84	22d
U.S.	1.46	3.11	4.45	

From 1980 to 1996, prisoners per 1,000 population increased by 210%, versus a U.S. increase of 205%.

HEALTH CARE

Health-Care Spending

New York's per capita state and local health-care spending registered $210 in 1996, ranking 8th in the nation and topping the U.S. average of $151 by 39%. From 1962 to 1996, New York's real per capita state and local health-care spending increased by 813%, versus an increase of 739% in the U.S. average.

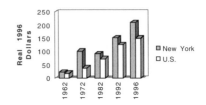

Real Per Capita State and Local Health Care Spending: New York vs. U.S.

Hospital Spending

New York's per capita state and local hospital spending registered $468 in 1996, ranking 7th in the nation and exceeding the U.S. average of $266 by 76%. From 1962 to 1996, New York's real per capita state and local hospital spending increased by 200%, as opposed to an increase of 189% in the U.S. average.

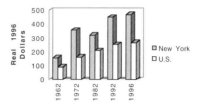

Real Per Capita State and Local Hospital Spending: New York vs. U.S.

Medicaid, 1997

	Spending Per Recipient	Ranking
N.Y.	$6,770	2d
U.S.	$3,681	

New York's per-recipient Medicaid spending exceeded the U.S. average by 84%.

ENVIRONMENT

Parks and Recreation Spending

New York's per capita state and local parks and recreation spending registered $75 in 1996, ranking 21st in the nation and outpacing the U.S. average of $72 by 4%. From 1962 to 1996, real per capita state and local parks and recreation spending increased by 134%, versus a 213% increase in the U.S. average.

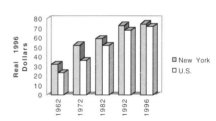

Real Per Capita State and Local Parks and Recreation Spending: New York vs. U.S.

State and Local Natural Resources Spending, 1996

	Per Capita	Ranking
N.Y.	$21	49th
U.S.	$60	

Per capita state and local natural resources spending in New York trailed the U.S. average by 65%.

State Parks Revenues as a Share of Operating Expenses, 1997

	Percent	Rank
N.Y.	26	38th
U.S.	42	

Percentage of Land Owned by the Federal Government, 1996

	Percent	Rank
N.Y.	0.6	47th
U.S.	24.8	

SOCIETY AND DEMOGRAPHICS

Population

New York's 1998 population of 18.175 million ranked 3d in the nation.

Population Growth, 1990–98

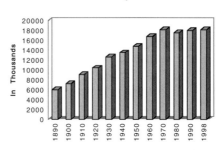

New York Population

	Percentage Change in Population	Ranking
N.Y.	1.02	45th
U.S.	8.66	

	Net International Migration	Ranking
N.Y.	1,021,218	2d

	Net Domestic Migration	Ranking
N.Y.	−1,722,451	50th

Infant Mortality Rate, 1997

	Percent	Rank
N.Y.	6.2	37th

Percentage of Births of Low Birthweight, 1997

	Percent	Rank
N.Y.	7.8	18th
U.S.	7.5	

Percentage of Live Births to Unmarried Women, 1997

	Percent	Rank
N.Y.	35.0	11th
U.S.	32.4	

Abortion Rate—Abortions Per 1,000 Women Ages 15–44, 1995

	Rate	Rank
N.Y.	42.8	3d
U.S.	22.9	

LIFESTYLE

Percentage of Households with Computers, 1998

	Percent	Rank
N.Y.	37.3	42d

Percentage of Households with Internet Access, 1998

	Percent	Rank
N.Y.	23.7	36th

State Arts Agency Spending, 1999

	Per Capita	Rank
N.Y.	$2.51	5th
U.S.	$1.35	

Per capita state arts spending in 1999 topped the U.S. average by 86%.

Major League Sports Facilities

Year Opened/ Refurb.	Stadium/ Arena	Home Team	Millions of Nominal Dollars		Millions of Real 1997 Dollars	
			Estimated Total Cost	Estimated Taxpayer Cost	Estimated Total Cost	Estimated Taxpayer Cost
1911	Polo Grounds	Giants (MLB) 1911–57 Yankees (MLB) 1913–22 Mets (MLB) 1962–63 Giants (NFL) 1925–55 Jets (AFL) 1960–63	$0.25	$0.0	$4.3	$0.0
1913	Ebbets Field	Dodgers (MLB) 1913–57	$0.75	$0.0	$12.1	$0.0
1923	Yankee Stadium	Yankees (MLB) 1923–present (except for 1974–75)	$3.1	$0.0	$29.2	$0.0
1976	Yankee Stadium (re)		$160.0	$160.0	$450.7	$450.7
1925	Madison Square Garden III	Knicks (NBA) 1946–68 Rangers (NHL) 1925–68	NA	$0.0	NA	$0.0
1937	War Memorial Stadium	Bills (AFL/NFL) 1960–72	$3.0	$3.0	$30.6	$30.6
1960	War Memorial Stadium (re)		$0.75	$0.75	$4.1	$4.1
1964	War Memorial Stadium (re)		$1.5	$1.5	$7.8	$7.8
1939	The Aud	Sabres (NHL) 1970–96 Braves (NBA) 1970–78	NA	NA	NA	NA

Year	Facility	Team(s)				
1964	Shea Stadium	Mets (MLB) 1964–present Yankees (MLB) 1974–75 Jets (AFL/NFL) 1964–83 Giants (NFL) 1975	$24.0	$24.0	$124.4	$124.4
1968	Madison Square Garden IV	Knicks (NBA) 1968–present Rangers (NHL) 1968–present	$133.0	$0.0	$612.9	$0.0
1991	Madison Square Garden IV(re)		$200.0	$0.0	$235.6	$0.0
1972	Nassau Coliseum	Islanders (NHL) 1972–present Nets (ABA) 1972–77	$28.0	$28.0	$107.7	$107.7
1973	Rich Stadium	Bills (NFL) 1973–present	$22.0	$22.0	$79.4	$79.4
1996	Marine Midland	Sabres (NHL) 1996–present	$127.5	$55.0	$130.4	$56.2

NORTH CAROLINA

A hand of urban centers across North Carolina—stretching from the Piedmont Triad in the north central part of the state, down through the Research Triangle region (so named because of its location between Raleigh, Durham, and Chapel Hill), to the Charlotte metropolitan area—is enjoying robust growth. Many North Carolinians in other parts of the state, however, who still depend on the old-line economy of textiles, manufacturing, and tobacco, have not been as fortunate. The result is two very different economies within one state.

"If you analyze North Carolina, and look at where the jobs are being generated, more than half are in the three major metropolitan areas," according to Gary Shoesmith, director of the Center for Economic Studies at the Wake Forest University Babcock Graduate School of Management.

As a whole, the state's economy has been booming. Performance has been high in terms of general economic and population growth, job creation, growth in disposable income, and new business incorporations.

A major reason why North Carolina is experiencing solid economic growth is the state's low property taxes. Property taxes that lag some 40% behind the U.S. average are quite seductive in terms of attracting people from high property-tax states like New York. In fact, according to an August 1999 report from the Empire Foundation for Policy Research in New York, North Carolina gained 65,689 taxpayers and more than $1.1 billion in income from New York between 1992 and 1997. During this period, North Carolina ranked third in terms of destinations for those fleeing New York.

However, tobacco farmers have been hit hard. North Carolina is the nation's leading tobacco-producing state—more than one third of the U.S. tobacco crop is grown there each year. In recent years, and especially since Big Tobacco's 1997 legal settlement with the states, demand for North Carolina's tobacco leaves has plummeted, and while the drop in the domestic demand was offset for a while by foreign sales, slumping economies in Asia and Russia have taken a toll on exports as well. It is not just the tobacco growers who are suffering; all farmers are feeling the pinch. Falling prices for crops such as sweet potatoes, corn, and cotton have driven agricultural income down.

North Carolina's textile industry, which employs 166,800 and is the largest in the United States, is also facing tough times. Because of improved technology and increased foreign production, textile employment is in the midst of a six-decade decline.

So, while the state's economy has performed quite well overall, policy improvements will be needed to spread growth, entrepreneurship, and diversification across the state. In fact, in terms of its overall public policy environment, for example, the Small Business Survival Committee ranks North Carolina quite poorly. In addition to the state's high crime rate, personal income, capital gains, and corporate income taxes are quite onerous. A 1997 study by North Carolina State University professor Michael Walden for North Carolina's John Locke Foundation concluded that the state's income taxes took a heavy toll on job growth and personal income in North Carolina.

The Locke Foundation also reported (October 28, 1998) that in fiscal year 1998–99, state general fund spending was scheduled to leap by a lofty 11 percent—light years ahead of the inflation rate—while tax relief was far smaller. In fact, the foundation estimated that in FY 1998–99, spending increases outweighed tax cuts by a ratio of 25–1. However, legislation phasing out the state's inheritance tax will have a positive impact on family businesses, farms, and the economy in general.

As for education, the state ranks average to below average on a wide array of performance measures. Again, the Locke Foundation offers some sound remedies, including implementing state deductions and credits for parents to establish education savings accounts to help cover various education expenses, lifting the cap on state charter schools, ending teacher tenure, and providing scholarships for students in the state's worst performing public schools for use in private schools.

North Carolina has much going for it, but given its high income tax and crime rates, as well as its mediocre schools, it could easily fall from its current lofty perch.

POLITICS

Registered Voters

54% Democrats
34% Republicans
12% Other

Federal Officials: Recent Election and Group Ratings

			ACU	ADA	SBSC
U.S. Senators:	Jesse Helms (R)		99	7	70
	1996 Helms (R)	52%			
	Gantt (D)	45%			
	John Edwards (D)		NA	NA	NA
	1998 Edwards (D)	51%			
	Faircloth (R)	47%			
U.S. Representatives:	Eva Clayton (D-1)		3	100	20
	1998 Clayton (D)	62%			
	Tyler (R)	37%			
	Bob Etheridge (D-2)		30	73	30
	1998 Etheridge (D)	57%			
	Page (R)	42%			
	Walter Jones Jr. (R-3)		99	36	90
	1998 Jones (R)	62%			
	Williams (D)	37%			

			ACU	ADA	SBSC
David Price (D-4)			2	75	25
1998	Price (D)	57%			
	Roberg (R)	42%			
Richard Burr (R-5)			93	5	90
1998	Burr (R)	68%			
	Robinson (D)	32%			
Howard Coble (R-6)			89	8	75
1998	Coble (R)	89%			
	Bentley (LBT)	11%			
Mike McIntyre (D-7)			56	50	30
1998	McIntyre (D)	91%			
	Meadows (LBT)	9%			
Robin Hayes (R-8)			NA	NA	NA
1998	Hayes (R)	51%			
	Taylor (D)	48%			
Sue Myrick (R-9)			96	5	100
1998	Myrick (R)	69%			
	Blake (D)	29%			
Cass Ballenger (R-10)			89	6	90
1998	Ballenger (R)	86%			
	Eddins (LBT)	14%			
Charles Taylor (R-11)			94	6	85
1998	Taylor (R)	57%			
	Young (D)	42%			
Melvin Watt (D-12)			4	82	15
1998	Watt (D)	56%			
	Keadle (R)	42%			

Electoral Votes: 14

1996 Presidential Results:

Clinton	44%
Dole	49%
Perot	7%

State Officials

Governor 1996 Election:

James Hunt Jr. (D)	56%
Robin Hayes (R)	43%

Lt. Governor: Dennis Wicker (D)
Attorney General: Mike Easley (D)
State Senate: 35 Democrats
15 Republicans
State House: 66 Democrats
54 Republicans

TAXES AND SPENDING

Total Revenues

North Carolina's per capita state and local total revenues registered $4,900 in 1996, ranking 38th in the nation and trailing the U.S. average of $5,706 by 14%. From 1962 to 1996, real per capita state and local revenues increased by 368%, compared with an increase in the national average of 297%.

Taxes

North Carolina's per capita state and local taxes registered $2,251 in 1996, ranking 34th in the nation and trailing the U.S. average of $2,597 by 13%. From 1962 to 1996, real per capita state and local taxes increased by 212%, compared with an increase of 152% in the U.S. average.

Property Taxes

North Carolina's per capita state and local property taxes equaled $472 in 1996, ranking 41st in the nation and trailing the U.S. average of $789 by 40%. From 1962 to 1996, real per capita state and local property taxes increased by 134%, versus a 67% increase in the U.S. average.

Sales and Gross Receipts Taxes

North Carolina's per capita state and local sales and gross receipts taxes came in at $835 in 1996, ranking 23d in the nation and trailing the U.S. average of $939 by 11%. From 1962 to 1996, real per capita state and local sales and gross receipts taxes increased by 184%, versus an increase of 214% in the U.S. average.

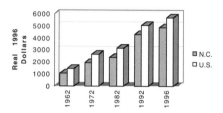

Real Per Capita State and Local Total Revenues: North Carolina vs. U.S.

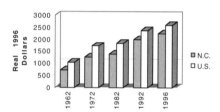

Real Per Capita State and Local Taxes: North Carolina vs. U.S.

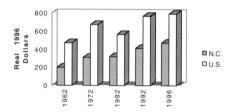

Real Per Capita State and Local Property Taxes: North Carolina vs. U.S.

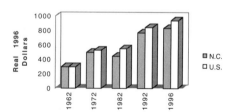

Real Per Capita State and Local Sales and Gross Receipts Taxes: North Carolina vs. U.S.

Income Taxes

North Carolina's per capita state and local income (individual and corporate) taxes registered $801 in 1996, ranking 15th in the nation and exceeding the U.S. average of $674 by 19%. From 1962 to 1996, real per capita state and local income taxes increased by 445%, versus a 567% increase in the U.S. average.

Personal Income Tax

A rate of 7.75%, ranking 41st in the nation (from lowest tax rate to highest), and comparing with the national average of 5.26%.

Capital Gains Tax

A rate of 7.75%, ranking 43d in the nation (from lowest tax rate to highest), and comparing with the national average of 4.68%.

Corporate Income Tax

A rate of 6.9%, ranking 25th in the nation (from lowest tax rate to highest), and comparing with the national average of 6.63%.

Total Expenditures

North Carolina's per capita state and local total spending registered $4,640 in 1996, ranking 36th in the nation and trailing the U.S. average of $5,268 by 12%. From 1962 to 1996, real per capita state and local total spending increased by 339%, versus an increase of 254% in the U.S. average.

Welfare Expenditures

North Carolina's per capita state and local public welfare spending registered $626 in 1996, ranking 31st in the nation and trailing the U.S. average of $729 by 14%. From 1962 to 1996, real per capita state and local public welfare spending increased by 240%, compared with a 488% increase in the U.S. average.

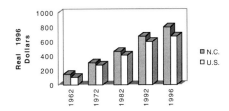

Real Per Capita State and Local Income Taxes: North Carolina vs. U.S.

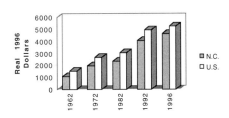

Real Per Capita State and Local Total Expenditures: North Carolina vs. U.S.

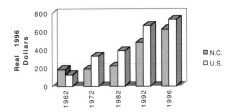

Real Per Capita State and Local Public Welfare Spending: North Carolina vs. U.S.

Welfare Recipients (in thousands)

	1980	1989	3/99	Change 1989–99
N.C.	202	216	139	−36%
U.S.	10,923	10,987	7,335	−33%

Interest on General Debt

North Carolina's per capita state and local interest on general debt registered $125 in 1996, ranking 47th in the nation and trailing the U.S. average of $222 by 44%. From 1962 to 1996, real per capita state and local interest on general debt increased by 443%, versus an increase of 335% in the U.S. average.

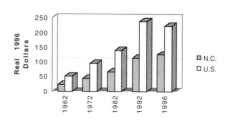

Real Per Capita State and Local Interest on General Debt: North Carolina vs. U.S.

Total Debt Outstanding

North Carolina's per capita state and local debt registered $2,936 in 1996, ranking 41st in the nation and trailing the U.S. average of $4,409 by 33%. From 1962 to 1996, real per capita state and local debt outstanding increased by 204%, versus an increase of 120% in the U.S. average.

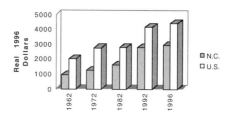

Real Per Capita State and Local Debt Outstanding: North Carolina vs. U.S.

Government Employees

North Carolina's state and local government employees (full-time equivalent, or FTE) per 10,000 population registered 560.0 in 1997, ranking 19th in the nation and exceeding the U.S. average of 531.1 by 5%. From 1962 to 1996, state and local FTE employees per 10,000 population increased by 103%, compared with an increase in the U.S average of 66%.

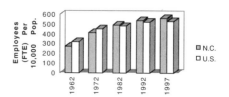

State and Local Government Employees (FTE) Per 10,000 Population: North Carolina vs. U.S.

Per Capita Federal Government Expenditures, 1998

	1998	Ranking
N.C.	$4,728	40th
U.S.	$5,491	

Per capita federal spending in North Carolina trailed the national average by 14%.

EDUCATION

Total Education Spending

North Carolina's per capita state and local education spending registered $1,397 in 1996, ranking 35th in the nation and trailing the U.S. average of $1,503 by 7%. From 1962 to 1996, real per capita total education spending increased by 207%, versus an increase in the U.S. average of 173%.

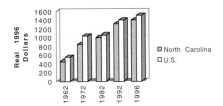

Real Per Capita State and Local Education Spending: North Carolina vs. U.S.

Per Pupil Spending

North Carolina's per pupil public school spending registered $4,983 in 1998, ranking 40th in the nation and trailing the U.S. average of $6,131 by 19%. From 1970 to 1998, North Carolina's real per pupil public school spending increased by 136%, compared with a 120% increase in the U.S. average.

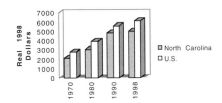

Real Per Pupil Public School Spending: North Carolina vs. U.S.

Average Public School Teacher Salaries (in 1997–98 dollars)

	1970	1980	1990	1998	1998 Ranking
N.C.	32,087	29,412	35,518	33,315	38th
U.S.	36,934	33,272	39,956	39,385	

In 1998, the average public school teacher salary in North Carolina trailed the U.S. average by 15%. From 1970 to 1998, the real average teacher salary in Alabama increased by 4%, versus an increase in the U.S. average of 7%.

Pupil/Teacher Ratio, Fall 1996

	Ratio	Rank
N.C.	16.1	23d
U.S.	17.1	

Teachers/Staff, Fall 1996

	Percent	Rank
N.C.	51.8	34th
U.S.	52.1	

Public School 4th-Grade Reading Proficiency, 1998

	Average	Rank (out of 40 states)
N.C.	217	16th
U.S.	215	

Public School 8th-Grade Reading Proficiency, 1998

	Average	Rank (out of 37 states)
N.C.	264	14th
U.S.	261	

Public School 4th-Grade Math Proficiency, 1996

	Average	Rank (out of 44 states)
N.C.	224	20th
U.S.	224	

Public School 8th-Grade Math Proficiency, 1996

	Average	Rank (out of 41 states)
N.C.	268	25th
U.S.	271	

Public School 8th-Grade Science Proficiency, 1996

	Average	Rank (out of 41 states)
N.C.	147	22d
U.S.	148	

Average Math SAT Scores

	1972	1982	1992	1998	Percentage Taking SAT in 1998
N.C.	468	462	479	492	62
U.S.	509	493	501	512	43

Average Verbal SAT Scores

	1972	1982	1992	1998	Percentage Taking SAT in 1998
N.C.	489	474	482	490	62
U.S.	530	504	500	505	43

Expenditures by Public Institutions of Higher Education Per Full-Time-Equivalent Student, 1996

	FTE Student Spending	Rank
N.C.	$12,819	21st
U.S.	$12,343	

Per-FTE-student spending in public institutions of higher education exceeded the U.S. average by 4%.

Per Full-Time-Equivalent Student Revenues from Federal, State, and Local Governments, for Public Institutions of Higher Education, 1996

	FTE Student Government Revenues	Rank
N.C.	$10,014	6th
U.S.	$8,101	

Per-FTE-student-government revenues in public institutions of higher education topped the U.S. average by 24%.

Average Salary for Full-Time Professors at Public Universities, 1997

	Average	Rank
N.C.	$79,294	6th
U.S.	$72,599	

The average full-time public university professor salary exceeded the U.S. average by 9%.

ECONOMY AND BUSINESS

Economic Growth

Over the period of 1977 to 1997, North Carolina's real gross state product (GSP) grew by 106.6%—ranking 8th in the nation—as compared with real U.S. gross domestic product (GDP), expanding by 70.1%.

At $218.9 billion in 1997, North Carolina's GSP ranked as 12th largest in the nation.

From 1993 to 1997, North Carolina's annual real GSP growth averaged 4.72%—ranking 11th in the nation—as compared with annual real U.S. GDP growth, averaging 3.08%.

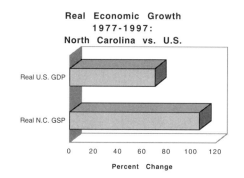

Real Economic Growth 1977-1997: North Carolina vs. U.S.

Job Growth

	Growth in Employee Payrolls (Nonagricultural) 1962–98	Ranking
N.C.	199.8%	12th
U.S.	126.5%	

	Average Annual Growth in Employee Payrolls (Nonagricultural) 1993–98	Ranking
N.C.	3.82%	10th
U.S.	2.98%	

Per Capita Disposable Income, 1997

	1997	Ranking
N.C.	$19,957	32d
U.S.	$21,607	

Per capita disposable income trailed the U.S. average by 8%.

	Real Growth 1962–97	Ranking
N.C.	166.4%	5th
U.S.	116.7%	

	Average Annual Real Growth 1993–97	Ranking
N.C.	2.23%	6th
U.S.	1.48%	

Number of Businesses

	1997	Percent with Fewer than 500 Employees
Businesses with Employees	159,745	98.0
Self-employed Individuals	277,000	

New Business Incorporations

	1980	1986	1992	1997
N.C.	8,758	12,654	12,580	19,078

Percentage Change in Annual New Business Incorporations, 1980 vs. 1997

	Percent	Ranking
N.C.	117.8	4th
U.S.	49.7	

State Merchandise Exports to the World, 1998 (in millions of dollars)

	1998	Rank
N.C.	$12,920	14th

Small Business Survival Index, 1999

North Carolina ranks a poor 39th in terms of its policy environment for entrepreneurship.

Fortune 500 Headquarters in 1999

A total of 9 (ranked 18th)

Labor Union Membership, 1983 vs. 1997

	Percentage of Workers		
	1983	1997	1997 Rank
N.C.	7.6	3.8	50th
U.S.	20.1	14.1	

Homeownership Rate, 1998

	Rate	Rank
N.C.	71.3	14th
U.S.	66.3	

CRIME

Crime Rates Per 100 Residents (rankings from best to worst crime rate)

Total Crime	1960	1970	1980	1990	1998	1998 Ranking
N.C.	0.70	1.86	4.64	5.49	5.32	38th
U.S.	1.04	2.74	5.90	5.82	4.62	

From 1960 to 1998, North Carolina's crime rate increased by 660%, versus a U.S. increase of 344%. From 1990 to 1998, North Carolina's crime rate fell by 3%, versus a U.S. decrease of 21%.

Violent Crime	1960	1970	1980	1990	1998	1998 Ranking
N.C.	0.22	0.36	0.46	0.62	0.58	36th
U.S.	0.14	0.36	0.58	0.73	0.57	

From 1960 to 1998, North Carolina's violent crime rate increased by 164%, versus a U.S. increase of 307%. From 1990 to 1998, North Carolina's violent crime rate decreased by 6%, compared with a national decline of 22%.

Property Crime	1960	1970	1980	1990	1998	1998 Ranking
N.C.	0.48	1.50	4.19	4.86	4.74	40th
U.S.	0.90	2.38	5.32	5.09	4.05	

From 1960 to 1998, North Carolina's property crime rate increased by 888%, versus a national increase of 350%. From 1990 to 1998, North Carolina's property crime rate increased by 2%, compared with a national decline of 20%.

Real Per Capita Police Protection Spending (in real 1996 dollars)

	1962	1972	1982	1992	1996	1996 Ranking
N.C.	28	59	80	113	136	29th
U.S.	51	95	114	148	168	

In 1996, per capita state and local police protection spending in North Carolina trailed the U.S. average by 19%. From 1962 to 1996, real per capita state and local police protection spending increased by 386%, versus an increase of 229% in the U.S. average.

Prisoners in State and Federal Prisons Per 1,000 Population

	1980	1990	1996	1996 Ranking
N.C.	2.64	2.78	4.19	18th
U.S.	1.46	3.11	4.45	

From 1980 to 1996, prisoners per 1,000 population increased by 59%, versus a U.S. increase of 205%.

HEALTH CARE

Health-Care Spending

North Carolina's per capita state and local health-care spending registered $177 in 1996, ranking 13th in the nation and exceeding the U.S. average of $151 by 17%. From 1962 to 1996, North Carolina's real per capita state and local health-care spending increased by 1,164%, versus an increase of 739% in the U.S. average.

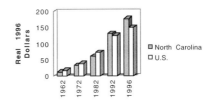

Real Per Capita State and Local Health Care Spending: North Carolina vs. U.S.

Hospital Spending

North Carolina's per capita state and local hospital spending registered $392 in 1996, ranking 9th in the nation and exceeding the U.S. average of $266 by 47%. From 1962 to 1996, North Carolina's real per capita state and local hospital spending increased by 468%, as opposed to an increase of 189% in the U.S. average.

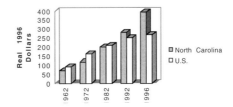

Real Per Capita State and Local Hospital Spending: North Carolina vs. U.S.

Medicaid, 1997

	Spending Per Recipient	Ranking
N.C.	$3,403	30th
U.S.	$3,681	

North Carolina's per-recipient Medicaid spending trailed the U.S. average by 8%.

ENVIRONMENT

Parks and Recreation Spending

North Carolina's per capita state and local parks and recreation spending registered $50 in 1996, ranking 35th in the nation and trailing the U.S. average of $72 by 31%. From 1962 to 1996, real per capita state and local parks and recreation spending increased by 900%, versus a 213% increase in the U.S. average.

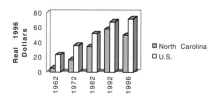

Real Per Capita State and Local Parks and Recreation Spending: North Carolina vs. U.S.

State and Local Natural Resources Spending, 1996

	Per Capita	Ranking
N.C.	$62	28th
U.S.	$60	

Per capita state and local natural resources spending in North Carolina topped the U.S. average by 3%.

State Parks Revenues as a Share of Operating Expenses, 1997

	Percent	Rank
N.C.	16	46th
U.S.	42	

Percentage of Land Owned by the Federal Government, 1996

	Percent	Rank
N.C.	6.5	22d
U.S.	24.8	

SOCIETY AND DEMOGRAPHICS

Population

North Carolina's 1998 population of 7.546 million ranked 11th in the nation.

Population Growth, 1990–98

North Carolina Population

	Percentage Change in Population	Ranking
N.C.	13.78	12th
U.S.	8.66	

	Net International Migration	Ranking
N.C.	49,418	19th

	Net Domestic Migration	Ranking
N.C.	500,989	5th

Infant Mortality Rate, 1998

	Percent	Rank
N.C.	9.5	6th
U.S.	6.4	

Percentage of Births of Low Birthweight, 1997

	Percent	Rank
N.C.	8.8	7th
U.S.	7.5	

Percentage of Live Births to Unmarried Women, 1997

	Percent	Rank
N.C.	32.2	25th
U.S.	32.4	

Abortion Rate—Abortions Per 1,000 Women Ages 15–44, 1995

	Rate	Rank
N.C.	21.0	17th
U.S.	22.9	

LIFESTYLE

Percentage of Households with Computers, 1998

	Percent	Rank
N.C.	35.0	46th

Percentage of Households with Internet Access, 1998

	Percent	Rank
N.C.	19.9	47th

State Arts Agency Spending, 1999

	Per Capita	Rank
N.C.	$0.78	29th
U.S.	$1.35	

Per capita state arts spending in 1999 trailed the U.S. average by 42%.

Major League Sports Facilities

Year Opened/ Refurb.	Stadium/ Arena	Home Team	Millions of Nominal Dollars		Millions of Real 1997 Dollars	
			Estimated Total Cost	Estimated Taxpayer Cost	Estimated Total Cost	Estimated Taxpayer Cost
1985	Charlotte Coliseum	Hornets (NBA) 1988–present	$58.0	$58.0	$86.6	$86.6
1996	Ericcson Stadium	Panthers (NFL) 1996–present	$248.0	$45.0	$253.6	$46.0
1999	Raleigh Entertainment & Sports Arena	Hurricanes (NHL) 1999–present	$152.0	$152.0	$146.7	$146.7

NORTH DAKOTA

North Dakota is one of those states that must drive education unions crazy.

Public school per pupil spending comes in almost $1,000 dollars less than the national average. The average public school teacher salary places 50th in the nation, not only lagging almost 30% behind the U.S. average but actually declining ever so slightly in real terms between 1970 and 1998. Recent student proficiency measures, however, show that North Dakota excels, ranking among the very best in the nation.

Beyond education, North Dakota's general tax and spending levels also tend to come in a bit below the U.S. averages—except for the number of state and local government employees as a share of population, per capita federal spending in the state (7th highest in the nation), and the corporate income tax rate, all of which run on the high side. In addition, while effective personal income and capital gains tax rates are fairly low, the state's income tax system is unnecessarily complex.

North Dakota also claims the third lowest crime rate in the nation and the very lowest violent crime rate, though it increased from 1990 to 1997 while the national rate declined. Meanwhile, per capita police spending and prisoners as a share of population each ranked 50th in the nation.

Let us see: a pretty good education at a relatively low cost, generally below-average government spending, and very little crime—sounds like a great place to live and work, right?

Actually, from 1990 to 1998, North Dakota was a net exporter of residents to other states, and the overall population fell. In fact, North Dakota's population has been more or less declining since 1930. Obviously, this ties in with the almost century-long decline in farm population as a restult of vast leaps in productivity. However, North Dakota has proven unable to diversify to stem a net population decline.

Indeed, the economy has been, to be very generous, sluggish in recent times. Real gross state product growth has badly fallen behind that of the nation, as has expansion in real disposable income. If new business incorporations are a trustworthy indicator, entrepreneurship in North Dakota has been stagnant as well.

What to do? Well, the state would do well to take lessons from its fellow Dakota to the south. South Dakota imposes no personal income, corporate income, or capital gains taxes, and its overall economic performance has been markedly better than that of North Dakota.

Combining a solid, proentrepreneur tax system, with the state's existing strengths in education performance and crime would be a formidable combination in helping to get North Dakota on the growth track into the 21st century.

POLITICS

Registered Voters

No party registration

Federal Officials: Recent Election and Group Ratings

			ACU	ADA	SBSC
U.S. Senators:	Kent Conrad (D)		19	80	20
	1994 Conrad (D)	58%			
	Clayburgh (R)	42%			
	Byron Dorgan (D)		18	83	20
	1998 Dorgan (D)	63%			
	Nalewaja (R)	35%			
U.S. Representatives:	Earl Pomeroy (D)		23	75	20
	1998 Pomeroy (D)	56%			
	Cramer (R)	41%			
Electoral Votes:	3				
1996 Presidential Results:	Clinton	40%			
	Dole	47%			
	Perot	12%			

State Officials

Governor 1996 Election:	Edward Schafer (R)	66%
	Lee Kaldor (D)	34%
Lt. Governor:	Rosemarie Myrdal (R)	
Attorney General:	Heidi Heitkamp (D)	
State Senate:	18 Democrats	
	31 Republicans	
State House:	34 Democrats	
	64 Republicans	

TAXES AND SPENDING

Total Revenues

North Dakota's per capita state and local total revenues registered $5,340 in 1996, ranking 25th in the nation and trailing the U.S. average of $5,706 by 6%. From 1962 to 1996, real per capita state and local revenues increased by 225%, compared with an increase in the national average of 297%.

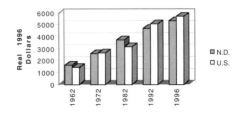

Real Per Capita State and Local Total Revenues: North Dakota vs. U.S.

Taxes

North Dakota's per capita state and local taxes registered $2,238 in 1996, ranking 35th in the nation and trailing the U.S. average of $2,597 by 14%. From 1962 to 1996, real per capita state and local taxes increased by 129%, compared with an increase of 152% in the U.S. average.

Property Taxes

North Dakota's per capita state and local property taxes equaled $641 in 1996, ranking 34th in the nation and trailing the U.S. average of $789 by 19%. From 1962 to 1996, real per capita state and local property taxes increased by 24%, versus a 67% increase in the U.S. average.

Sales and Gross Receipts Taxes

North Dakota's per capita state and local sales and gross receipts taxes came in at $928 in 1996, ranking 17th in the nation and trailing the U.S. average of $939 by 1%. From 1962 to 1996, real per capita state and local sales and gross receipts taxes increased by 254%, versus an increase of 214% in the U.S. average.

Income Taxes

North Dakota's per capita state and local income (individual and corporate) taxes registered $351 in 1996, ranking 41st in the nation and trailing the U.S. average of $674 by 48%. From 1962 to 1996, real per capita state and local income taxes rose by 485%, versus a 567% increase in the U.S. average.

Personal Income Tax

A rate of 5.544%, ranking 22d in the nation (from lowest tax rate to highest), and comparing with the national average of 5.26%.

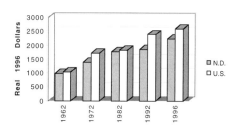

Real Per Capita State and Local Taxes: North Dakota vs. U.S.

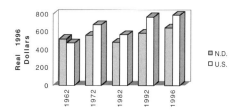

Real Per Capita State and Local Property Taxes: North Dakota vs. U.S.

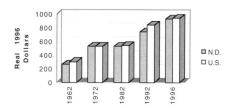

Real Per Capita State and Local Sales and Gross Receipts Taxes: North Dakota vs. U.S.

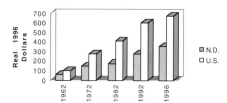

Real Per Capita State and Local Income Taxes: North Dakota vs. U.S.

Capital Gains Tax

A rate of 2.8%, ranking 13th in the nation (from lowest tax rate to highest), and comparing with the national average of 4.68%.

Corporate Income Tax

A rate of 6.825%, ranking 24th in the nation (from lowest tax rate to highest), and comparing with the national average of 6.63%.

Total Expenditures

North Dakota's per capita state and local total spending registered $4,593 in 1996, ranking 38th in the nation and trailing the U.S. average of $5,268 by 13%. From 1962 to 1996, real per capita state and local total spending increased by 165%, versus an increase of 254% in the U.S. average.

Welfare Expenditures

North Dakota's per capita state and local public welfare spending registered $613 in 1996, ranking 33d in the nation and trailing the U.S. average of $729 by 16%. From 1962 to 1996, real per capita state and local public welfare spending increased by 415%, compared with a 488% increase in the U.S. average.

Welfare Recipients (in thousands)

	1980	1989	3/99	Change 1989–99
N. Dak.	13	16	8	−50%
U.S.	10,923	10,987	7,335	−33%

Interest on General Debt

North Dakota's per capita state and local interest on general debt registered $169 in 1996, ranking 35th in the nation and trailing the U.S. average of $222 by 24%. From 1962 to 1996, real per capita state and local interest on general debt increased by 428%, versus an increase of 335% in the U.S. average.

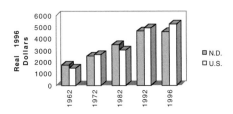

Real Per Capita State and Local Total Expenditures: North Dakota vs. U.S.

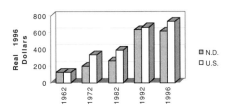

Real Per Capita State and Local Public Welfare Spending: North Dakota vs. U.S.

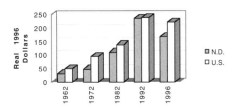

Real Per Capita State and Local Interest on General Debt: North Dakota vs. U.S.

Total Debt Outstanding

North Dakota's per capita state and local debt registered $2,704 in 1996, ranking 44th in the nation and trailing the U.S. average of $4,409 by 39%. From 1962 to 1996, real per capita state and local debt outstanding increased by 128%, versus an increase of 120% in the U.S. average.

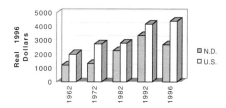

Real Per Capita State and Local Debt Outstanding: North Dakota vs. U.S.

Government Employees

North Dakota's state and local government employees (full-time equivalent, or FTE) per 10,000 population registered 571 in 1997, ranking 17th in the nation and exceeding the U.S. average of 531.1 by 8%. From 1962 to 1996, state and local FTE employees per 10,000 population increased by 67%, compared with an increase in the U.S. average of 66%.

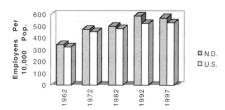

State and Local Government Employees (FTE) Per 10,000 Population: North Dakota vs. U.S.

Per Capita Federal Government Expenditures, 1998

	1998	Ranking
N. Dak.	$6,475	7th
U.S.	$5,491	

Per capita federal spending in North Dakota exceeded the national average by 18%.

EDUCATION

Total Education Spending

North Dakota's per capita state and local education spending registered $1,584 in 1996, ranking 19th in the nation and topping the U.S. average of $1,503 by 5%. From 1962 to 1996, real per capita total education spending increased by 143%, versus an increase in the U.S. average of 173%.

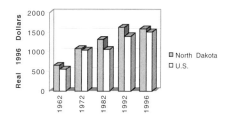

Real Per Capita State and Local Education Spending: North Dakota vs. U.S.

Per Pupil Spending

North Dakota's per pupil public school spending registered $5,214 in 1998, ranking 36th in the nation and trailing the U.S. average of $6,131 by 15%. From 1970 to 1998, North Dakota's real per pupil public school spending increased by 113%, compared with a 120% increase in the U.S. average.

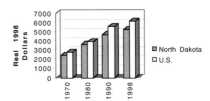

Real Per Pupil Public School Spending: North Dakota vs. U.S.

Average Public School Teacher Salaries (in 1997–98 dollars)

	1970	1980	1990	1998	1998 Ranking
N. Dak.	28,670	27,632	29,318	28,230	50th
U.S.	36,934	33,272	39,956	39,385	

In 1998, the average public school teacher salary in North Dakota trailed the U.S. average by 28%. From 1970 to 1998, the real average teacher salary in North Dakota decreased by 0.2%, versus an increase in the U.S. average of 7%.

Pupil/Teacher Ratio, Fall 1996

	Ratio	Rank
N. Dak.	15.2	15th
U.S.	17.1	

Teachers/Staff, Fall 1996

	Percent	Rank
N. Dak.	54.2	14th
U.S.	52.1	

Public School 4th-Grade Math Proficiency, 1996

	Average	Rank (out of 44 states)
N. Dak.	231	4th
U.S.	224	

Public School 8th-Grade Math Proficiency, 1996

	Average	Rank (out of 41 states)
N. Dak.	284	1st
U.S.	271	

Public School 8th-Grade Science Proficiency, 1996

	Average	Rank (out of 41 states)
N. Dak.	162	2d
U.S.	148	

Average Math SAT Scores

	1972	1982	1992	1998	Percentage Taking SAT in 1998
N. Dak.	579	577	580	599	5
U.S.	509	493	501	512	43

Average Verbal SAT Scores

	1972	1982	1992	1998	Percentage Taking SAT in 1998
N. Dak.	599	580	576	590	5
U.S.	530	504	500	505	43

Expenditures by Public Institutions of Higher Education Per Full-Time-Equivalent Student, 1996

	FTE Student Spending	Rank
N. Dak.	$11,670	34th
U.S.	$12,343	

Per-FTE-student spending in public institutions of higher education trailed the U.S. average by 5%.

Per Full-Time-Equivalent Student Revenues from Federal, State, and Local Governments, for Public Institutions of Higher Education, 1996

	FTE Student Government Revenues	Rank
N. Dak.	$6,921	40th
U.S.	$8,101	

Per-FTE-student-government revenues in public institutions of higher education trailed the U.S. average by 15%.

Average Salary for Full-Time Professors at Public Universities, 1997

	Average	Rank
N. Dak.	$49,892	49th
U.S.	$72,599	

The average full-time public university professor salary trailed the U.S. average by 31%.

ECONOMY AND BUSINESS

Economic Growth

Over the period of 1977 to 1997, North Dakota's real gross state product (GSP) grew by 35.2%—ranking 46th in the nation—as compared with real U.S. gross domestic product (GDP) expanding by 70.1%.

At $15.8 billion in 1997, North Dakota's GSP ranked as 50th largest in the nation.

From 1993 to 1997, North Dakota's annual real GSP growth averaged 2.71%—ranking 39th in the nation—as compared with annual real U.S. GDP growth averaging 3.08%.

Real Economic Growth 1977-1997: North Dakota vs. U.S.

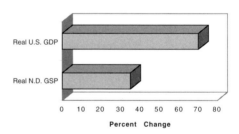

Percent Change

Job Growth

	Growth in Employee Payrolls (Nonagricultural) 1962–98	Ranking
N. Dak.	142.0%	27th
U.S.	126.5%	

Average Annual Growth in Employee Payrolls (Nonagricultural) 1993–98	Ranking
N. Dak.	2.76%	32d
U.S.	2.98%	

Per Capita Disposable Income

	1997	Ranking
N. Dak.	$17,878	42d
U.S.	$21,607	

Per capita disposable income trailed the U.S. average by 17%.

	Real Growth 1962–97	Ranking
N. Dak.	80.2%	49th
U.S.	116.7%	

	Average Annual Real Growth 1993–97	Ranking
N. Dak.	1.39%	39th
U.S.	1.48%	

Number of Businesses

	1997	Percent with Fewer than 500 Employees
Businesses with Employees	18,831	97.2
Self-employed Individuals	52,000	

New Business Incorporations

	1980	1986	1992	1997
N. Dak.	1,011	930	984	933

Percentage Change in Annual New Business Incorporations, 1980 vs. 1997

	Percent	Ranking
N. Dak.	−7.7	46th
U.S.	49.7	

State Merchandise Exports to the World, 1998 (in millions of dollars)

	1998	Rank
N. Dak.	$657	47th

Small Business Survival Index, 1999

North Dakota ranks a favorable 11th in the nation in terms of its policy environment for entrepreneurship.

Fortune 500 Headquarters in 1999

None

Labor Union Membership, 1983 vs. 1997

	Percentage of Workers		
	1983	1997	1997 Rank
N. Dak.	13.2	8.6	33d
U.S.	20.1	14.1	

Homeownership Rate, 1998

	Rate	Rank
N. Dak.	68.0	31st
U.S.	66.3	

CRIME

Crime Rates Per 100 Residents (rankings from best to worst crime rate)

Total Crime	1960	1970	1980	1990	1998	1998 Ranking
N. Dak.	0.37	0.85	2.96	2.92	2.68	4th
U.S.	1.04	2.74	5.90	5.82	4.62	

From 1960 to 1998, North Dakota's crime rate increased by 624%, versus a U.S. increase of 344%. From 1990 to 1998, North Dakota's crime rate decreased by 8%, versus a U.S. decrease of 21%.

Violent Crime	1960	1970	1980	1990	1998	1998 Ranking
N. Dak.	0.01	0.03	0.05	0.07	0.09	1st
U.S.	0.14	0.36	0.58	0.73	0.57	

From 1960 to 1998, North Dakota's violent crime rate increased by 800%, versus a U.S. increase of 307%. From 1990 to 1997, North Dakota's violent crime rate increased by 29%, compared with a national decline of 22%.

Property Crime	1960	1970	1980	1990	1998	1998 Ranking
N. Dak.	0.36	0.81	2.91	2.85	2.59	4th
U.S.	0.90	2.38	5.32	5.09	4.05	

From 1960 to 1998, North Dakota's property crime rate increased by 619%, versus a national increase of 350%. From 1990 to 1998, North Dakota's property crime rate decreased by 9%, compared with a national decline of 20%.

Real Per Capita Police Protection Spending (in real 1996 dollars)

	1962	1972	1982	1992	1996	1996 Ranking
N. Dak.	28	49	72	73	83	50th
U.S.	51	95	114	148	168	

In 1996, per capita state and local police protection spending in North Dakota trailed the U.S. average by 51%. From 1962 to 1996, real per capita state and local police protection spending increased by 196%, versus an increase of 229% in the U.S. average.

Prisoners in State and Federal Prisons Per 1,000 Population

	1980	1990	1996	1996 Ranking
N. Dak.	0.39	0.76	1.12	50th
U.S.	1.46	3.11	4.45	

From 1980 to 1996, prisoners per 1,000 population increased by 187%, versus a U.S. increase of 205%.

HEALTH CARE

Health-Care Spending

North Dakota's per capita state and local health-care spending registered $57 in 1996, ranking 51st in the nation and trailing the U.S. average of $151 by 62%. From 1962 to 1996, North Dakota's real per capita state and local health-care spending increased by 307%, versus an increase of 739% in the U.S. average.

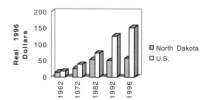
Real Per Capita State and Local Health Care Spending: North Dakota vs. U.S.

Hospital Spending

North Dakota's per capita state and local hospital spending registered $67 in 1996, ranking 48th in the nation and trailing the U.S. average of $266 by 75%. From 1962 to 1996, North Dakota's real per capita state and local hospital spending increased by 46%, as opposed to an increase of 189% in the U.S. average.

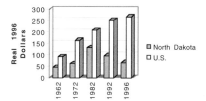
Real Per Capita State and Local Hospital Spending: North Dakota vs. U.S.

Medicaid, 1997

	Spending Per Recipient	Ranking
N. Dak.	$5,377	9th
U.S.	$3,681	

North Dakota's per-recipient Medicaid spending topped the U.S. average by 46%.

ENVIRONMENT

Parks and Recreation Spending

North Dakota's per capita state and local parks and recreation spending registered $75 in 1996, ranking 21st in the nation and exceeding the U.S. average of $72 by 4%. From 1962 to 1996, real per capita state and local parks and recreation spending increased by 436%, versus a 213% increase in the U.S. average.

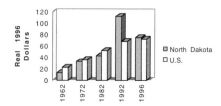
Real Per Capita State and Local Parks and Recreation Spending: North Dakota vs. U.S.

State and Local Natural Resources Spending, 1996

	Per Capita	Ranking
N. Dak.	$163	3d
U.S.	$60	

Per capita state and local natural resources spending in North Dakota exceeded the U.S. average by 172%.

State Parks Revenues as a Share of Operating Expenses, 1997

	Percent	Rank
N. Dak.	37	30th
U.S.	42	

Percentage of Land Owned by the Federal Government, 1996

	Percent	Rank
N. Dak.	3.2%	33d
U.S.	24.8%	

SOCIETY AND DEMOGRAPHICS

Population

North Dakota's 1998 population of .638 million ranked 47th in the nation.

Population Growth 1990–98

	Percentage Change in Population	Ranking
N. Dak.	−0.16	48th
U.S.	8.66	

	Net International Migration	Ranking
N. Dak.	4,493	45th

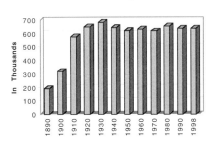

North Dakota Population

	Net Domestic Migration	Ranking
N. Dak.	−30,242	37th

Infant Mortality Rate, 1998

	Percent	Rank
N. Dak.	7.4	19th
U.S.	6.4	

Percentage of Births of Low Birthweight, 1997

	Percent	Rank
N. Dak.	6.2	43d
U.S.	7.5	

Percentage of Live Births to Unmarried Women, 1997

	Percent	Rank
N. Dak.	26.0	44th
U.S.	32.4	

Abortion Rate—Abortions Per 1,000 Women Ages 15–44, 1995

	Rate	Rank
N. Dak.	9.6	42d
U.S.	22.9	

LIFESTYLE

Percentage of Households with Computers, 1998

	Percent	Rank
N. Dak.	40.2	37th

Percentage of Households with Internet Access, 1998

	Percent	Rank
N. Dak.	20.6	45th

State Arts Agency Spending, 1999

	Per Capita	Rank
N. Dak.	$0.61	37th
U.S.	$1.35	

Per capita state arts spending in 1999 trailed the U.S. average by 55%.

Major League Sports Facilities

None

OHIO

In Cleveland, low-income parents of children using state vouchers to attend private schools are more satisfied with their children's education than are parents with children in the city's public schools. That is what a 1999 study from Harvard University's Program on Education Policy and Governance found in a survey undertaken after the first two years of Ohio's pilot school choice program in Cleveland. The program, passed by the Ohio state legislature in 1995, provides 4,000 low-income students in Cleveland with vouchers worth up to $2,500 for tuition purposes.

The study's findings were summarized in the Heartland Institute's monthly *School Reform News* (August, 1999):

- "Nearly half of the parents with students in choice schools reported being 'very satisfied' with the academic program of their child's school. By contrast, less than 30 percent of public school parents felt that way."
- "Similarly, half of scholarship parents, but just over 30 percent of public school parents, were 'very satisfied' with school safety."
- "Half of the scholarship parents were 'very satisfied' with school discipline, compared to only one-quarter of public school parents."
- "Public school parents report levels of involvement in school activities and the education of their children at home just as high as levels reported by parents of scholarship recipients."
- "In another rebuke to choice critics, who charge that choice programs benefit the better-off at the expense of the poor, the new survey shows that voucher recipients were more likely to be economically disadvantaged than the average public school family. Voucher families had lower incomes and were more likely to have only one parent in the home."

The Ohio Supreme Court ruled in 1999 that the program did not violate the separation of church and state; however, the court further ruled that the program needed legislative reauthorization because of the way it was passed. The legislature accordingly reauthorized it. One day before school opened in August 1999, Federal District Court Judge Solomon Oliver Jr. issued an injunction against the program, declaring that the pilot program had "the primary effect of advancing religion." Parents with children in the voucher program were thrown into chaos, though several days later Oliver graciously decreed that children who had participated in the program in earlier years would be allowed to continue until a decision was made. As for new students, the judge sent a clear message: Too bad.

Oliver seemed intent on declaring the Cleveland program unconstitutional, and did so in December. However, the voucher plan continued with an appeal headed for the Sixth Circuit Court of Appeals. In the end, the Cleveland voucher program should survive. The courts have been running strongly against such judicial activism. For example, the Wisconsin State Supreme Court upheld a Milwaukee school choice program that included religious schools, and in 1998 the U.S. Supreme Court let the decision stand by refusing to hear an appeal.

Once the Cleveland program is affirmed by the U.S. Supreme Court, Ohio would be wise to empower parents across the state with the ability to choose the best school for their children.

The same notion goes for a host of other issues critical to Ohio—disarm government bureaucrats and embolden individuals, families, entrepreneurs, and businesses.

For example, the state's rather lofty personal income, corporate income, and capital gains tax rates cry out to be slashed. Remember, as recently as 1970, Ohio imposed no income taxes. Incidentally, ever since Ohio instituted income taxes in 1971, the state's population has stagnated.

Make no mistake, steps to reduce the size of government and enhance incentives for working and risk taking are necessary, given Ohio's poor economic performance. As noted below, economic, population, job, and disposable income growth have been woeful in recent years.

Ohio's Buckeye Institute for Public Policy Solutions has been out front in arguing for progrowth policy reforms. In a recent publication, the group offers hope: "Perhaps the climate for change will benefit from Ohio's last major political reform: term limits. Significantly, most proposals to reduce government are coming from younger members of the Ohio legislature, and in the year 2000, more than a third of the current legislators will be ineligible to run for reelection. An infusion of new blood into the General Assembly could be just what the doctor—and a growing number of economists—have prescribed."

Let us hope so. The far more competitive and opportunity-laden 21st century will require such changes if Ohio is to prosper.

POLITICS

Registered Voters

14% Democrats
16% Republicans
71% Other

Federal Officials: Recent Election and Group Ratings

			ACU	ADA	SBSC
U.S. Senators:	Mike DeWine (R)		83	10	75
	1998 DeWine (R)	53%			
	Hyatt (D)	39%			
	George Voinovich (R)		NA	NA	NA
	1998 Voinovich (R)	56%			
	Boyle (D)	44%			
U.S. Representatives:	Steve Chabot (R-1)		98	9	100
	1998 Chabot (R)	53%			
	Qualls (D)	47%			

			ACU	ADA	SBSC
Rob Portman (R-2)			90	9	100
1998	Portman (R)	76%			
	Sanders (D)	24%			
Tony Hall (D-3)			16	72	20
1998	Hall (D)	69%			
	Shondel (R)	31%			
Michael Oxley (R-4)			88	6	95
1998	Oxley (R)	64%			
	McClain (D)	36%			
Paul Gillmor (R-5)			80	11	75
1998	Gillmor (R)	67%			
	Darrow (D)	33%			
Ted Strickland (D-6)			24	83	10
1998	Strickland (D)	57%			
	Hollister (R)	43%			
David Hobson (R-7)			80	10	95
1998	Hobson (R)	67%			
	Minor (D)	28%			
John Boehner (R-8)			95	1	95
1998	Boehner (R)	71%			
	Griffin (D)	29%			
Marcy Kaptur (D-9)			13	75	10
1998	Kaptur (D)	81%			
	Emery (R)	19%			
Dennis Kucinich (D-10)			18	90	15
1998	Kucinich (D)	67%			
	Slovenec (R)	33%			
Stephanie Tubbs Jones (D-11)			NA	NA	NA
1998	Jones (D)	80%			
	Hereford (R)	13%			
John Kasich (R-12)			87	10	95
1998	Kasich (R)	67%			
	Brown (D)	33%			
Sherrod Brown (D-13)			12	92	10
1998	Brown (D)	62%			
	Drake (R)	38%			

			ACU	ADA	SBSC
Thomas Sawyer (D-14)			3	91	20
1998	Sawyer (D)	63%			
	Watkins (R)	37%			
Deborah Pryce (R-15)			78	10	75
1998	Pryce (R)	66%			
	Miller (D)	28%			
Ralph Regula (R-16)			56	23	75
1998	Regula (R)	64%			
	Ferguson (D)	36%			
James Traficant Jr. (D-17)			27	73	50
1998	Traficant (D)	68%			
	Alberty (R)	32%			
Robert Ney (R-18)			79	14	75
1998	Ney (R)	60%			
	Burch (D)	40%			
Steven Latourette (R-19)			70	25	60
1998	Latourette (R)	66%			
	Kelley (D)	34%			

Electoral Votes: 21

1996 Presidential Results:

Clinton	47%
Dole	41%
Perot	11%

State Officials

Governor 1998 Election:

Robert Taft (R)	50%
Lee Fisher (D)	45%

Lt. Governor: Maureen O'Connor (R)
Attorney General: Betty Montgomery (R)
State Senate: 12 Democrats
21 Republicans

State House: 40 Democrats
59 Republicans

TAXES AND SPENDING

Total Revenues

Ohio's per capita state and local total revenues registered $5,776 in 1996, ranking 18th in the nation and topping the U.S. average of $5,706 by 1%. From 1962 to 1996, real per capita state and local revenues increased by 351%, compared with an increase in the national average of 297%.

Taxes

Ohio's per capita state and local taxes registered $2,503 in 1996, ranking 22d in the nation and lagging behind the U.S. average of $2,597 by 4%. From 1962 to 1996, real per capita state and local taxes increased by 177%, compared with an increase of 152% in the U.S. average.

Property Taxes

Ohio's per capita state and local property taxes equaled $713 in 1996, ranking 30th in the nation and trailing the U.S. average of $789 by 10%. From 1962 to 1996, real per capita state and local property taxes increased by 52%, versus a 67% increase in the U.S. average.

Sales and Gross Receipts Taxes

Ohio's per capita state and local sales and gross receipts taxes came in at $772 in 1996, ranking 37th in the nation and trailing the U.S. average of $939 by 18%. From 1962 to 1996, real per capita state and local sales and gross receipts taxes increased by 151%, versus a 214% increase in the U.S. average.

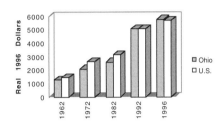

Real Per Capita State and Local Total Revenues: Ohio vs. U.S.

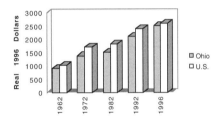

Real Per Capita State and Local Taxes: Ohio vs. U.S.

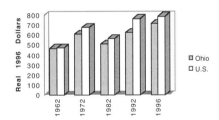

Real Per Capita State and Local Property Taxes: Ohio vs. U.S.

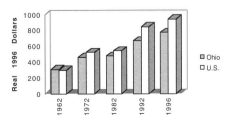

Real Per Capita State and Local Sales and Gross Receipts Taxes: Ohio vs. U.S.

Income Taxes

Ohio's per capita state and local income (individual and corporate) taxes registered $863 in 1996, ranking 11th in the nation and outpacing the U.S. average of $674 by 28%. From 1962 to 1996, U.S. average real per capita state and local income taxes increased by 567%, while Ohio imposed no income levies until 1971. From 1972 to 1996, Ohio's real per capita income taxes increased by 1,051%, versus a U.S. increase of 145%.

Personal Income Tax

A rate of 6.799%, ranking 37th in the nation (from lowest tax rate to highest), and comparing with the national average of 5.26%.

Capital Gains Tax

A rate of 6.799%, ranking 40th in the nation (from lowest tax rate to highest), and comparing with the national average of 4.68%.

Corporate Income Tax

A rate of 8.5%, ranking 37th in the nation (from lowest tax rate to highest), and comparing with the national average of 6.63%.

Total Expenditures

Ohio's per capita state and local total spending registered $4,926 in 1996, ranking 25th in the nation and trailing the U.S. average of $5,268 by 6%. From 1962 to 1996, real per capita state and local total spending increased by 274%, versus a 254% increase in the U.S. average.

Welfare Expenditures

Ohio's per capita state and local public welfare spending registered $707 in 1996, ranking 20th in the nation and trailing the U.S. average of $729 by 3%. From 1962 to 1996, real per capita state and local public welfare spending increased by 494%, compared with a 488% increase in the U.S. average.

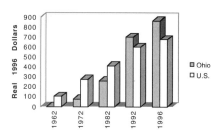

Real Per Capita State and Local Income Taxes: Ohio vs. U.S.

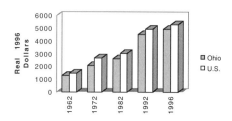

Real Per Capita State and Local Total Expenditures: Ohio vs. U.S.

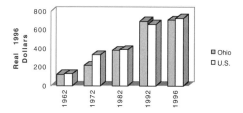

Real Per Capita State and Local Public Welfare Spending: Ohio vs. U.S.

Welfare Recipients (in thousands)

	1980	1989	3/99	Change 1989–99
Ohio	572	623	282	−55%
U.S.	10,923	10,987	7,335	−33%

Interest on General Debt

Ohio's per capita state and local interest on general debt registered $150 in 1996, ranking 37th in the nation and trailing the U.S. average of $222 by 32%. From 1962 to 1996, real per capita state and local interest on general debt increased by 226%, versus an increase of 335% in the U.S. average.

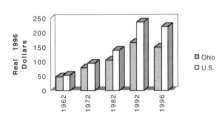

Real Per Capita State and Local Interest on General Debt: Ohio vs. U.S.

Total Debt Outstanding

Ohio's per capita state and local debt registered $2,591 in 1996, ranking 46th in the nation and trailing the U.S. average of $4,409 by 41%. From 1962 to 1996, real per capita state and local debt outstanding increased by 57%, versus an increase of 120% in the U.S. average.

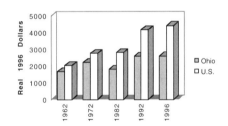

Real Per Capita State and Local Debt Outstanding: Ohio vs. U.S.

Government Employees

Ohio's state and local government employees (full-time equivalent, or FTE) per 10,000 population registered 501.7 in 1997, ranking 41st in the nation and trailing the U.S. average of 531.1 by 6%. From 1962 to 1996, state and local FTE employees per 10,000 population increased by 70%, compared with an increase in the U.S. average of 66%.

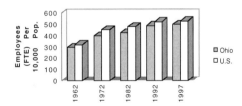

State and Local Government Employees (FTE) Per 10,000 Population: Ohio vs. U.S.

Per Capita Federal Government Expenditures, 1998

	1998	Ranking
Ohio	$4,640	42d
U.S.	$5,491	

Per capita federal spending in Ohio trailed the national average by 15%.

EDUCATION

Total Education Spending

Ohio's per capita state and local education spending registered $1,488 in 1996, ranking 28th in the nation and trailing the U.S. average of $1,503 by 1%. From 1962 to 1996, real per capita total education spending increased by 200%, versus an increase in the U.S. average of 173%.

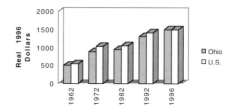

Real Per Capita State and Local Education Spending: Ohio vs. U.S.

Per Pupil Spending

Ohio's per pupil public school spending registered $6,020 in 1998, ranking 23d in the nation and trailing the U.S. average of $6,131 by 2%. From 1970 to 1998, Ohio's real per pupil public school spending increased by 140%, compared with a 120% increase in the U.S. average.

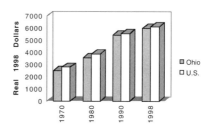

Real Per Pupil Public School Spending: Ohio vs. U.S.

Average Public School Teacher Salaries (in 1997–98 dollars)

	1970	1980	1990	1998	1998 Ranking
Ohio	35,538	31,812	39,766	38,977	18th
U.S.	36,934	33,272	39,956	39,385	

In 1998, the average public school teacher salary in Ohio trailed the U.S. average by 1%. From 1970 to 1998, the real average teacher salary in Ohio increased by 10%, versus an increase in the U.S. average of 7%.

Pupil/Teacher Ratio, Fall 1996

	Ratio	Rank
Ohio	17.0	31st
U.S.	17.1	

Teachers/Staff, Fall 1996

	Percent	Rank
Ohio	55.1	9th
U.S.	52.1	

Average Math SAT Scores

	1972	1982	1992	1998	Percentage Taking SAT in 1998
Ohio	519	525	523	540	24
U.S.	509	493	501	512	43

Average Verbal SAT Scores

	1972	1982	1992	1998	Percentage Taking SAT in 1998
Ohio	538	533	527	536	24
U.S.	530	504	500	505	43

Expenditures by Public Institutions of Higher Education Per Full-Time-Equivalent Student, 1996

	FTE Student Spending	Rank
Ohio	$12,409	23d
U.S.	$12,343	

Per-FTE-student spending in public institutions of higher education exceeded the U.S. average by 1%.

Per Full-Time-Equivalent Student Revenues from Federal, State, and Local Governments for Public Institutions of Higher Education, 1996

	FTE Student Government Revenues	Rank
Ohio	$6,768	42d
U.S.	$8,101	

Per-FTE-student-government revenues in public institutions of higher education trailed the U.S. average by 16%.

Average Salary for Full-Time Professors at Public Universities, 1997

	Average	Rank
Ohio	$71,830	21st
U.S.	$72,599	

The average full-time public university professor salary trailed the U.S. average by 1%.

ECONOMY AND BUSINESS

Economic Growth

Over the period of 1977 to 1997, Ohio's real gross state product (GSP) grew by 46.2%—ranking 43d in the nation—as compared with real U.S. gross domestic product (GDP), expanding by 70.1%.

At $320.5 billion in 1997, Ohio's GSP ranked as 7th largest in the nation.

From 1993 to 1997, Ohio's annual real GSP growth averaged 3.48%—ranking 30th in the nation—as compared with annual real U.S. GDP growth, averaging 3.08%.

**Real Economic Growth
1977-1997: Ohio vs. U.S.**

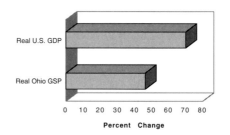

Job Growth

	Growth in Employee Payrolls (Nonagricultural) 1962–98	Ranking
Ohio	76.6%	43d
U.S.	120.1%	

	Average Annual Growth in Employee Payrolls (Nonagricultural) 1993–98	Ranking
Ohio	2.46%	37th
U.S.	2.98%	

Per Capita Disposable Income, 1997

	1997	Ranking
Ohio	$20,657	23d
U.S.	$21,607	

Per capita disposable income trailed the U.S. average by 4%.

	Real Growth 1962–97	Ranking
Ohio	101.5%	41st
U.S.	116.7%	

	Average Annual Real Growth 1993–97	Ranking
Ohio	1.61%	29th
U.S.	1.48%	

Number of Businesses

	1997	Percent with Fewer than 500 Employees
Businesses with Employees	228,772	98.4
Self-employed Individuals	361,000	

New Business Incorporations

	1980	1986	1992	1997
Ohio	15,870	18,410	18,730	20,105

Percentage Change in Annual New Business Incorporations, 1980 vs. 1997

	Percent	Ranking
Ohio	26.7	31st
U.S.	49.7	

State Merchandise Exports to the World, 1998 (in millions of dollars)

	1998	Rank
Ohio	$24,815	7th

Small Business Survival Index, 1999

Ohio ranks a sad 43d in terms of its policy environment for entrepreneurship.

Fortune 500 Headquarters in 1999

A total of 27 (ranked 5th), with Cleveland ranked 9th among U.S. cities, with 7 headquarters

Labor Union Membership, 1983 vs. 1997

	Percentage of Workers		
	1983	1997	1997 Rank
Ohio	25.1	18.9	9th
U.S.	20.1	14.1	

Homeownership Rate, 1998

	Rate	Rank
Ohio	70.7	19th
U.S.	66.3	

CRIME

Crime Rates Per 100 Residents (rankings from best to worst crime rate)

Total Crime	1960	1970	1980	1990	1998	1998 Ranking
Ohio	0.75	2.38	5.43	4.84	4.33	23d
U.S.	1.04	2.74	5.90	5.82	4.62	

From 1960 to 1998, Ohio's crime rate increased by 477%, versus a U.S. increase of 344%. From 1990 to 1998, Ohio's crime rate decreased by 11%, versus a U.S. decrease of 21%.

Violent Crime	1960	1970	1980	1990	1998	1998 Ranking
Ohio	0.08	0.28	0.50	0.51	0.36	18th
U.S.	0.14	0.36	0.58	0.73	0.57	

From 1960 to 1998, Ohio's violent crime rate increased by 350%, versus a U.S. increase of 307%. From 1990 to 1998, Ohio's violent crime rate decreased by 29%, compared with a national decline of 22%.

Property Crime	1960	1970	1980	1990	1998	1998 Ranking
Ohio	0.67	2.09	4.93	4.34	3.97	25th
U.S.	0.90	2.38	5.32	5.09	4.05	

From 1960 to 1998, Ohio's property crime rate increased by 493%, versus a national increase of 350%. From 1990 to 1998, Ohio's property crime rate decreased by 9%, compared with a national decline of 20%.

Real Per Capita Police Protection Spending (in real 1996 dollars)

	1962	1972	1982	1992	1996	1996 Ranking
Ohio	41	79	97	133	154	21st
U.S.	51	95	114	148	168	

In 1996, per capita state and local police protection spending in Ohio trailed the U.S. average by 8%. From 1962 to 1996, real per capita state and local police protection spending increased by 276%, versus an increase of 229% in the U.S. average.

Prisoners in State and Federal Prisons Per 1,000 Population

	1980	1990	1996	1996 Ranking
Ohio	1.25	2.93	4.14	20th
U.S.	1.46	3.11	4.45	

From 1980 to 1996, prisoners per 1,000 population increased by 231%, versus a U.S. increase of 205%.

HEALTH CARE

Health-Care Spending

Ohio's per capita state and local health-care spending registered $189 in 1996 ranking 12th in the nation and topping the U.S. average of $151 by 25%. From 1962 to 1996, Ohio's real per capita state and local health-care spending increased by 1,250%, versus an increase of 739% in the U.S. average.

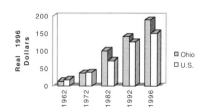

Real Per Capita State and Local Health Care Spending: Ohio vs. U.S.

Hospital Spending

Ohio's per capita state and local hospital spending registered $149 in 1996, ranking 36th in the nation and trailing the U.S. average of $266 by 44%. From 1962 to 1996, Ohio's real per capita state and local hospital spending increased by 116%, as opposed to an increase of 189% in the U.S. average.

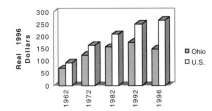

Real Per Capita State and Local Hospital Spending: Ohio vs. U.S.

Medicaid, 1997

	Spending Per Recipient	Ranking
Ohio	$4,189	18th
U.S.	$3,681	

Ohio's per-recipient Medicaid spending exceeded the U.S. average by 14%.

ENVIRONMENT

Parks and Recreation Spending

Ohio's per capita state and local parks and recreation spending registered $52 in 1996, ranking 34% in the nation and trailing the U.S. average of $72 by 28%. From 1962 to 1996, real per capita state and local parks and recreation spending increased by 271%, versus a 213% increase in the U.S. average.

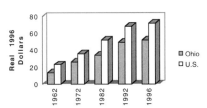

Real Per Capita State and Local Parks and Recreation Spending: Ohio vs. U.S.

State and Local Natural Resources Spending, 1996

	Per Capita	Ranking
Ohio	$28	44th
U.S.	$60	

Per capita state and local natural resources spending in Ohio trailed the U.S. average by 53%.

State Parks Revenues as a Share of Operating Expenses, 1997

	Percent	Rank
Ohio	41	26th
U.S.	42	

Percentage of Land Owned by the Federal Government, 1996

	Percent	Rank
Ohio	1.1	41st
U.S.	24.8	

SOCIETY AND DEMOGRAPHICS

Population

Ohio's 1998 population of 11.209 million ranked 7th in the nation.

Population Growth, 1990–98

	Percentage Change in Population	Ranking
Ohio	3.34	41st
U.S.	8.66	

	Net International Migration	Ranking
Ohio	48,238	20th

	Net Domestic Migration	Ranking
Ohio	−143,533	43d

Ohio Population

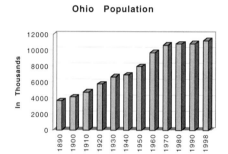

Infant Mortality Rate, 1998

	Percent	Rank
Ohio	7.5	18th
U.S.	6.4	

Percentage of Births of Low Birthweight, 1997

	Percent	Rank
Ohio	7.7	21st
U.S.	7.5	

Percentage of Live Births to Unmarried Women, 1997

	Percent	Rank
Ohio	33.9	14th
U.S.	32.4	

Abortion Rate—Abortions Per 1,000 Women Ages 15–44, 1995

	Rate	Rank
Ohio	16.2	25th
U.S.	22.9	

LIFESTYLE

Percentage of Households with Computers, 1998

	Percent	Rank
Ohio	40.7	35th

Percentage of Households with Internet Access, 1998

	Percent	Rank
Ohio	24.6	30th

State Arts Agency Spending, 1999

	Per Capita	Rank
Ohio	$1.33	17th
U.S.	$1.35	

Per capita state arts spending in 1999 trailed the U.S. average by 1.5%.

Major League Sports Facilities

Year Opened/ Refurb.	Stadium/ Arena	Home Team	Millions of Nominal Dollars		Millions of Real 1997 Dollars	
			Estimated Total Cost	Estimated Taxpayer Cost	Estimated Total Cost	Estimated Taxpayer Cost
1901	League Park	Indians (MLB) 1901–46	NA	$0.0	NA	$0.0
1912	Crosley Field	Reds (MLB) 1912–70	$0.4	$0.0	$6.7	$0.0
1931	Municipal Stadium	Indians (MLB) 1932–93 Browns (NFL) 1946–95	$3.0	$3.0	$31.6	$31.6
1970	Riverfront Stadium	Reds (MLB) 1970–present Bengals (NFL) 1970–present	$54.5	$54.5	$225.2	$225.2
1974	Richfield Coliseum	Cavaliers (NBA) 1974–94	$45.0	$45.0	$146.6	$146.6
1994	Cleveland Gateway Jacobs Field Gund Arena	Indians (MLB) 1994–present Cavaliers (NBA) 1994–present	$462.0	$305.0	$500.5	$330.4

OKLAHOMA

The Rodgers and Hammerstein musical asserts that Oklahoma is "okay." Is that the case today? The answer is mixed.

In the early 1980s, when Reaganomics spurred a nationwide recovery following the downward economic spiral of the Nixon-Ford-Carter years, Oklahoma remained economically depressed. Even when the oil industry recovered in neighboring Texas, Oklahoma was slow to feel the positive effects. In recent years, oil, gas, and farming have all faced economic difficulties.

Looking at recent economic growth, job creation, disposable income, population growth, and new business incorporation numbers, one can conclude that Oklahoma's economy is okay, but not much better than okay.

While overall government spending and revenues come in below U.S. averages—property taxes are particularly low (ranked 48th in the nation)—there is room for improvement that would help the economy. For example, it is somewhat surprising that Oklahoma's income tax rates are definitely on the high side, and reductions there would have salutary effects on entrepreneurship and investment.

On the political front, Republicans rule. Though Oklahoma remains Democratic in terms of voter registration, there is no question that at the ballot box the state has become increasingly dominated by the GOP. Every federal office is held by a Republican, and the state has voted for the Republican nominee for president 11 out of the last 12 times. The governor and lieutenant governor are Republicans, and the GOP has made progress down-ballot as well, achieving a net gain of three statewide secondary offices as well as picking up two senate seats and nine house seats in the state legislature since 1994.

Republicans in Oklahoma are perhaps some of the most conservative in the entire nation. The state's two senators and six congressmen average a "96" lifetime approval rating by the American Conservative Union.

The legislature, which meets February through May each year, "is the last stand for the Democrats here," observes Sharon Caldwell, a principal in the Oklahoma City consulting firm, Cole, Snodgrass, Hardgrove, and Associates. Democrats hold 33 of the 48 state senate seats and 61 of the 101 state house seats. "Many issues don't cut along party lines in the state legislature," Caldwell comments. "Heated disagreements" she adds, are more likely to be "urban versus rural." Underscoring this observation is the makeup of the legislature itself. Marie Price, writing in Oklahoma City's *Journal Record*, of August 9, 1999, reported that only 13 of the 48 senators and 9 of the 101 state representatives are lawyers. By contrast, the most prevalent occupation, farming or ranching, is listed by 30 members.

Governor Frank Keating (no relation to this book's coauthor), who comfortably won reelection in 1998 with 58% of the vote, has made education and crime his two showcase issues. The thrust of his education program called for all high school students to successfully complete four years of math, four years of English, four years of science, and four years of social studies. Though unsuccessful in convincing the legislature to pass his full plan known as "Four by Four," he has succeeded in getting a modified version signed into law. Even the modified version was the subject of great protest by the teachers' unions and school administrators. "I hate to see us have a requirement that makes kids miserable at the best and makes them drop out at the worst," states Randall Raburn, Executive Director of the Cooperative Council of Oklahoma School Administrators, in the *Oklahoma* (March 18, 1999).

While the overall crime rate has decreased 11% in Oklahoma during most of the 1990s, the decline has lagged behind the total U.S. crime rate, which was down 21% during the same period. It is hard to say whether this statistic is central to Keating's determination to reduce crime in his state. Whatever the reason, the governor has made it clear which side of the classic argument he is on, placing a priority on building more prisons rather than on criminal rehabilitation programs. Not surprisingly, Oklahoma ranks near the top of the list (sixth) of prisoners in state and federal prisons as a share of the population, with an increase of 274% from 1980 to 1996.

Other criminal deterrents in Oklahoma, where the National Rifle Association is extremely popular, include a right-to-carry gun law (known as "concealed carry" by its opponents), which was passed in 1995, and the state's even newer, unique "make my day law" that acknowledges property owners' right to shoot-to-kill anyone coming on their property with the intent to commit a crime.

With trying to improve its economy, and with a popular governor and united elected officials, Oklahoma has embarked on a "renaissance of sorts," comments Sharon Caldwell.

POLITICS

Registered Voters

59% Democrats
35% Republicans
6% Other

Federal Officials: Recent Election and Group Ratings

			ACU	ADA	SBSC
U.S. Senators:	Don Nickles (R)		95	2	90
	1998 Nickles (R)	66%			
	Carroll (D)	31%			
	James Inhofe (R)		98	3	90
	1996 Inhofe (R)	56%			
	Boren (D)	40%			
U.S. Representatives:	Steve Largent (R-1)		97	6	95
	1998 Largent (R)	62%			
	Plowman (D)	38%			

			ACU	ADA	SBSC
Tom Coburn (R-2)			96	5	85
1998	Coburn (R)	58%			
	Pharaoh (D)	40%			
Wes Watkins (R-3)			96	3	85
1998	Watkins (R)	62%			
	Roberts (D)	38%			
J.C. Watts (R-4)			95	3	80
1998	Watts (R)	62%			
	Odom (D)	38%			
Ernest Jim Istook Jr. (R-5)			98	5	85
1998	Istook (R)	68%			
	Smothermon (D)	32%			
Frank Lucas (R-6)			96	0	95
1998	Lucas (R)	65%			
	Barby (D)	33%			

Electoral Votes: 8

1996 Presidential Results:

Clinton	40%
Dole	48%
Perot	11%

State Officials

Governor 1998 Election:

Frank Keating (R)	58%
Laura Boyd (D)	41%

Lt. Governor: Mary Fallin (R)

Attorney General: Drew Edmondson (D)

State Senate: 33 Democrats
15 Republicans

State House: 61 Democrats
40 Republicans

TAXES AND SPENDING

Total Revenues

Oklahoma's per capita state and local total revenues registered $4,543 in 1996, ranking 49th in the nation and lagging behind the U.S. average of $5,706 by 20%. From 1962 to 1996, real per capita state and local revenues increased by 221%, compared with an increase in the national average of 297%.

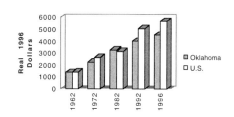

Real Per Capita State and Local Total Revenues: Oklahoma vs. U.S.

Taxes

Oklahoma's per capita state and local taxes registered $1,987 in 1996, ranking 44th in the nation and lagging behind the U.S. average of $2,597 by 23%. From 1962 to 1996, real per capita state and local taxes increased by 131%, compared with an increase of 152% in the U.S. average.

Property Taxes

Oklahoma's per capita state and local property taxes equaled $307 in 1996, ranking 48th in the nation and trailing the U.S. average of $789 by 61%. From 1962 to 1996, real per capita state and local property taxes increased by 15%, versus a 67% increase in the U.S. average.

Sales and Gross Receipts Taxes

Oklahoma's per capita state and local sales and gross receipts taxes came in at $837 in 1996, ranking 30th in the nation and trailing the U.S. average of $939 by 11%. From 1962 to 1996, real per capita state and local sales and gross receipts taxes increased by 160%, versus a 214% increase in the U.S. average.

Income Taxes

Oklahoma's per capita state and local income (individual and corporate) taxes registered $508 in 1996, ranking 37th in the nation and trailing the U.S. average of $674 by 25%. From 1962 to 1996, real per capita state and local income taxes increased by 512%, versus a 567% increase in the U.S. average.

Personal Income Tax

A rate of 6.75%, ranking 35th in the nation (from lowest tax rate to highest), and comparing with the national average of 5.26%.

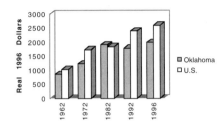

Real Per Capita State and Local Taxes: Oklahoma vs. U.S.

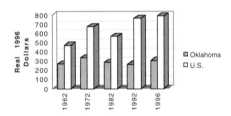

Real Per Capita State and Local Property Taxes: Oklahoma vs. U.S.

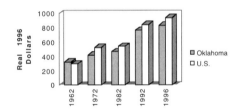

Real Per Capita State and Local Sales and Gross Receipts Taxes: Oklahoma vs. U.S.

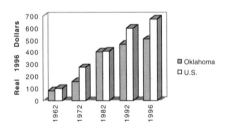

Real Per Capita State and Local Income Taxes: Oklahoma vs. U.S.

Capital Gains Tax

A rate of 6.75%, ranking 39th in the nation (from lowest tax rate to highest), and comparing with the national average of 4.68%.

Corporate Income Tax

A rate of 6.0%, ranking 16th in the nation (from lowest tax rate to highest), and comparing with the national average of 6.63%

Total Expenditures

Oklahoma's per capita state and local total spending registered $4,110 in 1996, ranking 49th in the nation and trailing the U.S. average of $5,268 by 22%. From 1962 to 1996, real per capita state and local total spending increased by 199%, versus a 254% increase in the U.S. average.

Welfare Expenditures

Oklahoma's per capita state and local public welfare spending registered $493 in 1996, ranking 46th in the nation trailing the U.S. average of $729 by 32%. From 1962 to 1996, real per capita state and local public welfare spending increased by 85%, compared with a 488% increase in the U.S. average.

Welfare Recipients (in thousands)

	1980	1989	3/99	Change 1989–99
Okla.	92	105	57	−46%
U.S.	10,923	10,987	7,335	−33%

Interest on General Debt

Oklahoma's per capita state and local interest on general debt registered $137 in 1996, ranking 41st in the nation and trailing the U.S. average of $222 by 38%. From 1962 to 1996, real per capita state and local interest on general debt increased by 270%, versus an increase of 335% in the U.S. average.

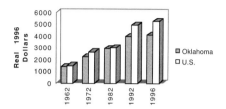

Real Per Capita State and Local Total Expenditures: Oklahoma vs. U.S.

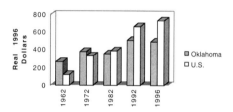

Real Per Capita State and Local Public Welfare Spending: Oklahoma vs. U.S.

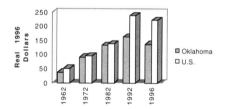

Real Per Capita State and Local Interest on General Debt: Oklahoma vs. U.S.

Total Debt Outstanding

Oklahoma's per capita state and local debt registered $2,716 in 1996, ranking 43d in the nation and trailing the U.S average of $4,409 by 41%. From 1962 to 1996, real per capita state and local debt outstanding increased by 63%, versus an increase of 120% in the U.S. average.

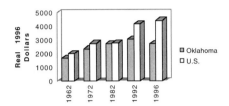

Real Per Capita State and Local Debt Outstanding: Oklahoma vs. U.S.

Government Employees

Oklahoma's state and local government employees (full-time equivalent, or FTE) per 10,000 population registered 607.6 in 1997, ranking 10th in the nation and topping the U.S. average of 531.1 by 14%. From 1962 to 1996, state and local FTE employees per 10,000 population increased by 89%, compared with an increase in the U.S. average of 66%.

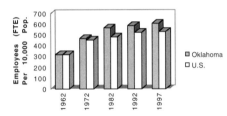

State and Local Government Employees (FTE) Per 10,000 Population: Oklahoma vs. U.S.

Per Capita Federal Government Expenditures

	1998	Ranking
Okla.	$5,440	25th
U.S.	$5,491	

Per capita federal spending in Oklahoma trailed the national average by 1%.

EDUCATION

Total Education Spending

Oklahoma's per capita state and local education spending registered $1,371 in 1996, ranking 39th in the nation and trailing the U.S. average of $1,503 by 9%. From 1962 to 1996, real per capita total education spending increased by 176%, versus an increase in the U.S. average of 173%.

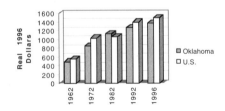

Real Per Capita State and Local Education Spending: Oklahoma vs. U.S.

Per Pupil Spending

Oklahoma's per pupil public school spending registered $5,071 in 1998, ranking 39th in the nation and trailing the U.S. average of $6,131 by 17%. From 1970 to 1998, Oklahoma's real per pupil public school spending increased by 147%, compared with a 120% increase in the U.S. average.

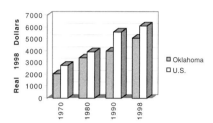

Real Per Pupil Public School Spending: Oklahoma vs. U.S.

Average Public School Teacher Salaries (in 1997–98 dollars)

	1970	1980	1990	1998	1998 Ranking
Okla.	29,467	27,307	29,387	30,606	45th
U.S.	36,934	33,272	39,956	39,385	

In 1998, the average public school teacher salary in Oklahoma trailed the U.S. average by 22%. From 1970 to 1998, the real average teacher salary in Oklahoma increased by 4%, versus an increase in the U.S. average of 7%.

Pupil/Teacher Ratio, Fall 1996

	Ratio	Rank
Okla.	15.7	20th
U.S.	17.1	

Teachers/Staff, Fall 1996

	Percent	Rank
Okla.	47.3	49th
U.S.	52.1	

Public School 4th-Grade Reading Proficiency, 1998

	Average	Rank (out of 40 states)
Okla.	220	11th
U.S.	215	

Public School 8th-Grade Reading Proficiency, 1998

	Average	Rank (out of 37 states)
Okla.	265	11th
U.S.	261	

Average Math SAT Scores

	1972	1982	1992	1998	Percentage Taking SAT in 1998
Okla.	542	539	546	564	8
U.S.	509	493	501	512	43

Average Verbal SAT Scores

	1972	1982	1992	1998	Percentage Taking SAT in 1998
Okla.	570	559	556	568	8
U.S.	530	504	500	505	43

Expenditures by Public Institutions of Higher Education Per Full-Time-Equivalent Student, 1996

	FTE Student Spending	Rank
Okla.	$9,199	51st
U.S.	$12,343	

Per-FTE-student spending in public institutions of higher education trailed the U.S. average by 25%.

Per Full-Time-Equivalent Student Revenues from Federal, State, and Local Governments for Public Institutions of Higher Education, 1996

	FTE Student Government Revenues	Rank
Okla.	$7,351	33d
U.S.	$8,101	

Per-FTE-student-government revenues in public institutions of higher education trailed the U.S. average by 9%.

Average Salary for Full-Time Professors at Public Universities, 1997

	Average	Rank
Okla.	$63,279	39th
U.S.	$72,599	

The average full-time public university professor salary trailed the U.S. average by 13%.

ECONOMY AND BUSINESS

Economic Growth

Over the period of 1977 to 1997, Oklahoma's real gross state product (GSP) grew by 37.7%—ranking 45th in the nation—as compared with real U.S. gross domestic product (GDP), expanding by 70.1%.

At $76.6 billion in 1997, Oklahoma's GSP ranked as 30th largest in the nation.

From 1993 to 1997, Oklahoma's annual real GSP growth averaged 2.63%—ranking 40th in the nation—as compared with annual real U.S. GDP growth, averaging 3.08%.

**Real Economic Growth
1977-1997: Oklahoma vs. U.S.**

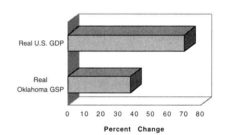

Percent Change

Job Growth

	Growth in Employee Payrolls (Nonagricultural) 1962–98	Ranking
Okla.	141.6%	28th
U.S.	126.5%	

	Average Annual Growth in Employee Payrolls (Nonagricultural) 1993–98	Ranking
Okla.	3.35%	13th
U.S.	2.98%	

Per Capita Disposable Income, 1997

	1997	Ranking
Okla.	$17,661	45th
U.S.	$21,607	

Per capita disposable income trailed the U.S. average by 18%.

	Real Growth 1962–97	Ranking
Okla.	112.8%	32d
U.S.	116.7%	

	Average Annual Real Growth 1993–97	Ranking
Okla.	1.19%	45th
U.S.	1.48%	

Number of Businesses

	1997	Percent with Fewer than 500 Employees
Businesses with Employees	72,648	97.6
Self-employed Individuals	161,000	

New Business Incorporations

	1980	1986	1992	1997
Okla.	5,453	7,565	7,207	8,162

Percentage Change in Annual New Business Incorporations, 1980 vs. 1997

	Percent	Ranking
Okla.	49.7	23d

State Merchandise Exports to the World, 1998 (in millions of dollars)

	1998	Rank
Okla.	$2,623	35th

Small Business Survival Index, 1999

Oklahoma ranks 34th in terms of its policy environment for entrepreneurship.

Fortune 500 Headquarters in 1999

A total of 3 (ranked 28th)

Labor Union Membership, 1983 vs. 1997

| | Percentage of Workers | | |
	1983	1997	1997 Rank
Okla.	11.5	8.4	37th
U.S.	20.1	14.1	

Homeownership Rate, 1998

	Rate	Rank
Okla.	69.7	24th
U.S.	66.3	

CRIME

Crimes Rates Per 100 Residents (rankings from best to worst crime rate)

Total Crime	1960	1970	1980	1990	1998	1998 Ranking
Okla.	1.07	1.95	5.05	5.60	5.00	34th
U.S.	1.04	2.74	5.90	5.82	4.62	

From 1960 to 1998, Oklahoma's crime rate increased by 367%, versus a U.S. increase of 344%. From 1990 to 1998, Oklahoma's crime rate decreased by 11%, versus a U.S. decrease of 21%.

Violent Crime	1960	1970	1980	1990	1998	1998 Ranking
Okla.	0.10	0.20	0.42	0.55	0.54	31st
U.S.	0.14	0.36	0.58	0.73	0.57	

From 1960 to 1998, Oklahoma's violent crime rate increased by 440% versus a U.S. increase of 307%. From 1990 to 1998, Oklahoma's violent crime rate decreased by 2%, compared with a national decline of 22%.

Property Crime	1960	1970	1980	1990	1998	1998 Ranking
Okla.	0.98	1.75	4.63	5.05	4.46	34th
U.S.	0.90	2.38	5.32	5.09	4.05	

From 1960 to 1998, Oklahoma's property crime rate increased by 355%, versus a national increase of 350%. From 1990 to 1998, Oklahoma's property crime rate decreased by 12%, compared with a national decline of 20%.

Real Per Capita Police Protection Spending (in real 1996 dollars)

	1962	1972	1982	1992	1996	1996 Ranking
Okla.	32	52	84	100	122	37th
U.S.	51	95	114	148	168	

In 1996, per capita state and local police protection spending in Oklahoma trailed the U.S. average by 27%. From 1962 to 1996, real per capita state and local police protection spending increased by 281%, versus an increase of 229% in the U.S. average.

Prisoners in State and Federal Prisons Per 1,000 Population

	1980	1990	1996	1996 Ranking
Okla.	1.59	3.90	5.95	6th
U.S.	1.46	3.11	4.45	

From 1980 to 1996, prisoners per 1,000 population increased by 274%, versus a U.S. increase of 205%.

HEALTH CARE

Health-Care Spending

Oklahoma's per capita state and local health-care spending registered $95 in 1996, ranking 41st in the nation and trailing the U.S. average of $151 by 37%. From 1962 to 1996, Oklahoma's real per capita state and local health-care spending increased by 956%, versus an increase of 739% in the U.S. average.

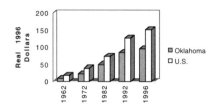

Real Per Capita State and Local Health Care Spending: Oklahoma vs. U.S.

Hospital Spending

Oklahoma's per capita state and local hospital spending registered $276 in 1996, ranking 19th in the nation and topping the U.S. average of $266 by 10%. From 1962 to 1996, Oklahoma's real per capita state and local hospital spending increased by 331%, as opposed to an increase of 189% in the U.S. average.

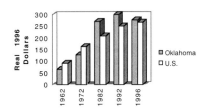

Real Per Capita State and Local Hospital Spending: Oklahoma vs. U.S.

Medicaid, 1997

	Spending Per Recipient	Ranking
Okla.	$3,284	32d
U.S.	$3,681	

Oklahoma's per-recipient Medicaid spending trailed the U.S. average by 11%.

ENVIRONMENT

Parks and Recreation Spending

Oklahoma's per capita state and local parks and recreation spending registered $59 in 1996, ranking 30th in the nation and trailing the U.S. average of $72 by 18%. From 1962 to 1996, real per capita state and local parks and recreation spending increased by 556%, versus a 213% increase in the U.S. average.

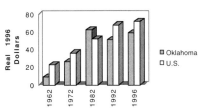

Real Per Capita State and Local Parks and Recreation Spending: Oklahoma vs. U.S.

State and Local Natural Resources Spending, 1996

	Per Capita	Ranking
Okla.	$39	39th
U.S.	$60	

Per capita state and local natural resources spending in Oklahoma trailed the U.S. average by 35%.

State Parks Revenues as a Share of Operating Expenses, 1997

	Percent	Rank
Okla.	98	2d
U.S.	42	

Percentage of Land Owned by the Federal Government, 1996

	Percent	Rank
Okla.	1.5	39th
U.S.	24.8	

SOCIETY AND DEMOGRAPHICS

Population

Oklahoma's 1998 population of 3.347 million ranked 29th in the nation.

Population Growth, 1990–98

	Percentage Change in Population	Ranking
Okla.	6.39	31st
U.S.	8.66	

	Net International Migration	Ranking
Okla.	26,153	28th

	Net Domestic Migration	Ranking
Okla.	47,774	24th

Oklahoma Population

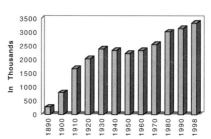

Infant Mortality Rate, 1998

	Percent	Rank
Okla.	6.0	37th
U.S.	6.4	

Percentage of Births of Low Birthweight, 1997

	Percent	Rank
Okla.	7.3	29th
U.S.	7.5	

Percentage of Live Births to Unmarried Women, 1997

	Percent	Rank
Okla.	32.3	24th
U.S.	32.4	

Abortion Rate—Abortions Per 1,000 Women Ages 15–44, 1995

	Rate	Rank
Okla.	12.9	34th
U.S.	22.9	

LIFESTYLE

Percentage of Households with Computers, 1998

	Percent	Rank
Okla.	37.8	40th

Percentage of Households with Internet Access, 1998

	Percent	Rank
Okla.	20.4	46th

State Arts Agency Spending, 1999

	Per Capita	Rank
Okla.	$1.20	18th
U.S.	$1.35	

Per capita state arts spending in 1999 trailed the U.S. average by 11%.

Major League Sports Facilities

None

$\boldsymbol{O}$REGON

Oregon seems to be vying to become North America's Sweden.

From the 1960s to the 1980s, Sweden served as one of the Left's favorite countries. Liberals asserted that Sweden showed that people could prosper when big government was done right. Sweden's government supposedly could raise taxes, endlessly expand the social welfare state, and run businesses with impunity.

However, while Sweden brandished an impressive economic performance during the 1960s, economic reality soon caught up to Europe's most famous example of democratic socialism. From the mid-1970s to the late 1980s, Sweden's economy languished, and in the late 1980s and early 1990s, the weight of big government came crashing down in full.

In recent years, Oregon, like the Sweden of old, has assumed that living the liberal dream of expanding government can be attained without paying a price. Oregon's per capita state and local government spending levels generally run ahead of the national averages. Government revenues also outpace the U.S. average, and the state imposes the fifth highest personal income tax rate and the third highest capital gains tax rate among the states. (However, there is no state sales tax). In addition, over half the land in the state is owned by the federal government.

Just to show how strange Oregon can get, Washington County in the Portland area set up a rather bizarre deal with Intel Corporation. As the *New York Times* reported (June 9, 1999), in exchange for property tax breaks, Intel would invest in equipment and plant upgrades. So far, this just seems like another case of corporate welfare. However, Intel faces a job creation cap of 1,000 new jobs. If the company creates more jobs, it would have to pay an annual $1,000 per excess worker fee. Not only are these local politicians arrogant enough to assume that they can and should pick winners and losers in the marketplace with taxpayer subsidies, but they also think they know exactly how many new jobs should be created.

These are just a few examples of statism run amok in "North America's Sweden," which also includes government micromanagement of health care, as well as voter approval of two referenda for physician-assisted suicide (that is, state-sanctioned murder) during the 1990s.

In the face of such flagrant statist overreach, Oregon's economy nevertheless has been chugging along in recent years. Real disposable income and economic growth have been running well, and jobs and population apparently are advancing at a pace just too fast for some politicians. Oregon of the 1990s was like Sweden of the 1960s.

Similarly, the liberal dream in "North America's Sweden" will soon begin to fade and eventually turn into a nightmare. Sweden had to slash taxes (the top tax rate went from a crushing 98% to a still-too-high 56%), privatize industries, and drastically reduce government expenditures in order to recover from its long, severe economic downturn.

When economic reality catches up to Oregon, it too will be forced to cut taxes, reduce spending, and pull back from its micromanagement of the private sector.

Will Oregon's politician's catch on early and take some steps toward sound fiscal and economic policies before the crash comes? Quite frankly, we doubt it. None of the state's leading politicians seem to get it.

POLITICS

Registered Voters

41% Democrats
36% Republicans
23% Other

Federal Officials: Recent Election and Group Ratings

			ACU	ADA	SBSC
U.S. Senators:	Ron Wyden (D)		10	92	25
	1998 Wyden (D)	61%			
	Lim (R)	34%			
	Gordon Smith (R)		72	15	85
	1996 Smith (D)	49%			
	Bruggere (D)	45%			
U.S. Representatives:	David Wu (D-1)		NA	NA	NA
	1998 Wu (D)	50%			
	Bordonaro (R)	47%			
	Greg Walden (R-2)		NA	NA	NA
	1998 Walden (R)	61%			
	Campbell (D)	35%			
	Earl Blumenauer (D-3)		4	89	15
	1998 Blumenauer (D)	84%			
	Knight (LBT)	9%			
	Peter DeFazio (D-4)		11	89	10
	1998 DeFazio (D)	70%			
	Webb (R)	29%			
	Darlene Hooley (D-5)		14	93	20
	1998 Hooley (D)	55%			
	Shannon (R)	41%			

Electoral Votes: 7

1996 Presidential Results:

Clinton	47%
Dole	39%
Perot	9%

State Officials

Governor 1998 Election:	John Kitzhaber (D)	64%
	Bill Sizemore (R)	30%
Attorney General:	Hardy Myers (D)	
State Senate:	12 Democrats	
	17 Republicans	
	1 Independent	
State House:	25 Democrats	
	34 Republicans	
	1 Independent	

TAXES AND SPENDING

Total Revenues

Oregon's per capita state and local total revenues registered $6,906 in 1996, ranking 5th in the nation and exceeding the U.S. average of $5,706 by 21%. From 1962 to 1996, real per capita state and local revenues increased by 311%, compared with an increase in the national average of 297%.

Taxes

Oregon's per capita state and local taxes registered $2,259 in 1996, ranking 32d in the nation and trailing the U.S. average of $2,597 by 13%. From 1962 to 1996, real per capita state and local taxes increased by 113%, compared with an increase of 152% in the U.S. average.

Property Taxes

Oregon's per capita state and local property taxes equaled $728 in 1996, ranking 26th in the nation and trailing the U.S. average of $789 by 8%. From 1962 to 1996, real per capita state and local property taxes increased by 44%, versus a 67% increase in the U.S. average.

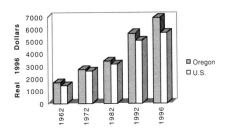

Real Per Capita State and Local Total Revenues: Oregon vs. U.S.

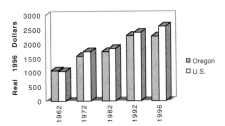

Real Per Capita State and Local Taxes: Oregon vs. U.S.

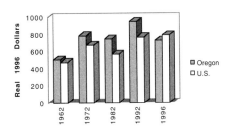

Real Per Capita State and Local Property Taxes: Oregon vs. U.S.

Sales and Gross Receipts Taxes

Oregon's per capita state and local sales and gross receipts taxes came in at $231 in 1996, ranking 51st in the nation and trailing the U.S. average of $939 by 75%. From 1962 to 1996, real per capita state and local sales and gross receipts taxes increased by 86%, versus an increase of 214% in the U.S. average.

Income Taxes

Oregon's per capita state and local income (individual and corporate) taxes registered $975 in 1996, ranking 8th in the nation and topping the U.S. average of $674 by 45%. From 1962 to 1996, real per capita state and local income taxes increased by 242%, versus a 567% increase in the U.S. average.

Personal Income Tax

A rate of 9.0%, ranking 47th in the nation (from lowest tax rate to highest), and comparing with the national average of 5.26%.

Capital Gains Tax

A rate of 9.0%, ranking 49th in the nation (from lowest tax rate to highest), and comparing with the national average of 4.68%.

Corporate Income Tax

A rate of 6.6%, ranking 22d in the nation (from lowest tax rate to highest), and comparing with the national average of 6.63%.

Total Expenditures

Oregon's per capita state and local total spending registered $5,761 in 1996, ranking 13th in the nation and exceeding the U.S. average of $5,268 by 9%. From 1962 to 1996, real per capita state and local total spending increased by 223%, versus an increase of 254% in the U.S. average.

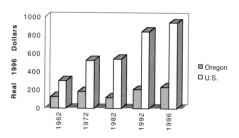

Real Per Capita Sales and Gross Receipts Taxes: Oregon vs. U.S.

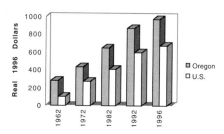

Real Per Capita State and Local Income Taxes: Oregon vs. U.S.

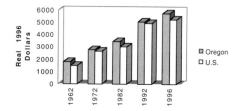

Real Per Capita State and Local Total Expenditures: Oregon vs. U.S.

Welfare Expenditures

Oregon's per capita state and local public welfare spending registered $664 in 1996, ranking 26th in the nation and trailing the U.S. average of $729 by 9%. From 1962 to 1996, real per capita state and local public welfare spending increased by 415%, compared with a 488% increase in the U.S. average.

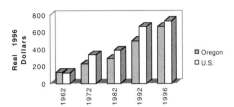

Real Per Capita State and Local Public Welfare Spending: Oregon vs. U.S.

Welfare Recipients (in thousands)

	1980	1989	3/99	Change 1989–99
Oreg.	94	87	45	−48%
U.S.	10,9 3	10,987	7,335	−33%

Interest on General Debt

Oregon's per capita state and local interest on general debt registered $193 in 1996, ranking 30th in the nation and trailing the U.S. average of $222 by 13%. From 1962 to 1996, real per capita state and local interest on general debt increased by 371%, versus an increase of 335% in the U.S. average. From 1992 to 1996, Oregon's real per capita interest on debt fell by 47%.

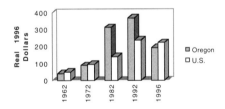

Real Per Capita State and Local Interest on General Debt: Oregon vs. U.S.

Total Debt Outstanding

Oregon's per capita state and local debt registered $3,886 in 1996, ranking 26th in the nation and lagging behind the U.S. average of $4,409 by 12%. From 1962 to 1996, real per capita state and local debt outstanding increased by 103%, versus an increase of 120% in the U.S. average. From 1982 to 1996, Oregon's real per capita debt fell by 25%.

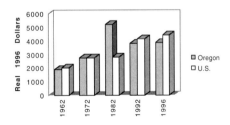

Real Per Capita State and Local Debt Outstanding: Oregon vs. U.S.

Government Employees

Oregon's state and local government
employees (full-time equivalent, or FTE) per
10,000 population registered 529.5 in 1997,
ranking 29th in the nation and running just
behind the U.S. average of 531.1 by 0.3%.
From 1962 to 1996, state and local FTE
employees per 10,000 population increased by
36%, compared with an increase in the U.S.
average of 66%.

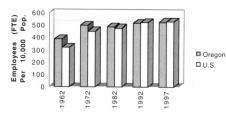

State and Local Government
Employees (FTE) Per 10,000
Population: Oregon vs. U.S.

Per Capita Federal Government Expenditures, 1998

	1998	Ranking
Oreg.	$4,607	43d
U.S.	$5,491	

Per capita federal spending in Oregon trailed the national average by 16%.

EDUCATION

Total Education Spending

Oregon's per capita state and local education
spending registered $1,653 in 1996, ranking
14th in the nation and topping the U.S.
average of $1,503 by 10%. From 1962 to 1996,
real per capita total education spending
increased by 131%, versus an increase in the
U.S. average of 173%.

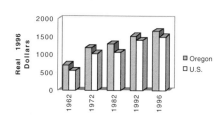

Real Per Capita State and
Local Education Spending:
Oregon vs. U.S.

Per Pupil Spending

Oregon's per pupil public school spending
registered $6,435 in 1998, ranking 14th in the
nation and exceeding the U.S. average of
$6,131 by 5%. From 1970 to 1998, Oregon's
real per pupil public school spending increased
by 106%, compared with a 120% increase in
the U.S. average.

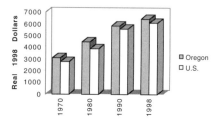

Real Per Pupil Public School
Spending: Oregon vs. U.S.

Average Public School Teacher Salaries (in 1997–98 dollars)

	1970	1980	1990	1998	1998 Ranking
Oreg.	37,756	33,889	39,284	42,150	13th
U.S.	36,934	33,272	39,956	39,385	

In 1998, the average public school teacher salary in Oregon exceeded the U.S. average by 7%. From 1970 to 1998, the real average teacher salary in Oregon increased by 12%, versus an increase in the U.S. average of 7%.

Pupil/Teacher Ratio, Fall 1996

	Ratio	Rank
Oreg.	20.1	48th
U.S.	17.1	

Teachers/Staff, Fall 1996

	Percent	Rank
Oreg.	51.2	37th
U.S.	52.1	

Public School 4th-Grade Reading Proficiency, 1998

	Average	Rank (out of 40 states)
Oreg.	214	25th
U.S.	215	

Public School 8th-Grade Reading Proficiency, 1998

	Average	Rank (out of 37 states)
Oreg.	266	7th
U.S.	261	

Public School 4th-Grade Math Proficiency, 1996

	Average	Rank (out of 44 states)
Oreg.	223	22d
U.S.	224	

Public School 8th-Grade Math Proficiency, 1996

	Average	Rank (out of 41 states)
Oreg.	276	14th
U.S.	271	

Public School 8th-Grade Science Proficiency, 1996

	Average	Rank (out of 41 states)
Oreg.	155	12th
U.S.	148	

Average Math SAT Scores

	1972	1982	1992	1998	Percentage Taking SAT in 1998
Oreg.	508	499	510	528	53
U.S.	509	493	501	512	43

Average Verbal SAT Scores

	1972	1982	1992	1998	Percentage Taking SAT in 1998
Oreg.	532	513	516	528	53
U.S.	530	504	500	505	43

Expenditures by Public Institutions of Higher Education Per Full-Time-Equivalent Student, 1996

	FTE Student Spending	Rank
Oreg.	$13,928	9th
U.S.	$12,343	

Per-FTE-student spending in public institutions of higher education exceeded the U.S. average by 13%.

Per Full-Time-Equivalent Student Revenues from Federal, State, and Local Governments for Public Institutions of Higher Education, 1996

	FTE Student Government Revenues	Rank
Oreg.	$8,595	11th
U.S.	$8,101	

Per-FTE-student-government revenues in public institutions of higher education outpaced the U.S. average by 6%.

Average Salary for Full-Time Professors at Public Universities, 1997

	Average	Rank
Oreg.	$60,405	43d
U.S.	$72,599	

The average full-time public university professor salary trailed the U.S. average by 17%.

ECONOMY AND BUSINESS

Economic Growth

Over the period of 1977 to 1997, Oregon's real gross state product (GSP) grew by 91.8%—ranking 14th in the nation—as compared with real U.S. gross domestic product (GDP), expanding by 70.1%.

At $98.4 billion in 1997, Oregon's GSP ranked as 27th largest in the nation.

From 1993 to 1997, Oregon's annual real GSP growth averaged 7.39%—ranking best in the nation—as compared with annual real U.S. GDP growth, averaging 3.08%.

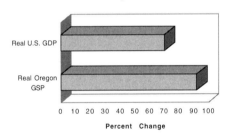

Real Economic Growth 1977-1997: Oregon vs. U.S.

Real U.S. GDP

Real Oregon GSP

0 10 20 30 40 50 60 70 80 90 100

Percent Change

Job Growth

	Growth in Employee Payrolls (Nonagricultural) 1962–98	Ranking
Oreg.	194.3%	14th
U.S.	126.5%	

Average Annual Growth in Employee Payrolls (Nonagricultural) 1993–98	Ranking
Oreg.	4.18%	9th
U.S.	2.98%	

Per Capita Disposable Income, 1997

	1997	Ranking
Oreg.	$20,160	29th
U.S.	$21,607	

Per capita disposable income exceeded the U.S. average by 7%.

	Real Growth 1962–97	Ranking
Oreg.	102.3%	40th
U.S.	116.7%	

	Average Annual Real Growth 1993–97	Ranking
Oreg.	2.45%	2d
U.S.	1.48%	

Number of Businesses

	1997	Percent with Fewer than 500 Employees
Businesses with Employees	97,147	97.8
Self-employed Individuals	175,000	

New Business Incorporations

	1980	1986	1992	1997
Oreg.	6,621	7,279	8,861	9,289

Percentage Change in Annual New Business Incorporations, 1980 vs. 1997

	Percent	Ranking
Oreg.	40.3	27th
U.S.	49.7	

State Merchandise Exports to the World, 1998 (in millions of dollars)

	1998	Rank
Oreg.	$8,144	22d

Small Business Survival Index, 1999

Oregon ranks a pathetic 46th in terms of its policy environment for entrepreneurship.

Fortune 500 Headquarters in 1999

A total of 4 (ranked 26th)

Labor Union Membership, 1983 vs. 1997

	Percentage of Workers		
	1983	1997	1997 Rank
Oreg.	22.3	17.6	13th
U.S.	20.1	14.1	

Homeownership Rate, 1998

	Rate	Rank
Oreg.	63.4	42d
U.S.	66.3	

CRIME

Crime Rates Per 100 Residents (rankings from best to worst crime rate)

Total Crime	1960	1970	1980	1990	1998	1998 Ranking
Oreg.	0.92	2.99	6.69	5.65	5.65	44th
U.S.	1.04	2.74	5.90	5.82	4.62	

From 1960 to 1998, Oregon's crime rate increased by 504%, versus a U.S. increase of 344%. From 1990 to 1998, Oregon's crime rate remained steady, versus a U.S. decrease of 21%.

Violent Crime	1960	1970	1980	1990	1998	1998 Ranking
Oreg.	0.07	0.26	0.49	0.51	0.42	23d
U.S.	0.14	0.36	0.58	0.73	0.57	

From 1960 to 1998, Oregon's violent crime rate increased by 500%, versus a U.S. increase of 307%. From 1990 to 1998, Oregon's violent crime rate decreased by 18%, compared with a national decline of 22%.

Property Crime	1960	1970	1980	1990	1998	1998 Ranking
Oreg.	0.85	2.73	6.20	5.14	5.23	45th
U.S.	0.90	2.38	5.32	5.09	4.05	

From 1960 to 1998, Oregon's property crime rate increased by 515%, versus a national increase of 350%. From 1990 to 1998, Oregon's property crime rate increased by 2%, compared with a national decline of 20%.

Real Per Capita Police Protection Spending (in real 1996 dollars)

	1962	1972	1982	1992	1996	1996 Ranking
Oreg.	51	88	116	133	166	15th
U.S.	51	95	114	148	168	

In 1996, per capita state and local police protection spending in Oregon trailed the U.S. average by 1%. From 1962 to 1996, real per capita state and local police protection spending increased by 225%, versus an increase of 229% in the U.S. average.

Prisoners in State and Federal Prisons Per 1,000 Population

	1980	1990	1996	1996 Ranking
Oreg.	1.21	2.28	2.71	38th
U.S.	1.46	3.11	4.45	

From 1980 to 1996, prisoners per 1,000 population increased by 124%, versus a U.S. increase of 205%.

HEALTH CARE

Health-Care Spending

Oregon's per capita state and local health-care spending registered $168 in 1996, ranking 16th in the nation and topping the U.S. average of $151 by 11%. From 1962 to 1996, Oregon's real per capita state and local health-care spending increased by 457%, versus an increase of 739% in the U.S. average.

Real Per Capita State and Local Health Care Spending: Oregon vs. U.S.

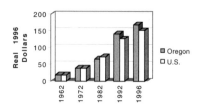

Hospital Spending

Oregon's per capita state and local hospital spending registered $224 in 1996, ranking 27th in the nation and lagging behind the U.S. average of $266 by 16%. From 1962 to 1996, Oregon's real per capita state and local hospital spending increased by 187%, as opposed to an increase of 189% in the U.S. average.

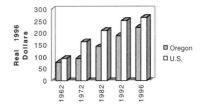

Real Per Capita State and Local Hospital Spending: Oregon vs. U.S.

Medicaid, 1997

	Spending Per Recipient	Ranking
Oreg.	$2,778	44th
U.S.	$3,681	

Oregon's per-recipient Medicaid spending trailed the U.S. average by 25%.

ENVIRONMENT

Parks and Recreation Spending

Oregon's per capita state and local parks and recreation spending registered $80 in 1996, ranking 19th in the nation and outpacing the U.S. average of $72 by 11%. From 1962 to 1996, real per capita state and local parks and recreation spending increased by 344%, versus a 213% increase in the U.S. average.

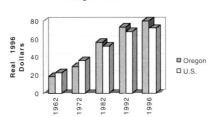

Real Per Capita State and Local Parks and Recreation Spending: Oregon vs. U.S.

State and Local Natural Resources Spending, 1996

	Per Capita	Ranking
Oreg.	$86	12th
U.S.	$60	

Per capita state and local natural resources spending in Oregon exceeded the U.S. average by 43%.

State Parks Revenues as a Share of Operating Expenses, 1997

	Percent	Rank
Oreg.	42	23d
U.S.	42	

Percentage of Land Owned by the Federal Government, 1996

	Percent	Rank
Oreg.	51.6	4th
U.S.	24.8	

SOCIETY AND DEMOGRAPHICS

Population

Oregon's 1998 population of 3.282 million ranked 28th in the nation.

Population Growth, 1990–98

	Percentage Change in Population	Ranking
Oreg.	15.48	9th
U.S.	8.66	

	Net International Migration	Ranking
Oreg.	58,050	16th

	Net Domestic Migration	Ranking
Oreg.	259,512	10th

Infant Mortality Rate, 1998

	Percent	Rank
Oreg.	5.9	38th
U.S.	6.4	

Percentage of Births of Low Birthweight, 1997

	Percent	Rank
Oreg.	5.5	50th
U.S.	7.5	

Oregon Population

Percentage of Live Births to Unmarried Women, 1997

	Percent	Rank
Oreg.	28.8	35th
U.S.	32.4	

Abortion Rate—Abortions Per 1,000 Women Ages 15–44, 1995

	Rate	Rank
Oreg.	22.6	14th
U.S.	22.9	

LIFESTYLE

Percentage of Households with Computers, 1998

	Percent	Rank
Oreg.	51.3	6th

Percentage of Households with Internet Access, 1998

	Percent	Rank
Oreg.	32.7	6th

State Arts Agency Spending, 1999

	Per Capita	Rank
Oreg.	$0.38	48th
U.S.	$1.35	

Per capita state arts spending in 1999 trailed the U.S. average by 72%.

Major League Sports Facilities

Year Opened/ Refurb.	Stadium/ Arena	Home Team	Millions of Nominal Dollars		Millions of Real 1997 Dollars	
			Estimated Total Cost	Estimated Taxpayer Cost	Estimated Total Cost	Estimated Taxpayer Cost
1995	Rose Garden	Trail Blazers (NBA) 1995–present	$262.0	$35.0	$275.8	$36.8

PENNSYLVANIA

If you love American history, then you have to love Pennsylvania.

Visit Philadelphia, for example, and walk where Jefferson, Madison, and Franklin walked. The city truly is the "Birthplace of Democracy," with the Declaration of Independence signed and the U.S. Constitution hammered out in Philadelphia. Of course, Philadelphia also served as our nation's capital from 1790 to 1800. Step in the doors of Independence Hall and be truly humbled.

Head west from Philadelphia, and stop at Gettysburg. Once again, Pennsylvania offers hallowed ground, with Gettysburg witnessing probably the most critical battle of the Civil War, giving birth to President Lincoln's "Gettysburg Address," and leading to the end of slavery and the salvation of the Union.

The state offers many other sites of historic significance, including Pittsburgh, one of the engines of the Industrial Revolution and the birthplace of Andrew Mellon, one of the nation's finest secretaries of the Treasury. Mellon's tax policies in the 1920s played a major role in sparking the economy and allowing the nation to recover from the many ravages of World War I.

Does Pennsylvania today stand up well to its storied past of upholding freedom and liberty? The numbers offer a very mixed verdict. For example, a majority of state and local government taxing, spending, and debt levels rose at a faster rate than the corresponding levels of the nation as a whole from the early 1960s into the late 1990s.

Pennsylvania also imposes the highest corporate income tax among the states. In fiscal year 2000, Governor Tom Ridge (R) and the state legislature pushed through some small business tax cuts. Most important was eliminating a restriction that prevented corporations already possessing S-corporation status at the federal level from being S-corporations under Pennsylvania law. Corporations now able to make the switch will see their tax rate plummet, since S-corporations are taxed under the personal income tax, which is far lower than the corporate rate in Pennsylvania. In addition, the state ranks 51st in the nation in terms of the number of state and local government employees as a share of population.

However, while the state personal income tax is low, Philadelphia and Pittsburgh pile on their own city income levies. Philadelphia's is particularly egregious, with the city imposing a 3.34% resident income tax and a 4.21% tax on nonresidents, while the Philadelphia School District imposes a 4.79% tax on residents' investment and nonbusiness incomes. In Pittsburgh, the city inflicts a 1% income tax on individuals, and the school district chimes in with another 1.875% tax. Not surprisingly, a Deloitte & Touche report, cited in the *Seattle Times* (August 8, 1999), estimated that Philadelphia and Pittsburgh ranked first and fourth heaviest among major U.S. cities in terms of their tax burdens on small business.

Meanwhile, the Keystone State's economy has performed quite poorly in recent times. Real economic growth and job creation have badly lagged behind those of the nation. Per capita disposable income comes in above the U.S. average, but its inflation-adjusted growth has been about average.

Overall population growth has stagnated since 1970, and from 1990 to 1998 Pennsylvania was the sixth largest net exporter of residents to other states.

Thankfully, the state's crime rate is fairly low, particularly for property crime.

While Pittsburgh and Philadelphia rank sixth and seventh, respectively, in terms of the number of Fortune 500 headquarters (Pennsylvania is fifth overall among the states), some serious policy changes will be needed if the state and its key cities are going to attract the start-ups and entrepreneurs that will build the Fortune 500 companies of tomorrow.

Building on the 1999 tax cut is vital. Philadelphia and Pittsburgh need to concentrate on the elimination of their city-based income taxes. Most of the large cities in America instituting a significant city income tax have suffered economically for such a choice, including Baltimore; Washington, D.C.; Detroit; New York; San Francisco; and St. Louis.

Indeed, eliminating city income taxes in Philadelphia and Pittsburgh alone would make an important contribution to economic and political history and set an exciting precedent at the dawn of the 21st century. If these cities could kill an egregious tax, then so could others. Philadelphia led the way to freedom once before . . . maybe it could again.

POLITICS

Registered Voters

49% Democrats
43% Republicans
8% Other

Federal Officials: Recent Election and Group Ratings

			ACU	ADA	SBSC
U.S. Senators:	Arlen Specter (R)		37	57	45
	1998 Specter (R)	61%			
	Lloyd (D)	35%			
	Rick Santorum (R)		83	9	90
	1994 Santorum (R)	49%			
	Wofford (D)	47%			
U.S. Representatives:	Robert Brady (D-1)		0	NA	9
	1998 Brady (D)	81%			
	Harrison (R)	17%			
	Chaka Fattah (D-2)		1	96	10
	1998 Fattah (D)	87%			
	Mulligan (R)	13%			

			ACU	ADA	SBSC
Robert Borski (D-3)			13	77	15
1998	Borski (D)	59%			
	Dougherty (R)	41%			
Ron Klink (D-4)			27	67	25
1998	Klink (D)	64%			
	Turzai (R)	36%			
John Peterson (R-5)			96	3	95
1998	Peterson (R)	85%			
	Belitskus (G)	15%			
Tim Holden (D-6)			43	26	15
1998	Holden (D)	61%			
	Meckley (R)	39%			
Curt Weldon (R-7)			67	NA	60
1998	Weldon (R)	72%			
	D'Urso (D)	28%			
Jim Greenwood (R-8)			61	28	65
1998	Greenwood (R)	63%			
	Tuthill (D)	33%			
Bud Shuster (R-9)			93	7	90
1998	Shuster (R)	NO			
Don Sherwood (R-10)			NA	NA	NA
1998	Sherwood (R)	49%			
	Casey (D)	48%			
Paul Kanjorski (D-11)			21	71	10
1998	Kanjorski (D)	67%			
	Urban (R)	33%			
John Murtha (D-12)			35	45	25
1998	Murtha (D)	68%			
	Holloway (R)	32%			
Joe Hoeffel (D-13)			NA	NA	NA
1998	Hoeffel (D)	52%			
	Fox (R)	47%			
William Coyne (D-14)			3	95	15
1998	Coyne (D)	61%			
	Ravotti (R)	38%			
Pat Toomey (R-15)			NA	NA	NA
1998	Toomey (R)	55%			
	Afflerbach (D)	45%			

			ACU	ADA	SBSC
Joseph Pitts (R-16)			96	3	95
1998	Pitts (R)	71%			
	Yorczyk (D)	29%			
George Gekas (R-17)			85	10	85
1998	Gekas (R)	NO			
Mike Doyle (D-18)			33	69	15
1998	Doyle (D)	68%			
	Walker (R)	32%			
William Goodling (R-19)			76	17	85
1998	Goodling (R)	68%			
	Ropp (D)	29%			
Frank Mascara (D-20)			31	73	15
1998	Mascara (D)	NO			
Phil English (R-21)			75	22	80
1998	English (R)	63%			
	Klemens (D)	37%			

Electoral Votes:	23	
1996 Presidential Results:	Clinton	49%
	Dole	40%
	Perot	10%

State Officials

Governor 1998 Election:	Tom Ridge (R)	57%
	Ivan Itkin (D)	31%
Lt. Governor:	Mark Schweiker (R)	
Attorney General:	Mike Fisher (R)	
State Senate:	20 Democrats	
	30 Republicans	
State House:	100 Democrats	
	103 Republicans	

TAXES AND SPENDING

Total Revenues

Pennsylvania's per capita state and local total revenues registered $5,345 in 1996, ranking 24th in the nation and trailing the U.S. average of $5,706 by 6%. From 1962 to 1996, real per capita state and local revenues increased by 328%, compared with an increase in the national average of 297%.

Taxes

Pennsylvania's per capita state and local taxes registered $2,512 in 1996, ranking 21st in the nation and trailing the U.S. average of $2,597 by 3%. From 1962 to 1996, real per capita state and local taxes increased by 167%, compared with an increase of 152% in the U.S. average.

Property Taxes

Pennsylvania's per capita state and local property taxes equaled $721 in 1996, ranking 28th in the nation and trailing the U.S. average of $789 by 9%. From 1962 to 1996, real per capita state and local property taxes increased by 121%, versus a 67% increase in the U.S. average.

Sales and Gross Receipts Taxes

Pennsylvania's per capita state and local sales and gross receipts taxes came in at $750 in 1996, ranking 39th in the nation and trailing the U.S. average of $939 by 20%. From 1962 to 1996, real per capita state and local sales and gross receipts taxes increased by 121%, versus an increase of 214% in the U.S. average.

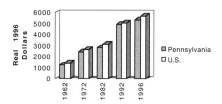

Real Per Capita State and Local Total Revenues: Pennsylvania vs. U.S.

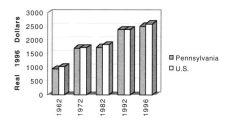

Real Per Capita State and Local Taxes: Pennsylvania vs. U.S.

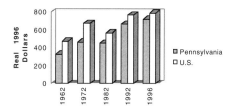

Real Per Capita State and Local Property Taxes: Pennsylvania vs. U.S.

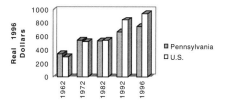

Real Per Capita State and Local Sales and Gross Receipts Taxes: Pennsylvania vs. U.S.

Income Taxes

Pennsylvania's per capita state and local income (individual and corporate) taxes registered $734 in 1996, ranking 17th in the nation and topping the U.S. average of $674 by 9%. From 1962 to 1996, real per capita state and local income taxes increased by 1,123%, versus a 567% increase in the U.S. average.

Personal Income Tax

A rate of 2.8%, ranking 10th in the nation (from lowest tax rate to highest), and comparing with the national average of 5.26%.

Capital Gains Tax

A rate of 2.8%, ranking 13th in the nation (from lowest tax rate to highest), and comparing with the national average of 4.68%.

Corporate Income Tax

A rate of 9.999%, ranking last in the nation (from lowest tax rate to highest), and comparing with the national average of 6.63%.

Total Expenditures

Pennsylvania's per capita state and local total spending registered $5,006 in 1996, ranking 21st in the nation and trailing the U.S. average of $5,268 by 5%. From 1962 to 1996, real per capita state and local total spending increased by 289%, versus an increase of 254% in the U.S. average.

Welfare Expenditures

Pennsylvania's per capita state and local public welfare spending registered $818 in 1996, ranking 13th in the nation and outpacing the U.S. average of $729 by 12%. From 1962 to 1996, real per capita state and local public welfare spending increased by 644%, compared with a 488% increase in the U.S. average.

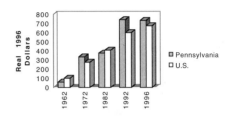

Real Per Capita State and Local Income Taxes: Pennsylvania vs. U.S.

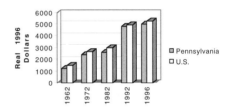

Real Per Capita State and Local Total Expenditures: Pennsylvania vs. U.S.

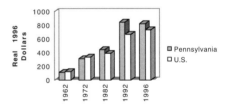

Real Per Capita State and Local Public Welfare Spending: Pennsylvania vs. U.S.

Welfare Recipients (in thousands)

	1980	1989	3/99	Change 1989–99
Pa.	637	508	312	−39%
U.S.	10,923	10,987	7,335	−33%

Interest on General Debt

Pennsylvania's per capita state and local interest on general debt registered $274 in 1996, ranking 14th in the nation and exceeding the U.S. average of $222 by 23%. From 1962 to 1996, real per capita state and local interest on general debt increased by 398%, versus an increase of 335% in the U.S. average.

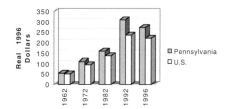

Real Per Capita State and Local Interest on General Debt: Pennsylvania vs. U.S.

Total Debt Outstanding

Pennsylvania's per capita state and local debt registered $4,852 in 1996, ranking 16th in the nation and exceeding the U.S. average of $4,409 by 10%. From 1962 to 1996, real per capita state and local debt outstanding increased by 143%, versus an increase of 120% in the U.S. average.

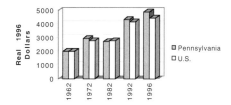

Real Per Capita State and Local Debt Outstanding: Pennsylvania vs. U.S.

Government Employees

Pennsylvania's state and local government employees (full-time equivalent, or FTE) per 10,000 population registered 429.2 in 1997, ranking 51st in the nation and lagging behind the U.S. average of 531.1 by 19%. From 1962 to 1996, state and local FTE employees per 10,000 population increased by 59%, compared with an increase in the U.S. average of 66%.

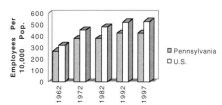

State and Local Government Employees (FTE) Per 10,000 Population: Pennsylvania vs. U.S.

Per Capita Federal Government Expenditures, 1998

	1998	Ranking
Pa.	$5,612	20th
U.S.	$5,491	

Per capita federal spending in Pennsylvania topped the national average by 2%.

EDUCATION

Total Education Spending

Pennsylvania's per capita state and local education spending registered $1,495 in 1996, ranking 27th in the nation and trailing the U.S. average of $1,503 by 1%. From 1962 to 1996, real per capita total education spending increased by 207%, versus an increase in the U.S. average of 173%.

Real Per Capita State and Local Education Spending: Pennsylvania vs. U.S.

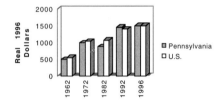

Per Pupil Spending

Pennsylvania's per pupil public school spending registered $7,669 in 1998, ranking 7th in the nation and exceeding the U.S. average of $6,131 by 25%. From 1970 to 1998, Pennsylvania's real per pupil public school spending increased by 154%, compared with a 120% increase in the U.S. average.

Real Per Pupil Public School Spending: Pennsylvania vs. U.S.

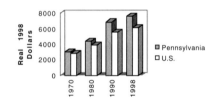

Average Public School Teacher Salaries (in 1997–98 dollars)

	1970	1980	1990	1998	1998 Ranking
Pa.	37,927	34,408	42,466	47,650	6th
U.S.	36,934	33,272	39,956	39,385	

In 1998, the average public school teacher salary in Pennsylvania exceeded the U.S. average by 21%. From 1970 to 1998, the real average teacher salary in Pennsylvania increased by 26%, versus an increase in the U.S. average of 7%.

Pupil/Teacher Ratio, Fall 1996

	Ratio	Rank
Pa.	17.0	31st
U.S.	17.1	

Teachers/Staff, Fall 1996

	Percent	Rank
Pa.	52.9	26th
U.S.	52.1	

Public School 4th-Grade Math Proficiency, 1996

	Average	Rank (out of 44 states)
Pa.	226	14th
U.S.	224	

Average Math SAT Scores

	1972	1982	1992	1998	Percentage Taking SAT in 1998
Pa.	504	489	487	495	71
U.S.	509	493	501	512	43

Average Verbal SAT Scores

	1972	1982	1992	1998	Percentage Taking SAT in 1998
Pa.	526	503	495	497	71
U.S.	530	504	500	505	43

Expenditures by Public Institutions of Higher Education Per Full-Time-Equivalent Student, 1996

	FTE Student Spending	Rank
Pa.	$13,698	12th
U.S.	$12,343	

Per-FTE-student spending in public institutions of higher education topped the U.S. average by 11%.

Per Full-Time-Equivalent Student Revenues from Federal, State, and Local Governments for Public Institutions of Higher Education, 1996

	FTE Student Government Revenues	Rank
Pa.	$6,995	38th
U.S.	$8,101	

Per-FTE-student-government revenues in public institutions of higher education trailed the U.S. average by 14%.

Average Salary for Full-Time Professors at Public Universities, 1997

	Average	Rank
Pa.	$81,139	5th
U.S.	$72,599	

The average full-time public university professor salary exceeded the U.S. average by 12%.

ECONOMY AND BUSINESS

Economic Growth

Over the period of 1977 to 1997, Pennsylvania's real gross state product (GSP) grew by 44.2%—ranking 44th in the nation—as compared with real U.S. gross domestic product (GDP), expanding by 70.1%.

At $339.9 billion in 1997, Pennsylvania's GSP ranked as 6th largest in the nation.

From 1993 to 1997, Pennsylvania's annual real GSP growth averaged 2.49%—ranking 42d in the nation—as compared with annual real U.S. GDP growth, averaging 3.08%.

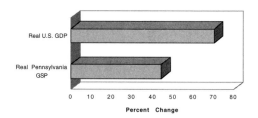

Real Economic Growth 1977-1997: Pennsylvania vs. U.S.

Job Growth

	Growth in Employee Payrolls (Nonagricultural) 1962–98	Ranking
Pa.	48.7%	49th
U.S.	126.5%	

	Average Annual Growth in Employee Payrolls (Nonagricultural) 1993–98	Ranking
Pa.	1.60%	46th
U.S.	2.98%	

Per Capita Disposable Income, 1997

	1997	Ranking
Pa.	$22,033	17th
U.S.	$21,607	

Per capita disposable income exceeded the U.S. average by 2%.

	Real Growth 1962–97	Ranking
Pa.	121.9%	24th
U.S.	116.7%	

	Average Annual Real Growth 1993–97	Ranking
Pa.	1.53%	31st
U.S.	1.48%	

Number of Businesses

	1997	Percent with Fewer than 500 Employees
Businesses with Employees	238,308	98.5
Self-employed Individuals	440,000	

New Business Incorporations

	1980	1986	1992	1997
Pa.	14,882	20,212	16,947	20,900

Percentage Change in Annual New Business Incorporations, 1980 vs. 1997

	Percent	Ranking
Pa.	40.4	26th
U.S.	49.7	

State Merchandise Exports to the World, 1998 (in millions of dollars)

	1998	Rank
Pa.	$19,139	10th

Small Business Survival Index, 1999

Pennsylvania ranks a very respectable 14th in terms of its policy environment for entrepreneurship.

Fortune 500 Headquarters in 1999

A total of 27 (ranked 5th); Pittsburgh ranked 6th among U.S. cities with 9 headquarters, and Philadelphia ranked 9th with 7 headquarters

Labor Union Membership, 1983 vs. 1997

| | Percentage of Workers | | |
	1983	1997	1997 Rank
Pa.	27.5	17.1	14th
U.S.	20.1	14.1	

Homeownership Rate, 1998

	Rate	Rank
Pa.	73.9	8th
U.S.	66.3	

CRIME

Crime Rates Per 100 Residents (rankings from best to worst crime rate)

Total Crime	1960	1970	1980	1990	1998	1998 Ranking
Pa.	0.75	1.54	3.74	3.48	3.27	8th
U.S.	1.04	2.74	5.90	5.82	4.62	

From 1960 to 1998, Pennsylvania's crime rate increased by 336%, versus a U.S. increase of 344%. From 1990 to 1998, Pennsylvania's crime rate dropped by 6%, versus a U.S. decrease of 21%.

Violent Crime	1960	1970	1980	1990	1998	1998 Ranking
Pa.	0.09	0.21	0.36	0.43	0.42	23d
U.S.	0.14	0.36	0.58	0.73	0.57	

From 1960 to 1998, Pennsylvania's violent crime rate increased by 367%, versus a U.S. increase of 307%. From 1990 to 1998, Pennsylvania's violent crime rate decreased by 2%, compared with a national decline of 22%.

Property Crime	1960	1970	1980	1990	1998	1998 Ranking
Pa.	0.65	1.33	3.37	3.05	2.85	7th
U.S.	0.90	2.38	5.32	5.09	4.05	

From 1960 to 1998, Pennsylvania's property crime rate increased by 338%, versus a national increase of 350%. From 1990 to 1998, Pennsylvania's property crime rate decreased by 7%, compared with a national decline of 20%.

Real Per Capita Police Protection Spending (in real 1996 dollars)

	1962	1972	1982	1992	1996	1996 Ranking
Pa.	51	85	92	113	144	25th
U.S.	51	95	114	148	168	

In 1996, per capita state and local police protection spending in Pennsylvania trailed the U.S. average by 14%. From 1962 to 1996, real per capita state and local police protection spending increased by 182%, versus an increase of 229% in the U.S. average.

Prisoners in State and Federal Prisons Per 1,000 Population

	1980	1990	1996	1996 Ranking
Pa.	0.69	1.88	2.87	35th
U.S.	1.46	3.11	4.45	

From 1980 to 1996, prisoners per 1,000 population increased by 316%, versus a U.S. increase of 205%.

HEALTH CARE

Health-Care Spending

Pennsylvania's per capita state and local health-care spending registered $129 in 1996, ranking 28th in the nation and lagging behind the U.S. average of $151 by 15%. From 1962 to 1996, Pennsylvania's real per capita state and local health-care spending increased by 821%, versus an increase of 739% in the U.S. average.

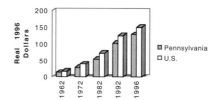

Real Per Capita State and Local Health Care Spending: Pennsylvania vs. U.S.

Hospital Spending

Pennsylvania's per capita state and local hospital spending registered $138 in 1996, ranking 40th in the nation and trailing the U.S. average of $266 by 48%. From 1962 to 1996, Pennsylvania's real per capita state and local hospital spending increased by 100%, as opposed to an increase of 189% in the U.S. average.

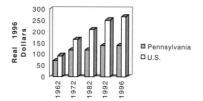

Real Per Capita State and Local Hospital Spending: Pennsylvania vs. U.S.

Medicaid, 1997

	Per Recipient	Ranking
Pa.	$4,575	14th
U.S.	$3,681	

Pennsylvania's per-recipient Medicaid spending exceeded the U.S. average by 24%.

ENVIRONMENT

Parks and Recreation Spending

Pennsylvania's per capita state and local parks and recreation spending registered $40 in 1996, ranking 44th in the nation and trailing the U.S. average of $72 by 44%. From 1962 to 1996, real per capita state and local parks and recreation spending increased by 122%, versus a 213% increase in the U.S. average.

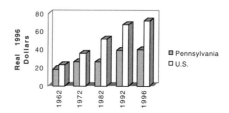

Real Per Capita State and Local Parks and Recreation Spending: Pennsylvania vs. U.S.

State and Local Natural Resources Spending, 1996

	Per Capita	Ranking
Pa.	$37	40th
U.S.	$60	

Per capita state and local natural resources spending in Pennsylvania trailed the U.S. average by 38%.

State Parks Revenues as a Share of Operating Expenses, 1997

	Percent	Rank
Pa.	20	45th
U.S.	42	

Percentage of Land Owned by the Federal Government, 1996

	Percent	Rank
Pa.	2.2	36th
U.S.	24.8	

SOCIETY AND DEMOGRAPHICS

Population

Pennsylvania's 1998 population of 12.001 million ranked 6th in the nation.

Population Growth, 1990–98

	Percentage Change in Population	Ranking
Pa.	0.99	47th
U.S.	8.66	

	Net International Migration	Ranking
Pa.	104,126	11th

	Net Domestic Migration	Ranking
Pa.	−219,072	46th

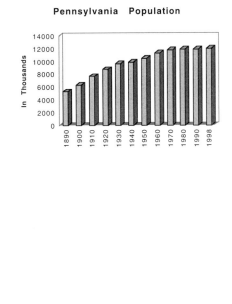

Pennsylvania Population

Infant Mortality Rate, 1998

	Percent	Rank
Pa.	6.6	31st
U.S.	6.4	

Percentage of Births of Low Birthweight, 1997

	Percent	Rank
Pa.	7.6	26th
U.S.	7.5	

Percentage of Live Births to Unmarried Women, 1997

	Percent	Rank
Pa.	32.8	21st
U.S.	32.4	

Abortion Rate—Abortions Per 1,000 Women Ages 15–44, 1995

	Rate	Rank
Pa.	15.5	27th
U.S.	22.9	

LIFESTYLE

Percentage of Households with Computers, 1998

	Percent	Rank
Pa.	39.3	39th

Percentage of Households with Internet Access, 1998

	Percent	Rank
Pa.	24.9	29th

State Arts Agency Spending, 1999

	Per Capita	Rank
Pa.	$0.88	24th
U.S.	$1.35	

Per capita state arts spending in 1999 trailed the U.S. average by 35%.

Major League Sports Facilities

Year Opened/ Refurb.	Stadium/ Arena	Home Team	Millions of Nominal Dollars		Millions of Real 1997 Dollars	
			Estimated Total Cost	Estimated Taxpayer Cost	Estimated Total Cost	Estimated Taxpayer Cost
1887	Baker Bowl	Phillies (MLB) 1895–1938 Eagles (NFL) 1933–35	$0.1	$0.0	$1.8	$0.0
1909	Shibe Park	A's (MLB) 1909–54 Phillies (MLB) 1938–70 Eagles (NFL) 1940, 1942, 1944–57	$0.3	$0.0	$5.6	$0.0
1909	Forbes Field	Pirates (MLB) 1909–70 Steelers (NFL) 1933–63	$2.0	$0.0	$35.7	$0.0
1961	Civic Arena	Penguins (NHL) 1967–present	$22.0	$22.0	$118.3	$118.3
1997 1967	Civic Arena (re) The Spectrum/ CoreStates	Flyers (NHL) 1967–96 76ers (NBA) 1967–96	$13.0 $12.0	$13.0 $0.0	$13.0 $58.0	$13.0 $0.0
1970	Three Rivers Stadium	Pirates (MLB) 1970–present Steelers (NFL) 1970–present	$55.0	$55.0	$227.3	$227.3

Year Opened/ Refurb.	Stadium/ Arena	Home Team	Millions of Nominal Dollars		Millions of Real 1997 Dollars	
			Estimated Total Cost	Estimated Taxpayer Cost	Estimated Total Cost	Estimated Taxpayer Cost
1971	Veterans Stadium	Phillies (MLB) 1971–present Eagles (NFL) 1971–present	$49.5	$49.5	$196.4	$196.4
1996	First Union Center	Flyers (NHL) 1996–present 76ers (NBA) 1996–present	$217.5	$32.0	$222.4	$32.7

RHODE ISLAND

A few years ago, one of us traveled to Rhode Island several times on a research project. In addition to touring a couple of the "summer cottages" in Newport—built before income and inheritance taxes—this co-author had lunch with Don Bousquet, one of the state's leading newspaper/political cartoonists, who graciously signed one of his books entitled *The Quahog Stops Here*. It is an amusing collection of cartoons about life in Rhode Island, though it probably helps to be a Rhode Islander to get all the jokes. What a quahog actually is also remained a mystery until *Webster's* later revealed it to be "an edible clam . . . having a very hard, solid shell."

The quahog turns out to be a fitting mascot for Rhode Island. To remain in the Ocean State, a very hard shell indeed is required. Apparently, though, many are too soft, as Rhode Island ranked dead last among the 50 states (excluding the District of Columbia) in terms of population growth between 1990 and 1998. In fact, Rhode Island actually lost population—with only Washington, D.C., Connecticut, and North Dakota also credited with such a dubious accomplishment. Over the same period, net domestic migration ranked a dismal 39th, with the state losing a net 63,503 people to the rest of the nation—a staggering figure in a state with fewer than 1 million residents.

Why the need for quahog-like skin? Well, government can be a nasty predator. Rhode Island carries heavy property and income tax burdens. In fact, even after scheduled reductions are implemented over the next two years, Rhode Island will still claim the highest personal income tax rate in the nation, and the corporate income tax rates fare little better. Similarly, state and local government debt and spending—including public welfare, health-care, and per pupil education expenditures—are quite robust as well.

The fallout from such policies is predictable. Not only has the state's population suffered, but so have Rhode Island's economic growth and job creation.

Some claim that Rhode Island was the birthplace of the Industrial Revolution. Talk about ancient history. Touring palatial "cottages" like the "Breakers" reminds one that Rhode Island was once quite hospitable to the entrepreneurs who built the nation's economy. Unfortunately, that hospitality has long since gone.

At the dawn of the 21st century, Rhode Island is not well positioned in terms of the size and reach of its government to capitalize on the current entrepreneurial revolution reshaping the global economy. Republican Governor Lincoln Almond, overwhelming Democratic majorities in the state legislature, and assorted big-government members of the state's congressional delegation seem unable to grasp the need to make Rhode Island friendlier to the private sector. Indeed, if efforts like the late GOP Senator John Chafee's mission to increase health-care costs or his support of environmental regulations (like those tied to the "Global Warming Treaty," agreed to by the Clinton administration in Kyoto, Japan, in December 1997) survive, matters will only grow worse.

One bright spot, however, is found in the state's fairly low crime rates, which have declined at a faster rate during the 1990s than what occurred nationally. The fact that Rhode Island government is able to do a relatively good job in protecting life, limb, and property is of obvious importance.

In the end, Rhode Island politicians would do well to remember that families, entrepreneurs, and businesses are not "quahogs." Right now, the motto that perhaps best reflects Rhode Island's tax and budget policies is, "Only economic quahogs need apply."

POLITICS

Registered Voters

No party registration

Federal Officials: Recent Election and Group Ratings

			ACU	ADA	SBSC
U.S. Senators:	John Chafee (R)*		30	55	55
	1994 Chafee (R)	65%			
	Kushner (D)	35%			
	Jack Reed (D)		0	98	20
	1996 Reed (D)	63%			
	Mayer (R)	35%			
U.S. Representatives:	Patrick Kennedy (D-1)		14	88	15
	1998 Kennedy (D)	67%			
	Santa (R)	28%			
	Robert Weygand (D-2)		23	80	20
	1998 Weygand (D)	72%			
	Matson (R)	25%			
Electoral Votes:	4				
1996 Presidential Results:	Clinton	60%			
	Dole	27%			
	Perot	11%			

State Officials

Governor 1998 Election:	Lincoln Almond (R)	57%
	Myrth York (D)	41%
Lt. Governor:	Charles J. Fogarty (D)	
Attorney General:	Sheldon Whitehouse (D)	

*Senator Chafee died in 1999, and his son, Lincoln Chafee, was named to fill out his term.

State Senate: 42 Democrats
8 Republicans

State House: 86 Democrats
13 Republicans
1 Independent

TAXES AND SPENDING

Total Revenues

Rhode Island's per capita state and local taxes registered $5,827 in 1996, ranking 17th in the nation and exceeding the U.S. average of $5,706 by 2%. From 1962 to 1996, real per capita state and local revenues increased by 356%, compared with an increase in the national average of 297%.

Taxes

Rhode Island's per capita state and local total revenues registered $2,738 in 1996, ranking 14th in the nation and exceeding the U.S. average of $2,597 by 5%. From 1962 to 1996, real per capita state and local taxes increased by 177%, compared with an increase of 152% in the U.S. average.

Property Taxes

Rhode Island's per capita state and local property taxes equaled $1,162 in 1996, ranking 6th in the nation and exceeding the U.S. average of $789 by 47%. From 1962 to 1996, real per capita state and local property taxes increased by 146%, versus a 67% increase in the U.S. average.

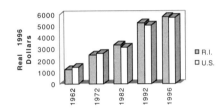

Real Per Capita State and Local Total Revenues: Rhode Island vs. U.S.

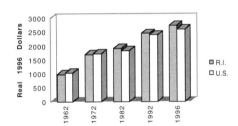

Real Per Capita State and Local Taxes: Rhode Island vs. U.S.

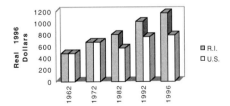

Real Per Capita State and Local Property Taxes: Rhode Island vs. U.S.

Sales and Gross Receipts Taxes

Rhode Island's per capita state and local sales and gross receipts taxes came in at $792 in 1996, ranking 35th in the nation and trailing the U.S. average of $939 by 16%. From 1962 to 1996, real per capita state and local sales and gross receipts taxes increased by 111%, versus an increase of 214% in the U.S. average.

Income Taxes

Rhode Island's per capita state and local income (individual and corporate) taxes registered $674 in 1996, ranking 22nd in the nation and equaling the U.S. average of $674. From 1962 to 1996, real per capita state and local income taxes increased by 1,222%, versus a 567% increase in the U.S. average.

Personal Income Tax

A rate of 10.296%, ranking 51st in the nation (from lowest tax rate to highest), and comparing with the national average of 5.26%.

Capital Gains Tax

A rate of 5.2%, ranking 27th in the nation (from lowest tax rate to highest), and comparing with the national average of 4.68%.

Corporate Income Tax

A rate of 9%, ranking 41st in the nation (from lowest tax rate to highest), and comparing with the U.S. average of 6.63%.

Total Expenditures

Rhode Island's per capita state and local total spending registered $5,638 in 1996, ranking 14th in the nation and exceeding the U.S. average of $5,268 by 7%. From 1962 to 1996, real per capita state and local total spending increased by 323%, versus an increase of 254% in the U.S. average.

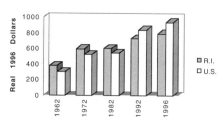

Real Per Capita State and Local Sales and Gross Receipts Taxes: Rhode Island vs. U.S.

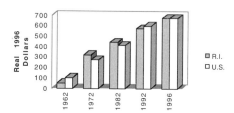

Real Per Capita State and Local Income Taxes: Rhode Island vs. U.S.

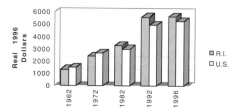

Real Per Capita State and Local Total Expenditures: Rhode Island vs. U.S.

Welfare Expenditures

Rhode Island's per capita state and local public welfare spending registered $876 in 1996, ranking 9th in the nation and outpacing the U.S. average of $729 by 20%. From 1962 to 1996, real per capita state and local public welfare spending increased by 535%, compared with a 488% increase in the U.S. average.

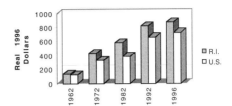

Real Per Capita State and Local Public Welfare Spending: Rhode Island vs. U.S.

Welfare Recipients (in thousands)

	1980	1989	3/99	Change 1989–99
R.I.	54	44	54	+ 23%
U.S.	10,923	10,987	7,335	− 33%

Interest on General Debt

Rhode Island's per capita state and local interest on general debt registered $348 in 1996, ranking 7th in the nation and exceeding the U.S. average of $222 by 57%. From 1962 to 1996, real per capita state and local interest on general debt increased by 657%, versus an increase of 335% in the U.S. average.

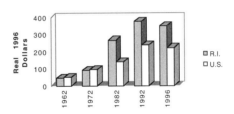

Real Per Capita State and Local Interest on General Debt: Rhode Island vs. U.S.

Total Debt Outstanding

Rhode Island's per capita state and local debt registered $6,583 in 1996, ranking 7th in the nation and outrunning the U.S. average of $4,409 by 49%. From 1962 to 1996, real per capita state and local debt outstanding increased by 256%, versus an increase of 120% in the U.S. average.

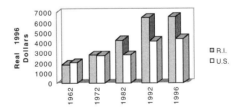

Real Per Capita State and Local Debt Outstanding: Rhode Island vs. U.S.

Government Employees

Rhode Island's state and local government employees (full-time equivalent, or FTE) per 10,000 population registered 499.3 in 1997, ranking 42nd in the nation and trailing the U.S. average of 531.1 by 6%. From 1962 to 1996, state and local FTE employees per 10,000 population increased by 70%, compared with an increase in the U.S. average of 66%.

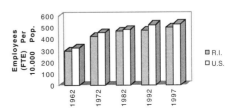

State and Local Government Employees (FTE) Per 10,000 Population: Rhode Island vs. U.S.

Per Capita Federal Government Expenditures, 1998

	1998	Ranking
R.I.	$6,112	9th
U.S.	$5,491	

Per capita federal spending in Rhode Island exceeded the national average by 11%.

EDUCATION

Total Education Spending

Rhode Island's per capita state and local education spending registered $1,511 in 1996, ranking 25th in the nation and exceeding the U.S. average of $1,503 by 0.5%. From 1962 to 1996, real per capita total education spending increased by 247%, versus an increase in the U.S. average of 173%.

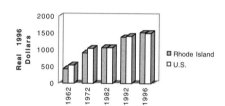

Real Per Capita State and Local Education Spending: Rhode Island vs. U.S.

Per Pupil Spending

Rhode Island's per pupil public school spending registered $7,363 in 1998, ranking 9th in the nation and exceeding the U.S. average of $6,131 by 20%. From 1970 to 1998, Rhode Island's real per pupil public school spending increased by 146%, compared with a 120% increase in the U.S. average.

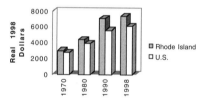

Real Per Pupil Public School Spending: Rhode Island vs. U.S.

Average Public School Teacher Salaries (in 1997–98 dollars)

	1970	1980	1990	1998	1998 Ranking
R.I.	37,576	37,506	45,930	44,300	8th
U.S.	36,934	33,272	39,956	39,385	

In 1998, the average public school teacher salary in Rhode Island outpaced the U.S. average by 12%. From 1970 to 1998, the real average teacher salary in Rhode Island increased by 18%, versus an increase in the U.S. average of 7%.

Pupil/Teacher Ratio, Fall 1996

	Ratio	Rank
R.I.	14.2	4th
U.S.	17.1	

Teachers/Staff, Fall 1996

	Percent	Rank
R.I.	63.3	1st
U.S.	52.1	

Public School 4th-Grade Reading Proficiency, 1998

	Average	Rank (out of 40 states)
R.I.	218	13th
U.S.	215	

Public School 8th-Grade Reading Proficiency, 1998

	Average	Rank (out of 37 states)
R.I.	262	17th
U.S.	261	

Public School 4th-Grade Math Proficiency, 1996

	Average	Rank (out of 44 states)
R.I.	220	28th
U.S.	224	

Public School 8th-Grade Math Proficiency, 1996

	Average	Rank (out of 41 states)
R.I.	269	24th
U.S.	271	

Public School 8th-Grade Science Proficiency, 1996

	Average	Rank (out of 41 states)
R.I.	149	20th
U.S.	148	

Average Math SAT Scores

	1972	1982	1992	1998	Percentage Taking SAT in 1998
R.I.	503	485	487	495	72
U.S.	509	493	501	512	43

Average Verbal SAT Scores

	1972	1982	1992	1998	Percentage Taking SAT in 1998
R.I.	529	498	498	501	72
U.S.	530	504	500	505	43

Expenditures by Public Institutions of Higher Education Per Full-Time-Equivalent Student, 1996

	FTE Student Spending	Rank
R.I.	$12,037	29th
U.S.	$12,343	

Per-FTE-student spending in public institutions of higher education trailed the U.S. average by 2%.

Per Full-Time-Equivalent Student Revenues from Federal, State, and Local Governments for Public Institutions of Higher Education, 1996

	FTE Student Government Revenues	Rank
R.I.	$6,710	45th
U.S.	$8,101	

Per-FTE-student-government revenues in public institutions of higher education lagged behind the U.S. average by 17%.

Average Salary for Full-Time Professors at Public Universities, 1997

	Average	Rank
R.I.	$68,840	27th
U.S.	$72,599	

The average full-time public university professor salary trailed the U.S. average by 9%.

ECONOMY AND BUSINESS

Economic Growth

Over the period of 1977 to 1997, Rhode Island's real gross state product (GSP) grew by 55.5%—ranking 33d in the nation—as compared with real U.S. gross domestic product (GDP), expanding by 70.1%.

At $27.8 billion in 1997, Rhode Island's GSP ranked as 45th largest in the nation.

From 1993 to 1997, Rhode Island's annual real GSP growth averaged 1.97%—ranking 47th in the nation—as compared with annual real U.S. GDP growth, averaging 3.08%.

Real Economic Growth 1977-1997: Rhode Island vs. U.S.

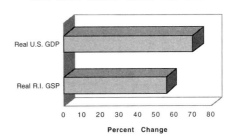

Job Growth

	Growth in Employee Payrolls (Nonagricultural) 1962–98	Ranking
R.I.	53.5%	48th
U.S.	126.5%	

	Average Annual Growth in Employee Payrolls (Nonagricultural) 1993–98	Ranking
R.I.	1.52%	47th
U.S.	2.98%	

Per Capita Disposable Income, 1997

	1997	Ranking
R.I.	$22,248	13th
U.S.	$21,607	

Per capita disposable income exceeded the U.S. average by 3%.

	Real Growth 1962–97	Ranking
R.I.	121.4%	25th
U.S.	116.7%	

	Average Annual Real Growth 1993–97	Ranking
R.I.	1.69%	23d
U.S.	1.48%	

Number of Businesses

	1997	Percent with Fewer than 500 Employees
Businesses with Employees	31,155	96.9
Self-employed Individuals	25,000	

New Business Incorporations

	1980	1986	1992	1997
R.I.	2,282	3,471	2,553	2,649

Percentage Change in Annual New Business Incorporations, 1980 vs. 1997

	Percent	Ranking
R.I.	16.1	37th
U.S.	49.7	

State Merchandise Exports to the World, 1998 (in millions of dollars)

	1998	Rank
R.I.	$1,113	44th

Small Business Survival Index, 1999

Rhode Island ranks among the very worst—49th—in terms of its policy environment for entrepreneurship.

Fortune 500 Headquarters in 1999

A total of 3 (ranked 28th)

Labor Union Membership, 1983 vs. 1997

| | Percentage of Workers | | |
	1983	1997	1997 Rank
R.I.	21.5	18.7	11th
U.S.	20.1	14.1	

Homeownership Rate, 1998

	Rate	Rank
R.I.	59.8	47th
U.S.	66.3	

CRIME

Crime Rates Per 100 Residents (rankings from best to worst crime rate)

Total Crime	1960	1970	1980	1990	1998	1998 Ranking
R.I.	1.27	2.93	5.93	5.35	3.52	11th
U.S.	1.04	2.74	5.90	5.82	4.62	

From 1960 to 1998, Rhode Island's crime rate increased by 177%, versus a U.S. increase of 344%. From 1990 to 1998, Rhode Island's crime rate dropped by 34%, versus 21% U.S. decline.

Violent Crime	1960	1970	1980	1990	1998	1998 Ranking
R.I.	0.04	0.20	0.41	0.43	0.31	13th
U.S.	0.14	0.36	0.58	0.73	0.57	

From 1960 to 1998, Rhode Island's violent crime rate increased by 675%, versus a U.S. increase of 307%. From 1990 to 1998, Rhode Island's violent crime rate decreased by 28%, compared with a national decline of 22%.

Property Crime	1960	1970	1980	1990	1998	1998 Ranking
R.I.	1.24	2.72	5.52	4.92	3.21	12th
U.S.	0.90	2.38	5.32	5.09	4.05	

From 1960 to 1998, Rhode Island's property crime rate increased by 159%, versus a national increase of 350%. From 1990 to 1998, Rhode Island's property crime rate decreased by 35%, compared with a national decline of 20%.

Real Per Capita Police Protection Spending (in real 1996 dollars)

	1962	1972	1982	1992	1996	1996 Ranking
R.I.	55	82	111	140	166	15th
U.S.	51	95	114	148	168	

In 1996, per capita state and local police protection spending in Rhode Island trailed the U.S. average by 1%. From 1962 to 1996, real per capita state and local police protection spending increased by 202%, versus an increase of 229% in the U.S. average.

Prisoners in State and Federal Prisons Per 1,000 population

	1980	1990	1996	1996 Ranking
R.I.	0.86	2.38	3.31	27th
U.S.	1.46	3.11	4.45	

From 1980 to 1996, prisoners per 1,000 population increased by 285%, versus a U.S. increase of 205%.

HEALTH CARE

Health-Care Spending

Rhode Island's per capita state and local health-care spending registered $274 in 1996, ranking 2d in the nation and exceeding the U.S. average of $151 by 81%. From 1962 to 1996, Rhode Island's real per capita state and local health-care spending increased by 1,422%, versus an increase of 739% in the U.S. average.

Real Per Capita State and Local Health Care Spending: Rhode Island vs. U.S.

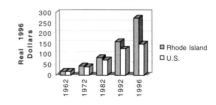

Hospital Spending

Rhode Island's per capita state and local hospital spending registered $91 in 1996, ranking 43d in the nation and trailing the U.S. average of $266 by 66%. From 1962 to 1996, Rhode Island's real per capita state and local hospital spending increased by 17%, as opposed to an increase of 189% in the U.S. average.

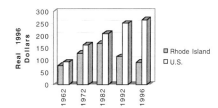

Real Per Capita State and Local Hospital Spending: Rhode Island vs. U.S.

Medicaid, 1997

	Spending Per Recipient	Ranking
R.I.	$6,308	5th
U.S.	$3,681	

Rhode Island's per-recipient Medicaid spending exceeded the U.S. average by 71%.

ENVIRONMENT

Parks and Recreation Spending

Rhode Island's per capita state and local parks and recreation spending registered $60 in 1996, ranking 27th in the nation and lagging behind the U.S. average of $72 by 17%. From 1962 to 1996, real per capita state and local parks and recreation spending increased by 329%, versus a 213% increase in the U.S. average.

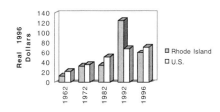

Real Per Capita State and Local Parks and Recreation Spending: Rhode Island vs. U.S.

State and Local Natural Resources Spending, 1996

	Per Capita	Ranking
R.I.	$28	44th
U.S.	$60	

Per capita state and local natural resources spending in Rhode Island trailed the U.S. average by 53%.

State Parks Revenues as a Share of Operating Expenses, 1997

	Percent	Rank
R.I.	51	17th
U.S.	42	

Percentage of Land Owned by the Federal Government, 1996

	Percent	Rank
R.I.	0.5	48th
U.S.	24.8	

SOCIETY AND DEMOGRAPHICS

Population

Rhode Island's 1998 population of .988 million ranked 43d in the nation.

Population Growth, 1990–98

	Percentage Change in Population	Ranking
R.I.	−1.50	50th
U.S.	8.66	

	Net International Migration	Ranking
R.I.	15,994	34th

	Net Domestic Migration	Ranking
R.I.	−63,503	39th

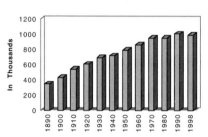

Rhode Island Population

Infant Mortality Rate, 1998

	Percent	Rank
R.I.	7.1	24th
U.S.	6.4	

Percentage of Births of Low Birthweight, 1997

	Percent	Rank
R.I.	7.4	28th
U.S.	7.5	

Percentage of Live Births to Unmarried Women, 1997

	Percent	Rank
R.I.	33.0	20th
U.S.	32.4	

Abortion Rate—Abortions Per 1,000 Women Ages 15–44, 1995

	Rate	Rank
R.I.	25.5	12th
U.S.	22.9	

LIFESTYLE

Percentage of Households with Computers, 1998

	Percent	Rank
R.I.	41.0	32d

Percentage of Households with Internet Access, 1998

	Percent	Rank
R.I.	27.1	19th

State Arts Agency Spending, 1999

	Per Capita	Rank
R.I.	$0.89	23d
U.S.	$1.35	

Per capita state arts spending in 1999 trailed the U.S. average by 35%.

Major League Sports Facilities

None

SOUTH CAROLINA

Myrtle Beach and Hilton Head Island lie inside the state of South Carolina. Why are these two places of immense importance? Golf.

Myrtle Beach bills itself as the "Seaside Golf Capital of the World," while Hilton Head Island also is blessed with several golf courses, including Harbour Town Golf Links, which is known around the world.

Normally the state's notable position in the golfing world would be enough for us to give a big thumbs up to South Carolina. Keep the fairways cut, the greens running smoothly, and the foursomes moving along, and who could possibly ask for more in the 21st century? Well, there is more.

South Carolina carries some of the lowest per capita tax burdens—particularly property and sales taxes—in the nation. While the state's personal income tax rate runs high, both the corporate income and capital gains tax rates are fairly low. Government debt numbers are favorable as well.

Meanwhile, on the spending side of the government equation in South Carolina, other than very high per capita health and hospital expenditures, most expenditure levels generally run a bit below the national average.

The result has been a dynamic economy. For example, growth rates in real gross state product, real disposable income, and new business incorporations have been robust in recent times. Job creation has been pretty solid, and South Carolina has experienced above-average population growth, with the state being a big net importer of residents from other states. Between 1989 and March 1999, the state's welfare rolls dropped by 59%, far ahead of the 33% decline nationally. South Carolina also claims the highest home ownership rate in the nation.

However, all is not as sweet as draining a 20-foot birdie putt on number 18. Crime remains a serious issue. The state's crime rates rank among the nation's worst.

Some other societal indicators are worrisome as well, such as high rates of infant mortality, low birth-weight babies, and illegitimacy.

When it comes to the economy and state and local government taxing and spending, however, South Carolina seems very well positioned to prosper in the 21st century. With low property, corporate income, and capital gains taxes, if state politicians would reduce the personal income tax, South Carolina would likely become the favorite destination for golf-loving supply-side economists (with one of this book's coauthors answering to such a description) across this great nation. Fore!

POLITICS

Registered Voters

No party registration

Federal Officials: Recent Election and Group Ratings

			ACU	ADA	SBSC
U.S. Senators:	Strom Thurmond (R)		90	4	85
	1996 Thurmond (R)	53%			
	Close (D)	44%			
	Ernest Hollings (D)		41	44	30
	1998 Hollings (D)	53%			
	Inglis (R)	46%			
U.S. Representatives:	Mark Sanford Jr. (R-1)		86	18	85
	1998 Sanford (R)	91%			
	Innella (NL)	9%			
	Floyd Spence (R-2)		89	6	85
	1998 Spence (R)	58%			
	Frederick (D)	41%			
	Lindsey Graham (R-3)		93	6	90
	1998 Graham (R)	NO			
	Jim Demint (R-4)		NA	NA	NA
	1998 Demint (R)	58%			
	Reese (D)	40%			
	John Spratt Jr. (D-5)		23	63	20
	1998 Spratt (D)	58%			
	Burkhold (R)	40%			
	James Clyburn (D-6)		12	89	10
	1998 Clyburn (D)	73%			
	McLeod (R)	26%			

Electoral Votes: 8
1996 Presidential Results:

Clinton	44%
Dole	50%
Perot	6%

State Officials

Governor 1998 Election:	Jim Hodges (D)	53%
	David Beasley (R)	45%
Lt. Governor:	Bob Peeler (R)	
Attorney General:	Charlie Condon (R)	
State Senate:	26 Democrats	
	20 Republicans	
State House:	68 Republicans	
	56 Democrats	

TAXES AND SPENDING

Total Revenues

South Carolina's per capita state and local total revenues registered $4,966 in 1996, ranking 35th in the nation and trailing the U.S. average of $5,706 by 13%. From 1962 to 1996, real per capita state and local revenues increased by 420%, compared with an increase in the national average of 297%.

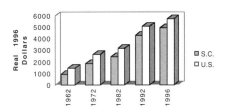

Real Per Capita State and Local Total Revenues: South Carolina vs. U.S.

Taxes

South Carolina's per capita state and local taxes registered $1,981 in 1996, ranking 45th in the nation and trailing the U.S. average of $2,597 by 24%. From 1962 to 1996, real per capita state and local taxes increased by 220%, compared with an increase of 152% in the U.S. average.

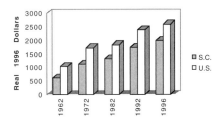

Real Per Capita State and Local Taxes: South Carolina vs. U.S.

Property Taxes

South Carolina's per capita state and local property taxes equaled $528 in 1996, ranking 37th in the nation and trailing the U.S. average of $789 by 33%. From 1962 to 1996, real per capita state and local property taxes increased by 247%, versus a 67% increase in the U.S. average.

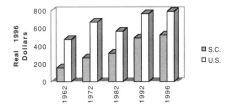

Real Per Capita State and Local Property Taxes: South Carolina vs. U.S.

Sales and Gross Receipts Taxes

South Carolina's per capita state and local sales and gross receipts taxes came in at $732 in 1996, ranking 41st in the nation and trailing the U.S. average of $939 by 22%. From 1962 to 1996, real per capita state and local sales and gross receipts taxes increased by 121%, versus an increase of 214% in the U.S. average.

Income Taxes

South Carolina's per capita state and local income (individual and corporate) taxes registered $558 in 1996, ranking 31st in the nation and trailing the U.S. average of $674 by 17%. From 1962 to 1996, real per capita state and local income taxes increased by 541%, versus a 567% increase in the U.S. average.

Personal Income Tax

A rate of 7.0%, ranking 40th in the nation (from lowest tax rate to highest), and comparing with the national average of 5.26%.

Capital Gains Tax

A rate of 3.92%, ranking 18th in the nation (from lowest tax rate to highest), and comparing with the national average of 4.68%.

Corporate Income Tax

A rate of 5.0%, ranking 8th in the nation (from lowest tax rate to highest), and comparing with the national average of 6.69%.

Total Expenditures

South Carolina's per capita state and local total spending registered $4,829 in 1996, ranking 29th in the nation and trailing the U.S. average of $5,268 by 8%. From 1962 to 1996, real per capita state and local total spending increased by 420%, versus an increase of 254% in the U.S. average.

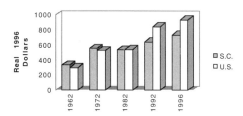

Real Per Capita State and Local Sales and Gross Receipts Taxes: South Carolina vs. U.S.

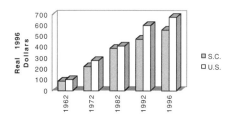

Real Per Capita State and Local Income Taxes: South Carolina vs. U.S.

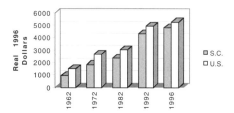

Real Per Capita State and Local Total Expenditures: South Carolina vs. U.S.

Welfare Expenditures

South Carolina's per capita state and local public welfare spending registered $692 in 1996, ranking 22d in the nation and trailing the U.S. average of $729 by 5%. From 1962 to 1996, real per capita state and local public welfare spending increased by 981%, compared with a 488% increase in the U.S. average.

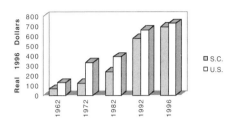

Real Per Capita State and Local Public Welfare Spending: South Carolina vs. U.S.

Welfare Recipients (in thousands)

	1980	1989	3/99	Change 1989–99
S.C.	156	105	43	−59%
U.S.	10,923	10,987	7,335	−33%

Interest on General Debt

South Carolina's per capita state and local interest on general debt registered $125 in 1996, ranking 47th in the nation and trailing the U.S. average of $222 by 44%. From 1962 to 1996, real per capita state and local interest on general debt increased by 594%, versus an increase of 335% in the U.S. average.

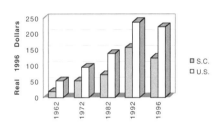

Real Per Capita State and Local Interest on General Debt: South Carolina vs. U.S.

Total Debt Outstanding

South Carolina's per capita state and local debt registered $3,272 in 1996, ranking 37th in the nation and trailing the U.S. average of $4,409 by 26%. From 1962 to 1996, real per capita state and local debt outstanding increased by 238%, versus an increase of 120% in the U.S. average.

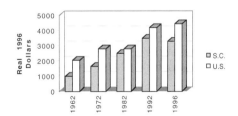

Real Per Capita State and Local Debt Outstanding: South Carolina vs. U.S.

Government Employees

South Carolina's state and local government employees (full-time equivalent, or FTE) per 10,000 population registered 589.7 in 1997, ranking 13th in the nation and exceeding the U.S. average of 531.1 by 11%. From 1962 to 1996, state and local FTE employees per 10,000 population increased by 118%, compared with an increase in the U.S. average of 66%.

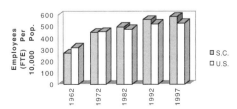

State and Local Government Employees (FTE) Per 10,000 Population: South Carolina vs. U.S.

Per Capita Federal Government Expenditures, 1998

	1998	Ranking
S.C.	$5,180	28th
U.S.	$5,491	

Per capita federal spending in South Carolina trailed the national average by 6%.

EDUCATION

Total Education Spending

South Carolina's per capita state and local education spending registered $1,430 in 1996, ranking 33d in the nation and trailing the U.S. average of $1,503 by 5%. From 1962 to 1996, real per capita total education spending increased by 275%, versus an increase in the U.S. average of 173%.

Real Per Capita State and Local Education Spending: South Carolina vs. U.S.

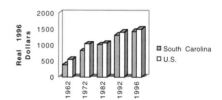

Per Pupil Spending

South Carolina's per pupil public school spending registered $5,204 in 1998, ranking 37th in the nation and trailing the U.S. average of $6,131 by 15%. From 1970 to 1998, South Carolina's real per pupil public school spending increased by 148%, compared with a 120% increase in the U.S. average.

Real Per Pupil Public School Spending: South Carolina vs. U.S.

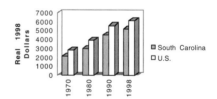

Average Public School Teacher Salaries (in 1997–98 dollars)

	1970	1980	1990	1998	1998 Ranking
S.C.	29,659	27,216	34,669	33,608	36th
U.S.	36,934	33,272	39,956	39,385	

In 1998, the average public school teacher salary in South Carolina trailed the U.S. average by 15%. From 1970 to 1998, the real average teacher salary in South Carolina increased by 13%, versus an increase in the U.S. average of 7%.

Pupil/Teacher Ratio, Fall 1996

	Ratio	Rank
S.C.	15.7	20th
U.S.	17.1	

Teachers/Staff, Fall 1996

	Ratio	Rank
S.C.	53.9	16th
U.S.	52.1	

Public School 4th-Grade Reading Proficiency, 1998

	Average	Rank (out of 40 states)
S.C.	210	29th
U.S.	215	

Public School 8th-Grade Reading Proficiency, 1998

	Average	Rank (out of 37 states)
S.C.	255	30th
U.S.	261	

Public School 4th-Grade Math Proficiency, 1996

	Average	Rank (out of 44 states)
S.C.	213	39th
U.S.	224	

Public School 8th-Grade Math Proficiency, 1996

	Average	Rank (out of 41 states)
S.C.	261	37th
U.S.	271	

Public School 8th-Grade Science Proficiency, 1996

	Average	Rank (out of 41 states)
S.C.	139	35th
U.S.	148	

Average Math SAT Scores

	1972	1982	1992	1998	Percentage Taking SAT in 1998
S.C.	455	443	467	473	61
U.S.	509	493	501	512	43

Average Verbal SAT Scores

	1972	1982	1992	1998	Percentage Taking SAT in 1998
S.C.	477	456	471	478	61
U.S.	530	504	500	505	43

Expenditures by Public Institutions of Higher Education Per Full-Time-Equivalent Student, 1996

	FTE Student Spending	Rank
S.C.	$12,427	22d
U.S.	$12,343	

Per-FTE-spending in public institutions of higher education topped the U.S. average by 1%.

Per Full-Time-Equivalent Student Revenues from Federal, State, and Local Governments for Public Institutions of Higher Education, 1996

	FTE Student Government Revenues	Rank
S.C.	$7,880	26th
U.S.	$8,101	

Per-FTE-student-government revenues in public institutions of higher education trailed the U.S. average by 3%.

Average Salary for Full-Time Professors at Public Universities, 1997

	Average	Rank
S.C.	$68,422	29th
U.S.	$72,599	

The average full-time public university professor salary trailed the U.S. average by 6%.

ECONOMY AND BUSINESS

Economic Growth

Over the period of 1977 to 1997, South Carolina's real gross state product (GSP) grew by 105.2%—ranking 9th in the nation—as compared with real U.S. gross domestic product (GDP), expanding by 70.1%.

At $93.2 billion in 1997, South Carolina's GSP ranked as 28th largest in the nation.

From 1993 to 1997, South Carolina's annual real GSP growth averaged 3.73%—ranking 24th in the nation—as compared with annual real U.S. GDP growth, averaging 3.08%

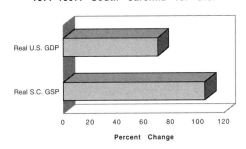

Real Economic Growth 1977-1997: South Carolina vs. U.S.

Job Growth

	Growth in Employee Payrolls (Nonagricultural) 1962–98	Ranking
S.C.	193.1%	15th
U.S.	126.5%	

	Average Annual Growth in Employee Payrolls (Nonagricultural) 1993–98	Ranking
S.C.	3.18%	21st
U.S.	2.98%	

Per Capita Disposable Income, 1997

	1997	Ranking
S.C.	$18,037	41st
U.S.	$21,607	

Per capita disposable income trailed the U.S. average by 17%.

	Real Growth 1962–97	Ranking
S.C.	168.6%	3d
U.S.	116.7%	

	Average Annual Real Growth 1993–97	Ranking
S.C.	1.90%	10th
U.S.	1.48%	

Number of Businesses

	1997	Percent with Fewer than 500 Employees
Businesses with Employees	82,673	97.4
Self-employed Individuals	109,000	

New Business Incorporations

	1980	1986	1992	1997
S.C.	4,095	6,176	6,189	8,149

Percentage Change in Annual New Business Incorporations, 1980 vs. 1997

	Percent	Ranking
S.C.	99.0	9th
U.S.	49.7	

State Merchandise Exports to the World, 1998 (in millions of dollars)

	1998	Rank
S.C.	$5,857	25th

Small Business Survival Index, 1999

South Carolina ranks 17th in terms of its policy environment for entrepreneurship.

Fortune 500 Headquarters in 1999

None

Labor Union Membership, 1983 vs. 1997

| | Percentage of Workers | | |
	1983	1997	1997 Rank
S.C.	5.9	3.7	51st
U.S.	20.1	14.1	

Homeownership Rate, 1998

	Rate	Rank
S.C.	76.6	1st
U.S.	66.3	

CRIME

Crime Rates Per 100 Residents (rankings from best to worst crime rate)

Total Crime	1960	1970	1980	1990	1998	1998 Ranking
S.C.	0.84	2.07	5.44	6.05	5.78	45th
U.S.	1.04	2.74	5.90	5.82	4.62	

From 1960 to 1998, South Carolina's crime rate increased by 588%, versus a U.S. increase of 344%. From 1990 to 1998, South Carolina's crime rate decreased by 4%, versus a U.S. decrease of 21%.

Violent Crime	1960	1970	1980	1990	1998	1998 Ranking
S.C.	0.15	0.29	0.66	0.98	0.90	48th
U.S.	0.14	0.36	0.58	0.73	0.57	

From 1960 to 1998, South Carolina's violent crime rate increased by 500%, versus as U.S. increase of 307%. From 1990 to 1998, South Carolina's violent crime rate decreased by 8%, compared with a national decline of 22%.

Property Crime	1960	1970	1980	1990	1998	1998 Ranking
S.C.	0.69	1.78	4.78	5.07	4.87	41st
U.S.	0.90	2.38	5.32	5.09	4.05	

From 1960 to 1998, South Carolina's property crime rate increased by 606%, versus a national increase of 350%. From 1990 to 1998, South Carolina's property crime rate decreased by 4%, compared with a national decline of 20%.

Real Per Capita Police Protection Spending (in real 1996 dollars)

	1962	1972	1982	1992	1996	1996 Ranking
S.C.	28	56	70	100	121	38th
U.S.	51	95	114	148	168	

In 1996, per capita state and local police protection spending in South Carolina trailed the U.S. average by 28%. From 1962 to 1996, real per capita state and local police protection spending increased by 332%, versus an increase of 229% in the U.S. average.

Prisoners in State and Federal Prisons Per 1,000 population

	1980	1990	1996	1996 Ranking
S.C.	2.52	4.97	5.50	7th
U.S.	1.46	3.11	4.45	

From 1980 to 1996, prisoners per 1,000 population increased by 118%, versus a U.S. increase of 205%.

HEALTH CARE

Health-Care Spending

South Carolina's per capita state and local health-care spending registered $199 in 1996, ranking 11th in the nation and topping the U.S. average of $151 by 32%. From 1962 to 1996, South Carolina's real per capita state and local health-care spending increased by 2,111%, versus an increase of 739% in the U.S. average.

Real Per Capita State and Local Health Care Spending: South Carolina vs. U.S.

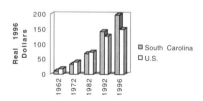

Hospital Spending

South Carolina's per capita state and local hospital spending registered $523 in 1996, ranking 2d in the nation and exceeding the U.S. average of $266 by 97%. From 1962 to 1996, South Carolina's real per capita state and local hospital spending increased by 571%, as opposed to an increase of 189% in the U.S. average.

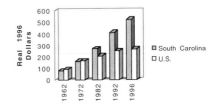

Real Per Capita State and Local Hospital Spending: South Carolina vs. U.S.

Medicaid, 1997

	Spending Per Recipient	Ranking
S.C.	$3,090	37th
U.S.	$3,681	

South Carolina's per-recipient Medicaid spending trailed the U.S. average by 16%.

ENVIRONMENT

Parks and Recreation Spending

South Carolina's per capita state and local parks and recreation spending registered $45 in 1996, ranking 39th in the nation and trailing the U.S. average of $72 by 38%. From 1962 to 1996, real per capita state and local parks and recreation spending increased by 800%, versus a 213% increase in the U.S. average.

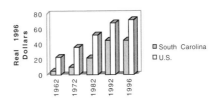

Real Per Capita State and Local Parks and Recreation Spending: South Carolina vs. U.S.

State and Local Natural Resources Spending, 1996

	Per Capita	Ranking
S.C.	$47	34th
U.S.	$60	

Per capita state and local natural resources spending in South Carolina trailed the U.S. average by 22%.

State Parks Revenues as a Share of Operating Expenses, 1997

	Percent	Rank
S.C.	69	8th
U.S.	42	

Percentage of Land Owned by the Federal Government, 1996

	Percent	Rank
S.C.	4.8	27th
U.S.	24.8	

SOCIETY AND DEMOGRAPHICS

Population

South Carolina's 1998 population of 3.836 million ranked 26th in the nation.

Population Growth, 1990–98

	Percentage of Change in Population	Ranking
S.C.	10.04	18th
U.S.	8.66	

	Net International Migration	Ranking
S.C.	15,789	35th

	Net Domestic Migration	Ranking
S.C.	118,895	12th

Infant Mortality Rate, 1998

	Percent	Rank
S.C.	9.1	7th
U.S.	6.4	

South Carolina Population

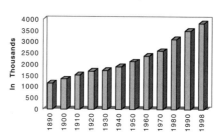

Percentage of Births of Low Birthweight, 1997

	Percent	Rank
S.C.	9.2	4th
U.S.	7.5	

Percentage of Live Births to Unmarried Women, 1997

	Percent	Rank
S.C.	38.0	5th
U.S.	32.4	

Abortion Rate—Abortions Per 1,000 Women Ages 15–44, 1995

	Rate	Rank
S.C.	12.9	34th
U.S.	22.9	

LIFESTYLE

Percentage of Households with Computers, 1998

	Percent	Rank
S.C.	35.7	45th

Percentage of Households with Internet Access, 1998

	Percent	Rank
S.C.	21.4	42d

State Arts Agency Spending, 1999

	Per Capita	Rank
S.C.	$1.09	22d
U.S.	$1.35	

Per capita state arts spending in 1999 trailed the U.S. average by 19%.

Major League Sports Facilities

None

SOUTH DAKOTA

Politically speaking, South Dakota is essentially two states in one, but the split has nothing to do with geography.

In-state elected officials are overwhelmingly Republican. For example, GOP Governor William Janklow won reelection by big numbers in 1998, and both houses of the state legislature carry large Republican majorities. In addition, South Dakotans went for the Democrat just four times in presidential contests since 1892. Heck, even the rather inept Bob Dole carried the state in 1998.

Similarly, state policies tend to be of a fairly free-market variety. The state imposes no individual income, capital gains, or corporate income taxes. The state and local tax burden comes in well below the U.S. average, as do government spending (but for natural resources and parks and recreation expenditures) and debt levels. Crime also is quite low in South Dakota.

In recent years, the economy has picked up considerably. Real state economic growth, job creation, and increases in disposable income have outpaced the U.S. averages. New business incorporations have shown solid progress, while the Small Business Survival Committee says South Dakota offers the best policy environment for entrepreneurship in the nation.

Meanwhile, the politicians that voters send to Washington, D.C. tend to be Democrats, and rather liberal ones at that. Just think back to former Senator George McGovern. Most prominent today, of course, is Senate Minority Leader Tom Daschle, who rates among the Senate's most left-leaning members. Free markets obviously do not get as much play with South Dakota's congressional delegation.

Why the dichotomy? Well, in a May 1999 column, George Will asserted that the job of South Dakota's members of Congress is "to deflect a stream of other states' dollars to South Dakota." Presumably, Democrats are pretty good at such things, but we thought that was the bipartisan purpose of almost all members of Congress.

Indeed, one has to wonder if Democratic dominance over federal offices in South Dakota may soon come to an end. As Republicans have proven time and again since taking control of Congress, GOPers are just as adept at bringing home the bacon as Democrats.

South Dakota's at-large Congressman John Thune is a Republican, and a pretty conservative one too, except for his ability to bring home federal dollars. One can easily envision Republicans succeeding Senators Daschle and Johnson when they finally decide to retire (of course, depending on the quality of the candidates).

For many South Dakotans, unfortunately, that is the best of both worlds—conservatives who make an exception when it comes to pork. Tragically, this GOP breed is not unique to South Dakota.

POLITICS

Registered Voters

40% Democrats
49% Republicans
11% Other

Federal Officials: Recent Election and Group Ratings

			ACU	ADA	SBSC
U.S. Senators:	Thomas Daschle (D)		15	85	15
	1998 Daschle (D)	62%			
	Schmidt (R)	36%			
	Tim Johnson (D)		1	85	15
	1996 Johnson (D)	51%			
	Pressler (R)	48%			
U.S. Representatives:	John Thune (R)		90	5	95
	1998 Thune (R)	75%			
	Moser (D)	25%			
Electoral Votes:	3				
1996 Presidential Results:	Clinton	43%			
	Dole	46%			
	Perot	10%			

State Officials

Governor 1998 Election:	William Janklow (R)	64%
	Bernie Hunhoff (D)	33%
Lt. Governor:	Carole Hillard (R)	
Attorney General:	Mark Barnett (R)	
State Senate:	13 Democrats	
	22 Republicans	
State House:	19 Democrats	
	51 Republicans	

TAXES AND SPENDING

Total Revenues

South Dakota's per capita state and local total revenues registered $4,707 in 1996, ranking 44th in the nation and trailing the U.S. average of $5,706 by 18%. From 1962 to 1996, real per capita state and local revenues increased by 196%, compared with an increase in the national average of 297%.

Taxes

South Dakota's per capita state and local taxes registered $1,965 in 1996, ranking 46th in the nation and trailing the U.S. average of $2,597 by 24%. From 1962 to 1996, real per capita state and local taxes increased by 103%, compared with an increase of 152% in the U.S. average.

Property Taxes

South Dakota's per capita state and local property taxes equaled $762 in 1996, ranking 22nd in the nation and trailing the U.S. average of $789 by 3%. From 1962 to 1996, real per capita state and local property taxes increased by 35%, versus a 67% increase in the U.S. average.

Sales and Gross Receipts Taxes

South Dakota's per capita state and local sales and gross receipts taxes came in at $950 in 1996, ranking 16th in the nation and outpacing the U.S. average of $939 by 1%. From 1962 to 1996, real per capita state and local sales and gross receipts taxes increased by 229%, versus an increase of 214% in the U.S. average.

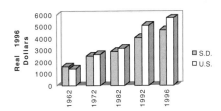

Real Per Capita State and Local Total Revenues: South Dakota vs. U.S.

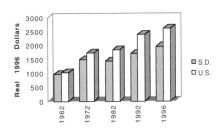

Real Per Capita State and Local Taxes: South Dakota vs. U.S.

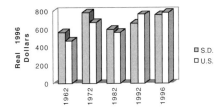

Real Per Capita State and Local Property Taxes: South Dakota vs. U.S.

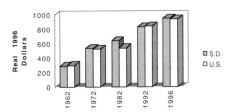

Real Per Capita State and Local Sales and Gross Receipts Taxes: South Dakota vs. U.S.

Income Taxes

South Dakota's per capita state and local income (individual and corporate) taxes registered $52 in 1996, ranking 47th in the nation and trailing the U.S. average of $674 by 92%. From 1962 to 1996, real per capita state and local income taxes increased by 940%, versus an increase of 214% in the U.S. average.

Personal Income Tax

A rate of 0%, ranking best in the nation (from lowest tax rate to highest), and comparing with the national average of 5.26%.

Capital Gains Tax

A rate of 0%, ranking best in the nation (from lowest tax rate of highest), and comparing with the national average of 4.68%.

Corporate Income Tax

A rate of 0%, ranking best in the nation (from lowest tax rate to highest), and comparing with the national average of 6.69%.

Total Expenditures

South Dakota's per capita state and local total spending registered $4,211 in 1996, ranking 47th in the nation and trailing the U.S. average of $5,268 by 11%. From 1962 to 1996, real per capita state and local total spending increased by 175% versus an increase of 254% in the U.S. average.

Welfare Expenditures

South Dakota's per capita state and local public welfare spending registered $559 in 1996, ranking 39th in the nation and trailing the U.S. average of $729 by 23%. From 1962 to 1996, real per capita state and local public welfare spending increased by 453%, compared with a 488% increase in the U.S. average.

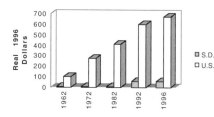

Real Per Capita State and Local Income Taxes: South Dakota vs. U.S.

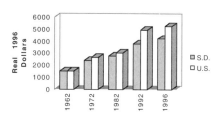

Real Per Capita State and Local Total Expenditures: South Dakota vs. U.S.

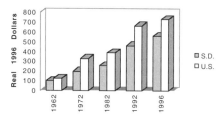

Real Per Capita State and Local Public Welfare Spending: South Dakota vs. U.S.

Welfare Recipients (in thousands)

	1980	1989	3/99	Change 1989–99
S. Dak.	19	19	8	−58%
U.S.	10,923	10,987	7,335	−33%

Interest on General Debt

South Dakota's per capita state and local interest on general debt registered $196 in 1996, ranking 29th in the nation and trailing the U.S. average of $222 by 12%. From 1962 to 1996, real per capita state and local interest on general debt increased by 2,078%, versus an increase of 335% in the U.S. average.

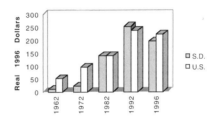

Real Per Capita State and Local Interest on General Debt: South Dakota vs. U.S.

Total Debt Outstanding

South Dakota's per capita state and local debt registered $3,287 in 1996, ranking 36th in the nation and trailing the U.S. average of $4,409 by 25%. From 1962 to 1996, real per capita state and local debt outstanding increased by 645%, versus an increase of 120% in the U.S. average.

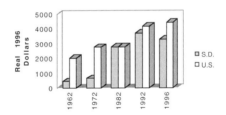

Real Per Capita State and Local Debt Outstanding: South Dakota vs. U.S.

Government Employees

South Dakota's state and local government employees (full-time equivalent, or FTE) per 10,000 population registered 539.8 in 1997, ranking 25th in the nation and topping the U.S. average of 531.1 by 2%. From 1962 to 1996, state and local FTE employees per 10,000 population increased by 64%, compared with an increase in the U.S. average of 66%.

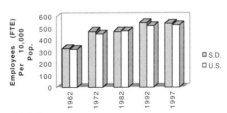

State and Local Government Employees (FTE) Per 10,000 Population: South Dakota vs. U.S.

Per Capita Federal Government Expenditures, 1998

	1998	Ranking
S. Dak.	$5,852	16th
U.S.	$5,491	

Per capita federal spending in South Dakota exceeded the national average by 7%.

EDUCATION

Total Education Spending

South Dakota's per capita state and local education spending registered $1,299 in 1996, ranking 45th in the nation and trailing the U.S. average of $1,503 by 14%. From 1962 to 1996, real per capita total education spending increased by 140%, versus an increase in the U.S. average of 173%.

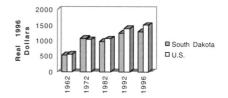

Real Per Capita State and Local Education Spending: South Dakota vs. U.S.

Per Pupil Spending

South Dakota's per pupil public school spending registered $4,581 in 1998, ranking 43d in the nation and trailing the U.S. average of $6,131 by 25%. From 1970 to 1998, South Dakota's real per pupil public school spending increased by 89%, compared with a 120% increase in the U.S. average.

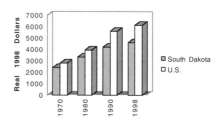

Real Per Pupil Public School Spending: South Dakota vs. U.S.

Average Public School Teacher Salaries (in 1997–98 dollars)

	1970	1980	1990	1998	1998 Ranking
S. Dak.	27,416	25,726	27,132	27,341	51st
U.S.	36,934	33,272	39,956	39,385	

In 1998, the average public school teacher salary in South Dakota trailed the U.S. average by 31%. From 1970 to 1998, the real average teacher salary in South Dakota decreased by 0.3%, versus an increase in the U.S. average of 7%.

Pupil/Teacher Ratio, Fall 1996

	Ratio	Rank
S. Dak.	14.9	11th
U.S.	17.1	

Teachers/Staff, Fall 1996

	Percent	Rank
S. Dak.	53.2	19th
U.S.	52.1	

Average Math SAT Scores

	1972	1982	1992	1998	Percentage Taking SAT in 1998
S. Dak.	563	568	565	581	5
U.S.	509	493	501	512	43

Average Verbal SAT Scores

	1972	1982	1992	1998	Percentage Taking SAT in 1998
S. Dak.	587	596	565	584	5
U.S.	530	504	500	505	43

Expenditures by Public Institutions of Higher Education Per Full-Time-Equivalent Student, 1996

	FTE Student Spending	Rank
S. Dak.	$9,759	50th
U.S.	$12,343	

Per-FTE-student spending in public institutions of higher education trailed the U.S. average by 21%.

Per Full-Time-Equivalent Student Revenues from Federal, State and Local Government for Public Institutions of Higher Education, 1996

	FTE Student Government Revenues	Rank
S.Dak.	$6,759	43d
U.S.	$8,101	

Per-FTE-student-government revenues in public institutions of higher education lagged behind the U.S. average by 17%.

Average Salary for Full-Time Professors at Public Universities, 1997

	Average	Rank
S. Dak.	$47,584	50th
U.S.	$72,599	

The average full-time public university professor salary trailed the U.S. average by 34%.

ECONOMY AND BUSINESS

Economic Growth

Over the period of 1977 to 1997, South Dakota's real gross state product (GSP) grew by 70.1%—ranking 25th in the nation—as compared with real U.S. gross domestic product (GDP), expanding by 70.1%.

At $20.2 billion in 1997, South Dakota's GSP ranked as 47th largest in the nation.

From 1993 to 1997, South Dakota's annual real GSP growth averaged 3.60%—ranking 28th in the nation—as compared with annual real U.S. GDP growth, averaging 3.08%.

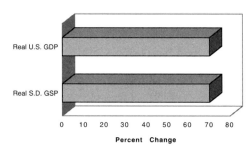

Real Economic Growth 1977-1997: South Dakota vs. U.S.

Job Growth

	Growth in Employee Payrolls (Nonagricultural) 1962–98	Ranking
S. Dak.	134.8%	32nd
U.S.	126.5%	

	Average Annual Growth in Employee Payrolls (Nonagricultural) 1993–98	Ranking
S. Dak.	3.19%	19th
U.S.	2.98%	

Per Capita Disposable Income

	1997	Ranking
S. Dak.	$19,060	36th
U.S.	$21,607	

Per capita disposable income trailed the U.S. average by 12%.

	Real Growth 1962–97	Ranking
S. Dak.	113.0%	31st
U.S.	116.7%	

	Average Annual Real Growth 1993–97	Ranking
S. Dak.	2.20%	7th
U.S.	1.48%	

Number of Businesses

	1997	Percent with Fewer than 500 Employees
Businesses with Employees	21,370	97.3
Self-employed Individuals	53,000	

New Business Incorporations

	1980	1986	1992	1997
S. Dak.	910	973	1,218	1,440

Percentage Change in Annual New Business Incorporations, 1980 vs. 1997

	Percent	Ranking
S. Dak.	58.2	20th
U.S.	49.7	

State Merchandise Exports to the World, 1998 (in millions of dollars)

	1998	Rank
S. Dak.	$373.5	49th

Small Business Survival Index, 1999

South Dakota ranks as the very best policy environment for entrepreneurship in the nation.

Fortune 500 Headquarters in 1999

None

Labor Union Membership, 1983 vs. 1997

| | Percentage of Workers | | |
	1983	1997	1997 Rank
S. Dak.	11.5	6.9	44th
U.S.	20.1	14.1	

Homeownership Rate, 1998

	Rate	Rank
S. Dak.	67.3	33d
U.S.	66.3	

CRIME

Crime Rates Per 100 Residents (rankings from best to worst crime rate)

Total Crime	1960	1970	1980	1990	1998	1998 Ranking
S. Dak.	0.57	1.15	3.24	2.91	2.62	3d
U.S.	1.04	2.74	5.90	5.82	4.62	

From 1960 to 1998, South Dakota's crime rate increased by 360%, versus a U.S. increase of 344%. From 1990 to 1998, South Dakota's crime rate decreased by 10%, versus a U.S. decrease of 21%.

Violent Crime	1960	1970	1980	1990	1998	1998 Ranking
S. Dak.	0.03	0.09	0.13	0.16	0.15	6th
U.S.	0.14	0.36	0.58	0.73	0.57	

From 1960 to 1998, South Dakota's violent crime rate increased by 400%, versus a U.S. increase of 307%. From 1990 to 1998, South Dakota's violent crime rate decreased by 6%, compared with a national decline of 22%.

Property Crime	1960	1970	1980	1990	1998	1998 Ranking
S. Dak.	0.53	1.06	3.12	2.75	2.47	3d
U.S.	0.90	2.38	5.32	5.09	4.05	

From 1960 to 1998, South Dakota's property crime rate increased by 366%, versus a national increase of 379%. From 1990 to 1998, South Dakota's property crime rate decreased by 10%, compared with a national decline of 20%.

Real Per Capita Police Protection Spending (in real 1996 dollars)

	1962	1972	1982	1992	1996	1996 Ranking
S. Dak.	28	46	70	87	110	43d
U.S.	51	95	114	148	168	

In 1996, per capita state and local police protection spending in South Dakota trailed the U.S. average by 35%. From 1962 to 1996, real per capita state and local police protection spending increased by 293%, versus an increase of 229% in the U.S. average.

Prisoners in State and Federal Prisons Per 1,000 Population

	1980	1990	1996	1996 Ranking
S. Dak.	0.92	1.93	2.80	36th
U.S.	1.46	3.11	4.45	

From 1980 to 1996, prisoners per 1,000 population increased by 204%, versus a U.S. increase of 205%.

HEALTH CARE

Health-Care Spending

South Dakota's per capita state and local health-care spending registered $97 in 1996, ranking 39th in the nation and trailing the U.S. average of $151 by 36%. From 1962 to 1996, South Dakota's real per capita state and local health-care spending increased by 593%, versus an increase of 739% in the U.S. average.

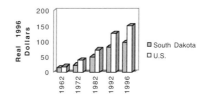

Real Per Capita State and Local Health Care Spending: South Dakota vs. U.S.

Hospital Spending

South Dakota's per capita state and local hospital spending registered $99 in 1996, ranking 42d in the nation and lagging behind the U.S. average of $266 by 63%. From 1962 to 1996, South Dakota's real per capita state and local hospital spending increased by 168%, as opposed to an increase of 189% in the U.S. average.

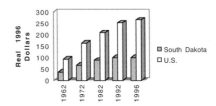

Real Per Capita State and Local Hospital Spending: South Dakota vs. U.S.

Medicaid, 1997

	Spending Per Recipient	Ranking
S. Dak.	$4,240	17th
U.S.	$3,681	

South Dakota's per-recipient Medicaid spending exceeded the U.S. average by 15%.

ENVIRONMENT

Parks and Recreation Spending

South Dakota's per capita state and local parks and recreation spending registered $105 in 1996, ranking 8th in the nation and exceeding the U.S average of $72 by 46%. From 1962 to 1996, real per capita state and local parks and recreation spending increased by 650%, versus a 213% increase in the U.S. average.

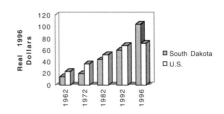

Real Per Capita State and Local Parks and Recreation Spending: South Dakota vs. U.S.

State and Local Natural Resources Spending, 1996

	Per Capita	Ranking
S. Dak.	$113	7th
U.S.	$60	

Per capita state and local natural resources spending in South Dakota topped the U.S. average by 88%.

State Parks Revenues as a Share of Operating Expenses, 1997

	Percent	Rank
S. Dak.	77	5th
U.S.	42	

Percentage of Land Owned by the Federal Government, 1996

	Percent	Rank
S. Dak.	5.3	25th
U.S.	24.8	

SOCIETY AND DEMOGRAPHICS

Population

South Dakota's 1998 population of .738 million ranked 46th in the nation.

Population Growth, 1990–98

	Percentage Change in Population	Ranking
S. Dak.	6.03	34th
U.S.	8.66	

	Net International Migration	Ranking
S. Dak.	4,203	47th

	Net Domestic Migration	Ranking
S. Dak.	5,943	29th

Infant Mortality Rate, 1998

	Percent	Rank
S. Dak.	8.4	10th
U.S.	6.4	

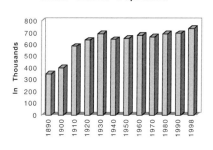

South Dakota Population

Percentage of Births of Low Birthweight, 1997

	Percent	Rank
S. Dak.	5.5	50th
U.S.	7.5	

Percentage of Live Births to Unmarried Women, 1997

	Percent	Rank
S. Dak.	31.1	28th
U.S.	32.4	

Abortion Rate—Abortions Per 1,000 Women Ages 15–44, 1995

	Rate	Rank
S. Dak.	6.6	48th
U.S.	22.9	

LIFESTYLE

Percentage of Households with Computers, 1998

	Percent	Rank
S. Dak.	41.6	29th

Percentage of Households with Internet Access, 1998

	Percent	Rank
S. Dak.	23.9	35th

State Arts Agency Spending, 1999

	Per Capita	Rank
S. Dak.	$0.64	35th
U.S.	$1.35	

Per capita state arts spending in 1999 trailed the U.S. average by 53%.

Major League Sports Facilities

None

TENNESSEE

It is very hard not to notice that the country music emanating from Nashville in recent years has carried a different tone, if you will.

In the old days, country music tended to be a bit twangy, and much of it centered around broken hearts, cheatin' hearts, and drowning one's sorrows. It was kind of gloomy.

Today, country music has come a long way. Sure, those broken-heart songs are still around, but now those tunes really move. Just compare Hank Williams Sr., and Patsy Cline to Garth Brooks and Shania Twain, and you will see what we mean. Country music folks just seem to be a happier bunch these days.

Of course, the fact that country music's popularity has been rapidly spreading to all corners of the nation, not to mention around the globe, provides good reason to rejoice. As reported in the U.S. Census Bureau's annual *Statistical Abstract of the United States,* consumer spending on country music recordings jumped by 50% between 1990 and 1997, while spending on rock, R&B, and pop recordings each declined over the same period. The country music business certainly has been booming.

However, there are other reasons to be whistling happier tunes if you live and do business in Tennessee. Heck, even if you do not like country music and are not too crazy about native son Al Gore, you can still embrace Tennessee.

For example, individuals pay no general personal income or capital gains taxes. Property taxes are very low. Even the number of Tennessee government bureaucrats as a share of population comes in below the U.S. average. Now these are good reasons to kick up your heels, and that is exactly what Tennessee residents have been doing.

The economy, disposable income, employment, and population have all posted solid gains in recent years.

Of late, however, politicians have been threatening the state's progrowth, proentrepreneurial environment. State spending has been moving ahead quite robustly under Republican Governor Don Sundquist. As the *Wall Street Journal* reported (August 20, 1999), Sundquist also has shifted his position from "never" supporting a state income tax to admitting a new willingness to campaign for one if the state legislature decides it is needed. In fact, his original budget proposal offered earlier in the year actually included a thinly disguised income tax—new taxes on company payrolls and on profits—that fortunately was not instituted. In November, Sundquist called the state legislature into session for the specific purpose of instituting a personal income tax. Fortunately, this effort failed, as legislators deadlocked.

The economics are plain: without personal income and capital gains taxes, Tennessee will be well positioned to attract labor and capital to keep its economy chugging along far into the 21st century. If an income tax is imposed, however, incentives for living, working, and investing in Tennessee will be diminished; more revenues will pour into state coffers, only to be wasted; and the state's economy will take a major hit.

Sundquist is term limited, so he cannot run for reelection in 2002. Let us hope his newfound income tax proclivities will continue to be restrained until he leaves office.

POLITICS

Registered Voters

No party registration

Federal Officials: Recent Election and Group Ratings

			ACU	ADA	SBSC
U.S. Senators:	William Frist (R)		80	4	85
	1994　Frist (R)	56%			
	Sasser (D)	42%			
	Fred Thompson (R)		85	4	85
	1996　Thompson (R)	61%			
	Gordon (D)	36%			
U.S. Representatives:	William Jenkins (R-1)		94	5	90
	1998　Jenkins (R)	69%			
	White (D)	31%			
	John Duncan Jr. (R-2)		87	18	85
	1998　Duncan (R)	89%			
	Watson (I)	4%			
	Zach Wamp (R-3)		93	9	80
	1998　Wamp (R)	66%			
	Lewis (D)	33%			
	Van Hilleary (R-4)		98	3	80
	1998　Hilleary (R)	60%			
	Cooper (D)	40%			
	Bob Clement (D-5)		27	55	25
	1998　Clement (D)	83%			
	Lancaster (I)	7%			
	Bart Gordon (D-6)		23	67	25
	1998　Gordon (D)	55%			
	Massey (R)	45%			
	Ed Bryant (R-7)		100	1	95
	1998　Bryant (R)	NO			
	John Tanner (D-8)		43	44	30
	1998　Tanner (D)	NO			
	Harold Ford (D-9)		11	81	15
	1998　Ford (D)	79%			
	Burdikoff (R)	19%			

Electoral Votes:	11	
1996 Presidential Results:	Clinton	48%
	Dole	46%
	Perot	6%

State Officials

Governor 1998 Election:	Don Sundquist (R)	69%
	John Jay Hooker (D)	29%
Lt. Governor:	John Wilder (D)	
Attorney General:	Paul Summers (nonpartisan)	
State Senate:	18 Democrats	
	15 Republicans	
State House:	59 Democrats	
	40 Republicans	

TAXES AND SPENDING

Total Revenues

Tennessee's per capita state and local total revenues registered $5,112 in 1996, ranking 30th in the nation and trailing the U.S. average of $5,706 by 10%. From 1962 to 1996, real per capita state and local revenues increased by 399%, compared with an increase in the national average of 297%.

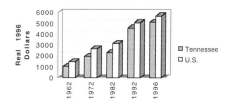

Real Per Capita State and Local Total Revenues: Tennessee vs. U.S.

Taxes

Tennessee's per capita state and local taxes registered $1,878 in 1996, ranking 50th in the nation and trailing the U.S. average of $2,597 by 28%. From 1962 to 1996, real per capita state and local taxes increased by 182%, compared with an increase of 152% in the U.S. average.

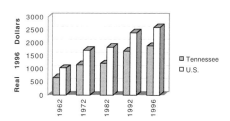

Real Per Capita State and Local Taxes: Tennessee vs. U.S.

Property Taxes

Tennessee's per capita state and local property taxes equaled $426 in 1996, ranking 43d in the nation and trailing the U.S. average of $789 by 46%. From 1962 to 1996, real per capita state and local property taxes increased by 94%, versus a 67% increase in the U.S. average.

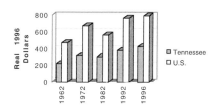

Real Per Capita State and Local Property Taxes: Tennessee vs. U.S.

Sales and Gross Receipts Taxes

Tennessee's per capita state and local sales and gross receipts taxes came in at $1,142 in 1996, ranking 8th in the nation and exceeding the U.S. average of $939 by 22%. From 1962 to 1996, real per capita state and local sales and gross receipts taxes increased by 288%, versus an increase of 214% in the U.S. average.

Income Taxes

Tennessee's per capita state and local income (individual and corporate) taxes registered $122 in 1996, ranking 45th in the nation and trailing the U.S. average of $674 by 82%. From 1962 to 1996, real per capita state and local income taxes increased by 230%, versus a 567% increase in the U.S. average.

Personal Income Tax

A rate of 0%, ranking best in the nation (from lowest tax rate to highest), and comparing with the national average of 5.26%.

Capital Gains Tax

A rate of 0%, ranking best in the nation (from lowest tax rate to highest), and comparing with the national average of 4.68%.

Corporate Income Tax

A rate of 6.0%, ranking 15th in the nation (from lowest tax rate to highest), and comparing with the national average of 6.69%.

Total Expenditures

Tennessee's per capita state and local total spending registered $4,842 in 1996, ranking 27th in the nation and trailing the U.S. average of $5,268 by 8%. From 1962 to 1996, real per capita state and local total spending increased by 335%, versus an increase of 254% in the U.S. average.

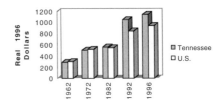

Real Per Capita State and Local Sales and Gross Receipts Taxes: Tennessee vs. U.S.

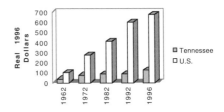

Real Per Capita State and Local Income Taxes: Tennessee vs. U.S.

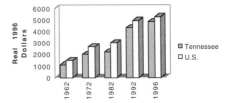

Real Per Capita State and Local Total Expenditures: Tennessee vs. U.S.

Welfare Expenditures

Tennessee's per capita state and local public welfare spending registered $709 in 1996, ranking 19th in the nation and trailing the U.S. average of $729 by 3%. From 1962 to 1996, real per capita state and local public welfare spending increased by 754%, compared with a 488% increase in the U.S. average.

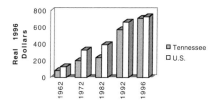

Real Per Capita State and Local Public Welfare Spending: Tennessee vs. U.S.

Welfare Recipients (in thousands)

	1980	1989	3/99	Change 1989–99
Tenn.	174	207	153	−26%
U.S.	10,923	10,987	7,335	−33%

Interest on General Debt

Tennessee's per capita state and local interest on general debt registered $132 in 1996, ranking 42d in the nation and trailing the U.S. average of $222 by 41%. From 1962 to 1996, real per capita state and local interest on general debt increased by 313%, versus an increase of 335% in the U.S. average.

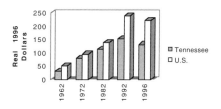

Real Per Capita State and Local Interest on General Debt: Tennessee vs. U.S.

Total Debt Outstanding

Tennessee's per capita state and local debt registered $4,227 in 1996, ranking 23d in the nation and trailing the U.S. average of $4,409 by 4%. From 1962 to 1996, real per capita state and local debt outstanding increased by 140%, versus an increase of 120% in the U.S. average.

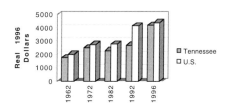

Real Per Capita State and Local Debt Outstanding: Tennessee vs. U.S.

Government Employees

Tennessee's state and local government employees (full-time equivalent, or FTE) per 10,000 population registered 514.2 in 1997, ranking 36th in the nation and trailing the U.S. average of 531.1 by 3%. From 1962 to 1996, state and local FTE employees per 10,000 population increased by 69%, compared with an increase in the U.S. average of 66%.

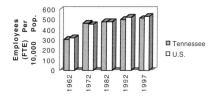

State and Local Government Employees (FTE) Per 10,000 Population: Tennessee vs. U.S.

Per Capita Federal Government Expenditures

	1998	Ranking
Tenn.	$5,615	19th
U.S.	$5,491	

Per capita federal spending in Tennessee exceeded the national average by 2%.

EDUCATION

Total Education Spending

Tennessee's per capita state and local education spending registered $1,199 in 1996, ranking 51st in the nation and trailing the U.S. average of $1,503 by 20%. From 1962 to 1996, real per capita total education spending increased by 222%, versus an increase in the U.S. average of 173%.

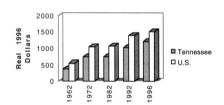

Real Per Capita State and Local Education Spending: Tennessee vs. U.S.

Per Pupil Spending

Tennessee's per pupil public school spending registered $4,322 in 1998, ranking 48th in the nation and trailing the U.S. average of $6,131 by 30%. From 1970 to 1998, Tennessee's real per pupil public school spending increased by 120%, mirroring a 120% increase in the U.S. average.

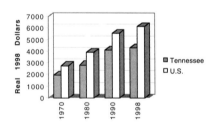

Real Per Pupil Public School Spending: Tennessee vs. U.S.

Average Public School Teacher Salaries (in 1997–98 dollars)

	1970	1980	1990	1998	1998 Ranking
Tenn.	30,186	29,110	34,459	35,340	28th
U.S.	36,934	33,272	39,956	39,385	

In 1998, the average public school teacher salary in Tennessee trailed the U.S. average by 10%. From 1970 to 1998, the real average teacher salary in Tennessee increased by 17%, versus an increase in the U.S. average of 7%.

Pupil/Teacher Ratio, Fall 1996

	Ratio	Rank
Tenn.	16.5	25th
U.S.	17.1	

Teachers/Staff, Fall 1996

	Percent	Rank
Tenn.	54.0	15th
U.S.	52.1	

Public School 4th-Grade Reading Proficiency, 1998

	Average	Rank (out of 40 states)
Tenn.	212	26th
U.S.	215	

Public School 8th-Grade Reading Proficiency, 1998

	Average	Rank (out of 37 states)
Tenn.	259	24th
U.S.	261	

Public School 4th-Grade Math Proficiency, 1996

	Average	Rank (out of 44 states)
Tenn.	219	30th
U.S.	224	

Public School 8th-Grade Math Proficiency, 1996

	Average	Rank (out of 41 states)
Tenn.	263	31st
U.S.	271	

Public School 8th-Grade Science Proficiency, 1996

	Average	Rank (out of 41 states)
Tenn.	143	30th
U.S.	148	

Average Math SAT Scores

	1972	1982	1992	1998	Percentage Taking SAT in 1998
Tenn.	530	539	548	557	13
U.S.	509	493	501	512	43

Average Verbal SAT Scores

	1972	1982	1992	1998	Percentage Taking SAT in 1998
Tenn.	555	556	559	564	13
U.S.	530	504	500	505	43

Expenditures by Public Institutions of Higher Education Per Full-Time-Equivalent Student, 1996

	FTE Student Spending	Rank
Tenn.	$11,283	40th
U.S.	$12,343	

Per-FTE-student spending in public institutions of higher education trailed the U.S. average by 9%.

Per Full-Time-Equivalent Student Revenues from Federal, State, and Local Governments for Public Institutions of Higher Education, 1996

	FTE Student Government Revenues	Rank
Tenn.	$7,482	32d
U.S.	$8,101	

Per-FTE-student-government revenues in public institutions of higher education trailed the U.S. average by 8%.

Average Salary for Full-Time Professors at Public Universities, 1997

	Average	Rank
Tenn.	$65,579	33d
U.S.	$72,599	

The average full-time public university professor salary trailed the U.S. average by 10%.

ECONOMY AND BUSINESS

Economic Growth

Over the period of 1977 to 1997, Tennessee's real gross state product (GSP) grew by 90.8%—ranking 15th in the nation—as compared with real U.S. gross domestic product (GDP), expanding by 70.1%.

At $147.0 billion in 1997, Tennessee's GSP ranked as 20th largest in the nation.

From 1993 to 1997, Tennessee's annual real GSP growth averaged 4.01%—ranking 17th in the nation—as compared with annual real U.S. GDP growth, averaging 3.08%.

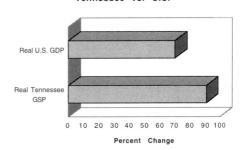

Real Economic Growth 1977-1997: Tennessee vs. U.S.

Job Growth

	Growth in Employee Payrolls (Nonagricultural) 1962–98	Ranking
Tenn.	172.0%	18th
U.S.	126.5%	

	Average Annual Growth in Employee Payrolls (Nonagricultural) 1993–98	Ranking
Tenn.	3.26%	17th
U.S.	2.98%	

Per Capita Disposable Income, 1997

	1997	Ranking
Tenn.	$20,117	30th
U.S.	$21,607	

Per capita disposable income trailed the U.S. average by 7%.

	Real Growth 1962–97	Ranking
Tenn.	174.1%	2d
U.S.	116.7%	

	Average Annual Real Growth 1993–97	Ranking
Tenn.	1.82%	14th
U.S.	1.48%	

Number of Businesses

	1997	Percent with Fewer than 500 Employees
Businesses with Employees	108,263	97.4
Self-employed Individuals	268,000	

New Business Incorporations

	1980	1986	1992	1997
Tenn.	6,544	9,339	8,514	7,495

Percentage Change in Annual New Business Incorporations, 1980 vs. 1997

	Percent	Ranking
Tenn.	14.5	39th
U.S.	49.7	

State Merchandise Exports to the World, 1998 (in millions of dollars)

	1998	Rank
Tenn.	$9,873	20th

Small Business Survival Index, 1999

Tennessee ranks 9th best in terms of its policy environment for entrepreneurship.

Fortune 500 Headquarters in 1999

A total of 7 (ranked 20th)

Labor Union Membership, 1983 vs. 1997

| | Percentage of Workers | | |
	1983	1997	1997 Rank
Tenn.	15.1	8.6	33d
U.S.	20.1	14.1	

Homeownership Rate, 1998

	Rate	Rank
Tenn.	71.3	14th
U.S.	66.3	

CRIME

Crime Rates Per 100 Residents (rankings from best to worst crime rate)

Total Crime	1960	1970	1980	1990	1998	1998 Ranking
Tenn.	0.83	1.89	4.50	5.05	5.03	35th
U.S.	1.04	2.74	5.90	5.82	4.62	

From 1960 to 1998, Tennessee's crime rate increased by 506%, versus a U.S. increase of 344%.
From 1990 to 1998, Tennessee's crime rate decreased by 0.4%, versus a U.S. decrease of 21%.

Violent Crime	1960	1970	1980	1990	1998	1998 Ranking
Tenn.	0.09	0.27	0.46	0.67	0.72	43d
U.S.	0.14	0.36	0.58	0.73	0.57	

From 1960 to 1998, Tennessee's violent crime rate increased by 700%, versus a U.S. increase of 307%.
From 1990 to 1998, Tennessee's violent crime rate increased by 7%, compared with a national decline of 22%.

Property Crime	1960	1970	1980	1990	1998	1998 Ranking
Tenn.	0.73	1.61	4.04	4.38	4.32	33d
U.S.	0.90	2.38	5.32	5.09	4.05	

From 1960 to 1998, Tennessee's property crime rate increased by 492%, versus a national increase of 350%. From 1990 to 1998, Tennessee's property crime rate decreased by 1%, compared with a national decline of 20%.

Real Per Capita Police Protection Spending (in real 1996 dollars)

	1962	1972	1982	1992	1996	1996 Ranking
Tenn.	32	56	80	102	124	36th
U.S.	51	95	114	148	168	

In 1996, per capita state and local police protection spending in Tennessee trailed the U.S. average by 26%. From 1962 to 1996, real per capita state and local police protection spending increased by 288%, versus an increase of 229% in the U.S. average.

Prisoners in State and Federal Prisons Per 1,000 Population

	1980	1990	1996	1996 Ranking
Tenn.	1.53	2.13	2.94	33d
U.S.	1.46	3.11	4.45	

From 1980 to 1996, prisoners per 1,000 population increased by 92%, versus a U.S. increase of 205%.

HEALTH CARE

Health-Care Spending

Tennessee's per capita state and local health-care spending registered $132 in 1996, ranking 26th in the nation and trailing the U.S. average of $151 by 13%. From 1962 to 1996, Tennessee's real per capita state and local health-care spending increased by 843%, versus an increase of 739% in the U.S. average.

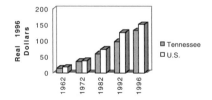

Real Per Capita State and Local Health Care Spending: Tennessee vs. U.S.

Hospital Spending

Tennessee's per capita state and local hospital spending registered $350 in 1996, ranking 11th in the nation and exceeding the U.S. average of $266 by 32%. From 1962 to 1996, Tennessee's real per capita state and local hospital spending increased by 379%, as opposed to an increase of 189% in the U.S. average.

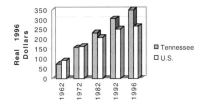

Real Per Capita State and Local Hospital Spending: Tennessee vs. U.S.

Medicaid, 1996

	Spending Per Recipient	Ranking
Tenn.	$2,073	49th
U.S.	$3,681	

Tennessee's per-recipient Medicaid spending trailed the U.S. average by 44%.

ENVIRONMENT

Parks and Recreation Spending

Tennessee's per capita state and local parks and recreation spending registered $62 in 1996, ranking 25th in the nation and trailing the U.S. average of $72 by 14%. From 1962 to 1996, real per capita state and local parks and recreation spending increased by 589%, versus a 213% increase in the U.S. average.

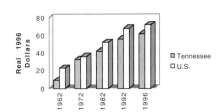

Real Per Capita State and Local Parks and Recreation Spending: Tennessee vs. U.S.

State and Local Natural Resources Spending, 1996

	Per Capita	Ranking
Tenn.	$40	38th
U.S.	$60	

Per capita state and local natural resources spending in Tennessee trailed the U.S. average by 33%.

State Parks Revenues as a Share of Operating Expenses, 1997

	Percent	Rank
Tenn.	53	15th
U.S.	42	

Percentage of Land Owned by the Federal Government, 1996

	Percent	Rank
Tenn.	5.9	24th
U.S.	24.8	

SOCIETY AND DEMOGRAPHICS

Population

Tennessee's 1998 population of 5.431 million ranked 17th in the nation.

Population Growth, 1990–98

	Percentage Change in Population	Ranking
Tenn.	11.36	15th
U.S.	8.66	

	Net International Migration	Ranking
Tenn.	27,279	26th

	Net Domestic Migration	Ranking
Tenn.	337,630	9th

Infant Mortality Rate, 1998

	Percent	Rank
Tenn.	8.5	8th
U.S.	6.4	

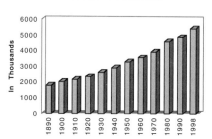

Tennessee Population

Percentage of Births of Low Birthweight, 1997

	Percent	Rank
Tenn.	8.8	7th
U.S.	7.5	

Percentage of Live Births to Unmarried Women, 1997

	Percent	Rank
Tenn.	34.1	13th
U.S.	32.4	

Abortion Rate—Abortions Per 1,000 Women Ages 15–44, 1995

	Rate	Rank
Tenn.	15.2	28th
U.S.	22.9	

LIFESTYLE

Percentage of Households with Computers, 1998

	Percent	Rank
Tenn.	37.5	41st

Percentage of Households with Internet Access, 1998

	Percent	Rank
Tenn.	21.3	43d

State Arts Agency Spending, 1999

	Per Capita	Rank
Tenn.	$0.52	44th
U.S.	$1.35	

Per capita state arts spending in 1999 trailed the U.S. average by 61%.

Major League Sports Facilities

| Year Opened/ Refurb. | Stadium/ Arena | Home Team | Millions of Nominal Dollars | | Millions of Real 1997 Dollars | |
			Estimated Total Cost	Estimated Taxpayer Cost	Estimated Total Cost	Estimated Taxpayer Cost
1994	Nashville Arena	Predators (NHL) 1998–present	$143.0	$143.0	$154.9	$154.9
1999	Adelphia Stadium	Titans (NFL) 1999–present	$292.0	$227.0	$281.9	$219.1

TEXAS

In a *Texas Monthly* article (July 1998), Texas Governor George W. Bush was quoted laying out a very important plank in his "compassionate conservative" agenda: "Baseball should always be played outdoors with wooden bats." If only politicians were so clear thinking on political issues as well!

In fact, even the purity of baseball can be muddied by politics. George W. Bush serves as an example. When he was managing partner of the Texas Rangers in the early 1990s, Bush led the charge to build a new ballpark for the Rangers. Opened in 1994, the Ballpark at Arlington is a glorious addition to the growing list of new ballparks, with all the modern amenities with an old-time feel as well. However, this facility was not a model of a successful private-sector venture, but instead just another example of wealthy baseball team owners and players being subsidized by the taxpayers, who picked up about $143 million of the $191 million cost. We guess "compassionate conservatism" includes corporate welfare for sports teams, too.

Obviously, there is more to the Texas governor's policy agenda. When one brings together the name "Bush" with the word "taxes," sirens and warning lights tend to go off for those favoring tax relief, and for good reason, thanks to former President George Bush's notorious breaking of his "no new taxes" pledge.

George W.'s support for a sales tax hike to fund the Rangers's new ballpark is not reassuring. In addition, in 1997 Bush escaped the fallout from problems with his own tax proposal. The good news was that Bush called for a $3 billion property tax cut. The bad news was that it would have been partially offset by a $2 billion tax increase covering a variety of taxes and fees, including an extension of the state's corporate income tax (imposed by his predecessor, Ann Richards) to include nonincorporated partnerships. So, while Bush was emphasizing that he would never impose a personal income tax in Texas, in fact he was trying to do so for partnerships. In the end, after storms of protest from taxpayers and business groups, a straight $1 billion property tax cut was passed. Of course, like a good politician, Bush claims he succeeded in passing a $1 billion tax cut.

Unlike his father, however, George W. may be able to learn from experience. He proposed and got a sizeable, clean state tax cut in 1999 (though after the legislature was done, it wound up being smaller than Bush had originally called for). Disappointingly, Bush never seized on the opportunity to roll back the corporate income tax imposed by Richards.

Bush has spoken favorably of cutting capital gains taxes and marginal income tax rates at the federal level. It is hard to imagine a President George W. Bush repeating the mistake of his father and raising taxes. However, it may be equally difficult to envision a revolutionary, progrowth plan to overhaul our current messy, complicated tax system, or to even get personal income tax rates back down to where they were before Presidents Bush and Clinton raised them.

On education, like most GOPers today, George W. favors massive increases in spending and believes that the federal role should be limited to sending dollars to the states with no strings attached. However, he supports school choice and phonics, distrusts national standards and tests, and calls for

803

ending social promotion in schools. As governor, some of his biggest successes have come on the education front, including cutting regulations, boosting standards, and establishing charter schools and public-school choice.

As for Bush's "law-and-order" agenda, crime has fallen in Texas during Bush's governorship, and he strongly supports the death penalty. In fact, according to a report in *Newsday* (August 16, 1999), from the time he took office in 1995 to August 1999 Bush signed 95 death warrants. He also has toughened juvenile-justice laws and given Charles Colson's Prison Fellowship a contract to run part of a state prison. Bush also signed legislation allowing the right to carry concealed fire arms in Texas.

On the international and defense fronts, where would a President George W. Bush position himself? Bush's profree trade, proimmigration, and protrade with Mexico positions are a refreshing contrast to the isolationist, protectionist likes of Pat Buchanan. Bush seems to strongly support rebuilding our defense after years of neglect by the Clinton administration and, quite frankly, a Republican-led Congress.

"Dubya," as Bush is often called, is generally conservative, unabashedly optimistic, affable, and has a sense of humor. The real questions center on substance. Is his "compassionate conservatism" substantive or just an update on the previous Bush's "kinder, gentler" fiasco or some kind of response to Clintonian "feel your pain" psychobabble? Myron Magnet's attempt to explain "compassionate conservatism," in a *Wall Street Journal* op-ed (February 5, 1999), fell rather flat as a major break with Republican programs of the past. Magnet's piece essentially said that "compassionate conservatism" is neoconservatism with a new name (which is fine, if that is the case). Some see the "compassionate conservatism" of George W. as an effort to take fundamentally conservative ideas to groups that may not have been exposed previously, such as immigrants and minorities. In this sense, it is rather Jack Kemp-like—ironic, considering that Bush the father and Kemp mix like oil and water.

Bush certainly is no policy wonk—which can be a positive for a president, as long as he has a set of core principles and ideas. Meanwhile, one free-market critic in Texas accuses Dubya of not being strongly principled and says that he is "not willing to anger anyone"—concluding that it is all "very President Bush-ish."

For the Lone Star State, one can honestly conclude that Bush generally has improved the state of affairs for Texas. Compared with the other states, Texas claims below-average government spending and debt burdens, low taxes, a dramatic decline in welfare rolls over the past decade, and rock-solid growth in population, the economy, jobs, and disposable income. Though state crime levels remains on the high side compared with the rest of the nation, Texas has shown dramatic improvement in recent years.

Texas is well positioned to continue this overall success story in the 21st century.

POLITICS

Registered Voters

No party registration

Federal Officials: Recent Election and Group Ratings

			ACU	ADA	SBSC
U.S. Senators:	Phil Gramm (R)		93	1	85
	1996 Gramm (R)	54%			
	Morales (D)	43%			
	Kay Bailey Hutchinson (R)		93	6	85
	1994 Hutchinson (R)	61%			
	Fisher (D)	38%			
U.S. Representatives:	Max Sandlin Jr. (D-1)		38	70	20
	1998 Sandlin (D)	59%			
	Boerner (R)	41%			
	Jim Turner (D-2)		48	58	25
	1998 Turner (D)	58%			
	Babin (R)	41%			
	Sam Johnson (R-3)		98	3	95
	1998 Johnson (R)	91%			
	Ashby (D)	9%			
	Ralph Hall (D-4)		81	14	85
	1998 Hall (D)	58%			
	Lohmeyer (R)	41%			
	Pete Sessions (R-5)		100	0	95
	1998 Sessions (R)	56%			
	Morales (D)	43%			
	Joe Barton (R-6)		94	5	90
	1998 Barton (R)	73%			
	Boothe (D)	26%			
	Bill Archer (R-7)		96	3	95
	1998 Archer (R)	93%			
	Parks (LBT)	7%			
	Kevin Brady (R-8)		98	3	90
	1998 Brady (R)	93%			
	Richards (D)	7%			
	Nick Lampson (D-9)		20	83	5
	1998 Lampson (D)	64%			
	Cottar (R)	36%			
	Lloyd Doggett (D-10)		10	91	15
	1998 Doggett (D)	85%			
	May (LBT)	15%			

			ACU	ADA	SBSC
Chet Edwards (D-11)			29	54	25
1998	Edwards (D)	82%			
	Hanke (LBT)	18%			
Kay Granger (R-12)			88	3	95
1998	Granger (R)	62%			
	Hall (D)	36%			
Mac Thornberry (R-13)			98	3	95
1998	Thornberry (R)	68%			
	Harmon (D)	31%			
Ron Paul (R-14)			84	25	75
1998	Paul (R)	55%			
	Sneary (D)	44%			
Ruben Hinojosa (D-15)			23	85	15
1998	Hinojosa (D)	58%			
	Haughey (R)	42%			
Silvestre Reyes (D-16)			26	73	15
1998	Reyes (D)	88%			
	Nance (LBT)	7%			
Charles Stenholm (D-17)			75	18	50
1998	Stenholm (D)	54%			
	Izzard (R)	45%			
Sheila Jackson Lee (D-18)			7	91	10
1998	Lee (D)	90%			
	Galvan (LBT)	10%			
Larry Combest (R-19)			98	3	90
1998	Combest (R)	84%			
	Blankenship (D)	16%			
Charles Gonzalez (D-20)			14	71	0
1998	Gonzalez (D)	63%			
	Walker (R)	36%			
Lamar Smith (R-21)			92	6	90
1998	Smith (R)	91%			
	Blunt (LBT)	9%			
Thomas DeLay (R-22)			96	2	100
1998	DeLay (R)	65%			
	Kemp (D)	34%			

			ACU	ADA	SBSC
Henry Bonilla (R-23)			92	4	85
1998	Bonilla (R)	64%			
	Jones (D)	35%			
Martin Frost (D-24)			18	67	20
1998	Frost (D)	57%			
	Terry (R)	41%			
Ken Bensten (D-25)			9	82	20
1998	Bensten (D)	58%			
	Sanchez (R)	41%			
Richard Armey (R-26)			97	2	100
1998	Armey (R)	88%			
	Turner (LBT)	12%			
Solomon Ortiz (D-27)			31	54	20
1998	Ortiz (D)	63%			
	Stone (R)	35%			
Ciro Rodriguez (D-28)			15	88	10
1998	Rodriguez (D)	91%			
	Elmer (LBT)	9%			
Gene Green (D-29)			24	82	20
1998	Green (D)	93%			
	Sherman (I)	4%			
Eddie Bernice Johnson (D-30)			8	88	15
1998	Johnson (D)	72%			
	Kelleher (R)	27%			

Electoral Votes:	32	
1996 Presidential Results:	Clinton	44%
	Dole	49%
	Perot	7%

State Officials

Governor 1998 Election:	George W. Bush (R)	68%
	Garry Mauro (D)	31%
Lt. Governor:	Rick Perry (R)	
Attorney General:	John Cornyn (R)	
State Senate:	15 Democrats	
	16 Republicans	
State House:	79 Democrats	
	71 Republicans	

TAXES AND SPENDING

Total Revenues

Texas's per capita state and local total revenues registered $4,669 in 1996, ranking 46th in the nation and trailing the U.S. average of $5,706 by 18%. From 1962 to 1996, real per capital state and local revenues increased by 277%, compared with an increase in the national average of 297%.

Taxes

Texas's per capita state and local taxes registered $2,128 in 1996, ranking 41st in the nation and trailing the U.S. average of $2,597 by 18%. From 1962 to 1996, real per capita state and local taxes increased by 153%, compared with an increase of 152% in the U.S. average.

Property Taxes

Texas's per capita state and local property taxes equaled $797 in 1996, ranking 20th in the nation and topping the U.S. average of $789 by 1%. From 1962 to 1996, real per capita state and local property taxes increased by 109%, versus a 67% increase in the U.S. average.

Sales and Gross Receipts Taxes

Texas's per capita state and local sales and gross receipts taxes came in at $1,079 in 1996, ranking 9th in the nation and exceeding the U.S. average of $939 by 15%. From 1962 to 1996, real per capita state and local sales and gross receipts taxes increased by 312%, versus an increase of 214% in the U.S. average.

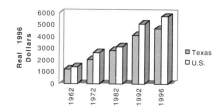

Real Per Capita State and Local Total Revenues: Texas vs. U.S.

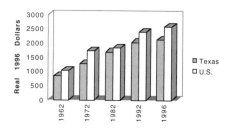

Real Per Capita State and Local Taxes: Texas vs. U.S.

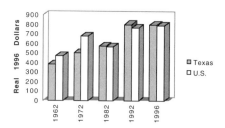

Real Per Capita State and Local Property Taxes: Texas vs. U.S.

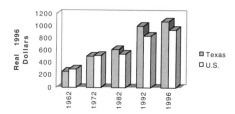

Real Per Capita State and Local Sales and Gross Receipts Taxes: Texas vs. U.S.

Income Taxes

According to Census Bureau data, Texas's per capita state and local income (individual and corporate) taxes registered $0 in 1996, ranking last in the nation and trailing the U.S. average of $674. From 1962 to 1996, real per capita state and local income taxes increased by 0%, versus a 567% increase in the U.S. average. However, these numbers are deceptive in that Texas imposes a corporate income tax, but U.S. Census Bureau data ranks it as a gross receipts tax.

Personal Income Tax

A rate of 0%, ranking best in the nation (from lowest tax rate to highest), and comparing with the national average of 5.26%.

Capital Gains Tax

A rate of 0%, ranking best in the nation (from lowest tax rate to highest), and comparing with the national average of 4.68%.

Corporate Income Tax

A rate of 4.5%, ranking 7th in the nation (from lowest tax rate to highest), and comparing with the national average of 6.69%.

Total Expenditures

Texas's per capita state and local total spending registered $4,365 in 1996, ranking 42d in the nation and trailing the U.S. average of $5,268 by 17%. From 1962 to 1996, real per capita state and local total spending increased by 256%, versus a 254% increase in the U.S. average.

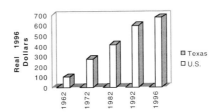

Real Per Capita State and Local Income Taxes: Texas vs. U.S.

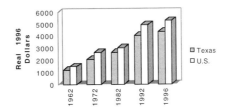

Real Per Capita State and Local Total Expenditures: Texas vs. U.S.

Welfare Expenditures

Texas's per capita state and local public welfare spending registered $535 in 1996, ranking 43d in the nation and trailing the U.S average of $729 by 27%. From 1962 to 1996, real per capita state and local public welfare spending increased by 457%, compared with a 488% increase in the U.S. average.

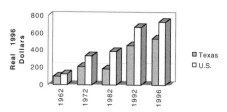

Real Per Capita State and Local Public Welfare Spending: Texas vs. U.S.

Welfare Recipients (in thousands)

	1980	1989	3/99	Change 1989–99
Tex.	320	581	314	−46%
U.S.	10,923	10,987	7,335	−33%

Interest on General Debt

Texas's per capita state and local interest on general debt registered $184 in 1996, ranking 32d in the nation and trailing the U.S. average of $222 by 17%. From 1962 to 1996, real per capita state and local interest on general debt increased by 300%, versus an increase of 335% in the U.S. average.

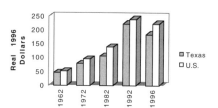

Real Per Capita State and Local Interest on General Debt: Texas vs. U.S.

Total Debt Outstanding

Texas's per capita state and local debt registered $3,973 in 1996, ranking 24th in the nation and trailing the U.S. average of $4,409 by 10%. From 1962 to 1996, real per capita state and local debt outstanding increased by 109%, versus an increase of 120% in the U.S. average.

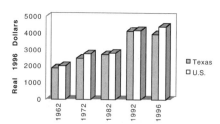

Real Per Capita State and Local Debt Outstanding: Texas vs. U.S.

Government Employees

Texas's state and local government employees (full-time equivalent, or FTE) per 10,000 population registered 572.2 in 1997, ranking 16th in the nation and exceeding the U.S. average of 531.1 by 8%. From 1962 to 1996, state and local FTE employees per 10,000 population increased by 87%, compared with an increase in the U.S. average of 66%.

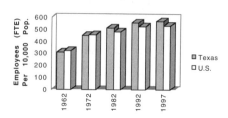

State and Local Government Employees (FTE) Per 10,000 Population: Texas vs. U.S.

Per Capita Federal Government Expenditures

	1998	Ranking
Tex.	$4,657	41st
U.S.	$5,491	

Per capita federal spending in Texas trailed the national average by 15%.

EDUCATION

Total Education Spending

Texas's per capita state and local education spending registered $1,456 in 1996, ranking 30th in the nation and trailing the U.S. average of $1,503 by 3%. From 1962 to 1996, real per capita total education spending increased by 196%, versus an increase in the U.S. average of 173%.

Real Per Capita State and Local Education Spending: Texas vs. U.S.

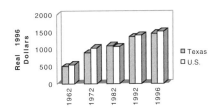

Per Pupil Spending

Texas's per pupil public school spending registered $5,851 in 1998, ranking 29th in the nation and trailing the U.S. average of $6,131 by 5%. From 1970 to 1998, Texas's real per pupil public school spending increased by 187%, compared with a 120% increase in the U.S. average.

Real Per Pupil Public School Spending: Texas vs. U.S.

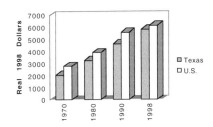

Average Public School Teacher Salaries (in 1997–98 dollars)

	1970	1980	1990	1998	1998 Ranking
Tex.	31,064	29,443	35,025	33,648	35th
U.S.	36,934	33,272	39,956	39,385	

In 1998, the average public school teacher salary in Texas trailed the U.S. average by 15%. From 1970 to 1998, the real average teacher salary in Texas increased by 8%, versus an increase in the U.S. average of 7%.

Pupil/Teacher Ratio, Fall 1996

	Ratio	Rank
Tex.	15.5	18th
U.S.	17.1	

Teachers/Staff, Fall 1996

	Ratio	Rank
Tex.	51.8	34th
U.S.	52.1	

Public School 4th-Grade Reading Proficiency, 1998

	Average	Rank (out of 40 states)
Tex.	217	16th
U.S.	215	

Public School 8th-Grade Reading Proficiency, 1998

	Average	Rank (out of 37 states)
Tex.	262	17th
U.S.	261	

Public School 4th-Grade Math Proficiency, 1996

	Average	Rank (out of 44 states)
Tex.	229	6th
U.S.	224	

Public School 8th-Grade Math Proficiency, 1996

	Average	Rank (out of 41 states)
Tex.	270	20th
U.S.	271	

Public School 8th-Grade Science Proficiency, 1996

	Average	Rank (out of 41 states)
Tex.	145	26th
U.S.	148	

Average Math SAT Scores

	1972	1982	1992	1998	Percentage Taking SAT in 1998
Tex.	502	481	493	501	51
U.S.	509	493	501	512	43

Average Verbal SAT Scores

	1972	1982	1992	1998	Percentage Taking SAT in 1998
Tex.	523	493	487	494	51
U.S.	530	504	500	505	43

Expenditures by Public Institutions of Higher Education Per Full-Time-Equivalent Student, 1996

	FTE Student Spending	Rank
Tex.	$12,155	26th
U.S.	$12,343	

Per-FTE-student spending in public institutions of higher education trailed the U.S. average by 2%.

Per Full-Time-Equivalent Student Revenues from Federal, State, and Local Governments for Public Institutions of Higher Education, 1996

	FTE Student Government Revenues	Rank
Tex.	$8,783	9th
U.S.	$8,101	

Per-FTE-student-government revenues in public institutions of higher education exceeded the U.S. average by 8%.

Average Salary for Full-Time Professors at Public Universities, 1997

	Average	Rank
Tex.	$72,418	20th
U.S.	$72,599	

The average full-time public university professor salary trailed the U.S. average by 0.2%.

ECONOMY AND BUSINESS

Economic Growth

Over the period of 1977 to 1997, Texas's real gross state product (GSP) grew by 90.7%—ranking 16th in the nation—as compared with real U.S. gross domestic product (GDP), expanding by 70.1%.

At $601.6 billion in 1997, Texas's GSP ranked as 3d largest in the nation.

From 1993 to 1997, Texas's annual real GSP growth averaged 5.09%—ranking 10th in the nation—as compared with annual real U.S. GDP growth, averaging 3.08%.

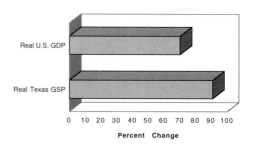

Real Economic Growth 1977-1997: Texas vs. U.S.

Job Growth

	Growth in Employee Payrolls (Nonagricultural) 1962–98	Ranking
Tex.	239.7%	8th
U.S.	126.5%	

	Average Annual Growth in Employee Payrolls (Nonagricultural) 1993–98	Ranking
Tex.	4.21%	8th
U.S.	2.98%	

Per Capita Disposable Income, 1997

	1997	Ranking
Tex.	$20,927	22d
U.S.	$21,607	

Per capita disposable income trailed the U.S. average by 3%.

	Real Growth 1962–97	Ranking
Tex.	143.4%	11th
U.S.	116.7%	

	Average Annual Real Growth 1993–97	Ranking
Tex.	2.08%	8th
U.S.	1.48%	

Number of Businesses

	1997	Percent with Fewer than 500 Employees
Businesses with Employees	375,357	98.7
Self-employed Individuals	845,000	

New Business Incorporations

	1980	1986	1992	1997
Tex.	37,275	38,796	34,011	39,298

Percentage Change in Annual New Business Incorporations, 1980 vs. 1997

	Percent	Ranking
Tex.	5.4	42d
U.S.	49.7	

State Merchandise Exports to the World, 1998 (in millions of dollars)

	1998	Rank
Tex.	$59,029	2d

Small Business Survival Index, 1999

Texas ranks 5th best in terms of its policy environment for entrepreneurship.

Fortune 500 Headquarters in 1999

A total of 36 (ranked 4th), with Houston ranked 3d among U.S. cities with 13 and Dallas ranked 6th with 9 headquarters

Labor Union Membership, 1983 vs. 1997

| | Percentage of Workers | | Rank |
	1983	1997	
Tex.	9.7	6.4	47th
U.S.	20.1	14.1	

Homeownership Rate, 1998

	Rate	Rank
Tex.	62.5	44th
U.S.	66.3	

CRIME

Crime Rates Per 100 Residents (rankings from best to worst crime rate)

Total Crime	1960	1970	1980	1990	1998	1998 Ranking
Tex.	1.15	2.71	6.14	7.83	5.11	36th
U.S.	1.04	2.74	5.90	5.82	4.62	

From 1960 to 1998, Texas's crime rate increased by 344%, the same as a U.S. increase of 344%. From 1990 to 1998, Texas's crime rate dropped by 35%, versus a U.S. decrease of 21%

Violent Crime	1960	1970	1980	1990	1998	1998 Ranking
Tex.	0.16	0.36	0.55	0.76	0.56	32d
U.S.	0.14	0.36	0.58	0.73	0.57	

From 1960 to 1998, Texas's violent crime rate increased by 250%, versus a U.S. increase of 307%. From 1990 to 1998, Texas's violent crime rate decreased by 26%, compared with a national decline of 22%

Property Crime	1960	1970	1980	1990	1998	1998 Ranking
Tex.	0.99	2.34	5.59	7.07	4.55	36th
U.S.	0.90	2.38	5.32	5.09	4.05	

From 1960 to 1998, Texas's property crime rate increased by 360%, versus a national increase of 350%. From 1990 to 1998, Texas's property crime rate decreased by 36%, compared with a national decline of 20%.

Real Per Capita Police Protection Spending (in real 1996 dollars)

	1962	1972	1982	1992	1996	1996 Ranking
Tex.	41	66	91	120	135	31st
U.S.	51	95	114	148	168	

In 1996, per capita state and local police protection spending in Texas trailed the U.S. average by 20%. From 1962 to 1996, real per capita state and local police protection spending increased by 229%, mirroring an increase of 229% in the U.S. average.

Prisoners in State and Federal Prisons Per 1,000 Population

	1980	1990	1996	1996 Ranking
Tex.	2.10	2.95	6.93	3d
U.S.	1.46	3.11	4.45	

From 1980 to 1996, prisoners per 1,000 population increased by 230%, versus a U.S. increase of 205%.

HEALTH CARE

Health-Care Spending

Texas's per capita state and local health-care spending registered $93 in 1996, ranking 43d in the nation and lagging behind the U.S. average of $151 by 38%. From 1962 to 1996, Texas's real per capita state and local health-care spending increased by 933%, versus an increase of 739% in the U.S. average.

Real Per Capita State and Local Health Care Spending: Texas vs. U.S.

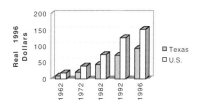

Hospital Spending

Texas's per capita state and local hospital spending registered $319 in 1996, ranking 13th in the nation and exceeding the U.S. average of $266 by 20%. From 1962 to 1996, Texas's real per capita state and local hospital spending increased by 432%, as opposed to an increase of 189% in the U.S. average.

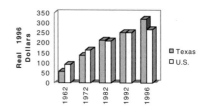

Real Per Capita State and Local Hospital Spending: Texas vs. U.S.

Medicaid, 1997

	Spending Per Recipient	Ranking
Tex.	$2,893	40th
U.S.	$3,681	

Texas's per-recipient Medicaid spending trailed the U.S. average by 21%.

ENVIRONMENT

Parks and Recreation Spending

Texas's per capita state and local parks and recreation spending registered $44 in 1996, ranking 40th in the nation and trailing the U.S. average of $72 by 39%. From 1962 to 1996, real per capita state and local parks and recreation spending increased by 214%, versus a 213% increase in the U.S. average.

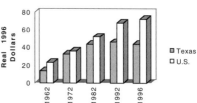

Real Per Capita State and Local Parks and Recreation Spending: Texas vs. U.S.

State and Local Natural Resources Spending, 1996

	Per Capita	Ranking
Tex.	$43	35th
U.S.	$60	

Per capita state and local natural resources spending in Texas trailed the U.S. average by 28%.

State Parks Revenues as a Share of Operating Expenses, 1997

	Percent	Rank
Tex.	66	9th
U.S.	42	

Percentage of Land Owned by the Federal Government, 1996

	Percent	Rank
Tex.	1.2	40th
U.S.	24.8	

SOCIETY AND DEMOGRAPHICS

Population

Texas's 1998 population of 19.760 million ranked 2d in the nation.

Population Growth, 1990–98

	Percentage Change in Population	Ranking
Tex.	16.33	8th
U.S.	8.66	

	Net International Migration	Ranking
Tex.	655,666	3d

	Net Domestic Migration	Ranking
Tex.	541,020	3d

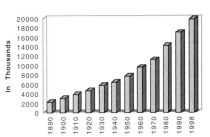

Texas Population

Infant Mortality Rate, 1998

	Percent	Rank
Tex.	6.5	32d
U.S.	6.4	

Percentage of Births of Low Birthweight, 1997

	Percent	Rank
Tex.	7.3	29th
U.S.	7.5	

Percentage of Live Births to Unmarried Women, 1997

	Percent	Rank
Tex.	30.7	29th
U.S.	32.4	

Abortion Rate—Abortions Per 1,000 Women Ages 15–44, 1995

	Rate	Rank
Tex.	20.5	18th
U.S.	22.9	

LIFESTYLE

Percentage of Households with Computers, 1998

	Percent	Rank
Tex.	40.9	34th

Percentage of Households with Internet Access, 1998

	Percent	Rank
Tex.	24.5	31st

State Arts Agency Spending, 1999

	Per Capita	Rank
Tex.	$0.26	51st
U.S.	$1.35	

Per capita state arts spending in 1999 lagged behind the U.S. average by 81%.

Major League Sports Facilities

Year Opened/Refurb.	Stadium/Arena	Home Team	Millions of Nominal Dollars		Millions of Real 1997 Dollars	
			Estimated Total Cost	Estimated Taxpayer Cost	Estimated Total Cost	Estimated Taxpayer Cost
1962	Colt Stadium	Colt '45s (MLB) 1962–64	$2.0	$0.0	$10.6	$0.0
1964	Arlington Stadium	Rangers (MLB) 1972–93	$1.9	$1.9	$9.9	$9.9
1972	Arlington Stad. (re)		$19.0	$19.0	$73.1	$73.1
1983	Arlington Stad. (re)		$3.0	$3.0	$4.8	$4.8
1965	Astrodome	Astros (MLB) 1965–1999 Oilers (AFL/NFL) 1968–96	$38.0	$38.0	$193.9	$193.9
1987	Astrodome (re)		$67.0	$67.0	$94.6	$94.6
1971	Texas Stadium	Cowboys (NFL) 1971–present	$25.0	$25.0	$99.2	$99.2
1975	The Summit/ Compaq Center	Rockets (NBA) 1975–present	$18.0	$18.0	$53.4	$53.4
1994	The Summit (re)		$6.2	$6.2	$6.7	$6.7
1980	Reunion Arena	Mavericks (NBA) 1980–present Stars (NHL) 1993–present	$27.0	$27.0	$52.6	$52.6
1993	Reunion Arena (re)		$5.0	$5.0	$5.6	$5.6
1993	Alamodome	Spurs (NBA) 1993–present	$195.0	$195.0	$216.7	$216.7
1994	Ballpark at Arlington	Rangers (MLB) 1994–present	$191.0	$143.0	$206.9	$154.9
2000	Enron Field	Astros (MLB) 2000–present	$248.1	$181.0	$234.3	$170.9

UTAH

Utah was prominently elevated to the national stage twice between 1996 and 1999. In neither instance was the news good.

In 1996, Utah was another victim of the political ambitions of President Clinton and of the desires of environmental extremists. During the 1996 presidential campaign, Clinton announced a monumental federal government land grab under the obscure 1906 Antiquities Act. Bypassing Congress, failing to consult the good people of Utah, and announcing his actions while in Arizona, Clinton irresponsibly turned some 1.7 million acres in Utah (reportedly consuming about 80 percent of Kane County) into a national monument.

According to Liz Arnold of the People for the West, writing in the *Washington Times* (October 5, 1996): "The land is a hodgepodge of private, state and public land differentiated by wilderness areas, multiple-use and mineral-development areas and land needed for state tax revenues." This was not endangered land; it was politically convenient land.

The reason for Clinton's action was, first, to appease some environmentalists who oppose mining huge coal deposits. However, not only would such development create hundreds, if not thousands, of new jobs; this particular deposit, according to numerous reports, happens to be low-sulphur, clean-burning coal, which helps fight pollution. So much for the environment.

Second, Clinton was trolling for votes. While Utah was not about to vote for Clinton in 1996 (they did not), Arizona certainly was in play (he won it). Clinton also would gain favor with those urban folks who care so much about open spaces far from where they themselves live.

Legislative efforts to reel in the 1906 Antiquities Act, which allowed Presidents Franklin Delano Roosevelt and Jimmy Carter to partake in their own land grabs as well, have gone nowhere. However, a lawsuit brought by the Utah Association of Counties and the Mountain States Legal Defense Fund, that accuses the president of overstepping his authority is proceeding.

Incidentally, before Clinton's action, the federal government had owned more than 64% of the land in Utah.

Utah's other dark story has its origins in the big city. When Salt Lake City captured the 2002 Winter Olympics, most assumed it would be a big economic and public relations boost to Utah. However, the November 1998 revelation of a bribery scheme to win the Games has raised serious doubts. Until people see the first ski hit the snow and the first skate on the ice in 2002, almost every story and report about the 2002 Winter Games will reference the scandal.

We love watching athletes compete in the Olympics and certainly hope that the people of Salt Lake City come out okay in the end. It should be noted that subsequent investigations have raised questions about unsavory dealings by other cities to lure the Olympics as well. In March 1999, the Mitchell report, produced by a panel headed up by former U.S. Senator George Mitchell, lambasted the International Olympic Committee for a culture of corruption. However, when you are talking about elected officials competing for a sporting event that will put their city in the global spotlight, quite frankly no one should be surprised by bribes and other shenanigans. After all, it is politics.

Beyond Clinton and the Olympics, however, the news about Utah is overwhelmingly good news that is far more important to the average family and business owner.

This very Republican state imposes fairly low taxes overall—with property taxes quite low but income levies leaving room for improvement—as well as below-average government spending and employee levels. Utah's education numbers are particularly exciting. The state actually ranks last in the nation in terms of per pupil public school spending, but student performance is quite good.

The state's economy has been quite healthy. Growth in real gross state product ranks among the very best in the nation, as do job growth and increases in new business incorporations. Population growth also rates among the nation's most vibrant, and in recent years real per capita disposable income growth has registered a top level of performance.

The truly big stories in Utah are about getting a good education at low costs and benefiting from robust entrepreneurship and economic dynamism. Utah will do well in the 21st century as long as politicians refrain from going on any spending and taxing sprees—no matter how well or poorly the 2002 Winter Games do.

POLITICS

Registered Voters

No party registration

Federal Officials: Recent Election and Group Ratings

			ACU	ADA	SBSC
U.S. Senators:	Orrin Hatch (R)		90	7	95
	1994 Hatch (R)	69%			
	Shea (D)	28%			
	Robert Bennett (R)		82	6	80
	1998 Bennett (R)	64%			
	Leckman (D)	33%			
U.S. Representatives:	James Hansen (R-1)		94	1	95
	1998 Hansen (R)	68%			
	Beierlein (D)	30%			
	Merrill Cook (R-2)		86	10	85
	1998 Cook (R)	53%			
	Eskelsen (D)	43%			
	Chris Cannon (R-3)		96	8	65
	1998 Cannon (R)	77%			
	Christensen (IAP)	16%			

Electoral Votes:	5	
1996 Presidential Results:	Clinton	33%
	Dole	54%
	Perot	10%

State Officials

Governor 1996 Election:	Michael Leavitt (R)	75%
	Jim Bradley (D)	23%
Lt. Governor:	Olene Walker (R)	
Attorney General:	Jan Graham (D)	
State Senate:	11 Democrats	
	18 Republicans	
State House:	21 Democrats	
	54 Republicans	

TAXES AND SPENDING

Total Revenues

Utah's per capita state and local total revenues registered $5,230 in 1996, ranking 26th in the nation and trailing the U.S. average of $5,706 by 8%. From 1962 to 1996, real per capita state and local revenues increased by 252%, compared with an increase in the national average of 297%.

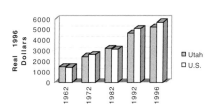

Real Per Capita State and Local Total Revenues: Utah vs. U.S.

Taxes

Utah's per capita state and local total revenues registered $2,147 in 1996, ranking 39th in the nation and trailing the U.S. average of $2,597 by 17%. From 1962 to 1996, real per capita state and local taxes increased by 118%, compared with an increase of 152% in the U.S. average.

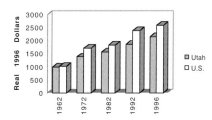

Real Per Capita State and Local Taxes: Utah vs. U.S.

Property Taxes

Utah's per capita state and local property taxes equaled $504 in 1996, ranking 39th in the nation and trailing the U.S. average of $789 by 36%. From 1962 to 1996, real per capita state and local property taxes increased by 16%, versus a 67% increase in the U.S. average.

Sales and Gross Receipts Taxes

Utah's per capita state and local sales and gross receipts taxes came in at $893 in 1996, ranking 27th in the nation and trailing the U.S. average of $939 by 5%. From 1962 to 1996, real per capita state and local sales and gross receipts taxes increased by 182%, versus an increase of 214% in the U.S. average.

Income Taxes

Utah's per capita state and local income (individual and corporate) taxes registered $658 in 1996, ranking 23d in the nation and trailing the U.S. average of $674 by 2%. From 1962 to 1996, real per capita state and local income taxes increased by 472%, versus a 567% increase in the U.S. average.

Personal Income Tax

A rate of 5.614%, ranking 23d in the nation (from lowest tax rate to highest), and comparing with the national average of 5.26%.

Capital Gains Tax

A rate of 6.3%, ranking 34th in the nation (from lowest tax rate to highest), and comparing with the national average of 4.68%.

Corporate Income Tax

A rate of 5.0%, ranking 8th in the nation (from lowest tax rate to highest), and comparing with the national average of 6.69%.

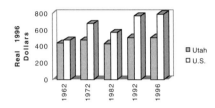

Real Per Capita State and Local Property Taxes: Utah vs. U.S.

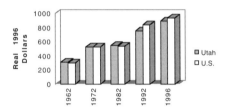

Real Per Capita State and Local Sales and Gross Receipts Taxes: Utah vs. U.S.

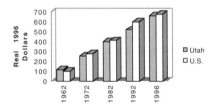

Real Per Capita State and Local Income Taxes: Utah vs. U.S.

Total Expenditures

Utah's per capita state and local total spending registered $4,942 in 1996, ranking 23d in the nation and trailing the U.S. average of $5,268 by 6%. From 1962 to 1996, real per capita state and local total spending increased by 216%, versus an increase of 254% in the U.S. average.

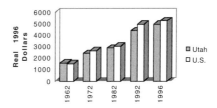

Real Per Capita State and Local Total Expenditures: Utah vs. U.S.

Welfare Expenditures

Utah's per capita state and local public welfare spending registered $480 in 1996, ranking 48th in the nation and trailing the U.S. average of $729 by 34%. From 1962 to 1996, real per capita state and local public welfare spending increased by 375%, compared with a 488% increase in the U.S. average.

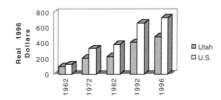

Real Per Capita State and Local Public Welfare Spending: Utah vs. U.S.

Welfare Recipients (in thousands)

	1980	1989	3/99	Change 1989–99
Utah	44	45	26	−42%
U.S.	10,923	10,987	7,335	−33%

Interest on General Debt

Utah's per capita state and local interest on general debt registered $150 in 1996, ranking 37th in the nation and trailing the U.S. average of $222 by 32%. From 1962 to 1996, real per capita state and local interest on general debt increased by 733%, versus an increase of 335% in the U.S. average.

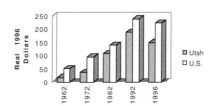

Real Per Capita State and Local Interest on General Debt: Utah vs. U.S.

Total Debt Outstanding

Utah's per capita state and local debt registered $5,739 in 1996, ranking 11th in the nation and topping the U.S. average of $4,409 by 30%. From 1962 to 1996, real per capita state and local debt outstanding increased by 340%, versus an increase of 120% in the U.S. average.

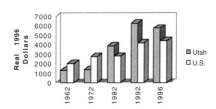

Real Per Capita State and Local Debt Outstanding: Utah vs. U.S.

Government Employees

Utah's state and local government employees (full-time equivalent, or FTE) per 10,000 population registered 529.5 in 1997, ranking 29th in the nation and trailing the U.S. average of 531.1 by 0.3%. From 1962 to 1996, state and local FTE employees per 10,000 population increased by 53%, compared with an increase in the U.S. average of 66%.

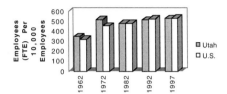

State and Local Government Employees (FTE) Per 10,000 Population: Utah vs. U.S.

Per Capita Federal Government Expenditures, 1998

	1998	Ranking
Utah	$4,156	51st
U.S.	$5,491	

Per capita federal spending in Utah trailed the national average by 24%.

EDUCATION

Total Education Spending

Utah's per capita state and local education spending registered $1,714 in 1996, ranking 10th in the nation and exceeding the U.S. average of $1,503 by 14%. From 1962 to 1996, real per capita total education spending increased by 123%, versus an increase in the U.S. average of 173%.

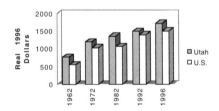

Real Per Capita State and Local Education Spending: Utah vs. U.S.

Per Pupil Spending

Utah's per pupil public school spending registered $3,940 in 1998, ranking 51st in the nation and trailing the U.S. average of $6,131 by 36%. From 1970 to 1998, Utah's real per pupil public school spending increased by 79%, compared with a 120% increase in the U.S. average.

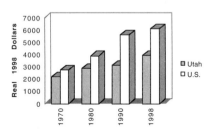

Real Per Pupil Public School Spending: Utah vs. U.S.

Average Public School Teacher Salaries (in 1997–98 dollars)

	1970	1980	1990	1998	1998 Ranking
Utah	32,729	31,062	30,171	32,950	39th
U.S.	36,934	33,272	39,956	39,385	

In 1998, the average public school teacher salary in Utah trailed the U.S. average by 16%. From 1970 to 1998, the real average teacher salary in Utah increased by 1%, versus an increase in the U.S. average of 7%.

Pupil/Teacher Ratio, Fall 1996

	Ratio	Rank
Utah	24.4	51st
U.S.	17.1	

Teachers/Staff, Fall 1996

	Percent	Rank
Utah	52.7	29th
U.S.	52.1	

Public School 4th-Grade Reading Proficiency, 1998

	Average	Rank (out of 40 states)
Utah	215	23d
U.S.	215	

Public School 8th-Grade Reading Proficiency, 1998

	Average	Rank (out of 37 states)
Utah	265	11th
U.S.	261	

Public School 4th-Grade Math Proficiency, 1996

	Average	Rank (out of 44 states)
Utah	227	12th
U.S.	224	

Public School 8th-Grade Math Proficiency, 1996

	Average	Rank (out of 41 states)
Utah	277	12th
U.S.	271	

Public School 8th-Grade Science Proficiency, 1996

	Average	Rank (out of 41 states)
Utah	156	11th
U.S.	148	

Average Math SAT Scores

	1972	1982	1992	1998	Percentage Taking SAT in 1998
Utah	570	547	562	570	4
U.S.	509	493	501	512	43

Average Verbal SAT Scores

	1972	1982	1992	1998	Percentage Taking SAT in 1998
Utah	599	569	570	572	4
U.S.	530	504	500	505	43

Expenditures by Public Institutions of Higher Education Per Full-Time-Equivalent Student, 1996

	FTE Student Spending	Rank
Utah	$13,029	18th
U.S.	$12,343	

Per-FTE-student spending in public institutions of higher education topped the U.S. average by 6%.

Per Full-Time-Equivalent Student Revenues from Federal, State, and Local Governments for Public Institutions of Higher Education, 1996

	FTE Student Government Revenues	Rank
Utah	$7,987	24th
U.S.	$8,101	

Per-FTE-student-government revenues in public institutions of higher education trailed the U.S. average by 1%.

Average Salary for Full-Time Professors at Public Universities, 1997

	Average	Rank
Utah	$65,870	32d
U.S.	$72,599	

The average full-time public university professor salary trailed the U.S. average by 9%.

ECONOMY AND BUSINESS

Economic Growth

Over the period of 1977 to 1997, Utah's real gross state product (GSP) grew by 124.2%—ranking 6th in the nation—as compared with real U.S. gross domestic product (GDP), expanding by 70.1%.

At $55.4 billion in 1997, Utah's GSP ranked as 35th largest in the nation.

From 1993 to 1997, Utah's annual real GSP growth averaged 7.10%—ranking 3d in the nation—as compared with annual real U.S. GDP growth, averaging 3.08%.

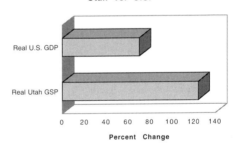

Real Economic Growth 1977-1997: Utah vs. U.S.

Job Growth

	Growth in Employee Payrolls (Nonagricultural) 1962–98	Ranking
Utah	257.9%	6th
U.S.	120.1%	

Average Annual Growth in Employee Payrolls (Nonagricultural) 1993–98	Ranking
Utah	5.88%	3d
U.S.	2.98%	

Per Capita Disposable Income, 1997

	1997	Ranking
Utah	$17,320	47th
U.S.	$21,607	

Per capita disposable income trailed the U.S. average by 20%.

	Real Growth 1962–97	Ranking
Utah	88.6%	46th
U.S.	116.7%	

	Average Annual Real Growth 1993–97	Ranking
Utah	2.66%	1st
U.S.	1.48%	

Number of Businesses

	1997	Percent with Fewer than 500 Employees
Businesses with Employees	47,465	96.5
Self-employed Individuals	80,000	

New Business Incorporations

	1980	1986	1992	1997
Utah	3,755	3,865	4,582	7,301

Percentage Change in Annual New Business Incorporations, 1980 vs. 1997

	Percent	Ranking
Utah	94.4	11th
U.S.	49.7	

State Merchandise Exports to the World, 1998 (in millions of dollars)

	1998	Rank
Utah	$3,099	33d

Small Business Survival Index, 1999

Utah ranks 23d in terms of its policy environment for entrepreneurship.

Fortune 500 Headquarters in 1999

A total of 2 (ranked 34th)

Labor Union Membership, 1983 vs. 1997

| | Percentage of Workers | | Rank |
	1983	1997	
Utah	15.2	8.3	39th
U.S.	20.1	14.1	

Homeownership Rate, 1998

	Rate	Rank
Utah	73.7	9th
U.S.	66.3	

CRIME

Crime Rates Per 100 Residents (rankings from best to worst crime rate)

Total Crime	1960	1970	1980	1990	1998	1998 Ranking
Utah	0.88	2.37	5.88	5.66	5.51	43d
U.S.	1.04	2.74	5.90	5.82	4.62	

From 1960 to 1998, Utah's crime rate increased by 526%, versus a U.S. increase of 344%. From 1990 to 1998, Utah's crime rate decreased by 3%, versus a U.S. decrease of 21%.

Violent Crime	1960	1970	1980	1990	1998	1998 Ranking
Utah	0.05	0.14	0.30	0.28	0.31	13th
U.S.	0.14	0.36	0.58	0.73	0.57	

From 1960 to 1998, Utah's violent crime rate increased by 520%, versus a U.S. increase of 307%. From 1990 to 1998, Utah's violent crime rate increased by 11%, compared with a national decline of 22%.

Property Crime	1960	1970	1980	1990	1998	1998 Ranking
Utah	0.83	2.24	5.58	5.38	5.19	44th
U.S.	0.90	2.38	5.32	5.09	4.05	

From 1960 to 1998, Utah's property crime rate increased by 525%, versus a national increase of 350%. From 1990 to 1998, Utah's property crime rate decreased by 4%, compared with a national decline of 20%.

Real Per Capita Police Protection Spending (in real 1996 dollars)

	1962	1972	1982	1992	1996	1996 Ranking
Utah	37	59	106	105	132	33d
U.S.	51	95	114	148	168	

In 1996, per capita state and local police protection spending in Utah trailed the U.S. average by 38%. From 1962 to 1996, real per capita state and local police protection spending increased by 257%, versus an increase of 229% in the U.S. average.

Prisoners in State and Federal Prisons Per 1,000 Population

	1980	1990	1996	1996 Ranking
Utah	0.64	1.45	1.97	44th
U.S.	1.46	3.11	4.45	

From 1980 to 1996, prisoners per 1,000 population increased by 208%, versus a U.S. increase of 205%.

HEALTH CARE

Health-Care Spending

Utah's per capita state and local health-care spending registered $127 in 1996, ranking 29th in the nation and lagging behind the U.S. average of $151 by 16%. From 1962 to 1996, Utah's real per capita state and local health-care spending increased by 807%, versus an increase of 739% in the U.S. average.

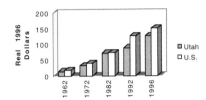

Real Per Capita State and Local Health Care Spending: Utah vs. U.S.

Hospital Spending

Utah's per capita state and local hospital spending registered $151 in 1996, ranking 35th in the nation and trailing the U.S. average of $266 by 43%. From 1962 to 1996, Utah's real per capita state and local hospital spending increased by 196%, as opposed to an increase of 189% in the U.S. average.

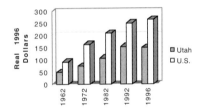

Real Per Capita State and Local Hospital Spending: Utah vs. U.S.

Medicaid, 1997

	Spending Per Recipient	Ranking
Utah	$2,924	39th
U.S.	$3,681	

Utah's per-recipient Medicaid spending trailed the U.S. average by 21%.

ENVIRONMENT

Parks and Recreation Spending

Utah's per capita state and local parks and recreation spending registered $95 in 1996, ranking 11th in the nation and topping the U.S. average of $72 by 32%. From 1962 to 1996, real per capita state and local parks and recreation spending increased by 428%, versus a 213% increase in the U.S. average.

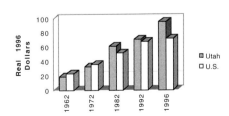

Real Per Capita State and Local Parks and Recreation Spending: Utah vs. U.S.

State and Local Natural Resources Spending, 1996

	Per Capita	Ranking
Utah	$71	22d
U.S.	$60	

Per capita state and local natural resources spending in Utah topped the U.S. average by 18%.

State Parks Revenues as a Share of Operating Expenses, 1997

	Percent	Rank
Utah	35	33d
U.S.	42	

Percentage of Land Owned by the Federal Government, 1996

	Percent	Rank
Utah	64.3	2d
U.S.	24.8	

SOCIETY AND DEMOGRAPHICS

Population

Utah's 1998 population of 2.100 million ranked 34th in the nation.

Population Growth, 1990–98

	Percentage Change in Population	Ranking
Utah	21.88	4th
U.S.	8.66	

	Net International Migration	Ranking
Utah	26,911	27th

	Net Domestic Migration	Ranking
Utah	86,168	17th

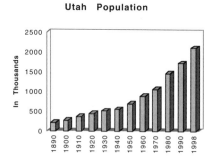

Utah Population

Infant Mortality Rate, 1998

	Percent	Rank
Utah	5.7	40th
U.S.	6.4	

Percentage of Births of Low Birthweight, 1997

	Percent	Rank
Utah	6.6	37th
U.S.	7.5	

Percentage of Live Births to Unmarried Women, 1997

	Percent	Rank
Utah	18.6	51st
U.S.	32.4	

Abortion Rate—Abortions Per 1,000 Women Ages 15–44, 1995

	Rate	Rank
Utah	8.1	46th
U.S.	22.9	

LIFESTYLE

Percentage of Households with Computers, 1998

	Percent	Rank
Utah	60.1	2d

Percentage of Households with Internet Access, 1998

	Percent	Rank
Utah	35.8	4th

State Arts Agency Spending, 1999

	Per Capita	Rank
Utah	$1.39	19th
U.S.	$1.35	

Per capita state arts spending in 1999 topped the U.S. average by 3%.

Major League Sports Facilities

Year Opened/ Refurb.	Stadium/ Arena	Home Team	Millions of Nominal Dollars		Millions of Real 1997 Dollars	
			Estimated Total Cost	Estimated Taxpayer Cost	Estimated Total Cost	Estimated Taxpayer Cost
1969	Salt Palace	Jazz (NBA) 1979–91	$17.0	$17.0	$74.2	$74.2
1991	Delta Center	Jazz (NBA) 1991–present	$102.6	$24.6	$120.8	$29.0

VERMONT

Some of the nagging philosophical questions of our time include:

- What is the meaning of life?
- Can we find true happiness?
- Are there any conservatives in Vermont?

That last query may be the toughest to answer. Indeed, it is highly debatable that a conservative could even survive in the harsh climate of Vermont these days—and we are not talking about the snow.

Just look at whom Vermonters have put into office in recent years. Governor Howard Dean (D) provided President Clinton and the first lady with all sorts of bad ideas for their failed attempt at a government takeover of the health-care industry in the early 1990s. Senator Patrick Leahy is a hard-core liberal whose opponent in 1998 was a 77-year-old dairy farmer named Fred Tuttle. Tuttle's campaign was nothing more than a publicity stunt, but alas so is much of Vermont's GOP. The state's junior senator, Jim Jeffords is really a Republican in name only, as is clear from his voting record.

Perhaps the best symbol of Vermont's quixotic fixation with liberalism is the state's sole member of the House of Representatives. Congressman Bernie Sanders is not just a liberal, he is a socialist—the only one in Congress—and he has a voting record to prove it.

Since his election to the House in 1990, Sanders has championed some of the most bizarre causes and taken positions that have left him on the short end of some of the most lop sided congressional votes. He not only voted against Operation Desert Storm, he was one of only 6 congressmen out of 435 who refused to support a resolution expressing support for American troops. He voted against a bill to prohibit Russia from sending American aid dollars to Cuba and voted in favor of giving U.S. tax dollars to the South African Communist Party. Sanders supported giving Pell Grants to imprisoned felons, and he voted to effectively do away with the death penalty. Nonetheless, Sanders has been sent back to Washington repeatedly by Vermont voters.

Could there actually be a conservative backlash against Sanders's ultraliberal voting record? While we do not think that is likely, we are encouraged by a minor uprising that has taken place since Vermont enacted one of the most unfair and confiscatory property tax schemes we have ever seen, known in-state as Act 60.

Basically, Act 60 created a burdensome new statewide property tax and gave local governments authority to pile on as well. The goal of the plan was to essentially take money from the wealthier localities—so-called "gold towns"—and give it to less wealthy towns to help pay for education. Not surprisingly, residents in the "gold towns" have refused to play along with this redistribution scheme. Several lawsuits have been filed against Act 60. Unfortunately, none have been successful so far, so many of the hardest-hit towns are simply refusing to hand over the loot to the state government.

It certainly will be interesting to see how the full drama plays out. The 1998 state elections might provide a clue. The Democratic Party, which championed Act 60, suffered major losses. Republicans are hopeful that they will gain the handful of seats necessary to actually take control of the House in the next election cycle.

"We changed the balance in the legislature so that we were able to scale back a lot of the stuff that they [the Democrats] had pushed through," said Vermont political consultant George McNeil, "and we also kept them from going further than they had already gone."

Until some major reforms are enacted, though, Vermont will continue to suffer under one of the most punitive property taxes in the nation, the second highest personal income tax rate, and the fifth highest corporate income levy. While many other states were cutting taxes in 1997, Vermont hiked its corporate income tax, as well as the state sales tax.

All this big government seems to have taken a real toll on Vermont. In the most recent years for which we have data, key measures like economic growth, job creation, disposable income, new business incorporations, and population growth have all fallen below national averages.

Conservatives remain an endangered species in Vermont. Without a serious conservative counterbalance to offset Vermont's extreme liberalism, the state's entire economy is placed at serious risk as we move into the 21st century.

POLITICS

Registered Voters

No party registration

Federal Officials: Recent Election and Group Ratings

			ACU	ADA	SBSC
U.S. Senators:	Patrick Leahy (D)		6	89	15
	1998　Leahy (D)	72%			
	Tuttle (R)	22%			
	James Jeffords (R)		29	59	50
	1998　Jeffords (R)	50%			
	Backus (D)	41%			
U.S. Representatives:	Bernard Sanders (Ind)		7	98	10
	1998　Sanders (I)	63%			
	Candon (R)	33%			
Electoral Votes:	3				
1996 Presidential Results:	Clinton	53%			
	Dole	31%			
	Perot	12%			

State Officials

Governor 1998 Election:	Howard Dean (D)	56%
	Ruth Dwyer (R)	41%
Lt. Governor:	Doug Racine (D)	
Attorney General:	William Sorrell (D)	
State Senate:	17 Democrats	
	13 Republicans	
State House:	77 Democrats	
	67 Republicans	
	4 Progressives	
	2 Independents	

TAXES AND SPENDING

Total Revenues

Vermont's per capita state and local total revenues registered $5,414 in 1996, ranking 22d in the nation and trailing the U.S. average of $5,706 by 5%. From 1962 to 1996, real per capita state and local revenues increased by 211%, compared with an increase in the national average of 297%.

Taxes

Vermont's per capita state and local taxes registered $2,577 in 1996, ranking 19th in the nation and trailing the U.S. average of $2,597 by 1%. From 1962 to 1996, real per capita state and local taxes increased by 136%, compared with an increase of 152% in the U.S. average.

Property Taxes

Vermont's per capita state and local property taxes equaled $1,155 in 1996, ranking 7th in the nation and topping the U.S. average of $789 by 46%. From 1962 to 1996, real per capita state and local property taxes increased by 133%, versus a 67% increase in the U.S. average.

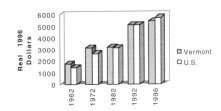

Real Per Capita State and Local Total Revenues: Vermont vs. U.S.

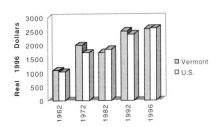

Real Per Capita State and Local Taxes: Vermont vs. U.S.

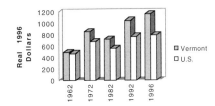

Real Per Capita State and Local Property Taxes: Vermont vs. U.S.

Sales and Gross Receipts Taxes

Vermont's per capita state and local sales and gross receipts taxes came in at $688 in 1996, ranking 44th in the nation and trailing the U.S. average of $939 by 27%. From 1962 to 1996, real per capita state and local sales and gross receipts taxes increased by 159%, versus an increase of 214% in the U.S. average.

Income Taxes

Vermont's per capita state and local income (individual and corporate) taxes registered $553 in 1996, ranking 33d in the nation and trailing the U.S. average of $674 by 18%. From 1962 to 1996, real per capita state and local income taxes increased by 209%, versus a 567% increase in the U.S. average.

Personal Income Tax

A rate of 9.9%, ranking 50th in the nation (from lowest tax rate to highest), and comparing with the national average of 5.26%.

Capital Gains Tax

A rate of 5.0%, ranking 25th in the nation (from lowest tax rate to highest), and comparing with the national average of 4.68%.

Corporate Income Tax

A rate of 9.75%, ranking 47th in the nation (from lowest tax rate to highest), and comparing with the national average of 6.69%.

Total Expenditures

Vermont's per capita state and local total spending registered $4,932 in 1996, ranking 24th in the nation and trailing the U.S. average of $5,268 by 6%. From 1962 to 1996, real per capita state and local total spending increased by 183%, versus an increase of 254% in the U.S. average.

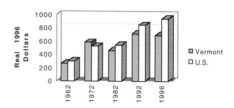

Real Per Capita State and Local Sales and Gross Receipts Taxes: Vermont vs. U.S.

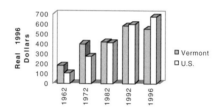

Real Per Capita State and Local Income Taxes: Vermont vs. U.S.

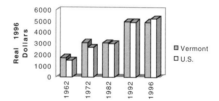

Real Per Capita State and Local Total Expenditures: Vermont vs. U.S.

Welfare Expenditures

Vermont's per capita state and local public welfare spending registered $857 in 1996, ranking 12th in the nation and exceeding the U.S. average of $729 by 18%. From 1962 to 1996, real per capita state and local public welfare spending increased by 591%, compared with a 488% increase in the U.S. average.

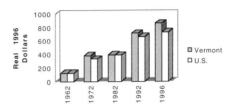

Real Per Capita State and Local Public Welfare Spending: Vermont vs. U.S.

Welfare Recipients (in thousands)

	1980	1989	3/99	Change 1989–99
Vt.	24	21	18	−14%
U.S.	10,923	10,987	7,335	−33%

Interest on General Debt

Vermont's per capita state and local interest on general debt registered $206 in 1996, ranking 24th in the nation and trailing the U.S. average of $222 by 7%. From 1962 to 1996, real per capita state and local interest on general debt increased by 544%, versus an increase of 335% in the U.S. average.

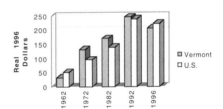

Real Per Capita State and Local Interest on General Debt: Vermont vs. U.S.

Total Debt Outstanding

Vermont's per capita state and local debt registered $3,831 in 1996, ranking 27th in the nation and trailing the U.S. average of $4,409 by 13%. From 1962 to 1996, real per capita state and local debt outstanding increased by 210%, versus an increase of 120% in the U.S. average.

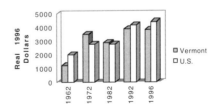

Real Per Capita State and Local Debt Outstanding: Vermont vs. U.S.

Government Employees

Vermont's state and local government employees (full-time equivalent, or FTE) per 10,000 population registered 513.9 in 1997, ranking 37th in the nation and trailing the U.S. average of 531.1 by 3%. From 1962 to 1996, state and local FTE employees per 10,000 population increased by 60%, compared with an increase in the U.S. average of 66%.

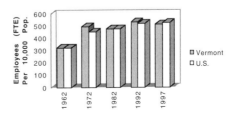

State and Local Government Employees (FTE) Per 10,000 Population: Vermont vs. U.S.

Per Capita Federal Government Expenditures, 1998

	1998	Ranking
Vt.	$4,898	36th
U.S.	$5,491	

Per capita federal spending in Vermont trailed the national average by 11%.

EDUCATION

Total Education Spending

Vermont's per capita state and local education spending registered $1,771 in 1996, ranking 9th in the nation and exceeding the U.S. average of $1,503 by 18%. From 1962 to 1996, real per capita total education spending increased by 201%, versus an increase in the U.S. average of 173%.

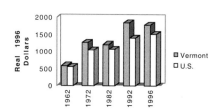

Real Per Capita State and Local Education Spending: Vermont vs. U.S.

Per Pupil Spending

Vermont's per pupil public school spending registered $6,397 in 1998, ranking 16th in the nation and exceeding the U.S. average of $6,131 by 4%. From 1970 to 1998, Vermont's real per pupil public school spending increased by 164%, compared with a 120% increase in the U.S. average.

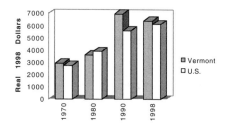

Real Per Pupil Public School Spending: Vermont vs. U.S.

Average Public School Teacher Salaries (in 1997–98 dollars)

	1970	1980	1990	1998	1998 Ranking
Vt.	34,117	26,009	36,956	36,299	27th
U.S.	36,934	33,272	39,956	39,385	

In 1998, the average public school teacher salary in Vermont trailed the U.S. average by 8%. From 1970 to 1998, the real average teacher salary in Vermont increased by 6%, versus an increase in the U.S. average of 7%.

Pupil/Teacher Ratio, Fall 1996

	Ratio	Rank
Vt.	13.7	2d
U.S.	17.1	

Teachers/Staff, Fall 1996

	Percent	Rank
Vt.	49.4	45th
U.S.	52.1	

Public School 4th-Grade Math Proficiency, 1996

	Average	Rank (out of 44 states)
Vt.	225	17th
U.S.	224	

Public School 8th-Grade Math Proficiency, 1996

	Average	Rank (out of 41 states)
Vt.	279	9th
U.S.	271	

Public School 8th-Grade Science Proficiency, 1996

	Average	Rank (out of 41 states)
Vt.	157	8th
U.S.	148	

Average Math SAT Scores

	1972	1982	1992	1998	Percentage Taking SAT in 1998
Vt.	508	498	495	504	71
U.S.	509	493	501	512	43

Average Verbal SAT Scores

	1972	1982	1992	1998	Percentage Taking SAT in 1998
Vt.	531	511	506	508	71
U.S.	530	504	500	505	43

Expenditures by Public Institutions of Higher Education Per Full-Time-Equivalent Student, 1996

	FTE Student Spending	Rank
Vt.	$18,813	2d
U.S.	$12,343	

Per-FTE-student spending in public institutions of higher education topped the U.S. average by 52%.

Per Full-Time-Equivalent Student Revenues from Federal, State, and Local Governments for Public Institutions of Higher Education, 1996

	FTE Student Government Revenues	Rank
Vt.	$5,753	50th
U.S.	$8,101	

Per-FTE-student-government revenues in public institutions of higher education trailed the U.S. average by 29%.

Average Salary for Full-Time Professors at Public Universities, 1997

	Average	Rank
Vt.	$64,822	34th
U.S.	$72,599	

The average full-time public university professor salary trailed the U.S. average by 11%.

ECONOMY AND BUSINESS

Economic Growth

Over the period of 1977 to 1997, Vermont's real gross state product (GSP) grew by 98.4%—ranking 10th in the nation—as compared with real U.S. gross domestic product (GDP), expanding by 70.1%.

At $15.2 billion in 1997, Vermont's GSP ranked as smallest in the nation.

From 1993 to 1997, Vermont's annual real GSP growth averaged 2.47%—ranking 43d in the nation—as compared with annual real U.S. GDP growth, averaging 3.08%.

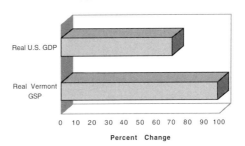

Real Economic Growth 1977-1997: Vermont vs. U.S.

Real U.S. GDP

Real Vermont GSP

0 10 20 30 40 50 60 70 80 90 100

Percent Change

Job Growth

	Growth in Employee Payrolls (Nonagricultural) 1962–98	Ranking
Vt.	158.7%	24th
U.S.	126.5%	

	Average Annual Growth in Employee Payrolls (Nonagricultural) 1993–98	Ranking
Vt.	2.63%	34th
U.S.	2.98%	

Per Capita Disposable Income, 1997

	1997	Ranking
Vt.	$19,908	33d
U.S.	$21,607	

Per capita disposable income trailed the U.S. average by 8%.

	Real Growth 1962–97	Ranking
Vt.	130.9%	17th
U.S.	116.7%	

	Average Annual Real Growth 1993–97	Ranking
Vt.	1.45%	36th
U.S.	1.48%	

Number of Businesses

	1997	Percent with Fewer than 500 Employees
Businesses with Employees	20,014	97.2
Self-employed Individuals	40,000	

New Business Incorporations

	1980	1986	1992	1997
Vt.	1,171	1,802	1,589	1,417

Percentage Change in Annual New Business Incorporations, 1980 vs. 1997

	Percent	Ranking
Vt.	21.0	34th
U.S.	49.7	

State Merchandise Exports to the World, 1998 (in millions of dollars)

	1998	Rank
Vt.	$2,758	34th

Small Business Survival Index, 1999

Vermont ranks a poor 38th in terms of its policy environment for entrepreneurship.

Fortune 500 Headquarters in 1999

None

Labor Union Membership, 1983 vs. 1997

| | Percentage of Workers | | |
	1983	1997	Rank
Vt.	12.6	8.5	35th
U.S.	20.1	14.1	

Homeownership Rate, 1998

	Rate	Rank
Vt.	69.1	28th
U.S.	66.3	

CRIME

Crime Rates Per 100 Residents (rankings from best to worst crime rate)

Total Crime	1960	1970	1980	1990	1998	1998 Ranking
Vt.	0.54	1.27	4.99	4.34	3.14	7th
U.S.	1.04	2.74	5.90	5.82	4.62	

From 1960 to 1998, Vermont's crime rate increased by 481%, versus a U.S. increase of 344%.
From 1990 to 1998, Vermont's crime rate decreased by 28%, versus a U.S. decrease of 21%.

Violent Crime	1960	1970	1980	1990	1998	1998 Ranking
Vt.	0.01	0.07	0.18	0.13	0.11	2d
U.S.	0.14	0.36	0.58	0.73	0.57	

From 1960 to 1998, Vermont's violent crime rate increased by 1,000%, versus a U.S. increase of 307%.
From 1990 to 1998, Vermont's violent crime rate decreased by 15%, compared with a national decline of 22%.

Property Crime	1960	1970	1980	1990	1998	1998 Ranking
Vt.	0.53	1.89	4.31	4.09	3.03	10th
U.S.	0.90	2.38	5.32	5.09	4.05	

From 1960 to 1998, Vermont's property crime rate increased by 472%, versus a national increase of 350%. From 1990 to 1998, Vermont's property crime rate decreased by 26%, compared with a national decline of 20%.

Real Per Capita Police Protection Spending (in real 1996 dollars)

	1962	1972	1982	1992	1996	1996 Ranking
Vt.	28	69	75	105	114	42d
U.S.	51	95	114	148	168	

In 1996, per capita state and local police protection spending in Vermont trailed the U.S. average by 32%. From 1962 to 1996, real per capita state and local police protection spending increased by 307%, versus an increase of 229% in the U.S. average.

Prisoners in State and Federal Prisons Per 1,000 Population

	1980	1990	1996	1996 Ranking
Vt.	0.94	1.86	1.91	46th
U.S.	1.46	3.11	4.45	

From 1980 to 1996, prisoners per 1,000 population increased by 103%, versus a U.S. increase of 205%.

HEALTH CARE

Health-Care Spending

Vermont's per capita state and local health-care spending registered $94 in 1996, ranking 42d in the nation and lagging behind the U.S. average of $151 by 38%. From 1962 to 1996, Vermont's real per capita state and local health-care spending increased by 309%, versus an increase of 739% in the U.S. average.

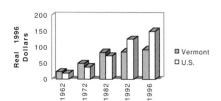

Real Per Capita State and Local Health Care Spending: Vermont vs. U.S.

Hospital Spending

Vermont's per capita state and local hospital spending registered $16 in 1996, ranking 51st in the nation and trailing the U.S. average of $266 by 94%. From 1962 to 1996, Vermont's real per capita state and local hospital spending decreased by 73%, as opposed to an increase of 189% in the U.S. average.

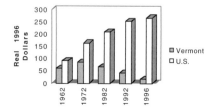

Real Per Capita State and Local Hospital Spending: Vermont vs. U.S.

Medicaid, 1997

	Spending Per Recipient	Ranking
Vt.	$2,835	42d
U.S.	$3,681	

Vermont's per-recipient Medicaid spending trailed the U.S. average by 23%.

ENVIRONMENT

Parks and Recreation Spending

Vermont's per capita state and local parks and recreation spending registered $35 in 1996, ranking 47th in the nation and trailing the U.S. average of $72 by 51%. From 1962 to 1996, real per capita state and local parks and recreation spending increased by 600%, versus a 213% increase in the U.S. average.

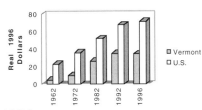

Real Per Capita State and Local Parks and Recreation Spending: Vermont vs. U.S.

State and Local Natural Resources Spending, 1996

	Per Capita	Ranking
Vt.	$85	14th
U.S.	$60	

Per capita state and local natural resources spending in Vermont exceeded the U.S. average by 42%.

State Parks Revenues as a Share of Operating Expenses, 1997

	Percent	Rank
Vt.	93	3d
U.S.	42	

Percentage of Land Owned by the Federal Government, 1996

	Percent	Rank
Vt.	6.3	23d
U.S.	24.8	

SOCIETY AND DEMOGRAPHICS

Population

Vermont's 1998 population of 0.591 million ranked 49th in the nation.

Population Growth, 1990–98

	Percentage Change in Population	Ranking
Vt.	4.97	39th
U.S.	8.66	

	Net International Migration	Ranking
Vt.	4,212	46th

	Net Domestic Migration	Ranking
Vt.	4,835	30th

Infant Mortality Rate, 1998

	Percent	Rank
Vt.	5.7	40th
U.S.	6.4	

Percentage of Births of Low Birthweight, 1997

	Percent	Rank
Vt.	6.3	40th
U.S.	7.5	

Percentage of Live Births to Unmarried Women, 1997

	Percent	Rank
Vt.	28.1	36th
U.S.	32.4	

Vermont   Population

Abortion Rate—Abortions Per 1,000 Women Ages 15–44, 1995

	Rate	Rank
Vt.	17.9	24th
U.S.	22.9	

LIFESTYLE

Percentage of Households with Computers, 1998

	Percent	Rank
Vt.	48.7	8th

Percentage of Households with Internet Access, 1998

	Percent	Rank
Vt.	31.8	8th

State Arts Agency Spending, 1999

	Per Capita	Rank
Vt.	$1.15	19th
U.S.	$1.35	

Per capita state arts spending in 1999 trailed the U.S. average by 15%.

Major League Sports Facilities

None

VIRGINIA

Governor Jim Gilmore (R) wants Virginia to be known as the "Internet State." In fact, Virginia is developing into one of the leading high-technology centers for computer software, information technology, and telecommunications. According to the American Electronics Association, Virginia is now the third-fastest-growing high-tech state in the country.

"We're using the Internet as a defining point for Virginia," observed Donald Upson, the state's technology secretary, in a *Virginian-Pilot* story (April 12, 1999). The vast majority of the state's high-tech industry is located in the Northern Virginia region. For years, some in this business community were seen as "beltway bandits," that is, systems and analysis firms living off government and defense contracts. While such enterprises still exist, they are being overshadowed by the likes of America Online and MCI Worldcom, which have transformed the region into the so-called "Silicon Dominion."

To meet the growing demand for skilled workers, and to keep their corporate neighbors happy, local government officials in Northern Virginia have launched a full-scale recruiting drive in the Silicon Valley, using Virginia's lower cost of living as the bait. "When you're making more at your job and wasting less on your mortgage, you'll be endlessly tempted to spend the difference on yourself," whispers an advertisement for Fairfax County in *Wired* magazine. Of course, the notion that taxpayers should be picking up part of the tab for recruitment efforts for certain Virginia industries and businesses is not only unfair, but such government subsidies always make for bad economic policy. Obviously, government cannot pick winners and losers in the marketplace, and cracking the door open to subsidies guarantees that recipients will be back for more later.

There is home-grown talent. For example, technology-related degrees conferred by Virginia's colleges and universities jumped 24% between 1990 and 1996, while nationwide that number actually declined 5% in the same period, according to the American Electronics Association.

For his part, Gilmore has been one of the country's leading executives in setting a probusiness, pro-technology agenda. As a member of the federal Advisory Commission on Electronic Commerce, Gilmore was an outspoken advocate of the Internet Tax Freedom Act, a 1998 federal law that placed a three-year moratorium on Internet taxes. The Electronic Industries Association recently gave the governor its "State Technology Policy" award for his efforts on behalf of the high-tech industry. Overall, in recent years, rates of real economic growth and job creation in Virginia have outpaced the national averages.

Because its most famous private employer is Newport News Shipbuilding, however, Hampton Roads is widely perceived to be ideal for lower-paying, blue collar industries, not for high-dollar, high-tech corporations. Overall, the workforce is less educated than Northern Virginia's (although with NASA's Langley facility, there are a large number of scientists and researchers in the area). Virginia's poorest region, located along the Blue Ridge mountains in the southwest portion of the state, also is making a pitch to get a piece of the info-tech pie.

For these reasons and others, Virginia has been subject to a growing sense of regionalism. Legislators from Northern Virginia want more money for roads and other improvements to break the traffic gridlock clogging area roads, and they are open to increasing taxes to fund such projects. Representatives from more rural areas are adamantly opposed to new taxes and want more help from the state government in attracting new business.

Another dividing line has been drawn on the issue of so-called "sprawl." Northern Virginia is a hotbed for this increasingly prominent issue in areas experiencing good economic times. Interestingly, sprawl does not seem to know any boundaries when it comes to political parties and even philosophies. Just look at the two coauthors of this book. The sprawl issue is one where we part ways, and we thought it would be of interest to read our separate thoughts on this issue.

Edmonds on Sprawl. While the high-tech boom has saved thousands of jobs that not long ago were threatened by Department of Defense cutbacks and put more money into the pockets of its residents, reaction among Northern Virginians has not been all positive. Many of the area's rolling green hills are being plowed under to make way for gleaming high rises and office parks, new subdivisions seem to sprout up on virtually every unused acre of real estate, and traffic congestion in the area is second only to that of Los Angeles. Critics of the growth decry the so-called "sprawl," claiming that shopping centers and "cookie-cutter" new communities are depriving Virginia of its heritage and southern charm.

People I have spoken with in Virginia and elsewhere in the nation see sprawl as a problem, but many disagree over its full content and what to do about it. For example, Rick Ridder, a Democratic political consultant in Denver and current president of the International Association of Political Consultants, notes that sprawl is an issue even in Colorado today. "Sprawl means a whole series of different things" observes Ridder, "Traffic, crowded schools, quality of life, and unfulfilled expectations. But more than anything else, it is a loss of identity. We used to identify where we came from by the town or city in which we grew up. Today, ask any school kid where he is from, and he will answer with 'I attend such and such a school.'"

The seeds of the sprawl issue, which promises to dominate local politics in communities across the nation, can be traced to unfortunate decisions made in the post-World War II era. Auto manufacturers, developers, and the government planners in their wisdom decided that we should separate homes, schools, stores, and the workplace. Now, by design, we have a country where our kids cannot walk to school and we must fire up the SUV if we need an extra loaf of bread. Our nation's love affair with the auto has been reduced to massive parking lots, busy service roads, and interminable commutes.

Local and county governments also have added to the problem. They have created their own death spiral. Many must grant new building permits to generate revenue to pay for the infrastructure for the new homes just being completed. When things seem bleak, they try micromanaging the economy by requiring multiacre lots as opposed to dense construction. The result is often only a temporary solution with less density and farther flung sprawl.

The intensity of the backlash has caused developers and government alike to question the wisdom of the "Levittown" blueprint. Older, integrated planned communities like Reston, Virginia, and Columbia, Maryland, are being joined by new variations on the theme like Florida's Celebration.

Perhaps America in the 21st century will discover that a true convenience store is one you can walk to.

Keating on Sprawl. A hodgepodge of folks—including environmentalists, antipopulation advocates, NIMBYists, and general social engineers—have come together to oppose urban or suburban "sprawl" and offer the solution of "smart growth." Once you get beyond the labels, the bottom line is that the "smart-growth" agenda is a no-growth agenda that is opposed to enhanced economic opportunity and fulfillment of the American Dream of owning one's own business and home.

The antisprawlers grab at any straw to advance their cause. Some scream that building more businesses and homes will hurt the environment. Meanwhile, they offer nothing more than pseudoscience to back up their claims. Others rant about a nebulous overcrowding. Some point to traffic congestion, without mentioning how today's government planners will undo the traffic problems created by yesterday's government planners.

The more high-minded and snobbish raise aesthetic questions regarding signs, parking lots, strip malls, and fast-food establishments. Some antisprawlers have suddenly fallen in love with agriculture and cite the need "to save our rural way of life."

Still others tap into taxpayer angst by saying that allowing more homes to be built will only mean that families will move into those homes, and that means higher school taxes. Therefore, it is cheaper just to have taxpayers cough up their hard-earned dollars to "preserve open space." In many communities, the costs of public schools are so out of control that this antifamilies, antichildren message has some resonance. Rather than seriously addressing the issue of burdensome taxes, the antisprawlers manipulate it to their advantage.

The entire "sprawl" agenda is just another manufactured crisis; it is a solution in search of a problem. After all, more than 96% of land in the United States is undeveloped, according to the Census Bureau.

The "sprawl" micromanagers refuse to accept several key facts of life: (1) that different people choose different sorts of living arrangements (some like small towns, some like the suburbs, and others enjoy big cities), (2) that there are costs and benefits to any decision in life, (3) that economic change does occur and, again, there are a few costs that come with the enormous benefits, and (4) that people have a basic right to private property, without the government dictating who can build what and where.

In the end, "smart growth" will amount to nothing more than added government spending and planning, higher taxes, increased regulation, and more government ownership of land.

"I think we're moving away from political parties being that important [in state politics]," says veteran Virginia political operative Ed Debolt. "I really think regions will dominate. They won't be fighting partisan battles; they'll be fighting economic share battles and turf battles."

Thus far, Governor Gilmore has sided with the more fiscally conservative regions of the state. Though sympathetic to Northern Virginia's concerns, Gilmore, who was elected on a pledge to end the state's annual motor vehicle tax, has adamantly opposed raising taxes for any reason.

However, to secure the goal of keeping Virginia at the cutting edge of the 21st century high-tech economy, more serious tax relief should be undertaken—with capital gains tax reduction topping the recommended list. Capital gains taxes merely raise the costs of entrepreneurship and investment. Eleven other states have seen the wisdom of not taxing capital gains at all, not taxing long-term capital gains, or not taxing in-state capital gains. Eliminating capital gains in Virginia would position the state well to attract capital—the lifeblood of any economy.

Finally, of note on the education front, school choice efforts have not gotten very far, despite the fact that Gilmore's predecessor, George Allen (R), was a fairly strong advocate for more choice and competition in education. However, Virginia has gained very high marks for its state history standards, which were finalized in 1995. For example, in a February 1998 assessment of history standards in 37 states and Washington, D.C., performed by David Warren Saxe for the Thomas Fordham Foundation, Virginia was the only state to receive a grade of "A." Saxe writes: "Virginia has developed outstanding history standards. They are clearly written and provide solid content. Standards-setters from other states should carefully review them."

As the *Washington Post* reported (August 14, 1999), only 6.5% of Virginia public schools met state standards on achievement tests in the spring of 1999, though this was an improvement over the previous year. The history tests reportedly resulted in the poorest student performance rates. The general responses quoted by the *Post* to this high failure rate were quite predictable. The Fairfax School superintendent was looking for more state money, while others complained about the tests themselves and that students were required to remember too many facts. Suggesting that schools, teachers, parents, and students might have to work harder, or that competition should be used to spur performance forward naturally, were not mentioned.

Given its rich history—most notably that Virginia gave the nation seven U.S. presidents, including George Washington, James Madison, and Thomas Jefferson—it is particularly fitting that Virginia should offer the top-rated history standards in the nation.

Looking ahead to a robust, high-tech future, while possessing a solid respect for history—now that is not a bad combination for the state of Virginia at the dawn of a new century.

POLITICS

Registered Voters

No party registration

Federal Officials: Recent Election and Group Ratings

			ACU	ADA	SBSC
U.S. Senators:	John Warner (R)		80	13	90
	1996 Warner (R)	52%			
	Warner (D)	47%			
	Charles Robb (D)		20	68	25
	1994 Robb (D)	46%			
	North (R)	43%			
U.S. Representatives:	Herbert Bateman (R-1)		79	8	85
	1998 Bateman (R)	76%			
	Phillips (I)	13%			
	Owen Pickett (D-2)		39	46	40
	1998 Pickett (D)	NO			
	Robert Scott (D-3)		11	90	25
	1998 Scott (D)	76%			
	Barnett (I)	23%			

			ACU	ADA	SBSC
Norman Sisisky (D-4)			39	47	35
1998	Sisisky (D)	NO			
Virgil Goode Jr. (D-5)			84	28	70
1998	Goode (D)	NO			
Bob Goodlatte (R-6)			91	5	95
1998	Goodlatte (R)	69%			
	Bowers (D)	31%			
Tom Bliley Jr. (R-7)			91	4	90
1998	Bliley (R)	79%			
	Evans (I)	21%			
James Moran (D-8)			14	70	30
1998	Moran (D)	67%			
	Miller (R)	33%			
Rick Boucher (D-9)			12	74	10
1998	Boucher (D)	61%			
	Barta (R)	39%			
Frank Wolf (R-10)			83	11	85
1998	Wolf (R)	72%			
	Brooks (D)	25%			
Thomas Davis III (R-11)			70	27	85
1998	Davis (R)	82%			
	Levy (I)	17%			

Electoral Votes:	13	
1996 Presidential Results:	Clinton	45%
	Dole	47%
	Perot	7%

State Officials

Governor 1997 Election:	Jim Gilmore (R)	56%
	Don Beyer Jr. (D)	43%
Lt. Governor:	John Hager (R)	
Attorney General:	Mark Earley (R)	
State Senate:	19 Democrats	
	21 Republicans	
State House of Delegates:	50 Democrats	
	49 Republicans	
	1 Independent	

TAXES AND SPENDING

Total Revenues

Virginia's per capita state and local total revenues registered $4,744 in 1996, ranking 43d in the nation and trailing the U.S. average of $5,706 by 17%. From 1962 to 1996, real per capita state and local revenues increased by 365%, compared with an increase in the national average of 297%.

Taxes

Virginia's per capita state and local taxes registered $2,341 in 1996, ranking 28th in the nation and trailing the U.S. average of $2,597 by 10%. From 1962 to 1996, real per capita state and local taxes increased by 247%, compared with an increase of 152% in the U.S. average.

Property Taxes

Virginia's per capita state and local property taxes equaled $726 in 1996, ranking 25th in the nation and lagging behind the U.S. average of $789 by 8%. From 1962 to 1996, real per capita state and local property taxes increased by 199%, versus a 67% increase in the U.S. average.

Sales and Gross Receipts Taxes

Virginia's per capita state and local sales and gross receipts taxes came in at $728 in 1996, ranking 42d in the nation and trailing the U.S. average of $939 by 22%. From 1962 to 1996, real per capita state and local sales and gross receipts taxes increased by 307%, versus an increase of 214% in the U.S. average.

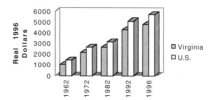

Real Per Capita State and Local Total Revenues: Virginia vs. U.S.

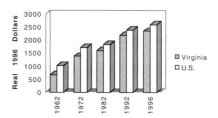

Real Per Capita State and Local Taxes: Virginia vs. U.S.

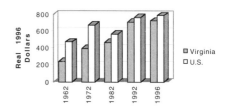

Real Per Capita State and Local Property Taxes: Virginia vs. U.S.

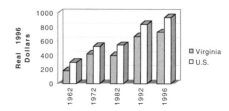

Real Per Capita State and Local Sales and Gross Receipts Taxes: Virginia vs. U.S.

Income Taxes

Virginia's per capita state and local income (individual and corporate) taxes registered $699 in 1996, ranking 19th in the nation and topping the U.S. average of $674 by 4%. From 1962 to 1996, real per capita state and local income taxes increased by 426%, versus a 567% increase in the U.S. average.

Personal Income Tax

A rate of 5.75%, ranking 24th in the nation (from lowest tax rate to highest), and comparing with the national average of 5.26%.

Capital Gains Tax

A rate of 5.75%, ranking 28th in the nation (from lowest tax rate to highest), and comparing with the national average of 4.68%.

Corporate Income Tax

A rate of 6.0%, ranking 15th in the nation (from lowest tax rate to highest), and comparing with the national average of 6.69%.

Total Expenditures

Virginia's per capita state and local total spending registered $4,349 in 1996, ranking 43d in the nation and trailing the U.S. average of $5,268 by 17%. From 1962 to 1996, real per capita state and local total spending increased by 277%, versus an increase of 254% in the U.S. average.

Welfare Expenditures

Virginia's per capita state and local public welfare spending registered $493 in 1996, ranking 47th in the nation and trailing the U.S. average of $729 by 32%. From 1962 to 1996, real per capita state and local public welfare spending increased by 867%, compared with a 488% increase in the U.S. average.

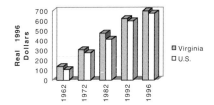

Real Per Capita State and Local Income Taxes: Virginia vs. U.S.

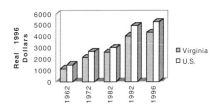

Real Per Capita State and Local Total Expenditures: Virginia vs. U.S.

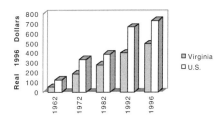

Real Per Capita State and Local Public Welfare Spending: Virginia vs. U.S.

Welfare Recipients (in thousands)

	1980	1989	3/99	Change 1989–99
Va.	176	150	89	−41%
U.S.	10,923	10,987	7,335	−33%

Interest on General Debt

Virginia's per capita state and local interest on general debt registered $193 in 1996, ranking 30th in the nation and trailing the U.S. average of $222 by 13%. From 1962 to 1996, real per capita state and local interest on general debt increased by 371%, versus an increase of 335% in the U.S. average.

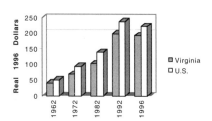

Real Per Capita State and Local Interest on General Debt: Virginia vs. U.S.

Total Debt Outstanding

Virginia's per capita state and local debt registered $3,630 in 1996, ranking 32d in the nation and trailing the U.S. average of $4,409 by 18%. From 1962 to 1996, real per capita state and local debt outstanding increased by 157%, versus an increase of 120% in the U.S. average.

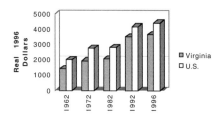

Real Per Capita State and Local Debt Outstanding: Virginia vs. U.S.

Government Employees

Virginia's state and local government employees (full-time equivalent, or FTE) per 10,000 population registered 532.7 in 1997, ranking 28th in the nation and exceeding the U.S. average of 531.1 by 0.3%. From 1962 to 1996, state and local FTE employees per 10,000 population increased by 91%, compared with an increase in the U.S. average of 66%.

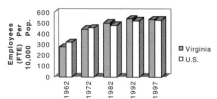

State and Local Government Employees (FTE) Per 10,000 Population: Virginia vs. U.S.

Per Capita Federal Government Expenditures, 1998

	1998	Ranking
Va.	$8,221	2d
U.S.	$5,491	

Per capita spending in Virginia topped the national average by 50%.

EDUCATION

Total Education Spending

Virginia's per capita state and local education spending registered $1,501 in 1996, ranking 26th in the nation and trailing the U.S. average of $1,503 by 0.1%. From 1962 to 1996, real per capita total education spending increased by 247%, versus an increase in the U.S. average of 173%.

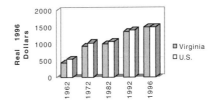

Real Per Capita State and Local Education Spending: Virginia vs. U.S.

Per Pupil Spending

Virginia's per pupil public school spending registered $5,571 in 1998, ranking 32d in the nation and trailing the U.S. average of $6,131 by 9%. From 1970 to 1998, Virginia's real per pupil public school spending increased by 130%, compared with a 120% increase in the U.S. average.

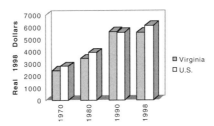

Real Per Pupil Public School Spending: Virginia vs. U.S.

Average Public School Teacher Salaries (in 1997–98 dollars)

	1970	1980	1990	1998	1998 Ranking
Va.	34,553	29,293	39,409	36,654	25th
U.S.	36,934	33,272	39,956	39,385	

In 1998, the average public school teacher salary in Virginia trailed the U.S. average by 7%. From 1970 to 1998, the real average teacher salary in Virginia increased by 6%, versus an increase in the U.S. average of 7%.

Pupil/Teacher Ratio, Fall 1996

	Ratio	Rank
Va.	14.7	9th
U.S.	17.1	

Teachers/Staff, Fall 1996

	Percent	Rank
Va.	53.5	17th
U.S.	52.1	

Public School 4th-Grade Reading Proficiency, 1998

	Average	Rank (out of 40 states)
Va.	218	13th
U.S.	215	

Public School 8th-Grade Reading Proficiency, 1998

	Average	Rank (out of 37 states)
Va.	266	7th
U.S.	261	

Public School 4th-Grade Math Proficiency, 1996

	Average	Rank (out of 44 states)
Va.	223	22d
U.S.	224	

Public School 8th-Grade Math Proficiency, 1996

	Average	Rank (out of 41 states)
Va.	270	20th
U.S.	271	

Public School 8th-Grade Science Proficiency, 1996

	Average	Rank (out of 41 states)
Va.	149	20th
U.S.	148	

Average Math SAT Scores

	1972	1982	1992	1998	Percentage Taking SAT in 1998
Va.	501	489	494	499	56
U.S.	509	493	501	512	43

Average Verbal SAT Scores

	1972	1982	1992	1998	Percentage Taking SAT in 1998
Va.	521	504	501	507	56
U.S.	530	504	500	505	43

Expenditures by Public Institutions of Higher Education Per Full-Time-Equivalent Student, 1996

	FTE Student Spending	Rank
Va.	$11,121	41st
U.S.	$12,343	

Per-FTE-student spending in public institutions of higher education trailed the U.S. average by 10%.

Per Full-Time-Equivalent Student Revenues from Federal, State, and Local Governments for Public Institutions of Higher Education, 1996

	FTE Student Government Revenues	Rank
Va.	$6,058	48th
U.S.	$8,101	

Per-FTE-student-government revenues in public institutions of higher education trailed the U.S. average by 25%.

Average Salary for Full-Time Professors at Public Universities, 1997

	Average	Rank
Va.	$73,057	17th
U.S.	$72,599	

The average full-time public university professor salary exceeded the U.S. average by 0.6%.

ECONOMY AND BUSINESS

Economic Growth

Over the period of 1977 to 1997, Virginia's real gross state product (GSP) grew by 86.2%—ranking 21st in the nation—as compared with real U.S. gross domestic product (GDP), expanding by 70.1%.

At $211.3 billion in 1997, Virginia's GSP ranked as 13th largest in the nation.

From 1993 to 1997, Virginia's annual real GSP growth averaged 3.34%—ranking 32d in the nation—as compared with annual real U.S. GDP growth, averaging 3.08%.

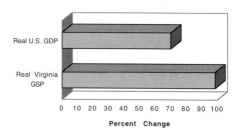

Real Economic Growth 1977-1997: Virginia vs. U.S.

Job Growth

	Growth in Employee Payrolls (Nonagricultural) 1962–1998	Ranking
Va.	205.9%	10th
U.S.	126.5%	

	Average Annual Growth in Employee Payrolls (Nonagricultural) 1993–98	Ranking
Va.	3.04%	27th
U.S.	2.98%	

Per Capita Disposable Income, 1997

	1997	Ranking
Va.	$22,192	16th
U.S.	$21,607	

Per capita disposable income exceeded the U.S. average by 3%.

	Real Growth 1962–97	Ranking
Va.	156.2%	8th
U.S.	116.7%	

	Average Annual Real Growth 1993–97	Ranking
Va.	1.42%	37th
U.S.	1.48%	

Number of Businesses

	1997	Percent with Fewer than 500 Employees
Businesses with Employees	152,460	97.9
Self-employed Individuals	196,000	

New Business Incorporations

	1980	1986	1992	1997
Va.	10,845	16,726	16,936	18,704

Percentage Change in Annual New Business Incorporations, 1980 vs. 1997

	Percent	Ranking
Va.	72.5	15th
U.S.	49.7	

State Merchandise Exports to the World, 1998 (in millions of dollars)

	1998	Rank
Va.	$11,460	16th

Small Business Survival Index, 1999

Virginia ranks 18th in terms of its policy environment for entrepreneurship.

Fortune 500 Headquarters in 1999

A total of 18 (ranked 8th), with Richmond ranked 11th among U.S. cities with 6 headquarters

Labor Union Membership, 1983 vs. 1997

	Percentage of Workers 1983	1997	Rank
Va.	11.7	6.5	46th
U.S.	20.1	14.1	

Homeownership Rate, 1998

	Rate	Rank
Va.	69.4	26th
U.S.	66.3	

CRIME

Crime Rates Per 100 Residents (rankings from best to worst crime rate)

Total Crime	1960	1970	1980	1990	1998	1998 Ranking
Va.	0.82	2.15	4.62	4.44	3.66	15th
U.S.	1.04	2.74	5.90	5.82	4.62	

From 1960 to 1998, Virginia's crime rate increased by 346%, versus a U.S. increase of 344%. From 1990 to 1998, Virginia's crime rate dropped by 18%, compared with the U.S. decrease of 21%.

Violent Crime	1960	1970	1980	1990	1998	1998 Ranking
Va.	0.14	0.26	0.31	0.35	0.33	17th
U.S.	0.14	0.36	0.58	0.73	0.57	

From 1960 to 1998, Virginia's violent crime rate increased by 136%, versus a U.S. increase of 307%. From 1990 to 1998, Virginia's violent crime rate decreased by 6%, compared with a national decline of 22%.

Property Crime	1960	1970	1980	1990	1998	1998 Ranking
Va.	0.68	1.89	4.31	4.09	3.33	15th
U.S.	0.90	2.38	5.32	5.09	4.05	

From 1960 to 1998, Virginia's property crime rate increased by 390%, versus a national increase of 350%. From 1990 to 1998, Virginia's property crime rate decreased by 19%, compared with a national decline of 20%.

Real Per Capita Police Protection Spending (in real 1996 dollars)

	1962	1972	1982	1992	1996	1996 Ranking
Va.	37	69	94	126	136	29th
U.S.	51	95	114	148	168	

In 1996, per capita state and local police protection spending in Virginia trailed the U.S. average by 19%. From 1962 to 1996, real per capita state and local police protection spending increased by 268%, versus an increase of 229% in the U.S. average.

Prisoners in State and Federal Prisons Per 1,000 Population

	1980	1990	1996	1996 Ranking
Va.	1.67	2.84	4.15	29th
U.S.	1.46	3.11	4.45	

From 1980 to 1996, prisoners per 1,000 population increased by 149%, versus a U.S. increase of 205%.

HEALTH CARE

Health-Care Spending

Virginia's per capita state and local health-care spending registered $96 in 1996, ranking 40th in the nation and trailing the U.S. average of $151 by 36%. From 1962 to 1996, Virginia's real per capita state and local health-care spending increased by 586%, versus an increase of 739% in the U.S. average.

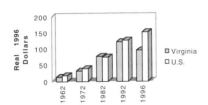

Real Per Capita State and Local Health Care Spending: Virginia vs. U.S.

Hospital Spending

Virginia's per capita state and local hospital spending registered $191 in 1996, ranking 31st in the nation and trailing the U.S. average of $266 by 28%. From 1962 to 1996, Virginia's real per capita state and local hospital spending increased by 218%, as opposed to an increase of 189% in the U.S. average.

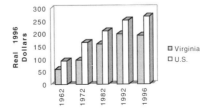

Real Per Capita State and Local Hospital Spending: Virginia vs. U.S.

Medicaid, 1997

	Spending Per Recipient	Ranking
Va.	$3,123	36th
U.S.	$3,681	

Virginia's per-recipient Medicaid spending trailed the U.S. average by 15%.

ENVIRONMENT

Parks and Recreation Spending

Virginia's per capita state and local parks and recreation spending registered $60 in 1996, ranking 27th in the nation and trailing the U.S. average of $72 by 17%. From 1962 to 1996, real per capita state and local parks and recreation spending increased by 567%, versus a 213% increase in the U.S. average.

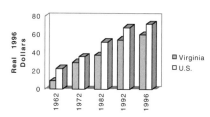

Real Per Capita State and Local Parks and Recreation Spending: Virginia vs. U.S.

State and Local Natural Resources Spending, 1996

	Per Capita	Ranking
Va.	$25	46th
U.S.	$60	

Per capita state and local natural resources spending in Virginia trailed the U.S. average by 58%.

State Parks Revenues as a Share of Operating Expenses, 1997

	Percent	Rank
Va.	42	23d
U.S.	42	

Percentage of Land Owned by the Federal Government, 1996

	Percent	Rank
Va.	8.9	16th
U.S.	24.8	

SOCIETY AND DEMOGRAPHICS

Population

Virginia's 1998 population of 6.791 million ranked 12th in the nation.

Population Growth, 1990–98

	Percentage Change in Population	Ranking
Va.	9.73	19th
U.S.	8.66	

	Net International Migration	Ranking
Va.	131,471	9th

	Net Domestic Migration	Ranking
Va.	67,977	21st

Virginia   Population

Infant Mortality Rate, 1998

	Percent	Rank
Va.	7.4	19th
U.S.	6.4	

Percentage of Births of Low Birthweight, 1997

	Percent	Rank
Va.	7.7	21st
U.S.	7.5	

Percentage of Live Births to Unmarried Women, 1997

	Percent	Rank
Va.	29.3	34th
U.S.	32.4	

Abortion Rate—Abortions Per 1,000 Women Ages 15–44, 1995

	Rate	Rank
Va.	20.0	20th
U.S.	22.9	

LIFESTYLE

Percentage of Households with Computers, 1998

	Percent	Rank
Va.	46.4	12th

Percentage of Households with Internet Access, 1998

	Percent	Rank
Va.	27.9	15th

State Arts Agency Spending, 1999

	Per Capita	Rank
Va.	$0.56	40th
U.S.	$1.35	

Per capita state arts spending in 1999 trailed the U.S. average by 59%.

Major League Sports Facilities

None

WASHINGTON

The state of Washington ranks third in both the percentage of households with computers and the percentage of households with Internet access. High numbers are exactly what you would expect, since Microsoft calls the state of Washington home. The Redmond-based firm is a fantastic story of entrepreneurial success and ranks as the world's largest software producer.

Over the past decade, the people of Washington have gotten a first-hand look at how the federal government treats a global business success. Rather than holding up Microsoft as a stellar example of a business that gained economic leadership by serving customers well, the federal government—mainly, the U.S. Department of Justice—instead launched an antitrust assault.

If a company wildly succeeds or attempts to merge with another business, then it may be ripe for antitrust action.

In the end, antitrust regulation is fundamentally contradictory. It supposedly protects consumers from evil monopolies, but it actually overrides the decisions made by consumers in the marketplace, supplanting them with the dictates of government bureaucrats.

The Microsoft antitrust case suffered from some glaring weaknesses. Most prominent was the simple fact that Microsoft is not a monopoly. The company competes against present and future competitors. Current competitors are lurking and have made real inroads. For example, in a *Wall Street Journal* article (April 9, 1999), Hudson Institute economist Alan Reynolds revealed that the Department of Justice's claim that Microsoft controls more than 90% of the computer operating systems market includes "only single-user computers with Intel microprocessors." Reynolds notes, "That definition turns out to exclude Microsoft's most famous rivals." Factor in workstations; business networks; Apple PCs; subnotebooks; handheld computers; TV set devices; Intel-based operating systems like Linux, Free BSD, and BeOS 4.0; as well as Intel-based PCs shipped without operating systems and Microsoft's market share turns out to be a "much smaller" 70%.

Most critically, consumer harm should provide the foundation of any government antitrust action. However, consumers clearly are being well served in today's dynamic computer marketplace. In reality, the source of most antitrust investigations is not the consumer but the targeted company's competitors who failed to keep up.

Washington residents would do well to keep in mind the federal government's inability to understand the computer industry when looking at other government ventures at the federal, state, and local levels. There would seem to be reason for some concern in-state, for example, as per capita state and local spending, taxing, and debt outpace the U.S. averages.

At the same time, however, the lack of state personal income, corporate income, and capital gains taxes provide a sound foundation for Washington's economy. In fact, economic growth, job creation, and population growth have outdistanced the nation as a whole in recent times. From 1990 to 1998, Washington was a particularly large importer of people from other states and around the world.

While the lack of state income taxes is a big plus for Washington upon entering the 21st century, much work needs to be done in getting overall spending and property taxes under control. Just a little bit of frugality on the government's part (never an easy task) would only add to the allure of Washington—and perhaps would attract the next Microsoft to the state.

POLITICS

Registered Voters

No party registration

Federal Officials: Recent Election and Group Ratings

			ACU	ADA	SBSC
U.S. Senators:	Slade Gorton (R)		62	18	65
	1994 Gorton (R)	56%			
	Sims (D)	44%			
	Patty Murray (D)		1	91	30
	1998 Murray (D)	58%			
	Smith (R)	41%			
U.S. Representatives:	Jay Inslee (D-1)		NA	NA	NA
	1998 Inslee (D)	50%			
	White (R)	44%			
	Jack Metcalf (R-2)		89	10	65
	1998 Metcalf (R)	55%			
	Cammermeyer (D)	45%			
	Brian Baird (D-3)		NA	NA	NA
	1998 Baird (D)	55%			
	Benton (R)	45%			
	Richard (Doc) Hastings (R-4)		96	0	95
	1998 Hastings (R)	69%			
	Pross (D)	24%			
	George Nethercutt (R-5)		93	1	90
	1998 Nethercutt (R)	57%			
	Lyons (D)	38%			
	Norman Dicks (D-6)		10	74	20
	1998 Dicks (D)	68%			
	Lawrence (R)	32%			

				ACU	ADA	SBSC
Jim McDermott (D-7)				2	93	15
1998	McDermott (D)	88%				
	Lippman (REF)	9%				
Jennifer Dunn (R-8)				91	3	95
1998	Dunn (R)	60%				
	Behrens-Benedict (D)	40%				
Adam Smith (D-9)				10	90	20
1998	Smith (D)	65%				
	Taber (R)	35%				

Electoral Votes:	11	
1996 Presidential Results:	Clinton	50%
	Dole	37%
	Perot	9%

State Officials

Governor 1996 Election:	Gary Locke (D)	58%
	Ellen Craswell (R)	42%
Lt. Governor:	Brad Owen (D)	
Attorney General:	Christine Gregoire (D)	
State Senate:	27 Democrats	
	22 Republicans	
State General Assembly:	49 Democrats	
	49 Republicans	

TAXES AND SPENDING

Total Revenues

Washington's per capita state and local total revenues registered $6,788 in 1996, ranking 6th in the nation and topping the U.S. average of $5,706 by 19%. From 1962 to 1996, real per capita state and local revenues increased by 288%, compared with an increase in the national average of 297%.

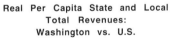

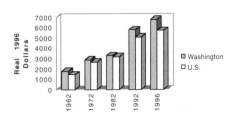

Taxes

Washington's per capita state and local taxes registered $2,795 in 1996, ranking 11th in the nation and exceeding the U.S. average of $2,597 by 8%. From 1962 to 1996, real per capita state and local taxes increased by 141%, compared with an increase of 152% in the U.S. average.

Property Taxes

Washington's per capita state and local property taxes equaled $845 in 1996, ranking 17th in the nation and exceeding the U.S. average of $789 by 7%. From 1962 to 1996, real per capita state and local property taxes increased by 136%, versus a 67% increase in the U.S. average.

Sales and Gross Receipts Taxes

Washington's per capita state and local sales and gross receipts taxes came in at $1,689 in 1996, ranking 2d in the nation and exceeding the U.S. average of $939 by 80%. From 1962 to 1996, real per capita state and local sales and gross receipts taxes increased by 156%, versus an increase of 214% in the U.S. average.

Income Taxes

Washington's per capita state and local income (individual and corporate) taxes registered $0 in 1996, ranking last in the nation and trailing the U.S. average of $674. From 1962 to 1996, U.S. real per capita state and local income taxes increased by 567%.

Personal Income Tax

A rate of 0%, ranking best in the nation (from lowest tax rate to highest), and comparing with the national average of 5.26%.

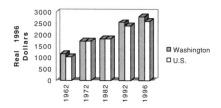

Real Per Capita State and Local Taxes: Washington vs. U.S.

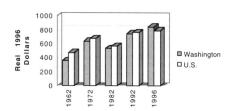

Real Per Capita State and Local Property Taxes: Washington vs. U.S.

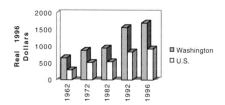

Real Per Capita State and Local Sales and Gross Receipts Taxes: Washington vs. U.S.

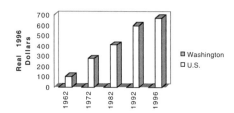

Real Per Capita State and Local Income Taxes: Washington vs. U.S.

Capital Gains Tax

A rate of 0%, ranking best in the nation (from lowest tax rate to highest), and comparing with the national average of 4.68%.

Corporate Income Tax

A rate of 0%, ranking best in the nation (from lowest tax rate to highest), and comparing with the national average of 6.69%.

Total Expenditures

Washington's per capita state and local total spending registered $6,255 in 1996, ranking 6th in the nation and outpacing the U.S. average of $5,268 by 19%. From 1962 to 1996, real per capita state and local total spending increased by 249%, versus an increase of 254% in the U.S. average.

Welfare Expenditures

Washington's per capita state and local public welfare spending registered $687 in 1996, ranking 23d in the nation and trailing the U.S. average of $729 by 6%. From 1962 to 1996, real per capita state and local public welfare spending increased by 316%, compared with a 488% increase in the U.S. average.

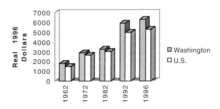

Real Per Capita State and Local Total Expenditures: Washington vs. U.S.

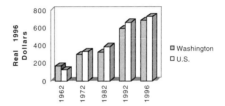

Real Per Capita State and Local Public Welfare Spending: Washington vs. U.S.

Welfare Recipients (in thousands)

	1980	1989	3/99	Change 1989–99
Wash.	173	225	174	−23%
U.S.	10,923	10,987	7,335	−33%

Interest on General Debt

Washington's per capita state and local interest on general debt registered $214 in 1996, ranking 22d in the nation and trailing the U.S. average of $222 by 4%. From 1962 to 1996, real per capita state and local interest on general debt increased by 289%, versus an increase of 335% in the U.S. average.

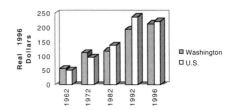

Real Per Capita State and Local Interest on General Debt: Washington vs. U.S.

Total Debt Outstanding

Washington's per capita state and local debt registered $5,742 in 1996, ranking 10th in the nation and topping the U.S. average of $4,409 by 30%. From 1962 to 1996, real per capita state and local debt outstanding increased by 59%, versus an increase of 120% in the U.S. average.

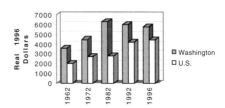

Real Per Capita State and Local Debt Outstanding: Washington vs. U.S.

Government Employees

Washington's state and local government employees (full-time equivalent, or FTE) per 10,000 population registered 522.7 in 1997, ranking 34th in the nation and trailing the U.S. average of 531.1 by 2%. From 1962 to 1996, state and local FTE employees per 10,000 population increased by 43%, compared with an increase in the U.S. average of 66%.

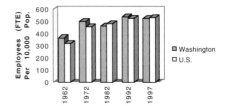

State and Local Government Employees (FTE) Per 10,000 Population: Washington vs. U.S.

Per Capita Federal Government Expenditures, 1998

	1998	Ranking
Wash.	$5,482	24th
U.S.	$5,491	

Per capita federal spending in Washington trailed the national average by 0.2%.

EDUCATION

Total Education Spending

Washington's per capita state and local education spending registered $1,704 in 1996, ranking 12th in the nation and topping the U.S. average of $1,503 by 13%. From 1962 to 1996, real per capita total education spending increased by 135%, versus an increase in the U.S. average of 173%.

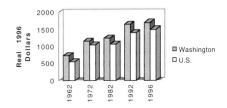

Real Per Capita State and Local Education Spending: Washington vs. U.S.

Per Pupil Spending

Washington's per pupil public school spending registered $6,663 in 1998, ranking 12th in the nation and exceeding the U.S. average of $6,131 by 9%. From 1970 to 1998, Washington's real per pupil public school spending increased by 111%, compared with a 120% increase in the U.S. average.

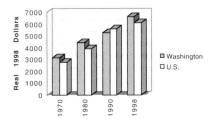

Real Per Pupil Public School Spending: Washington vs. U.S.

Average Public School Teacher Salaries (in 1997–98 dollars)

	1970	1980	1990	1998	1998 Ranking
Wash.	39,499	39,210	38,796	38,788	19th
U.S.	36,934	33,272	39,956	39,385	

In 1998, the average public school teacher salary in Washington trailed the U.S. average by 2%. From 1970 to 1998, the real average teacher salary in Washington decreased by 2%, versus an increase in the U.S. average of 7%.

Pupil/Teacher Ratio, Fall 1996

	Ratio	Rank
Wash.	20.2	49th
U.S.	17.1	

Teachers/Staff, Fall 1996

	Percent	Rank
Wash.	51.0	39th
U.S.	52.1	

Public School 4th-Grade Reading Proficiency, 1998

	Average	Rank (out of 40 states)
Wash.	217	16th
U.S.	215	

Public School 8th-Grade Reading Proficiency, 1998

	Average	Rank (out of 37 states)
Wash.	265	11th
U.S.	261	

Public School 4th-Grade Math Proficiency, 1996

	Average	Rank (out of 44 states)
Wash.	225	17th
U.S.	224	

Public School 8th-Grade Math Proficiency, 1996

	Average	Rank (out of 41 states)
Wash.	276	14th
U.S.	271	

Public School 8th-Grade Science Proficiency, 1996

	Average	Rank (out of 41 states)
Wash.	150	19th
U.S.	148	

Average Math SAT Scores

	1972	1982	1992	1998	Percentage Taking SAT in 1998
Wash.	541	532	509	526	53
U.S.	509	493	501	512	43

Average Verbal SAT Scores

	1972	1982	1992	1998	Percentage Taking SAT in 1998
Wash.	568	545	509	524	53
U.S.	530	504	500	505	43

Expenditures by Public Institutions of Higher Education Per Full-Time-Equivalent Student, 1996

	FTE Student Spending	Rank
Wash.	$12,311	25th
U.S.	$12,343	

Per-FTE-student spending in public institutions of higher education trailed the U.S. average by 0.3%.

Per Full-Time-Equivalent Student Revenues from Federal, State, and Local Governments for Public Institutions of Higher Education, 1996

	FTE Student Government Revenues	Rank
Wash.	$8,464	18th
U.S.	$8,101	

Per-FTE-student-government revenues in public institutions of higher education topped the U.S. average by 4%.

Average Salary for Full-Time Professors at Public Universities, 1997

	Average	Rank
Wash.	$68,166	31st
U.S.	$72,599	

The average full-time public university professor salary trailed the U.S. average by 6%.

ECONOMY AND BUSINESS

Economic Growth

Over the period of 1977 to 1997, Washington's real gross state product (GSP) grew by 94.4%—ranking 13th in the nation—as compared with real U.S. gross domestic product (GDP), expanding by 70.1%.

At $172.2 billion in 1997, Washington's GSP ranked as 14th largest in the nation.

From 1993 to 1997, Washington's annual real GSP growth averaged 3.41%—ranking 31st in the nation—as compared with annual real U.S. GDP growth, averaging 3.08%.

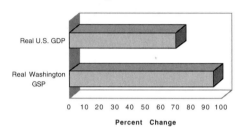

Real Economic Growth 1977-1997: Washington vs. U.S.

Real U.S. GDP

Real Washington GSP

0 10 20 30 40 50 60 70 80 90 100

Percent Change

Job Growth

	Growth in Employee Payrolls (Nonagricultural) 1962–98	Ranking
Wash.	203.0%	11th
U.S.	126.5%	

	Average Annual Growth in Employee Payrolls (Nonagricultural) 1993–98	Ranking
Wash.	3.16%	22d
U.S.	2.98%	

Per Capita Disposable Income, 1997

	1997	Ranking
Wash.	$22,872	10th
U.S.	$21,607	

Per capita disposable income exceeded the U.S. average by 6%.

	Real Growth 1962–97	Ranking
Wash.	106.9%	37th
U.S.	116.7%	

	Average Annual Real Growth 1993–97	Ranking
Wash.	1.63%	27th
U.S.	1.48%	

Number of Businesses

	1997	Percent with Fewer than 500 Employees
Businesses with Employees	174,516	98.3
Self-employed Individuals	269,000	

New Business Incorporations

	1980	1986	1992	1997
Wash.	8,396	9,914	12,500	12,487

Percentage Change in Annual New Business Incorporations, 1980 vs. 1997

	Percent	Ranking
Wash.	48.7	24th
U.S.	49.7	

State Merchandise Exports to the World, 1998 (in millions of dollars)

	1998	Rank
Wash.	$37,960	5th

Small Business Survival Index, 1999

Washington ranks 6th best in the nation in terms of its policy environment for entrepreneurship.

Fortune 500 Headquarters in 1999

A total of 10 (ranked 16th)

Labor Union Membership, 1983 vs. 1997

	Percentage of Workers		
	1983	1997	1997 Rank
Wash.	27.1	20.5	5th
U.S.	20.1	14.1	

Homeownership Rate, 1998

	Rate	Rank
Wash.	64.9	40th
U.S.	66.3	

CRIME

Crime Rates Per 100 Residents (rankings from best to worst crime rate)

Total Crime	1960	1970	1980	1990	1998	1998 Ranking
Wash.	1.03	3.16	6.92	6.22	5.87	46th
U.S.	1.04	2.74	5.90	5.82	4.62	

From 1960 to 1998, Washington's crime rate increased by 470%, versus a U.S. increase of 344%. From 1990 to 1998, Washington's crime rate decreased by 6%, versus a U.S. decrease of 21%

Violent Crime	1960	1970	1980	1990	1998	1998 Ranking
Wash.	0.05	0.22	0.46	0.50	0.43	25th
U.S.	0.14	0.36	0.58	0.73	0.57	

From 1960 to 1998, Washington's violent crime rate increased by 760%, versus a U.S. increase of 307%. From 1990 to 1998, Washington's violent crime rate decreased by 14%, compared with a national decline of 22%.

Property Crime	1960	1970	1980	1990	1998	1998 Ranking
Wash.	0.98	2.93	6.45	5.72	5.44	47th
U.S.	0.90	2.38	5.32	5.09	4.05	

From 1960 to 1998, Washington's property crime rate increased by 455%, versus a national increase of 350%. From 1990 to 1998, Washington's property crime rate decreased by 5%, compared with a national decline of 20%.

Real Per Capita Police Protection Spending (in real 1996 dollars)

	1962	1972	1982	1992	1996	1996 Ranking
Wash.	46	92	106	134	146	24th
U.S.	51	95	114	148	168	

In 1996, per capita state and local police protection spending in Washington trailed the U.S. average by 13%. From 1962 to 1996, real per capita state and local police protection spending increased by 217%, versus an increase of 229% in the U.S. average.

Prisoners in State and Federal Prisons Per 1,000 Population

	1980	1990	1996	1996 Ranking
Wash.	1.06	1.64	2.27	41st
U.S.	1.46	3.11	4.45	

From 1980 to 1996, prisoners per 1,000 population increased by 114%, versus a U.S. increase of 205%.

HEALTH CARE

Health-Care Spending

Washington's per capita state and local health-care spending registered $219 in 1996, ranking 6th in the nation and topping the U.S. average of $151 by 45%. From 1962 to 1996, Washington's real per capita state and local health-care spending increased by 1,464%, versus an increase of 739% in the U.S. average.

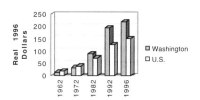

Real Per Capita State and Local Health Care Spending: Washington vs. U.S.

Hospital Spending

Washington's per capita state and local hospital spending registered $236 in 1996, ranking 26th in the nation and trailing the U.S. average of $266 by 11%. From 1962 to 1996, Washington's real per capita state and local hospital spending increased by 203%, as opposed to an increase of 189% in the U.S. average.

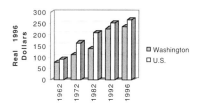

Real Per Capita State and Local Hospital Spending: Washington vs. U.S.

Medicaid, 1997

	Spending Per Recipient	Ranking
Wash.	$2,211	48th
U.S.	$3,681	

Washington's per-recipient Medicaid spending trailed the U.S. average by 40%.

ENVIRONMENT

Parks and Recreation Spending

Washington's per capita state and local parks and recreation spending registered $117 in 1996, ranking 6th in the nation and exceeding the U.S. average of $72 by 63%. From 1962 to 1996, real per capita state and local parks and recreation spending increased by 318%, versus a 213% increase in the U.S. average.

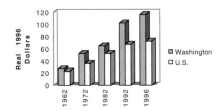

Real Per Capita State and Local Parks and Recreation Spending: Washington vs. U.S.

State and Local Natural Resources Spending, 1996

	Per Capita	Ranking
Wash.	$93	9th
U.S.	$60	

Per capita state and local natural resources spending in Washington exceeded the U.S. average by 55%.

State Parks Revenues as a Share of Operating Expenses, 1997

	Percent	Rank
Wash.	36	31st
U.S.	42	

Percentage of Land Owned by the Federal Government, 1996

	Percent	Rank
Wash.	28.0	11th
U.S.	24.8	

SOCIETY AND DEMOGRAPHICS

Population

Washington's 1998 population of 5.689 million ranked 15th in the nation.

Population Growth, 1990–98

	Percentage Change in Population	Ranking
Wash.	16.89	7th
U.S.	8.66	

	Net International Migration	Ranking
Wash.	121,317	9th

	Net Domestic Migration	Ranking
Wash.	373,946	7th

Infant Mortality Rate, 1998

	Percent	Rank
Wash.	5.4	44th
U.S.	6.4	

Percentage of Births of Low Birthweight, 1997

	Percent	Rank
Wash.	5.6	49th
U.S.	7.5	

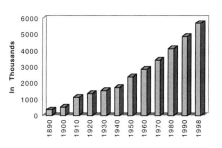

Washington Population

Percentage of Live Births to Unmarried Women, 1997

	Percent	Rank
Wash.	27.1	41st
U.S.	32.4	

Abortion Rate—Abortions Per 1,000 Women Ages 15–44, 1995

	Rate	Rank
Wash.	20.2	19th
U.S.	22.9	

LIFESTYLE

Percentage of Households with Computers, 1998

	Percent	Rank
Wash.	56.3	3d

Percentage of Households with Internet Access, 1998

	Percent	Rank
Wash.	36.6	3d

State Arts Agency Spending, 1999

	Per Capita	Rank
Wash.	$0.36	49th
U.S.	$1.35	

Per capita state arts spending in 1999 trailed the U.S. average by 73%.

Major League Sports Facilities

Year Opened/ Refurb.	Stadium/ Arena	Home Team	Millions of Nominal Dollars		Millions of Real 1997 Dollars	
			Estimated Total Cost	Estimated Taxpayer Cost	Estimated Total Cost	Estimated Taxpayer Cost
1938	Sick's Stadium	Pilots (MLB) 1969	$0.35	$0.0	$3.5	$0.0
1976	Kingdome	Mariners (MLB) 1977–present Seahawks (NFL) 1976–present	$67.0	$67.0	$188.7	$188.7
1995	Key Arena II	SuperSonics (NBA) 1995–present	$119.0	$74.5	$125.3	$78.4
1999	Safeco Field	Mariners (MLB) 1999–present	$517.0	$432.0	$499.0	$417.0

WEST VIRGINIA

West Virginia has long been one of the nation's worst-performing state economies.

Real gross state product growth, job creation, merchandise exports, and changes in annual new business incorporations all rank poorly. The state's population has been trending downward since 1950. Per capita disposable income ranks 50th in the nation and has recently been growing at a below-average pace. Household computer ownership and Internet access rank among the nation's worst.

The state's big bright spot is the second lowest crime rate in the nation. Though even when it comes to crime, West Virginia's violent crime rate leaped dramatically between 1990 and 1998, while the nation experienced a substantial decline.

The presumed remedy to West Virginia's woes has been more dollars and pork from the federal government. The state's two U.S. senators, Robert Byrd and John D. Rockefeller IV, stand out, respectively, for the ability to bring home the bacon and for strong liberal leanings. In 1998, per capita federal government spending in West Virginia ranked 14th highest in the United States. Revenues from the federal government flowing into government coffers in West Virginia accounted for 25% of total state and local revenues, compared to the U.S. average of only 16% (1996 data).

Years ago, one of this book's coauthors had the opportunity to engage the late governor of Virginia, Mills Godwin, on the constitutionality of West Virginia. The governor quickly whispered, "Shhh, we don't want it back."

What needs to be done? Given the state's recent history, half-measures will accomplish little. Cutting taxes just a little bit will have no impact. After all, on a per capita basis, taxes already are quite low (though in West Virginia's case it must be recognized that income levels are quite low as well).

West Virginia needs an initial bold stroke to make businesses, entrepreneurs, and investors stand up and take notice. The biggest bang for the buck would be accomplished by immediately doing away with capital gains taxes in West Virginia. That would put West Virginia in the company of 11 other visionary states that do not impose capital gains taxes in one way or another. In addition, the state's very high corporate income tax needs to be cut in half. These steps would remove significant obstacles to business development.

Sound risky? In the private sector, there is a tradeoff between risk and reward. The bigger the risk, the greater the potential rewards. When a state's economy performs as poorly as West Virginia's has for so long, policymakers must become risk takers. It is not easy, as all the incentives in government point to maintaining the status quo, relying on bigger budgets, and accumulating power and staff. What West Virginia needs is just the opposite. The status quo means the state continues to languish. More power, resources, and manpower in the hands of government will only serve to accelerate West Virginia's decline.

If West Virginia has any chance of thriving in the 21st century, dramatic change will be needed. As it did during the Civil War—breaking away from Virginia and staying in the Union—West Virginia needs to chart its own starkly different course. It is time to wean itself from federal largess and instead create an environment where investment and entrepreneurship, the true sources of growth and prosperity, have a chance to thrive.

POLITICS

Registered Voters

63% Democrats
30% Republicans
7% Other

Federal Officials: Recent Election and Group Ratings

			ACU	ADA	SBSC
U.S. Senators:	Robert Byrd (D)		27	55	10
	1994 Byrd (D)	69%			
	Klos (R)	31%			
	John D. Rockefeller IV (D)		10	82	15
	1996 Rockefeller (D)	76%			
	Burks (R)	23%			
U.S. Representatives:	Alan Mollohan (D-1)		31	59	25
	1998 Mollohan (D)	85%			
	Kerr (LBT)	15%			
	Robert Wise Jr. (D-2)		13	77	10
	1998 Wise (D)	73%			
	Kay (R)	21%			
	Nick Rahall II (D-3)		17	74	15
	1998 Rahall (D)	87%			
	Whelan (LBT)	13%			
Electoral Votes:	5				
1996 Presidential Results:	Clinton	52%			
	Dole	37%			
	Perot	11%			

State Officials

Governor 1996 Election:	Cecil Underwood (R)	52%
	Charlotte Pritt (D)	46%
Attorney General:	Darrell McGraw (D)	
State Senate:	29 Democrats	
	5 Republicans	
State House:	75 Democrats	
	25 Republicans	

TAXES AND SPENDING

Total Revenues

West Virginia's per capita state and local total revenues registered $4,789 in 1996, ranking 40th in the nation and trailing the U.S. average of $5,706 by 16%. From 1962 to 1996, real per capita state and local revenues increased by 314%, compared with an increase in the national average of 297%.

Taxes

West Virginia's per capita state and local taxes registered $1,995 in 1996, ranking 43d in the nation and trailing the U.S. average of $2,597 by 23%. From 1962 to 1996, real per capita state and local taxes increased by 154%, compared with an increase of 152% in the U.S. average.

Property Taxes

West Virginia's per capita state and local property taxes equaled $398 in 1996, ranking 45th in the nation and trailing the U.S. average of $789 by 50%. From 1962 to 1996, real per capita state and local property taxes increased by 89%, versus a 67% increase in the U.S. average.

Sales and Gross Receipts Taxes

West Virginia's per capita state and local sales and gross receipts taxes came in at $816 in 1996, ranking 33d in the nation and trailing the U.S. average of $939 by 13%. From 1962 to 1996, real per capita state and local sales and gross receipts taxes increased by 89%, versus an increase of 214% in the U.S. average.

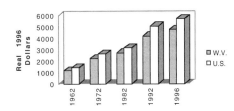

Real Per Capita State and Local Total Revenues: West Virginia vs. U.S.

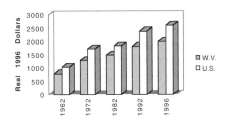

Real Per Capita State and Local Taxes: West Virginia vs. U.S.

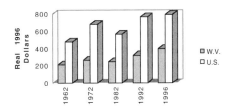

Real Per Capita State and Local Property Taxes: West Virginia vs. U.S.

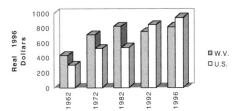

Real Per Capita State and Local Sales and Gross Receipts Taxes: West Virginia vs. U.S.

Income Taxes

West Virginia's per capita state and local income (individual and corporate) taxes registered $540 in 1996, ranking 34th in the nation and trailing the U.S. average of $674 by 20%. From 1962 to 1996, real per capita state and local income taxes increased by 882%, versus a 567% increase in the U.S. average.

Personal Income Tax

A rate of 6.5%, ranking 32d in the nation (from lowest tax rate to highest), and comparing with the national average of 5.26%.

Capital Gains Tax

A rate of 6.5%, ranking 37th in the nation (from lowest tax rate to highest), and comparing with the national average of 4.68%.

Corporate Income Tax

A rate of 9.0%, ranking 41st in the nation (from lowest tax rate to highest), and comparing with the national average of 6.69%.

Total Expenditures

West Virginia's per capita state and local total spending registered $4,620 in 1996, ranking 37th in the nation and trailing the U.S. average of $5,268 by 12%. From 1962 to 1996, real per capita state and local total spending increased by 296%, versus an increase of 254% in the U.S. average.

Welfare Expenditures

West Virginia's per capita state and local public welfare spending registered $870 in 1996, ranking 10th in the nation and exceeding the U.S. average of $729 by 19%. From 1962 to 1996, real per capita state and local public welfare spending increased by 440%, compared with a 488% increase in the U.S. average.

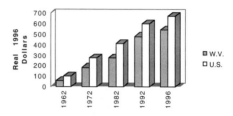

Real Per Capita State and Local Income Taxes: West Virginia vs. U.S.

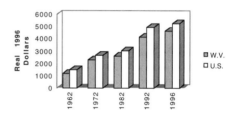

Real Per Capita State and Local Total Expenditures: West Virginia vs. U.S.

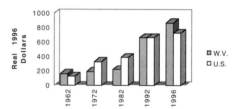

Real Per Capita State and Local Public Welfare Spending: West Virginia vs. U.S.

Welfare Recipients (in thousands)

	1980	1989	3/99	Change 1989–99
W. Va.	80	109	44	−60%
U.S.	10,923	10,987	7,335	−33%

Interest on General Debt

West Virginia's per capita state and local interest on general debt registered $222 in 1996, ranking 21st in the nation and equaling the U.S. average of $222. From 1962 to 1996, real per capita state and local interest on general debt increased by 594%, versus an increase of 335% in the U.S. average.

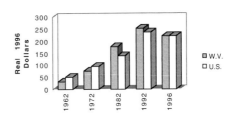

Real Per Capita State and Local Interest on General Debt: West Virginia vs. U.S.

Total Debt Outstanding

West Virginia's per capita state and local debt registered $3,559 in 1996, ranking 33d in the nation and trailing the U.S. average of $4,409 by 19%. From 1962 to 1996, real per capita state and local debt outstanding increased by 189%, versus an increase of 120% in the U.S. average.

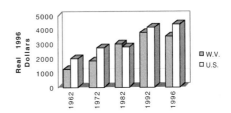

Real Per Capita State and Local Debt Outstanding: West Virginia vs. U.S.

Government Employees

West Virginia's state and local government employees (full-time equivalent, or FTE) per 10,000 population registered 508.1 in 1997, ranking 38th in the nation and trailing the U.S. average of 531.1 by 4%. From 1962 to 1996, state and local FTE employees per 10,000 population increased by 189%, compared with an increase in the U.S. average of 66%.

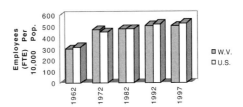

State and Local Government Employees (FTE) Per 10,000 Population: West Virginia vs. U.S.

Per Capita Federal Government Expenditures, 1998

	1998	Ranking
W. Va.	$5,906	14th
U.S.	$5,491	

Per capita federal spending in West Virginia exceeded the national average by 8%.

EDUCATION

Total Education Spending

West Virginia's per capita state and local education spending registered $1,453 in 1996, ranking 31st in the nation and trailing the U.S. average of $1,503 by 3%. From 1962 to 1996, real per capita total education spending increased by 229%, versus an increase in the U.S. average of 173%.

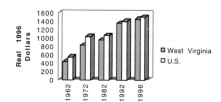

Real Per Capita State and Local Education Spending: West Virginia vs. U.S.

Per Pupil Spending

West Virginia's per pupil pubic school spending registered $6,342 in 1998, ranking 18th in the nation and topping the U.S. average of $6,131 by 3%. From 1970 to 1998, West Virginia's real per pupil public school spending increased by 176%, compared with a 120% increase in the U.S. average.

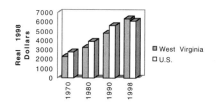

Real Per Pupil Public School Spending: West Virginia vs. U.S.

Average Public School Teacher Salaries (in 1997–98 dollars)

	1970	1980	1990	1998	1998 Ranking
W. Va.	32,755	28,564	29,096	33,398	37th
U.S.	36,934	33,272	39,956	39,385	

In 1998, the average public school teacher salary in West Virginia trailed the U.S. average by 15%. From 1970 to 1998, the real average teacher salary in West Virginia increased by 2%, versus an increase in the U.S. average of 7%.

Pupil/Teacher Ratio, Fall 1996

	Ratio	Rank
W. Va.	14.6	8th
U.S.	17.1	

Teachers/Staff, Fall 1996

	Percent	Rank
W. Va.	54.8	10th
U.S.	52.1	

Public School 4th-Grade Reading Proficiency, 1998

	Average	Rank (out of 40 states)
W. Va.	216	20th
U.S.	215	

Public School 8th-Grade Reading Proficiency, 1998

	Average	Rank (out of 37 states)
W. Va.	262	17th
U.S.	261	

Public School 4th-Grade Math Proficiency, 1996

	Average	Rank (out of 44 states)
W. Va.	223	22d
U.S.	224	

Public School 8th-Grade Math Proficiency, 1996

	Average	Rank (out of 41 states)
W. Va.	265	29th
U.S.	271	

Public School 8th-Grade Science Proficiency, 1996

	Average	Rank (out of 41 states)
W. Va.	147	22d
U.S.	148	

Average Math SAT Scores

	1972	1982	1992	1998	Percentage Taking SAT in 1998
W. Va.	522	528	509	513	18
U.S.	509	493	501	512	43

Average Verbal SAT Scores

	1972	1982	1992	1998	Percentage Taking SAT in 1998
W. Va	546	539	518	525	18
U.S.	530	504	500	505	43

Expenditures by Public Institutions of Higher Education Per Full-Time-Equivalent Student, 1996

	FTE Student Spending	Rank
W. Va.	$10,367	48th
U.S.	$12,343	

Per-FTE-student spending in public institutions of higher education trailed the U.S. average by 16%.

Per Full-Time-Equivalent Student Revenues from Federal, State, and Local Governments for Public Institutions of Higher Education, 1996

	FTE Student Government Revenues	Rank
W. Va.	$6,994	39th
U.S.	$8,101	

Per-FTE-student-government revenues in public institutions of higher education trailed the U.S. average by 14%.

Average Salary for Full-Time Professors at Public Universities, 1997

	Average	Rank
W. Va.	$60,938	42d
U.S.	$72,599	

The average full-time public university professor salary trailed the U.S. average by 16%.

ECONOMY AND BUSINESS

Economic Growth

Over the period of 1977 to 1997, West Virginia's real gross state product (GSP) grew by 29.6%—ranking 49th in the nation—as compared with real U.S. gross domestic product (GDP), expanding by 70.1%.

At $38.2 billion in 1997, West Virginia's GSP ranked as 39th largest in the nation.

From 1993 to 1997, West Virginia's annual real GSP growth averaged 3.13%—ranking 35th in the nation—as compared with annual real U.S. GDP growth, averaging 3.08%.

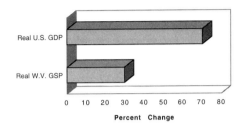

Real Economic Growth 1977-1997: West Virginia vs. U.S.

Real U.S. GDP

Real W.V. GSP

0   10   20   30   40   50   60   70   80

Percent Change

Job Growth

	Growth in Employee Payrolls (Nonagricultural) 1968–98	Ranking
W. Va.	60.6%	47th
U.S.	126.5%	

	Average Annual Growth in Employee Payrolls (Nonagricultural) 1993–98	Ranking
W. Va.	2.34%	39th
U.S.	2.98%	

Per Capita Disposable Income, 1997

	1997	Ranking
W. Va.	$16,660	50th
U.S.	$21,607	

Per capita disposable income trailed the U.S. average by 23%.

	Real Growth 1962–1997	Ranking
W. Va.	127.6%	21st
U.S.	116.7%	

	Average Annual Real Growth 1993–97	Ranking
W. Va.	1.12%	46th
U.S.	1.48%	

Number of Businesses

	1997	Percent with Fewer than 500 Employees
Businesses with Employees	37,970	96.9
Self-employed Individuals	54,000	

New Business Incorporations

	1980	1986	1992	1997
W. Va.	2,789	2,561	2,236	2,069

Percentage Change in Annual New Business Incorporations, 1980 vs. 1997

	Percent	Ranking
W. Va.	25.8	49th
U.S.	49.7	

State Merchandise Exports to the World, 1998 (in millions of dollars)

	1998	Rank
W. Va.	$1,178	43d

Small Business Survival Index, 1999

West Virginia ranks 31st in terms of its policy environment for entrepreneurship.

Fortune 500 Headquarters in 1999

None

Labor Union Membership, 1983 vs. 1997

	Percentage of Workers		1997 Rank
	1983	1997	1997 Rank
W. Va.	25.3	15.6	17th
U.S.	20.1	14.1	

Homeownership Rate, 1998

	Rate	Rank
W. Va.	74.8	5th
U.S.	66.3	

CRIME

Crime Rates Per 100 Residents (rankings from best to worst crime rate)

Total Crime	1960	1970	1980	1990	1998	1998 Ranking
W. Va.	0.46	0.96	2.55	2.50	2.55	2d
U.S.	1.04	2.74	5.90	5.82	4.62	

From 1960 to 1998, West Virginia's crime rate increased by 454%, versus a U.S. increase of 344%. From 1990 to 1998, West Virginia's crime rate increased by 2%, versus a U.S. decrease of 21%.

Violent Crime	1960	1970	1980	1990	1998	1998 Ranking
W. Va.	0.06	0.12	0.18	0.17	0.25	7th
U.S.	0.14	0.36	0.58	0.73	0.57	

From 1960 to 1998, West Virginia's violent crime rate increased by 317%, versus a U.S. increase of 307%. From 1990 to 1998, West Virginia's violent crime rate increased by 47%, compared with a national decline of 22%.

Property Crime	1960	1970	1980	1990	1998	1998 Ranking
W. Va.	0.40	0.84	2.37	2.33	2.30	1st
U.S.	0.90	2.38	5.32	5.09	4.05	

From 1960 to 1998, West Virginia's property crime rate increased by 475%, versus a national increase of 350%. From 1990 to 1998, West Virginia's property crime rate decreased by 1%, compared with a national decline of 20%.

Real Per Capita Police Protection Spending (in real 1996 dollars)

	1962	1972	1982	1992	1996	1996 Ranking
W. Va.	23	39	56	56	73	51st
U.S.	51	95	114	148	168	

In 1996, per capita state and local police protection spending in West Virginia trailed the U.S. average by 57%. From 1962 to 1996, real per capita state and local police protection spending increased by 217%, versus an increase of 229% in the U.S. average.

Prisoners in State and Federal Prisons Per 1,000 Population

	1980	1990	1996	1996 Ranking
W. Va.	0.64	0.87	1.51	48th
U.S.	1.46	3.11	4.45	

From 1980 to 1996, prisoners per 1,000 population increased by 136%, versus a U.S. increase of 205%.

HEALTH CARE

Health-Care Spending

West Virginia's per capita state and local health-care spending registered $98 in 1996, ranking 36th in the nation and trailing the U.S. average of $151 by 35%. From 1962 to 1996, West Virginia's real per capita state and local health-care spending increased by 989%, versus an increase of 739% in the U.S. average.

Real Per Capita State and Local Health Care Spending: West Virginia vs. U.S.

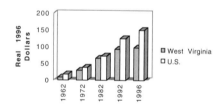

Hospital Spending

West Virginia's per capita state and local hospital spending registered $142 in 1996, ranking 38th in the nation and trailing the U.S. average of $266 by 47%. From 1962 to 1996, West Virginia's real per capita state and local hospital spending increased by 184%, as opposed to an increase of 189% in the U.S. average.

Real Per Capita State and Local Hospital Spending: West Virginia vs. U.S.

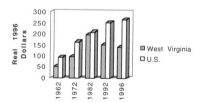

Medicaid, 1997

	Spending Per Recipient	Ranking
W. Va.	$3,501	27th
U.S.	$3,681	

West Virginia's per-recipient Medicaid spending trailed the U.S. average by 5%.

ENVIRONMENT

Parks and Recreation Spending

West Virginia's per capita state and local parks and recreation spending registered $41 in 1996, ranking 42d in the nation and trailing the U.S. average of $72 by 43%. From 1962 to 1996, real per capita state and local parks and recreation spending increased by 356%, versus a 213% increase in the U.S. average.

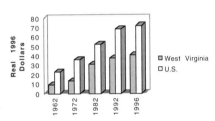

Real Per Capita State and Local Parks and Recreation Spending: West Virginia vs. U.S.

State and Local Natural Resources Spending, 1996

	Per Capita	Ranking
W. Va.	$80	16th
U.S.	$60	

Per capita state and local natural resources spending in West Virginia topped the U.S. average by 33%.

State Parks Revenues as a Share of Operating Expenses, 1997

	Percent	Rank
W. Va.	59	12th
U.S.	42	

Percentage of Land Owned by the Federal Government, 1996

	Percent	Rank
W. Va.	7	21st
U.S.	24	

SOCIETY AND DEMOGRAPHICS

Population

West Virginia's 1998 population of 1.811 million ranked 35th in the nation.

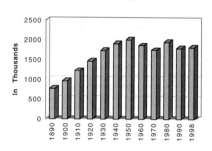

West Virginia Population

Population Growth, 1990–98

	Percentage Change in Population	Ranking
W. Va.	1.00	46th
U.S.	8.66	

	Net International Migration	Ranking
W. Va.	3,345	49th

	Net Domestic Migration	Ranking
W. Va.	8,023	28th

Infant Mortality Rate, 1998

	Percent	Rank
W. Va.	7.0	24th
U.S.	6.4	

Percentage of Births of Low Birthweight, 1997

	Percent	Rank
W. Va.	8.3	14th
U.S.	7.5	

Percentage of Live Births to Unmarried Women, 1997

	Percent	Rank
W. Va.	31.3	27th
U.S.	32.4	

Abortion Rate—Abortions Per 1,000 Women Ages 15–44, 1995

	Rate	Rank
W. Va.	7.6	47th
U.S.	22.9	

LIFESTYLE

Percentage of Households with Computers, 1998

	Percent	Rank
W. Va.	28.3	50th

Percentage of Households with Internet Access, 1998

	Percent	Rank
W. Va.	17.6	49th

State Arts Agency Spending, 1999

	Per Capita	Rank
W. Va.	$1.16	20th
U.S.	$1.35	

Per capita state arts spending in 1999 trailed the U.S. average by 14%.

Major League Sports Facilities

None

WISCONSIN

Throughout much of the 20th century, Wisconsin was a Progressive (that is, liberal) state. Indeed, considering that U.S. Senator Robert M. LaFollette, probably the leading Progressive politician of the early 20th century, hailed from Wisconsin, one might declare the state to be the official home of Progressivism.

Under the leadership of Governor Tommy Thompson since 1987, however, Wisconsin has gotten out front on some cutting-edge conservative reforms. For example, a school choice program for low-income families was established in Milwaukee in 1990 and was expanded in 1995 to include the ability to attend religious schools.

Thompson has become perhaps most famous across the nation for his welfare reform measures. Welfare experts Robert E. Rector and Sarah E. Youssef, in their Heritage Foundation book *The Impact of Welfare Reform: The Trend in State Caseloads 1985–1998*, observe, "Wisconsin has been the national leader in reducing welfare dependence." From 1989 to March 1999, Wisconsin's welfare rolls plummeted by an astounding 88%, as opposed to a national decline of 33%.

Ironically, however, per capita state and local public welfare expenditures recently have run above the U.S. average (according to the most recent comparative data). Also, while reforming welfare for the masses, Thompson was out front in favor of corporate welfare for the Milwaukee Brewers in the team's pursuit of a new taxpayer-funded ballpark.

Meanwhile, Thompson has reduced personal income and capital gains tax rates, thereby providing a boost to incentives for investing and working in the Badger State. The state's crime rate is low as well.

As a result of recent positive reforms, Wisconsin's economy has shrugged off much of its sluggishness. Real economic and disposable income growth recently have been running ahead of U.S. averages, and job creation has finally caught up to the rest of the country. In addition, from 1990 to 1998, Wisconsin was a rather aggressive importer of people from other states.

Apparently, though, decade upon decade of Progressive programs and inclinations do not stop and reverse themselves in a mere dozen years or so. The numbers below reveal that much work still needs to be done. Per capita state and local taxes, for example, are high pretty much across the board, and they increased at a rapid clip from the early 1960s into the late 1990s. Wisconsin's education spending also ranks very high among the states.

At the dawn of the 20th century, Wisconsin was in the firm grasp of Progressives; at the close, conservatives were battling for control of the state. If faith in free markets manages to trump faith in big government, Wisconsin will experience a far more prosperous 21st century.

POLITICS

Registered Voters

No state voter registration

Federal Officials: Recent Election and Group Ratings

				ACU	ADA	SBSC
U.S. Senators:	Herbert Kohl (D)			3	88	30
	1994	Kohl (D)	58%			
		Welch (R)	41%			
	Russell Feingold (D)			14	97	25
	1998	Feingold (D)	51%			
		Neumann (R)	48%			
U.S. Representatives:	Paul Ryan (R-1)			NA	NA	NA
	1998	Ryan (R)	57%			
		Spottswood (D)	43%			
	Tammy Baldwin (D-2)			NA	NA	NA
	1998	Baldwin (D)	52%			
		Musser (R)	47%			
	Ron Kind (D-3)			8	85	30
	1998	Kind (D)	71%			
		Brechler (R)	28%			
	Gerald Kleczka (D-4)			11	82	10
	1998	Kleczka (D)	58%			
		Reynolds (R)	42%			
	Thomas Barrett (D-5)			10	90	15
	1998	Barrett (D)	78%			
		Melvin (R)	22%			
	Thomas Petri (R-6)			76	23	80
	1998	Petri (R)	93%			
		Farness (UST)	7%			
	David Obey (D-7)			8	89	10
	1998	Obey (D)	61%			
		West (R)	39%			
	Mark Green (R-8)			NA	NA	NA
	1998	Green (R)	55%			
		Johnson (D)	45%			
	James Sensenbrenner Jr. (R-9)			86	15	100
	1998	Sensenbrenner (R)	91%			
		Gonyo (I)	9%			

Electoral Votes:	11	
1996 Presidential Results:	Clinton	49%
	Dole	38%
	Perot	10%

State Officials

Governor 1998 Election:	Tommy Thompson (R)	60%
	Ed Garvey (D)	39%
Lt. Governor:	Scott McCallum (R)	
Attorney General:	Jim Doyle (D)	
State Senate:	17 Democrats	
	16 Republicans	
State General Assembly:	44 Democrats	
	55 Republicans	

TAXES AND SPENDING

Total Revenues

Wisconsin's per capita state and local total revenues registered $6,556 in 1996, ranking 10th in the nation and leading the U.S. average of $5,706 by 15%. From 1962 to 1996, real per capita state and local revenues increased by 342%, compared with an increase in the national average of 297%.

Real Per Capita State and Local Total Revenues: Wisconsin vs. U.S.

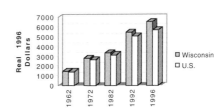

Taxes

Wisconsin's per capita state and local taxes registered $2,947 in 1996, ranking 9th in the nation and topping the U.S. average of $2,597 by 13%. From 1962 to 1996, real per capita state and local taxes increased by 164%, compared with an increase of 152% in the U.S. average.

Real Per Capita State and Local Taxes: Wisconsin vs. U.S.

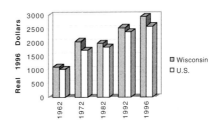

Property Taxes

Wisconsin's per capita state and local property taxes equaled $1,054 in 1996, ranking 12th in the nation and exceeding the U.S. average of $789 by 34%. From 1962 to 1996, real per capita state and local property taxes increased by 70%, versus a 67% increase in the U.S. average.

Sales and Gross Receipts Taxes

Wisconsin's per capita state and local sales and gross receipts taxes came in at $815 in 1996, ranking 34th in the nation and trailing the U.S. average of $939 by 13%. From 1962 to 1996, real per capita state and local sales and gross receipts taxes increased by 366%, versus an increase of 214% in the U.S. average.

Income Taxes

Wisconsin's per capita state and local income (individual and corporate) taxes registered $925 in 1996, ranking 9th in the nation and exceeding the U.S. average of $674 by 37%. From 1962 to 1996, real per capita state and local income taxes increased by 311%, versus a 567% increase in the U.S. average.

Personal Income Tax

A rate of 6.77%, ranking 36th in the nation (from lowest tax rate to highest), and comparing with the national average of 5.26%.

Capital Gains Tax

A rate of 2.708%, ranking 12th in the nation (from lowest tax rate to highest), and comparing with the national average of 4.68%.

Corporate Income Tax

A rate of 7.9%, ranking 32d in the nation (from lowest tax rate to highest), and comparing with the national average of 6.69%.

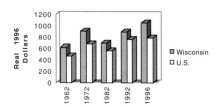

Real Per Capita State and Local Property Taxes: Wisconsin vs. U.S.

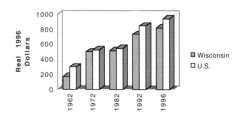

Real Per Capita State and Local Sales and Gross Receipts Taxes: Wisconsin vs. U.S.

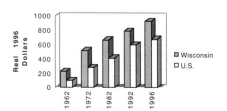

Real Per Capita State and Local Income Taxes: Wisconsin vs. U.S.

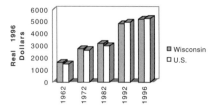

Real Per Capita State and Local Total Expenditures: Wisconsin vs. U.S.

Total Expenditures

Wisconsin's per capita state and local total spending registered $5,183 in 1996, ranking 16th in the nation and trailing the U.S. average of $5,268 by 2%. From 1962 to 1996, real per capita state and local total spending increased by 220%, versus an increase of 254% in the U.S. average.

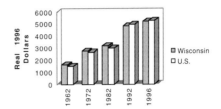

Real Per Capita State and Local Total Expenditures: Wisconsin vs. U.S.

Welfare Expenditures

Wisconsin's per capita state and local public welfare spending registered $761 in 1996, ranking 15th in the nation and exceeding the U.S. average of $729 by 4%. From 1962 to 1996, real per capita state and local public welfare spending increased by 539%, compared with a 488% increase in the U.S. average.

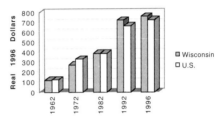

Real Per Capita State and Local Public Welfare Spending: Wisconsin vs. U.S.

Welfare Recipients (in thousands)

	1980	1989	3/99	Change 1989–99
Wisc.	232	237	29	−88%
U.S.	10,923	10,987	7,335	−33%

Interest on General Debt

Wisconsin's per capita state and local interest on general debt registered $210 in 1996, ranking 23d in the nation and trailing the U.S. average of $222 by 5%. From 1962 to 1996, real per capita state and local interest on general debt increased by 556%, versus an increase of 335% in the U.S. average.

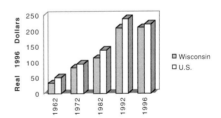

Real Per Capita State and Local Interest on General Debt: Wisconsin vs. U.S.

Total Debt Outstanding

Wisconsin's per capita state and local debt registered $3,816 in 1996, ranking 28th in the nation and trailing the U.S. average of $4,409 by 13%. From 1962 to 1996, real per capita state and local debt outstanding increased by 190%, versus an increase of 120% in the U.S. average.

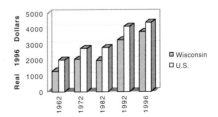

Real Per Capita State and Local Debt Outstanding: Wisconsin vs. U.S.

Government Employees

Wisconsin's state and local government employees (full-time equivalent, or FTE) per 10,000 population registered 515.2 in 1997, ranking 35th in the nation and trailing the U.S. average of 531.1 by 3%. From 1962 to 1996, state and local FTE employees per 10,000 population increased by 62%, compared with an increase in the U.S. average of 66%.

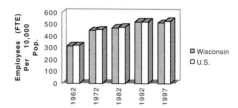

State and Local Government Employees (FTE) Per 10,000 Population: Wisconsin vs. U.S.

Per Capita Federal Government Expenditures, 1998

	1998	Ranking
Wisc.	$4,189	50th
U.S.	$5,491	

Per capita federal spending in Wisconsin trailed the national average by 24%.

EDUCATION

Total Education Spending

Wisconsin's per capita state and local education spending registered $1,774 in 1996, ranking 4th in the nation and topping the U.S. average of $1,503 by 18%. From 1962 to 1996, real per capita total education spending increased by 206%, versus an increase in the U.S. average of 173%.

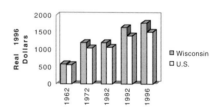

Real Per Capita State and Local Education Spending: Wisconsin vs. U.S.

Per Pupil Spending

Wisconsin's per pupil public school spending registered $7,045 in 1998, ranking 10th in the nation and topping the U.S. average of $6,131 by 15%. From 1970 to 1998, Wisconsin's real per pupil public school spending increased by 140%, compared with a 120% increase in the U.S. average.

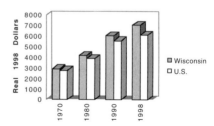

Real Per Pupil Public School Spending: Wisconsin vs. U.S.

Average Public School Teacher Salaries (in 1997–98 dollars)

	1970	1980	1990	1998	1998 Ranking
Wisc.	38,377	33,347	40,661	39,899	15th
U.S.	36,934	33,272	39,956	39,385	

In 1998, the average public school teacher salary in Wisconsin exceeded the U.S. average by 1%. From 1970 to 1998, the real average teacher salary in Wisconsin increased by 4%, versus an increase in the U.S. average of 7%.

Pupil/Teacher Ratio, Fall 1996

	Ratio	Rank
Wisc.	16.1	23d
U.S.	17.1	

Teachers/Staff, Fall 1996

	Percent	Rank
Wisc.	54.8	10th
U.S.	52.1	

Public School 4th-Grade Reading Proficiency, 1998

	Average	Rank (out of 40 states)
Wisc.	224	6th
U.S.	215	

Public School 8th-Grade Reading Proficiency, 1998

	Average	Rank (out of 37 states)
Wisc.	266	7th
U.S.	261	

Public School 4th-Grade Math Proficiency, 1996

	Average	Rank (out of 44 states)
Wisc.	231	4th
U.S.	224	

Public School 8th-Grade Math Proficiency, 1996

	Average	Rank (out of 41 states)
Wisc.	283	5th
U.S.	271	

Public School 8th-Grade Science Proficiency, 1996

	Average	Rank (out of 41 states)
Wisc.	160	4th
U.S.	148	

Average Math SAT Scores

	1972	1982	1992	1998	Percentage Taking SAT in 1998
Wisc.	560	553	564	594	7
U.S.	509	493	501	512	43

Average Verbal SAT Scores

	1972	1982	1992	1998	Percentage Taking SAT in 1998
Wisc.	577	553	556	581	7
U.S.	530	504	500	505	43

Expenditures by Public Institutions of Higher Education Per Full-Time-Equivalent Student, 1996

	FTE Student Spending	Rank
Wisc.	$13,888	11th
U.S.	$12,343	

Per-FTE-student spending in public institutions of higher education topped the U.S. average by 13%.

Per Full-Time-Equivalent Student Revenues from Federal, State, and Local Governments for Public Institutions of Higher Education, 1996

	FTE Student Government Revenues	Rank
Wisc.	$8,781	10th
U.S.	$8,101	

Per-FTE-student-government spending in public institutions of higher education topped the U.S. average by 8%.

Average Salary for Full-Time Professors at Public Universities, 1997

	Average	Rank
Wisc.	$71,625	22nd
U.S.	$72,599	

The average full-time public university professor salary trailed the U.S. average by 1%.

ECONOMY AND BUSINESS

Economic Growth

Over the period of 1977 to 1997, Wisconsin's real gross state product (GSP) grew by 66.9%—ranking 28th in the nation—as compared with real U.S. gross domestic product (GDP), expanding by 70.1%.

At $147.3 billion in 1997, Wisconsin's GSP ranked as 19th largest in the nation.

From 1993 to 1997, Wisconsin's annual real GSP growth averaged 4.01%—ranking 18th in the nation—as compared with annual real U.S. GDP growth, averaging 3.08%.

Real Economic Growth 1977-1997: Wisconsin vs. U.S.

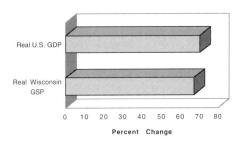

Job Growth

	Growth in Employee Payrolls (Nonagricultural) 1962–1998	Ranking
Wisc.	124.6%	34th
U.S.	126.5%	

Average Annual Growth in Employee Payrolls (Nonagricultural) 1993–98	Ranking
Wisc.	2.84%	30th
U.S.	2.98%	

Per Capita Disposable Income, 1997

	1997	Ranking
Wisc.	$20,362	28th
U.S.	$21,607	

Per capita disposable income trailed the U.S. average by 6%.

Real Growth 1962–1997	Ranking
Wisc.	108.1%	36th
U.S.	116.7%	

Average Annual Real Growth 1993–97	Ranking
Wisc.	1.72%	20th
U.S.	1.48%	

Number of Businesses

	1997	Percent with Fewer than 500 Employees
Businesses with Employees	118,766	98.1
Self-employed Individuals	232,000	

New Business Incorporations

	1980	1986	1992	1997
Wisc.	6,550	6,460	7,289	7,961

Percentage Change in Annual New Business Incorporations, 1980 vs. 1997

	Percent	Ranking
Wisc.	21.5	33d
U.S.	49.7	

State Merchandise Exports to the World, 1998 (in millions of dollars)

	1998	Rank
Wisc.	$9,221	21st

Small Business Survival Index, 1999

Wisconsin ranks 26th in terms of its policy environment for entrepreneurship.

Fortune 500 Headquarters in 1999

A total of 9 (ranked 18th)

Labor Union Membership, 1983 vs. 1997

	Percentage of Workers		
	1983	1997	1997 Rank
Wisc.	23.8	18.8	10th
U.S.	20.1	14.1	

Homeownership Rate, 1998

	Rate	Rank
Wisc.	70.1	21st
U.S.	66.3	

CRIME

Crime Rates Per 100 Residents (rankings from best to worst crime rate)

Total Crime	1960	1970	1980	1990	1998	1998 Ranking
Wisc.	0.51	1.51	4.80	4.40	3.54	12th
U.S.	1.04	2.74	5.90	5.82	4.62	

From 1960 to 1998, Wisconsin's crime rate increased by 594%, versus a U.S. increase of 344%. From 1990 to 1998, Wisconsin's crime rate decreased by 20%, versus a U.S. decrease of 21%.

Violent Crime	1960	1970	1980	1990	1998	1998 Ranking
Wisc.	0.03	0.09	0.18	0.27	0.25	8th
U.S.	0.14	0.36	0.58	0.73	0.57	

From 1960 to 1998, Wisconsin's violent crime rate increased by 733%, versus a U.S. increase of 307%. From 1990 to 1998, Wisconsin's violent crime rate decreased by 7%, compared with a national decline of 22%.

Property Crime	1960	1970	1980	1990	1998	1998 Ranking
Wisc.	0.48	1.43	4.62	4.13	3.29	14th
U.S.	0.90	2.38	5.32	5.09	4.05	

From 1960 to 1998, Wisconsin's property crime rate increased by 585%, versus a national increase of 350%. From 1990 to 1998, Wisconsin's property crime rate decreased by 20% equal to a national decline of 20%.

Real Per Capita Police Protection Spending (in real 1996 dollars)

	1962	1972	1982	1992	1996	1996 Ranking
Wisc.	55	85	137	152	169	14th
U.S.	51	95	114	148	168	

In 1996, per capita state and local police protection spending in Wisconsin topped the U.S. average by 1%. From 1962 to 1996, real per capita state and local police protection spending increased by 207%, versus an increase of 229% in the U.S. average.

Prisoners in State and Federal Prisons Per 1,000 Population

	1980	1990	1996	1996 Ranking
Wisc.	0.85	1.53	2.52	40th
U.S.	1.46	3.11	4.45	

From 1980 to 1996, prisoners per 1,000 population increased by 196%, versus a U.S. increase of 205%.

HEALTH CARE

Health-Care Spending

Wisconsin's per capita state and local health-care spending registered $137 in 1996, ranking 24th in the nation and trailing the U.S. average of $151 by 9%. From 1962 to 1996, Wisconsin's real per capita state and local health-care spending increased by 879%, versus an increase of 739% in the U.S. average.

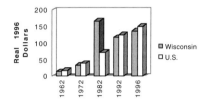

Real Per Capita State and Local Health Care Spending: Wisconsin vs. U.S.

Hospital Spending

Wisconsin's per capita state and local hospital spending registered $142 in 1996, ranking 38th in the nation and trailing the U.S. average of $266 by 47%. From 1962 to 1996, Wisconsin's real per capita state and local hospital spending increased by 54%, as opposed to an increase of 189% in the U.S. average.

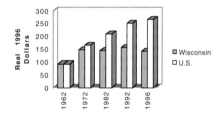

Real Per Capita State and Local Hospital Spending: Wisconsin vs. U.S.

Medicaid, 1997

	Spending Per Recipient	Ranking
Wisc.	$4,793	11th
U.S.	$3,681	

Wisconsin's per-recipient Medicaid spending topped the U.S. average by 30%.

ENVIRONMENT

Parks and Recreation Spending

Wisconsin's per capita state and local parks and recreation spending registered $77 in 1996, ranking 20th in the nation and exceeding the U.S. average of $72 by 7%. From 1962 to 1996, real per capita state and local parks and recreation spending increased by 108%, versus a 213% increase in the U.S. average.

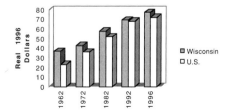

Real Per Capita State and Local Parks and Recreation Spending: Wisconsin vs. U.S.

State and Local Natural Resources Spending, 1996

	Per Capita	Ranking
Wisc.	$113	7th
U.S.	$60	

Per capita state and local natural resources spending in Wisconsin outpaced the U.S. average by 88%.

State Parks Revenues as a Share of Operating Expenses, 1997

	Percent	Rank
Wisc.	38	28th
U.S.	42	

Percentage of Land Owned by the Federal Government, 1996

	Percent	Rank
Wisc.	5.0	26th
U.S.	24.8	

SOCIETY AND DEMOGRAPHICS

Population

Wisconsin's 1998 population of 5.224 million ranked 18th in the nation.

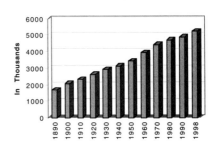

Wisconsin   Population

Population Growth, 1990–98

	Percentage Change in Population	Ranking
Wisc.	6.79	28th
U.S.	8.66	

	Net International Migration	Ranking
Wisc.	21,414	32d

	Net Domestic Migration	Ranking
Wisc.	84,398	18th

Infant Mortality Rate, 1998

	Percent	Rank
Wisc.	6.8	28th
U.S.	6.4	

Percentage of Births of Low Birthweight, 1997

	Percent	Rank
Wisc.	6.4	38th
U.S.	7.5	

Percentage of Live Births to Unmarried Women, 1997

	Percent	Rank
Wisc.	28.1	36th
U.S.	32.4	

Abortion Rate—Abortions Per 1,000 Women Ages 15–44, 1995

	Rate	Rank
Wisc.	11.6	38th
U.S.	22.9	

LIFESTYLE

Percentage of Households with Computers, 1998

	Percent	Rank
Wisc.	43.0	22d

Percentage of Households with Internet Access, 1998

	Percent	Rank
Wisc.	25.1	27th

State Arts Agency Spending, 1999

	Per Capita	Rank
Wisc.	$0.51	45th
U.S.	$1.35	

Per capita state arts spending in 1999 trailed the U.S. average by 62%.

Major League Sports Facilities

Year Opened/ Refurb.	Stadium/ Arena	Home Team	Millions of Nominal Dollars		Millions of Real 1997 Dollars	
			Estimated Total Cost	Estimated Taxpayer Cost	Estimated Total Cost	Estimated Taxpayer Cost
1953	County Stadium	Braves (MLB) 1953–1965 Brewers (MLB) 1970–present	$5.0	$5.0	$30.5	$30.5
1957	Lambeau Field	Packers (NFL) 1957–present	$1.0	$1.0	$5.5	$5.5
1988	Bradley Center	Bucks 1988–present	$53.0	$53.0	$71.9	$71.9

WYOMING

While vacationing in Massachusetts in August 1999, President Clinton, who hails from Arkansas, lives in Washington, D.C., and is moving to New York with his wife, announced that the federal government would spend $13 million to buy 9,000 acres of land adjacent to Yellowstone National Park in Wyoming. If this scenario does not raise questions about the relationship between the federal government and the states, few will.

Do not get us wrong. We love Yellowstone, and we are realistic enough to understand that a massive land privatization effort by the federal government is not about to happen any time soon. Republicans who love Teddy Roosevelt particularly feel faint when hearing notions about privatization. However, is it not enough that the federal government already owns about 25% of all land nationwide and nearly 50% of the state of Wyoming? Should taxpayer dollars from elsewhere in the nation be spent to buy up land in Wyoming, or any other state for that matter?

In addition, according to the National Wilderness Institute's periodical *NWI Resource* (Spring, 1995), the state owns at least another 6% of the land in Wyoming. However, ownership is only part of the story. Multiple use of the land is another dividing line. It pits snowmobilers against environmental groups and ranchers against bureaucrats. Until there is a change in the administration in Washington, D.C., these issues will not be resolved, and perhaps they will not be resolved even then.

The trend by which government taxes the many in order to fulfill the environmental and land-use desires of the few at the very least needs to be halted—and preferably reversed. Over the centuries, private owners have proven to be far better stewards than the government. Unfortunately, a whole generation of Wyoming ranchers are finding that inheritance taxes make it almost impossible to pass on family lands to the next generation.

On the political front, Wyoming is a strikingly Republican state—from the state legislature to the governor to its three members of Congress. "Republicans control virtually everything in this state, right down to the county courthouses," says Jan Larimer, Wyoming Republican Party Chairwoman. U.S. Senators Craig Thomas and Mike Enzi and at-large Representative Barbara Cubin rank among the most conservative in the Congress. Under the GOP hegemony, overall government spending (particularly hospital, education, natural resources, and parks and recreation expenditures) is on the high side, crime is low, and no income taxes are imposed.

Wyoming deserves kudos for a dramatic 86% decline in its welfare rolls between 1989 and March 1999. However, some of this credit is lost, due to the fact that, other than Washington, D.C., no state claims a larger number of state and local government employees as a share of population.

While some Wyoming economic indicators have lagged behind those of the nation over the long haul, in recent years new business incorporations and real economic growth have picked up considerably. Meanwhile, Wyoming rates second best in the nation in terms of the Small Business Survival Committee's "Small Business Survival Index."

The state would benefit further by diversifying and minimizing its dependence on oil and coal. Increased natural gas production and up-ticks in oil prices may have a short-term beneficial effect. A common complaint among business executives is air service. It is virtually impossible to fly from one city to another within the state without making connections in Salt Lake City or Denver.

Meanwhile, the lack of a state income tax may be one of the reasons that Hollywood stars and Fortune 500 executives have chosen to call Wyoming their "home." Most have settled in the resort areas near Jackson Hole, building such huge homes that the locals observe "the billionaires are pushing out the millionaires."

Of note on the societal front, Wyoming carries the lowest abortion rate in the nation.

With no income tax, few abortions, shrinking welfare rolls, Republican political control, and budding entrepreneurship, Wyoming has to rank as a favorite state for conservatives in America. Just get some of that land back in private hands, cut state and local spending, lure an intrastate commuter airline, and transplant many of those government workers to productive private-sector jobs, and Wyoming could become a conservative utopia.

POLITICS

Registered Voters

31% Democrats
58% Republicans
11% Other

Federal Officials: Recent Election and Group Ratings

			ACU	ADA	SBSC
U.S. Senators:	Craig Thomas (R)		86	6	90
	1994 Thomas (R)	59%			
	Sullivan (D)	39%			
	Mike Enzi (R)		90	5	85
	1996 Enzi (R)	54%			
	Karpan (D)	42%			
U.S. Representatives:	Barbara Cubin (R)		99	1	95
	1998 Cubin (R)	58%			
	Farris (D)	39%			
Electoral Votes:	3				
1996 Presidential Results:	Clinton	37%			
	Dole	50%			
	Perot	12%			

State Officials

Governor 1998 Election:	Jim Geringer (R)	56%
	John Vinich (D)	40%
Attorney General:	Gay Woodhouse (R)	
State Senate:	10 Democrats	
	20 Republicans	
State House:	17 Democrats	
	43 Republicans	

TAXES AND SPENDING

Total Revenues

Wyoming's per capita state and local total revenues registered $7,232 in 1996, ranking 4th in the nation and topping the U.S. average of $5,706 by 27%. From 1962 to 1996, real per capita state and local revenues increased by 222%, compared with an increase in the national average of 297%. Interestingly, from 1982 to 1996, Wyoming's real per capita total revenues actually fell by 1%, versus a national increase of 81%.

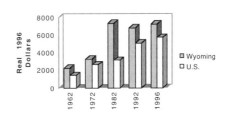

Real Per Capita State and Local Total Revenues: Wyoming vs. U.S.

Taxes

Wyoming's per capita state and local taxes registered $2,422 in 1996, ranking 25th in the nation and trailing the U.S. average of $2,597 by 7%. From 1962 to 1996, real per capita state and local taxes increased by 113%, compared with an increase of 152% in the U.S. average. From 1982 to 1996, Wyoming's real per capita taxes fell by 40%, versus a U.S. increase of 41%.

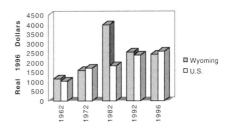

Real Per Capita State and Local Taxes: Wyoming vs. U.S.

Property Taxes

Wyoming's per capita state and local property taxes equaled $905 in 1996, ranking 14th in the nation and topping the U.S. average of $789 by 15%. From 1962 to 1996, real per capita state and local property taxes increased by 49%, versus a 67% increase in the U.S. average. From 1982 to 1996, Wyoming's real per capita property taxes fell by 36%, versus a U.S. increase of 40%.

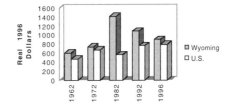

Real Per Capita State and Local Property Taxes: Wyoming vs. U.S.

Sales and Gross Receipts Taxes

Wyoming's per capita state and local sales and gross receipts taxes came in at $921 in 1996, ranking 22d in the nation and trailing the U.S. average of $939 by 2%. From 1962 to 1996, real per capita state and local sales and gross receipts taxes increased by 175%, versus an increase of 214% in the U.S. average.

Income Taxes

Wyoming's per capita state and local income (individual and corporate) taxes registered $0 in 1996, ranking lowest in the nation and trailing far behind the U.S. average of $674. Wyoming imposes no personal income, capital gains, or corporate income taxes.

Personal Income Tax

A rate of 0%, ranking best in the nation (from lowest tax rate to highest), and comparing with the national average of 5.26%.

Capital Gains Tax

A rate of 0%, ranking best in the nation (from lowest tax rate to highest), and comparing with the national average of 4.68%.

Corporate Income Tax

A rate of 0%, ranking best in the nation (from lowest tax rate to highest), and comparing with the national average of 6.69%.

Total Expenditures

Wyoming's per capita state and local total spending registered $6,326 in 1996, ranking 5th in the nation and topping the U.S. average of $5,268 by 20%. From 1962 to 1996, real per capita state and local total spending increased by 181%, versus an increase of 254% in the U.S. average.

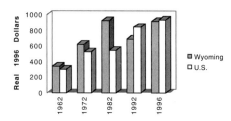

Real Per Capita State and Local Sales and Gross Receipts Taxes: Wyoming vs. U.S.

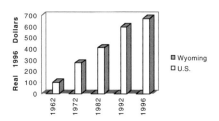

Real Per Capita State and Local Income Taxes: Wyoming vs. U.S.

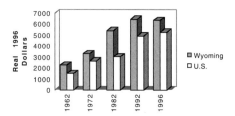

Real Per Capita State and Local Total Expenditures: Wyoming vs. U.S.

Welfare Expenditures

Wyoming's per capita state and local public welfare spending registered $533 in 1996, ranking 44th in the nation and trailing the U.S. average of $729 by 27%. From 1962 to 1996, real per capita state and local public welfare spending increased by 455%, compared with a 488% increase in the U.S. average.

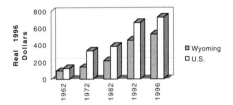

Real Per Capita State and Local Public Welfare Spending: Wyoming vs. U.S.

Welfare Recipients (in thousands)

	1980	1989	3/99	Change 1989–99
Wyo.	7	14	2	−86%
U.S.	10,923	10,987	7,335	−33%

Interest on General Debt

Wyoming's per capita state and local interest on general debt registered $253 in 1996, ranking 18th in the nation and exceeding the U.S. average of $222 by 14%. From 1962 to 1996, real per capita state and local interest on general debt increased by 691%, versus an increase of 335% in the U.S. average. From 1982 to 1996, Wyoming's real per capita interest paid fell by 30%, versus a U.S. increase of 60%.

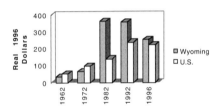

Real Per Capita State and Local Interest on General Debt: Wyoming vs. U.S.

Total Debt Outstanding

Wyoming's per capita state and local debt registered $3,889 in 1996, ranking 25th in the nation and trailing the U.S. average of $4,409 by 12%. From 1962 to 1996, real per capita state and local debt outstanding increased by 139%, versus an increase of 120% in the U.S. average. From 1982 to 1996, Wyoming's real per capita debt fell by 30%, versus a U.S. increase of 58%.

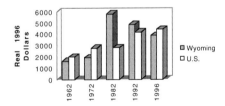

Real Per Capita State and Local Debt Outstanding: Wyoming vs. U.S.

Government Employees

Wyoming's state and local government employees (full-time equivalent, or FTE) per 10,000 population registered 800.9 in 1997, ranking 2d (behind Washington, D.C.) in the nation and topping the U.S. average of 531.1 by 51%. From 1962 to 1996, state and local FTE employees per 10,000 population increased by 79%, compared with an increase in the U.S. average of 66%.

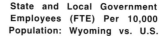

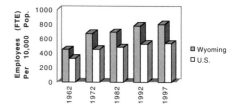

State and Local Government Employees (FTE) Per 10,000 Population: Wyoming vs. U.S.

Per Capita Federal Government Expenditures, 1998

	1998	Ranking
Wyo.	$5,702	18th
U.S.	$5,491	

Per capita federal spending in Wyoming exceeded the national average by 4%.

EDUCATION

Total Education Spending

Wyoming's per capita state and local education spending registered $2,015 in 1996, ranking 2d in the nation and exceeding the U.S. average of $1,503 by 34%. From 1962 to 1996, real per capita total education spending increased by 146%, versus an increase in the U.S. average of 173%.

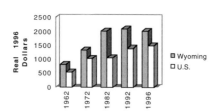

Real Per Capita State and Local Education Spending: Wyoming vs. U.S.

Per Pupil Spending

Wyoming's per pupil public school spending registered $6,366 in 1998, ranking 17th in the nation and outpacing the U.S. average of $6,131 by 4%. From 1970 to 1998, Wyoming's real per pupil public school spending increased by 114%, compared with a 120% increase in the U.S. average.

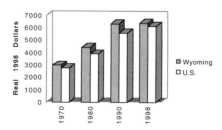

Real Per Pupil Public School Spending: Wyoming vs. U.S.

Average Public School Teacher Salaries (in 1997–98 dollars)

	1970	1980	1990	1998	1998 Ranking
Wyo.	35,247	33,360	35,846	32,022	43d
U.S.	36,934	33,272	39,956	39,385	

In 1998, the average public school teacher salary in Wyoming trailed the U.S. average by 19%. From 1970 to 1998, the real average teacher salary in Wyoming decreased by 9%, versus an increase in the U.S. average of 7%.

Pupil/Teacher Ratio, Fall 1996

	Ratio	Rank
Wyo.	14.7	9th
U.S.	17.1	

Teachers/Staff, Fall 1996

	Percent	Rank
Wyo.	50.5	42d
U.S.	52.1	

Public School 4th-Grade Reading Proficiency, 1998

	Average	Rank (out of 40 states)
Wyo.	219	12th
U.S.	215	

Public School 8th-Grade Reading Proficiency, 1998

	Average	Rank (out of 37 states)
Wyo.	262	17th
U.S.	261	

Public School 4th-Grade Math Proficiency, 1996

	Average	Rank (out of 44 states)
Wyo.	223	22d
U.S.	224	

Public School 8th-Grade Math Proficiency, 1996

	Average	Rank (out of 41 states)
Wyo.	275	18th
U.S.	271	

Public School 8th-Grade Science Proficiency, 1996

	Average	Rank (out of 41 states)
Wyo.	158	6th
U.S.	148	

Average Math SAT Scores

	1972	1982	1992	1998	Percentage Taking SAT in 1998
Wyo.	566	552	537	546	10
U.S.	509	493	501	512	43

Average Verbal SAT Scores

	1972	1982	1992	1998	Percentage Taking SAT in 1998
Wyo.	586	560	539	548	10
U.S.	530	504	500	505	43

Expenditures by Public Institutions of Higher Education Per Full-Time-Equivalent Student, 1996

	FTE Student Spending	Rank
Wyo.	$11,789	31st
U.S.	$12,343	

Per-FTE-student spending in public institutions of higher education trailed the U.S. average by 4%.

Per Full-Time-Equivalent Student Revenues from Federal, State, and Local Governments for Public Institutions of Higher Education, 1996

	FTE Student Government Revenues	Rank
Wyo.	$8,533	14th
U.S.	$8,101	

Per-FTE-student-government revenues in public institutions of higher education topped the U.S. average by 5%.

Average Salary for Full-Time Professors at Public Universities, 1997

	Average	Rank
Wyo.	$58,176	46th
U.S.	$72,599	

The average full-time public university professor salary trailed the U.S. average by 20%.

ECONOMY AND BUSINESS

Economic Growth

Over the period of 1977 to 1997, Wyoming's real gross state product (GSP) grew by 53.2%—ranking 36th in the nation—as compared with real U.S. gross domestic product (GDP), expanding by 70.1%.

At $17.6 billion in 1997, Wyoming's GSP ranked as 49th largest in the nation

From 1993 to 1997, Wyoming's annual real GSP growth averaged 3.76%—ranking 23d in the nation—as compared with annual real U.S. GDP growth, averaging 3.08%.

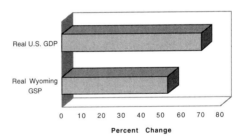

Real Economic Growth 1977-1997: Wyoming vs. U.S.

Percent Change

Job Growth

	Growth in Employee Payrolls (Nonagricultural) 1962–98	Ranking
Wyo.	138.5%	31st
U.S.	126.5%	

Average Annual Growth in Employee Payrolls (Nonagricultural) 1993–98	Ranking
Wyo.	2.07%	44th
U.S.	2.98%	

Per Capita Disposable Income, 1997

	1997	Ranking
Wyo.	$19,347	35th
U.S.	$21,607	

Per capita disposable income trailed the U.S. average by 10%.

	Real Growth 1962–97	Ranking
Wyo.	87.0%	47th
U.S.	116.7%	

	Average Annual Real Growth 1993–97	Ranking
Wyo.	0.92%	48th
U.S.	1.48%	

Number of Businesses

	1997	Percent with Fewer than 500 Employees
Businesses with Employees	18,000	96.7
Self-employed Individuals	30,000	

New Business Incorporations

	1980	1986	1992	1997
Wyo.	1,507	960	1,707	2,267

Percentage Change in Annual New Business Incorporations, 1980 vs. 1997

	Percent	Ranking
Wyo.	50.4	22d
U.S.	49.7	

State Merchandise Exports to the World, 1998 (in millions of dollars)

	1998	Rank
Wyo.	$158.4	51st

Small Business Survival Index, 1999

Wyoming ranks 2d best in the nation in terms of its policy environment for entrepreneurship.

Fortune 500 Headquarters in 1999

None

Labor Union Membership, 1983 vs. 1997

	Percentage of Workers		
	1983	1997	1997 Rank
Wyo.	13.9	9.3	31st
U.S.	20.1	14.1	

Homeownership Rate, 1998

	Rate	Rank
Wyo.	70.0	22d
U.S.	66.3	

CRIME

Crime Rates Per 100 Residents (rankings from best to worst crime rate)

Total Crime	1960	1970	1980	1990	1998	1998 Ranking
Wyo.	0.85	1.75	4.99	4.21	3.81	18th
U.S.	1.04	2.74	5.90	5.82	4.62	

From 1960 to 1998, Wyoming's crime rate increased by 348%, versus a U.S. increase of 344%. From 1990 to 1998, Wyoming's crime rate decreased by 10%, versus a U.S. decrease of 21%.

Violent Crime	1960	1970	1980	1990	1998	1998 Ranking
Wyo.	0.10	0.11	0.39	0.30	0.25	7th
U.S.	0.14	0.36	0.58	0.73	0.57	

From 1960 to 1998, Wyoming's violent crime rate increased by 150%, versus a U.S. increase of 307%. From 1990 to 1998, Wyoming's violent crime, decreased by 17%, compared with a national decline of 22%.

Property Crime	1960	1970	1980	1990	1998	1998 Ranking
Wyo.	0.75	1.63	4.59	3.91	3.56	18th
U.S.	0.90	2.38	5.32	5.09	4.05	

From 1960 to 1998, Wyoming's property crime rate increased by 375%, versus a national increase of 350%. From 1990 to 1998, Wyoming's property crime rate decreased by 9%, compared with a national decline of 20%.

Real Per Capita Police Protection Spending (in real 1996 dollars)

	1962	1972	1982	1992	1996	1996 Ranking
Wyo.	46	69	172	162	161	18th
U.S.	51	95	114	148	168	

In 1996, per capita state and local police protection spending in Wyoming trailed the U.S. average by 4%. From 1962 to 1996, real per capita state and local police protection spending increased by 250%, versus an increase of 229% in the U.S. average.

Prisoners in State and Federal Prisons Per 1,000 Population

	1980	1990	1996	1996 Ranking
Wyo.	1.14	2.44	3.12	31st
U.S.	1.46	3.11	4.45	

From 1980 to 1996, prisoners per 1,000 population increased by 174%, versus a U.S. increase of 205%.

HEALTH CARE

Health-Care Spending

Wyoming's per capita state and local health-care spending registered $151 in 1996, ranking 20th in the nation and equaling the U.S. average of $151. From 1962 to 1996, Wyoming's real per capita state and local health-care spending increased by 979%, versus an increase of 739% in the U.S. average.

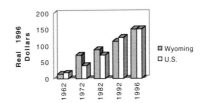

Real Per Capita State and Local Health Care Spending: Wyoming vs. U.S.

Hospital Spending

Wyoming's per capita state and local hospital spending registered $636 in 1996, ranking highest in the nation and exceeding the U.S. average of $266 by 139%. From 1962 to 1996, Wyoming's real per capita state and local hospital spending increased by 308%, as opposed to an increase of 189% in the U.S. average.

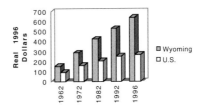

Real Per Capita State and Local Hospital Spending: Wyoming vs. U.S.

Medicaid, 1997

	Spending Per Recipient	Ranking
Wyo.	$3,755	23d
U.S.	$3,681	

Wyoming's per-recipient Medicaid spending exceeded the U.S. average by 2%.

ENVIRONMENT

Parks and Recreation Spending

Wyoming's per capita state and local parks and recreation spending registered $93 in 1996, ranking 13th in the nation and exceeding the U.S. average of $72 by 29%. From 1962 to 1996, real per capita state and local parks and recreation spending increased by 933%, versus a 213% increase in the U.S. average. From 1982 to 1996, Wyoming's real per capita parks and recreation spending declined by 28% versus a national increase of 38%.

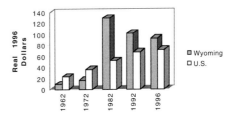

Real Per Capita State and Local Parks and Recreation Spending: Wyoming vs. U.S.

State and Local Natural Resources Spending, 1996

	Per Capita	Ranking
Wyo.	$177	2d
U.S.	$60	

Per capita state and local natural resources spending in Wyoming topped the U.S. average by 195%.

State Parks Revenues as a Share of Operating Expenses, 1997

	Percent	Rank
Wyo.	15	48th
U.S.	42	

Percentage of Land Owned by the Federal Government, 1996

	Percent	Rank
Wyo.	49.5	5th
U.S.	24.8	

SOCIETY AND DEMOGRAPHICS

Population

Wyoming's 1998 population of .481 million ranked 51st in the nation.

Population Growth, 1990–98

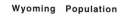

Wyoming Population

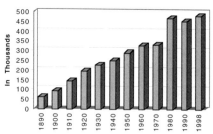

	Percentage Change in Population	Ranking
Wyo.	5.95	35th
U.S.	8.66	

	Net International Migration	Ranking
Wyo.	2,013	51st

	Net Domestic Migration	Ranking
Wyo.	−255	32d

Infant Mortality Rate, 1998

	Percent	Rank
Wyo.	5.2	47th
U.S.	6.4	

Percentage of Births of Low Birthweight, 1997

	Percent	Rank
Wyo.	9.0	6th
U.S.	7.5	

Percentage of Live Births to Unmarried Women, 1997

	Percent	Rank
Wyo.	27.3	40th
U.S.	32.4	

Abortion Rate—Abortions Per 1,000 Women Ages 15–44, 1995

	Rate	Rank
Wyo.	2.7	51st
U.S.	22.9	

LIFESTYLE

Percentage of Households with Computers, 1998

	Percent	Rank
Wyo.	46.1	14th

Percentage of Households with Internet Access, 1998

	Percent	Rank
Wyo.	22.7	38th

State Arts Agency Spending, 1999

	Per Capita	Rank
Wyo.	$0.71	32d
U.S.	$1.35	

Per capita state arts spending in 1999 trailed the U.S. average by 47%.

Major League Sports Facilities

None

DATA SOURCES

UNITED STATES CHAPTER

Politics

- Presidential election numbers from *Statistical Abstract of the United States*, annual (published by Bureau of the Census, U.S. Department of Commerce), *Historical Statistics of the United States: Colonial Times to 1970* (published by Bureau of the Census, U.S. Department of Commerce, in 1975), and *Encyclopedia of the American Presidency*, Volume 4 (edited by Leonard W. Levy and Louis Fisher, published by Simon & Schuster, New York, in 1994).
- Congress's political majorities and minorities from *Statistical Abstract of the United States*, annual (published by Bureau of the Census, U.S. Department of Commerce), and *Historical Statistics of the United States: Colonial Times to 1970* (published by Bureau of the Census, U.S., Department of Commerce, in 1975).
- Number of public bills enacted by Congress based on data from *The Federal Register* and *Vital Statistics on Congress 1997–98* (by Norman J. Orenstein, Thomas E. Mann and Michael J. Malbin, and published by Congressional Quarterly Inc., Washington, D.C., in 1998).

Taxes and Spending

- Government spending, revenue, and debt numbers, unless otherwise noted below, based on data from *Historical Statistics of the United States: Colonial Times to 1970* (published by Bureau of the Census, U.S. Department of Commerce, in 1975), the *Economic Report of the President*, annual (published by the United States Government Printing Office, Washington, D.C.) and *Budget of the United States Government*, annual (published by the U.S. Government Printing Office, Washington, D.C.).
- International numbers for central government revenues as a share of the economy based on data from *World Development Indicators 1999* (published by The World Bank, Washington, D.C., in 1999).
- Individual income tax for 1998, "Who Pays the Personal Income Tax?" and "The Tax Code" from "1999 Tax Facts," U.S. House of Representatives, Committee on Ways and Means, April 8, 1999.
- History of top personal income tax rate based on data and information from *Federal Tax Policy*, Fifth Edition (by Joseph A. Pechman, The Brookings Institution, Washington, D.C., 1987), and recent Internal Revenue Service forms.

- Corporate income tax for 1998 from the Internal Revenue Service's website at www.irs.ustreas.gov.
- History of top corporate income tax rate based on data and information from *Federal Tax Policy*, Fifth Edition (by Joseph A. Pechman, The Brookings Institution, Washington, D.C, 1987), and recent Internal Revenue Service forms.
- Top federal capital gains tax rates information from the American Council for Capital Formation (Washington, D.C.) and *The Labyrinth of Capital Gains Tax Policy* (by Leonard E. Burman, Brookings Institution Press, Washington, D.C., 1999).
- Social Security and Medicare payroll tax data from "1999 Tax Facts," U.S. House of Representatives, Committee on Ways and Means, April 8, 1999, and "1998 Green Book," U.S. House of Representatives, Committee on Ways and Means, May 19, 1998.
- International comparison of personal corporate income tax rates based on data from the *1999 Index of Economic Freedom* (by Bryan Johnson, Kim Holmes and Melanie Kirkpatrick, published by The Heritage Foundation and Dow Jones & Company, Inc. in 1999).
- International comparison of tax rates on capital gains, dividends and interest income, and death tax rates based on data from the American Council for Capital Formation.

Education

- Per pupil public school spending numbers based on data from the *Digest of Education Statistics*, annual (published annually by the National Center for Education Statistics, U.S. Department of Education).
- International per pupil spending on public and private institutions numbers from the Organization For Economic Cooperation and Development's website www.oecd.org.
- Average public school teacher salaries based on data from the *Digest of Education Statistics*, annual (published annually by the National Center for Education Statistics, U.S. Department of Education).
- International average public primary and high school teacher salaries from the Organization For Economic Cooperation and Development's website at www.oecd.org.
- International pupils per teacher in public and private schools based on data from the *Digest of Education Statistics*, annual (published annually by the National Center for Education Statistics, U.S. Department of Education).
- Hours spent on leisure activity each day for eight grade students from the *Digest of Education Statistics*, annual (published annually by the National Center for Education Statistics, U.S. Department of Education).
- Verbal and Math SAT scores from the College Board.
- Math and science scores from the *Digest of Education Statistics*, annual (published annually by the National Center for Education Statistics, U.S. Department of Education).
- Educational attainment from the Organization For Economic Cooperation and Development's website at www.oecd.org.

The Economy

- Economic growth numbers based on data from the *Economic Report of the President*, annual (published by the United States Government Printing Office, Washington, D.C.), *Historical Statistics 1960–1995* (published by the Organization For Economic Cooperation and Development in 1997), the Organization For Economic Cooperation and Development's website at www.oecd.org, *Historical Statistics of the United States: Colonial Times to 1970* (published by Bureau of the Census, U.S. Department of Commerce, in 1975), *World Tables 1995* (published for The World Bank by The Johns Hopkins University Press, Baltimore, in 1995), and Reuters News and Bloomberg Business News services.

- Employment numbers based on data from the U.S. Bureau of Labor Statistics, the *Economic Report of the President*, annual (published by the United States Government Printing Office, Washington, D.C.), *Historical Statistics of the United States: Colonial Times to 1970* (published by Bureau of the Census, U.S. Department of Commerce, in 1975), and *Economic Indicators*, monthly (prepared by the Council of Economic Advisers and published by the United States Government Printing Office).

- Labor force participation rates based on data from the *Handbook of U.S. Labor Statistics*, second edition (edited by Eva E. Jacobs and published by Bernan Press, Lanham, Maryland, in 1998).

- Labor union members numbers based on data from the U.S. Bureau of Labor Statistics, the Public Service Research Foundation, and *The Washington Post*, August 30, 1997.

- Industrial production and productivity numbers based on data from the *Economic Report of the President*, annual (published by the United States Government Printing Office, Washington, D.C.), and *Economic Indicators*, monthly (prepared by the Council of Economic Advisers and published by the United States Government Printing Office, Washington, D.C.).

- Consumer price and inflation numbers based on data from the *Economic Report of the President*, annual (published by the United States Government Printing Office, Washington, D.C.), *Historical Statistics 1960–1995* (published by the Organization For Economic Cooperation and Development in 1997), *Historical Statistics of the United States: Colonial Times to 1970* (published by Bureau of the Census, U.S. Department of Commerce, in 1975), *World Tables 1995* (published for The World Bank by The Johns Hopkins University Press, Baltimore, in 1995), and *Economic Indicators*, monthly (prepared by the Council of Economic Advisers and published by the United States Government Printing Office, Washington, D.C.).

- Bond yield numbers based on data from the *Economic Report of the President*, annual (published by the United States Government Printing Office, Washington, D.C.), *Historical Statistics of the United States: Colonial Times to 1970* (published by Bureau of the Census, U.S. Department of Commerce, in 1975), and *Economic Indicators*, monthly (prepared by the Council of Economic Advisers and published by the United States Government Printing Office, Washington, D.C.).

- Disposable income numbers based on data from the *Economic Report of the President*, annual (published by the United States Government Printing Office, Washington, D.C.), and *Economic Indicators*, monthly (prepared by the Council of Economic Advisers and published by the United States Government Printing Office, Washington, D.C.).

- S&P Composite Index numbers based on data from the *Economic Report of the President*, annual (published by the United States Government Printing Office, Washington, D.C.), *Historical Statistics of the United States: Colonial Times to 1970* (published by Bureau of the Census, U.S. Department of Commerce, in 1975), and *Economic Indicators*, monthly (prepared by the Council of Economic Advisers and published by the United States Government Printing Office, Washington, D.C.).

- Trade numbers based on data from the *Economic Report of the President*, annual (published by the United States Government Printing Office, Washington, D.C.), *Historical Statistics of the United*

States: Colonial Times to 1970 (published by Bureau of the Census, U.S. Department of Commerce, in 1975), *Economic Indicators*, monthly (prepared by the Council of Economic Advisers and published by the United States Government Printing Office, Washington, D.C.), and *World Development Indicators 1999* (published by The World Bank, Washington, D.C., in 1999).
- New business incorporations based on data from Dun & Bradstreet and the *Economic Report of the President*, annual (published by the United States Government Printing Office, Washington, D.C.). Number of businesses based on income tax filings from the Internal Revenue Service's quarterly *SOI Bulletin*.

Crime

- Crime numbers based on data from *Crime in the United States*, annual (published by the Federal Bureau of Investigations) and the *Statistical Abstract of the United States*, annual (published by Bureau of the Census, U.S. Department of Commerce).

Health Care

- Spending numbers based on data from *Health, United States, 1998* (published by the U.S. Department of Health and Human Services) and from the U.S. Bureau of the Census website at www.census.gov.

Environment

- Numbers regarding nationally protected areas based on data from *World Development Indicators 1999* (published by The World Bank, Washington, D.C., in 1999).
- Energy consumption numbers based on data from *Statistical Abstract of the United States 1998* (published by Bureau of the Census, U.S. Department of Commerce).
- Carbon dioxide numbers based on data from *World Development Indicators 1999* (published by The World Bank, Washington, D.C., in 1999).

Demographics and Society

- Population numbers from *Historical Statistics of the United States: Colonial Times to 1970* (published by Bureau of the Census, U.S. Department of Commerce, in 1975), *Statistical Abstract of the United States*, annual (published by Bureau of the Census, U.S. Department of Commerce), and the Census Bureau's website at www.census.gov.
- Age distribution and life expectancy numbers are based on data from *Statistical Abstract of the United States*, annual (published by Bureau of the Census, U.S. Department of Commerce), and *World Development Indicators 1999* (published by The World Bank, Washington, D.C., in 1999).
- Infant mortality rates based on data from *Statistical Abstract of the United States*, annual (published by Bureau of the Census, U.S. Department of Commerce), *Historical Statistics of the United States: Colonial Times to 1970* (published by Bureau of the Census, U.S. Department of Commerce, in 1975), and *World Development Indicators 1999* (published by The World Bank, Washington, D.C., in 1999).
- Birth numbers based on data from the *Statistical Abstract of the United States*, annual (published by Bureau of the Census, U.S. Department of Commerce), *Historical Statistics of the United States:*

Colonial Times to 1970 (published by Bureau of the Census, U.S. Department of Commerce, in 1975), and *Health, United States, 1998* (published by the U.S. Department of Health and Human Services).
- Abortion numbers based on data from the *Statistical Abstract of the United States*, annual (published by Bureau of the Census, U.S. Department of Commerce), and the National Right to Life Educational Trust Fund.

Lifestyle

- All numbers based on data from *World Development Indicators 1999* (published by The World Bank, Washington, D.C., in 1999) and the U.S. Bureau of the Census.

STATE CHAPTERS

Politics

- Registered voter percentages for 1996 and come from *National Journal's* "Cloakroom" website.
- Voting percentages for elections and state house breakdowns come from the Federal Election Commission (Washington, D.C.), the United States Congress, the National Governor's Association, the National Conference of State Legislatures, and various state sources.
- Group Ratings: Based on key congressional votes as identified and scored by three organizations. Each group rates 0 as the lowest score and 100 as the highest:
    ACU: American Conservative Union—lifetime ratings
    ADA: Americans for Democratic Action—estimated lifetime ratings
    SBSC: Small Business Survival Committee—ratings for the 105th Congress

Government Taxes and Spending

- Per capita state and local government revenue, spending and debt numbers, as well as state and local government employment numbers, based on data from the U.S. Bureau of the Census.

Education

- Except for data noted below, all state education numbers based on data from the National Center for Education Statistics, U.S. Department of Education, including the *Digest of Education Statistics*, annual.
- Per capita state and local education spending based on data from the U.S. Bureau of the Census
- Verbal and Math SAT scores from the College Board.

Economy and Business

- State economic growth numbers based on data from the Bureau of Economic Analysis, U.S. Department of Commerce.
- State job growth numbers based on data from the *Handbook of U.S. Labor Statistics*, Third Edition 1999 (edited by Eva E. Jacobs, Bernan Press, Lanham, MD, 1999).

- State per capita disposable income numbers based on data from *Business Statistics of the United States*, 1995 Edition (edited by Courtenay M. Slater, Bernan Press, Lanham, MD, 1996), and *Business Statistics of the United States*, 1998 Edition (edited by Courtenay M. Slater and Corneilia J. Strawser, Bernan Press, Lanham, MD, 1998).
- Number of businesses from the U.S. Small Business Administrator's "Small Business Profiles, 1998" (October 1998).
- New business incorporations numbers based on data from Dun & Bradstreet and the U.S. Small Business Administration.
- Export numbers based on data from the U.S. Department of Commerce.
- *Small Business Survival Index* is published annually by the Small Business Survival Committee (Washington, D.C.). The Index scores and ranks the states according to how friendly or unfriendly their public policy environment is for entrepreneurship. Raymond J. Keating, coauthor of this book, writes this study each year.
- Fortune 500 headquarters in 1999 from *Fortune* magazine, June 14, 1999.
- Labor union membership numbers based on data from the *Statistical Abstract of the United States*, annual (published by Bureau of the Census, U.S. Department of Commerce).
- Home ownership rate from the U.S. Bureau of the Census website at www.census.gov.

Crime

- Crime and prisoner numbers based on data from *Crime in the United States*, annual (published by the Federal Bureau of Investigations) and the *Statistical Abstract of the United States*, annual (published by Bureau of the Census, U.S. Department of Commerce).
- Per capita state and local police protection spending numbers based on data from the U.S. Bureau of the Census.

Health Care

- Per capita state and local health-care and hospital spending numbers based on data from the U.S. Bureau of the Census.
- Medicaid spending numbers based on data from the *Statistical Abstract of the United States*, annual (published by Bureau of the Census, U.S. Department of Commerce).

Environment

- Per capita state and local parks and recreation and natural resources spending numbers based on data from the U.S. Bureau of the Census.
- State parks revenues as a share of operating expenses from the Evergreen Freedom Foundation (Olympia, WA), "Toward a Self-Sufficient State Park System," December 9, 1998.
- Land owned by federal government based on data from the *Statistical Abstract of the United States*, annual (published by Bureau of the Census, U.S. Department of Commerce).

Society and Demographics

- Population numbers based on data from *Historical Statistics of the United States: Colonial Times to 1970* (published by Bureau of the Census, U.S. Department of Commerce, in 1975), *Statistical*

Abstract of the United States, annual (published by Bureau of the Census, U.S. Department of Commerce), and the Census Bureau's website at www.census.gov.
- Birth and infant mortality numbers based on data from the U.S. National Center for Health Statistics.
- Abortion numbers based on data from the *Statistical Abstract of the United States,* annual (published by Bureau of the Census, U.S. Department of Commerce).

Lifestyle

- Computer and Internet numbers from the National Telecommunications and Information Administration, U.S. Department of Commerce.
- State arts agency spending numbers based on data from the National Assembly of State Arts Agencies.
- Sports facilities numbers based on data from an April 5, 1999 study, "Sports Pork: The Costly Relationship Between Major League Sports and Government," written by Raymond J. Keating, coauthor of this book, for the Cato Institute (Washington, D.C.). The numbers have been updated and expanded based on a variety of wire and local news stories.

ABOUT THE AUTHORS

RAYMOND J. KEATING

Raymond J. Keating serves as chief economist with the Washington, D.C.-based Small Business Survival Committee (SBSC) and coauthors (with Matthew Carolan) a weekly newspaper column—"Carolan & Keating"—for *Newsday* in New York. Keating also writes a weekly cyber-column—"The Entrepreneurial View"—for SBSC's website at www.sbsc.org.

Keating's second book—*New York by the Numbers: State and City in Perpetual Crisis*—was published in May 1997. His first book, *D.C. by the Numbers: A State of Failure*, was coauthored with Thomas Edmonds and published in January 1995.

As a cofounder and principal of Capital Hill Research, Keating also writes political and economic analyses serving clients in the financial community.

Keating has written hundreds of policy studies and articles, published in such periodicals as the *Washington Post, The Wall Street Journal, The New York Times, National Review, Investor's Business Daily, Chicago Tribune, Policy Review,* the *Journal of Commerce, The Washington Times, New York Post, Daily News, Detroit Free Press, Indianapolis Star, Insight, Human Events,* the *City Journal,* and many more. In addition, Keating has been a guest or been featured on countless television and radio shows, including on NBC *Nightly News,* CNN/fn, CNBC, PBS, and WABC Radio in New York City. He also is a contributing editor to Foundation for Economic Education's monthly free-market magazine, the *Freeman.*

Keating holds an MA in economics from New York University, an MBA in banking and finance from Hofstra University, and a BS in business administration and economics from St. Joseph's College.

He lives on Long Island with his wife, Beth; and their son, David.

THOMAS N. EDMONDS

Tom Edmonds is a political media consultant. For 20 years his firm, Edmonds Associates, has developed and executed media campaigns for candidates at all levels of government. He also has implemented independent expenditure campaigns for a wide variety of national organizations.

In addition to his political work, Edmonds has produced several acclaimed documentaries, including the award-winning television documentary of the Reagan presidency, "Ronald Reagan: An American President."

Currently a director of the International Association of Political Consultants and a member of the advisory board of *Campaigns & Elections* magazine, Edmonds is also a past president of the bipartisan American Association of Political Consultants. He has provided political insight and commentary for CNN, *Nightline,* and National Public Radio. His work has been featured on *60 Minutes, 20/20, The*

Today Show, and the *NBC Nightly News,* among others. His articles and op-eds have appeared in the *Washington Post. Washington Times. Campaigns & Elections*, and *Advertising Age*.

As coauthor of *D.C. by the Numbers: A State of Failure*, the *Washington Post* dubbed Edmonds, "the man who wants to fix Washington."

He lives in Waterford, Virginia, with his wife, Schuyler, and son, Charlie.